SHAKESPEARE SURVEY

ADVISORY BOARD

SHAKESPEARE SURVEY

64

Shakespeare as Cultural Catalyst

EDITED BY

PETER HOLLAND

CAMBRIDGE
UNIVERSITY PRESS

CAMBRIDGE UNIVERSITY PRESS
Cambridge, New York, Melbourne, Madrid, Cape Town,
Singapore, São Paulo, Delhi, Tokyo, Mexico City

Cambridge University Press
The Edinburgh Building, Cambridge CB2 8RU, UK

Published in the United States of America by Cambridge University Press, New York

www.cambridge.org
Information on this title: www.cambridge.org/9781107011229

First published 2011

Printed in the United Kingdom at the University Press, Cambridge

A catalogue record for this publication is available from the British Library

ISBN 978-1-107-01122-9 Hardback

EDITOR'S NOTE

Volume 65, on '*A Midsummer Night's Dream*', will be at press by the time this volume appears. The theme of Volume 66 will be 'Working with Shakespeare' and of Volume 67 will be 'Shakespeare's Collaborative Plays'.

Submissions should be addressed to the Editor at The Shakespeare Institute, Church Street, Stratford-upon-Avon, Warwickshire, CV37 6HP, to arrive at the latest by 1 September 2012 for Volume 66 and 1 September 2013 for Volume 67. Pressures on space are heavy and priority is given to articles related to the theme of a particular volume. Please send a copy you do not wish to be returned. Submissions may also be made as attachments to e-mail to pholland@nd.edu. All articles submitted are read by the Editor and at least one member of the Advisory Board, whose indispensable assistance the Editor gratefully acknowledges.

Unless otherwise indicated, Shakespeare quotations and references are keyed to *The Complete Works*, ed. Stanley Wells, Gary Taylor, John Jowett and William Montgomery, 2nd edition (Oxford, 2005).

Review copies should be addressed to the Editor as above. In attempting to survey the ever-increasing bulk of Shakespeare publications our reviewers inevitably have to exercise some selection. We are pleased to receive offprints of articles which help to draw our reviewers' attention to relevant material.

P.D.H.

CONTRIBUTORS

PASCALE AEBISCHER, *University of Exeter*

STEPHEN COHEN, *Central Connecticut State University*

SUSANNE GREENHALGH, *Roehampton University*

DIANA E. HENDERSON, *Massachusetts Institute of Technology*

PETER HOLBROOK, *University of Queensland, Australia*

ADAM G. HOOKS, *University of Iowa*

ALEXANDER HUANG, *George Washington University*

SHOICHIRO KAWAI, *University of Tokyo*

BERNICE W. KLIMAN, *Nassau Community College*

DOUGLAS M. LANIER, *University of New Hampshire*

DAVID LINDLEY, *University of Leeds*

EMILY LINNEMANN, *University of Birmingham*

KATHLEEN MCLUSKIE, *University of Birmingham*

ROSHNI MOONEERAM, *University of Nottingham Ningbo, China*

RUTH MORSE, *University of Paris Diderot*

ANDREW MURPHY, *University of St Andrews*

JONOTHAN NEELANDS, *University of Warwick*

SHARON O'DAIR, *University of Alabama*

JACQUI O'HANLON, *Royal Shakespeare Company*

SARAH OLIVE, *University of York*

ROBERT ORMSBY, *Memorial University of Newfoundland, Canada*

MARTIN PROCHÁZKA, *Charles University, Prague*

KEVIN A. QUARMBY, *Shakespeare's Globe, London*

ERIC RASMUSSEN, *University of Nevada, Reno*

KATE RUMBOLD, *University of Birmingham*

CAROL CHILLINGTON RUTTER, *University of Warwick*

JULIE SANDERS, *University of Nottingham*

CHARLOTTE SCOTT, *Goldsmiths University of London*

JAMES SHAW, *University of Oxford*

FRAN TEAGUE, *University of Georgia*

OLWEN TERRIS, *British Universities Film & Video Council*

POONAM TRIVEDI, *University of Delhi*

JESÚS TRONCH-PÉREZ, *University of Valencia*

CONTENTS

CONTENTS

ILLUSTRATIONS

LIST OF ILLUSTRATIONS

THE COMMERCIAL BARD:
BUSINESS MODELS FOR
THE TWENTY-FIRST CENTURY

KATHLEEN McLUSKIE

Whether courting the Court of Queen Elizabeth, or relocating to save the finances of his co-investors, Shakespeare's entrepreneurial skill and nose for the market were as good as his writing.[1]

This, slightly unexpected, invocation of Shakespeare opens a report on 'The Entrepreneurial Museum', commissioned by the UK Museums and Libraries Association. The report provides a set of models for museum directors, urging them to embrace new business practices as a way of creating 'sustainable income through commercial activities' (p. 1). It urges museum managers to be aware of the commercial potential of the objects in their care and emphasizes the scope for creative association with commercial companies, offering examples of best practice such as 'the Natural History Museum's T-Rex pyjamas in M&S [Marks and Spencer], the John Lewis' V&A [Victoria and Albert Museum] secateurs, and the Science Museum's educational toys'.

In this context Shakespeare appears as an exemplar for contemporary cultural brokers, aware of and troubled by the traditional tension between commerce and the arts. It suggests that Shakespeare's aesthetic achievement was perfectly compatible with and perhaps even exemplified in his entrepreneurial role in the developing commercial theatre of early modern England. If there is no inconsistency between high value art (Shakespeare's writing) and the sharp management practice of the Globe's moonlight flitting, museum directors need not be concerned about any tension between the artistic and heritage values of

their collections and the interests of the reliable, middle-England, commercial partners who can help to market their assets and provide the financial resources that will ensure the continued success of their organizations.

At first glance this use of Shakespeare seems to fit the now familiar trope of a commodified Shakespeare, that Frederic Jameson described as yet another space in which something like the postmodern 'great transformation' can be read'.[2] However, the MLA report, along with other exemplars of the invocation of Shakespeare in the first decade of the twenty-first century, seems to offer a different take on the familiar connections between commerce and the arts. It proposes a new kind of relationship in which commercial activity is an enabling device, using the markets of mass production to protect rather than exploit artistic products that can use commercial support in order to survive the rigours of the market. The examples of successful collaboration, moreover, include products that use the arts for excellent design to create objects in perfect taste. They do not imitate or reference art works directly and are easily distinguishable from the tourist tat, mocked in late twentieth-century accounts of the Shakespeare trade,[3] or from the poisonous associations of armaments and cigarettes

---

[1] 'Intelligent Naivety, The Entrepreneurial Museum', Report commissioned by the Museums and Libraries Association, 2008 (www.IntelligentNaivety.com), p. 5.
[2] Fredric Jameson, 'Marxism and Postmodernism', *New Left Review*, 176 (1989), p. 40.
[3] Barbara Hodgdon, *The Shakespeare Trade* (Philadelphia, 1988).

1

that were used both in the 1980s critique of commercial sponsorship and in the radical denunciations, triggered by the 2010 drilling accident in the Gulf of Mexico, of BP's twenty-year sponsorship of the Tate Gallery.[4] The rhetorical strategies of the MLA report protected the value of the arts from the potentially controversial values of the market by literally and metaphorically separating out the space of cultural value in the gallery from the space of tasteful commerce in the surrounding shops or cafeterias or car parks.[5]

The protected space of cultural value was described as one of a direct communion between the art or artisanal craft work and the public: a space where the traditional artistic values of the heritage arts could flourish, where, in the words of the MLA document,

art and culture challenges the status quo, the mundane, the everyday, the ordinary. It elevates people to a higher ideal, a commonality of history or social bonds, or it dares to question the accepted norms of today.[6]

These values did not depend on the specific content of the 'art and culture' celebrated by the museums, which ranged from narrow boats to woodland crafts. Instead, the MLA document sought to manage the values of a generalized 'art and culture' by associating them with the desires and values of their audience. These values, which included challenging 'the accepted norms of today', could be kept clear of the market while ensuring that the resources to sustain their availability in a commercially competitive world could remain secure.

The MLA report is only one example of a number of attempts to reconfigure ideas of cultural value that were made in the first decade of the twenty-first century. Reports commissioned by arts organizations and government bodies also tried to negotiate the terrain between making a powerful case for the economic impact of the arts in generating revenue and employment and endorsing an idea of the arts as an autonomous and precious locus of a different kind of value. In order to do so, they too left the vexed questions of particular

aesthetic and ethical value to one side in order to keep it discursively separate from the arts' contribution to the national and regional economy, even while acknowledging that dependence in financial terms.

This contest between different forms of cultural production crossed over the boundary between commercial and state-funded arts to define a new arena for debates about cultural value. It effected an uneasy convergence between cultural values defined in terms of their content and origins (heritage values and new cultural forms), cultural value defined in terms of its contribution to the national economy and cultural value defined in terms of the diverse contributions of a multicultural society.

An important study, commissioned by Arts Council England from the consultancy group Demos, places these values in distinct categories: 'intrinsic, instrumental and institutional'. These locations of value, the Demos group argued, did not need to be in conflict because each different concept was acknowledged and successfully established within satisfactory distinctions, invoked by arts providers and arts managers alike.[7] The contests of twentieth-century *Kulturkritik* between high art and low, between culture as a way of life and culture as artistic production, between the needs of the populace and the tastes of the elite were bypassed in order to resolve ideological conflict and facilitate what Stuart Cunningham, the sociologist of culture, has described as 'public processes involved

---

[4] Discussed in Kathleen McLuskie, 'Shakespeare and the Millennial Market: The Commercial Bard', *Renaissance Drama*, 30 (2001), 161–82; for a discussion of the protest against the connection between BP and the Tate, see guardianonline.co.uk, 28 June 2010.
[5] The 'value chain' that connects the artistic and commercial sides of arts businesses is discussed in Emily Linnemann, 'The Cultural Value of Shakespeare in Twenty-First-Century Publicly-Funded Theatre in England', Ph.D. thesis, University of Birmingham, 2010. See also Stephen Preece, 'The Performing Arts Value Chain', *International Journal of Arts Management*, 8:1 (2005), 21–32.
[6] 'The Entrepreneurial Museum', p. 5.
[7] John Holden, *Cultural Value and the Crisis of Legitimacy* (London, 2006).

in formulating, implementing and contesting governmental intervention in and support of cultural activity'.[8]

Those changed cultural discourses replaced the complex abstractions of aesthetic and social analysis with the aspirations of public policy. In one public statement, for example, the culture secretary announced:

The whole process of stimulation through plays, books, films, works of art; the delight in design, in architecture, in crafts: all of this enlarges a country's capacity to be reflective, interested and bold. Dynamism in arts and culture creates dynamism in a nation. So when more children get access to the joy of art, it is not the art alone that they learn; it is the art of living, thinking and creating. They may never be, probably won't ever be, an artist or a dancer or a designer, but in whatever job, in whichever walk of life, they will carry an idea that is not just about the buying and selling, but about what makes the ordinary special. When people on low incomes can visit museums free of charge, and see great works of art, they take something of the inspiration with them. A nation that cares about art will not just be a better nation. In the early 21st Century it will be a more successful one.

Such policy statements[9] are less significant in their content than in what they signal about the struggle within the discourses of cultural value in the twenty-first century. They reflected the sense that sustaining a common 'culture' that embodies and communicates a set of abstracted common values may be the last and only hope of a divided society; they reiterated the commonplace distinction between 'great works of art' and 'buying and selling' and they aligned the aesthetic and emotive power of the arts with an idea of democracy achieved by widening access and the opening up of cultural institutions to the public as a whole. So the intrinsic value of 'great works of art' would be distinguished from the market value; free access to heritage institutions would ensure that this non-market value would become part of the national culture and the resulting 'dynamism and creativity' would contribute to the success of the nation.

The rhetorics surrounding those aspirations were both utopian and instrumental. Their utopian vision of a society inspired by the arts echoed, and in some cases explicitly quoted, Matthew Arnold, to agree that culture encompassed 'the best that has been thought and said'. The social critique that lay behind Arnold's own insistence on the distinct ethical value of the arts and its contrast with mechanistic commercial and political culture was subsumed into a generalized admiration for the collections of state-supported museums and galleries and an assumed consensus about the value of heritage and creativity. The more instrumental aim was to sustain public support for state funding of the arts and to manage the competition between different demands on the public purse, each of which required justification in terms of value for money.

The delicate balance was articulated by Tessa Jowell, arts minister from 2001 to 2007:

Value judgements, when fine judgements are required, are certainly to some degree subjective. But the kind of value judgement we make when we allocate millions to the Royal Shakespeare Company cannot be justified on subjective grounds: we need to be able to explain why it is right to do so to a critical bystander or a sceptical voter. We need to find a way to demonstrate the personal value-added which comes from engagement with complex art.[10]

By generalizing the value of the arts in terms of their inspirational impact on the society as a whole, these statements sought to avoid any focus on particular items of expenditure but they recognized the continuing power of oppositions between the canon of English artistic heritage and the cultural needs of minorities, or between high and low art. They could only be resolved by asserting the 'personal value-added which comes from

---

8 Stuart Cunningham, 'Cultural Studies from the Viewpoint of Cultural Policy', in Justin Lewis and Toby Miller, eds., *Critical Cultural Policy Studies: A Reader* (Oxford, 2003), p. 14.

9 For a fully archived range of research publications and ministerial statements, see www.culture.gov.uk/publications.

10 Tessa Jowell, 'Government and the Value of Culture' (2004), p. 5, accessed via www.shiftyparadigms.org/images/Cultural%20Policy/Tessa_Jowell.pdf, 2 December 2010.

engagement with complex art' and assuring the tax-paying public that those values could be available to the whole population.

Every arts policymaker and practitioner was aware that success in the arts had to be financially as well as critically rewarded and the rhetoric of public arts policy proposed that the arts could be assimilated into a managed economy whose primary aim is to provide the most efficient and effective distribution of goods, removing artificial barriers to participation and restricting the role of state intervention to managing the balance between a successful creative economy and the occasional requirement for protection against market failure. The arts were described as endowed with special values and accorded a special place in which to develop without being immediately and brutally channelled to meet the requirements of a demand-led market. This subsidized space, moreover, could be managed with the same economic and fiscal protocols as such other vulnerable commodities as new inventions or new services, which are managed by alternative departments of state in the interests of the wider economy.

As the then prime minister explained in 2007:

The model is a mixed economy. It combines public funding with private enterprise, subsidy and the box office together. It is characterised by partnerships between the creative sectors and private sponsors. Critically, the Arts Council operates as an arms-length body so the state is placed in the position of doing what it has historically done well – funding – and not what it has historically done very badly – control of the arts.[11]

Beyond championing what the culture minister called 'the complex arts', there was no need for either the regulator or the market to concern itself with the particular character of the culture or artistic activity being developed. Shakespeare, or narrow boats or woodland walks, were equally important in the enclosed sphere of 'intrinsic value', the place of 'commonality of history and social bonds' whose value would be enjoyed by everyone who engaged with any form of culture.

The role of the market was to ensure access to the whole of the cultural sphere, untrammelled by prejudices (in either direction) about high or low culture or an old-fashioned alignment of culture with social class. The role of government was to ensure that access to artistic production was not distorted by consumers' lack of knowledge of valued artistic products or that particular groups, such as children or poor people, were not excluded from the market by lack of funds. Arts Council policy was thus engaged in a balance between supply side intervention – subsidizing particular arts organizations – to demand side interventions such as the £10 ticket schemes for theatre or prioritizing audience development schemes and education in allocating funds to the complex mix of large-scale national organizations or community-focused providers.

II

This discursive and fiscal management of the arts market in twenty-first-century England[12] offered a characteristic New Labour attempt to go beyond the often bitter and hard-fought cultural conflicts of the twentieth century. The contest between high and low culture and between culture and the market that had dominated earlier debates about the value of the arts was replaced by a consensus that the arts in general constituted a social good that should be protected from a profit-seeking market. This consensus avoided the question of the aesthetic value of particular forms of art in order to exclude any suggestion of a hierarchy among them. The new, managed, arts market must be open to all in order to realize the double requirement of economic growth and of free, unrestrained access to the 'added value' that it offered.

The shift from conflict to consensus was in part a product of the politics of New Labour. However,

---

[11] For example, see Tony Blair's speech on culture at Tate Modern gallery, 6 March 2007, www.number10.gov.uk/Page11166. The balance that Tony Blair proposed in 2007 has of course been radically altered by policy reactions to the 2009 financial crisis and a change of UK government.

[12] Limiting the discussion to England is an attempt at precision rather than provincialism.

it also reflected fundamental changes in the economy of mass production. This subsidized market in cultural goods could avoid the closed competition over the value of particular products because it proposed a different economic model from that of older, closed commodity markets. The shifts in the rhetoric of government policy configured the arts as so-called 'non-rival goods' whose consumption by one group does not diminish the quantum available for others. When museum collections or theatre companies are part of the heritage assets of the nation their asset value is increased rather than diminished by the number of people who have access to them. Moreover, it can be further increased by investment into the asset since additional consumers of a high value non-rival good increase rather than diminish its value. Where most commodities exist in a market in which they are consumed and replaced by other commodities, (buying and selling) the value of non-rival goods can be quantified in terms of the number of consumers whose engagement does not diminish the supply of the goods concerned.

The concept of a non-rival good is a useful one for economists attempting to arrive at quantification of intangible assets. It acknowledges the complex accounting methods of contemporary markets for which the customer base is as much of an asset as the stock.[13] It can also be effectively aligned with the idea of democratic access without being caught up in ideologically fraught questions of social class or the old divisions between mass and popular culture.[14] The term is never explicitly used outside economics, but the concept underlies the management of the publicly funded arts which in the twenty-first century have routinely used complex customer surveys as a means both of arriving at the value of the arts and meeting the demands for public accountability.[15]

This form of market has had a much more significant impact on 'Shakespeare' than the 'assimilation of high culture into commodity production' identified by cultural critics such as Fredric Jameson in the very different cultural and economic moment of the late twentieth century.[16] As the MLA report demonstrated, 'Shakespeare' could be invoked as an exemplar of excellence because the mythologized historical positioning of his work resolved any residual anxiety about the relations between commerce and the arts, but the concept of Shakespeare was also usefully imprecise: the dramatic and poetic works, together with the historical figure, were corralled in an arena of 'excellence',[17] or 'heritage' without being tied to any specific production or object that might be the subject of commercially driven competition. This non-rival Shakespeare is the source of the value of all the particular objects and activities that exist in particular markets and each of those individual exemplars increases its non-rival value. The supply of those individual goods (this film, that theatre production) still requires financial resources but those financial resources are directed towards the value chain of additional goods and services that stretches from the non-rival Shakespeare to the final consumer.

The dynamic relationship between non-rival Shakespeare and particular 'Shakespeare' objects gives some sense of the complexity of Shakespeare's cultural value. It is a not a linear process in which some intrinsic aesthetic value held in the historic texts is transmitted to the present (the metaphor is telling). Rather it involves a circular, self-reinforcing process in which the dizzying

---

13 The most obvious example is Facebook, whose millions of participants make it a hugely valuable company in spite of an almost complete absence of cash flow.

14 A useful starting point for understanding non-rival goods is available at http://en.wikipedia.org/wiki/Rivalry_(economics). The importance of non-rival goods in sustaining relations of citizens rather than consumers in the modern world is eloquently argued in Michael Sandel's 2009 Reith Lecture, 'A New Citizenship', available at www.bbc.co.uk/radio4/features/the-reith-lectures/archive.

15 See www.dcms.gov.uk/research.

16 Fredric Jameson, 'Postmodernism, or the Cultural Logic of Late Capitalism', *New Left Review*, 146 (July–August, 1984), p. 56.

17 The word became a term of art in the 2008 Arts Council report that insisted on the 'excellence' of the arts production sponsored by the Council: its meaning depended on an opposition to 'instrumentality', the practice of prioritizing particular audiences. Excellence was a feature of the supply side; access and inclusivity the priorities of the demand side.

plurality of forms in which Shakespeare exists adds value to the non-rival Shakespeare and increases its value for the future.

The individual forms of Shakespeare's reproduction offer an almost infinite and ceaselessly renewed source of material in technologized production such as films (art-house and mall movies), theatre adaptations, rap music or interactive web 2.0 virtual worlds, but they also include the circulation of second-hand copies or amateur productions or YouTube videos. Each of these forms can be identified as 'Shakespeare', usually via overlaps of narrative or character but their relationships to one another and to the Shakespeare of the full texts that exist in multiple copies in European and North American libraries or on the free space of the World Wide Web[18] presents a considerable challenge to traditional ways of analysing the impact and the value of Shakespeare in the contemporary cultural economy.

As Richard Burt has clearly shown, the diversity of products known as Shakespeare is impossible to catalogue or analyse. Most of its exemplars lack what he calls the 'hermeneutic density' that would allow their persuasive analysis in literary critical terms or for their existence to be corralled into clearly differentiated categories of high and low culture or progressive and reactionary political interventions. Burt recognizes that they constitute a self-reinforcing cycle of products but, by identifying them as unitary commoditized products, he has no recourse to the idea of a value that might extend beyond them. He ignores the extensive intellectual, creative and technical work involved in creating a mediatized Shakespeare production and the value added by its hundreds or thousands or millions of viewers and instead identifies value purely in terms of the content and marketing. This allows him to offer the defiantly iconoclastic account of Shakespeare production as a process where 'there is trash Shakespeare and there is trash Shakespeare that attempts to distinguish itself from trash Shakespeare'.[19]

Like the strand of twentieth-century *Kulturkritik* that identified the mass market as a conspiracy against gullible consumers, Burt is able to dismiss the value that is repeatedly accorded to Shakespeare as mere delusion, a failure to see clearly the relentless logic of the market behind even the most valued individual product. The market in Shakespeare products undoubtedly exists but part of its process is to return value to non-rival Shakespeare by extending the range of values that can be associated with it. Those values include the representation of Shakespeare as accessible and ethically complex but even the trashiest of Burt's examples, such as the pornographic films, reinforce the value of non-rival Shakespeare as the source of the pleasures of iconoclasm.

It is important to distinguish these individual commercial forms from the non-rival Shakespeare that is the source and the recipient of their cultural value. This 'non-rival' Shakespeare exists in the public domain outside of particular markets and is constituted in a set of familiar narratives and quotations as well as a set of commonplace ideas about love and power. It is itself the product of centuries of cultural work that has not only kept Shakespeare's texts materially available in cheap print and theatrical traditions but also ensured that his plays were glossed, edited and rendered interpretable, the locus for the intellectual contest that could inform the innovation and adaptation that has made non-rival Shakespeare powerfully sustainable within the arts economy. However, the value of non-rival Shakespeare, which is different from the historical Shakespeare, is that it comprises only those ethical and aesthetic concepts that can be used as eloquent analogies for contemporary social preoccupations, as guarantor of their universality and their connection to the past.

In her critique of the banality of the 'Shakespeare' used to structure management training programmes, for example, Mary Polito observed that the trainers 'are entirely free to read for and utilize

---

[18] Extensive competition, of course, also exists among those libraries to digitize their holdings and to drive traffic to their sites accordingly.

[19] Richard Burt, ed., *Shakespeares after Shakespeare: An Encyclopedia of the Bard in Mass Media and Popular Culture* (Basingstoke, 2002), p. 10.

the affective potential of the plays and Shakespeare's name as a guarantor of value and ethics. There is no mechanism by which they are compelled to consider the critical tradition of the plays.'[20]

The trainers' 'freedom', of course, comes from the material fact that non-rival Shakespeare is out of copyright and therefore poses no initial costs on the value chain from non-rival Shakespeare to the expensive training event. Non-rival Shakespeare also offers a discursive freedom in which ideas and speeches created for a particular historical purpose have been opened out into meaningful statements about their larger significance by precisely the critical traditions that no longer need to be acknowledged. The analytic and hermeneutic activity that Mary Polito champions as the antithesis of an instrumental deployment of Shakespeare is itself a competitor in the process of creating the value of 'non-rival Shakespeare'. However, its weak position in the intellectual marketplace and its unprotected intellectual property allows it to be absorbed as another free element within non-rival Shakespeare that does not have to be acknowledged.

Non-rival Shakespeare can be used both to endorse commercial products ('trash Shakespeare that attempts to distinguish itself from trash Shakespeare') and to make a claim for values that transcend the commercial. Writing on behalf of the Arts and Humanities Research Council, in defence of the value of the research that they fund, Jonathan Bate invoked the moment in *Troilus and Cressida* where Troilus and Hector debate the 'value' of Helen of Troy. Bate opened his essay with Troilus's famous line 'what's ought but as 'tis valued' and concludes his reading of the passage with:

The relativism of Troilus (things only have value in so far as they are valued by particular people who prize them) is replaced by the proposition that there can be essential values, that a thing might be intrinsically valuable ('precious of itself').[21]

Professor Bate himself is well aware that the historical Shakespeare's articulation of this opposition arose in a theatrical and historical context where ideas of transcendent value were under quite specific pressure from social, religious and material change, not least in the theatre itself. Information about the precise historical circumstances of the plays' production or their formal articulation and about the theatricalisation of the debate is irrelevant to its particular rhetorical purpose. The Shakespeare that is being invoked has already been subject to the fundamental critical processes of interpretation and glossing in order to make it available for its new purpose in the cultural economy of state funding for academic research.

This process of transformation and redeployment is fundamental to the circulation of Shakespeare in contemporary cultural markets. It involves a highly mediated relationship between the semi-processed material of non-rival Shakespeare and the particular market relations that draw on and reinforce it. Those mediations range from the simplest form of rhetorical analogy to the complex value-chain of mediatized production and it is those mediations rather than the content of the individual products that determine the terms in which Shakespeare functions in the contemporary cultural economy. They are, however, most effectively deployed by institutions that can bring both the commercial resources of the value chain and the institutional assets that will make the resulting new products stand out.

III

In the spring of 2008, the Royal Shakespeare Company launched a new initiative called 'Stand up for Shakespeare'. The initiative was the culmination of a project in which RSC Learning (the education wing of the RSC) worked with schools from the public sector to train teachers to deliver Shakespeare lessons in ways that were informed by contemporary theatre practice. Teachers who received RSC training were put in touch with

[20] Mary Polito, '"Warriors for the Working Day": Shakespeare's Professionals', *Shakespeare*, 2 (2006), p. 18.

[21] Jonathan Bate, *Public Value in the Humanities* (London, 2011), p. 5.

up to ten schools each and were charged with communicating their learning across the sector. The learning culminated in a 'Schools mini complete works Shakespeare festival' that allowed 2,300 children to participate in a week-long series of performances, managed entirely by the youngsters themselves.

The strap-lines for the new project – 'Do it on your feet'; 'See it live'; Start it earlier' – indicated the core values of the project. They were to make the experience of 'doing Shakespeare' more dynamic, accessible and, above all, pleasurable. It would involve active learning using physical techniques and was explicitly contrasted with a view of existing education practice that was alleged to be, in the words of *The Independent* newspaper, 'a byword for boredom'. The project polarized what was described as 'academic' Shakespeare, 'deskbound', 'rote learning' with active learning that engaged the students' enthusiasm and innate love of and admiration for Shakespeare.

The antithesis between RSC learning and academic learning was perhaps more insisted upon by the press reaction to the 'Stand up for Shakespeare' project than the RSC itself. However, it indicated the discursive competition that accompanies the launch of new products in the cultural arts market. It would have been merely pedantic for academics to protest that what Styan described in 1977 as 'the Shakespeare Revolution'[22] had already rooted performed-Shakespeare in academic practice or that academic criticism had engaged enthusiastically with the polymorphous variety of contemporary Shakespeare production. The knowledge produced by their carefully researched and theorized analysis of past events has been assimilated into non-rival Shakespeare that informed the live, young, physical experience, which united the classroom and the rehearsal room as places of experiment and creativity.

Paradoxically, it is precisely that antithesis with authoritative but past knowledge that has allowed RSC Learning to create such a powerful new Shakespeare product.

The discursive contrast between knowledge, experience and creativity had important material effects. The RSC project was financially supported both by the 'Creative Partnerships' initiative that funded artists to support teachers in schools and by the Higher Education Funding Council that had supported innovation in teaching by establishing ring-fenced funding for 'Centres of Excellence in Learning and Teaching' (CETL) in selected universities. These state agencies were motivated less by the commercial imperative to market a unitary product than by a sense of crisis in an education system that they felt was not delivering the social goods of innovation and critical thinking required by modern economies. Working with the RSC offered these agencies the opportunity to support new forms of learning that would marshal the creative practice of the rehearsal room used by the flagship national Shakespeare company to produce new cultural goods in support of the transmission of other forms of knowledge. It would also provide high value endorsement of a government initiative through its link with the status of the Royal Shakespeare Company brand.

This authoritative endorsement provided more than funding. It allowed the company to cross organizational barriers and to change the relationships that had existed between 'Shakespeare in Schools' and Shakespeare in performance. As the project has developed since 2008, RSC Learning has collaborated with the University of Warwick Institute of Education to offer credit-bearing continuing professional development awards for teachers and extended its programme with the so-called 'Shakespeare challenge' that offers an accredited international award for young people, in collaboration with Trinity Guildhall, an international examinations board offering qualifications in English language and the performing arts. These collaborations offer an elegant and effective balance between the intrinsic good of personal engagement with Shakespeare and the instrumental need to work within the authoritative structures of existing institutions to diversify the economic base of a publicly funded company.

---

[22] J. L. Styan, *The Shakespeare Revolution* (Cambridge, 1977).

These developments extend the educational work undertaken by many arts organizations but their scale and organizational innovation indicate a significant change of direction in the role of Shakespeare in the twenty-first century arts economy. The 'Shakespeare' offered in this form does not need to compete explicitly with the multiple other forms of Shakespeare offered in new adaptations or new technologized forms. It insists on the use of 'original language' as the founding principle of the education provided.[23] However, the 'original language' (taken from edited texts and often adapted and cut, as is commonplace in performance) is made part of the teachers' and pupils' experience, thus building their confidence and making Shakespeare their own.

The evaluation of the work of the Learning and Performance Network asked candidates how far they felt able 'to make their own informed interpretive choices' and 'relate the experiences of Shakespeare's characters to modern events and personal experience'.[24] The resources for teachers on the RSC Learning website provides teachers with learning exercises that encourage independent thinking untrammelled by any acknowledgement of critical traditions or the historical distance between the early modern period and today. Its Shakespeare is always new because it is created afresh in each new direct encounter, encouraged and facilitated by the conduits to learning provided by the RSC.

One of the respondents to the evaluation further admired the 'personalised' approach. 'Too much INSET [In Service Educational Training] requires teachers to shut up, sit still and listen − the worst approach for effective learning! This INSET felt tailored to our needs, we could negotiate, we felt trusted...High challenge/low threat − Inspirational!'

The response assumed the virtue and the value of a kind of learning that prioritized personal growth over the command of knowledge and, in common with much recent educational writing, accordingly emphasized pedagogy over curriculum. High cultural assets no longer needed special pleading for their value or the guidance of authorities to make them accessible. They could be engaged with through a direct connection between the learner's experience and the material itself. Where earlier generations of progressive educationalists, such as the establishment figures who contributed to the Newbolt report or the teachers involved with the influential 'Shakespeare in Schools' project initiated by Rex Gibson,[25] had to argue a case for the role of the arts in education or the active engagement of children in their own learning, the RSC project and the national organizations that support it can safely invoke a universalized Shakespeare and an idealized image of the creative child or young person as the founding principles of their project.

The synergy between an idealized Shakespeare and an idealized child, together with the boundless creative enthusiasm of the teachers involved, made a significant contribution to the powerful impact of the 'Stand up for Shakespeare' project. It embodied, and was described in terms of, all the utopian aspirations of a free space of cultural engagement untrammelled by hierarchy and outside of the market. This illusion could be effectively maintained because the learning involved was, like the National Health Service, 'free at the point of access'. Neither the children nor the teachers and mentors trained in the project paid directly for the privilege of participation. The entire project was funded by a mix of state and grant funding that removed the direct connection between the cultural product and the market in which it functioned.

This non-commodified Shakespeare project was accompanied by more directly marketed products such as the print-based book of resources for teachers which took its place in a suite of Shakespeare products that included the co-branded *Complete*

---

[23] See the curriculum requirements provided at www.rsc.org. uk/education/award/shakespeare-challenge.aspx.

[24] Extract from the University of Warwick 'Impact Evaluation of the LPN/PG Cert Programme', slide 4. I am grateful to Jacqui O'Hanlon, director of RSC Learning for sharing this evaluation report with me.

[25] Discussed in Kathleen McLuskie, 'Dancing and Thinking', in G. B. Shand, ed., *Teaching Shakespeare: Passing It On* (Oxford, 2009), pp. 121–41.

Works of Shakespeare edited by Jonathan Bate and Eric Rasmussen, published by Macmillan, and the co-produced BBC production of *Hamlet* that was aired on Christmas Day 2009 and sold on DVD. These individual products allowed the RSC to monetize its past productions and secured their growing intellectual property in the ideas that drive their work, while leaving non-rival Shakespeare in the free space of cultural engagement.

These complex business models of the RSC Learning projects illustrate most clearly the different roles of non-rival Shakespeare and commercial Shakespeare products in the mixed economy of the arts in the UK. In each of them there is a value chain that involves expensive and highly qualified staff creating new Shakespeare experiences, together with the venues in which they take place and the organizational efforts required to secure their success. Their dependence on state and trust funding, and the small margin between price and cost, make a nonsense of any notion of a commercial commodity based on buying cheap and selling dear in order to make a profit. Their value, as with all rival goods, depends on engagement in which the number of people associated with the product becomes an asset in itself, even when they do not always result in sales. Levels of engagement, that can be quantified, become the direct justification and product for funding and investment, giving a reality to the aspirations for democracy and access to the arts.

Nor does this activity in any way diminish the quantum of non-rival Shakespeare available to other providers. In spite of the RSC's energetic efforts to associate themselves with the highest quality delivery of 'Shakespeare', both in the theatre and in education, there can be no question of their ability to operate as an exclusive supplier of 'Shakespeare'. Their emphasis on the face-to-face experience of Shakespeare is driven partly by their artistic and ideological preferences but it is also designed to create a special relationship with their audiences that cannot be so effectively reproduced by other providers.

The role of engaged participants that informs the RSC's rhetoric of a free Shakespeare is a critical dimension of the relationships established by Shakespeare institutions and non-rival Shakespeare. Although it is highly mediated by the value chain that provides the potential for free access, the idea of 'free Shakespeare' depends upon immediate and direct engagement between Shakespeare and the individual that does not require the mediation of the critical tradition. For the RSC, that immediate access is provided by the physical engagement using rehearsal techniques, but it can also be claimed for other forms of free access, including those provided by new technologies. The British Library's 2009 funding campaign imagined new ways of using the vast resources of information and knowledge held in its historic collections. The Library aimed to raise £50m over five years to extend its digitization of collections which already offers one million pages of historical newspapers, 4,000 hours of archival sound recordings and 100,000 out of copyright nineteenth-century books. The campaign document included a set of imagined scenarios in which this knowledge might be used including 'Imagine if Schools could encounter Shakespeare in a new dimension'. The new dimension is not theatre but comprises the 'wealth of contextual materials . . . formerly the privilege of adult researchers' that would be made directly accessible to students and school children. These images of the quartos of Shakespeare are currently available on the 'Turning the pages' section of the British Library website which will eventually include copies of the quartos held in collections worldwide.[26] The implications are that the former 'privilege' of academic researchers who have acted as conduits and mediators of knowledge for students and children will be removed and the knowledge will be available free, within the Library, to anyone who seeks it.

As with other heritage products, this 'free engagement' comes at a cost. The digitization of the British Library's heritage assets will add value to them, not only in engaging considerably larger numbers of people, but in pioneering new

---

[26] See www.bl.uk/onlinegallery/ttp.

business models that significantly modify the commercial relations of buying and selling. Controversially, their project to digitize up to 40 million pages of historic newspapers has involved a collaboration with the media company, brightsolid, who have invested in the costs of digitization. The resulting images will be available free within the Library but brightsolid will also market them using micropayments for viewing individual pages.[27] Heritage materials whose conservation and accessibility was formerly a cost, making the material a declining asset, can now become a growing asset, not only through the value-added of additional engagement but in real financial terms.

The new financial and technical models for disseminating heritage goods indicate the fundamental change in their circulation in the twenty-first century. When the engaged consumer is the source of the assets' growth, the construction of non-rival goods that are not diminished by each individual engagement is critical. The engagement can be created equally by a mix of intense face-to-face live experience and the sense of immediate access produced by digital platforms. The complex value chains that produce that sense of immediacy is rendered invisible, and the nature of the content is less significant than the experience that it provides.

For example, in 2009–10 the Shakespeare Birthplace Trust commissioned a 'Dig for Shakespeare' in the grounds of New Place, Shakespeare's last home in Stratford upon Avon. Though none of the sponsors of the dig, least of all the archaeologists commissioned from Birmingham Archaeology,[28] expected to find any specific artefact associated directly with Shakespeare, the dig aroused significant media interest, produced an exponential increase in the number of volunteers working with the Trust and provided a new 'offering' with which to refresh the core business of the Shakespeare Birthplace Trust's care and conservation of the Shakespeare houses.

'Shakespeare' provided the overarching rationale for the event by virtue of having lived in New Place but the artefacts that were unearthed – including an eighteenth-century bottle, a coin from 1640, a seventeenth-century fob seal – offered a tangible if unspecific connection to a sense of a past. This 'past' could not be commodified in any direct way but the excitement of engaging with it produced over 9,000 hours of volunteer labour and a level of community involvement with the Birthplace Trust that increased its local and regional visibility.

Unlike the British Library or the Royal Shakespeare Company, the Shakespeare Birthplace Trust does not receive direct state funding,[29] so there was no institutionally driven pressure to engage with particular groups in the population. Like those other institutional holders of 'Shakespeare' material, however, the Trust's widening engagement was a fundamental element in a strategy to make Shakespeare and the Trust better known and to extend that engagement to the whole population and a wider international audience. The 'Dig for Shakespeare', like 'Stand up for Shakespeare' or the British Library's Shakespeare site, offered a focus with which to attract existing generalized knowledge of Shakespeare and to identify each of those organizations as the place where that knowledge could be turned into a meaningful personal experience. That experience might or might not be monetized through the purchase of a particular item for sale but the ratio of engagement to sales was indirect and each of them took place in different parts of the organization, both physically and organizationally. The engagement with Shakespeare was part of the total cultural economy of those organizations: it required resources, both monetary and human; it contributed to the organizations' total assets and it sustained the continuing authority and standing of Shakespeare that was critical to their continued existence.

---

27 www.brightsolid.com/news.
28 The archaeologists' interest was in excavating a site that had a long history, with good records, including the records of the 1860 dig initiated by Halliwell-Phillips. Their findings about the structure of New Place and the artefacts that they did identify will add to the deep mapping of the material environment of the region.
29 It is, however, eligible for 'gift aid' which transfers 25 per cent from the tax revenues of all UK ticket buyers to the Trust.

The 'Shakespeare' involved was, as in all production, complexly and expensively mediated from the non-rival Shakespeare of interpretation and scholarship and bore an even more tenuous relation to the Shakespeare of early performances that have left not a rack behind. The version of Shakespeare in these cultural institutions, however, cannot be easily corralled either into the category of 'trash Shakespeare that attempts to distinguish itself from Shakespeare', the product of 'commodification', or into the fantasy of the transformative power of great art.

The deep suspicion of the instrumental effects of commerce that permeates critiques of the role of commercial sponsorship in the arts[30] continues to locate culture and the arts at the far end of a spectrum that separates intrinsic, unquantifiable and inalienable value at one end and instrumental profit-seeking, valuable only in financial terms, at the other. This polarization in value informs much of the discussion of Shakespeare's reproduction even when the polarities are stated in terms of further distinctions between 'mass' and 'popular' culture or celebrate (often through gritted teeth) the dispersal of high culture through the creative appropriation of Shakespeare in new artistic forms. At this stage in the twenty-first century, however, the complex structure and scale of the cultural economy calls those polarities into question. The worldwide ubiquity of Shakespeare in education, the overproduction of Shakespeare-referenced material and the now routine iconoclasm and parody that attends reproduction of his work makes any notion of a unitary commodified 'iconic' figure no more than a rhetorical gesture. Moreover, claims that align Shakespeare with other items in the cultural economy, however desirable or socially productive, must be seen as part of the same process of mediation that drives all reproduction of heritage goods.

The assimilation of Shakespeare and the valued arts of the past into the cultural logic of late capitalism requires a more complex account of competing values than the simple opposition between culture and commerce, or the more or less cynical or defiant rejection of one in favour of the other. It involves instead acknowledging the competing and contradictory drivers within the economy itself, when the business models include philanthropic and state sponsorship as well as direct sales, and the Shakespeare on offer may include forms of social engagement or creative innovation that both enhance the brand status or customer base of particular organizations and provide the opportunity for personal and individual pleasure that can be, but need not be, traded in the cultural market. These possibilities do require the affluent and secure markets and institutions of the early part of the twenty-first century that have provided the leisure, the surpluses and the trained personnel that assure the diverse contemporary market for Shakespeare. It is far from clear that they will continue in this form as the financial pressure on state and philanthropic resources reduces the funds available. However, the connection between non-rival Shakespeare and its creative engagement with an ever-expanding consumer base will dominate the process in spite of the reservations of those who hold on to the distinction between culture and commerce or insist on the primacy of the historical Shakespeare known only to those who study or research in academic institutions.

---

[30] See, for example, Chin Tao Wu, 'Embracing the Enterprise Culture: Art Institutions since the 1980s', *New Left Review*, 230 (1998), 28–57.

INTERNATIONAL INNOVATION? SHAKESPEARE AS INTERCULTURAL CATALYST

EMILY LINNEMANN

English publicly funded theatre in the twenty-first century, in which Shakespeare plays a considerable role, is becoming increasingly focused on the processes and products of innovation. The term 'innovation' has developed into something of a buzzword amongst cultural economists, policy-makers and practitioners.[1] Yet, notwithstanding the proliferation of cultural policy and think-tank documents discussing its merits, it is not always clear what form such innovation should take or even what constitutes innovation in the first place. In aesthetic terms innovation is not the same as 'novelty for its own sake'.[2] Instead, as defined by the *OED*, it is 'the alteration of what is established by the introduction of new elements or forms'. Idealized cultural innovation within publicly funded theatre thus operates as an alteration of established modes of production and the subsequent reinvigoration of resulting products. This understanding of innovation – as opposed to the alternative 'introduction of novelties' – is what permeates the policy work of John Holden (researcher for think-tank Demos), Brian McMaster (former artistic director of the Edinburgh Festival) and Arts Council England (the arms-length funding body for the arts). The process of innovation is assumed to be radical and risky, but, most importantly, value-generative.[3] It is thus part of an idealized process of production which ensures both aesthetic excellence and cultural value creation.

Cultural economists remind us that innovation is not the same thing as variety or diversity of work.[4] If a theatre simply produces a multitude of plays by different playwrights they are not necessarily

innovating. However, if the Royal Shakespeare Company only produces plays by Shakespeare but constantly reworks and redevelops the form and presentation of those plays it has the potential to be innovative. Innovation can thus occur within the performance of an established cultural product:

Few fans at a Rolling Stones concert want to see the Stones take an entirely new musical direction; most come to hear old favourites and relive youthful memories ... At the same time, the production technology and skill required to reproduce a simulacrum of a recorded disc in a live setting – or the character of earlier performances – is considerable, and may be regarded as innovative.[5]

In this sense, cultural innovation does not necessarily need to produce an entirely new product but it does need to embrace new technologies and new

The research for this essay was made possible through the support of the Arts and Humanities Research Council, UK.

1 Brian McMaster, *Supporting Excellence in the Arts: From Measurement to Judgement* (London, 2008); Arts Council England, *Great Art for Everyone* (London, 2008); Kate Oakley, Brooke Sperry and Andy Pratt, *The Art of Innovation: How Fine Art Graduates Contribute to Innovation*, ed. Hasan Bakhshi (London, 2008); David Throsby and Hasan Bakhshi, *Culture of Innovation: An Economic Analysis of Innovation in Arts and Cultural Organisations* (London, 2010).
2 Oakley, Sperry and Pratt, *Art of Innovation*, p. 26.
3 Maria Crealey, 'Applying New Product Development Models to the Performing Arts: Strategies for Managing Risk', *International Journal of Arts Management*, 5 (2003), 24–33.
4 Xavier Castañer and Lorenzo Campos, 'The Determination of Artistic Innovation: Bringing in the Role of Organizations', *Journal of Cultural Economics*, 26 (2002), 29–52.
5 Oakley, Sperry and Pratt, *Art of Innovation*, p. 26.

working methods in order to rework and redefine the modes of cultural production.

In its manifesto, *Great Art for Everyone*, Arts Council England suggests that, in the early twenty-first century, at least some innovation in publicly funded culture will come from working internationally and interculturally.[6] Their commitment to 'make sure [their] funding and processes challenge arts organizations to even greater ambition, whether they are working in traditional ways or discovering new ones', by encouraging 'greater exposure to international work and international influence', further emphasizes the perceived link between interculturalism and innovation.[7] The suggestion that intercultural work can help twenty-first-century arts organizations to innovate opens up an interesting realm of enquiry. Can Shakespeare operate as a catalyst or platform for intercultural innovation? If so, what effect does the reaction between the intercultural and the innovative have on the Shakespeare that is its vehicle?

Bonnie Marranca's critical definition of theatrical interculturalism provides a useful starting point for such an enquiry:

interculturalism... orients itself around the notion of 'people's theatre', in reaction to Western theatre convention and the more formalist, literary impulses of modernism. Generally this theatre demonstrates a less formal separation of performer and audience, independence from the dramatic text of a single author and disinterest in the work of an aesthetic object to be viewed.[8]

Marranca's identification of interculturalism as an antidote to Western theatrical convention demonstrates that activities labelled 'intercultural' may have less to do with an interaction between cultures and more to do with one culture providing a contrast and relief from another. Her recognition that intercultural theatre tends to flout Western conventions by breaking down the barrier between performer and spectator and by removing authorial voice from performance situates the interculturalism she is critiquing in the discourse of primitivism.

It is here that I begin to disagree with Marranca's assessment. She sees in interculturalism a break away from modernist impulses and a disinterest in aesthetics. I would argue that in fact, because of its primitivism and exoticism, intercultural endeavour tends to do the very opposite. As the case studies detailed below demonstrate, interculturalism is deeply embedded in and indebted to modernist ideals of consensual artistic realms, the 'complete' and authentic work of art and the ability of culture to reconnect the pieces of an increasingly fragmented society.

Underpinning this connection to modernism is an idealization of cultural authenticity. 'Authenticity' is a constructed and idealized cultural value. In the context of this discussion, the term is intended to relate not to an idea of an authentic Shakespeare but to an idealized cultural experience which is imagined to be more real and more connected to some form of inherent humanity. It is this idealized authenticity, linked to an essentialized concept of humanity, which Antonin Artaud imagines exists in Balinese theatre and which Theodor Adorno fears is lost when cultural goods become commodified.[9] This idea of authenticity is connected to a cultural product's perceived spontaneity and non-commerciality. It is, as Erik Cohen argues, 'a socially constructed concept' which is predicated on an over-generalized notion of itself as 'a quality of pre-modern life, and of cultural products produced prior to the penetration of modern Western influences'.[10] It is from this privileging of the 'pre-modern' as the site of authenticity that the connection with spontaneity and non-commerciality grows. Each of these idealized elements is mutually reaffirming. Spontaneity implies that an event

---

[6] *Great Art*, pp. 18–9.

[7] Arts Council England, *Theatre Assessment 2009* (London, 2009), p. 5.

[8] 'Thinking through Interculturalism', in Bonnie Marranca and Gautam Dasgupta, eds., *Interculturalism and Performance: Writings from PAJ* (New York, 1991), p. 14.

[9] Antonin Artaud, *The Theatre and its Double*, trans. by Victor Corti (London, 1970); Theodor Adorno, *The Culture Industry: Selected Essays on Mass Culture*, ed. J. M. Bernstein (London, 2001).

[10] 'Authenticity and Commoditization in Tourism', *Annals of Tourism Research*, 15 (1988), 371–86; pp. 374–5.

is unplanned. This explains its non-commercial nature since there is no infrastructure created in order to receive payment. The lack of commerciality itself becomes a precipitant of authenticity because an unplanned, unpaid-for event seems to avoid the apparently alienating process of monetary exchange, as elucidated by Dennis Kennedy in his analysis of cultural tourism.[11] Erik Cohen, however, questions the constructed and idealized nature of authenticity and suggests that commercialism can actually rescue cultures and cultural goods which would otherwise become obsolete and allow those cultures and goods to accrue new meanings. Equally, he argues that authenticity is a subjective rather than an objective value which can emerge from apparently 'inauthentic' experiences. Thus, although the concepts of authenticity and inauthenticity may seem to lie at opposing ends of a cultural value axis, that axis remains as a link between them. They are at once antithetical and mutually reaffirming.

Binaries or cultural tensions – such as those between authenticity and inauthenticity or commercial and non-commercial – circulate around the production of Shakespeare. They may be theoretically, and even ethically, unfashionable but they can be used in order to produce cultural value and innovation. Contradictions can be productive if they are seen as part of a mutually reaffirming relationship that can promote dialecticism, debate and negotiation. If, as Derrida suggests, we reconsider the oppositions on which our understanding of culture is founded we can start to see authenticity as 'the *différance* of the other' – in this case inauthenticity – 'as the other different and deferred in the economy of the same'.[12] Cultural binaries and tensions thus become, to invert Douglas Lanier's phrase, not just distinctions but links.[13] Within the theatre they create a dialectical space where 'inconsistent and contradictory attitudes can exist without synthesis' and audiences can be presented not with 'solutions, but knots'.[14]

Yet, although the relationship between authenticity and commoditization is nuanced and complex, it continues to be presented in the theatre as a simple binary. This is because entrenched and

constructed cultural values continue to inform the aesthetics of Shakespearian performance. It is the simplified tension between the local and the global or 'our local' and 'another's local' which dominates intercultural performances of Shakespeare. As Sonia Massai notes, these tensions are often part of a false dichotomy that reaffirms long-held values. However, despite generating what she describes as a 'critical impasse', the tension between local and global continues to influence the intercultural performance of Shakespeare's plays.[15] This is because working internationally encourages the exposure of contrasts between different cultures. It is only when these contrasts are dealt with as part of a dialectic rather than a dichotomy that value will be created. Some productions' relationships to the idea of local and global are more nuanced than others but, however they are presented, a drive towards innovation underpins them. If we think specifically about Shakespeare we can begin to understand how the idea of aesthetic innovation might become linked to internationalization and interculturalism.

Baxter Theatre's *Tempest* (2009) provides one example of the complex and sometimes fraught relationship between innovation and interculturalism. This production used the long-established connection between *The Tempest* and post-colonialism to make a political and social statement about the ending of apartheid in South Africa. Antony Sher played the white, colonialist Prospero who used magic to control the spirits and the people of the land he inhabited. Casting John Kani, an

---

[11] Dennis Kennedy, 'Shakespeare and Cultural Tourism', *Theatre Journal*, 50 (1998), 175–88.

[12] Jacques Derrida, *Margins of Philosophy*, trans. by Alan Bass (Hemel Hempstead, 1982), p. 17.

[13] Douglas Lanier, *Shakespeare and Modern Popular Culture* (Oxford, 2002), p. 3.

[14] Stephen Purcell, *Popular Shakespeare: Simulation and Subversion on the Modern Stage* (Basingstoke, 2009), p. 36; Eugenio Barba, *The Paper Canoe: A Guide to Theatre Anthropology*, trans. by Richard Fowler (London, 1995), p. 96.

[15] 'Defining Local Shakespeares', in Sonia Massai, ed., *Worldwide Shakespeares: Local Appropriations in Film and Performance* (London, 2005), p. 5.

actor widely known for his part in the cultural fight against apartheid, as Caliban made this approach, in places, both 'urgent (and poignant)'.[16] The impression of Prospero's dominance and manipulation of Caliban was further underlined by his exploitation of Ariel's powers. Ariel, in this production, was played by John Kani's son Atandwa.

This production had the potential to create a powerful *Tempest* that was politically and geographically specific and that could serve as an 'act of remembering', even as an exercise in reconciliation.[17] Yet, Honeyman's production frequently sentimentalized and generalized the 'Africa' in which it took place. Aesthetic effect was drawn from pan-African sources: the spirits which inhabited the isle and performed the wedding masque for Miranda and Ferdinand were transformed into brightly coloured puppets and the eponymous tempest was 'accomplished with the aid of a vast, slithering serpent which, in Zulu cosmology, embodies the force of nature'.[18] The tale of Ariel's imprisonment was performed to the audience, with Sycorax constructed as breasts, eyes and hands using giant puppets. To some extent, this could be seen as innovative, making 'this all-too-familiar play' unfamiliar.[19] However, it has also been described as representing 'the exhaustion of *The Tempest* as a vehicle' for post-colonial discourse and criticized for its presentation of a Disneyfied, exoticized version of 'Africa'.[20]

The internationalizing of Shakespeare is thus a paradoxical process. It focuses on providing innovative ways of staging and producing theatre but in order to perform this innovation it looks to the past and draws from the aesthetics of primitivist exoticism. Intercultural Shakespeare tends to innovate through tradition. *Macbeth*, directed by Grzegorz Bral and performed by his company Teatr Pieśń Kozła at the RSC's Complete Works Festival, provides an interesting example of this form of traditional innovation and elucidates further the use of 'authentic' theatricality and primitivism in twenty-first-century performance.

Teatr Pieśń Kozła's work has been described by theatre critic Mark Brown as sitting on the 'cusp between ancient ritual and theatrical

modernism'.[21] The metaphor of the 'cusp' binds together ancient ritual and theatrical modernism. It raises productive questions about the concepts of and relationship between 'ancient' and 'modern'. It asks us to consider how the seeming antitheses of the ancient and the modern are connected and suggests that ritual can tip over the cusp and become part of theatrical modernism. More specifically, in the case of Pieśń Kozła's *Macbeth*, the metaphor of the 'cusp' demands an examination of the role Shakespeare plays in negotiating between the ancient and the modern. It is the blending of these two disparate, tense elements which is paradigmatic of intercultural Shakespeare productions.

In Teatr Pieśń Kozła's work-in-progress, scenes from *Macbeth* were presented to the audience and intercut with short talks from the company's director, Grzegorz Bral. He identified his desire to create 'authentic' theatre as the overarching motivation for the production. In order to achieve authenticity he pared the script down to a small number of scenes, presented out of chronological sequence and without context. Every scene was accompanied by the background hum of polyphonic singing, lending the performance an eerie and esoteric quality. The songs themselves were based on those of an isolated Siberian village – dubbed the

[16] Carol Chillington Rutter, 'Shakespeare Performances in England 2009', in *Shakespeare Survey 63* (Cambridge, 2010), p. 356.

[17] Rutter, 'Shakespeare Performances', p. 356.

[18] Michael Billington, 'Myths and Metaphors Create Stunning African Tempest', *Guardian*, 19 February 2009, p. 38.

[19] Billington, 'Myths and Metaphors', p. 38.

[20] Anton Bosman, 'Cape of Storms: The Baxter Theatre Centre–RSC *Tempest* 2009', *Shakespeare Quarterly* 61 (2010), 108–17; pp. 109–10. See also, Rutter, 'Shakespeare Performances', p. 358, and Philip Holyman, 'The Tempest', *Whatsonstage.com*, 19 February 2009, www.whatsonstage.com/reviews/theatre/london/E8831235038970/The+Tempest+%28RSC%29.html (accessed 14 November 2010).

[21] Mark Brown, 'Grotowski in the 21st Century Theatre: Teatr Piesn Kozla (Song of the Goat Theatre), Wroclaw, Poland', *Critical Stages: The Webjournal of IATC*, 1 (2009), www.criticalstages.org/criticalstages/146?category=36, accessed 14 June 2010.

'Siberian Atlantis' – whose culture was nearly lost after serious flooding wiped out the population. Bral and his company had visited the village in order to save the cultural memories and reproduce them in their own work.

The key elements of this production were its status as work-in-progress, its absence of narrative, its emphasis on the non-verbal and its celebration of lost communities. It is in these elements that we can see the drive – successful or not – towards innovation. By flagging the production as a work-in-progress, Teatr Pieśń Kozła brought the creative process to the forefront of the theatre. Aesthetically it suggested that the piece was malleable and shifting. There was a sense that the actors and the audience were sharing the creative space within the theatre and taking part in the twenty-first-century process of 'co-creation'.[22] The work-in-progress nature of the production precipitated the performance's displacement of narrative. The scenes which the company performed were in non-chronological order and represented a series of symbolic and allegorical moments. Scenes were titled 'crown' or 'cauldron' and the company used the images of these objects in order to present the audience with polyphonic singing blended with a minimal amount of Shakespearian dialogue. *Macbeth* had been mined for its symbolism and metaphors rather than its narrative content. In Teatr Pieśń Kozła's case making Shakespeare innovative relied on a process whereby his plays are dismantled and reconstructed as a different, more abstract kind of cultural object.

This different cultural object, this Shakespeare 'different and deferred', resists the kind of co-creation which the production's status as work-in-progress tries to encourage. Instead of championing accessible theatre, Bral is keen to distance Pieśń Kozła from the easy-to-interpret and the banal. He relies on his audiences' abilities to unpick the symbolism of his productions: 'if you are intelligent enough or sensitive enough, you know what we are talking about'.[23] Pieśń Kozła's *Macbeth* operated in relation to its audience's cultural capital and hence ability to decode the play. Thus, the seemingly communal and inclusive nature of the

work-in-progress was disrupted by a simultaneous modernist elitism which denied the audience narrative satisfaction and, potentially, understanding. The work-in-progress, artisanal nature of the piece evokes Pieśń Kozła's link back to 'ancient' cultural forms, whilst their denial of easy accessibility aligns them with modernist sensibilities. The push for innovation which is evident in Pieśń Kozła's *Macbeth* was interrupted by the inability to reconcile these two elements of the production.

In order to make Shakespeare 'new', Bral blended his work with the Siberian 'old'. This was done not only to innovate but also to create an authentic performance, to innovate through authenticity. By blending Shakespeare's plays with the nearly lost songs of the Siberian Atlantis, Bral hoped to produce a play which could lay greater claim to authenticity than the work of a company that simply reproduced the Shakespearian text. Importantly, Bral was not trying to produce an authentic Shakespearian performance but rather an authentic theatrical experience. He was trying to create a production which was more than a play on a stage; a production which not only remade Shakespeare but remade the idea of performativity. In order to reinvigorate the theatrical cultural offer, Bral searched for solutions in ancient culture and ritual. Shakespeare was employed as a vehicle which allowed ancient Siberian culture to mix with modernist theatrical techniques.

Intercultural endeavour in general is governed by the tension between innovation and tradition and Shakespeare provides a potential mediator for this kind of cultural production. What is problematic about Bral's production is that in its quest for innovation and cultural authenticity it has lost sight of theatre's ability to entertain and to communicate a story to its audience. Further, the innovation which

---

22 C. K. Prahalad and Venkat Ramaswamy, 'Co-Creation Experiences: The Next Practice in Value Creation', *Journal of Interactive Marketing*, 18 (2004), 5–14.

23 Bral quoted in Mark Brown, 'Poetry in Motion', *New Statesman*, 2 August 2007, www.newstatesman.com/arts-and-culture/2007/08/goat-theatre-poland-song, accessed 16 June 2010.

Bral seems to have achieved in the privileging of metaphor and the blend of new and old culture is actually part of a long tradition. Using Shakespeare as the conceptual space in which the ancient and modern coalesce is a common paradigm of inter-cultural performance. The link between intercul-turalism and innovation is always one of paradox in which old cultural forms are used to create new cultural objects.

At its root, this treatment of the intercultural is linked to a primitivist reading of the 'other'. The 'lost' Siberian songs of *Macbeth* presented the audi-ence with a certain image of the originating cul-ture. Instead of focusing on highly sophisticated, complex cultural forms Bral had chosen to show-case what he read as 'simpler' folk culture. What is really intriguing about Bral's use of a primitive intercultural aesthetic to innovate Shakespearian performance is that it strives to make theatre more than valuable: to make it necessary. Peter Brook, one of intercultural theatre's most influential pro-ponents explains what he sees as the 'fundamental problem' of Western theatre:

How to make theatre absolutely and fundamentally *nec-essary* to people, as necessary as eating and sex? I mean a theatre which isn't a watered-down appendage or cul-tural decoration to life. I mean something that's a simple organic necessity – as theatre used to be and still is in certain societies. Make-believe is *necessity*. It's this qual-ity, lost to Western industrialized societies, I'm searching for.[24]

The contrast Brook creates here is clear. West-ern industrialized societies may create theatre which is beautiful, entertaining and even thought-provoking. What they are not doing – but what they should be doing according to Brook – is creating theatre which forms a necessary part of human existence. In trying to create theatre which meets this remit, theatre directors are simultane-ously asserting their belief in the value of culture and in their role as producers of it. Brook searched for necessary theatre in Africa whilst Bral believes he has found it in the lost songs of Siberia.

It should be evident from the quotation of Brook that Bral's *Macbeth* was not engaging with the intercultural in what could accurately be termed an innovative way. There were moments of the per-formance which had the potential to rework and reinvigorate Shakespeare. However, the mixture of primitivism and attempted innovation which char-acterized *Macbeth* is paradigmatic of a long-running encounter between Shakespeare and the cultural 'other'. This encounter, like that between intercul-turalism and innovation, is a paradoxical one. The twentieth-century development of this paradox can be illuminated by thinking of it as originating in a link between primitivism and avant-gardism.

According to Christopher Innes, whilst avant-gardism is seemingly forward-thinking it is char-acterized not by 'overtly modernist qualities' but 'primitivism'.[25] While avant-garde theatre was in the vanguard of twentieth-century cultural move-ments it was simultaneously beating a retreat into the past. Avant-garde theatre thus presents a prac-tical example of the way in which a negotia-tion between cultural value tensions – in this case 'new' and 'old' – can be a catalyst for cre-ativity. The cultural objects created through the avant-garde movement were prompted into being through a co-operation between ancient and mod-ern, new and old. This is, to some extent, to idealize the products of primitivism and to efface the problematic nature of that movement. How-ever, what I want to emphasize here is that, in spite of ethical problems, this kind of primitivism endures in twenty-first-century theatre and con-tinues to influence intercultural productions of Shakespeare.

Modernism, like avant-gardism, sought to find new ways to make art and to make art rele-vant to a modern society. Modernists saw art as the vehicle by which an increasingly fragmented society could be reunited and with which they could make sense of the commercial and alienated culture in which they lived. This drive towards a consensual, non-commercial, cultural utopia

---

24 Brook quoted in John Heilpern, *Conference of the Birds: The Story of Peter Brook in Africa* (Harmondsworth, 1977), p. 24.
25 Christopher Innes, *Avant Garde Theatre 1892–1992* (London, 1993), pp. 3, 8.

coalesced with a reading of primitive societies as authentic, communal and non-alienated. These idealized primitives offered a solution to modern 'problems' such as capitalism, commercialism and mass culture and, thus, a way to reach an idealized, modernist utopia. Modernism's connection between the primitive and the utopian – what I call utopian primitivism – informed cultural production, cultural critique and cultural valuation. According to Richard Halpern, it also informed modernism's reading of Shakespeare.[26]

As Halpern reminds us, the connection between Shakespeare and the primitive is frequently drawn in the work of modernists including T. S. Eliot, Wyndham Lewis, Lytton Strachey and Antonin Artaud. Eliot, for example, sees in Shakespeare's work a more refined expression of the primitive desire to beat a drum and create music: 'the next generation or civilization will find a more plausible reason for beating a drum. Shakespeare . . . found his own reason.' Comparing Shakespeare's version of drum beating with that of the twentieth century, Eliot evokes a sense of dispossession: 'we still have similar reasons but we have lost the drum'.[27] According to Eliot something is missing from twentieth-century culture and although the desire to beat a drum remains, the instruments with which to do it have been lost. Shakespeare provides a connection back to this disappearing cultural impetus. The solution to Eliot's sense of loss in his own community is to seek for the lost object in the communities of others. The culture of these 'other' communities leads him to end his poem of fragmentation and dissolution with the repetition of the word 'shantih shantih shantih'[28] and to imagine Shakespeare as the last, primitive, beater of the drum. Halpern contends that this reading continued to inform the cultural mediation of Shakespeare throughout the twentieth century.[29] Orson Welles's *Macbeth*, Peter Brook's *A Midsummer Night's Dream* or Ariane Mnouchkine's *King Lear* all constitute examples of this kind of mediation. Artaud's preoccupation with Balinese theatre and his belief that it could reinvigorate Western theatre is equally motivated by a utopian primitivist reading of other cultures. The treatment of

the encounter between interculturalism and Shakespeare in publicly funded theatre today – as evidenced by Pieśń Kozła's *Macbeth* – shows that utopian primitivism continues to be influential and informative in the production and dissemination of Shakespeare.

By the 1960s, the kind of intercultural dramatic work that Artaud endorses in *The Theatre and Its Double* had become widespread. It was prevalent enough in 1965 for M. C. Bradbrook to feel that before she could begin her address to the British Academy, she must dispel certain misunderstandings that may have arisen from her choice of the title *Shakespeare's Primitive Art*: 'today Bali rather than Athens supplies dramatic models, and the cult of the primitive theatre is so strong that it may have been suspected that I come to praise Shakespeare as a barbaric contemporary, after the fashion of Jan Kott – to enrol him in the theatre of cruelty'.[30]

Here, Bradbrook underlines the paradoxical connection between Shakespeare as primitive barbarian and Shakespeare as modern contemporary. The notion that Shakespeare becomes our contemporary through a connection to primitive theatre neatly embodies the paradox of utopian primitivization; reminding us that cultural innovation is frequently imagined to emerge from the action of looking back and searching into the cultural past. What is crucial about Bradbrook's recognition of the phenomenon is that it identifies an aesthetic thread running through the first half of the twentieth century.

This thread can be seen in Eugenio Barba's theatre anthropology, Ariane Mnouchkine's Théâtre du Soleil, Jerzy Grotowski's Poor Theatre and Richard Schechner's continued interest in the

---

[26] Richard Halpern, *Shakespeare Among the Moderns* (Ithaca, 1997), p. 16.

[27] T. S. Eliot, 'The Beating of a Drum', *Nation and Athenaeum*, 6 October 1923, pp. 11–12, as cited in Halpern, p. 16.

[28] T. S. Eliot, 'The Waste Land' in *The Waste Land, Prufrock and Other Poems* (Mineola, 1998), line 434.

[29] Halpern, *Among the Moderns*, p. 16.

[30] M. C. Bradbrook, *Shakespeare's Primitive Art*, Annual Shakespeare Lecture of the British Academy, 1965.

future of ritual.[31] Each of these directors' aesthetics has grown out of the avant-garde movement and the connection between utopian primitive interculturalism and innovation. Richard Schechner's preoccupation with ritual and ritualized theatre leads him to connect Shakespeare to other kinds of cultural performance: 'what is true of Shakespeare or clowning is also true of the Mass, an initiation rite of Australian aborigines, a Hindu puja, or a World Cup soccer match' (p. 230). Schechner's utopian primitivism is thus more nuanced than Brook's. He recognizes the inherent performativity of ritual and its unavoidably inauthentic nature. He sees the connection between Shakespeare and a puja but simultaneously aligns this sacred event with a World Cup football match. He is not idealizing the Hindu puja but is universalizing and essentializing the kind of human response it engenders.

It is this reading of the puja and of Shakespeare which lays Schechner's utopian primitivism open to criticism. Rustom Bharucha is a particularly vocal critic of his work and argues that 'our history is apparently of no concern to Euro-American interculturalists. It is our "tradition", our much glorified "past", to which they have turned to find revelations.'[32] What Bharucha is highlighting and what is evident in recent intercultural Shakespeare productions is that 'other' cultures presented to the English public are often merely gestured towards and generalized. The attempt to bring 'primitive' ritual and tradition into Western theatre often leads to a misrepresentation of both ritual practices and traditional performance, creating an unsatisfactory hybrid of diluted theatricalized ritual and Western performance conventions.

It is critiques like Bharucha's that have led, in the twenty-first century, to a move away from the discourse of interculturalism in the academy. The shifting treatment of this discourse can be mapped in *New Theatre Quarterly*. While articles published in the first six years of the journal are characterized by an admiration for Brook and his contemporaries, the tone begins to change in the last decade of the twentieth century. Rather than regarding Brook's work as groundbreaking, articles written in the 1990s and beyond tend to consider his work as a new form of colonialism. For some, Brook becomes anathema: 'I am not', says R. G. Davis, 'advocating what Peter Brook does which is to visit the native and revamp their culture in the frame of the Great Western European tradition, ripping off multitudes in his wake.'[33] John Russell Brown evokes a similar image when he argues against the 'theatrical pillage' of Asia.[34]

In a more complex analysis of interculturalism, Rustom Bharucha criticizes not only the colonizing propensities of Western theatre directors but also the collusion between intercultural events and the market when he states that 'a more nuanced position on the intercultural scenario would move beyond the strictures of domination to highlight the series of complicities between systems of power, which are ultimately determined by the state and increasingly by the market'.[35] Crucially, Bharucha refuses to criticize only the West as an exploiter of Eastern culture. Instead, he argues, it is the global economic opportunities afforded by intercultural endeavour that result in the exploitation and de-authenticization of localized cultures. Decontextualized 'folk' culture sells both in the West and – through tourism – in the countries from which it originates. Ironically, the marketability which Bharucha sees as the impetus for interculturalism undermines the idealization of the primitive as a realm where exchange value is disregarded. What Bharucha demonstrates

---

[31] See Barba, *The Paper Canoe*; Jerzy Grotowski, *Towards a Poor Theatre*, ed. Eugenio Barba (London, 1968); Richard Schechner, *The Future of Ritual: Writings on Culture and Performance* (London, 1993).

[32] *Theatre and the World: The Performance and Politics of Culture* (London, 1993), p. 4.

[33] 'Deep Culture: Thoughts on Third-World Theatre', *New Theatre Quarterly*, 6 (1990), 335–42; p. 338.

[34] John Russell Brown, 'Theatrical Pillage in Asia: Redirecting the Intercultural Traffic', *New Theatre Quarterly*, 14 (1998), 9–19.

[35] 'Under the Sign of the Onion: Intracultural Negotiations in Theatre', *New Theatre Quarterly*, 12 (1996), 116–29; p. 117.

is the lack of synergy between the ideal and the reality.

My own critique of utopian primitivism is inflected differently from the post-colonial approach and has to do with the potential it offers for cultural value creation and innovation. Intercultural endeavour is one of the ways that publicly funded theatres try to create innovative work from established cultural products. However, because of the kind of primitivist interculturalism that becomes connected to Shakespeare, it is not always innovation which arises from intercultural production. This is not only because utopian primitivist Shakespeare forms part of a long aesthetic tradition. It is also because, frequently, the lack of aesthetic innovation is mirrored in a lack of cultural value creation.

Innovation and interculturalism operate as part of a paradoxical, interconnected relationship. Utopian primitivism looks back to the past in order to innovate the culture of the present. In this sense, then, it embodies the kind of tension negotiation already identified as value-generative and potentially innovative. The problem with the utopian primitivist aesthetic is that, despite being defined by negotiation, it frequently treats tensions as confrontations. The twentieth- and twenty-first-century construction of the idealized primitive is predicated on such clashes, as Marianne Torgovnick explains: 'Is the present too materialistic? Primitive life is not – it is a precaptialist utopia in which only use value, never exchange value prevails. Is the present sexually repressed? Not primitive life.'[36]

In a performance which utilises the utopian primitivist aesthetic, these clashes will be brought to the fore. Shakespeare will be contrasted with folk culture, authentic with inauthentic, West with East. Even the Arts Council's projected innovation will form part of a confrontation as the utopian primitive privileges tradition and cultural heritage over modern cultural forms. Depending on how the production approaches Shakespeare, he will either be aligned with the primitive or stand in opposition to it. In either case, the traditional cultural values of Shakespeare: heritage, aesthetic quality, canonicity, authenticity, non-commerciality will be reaffirmed over the 'upstart' values of iconoclasm, inauthenticity and marketability. This reaffirmation denies Shakespeare's potential to accrue new value.

This is not to suggest that intercultural innovation is always an elusive concept. Companies and theatre directors can use it more effectively. Peter Brook's *A Midsummer Night's Dream* is one example of the kind of intercultural theatre which asks audience and performers to redefine their concept of traditional Shakespearian performance. If productions can negotiate between the fraught tensions thrown up by utopian primitivism then it is possible to reinvigorate and remake Shakespeare's cultural value.

I want to close by examining the more nuanced use of utopian primitivism in two productions: Dash Arts' *A Midsummer Night's Dream* and Nós do Morro's *Knock Against My Heart*. Neither of these plays' aesthetics is entirely unproblematic and they remain linked to a utopian primitivist reading of non-European culture. However, despite their problems, both plays created performances that were both visually and aurally beautiful. Either through adaptation (*Knock Against My Heart*) or through translation (*Dream*) they encouraged their audience to see and hear Shakespeare's plays in a new way. The productions did not lose sight of theatre's ability to entertain and did not operate as part of a simply binary relationship. Instead, they functioned as dialectical spaces in which tensions of cultural value could be expressed and, ultimately, questioned. In doing so, established modes of production could equally be rethought. *Dream* and *Knock Against My Heart* were able to offer their audience both theatrical and narrative pleasure and to use this to create further value for Shakespeare. In short, by managing cultural tensions and being at once innovative and traditional, simultaneously Shakespearian and Shakespeare-differed, they succeeded in redefining Shakespeare's cultural value.

---

[36] *Gone Primitive* (Chicago, 1990), pp. 8–9.

DASH ARTS' *A MIDSUMMER NIGHT'S DREAM*

The Indian culture of Tim Supple's *A Midsummer Night's Dream* (2006–7) is just one example of how utopian primitivism can be approached in a way that is more nuanced, does not wholly idealize other cultures and rather uses them to complicate and interrogate Shakespeare. The production brought together an eclectic mix of Indian art forms and a broad range of Indian languages. In many ways, Supple's production represents an archetypal engagement with utopian primitivism. The production used a mixture of rope work, music, acting, dancing and acrobatics and in doing so fully exploited the spectacular elements of Indian culture, thus enhancing the theatrical potential of Shakespeare's play. The production's many *coups de théâtre* resulted partly from Supple's reading of the Shakespearian text but largely from his assimilation of Indian performance techniques. As the scene shifted from the palace to the wood, fairies broke through the back of the set. As the lovers became increasingly disorientated in the forest, Puck created a cage for them out of elastic which made them stumble and lose their way. Titania, and later Hermia, slept in giant red scarves hanging from the ceiling of the theatre.

The theatrical richness of the performance was mirrored in the narrative pleasure provided in the marriages of the lovers and the reconcilement of Titania and Oberon. In Supple's production, these events were coupled with extra-textual intercultural work. The closing moments of the play were both aesthetically striking and the most overtly utopian as they celebrated the 'moment of extraordinary harmony' with which *Dream* ends.[37] In the extra-textual ending, the company of actors sang and danced together, surrounded by glowing candles and returned to the stage to sing again after the curtain call. This was no longer Shakespeare's *Dream*. It was, instead, a manifestation of the company's links to one another, of their enjoyment of their work and of the relationship they built with the audience during the performance. The audience willingly continued to participate in this moment of harmony, clapping the rhythm along with the drummers and thus demonstrating their communality with the actors. From this idealized, shared moment the cultural values of spontaneity and authenticity emerged which were a product of the intercultural utopianism. By allowing this moment to occur outside of Shakespeare's text, Supple was suggesting that the truly utopian emerges not from the play but the way it is presented to its audience.

This was further underlined by the translation of Shakespeare's language into seven different Indian dialects. This Babel of languages challenged the audience to access the play's meaning in new, potentially innovative ways. As the audience and performers worked together to re-create the play's meaning, so the cultural value of Shakespeare was negotiated and reinvigorated. The utopian primitivism of Supple's *Dream* enabled Dash Arts to present a challenge to Shakespeare's value as originator of the English language and offered the audience a spectacular, exotic, non-verbal Shakespeare – Shakespeare, in other words, who was differed and different from the kind of Shakespeare normally presented at the RSC. The Indian culture presented in *Dream* may have been part of an idealized aesthetic but it also complicated and challenged the audience's response to Shakespeare. In this way, Shakespeare's value was not only reaffirmed but reinvigorated through the process of performance.

NÓS DO MORRO'S *KNOCK AGAINST MY HEART*

Based on *The Tempest*, *Knock Against My Heart* tells the story of Hispanic Brazilian farmer and landowner Prospero whose land was acquired cheaply from Sycorax during a drought. The play's action centres on his plan to divert the river through his land so that he controls the water for

---

[37] Royal Shakespeare Company, interview with Tim Supple www.rsc.org.uk/explore/dream/1780.htm, accessed 17 May 2007.

the entire region. He has found a formidable opponent in Caliban, who as prince of the region fights
against the diversion and, at the same time, falls
in love with Prospero's daughter, Miranda. Nós do
Morro's play is not without its clichés and is, at
times, governed by an over-simplified reading of
The Tempest and post-colonialism. However, this
did not prevent the production from presenting its
audience with exciting and interesting moments of
theatre which were able to challenge and complicate Shakespeare's cultural authority and value.

Like Supple's *Dream*, *Knock Against My Heart*
used language to challenge the audience's response
to the performance and Shakespeare's play. Caliban
spoke only in Portuguese whilst the other characters used a mixture of Portuguese and English.
There were no surtitles used in the production
and so the audience had to interpret the physicality and musicality of the performance in order to
access its meaning. Adapting and then translating
Shakespeare's play generated new creative possibilities and aesthetic opportunities that would not
have been available if *Knock Against My Heart* had
remained *The Tempest*.

The music and physical movement of the piece
had two interrelated but separate outcomes: they
were a source of theatrical pleasure for the audience and a way in which to distinguish Caliban as
the archetypal utopian primitive. The play opened
with Caliban playing a berimbau – a stringed
instrument built from a gourd – which has its roots
in Southern African culture but has become incorporated into the Brazilian art of capoeira. With its
African roots and Brazilian associations, this instrument encapsulated and underlined the interculturalism of the play. The strangeness and difference
of Caliban's berimbau was redolent of the utopian
primitive ideals of authenticity and 'real' culture.
His ownership of the instrument recreated Caliban
as the utopian primitive hero of this new play.

Shakespeare's narrative was reinterpreted
through a privileging of Caliban-as-primitive
but this was not the only outcome of the play's
interculturalism. It also increased the potential
for theatrical pleasure offered by *The Tempest*.
William de Paula, the actor playing Caliban, used

capoeira to create a style of movement for his
character which was reminiscent of an animal
stalking its prey. The movement in the confined
space of the Birmingham Rep's studio theatre
was thrilling and beautiful to watch. Capoeira,
combined with the exotic and unusual notes
of the berimbau, thus contributed to the visual
and aural aesthetics of the play. The theatrical
pleasure which the audience derived from this
contributed to the value-generating potential of
the performative moment. The Brazilian setting
and intercultural reinterpretation of *The Tempest*
allowed for new performance styles to be attached
to this Shakespearian performance. As such, *Knock
Against My Heart* showed how intercultural Shakespeare can also be innovative, value-generating
Shakespeare.

The play's Shakespearian aesthetic was underlined by the title's allusion to *The Tempest*. *Knock
Against My Heart* is an extract from Miranda's line in
The Tempest 'O, the cry did knock/Against my very
heart!' Aside from this allusion, only three words
of the play echoed Shakespeare's 'brave new world'
(5.1.183). The contrast between the title, based on
relatively obscure lines from Miranda's lament on
the storm, and the frequently quoted 'brave new
world' is interesting. The title of the play avows its
links to Shakespeare without being explicit, whilst
the words chosen to remain at the core of the play
are now as frequently associated with Aldous Huxley. This fragmentary connection between Shakespeare, Huxley, primitivism and Nós do Morro,
opens up an interesting moment of nuance in the
production. *Knock Against My Heart* used utopian
primitivism to create an exciting performance but
the production contained within it the seeds of a
critique of such primitivism.

The line 'brave new world' thus provided an
interesting distortion of the utopian primitive presented by the production. Agboluaje's Prospero
stood for progress of the kind rued by Huxley,
whilst Miranda and Caliban remained immersed
in a primitive utopia and their 'brave new world'
was in fact figured in the rituals and traditions
of the past. In this respect, Miranda and Caliban
were far more closely aligned to the primitivism of

Artaud, Brook and Mnouchkine than the critique of primitivism Huxley provides. His depiction of the savages in *Brave New World* cannot be simply delineated as the utopian alternative to Lenina and Bernard's dystopian reality.[38] Instead, the savage reservation is violent and vengeful, unwilling to accept John's mother and prejudiced against John because of his parentage. The savage reservations seem little more attractive to the reader than the feely-house or the dormitories where children are indoctrinated by night. It is possible to accuse Huxley of xenophobia and certainly, as a member of the British Eugenic Society, he 'was not particularly interested in transcending cultural barriers'.[39] However, what Huxley recognizes is that both utopias and dystopias are fantasy worlds and as fictional as the works of Shakespeare in which John seeks solace. In Huxley's bleak reality, neither civilization nor primitivization provides a solution to the crisis of modernity. While *Knock Against My Heart* did not offer its audience such an obvious critique of primitivism it did allow its audience to create such a connection for themselves. In doing so, Nós do Morro opened up a dialectical space between idealization and reality, modernity and primitivism, utopia and dystopia.

In their rewriting of both Shakespeare's *Tempest* and Huxley's reading of primitivism, this Afro-Brazilian hybrid play could be seen as making the ultimate act of ownership. By refiguring, rewriting and creating a wholly new production, Nós do Morro are not only engaging with Shakespeare's text but exchanging it for their own; they are not dismissing Shakespeare but they are questioning his relevance in their culture and suggesting that there might be alternative ways of encountering him. They are creating a dialectical Shakespearian performance which makes full use of Shakespeare's role as catalyst in order to create further cultural value for both the theatre company and *The Tempest*.

The analysis of the performances above reveals that, often, the combination of Shakespeare, the intercultural and a drive towards innovation leads to a reductive reading of other cultures. This is partly because, far from being innovative, intercultural Shakespeare actually taps into a long-running tradition which has used the cultural other to recreate Western theatre. Utopian primitivism – as I have defined the tradition – assimilates idealized and often generalized readings of non-Western culture into its encounter with the Shakespearian cultural object. In doing so it frequently represents its inherent tensions – authentic/inauthentic, West/East, ancient/modern – as confrontations rather than negotiations. This is not to suggest that every intercultural Shakespeare production in publicly funded theatre is redundant or defunct. Some enable the redefinition of established cultural forms or, like the Rolling Stones' techno-roadies, reproduce 'old favourites' in an unfamiliar and refreshing way.[40] If the tensions within intercultural theatre can be treated as links rather than distinctions – such that intercultural Shakespeare is presented as both authentic and inauthentic, Western and Eastern, ancient and modern – then cultural value creation for Shakespeare and the cultural innovation of Shakespeare remain possible.

---

[38] Aldous Huxley, *Brave New World* (London, 1994).

[39] Carey Snyder, '"When the Indian was in Vogue": D. H. Lawrence, Aldous Huxley, and Ethnological Tourism in the Southwest', *Modern Fiction Studies*, 53 (2007), 662–96; p. 664.

[40] Oakley, Sperry and Pratt, *Art of Innovation*, p. 26.

BRAND SHAKESPEARE?

KATE RUMBOLD

NOT A BRAND . . .

In recent years, the notion of 'the Shakespeare brand' has provided scholars with a ready metaphor to describe Shakespeare's remarkable cultural and commercial purchase in the twenty-first century. Doug Lanier has titled Shakespeare 'the Coca-Cola of canonical culture',[1] and critics have explored the deployment of 'the Shakespeare brand' from the production of eighteenth-century editions to the marketing of twentieth-century screen adaptations of his plays.[2] Most recently, 'Deploying the Shakespeare Brand' was the topic of a lively seminar at the International Shakespeare Conference in Stratford-upon-Avon in 2010, that explored the commercial presence of 'Shakespeare' in, among other things, cartoons, crafts and film.

In many ways, 'brand' is a helpful term with which to understand Shakespeare's cultural purchase. With it, scholars can acknowledge that 'Shakespeare' has a symbolic function in the world quite separate from (if partly rooted in) the facts of his existence and the content of his plays. The range of associations 'Shakespeare' bears – from excellence to Englishness – can be deployed in new, profitable, ways. That his image graces 'bank cards, £20 notes (from 1970–93), beer, crockery, fishing tackle, book publishing, cigars, pubs, and breath mints'[3] is a familiar trope of reception studies. As critics have observed, too, 'Shakespeare', like any successful brand name, is attached to a seemingly endless series of new products, from stage and film adaptations to souvenir money-boxes, medallions and tea-towels,[4] and even the dizzying realms of ironic, academic kitsch – 'the Shakespeare beanie baby, the Shakespeare bobble-head, the Shakespeare action figure, or the Shakespeare celebriduck (a rubber bath duck adorned with the face of Shakespeare)'.[5] 'Brand' provides space for scholars to consider the meanings and values that Shakespeare brings to, and accrues in, these new settings. 'The Shakespeare brand' extends the opportunity, too, for scholars to reflect on Shakespeare's unusual leverage – for good or ill – in academic publishing, employment and student recruitment.

But there are serious limitations to the notion of 'the Shakespeare brand'. Taken literally, 'Shakespeare' is not a brand or brand-name, in the sense of being 'a trade or proprietary name'.[6] Shakespeare's name might appear to be a locus of commercial activity, and of a wide range of perceptions, but since no single organization or

---

[1] Doug Lanier, 'Shakespeare™: Myth and Biographical Fiction', in Robert Shaughnessy, ed., *The Cambridge Companion to Shakespeare and Popular Culture* (Cambridge, 2007), p. 93.

[2] Don-John Dugas, *Marketing the Bard: Shakespeare in Performance and Print 1660–1740* (Columbia and London, 2006); Emma French, *Selling Shakespeare to Hollywood: The Marketing of Filmed Shakespeare Adaptations from 1989 into the New Millennium* (Hatfield, 2006).

[3] Lanier, 'Shakespeare™', p. 93.

[4] Barbara Hodgdon, *The Shakespeare Trade: Performances and Appropriations* (Philadelphia, 1998), pp. 232–40.

[5] Lanier, 'Shakespeare™', p. 98.

[6] In 'brand, n.', *OED Online*, November 2010, Oxford University Press, www.oed.com/view/Entry/22627?redirectedFrom=brand-name.

individual is in control of that name, its products, or the revenue made from it, 'Shakespeare' cannot be described as a brand, in the same way that, say, Coca-Cola, Nike or Apple can. Despite Professor of Marketing Philip Kotler's expansive pronouncement that 'Everything is a brand: Coca-Cola, FedEx, Porsche, New York City, the United States, Madonna, and you – yes, you! A brand is any label that carries meaning and associations',[7] 'Shakespeare' still eludes this definition: while the name 'carries meaning and associations', 'Shakespeare', unlike 'Coca-Cola', 'Madonna', and even 'you', is neither a corporation, nor an individual, with any control over the presentation of those associations to the world. Likewise, while Leslie de Chernatony might proffer fourteen different interpretations of the word 'brand' (including 'logo', 'legal instrument' and 'cluster of values'), all of them concern the deliberate construction by an organization of its identity. Even if, as de Chernatony acknowledges, some of the associations that later accrue to a brand are partly beyond organizational control (including consumers' images of, and relationships with, the brand), companies are in charge of establishing the brand image at the outset.[8]

The use of the phrase 'Shakespeare brand' is, then, necessarily metaphorical: to speak of 'the Coca-Cola of canonical culture' is more to draw on a compelling analogy from a separate realm ('its most long-lived and widespread brand name') than to suggest a precise equivalent for Shakespeare's annual turnover. John Frow usefully notes that, while the reproduced signature of an author might have much in common with a brand – not least because the dead canonical author represents in the present 'the state of quality assurance that defines the successful brand' – brand remains a 'corporate rather than a personal' signature, the result of a company marshalling the semiotics of its advertising, more intensely than in even the most commercialized use of authors' names.[9] 'Shakespeare' is frequently 'marshalled' as a guarantee of quality, but only ever retrospectively.

Why, though, problematize a useful fiction that helps us to describe the unique status of an early modern dramatist in 2010? It is not that 'brand' cannot be a valuable metaphor; but rather that, by taking 'brand' literally, we might see where this analogy is most productive, and where it is stretched too far – specifically, when brand-as-metaphor is conflated with brand-as-phenomenon. Lanier's essay opens by discussing the similarities between author name and brand, but moves rapidly from comparison ('interesting *affiliations with* the phenomenon of branding' (my italics)) to adoption, albeit more self-consciously than most critics, of the language of branding ('the face of Shakespeare' has 'become' the 'trademark' of canonical culture (93)). I would contend that, while the image of Shakespeare might *enact* some of the legitimating functions of the trademark, it is not quite the same as being a trademark.

This is not to deny that 'brand' has a metaphorical function in business, too, where the word's original, literal meaning of a mark of ownership has become an abstraction. Nor is it to suggest that 'Shakespeare' exists only outside the market. Rather, it is to observe that the ready use of 'brand' as a metaphor can actually blanket over the more complex, interesting ways in which 'Shakespeare' functions in the marketplace. By speaking of a 'Shakespeare brand' as if it has agency, rather than of the range of companies and organizations that deploy the word 'Shakespeare' in their own corporate identities, this metaphor can occlude their work. I'm suggesting that it is their work that creates the *impression* of a Shakespeare brand.

This article contends that the impression of a Shakespeare 'brand' is retrospectively constructed. 'Shakespeare' might not be controlled by one commercial organization, but it has served a range of organizations well – from the Tonson cartel in

---

[7] 'Brands', in Philip Kotler, *Marketing Insights from A to Z: 80 Concepts Every Manager Needs to Know* (Hoboken, 2003), p. 90.

[8] Leslie de Chernatony, *From Brand Vision to Brand Evaluation: The Strategic Process of Growing and Strengthening Brands* (Oxford, 2001) (2nd edn 2006), pp. 27–61.

[9] John Frow, 'Signature and Brand', in Jim Collins, ed., *High-Pop: Making Culture into Popular Entertainment* (Malden, MA, 2002), pp. 56–74.

the eighteenth century to the Royal Shakespeare Company in the twenty-first – to seem as if they are desirable products of that overarching 'brand', at the same time that they developed their own commercial identities. My concern, then, is not so much the commercial production and consumption of Shakespeare as the symbolic function – and construction – of 'Shakespeare' in the marketplace. Ironically, the notion that Shakespeare is outside the market has been vital to the commercial success of a range of enterprises since shortly after his own lifetime. The very collocation 'Shakespeare brand' can contain a frisson of iconoclasm, holding in uneasy tension the apparently separate realms of culture and commerce. In a postmodern world where, as branding analysts imagine, 'former barriers fall, sacrosanct boundaries dissolve, irreconcilable opposites are successfully reconciled'[10] this distinction might seem to have less force. But in marketing ('brand culture') as much as in literary and cultural studies ('Shakespeare brand'), that sense of oxymoronic opposition persists. As Lanier notes, with reference to ironic novelty Shakespeare spin-offs, we should not underestimate the 'recuperative capacity of stratificational schemes and the residual usefulness of connotations of exclusivity, learnedness, and quality long attached to the Shakespeare trademark'.[11] I'll argue that the *perceived* opposition of culture and commerce, and of Shakespeare and brand, is a productive tension that generates new, creative possibilities on an even larger scale. It is this tension that makes Shakespeare a 'cultural catalyst' in the twenty-first century.

Finally, perhaps it is the otherness of 'brand' that appeals to Shakespeare scholars. Like other metaphors that reception studies already live by – from 'reception' itself, to the more active 'appropriation' – the very choice of this metaphor might be revealing. As well as promoting the study of a wider range of commercial products, 'the Shakespeare brand' might also signal the academy's aspiration to cultural significance (when Shakespeare and Coca-Cola are, in fact, produced and consumed on vastly different scales), or even a desire to control and demarcate as a 'brand' a protean 'Shakespeare' whose commercial deployments in film and advertising, let alone in new digital media, race effortlessly ahead of our best efforts to make meaning out of them.

CO-PRODUCING THE 'SHAKESPEARE BRAND'

To speak casually of 'the Shakespeare brand' is potentially to obscure a more complex symbolic relationship with the marketplace. If a 'Shakespeare brand' does not, in all accuracy, exist, what we can observe and describe instead in the marketplace is the idea or impression of a Shakespeare brand. This impression is generated by the organizations that treat 'Shakespeare' as a guarantor of the quality of their own products. The 'Shakespeare' brand does not pre-exist his commercial deployment, but is – and has been – retrospectively constructed by the organizations that appropriate and deploy Shakespeare's name for their own ends.

This impression of a 'Shakespeare' brand has a long history. Shakespeare's reception contains a series of important instances where his commercial deployment has not only contributed to the success of a new enterprise, but simultaneously constructed the impression of a larger Shakespeare 'brand'. The First Folio is perhaps the first commercial enterprise to trade on the impression of a coherent 'Shakespeare': John Heminges and Henry Condell emphasized that they were uniting for the first time multiple, disparate plays they had 'collected' together under the authenticating name of 'Mr William Shakespeare's Comedies, Histories and Tragedies'. Michael D. Bristol emphasizes the commercial, as much as literary, significance of this publication: Shakespeare's 'works were created not as autonomous works of literary or even dramatic art as we now understand such notions, but rather as a set of practical solutions to the exigencies of a heterogenous cultural market', and

---

[10] Stephen Brown, 'Ambi-brand Culture: On a Wing and a Swear with Ryanair', in Jonathan E. Schroeder and Miriam Salzer-Mörling, *Brand Culture* (London, 2006), p. 51.
[11] Lanier, 'Shakespeare^{TM}', p. 97.

seen in the context of an early and prototypical culture industry, the first folio is important as an assertion of the players' property rights and a shrewd device for capturing a share of what was already a profitable market for works by Shakespeare. More specifically, the first folio of Shakespeare's works is an effort to capture a portion of the up-scale market for printed books.[12]

Bristol suggests that the Folio's design and advertisement deliberately 'approximate the typical format in which other valued literary authors were marketed'. But the publication is also made to seem self-legitimating. The Folio creates the image, both visually, in the Droeshout portrait, and verbally, in its numerous dedicatory prefaces and poems, of a 'Shakespeare' who presides posthumously over the 'works', and whose much-vaunted absent-presence, rather than the book's physical similarity to other valued publications, is the guarantee of their quality. As Heminges and Condell claim, 'before, you were abused with divers stolen and surreptitious copies, maimed and deformed by the frauds and stealths of injurious impostors that exposed them, even those are now offered to your view cured and perfect of their limbs, and all the rest absolute in their numbers, as he conceived them'.[13] Proximity to Shakespeare's intentions, symbolized by the repeated presence of his image and name, is the signal of their value; and he their 'trademark'.

As a 'trademark', the clear linearity of the Droeshout portrait is at once compromised, and amplified, by the verbal images that surround it: Ben Jonson's poem evokes a protean 'Shakespeare' who flits between 'Swan of Avon', 'constellation' and 'star of poets'.[14] But it is precisely this elusiveness that means that 'Shakespeare' is increasingly located by the Folio in the works themselves: 'Read him.' 'Shakespeare' becomes at once brand and product – or, to pick up the ambiguity in early definitions, and in Shakespeare's own uses, of the word 'brand', the marking instrument, the act of marking and the object marked.[15] By occluding their own work ('who only gather his works and give them you'), Heminges and Condell reinforce this impression that the works are at once the product, and the symbol, of a Shakespeare brand.

This impression is expanded and confirmed in the early eighteenth century with the sequential production of sharply differentiated Shakespeare editions by the Tonson cartel. This competitive process develops, and continually refreshes, the Tonson brand. As Dugas acknowledges, the early Shakespeare editions were marketed as products of the already desirable Tonson brand: 'The edition of 1709 was specially packaged for the customers the Tonsons knew so well, customers who believed what they were buying was a high-quality product because it carried the Tonson imprint on its title-page.'[16] Yet Dugas observes, but underplays, the significance of a fascinating act of conflation whereby the Tonsons later adopt 'Shakespeare's head' as their trademark, merging their own brand with their chief product, to create the impression of a legitimating 'Shakespeare' brand;[17] Dugas buys into that conflation, noting that the Shakespeare product is 'their (now) flagship brand' (168). This 'brand' continues to sanction the publication of closely related products (Rowe, Pope, Theobald, etc.), differentiated by their various attempts to reach the emerging standard of 'Shakespeare'.

In 1769, the Jubilee celebrations staged by celebrity actor David Garrick in Shakespeare's honour in Stratford-upon-Avon would appear to perform that most valuable work of brand

---

12 Michael D. Bristol, *Big-time Shakespeare* (London, 1996), p. 49.
13 John Heminges and Henry Condell, 'To the Great Variety of Readers', *Comedies, Histories and Tragedies* (1623), in Stanley Wells and Gary Taylor, eds., *William Shakespeare: The Complete Works* (Oxford, 1988), p. xlv.
14 Ben Jonson, 'To the memory of my beloved, The AUTHOR, MASTER WILLIAM SHAKESPEARE, AND what he hath left us', *Comedies, Histories, Tragedies* (1623), in Wells and Taylor, p. xlvi.
15 4a. 'The mark made by burning with a hot iron.', 5. 'An iron instrument for making marks by burning' 'brand, n.', *OED Online*, November 2010, www.oed.com/view/Entry/22627?redirectedFrom=brand-name. See also Shakespeare: 'Cupid laid by his brand, and fell asleep' (Sonnet 153), and 'Brand not my forehead with thy piercing light' (*Rape of Lucrece* line 1091).
16 Dugas, *Marketing the Bard*, p. 159.
17 Dugas, *Marketing the Bard*, p. 166.

extension – detaching a brand name from its primary products, in order to permit the development of new ones.[18] Three days of pageantry, songs and poems – but, as critics are invariably moved to comment, no performances of his plays – served forcibly to detach the name 'Shakespeare' from its most obvious products. The event was built around the celebration of the *image* of Shakespeare – centring on the dedication of a new statue of the playwright – and, only to a much lesser extent, his words. Thus the Jubilee confirmed the impression of the 'immortal Shakespeare's' 'transcendence'[19] not just over the muddy festivities, but over his own works.

It is intriguing that all these early commercial enterprises worked to generate the impression that Shakespeare is above such monetary concerns. From the First Folio's claim that the collection is compiled 'without ambition of self-profit or fame, only to keep the memory of so worthy a friend alive as was our Shakespeare',[20] to the 'god of our idolatry' celebrated in Garrick's Jubilee Ode, these enterprises appear to lift Shakespeare above the mundanity of even their own commercial goals – but in a way that makes him ultimately more profitable. Garrick was criticized in the contemporary press for exploiting his Jubilee visitors. Satirical verses like 'so long as the world's full of nifeys and ninneys, / My mulberry-box will be full of good guineas' suggested that he was only out to make money out of the gullible Shakespeare pilgrims he attracted to Stratford.[21] However, the very suggestion that Garrick's commercial motives are unworthy of Shakespeare served to elevate the playwright. Bristol observes that 'paradoxically it is the belief in Shakespeare's transcendent worth that underwrites his currency in popular culture and secures his commercial value',[22] but, as my examples suggest, this impression of transcendence is in fact created by the market; it does not pre-exist his commercial deployment. While it might seem as if Shakespeare was a cultural icon that companies have subsequently commercialized, it is clear that the processes of making Shakespeare an icon and making him (appear to be) a brand actually happened in tandem.

We might say, then, that the impression of a Shakespeare brand is, and has long been, to use the terminology of marketing, 'co-produced' by the commercial and cultural organizations that deploy his image as if it is their trademark. Co-production, a term that describes the way that value is created by the service industries, has been used by marketing analysts to talk, for example, about the way that multiple organizations in a particular town or city work together in the pursuit of 'destination marketing', or the 'branding of places as tourism destinations'. A place is

comprised of an amalgamation of individual services, such as shopping and sports centres, theatres and museums as well as infrastructural services such as road and rail networks. The place product is therefore co-produced by a multiplicity of autonomous organisations, both public and private . . . [23]

'Co-production' refers here to the 'amalgamation' of multiple contributions, 'shopping and sports centres, theatres and museums' – to a 'place brand'. It might also helpfully articulate the way in which 'Shakespeare' is constructed by the operation of a range of commercial and cultural organizations: they, not Shakespeare, are the brands, but even as they compete with one another they help to render 'Shakespeare' an overarching 'brand' that legitimates their products.

Indeed, the twenty-first-century 'destination marketing' of Stratford-upon-Avon and its locale

---

[18] See Frow, 'Signature and Brand', pp. 64–5.

[19] Michael Dobson, *The Making of the National Poet: Shakespeare, Adaptation, and Authorship, 1660–1769* (Oxford, 1992), p. 219.

[20] John Heminges and Henry Condell, 'The Epistle Dedicatory', *Comedies, Histories, Tragedies* (1623), in Wells and Taylor, p. xliv.

[21] *The London Chronicle*, 15–17 August 1769, quoted in Johanne Stochholm, *Garrick's Folly: The Stratford Jubilee of 1769* (London, 1964), p. 38.

[22] Bristol, *Big-time Shakespeare*, p. 90.

[23] Graham Hankinson, 'The Management of Destination Brands: Five Guiding Principles Based on Recent Developments in Corporate Branding Theory', *Journal of Brand Management*, 14 (2007), 240–54. www.palgrave-journals.com/bm/journal/v14/n3/full/2550065a.html.

provides an excellent example of how the impression of a Shakespeare brand continues to be constructed and deployed to market very different products. The act of 'amalgamation' is exaggerated when 'place marketers . . . work together and combine two or more places together in order to provide a more attractive offer'. 'Shakespeare Country' is the trading name for 'South Warwickshire Tourism Ltd', a company whose marketing remit covers not only Stratford-upon-Avon, but also the towns, villages and countryside of the surrounding area:

Spend time in Shakespeare Country and leave with your own wonderful story to tell. You'll be sure to find something for everyone when you plan your short break or holiday in Shakespeare Country. Visit Stratford-upon-Avon – home of William Shakespeare, historic Warwick and Kenilworth with two of the most magnificent castles in English history and Royal Leamington Spa with its superb shopping in stunning Regency setting. Take time to explore the rolling green countryside of Warwickshire, dotted with an array of historic towns and villages. Journey to the south of Shakespeare Country and explore the Cotswolds with its classic landscape of honey-coloured cottages and gentle hills with dry stone walls and grazing sheep.[24]

Shakespeare Country uses 'Shakespeare' to unite as a destination the disparate offerings of Stratford and a number of other Warwickshire towns. Shakespeare's connection to the area's 'magnificent castles', 'superb shopping' and 'honey-coloured cottages' is, of course, tenuous, but his authorial reputation serves to join them in a coherent 'story' for visitors to take away.[25] 'Shakespeare' is proffered, then, as an overarching brand that confers value on all the products within a geographical area. Partly, this is an extension of the nostalgic rural aesthetic that has connected Shakespeare to the Stratford countryside since the eighteenth century. But just as adjectival praise like 'magnificent', 'superb', 'stunning' and 'classic' is transferred across from the discourse of Shakespeare's excellence to confer value on a range of anachronistic retail and leisure experiences, so too does 'Shakespeare' accrue from those diverse, up-to-date products a range of positive new associations.

Ironically, the failure of these organizations does not impinge on the success of the 'Shakespeare brand'. Just as Heminges and Condell distinguished between 'the reputation his, and the faults ours' (xlv), and the muddy disaster of the 1769 Jubilee appeared to fall short of the 'immortal Shakespeare', so commercial failure somehow serves to emphasize his elevated, abstract status. When, in 2010, 'Shakespeare Country' went into administration after council funding was withdrawn, its failure was attributed to changing technology and global economic crisis – not to the weakness of the 'Shakespeare' brand. Likewise, unsuccessful productions or film adaptations of Shakespeare's plays are not generally taken to diminish the strength of the 'Shakespeare' under whose name they seem to trade.

The Shakespeare 'brand', then, is a compelling impression produced by commercial organizations. But the symbolic meanings of 'Shakespeare' also complicate what it means to be a successful brand, with some organizations appearing to eschew, as well as seek, commercial success through his name. The Royal Shakespeare Company recently conducted a UK-wide survey to collect perceptions of their brand. They were declaredly delighted with the results: at least 80 per cent of people were aware of the RSC's name. They were pleased, too, with the associations the RSC's name triggered: 'high quality', 'successful' and 'entertaining' were the most popular selections from a range of possible responses.[26] However, a result to be greeted more cautiously was that 40 per cent of the public deemed the RSC 'upmarket' – a perception that, as Mary Butlin, Head of Market Planning at the RSC noted, most companies would be thrilled

---

[24] Shakespeare Country, www.shakespeare-country.co.uk/, accessed 29 November 2010.

[25] This goal is at least imaginatively realised in the viral computer game devised by 'Shakespeare Country', in which players help Romeo seek out Juliet in Stratford, passing, in the foreground, Shakespeare's houses, and, in the middle distance, Warwick and Kenilworth castles. http://romeo.viral-game.co.uk/.

[26] Mary Butlin, 'RSC Brand Values Research Executive Summary' (2010).

by, evoking as it does an aspirational level of quality and desirability. As a publicly funded organization, though, receiving around £14m of taxpayers' money per year, the RSC has a remit to engage with new, young and minority audiences. Being perceived as 'upmarket', as Butlin explains, risks undermining their espoused role of making 'Shakespeare for all'.

'Upmarket' evokes expensive, luxury brands like Tiffany & Co. and Mercedes, targeted at high-income customers.[27] Whether this impression emanates from Shakespeare's cultural status alone or from the high production values and polished visitor experience of the RSC is not specified. Either way, public funding, and the public good, complicate the idea of commercial success. The RSC's attempts to navigate the poles of desirable brand (their inclusion of 'upmarket' in their list of multiple-choice responses suggests that they are to some extent courting this perception, as well as rejecting it[28]) and valued public service, expose the complexities of how 'Shakespeare' operates symbolically in the marketplace. In this case, the state might be deemed the opposite of 'upmarket' exclusivity – representing the duty to provide for all. However, it has in recent decades been the state's intervention in the arts – through, for example, the establishment of the Arts Council of Great Britain, and the subsidizing of theatre and museums – that has been blamed for commodifying culture, because of its edicts about the kinds of value (economic, social or otherwise) that culture should produce.[29] If brand is, for many such critics, anathema to culture, then the public good can be at once something that helps culture to resist the market, and something that plays into that market.

Shakespeare's status as a public good – anchored, since the nineteenth century, in his place in compulsory education – can also be one of the most lucrative elements in his perceived 'brand'. It is not only major Shakespeare institutions that testify to the importance of their education departments as an income stream. Being 'good for you' is one of the most compelling perceptions associated with Shakespeare's name even in more wholly

commercial enterprises. In a 2010 advert for the energy drink Red Bull, a cartoon Shakespeare paces his study, fulsomely testing out lines that might soon become *Hamlet* – until his can of Red Bull is cleared away by a serving maid. His source of inspiration suddenly cut off, he sighs, 'and the rest is silence, it seems', before glumly signing his name, 'William Shakespeare'. If, as Shakespeare ruefully reflects in a final voiceover as the product shot fills the screen, 'genius does suffer without Red Bull', then, by being good for Shakespeare, Red Bull acquires by extension this lucrative 'good for you' status too (as well as a few of Shakespeare's

---

27 'Of merchandise, etc.: characteristic of or designed for the more expensive end of the market; superior, expensive, "quality"'. 'up-market, adj. and adv.', *OED Online*, November 2010, Oxford University Press, www.oed.com/view/Entry/220019?rskey=e0odAy&result=1&isAdvanced=false.

28 'Q8a: Please tell us which of these words or phrases you would use to describe RSC. Please click on as many or as few words as you wish, there are no right or wrong answers, it is just your personal opinion that we are interested in', Butlin, 'RSC Brand Values Research Executive Summary' (2010).

29 Cultural policy scholar Clive Gray describes the twentieth-century political process that turned the arts into 'commodities that can be judged by the same economic criteria that can be applied to cars, clothes or any other consumer good', by valuing them as 'products of public service' (Clive Gray, *The Politics of the Arts in Britain* (Basingstoke, 2000), pp. 6, 15). Cultural historian Robert Hewison blames in particular the 'value for money' edicts of the Thatcher government of the 1980s for creating a climate that encouraged traditional cultural organizations to think of themselves as commercial brands, greeting with horror the 1985 decision of the director of the Victoria and Albert Museum to accept and 'capitalise on what is a more market-oriented society' by merchandizing products based on the designs in the gallery, in the hope that 'the V&A could be the Laura Ashley of the 1990s' ('Towards a More Consumer-oriented V&A', Victoria and Albert Museum press release, 31 October 1985, 2, quoted in Robert Hewison, *Culture and Consensus: England, Art and Politics since 1940* (London, 1995), p. 269). This tension did not necessarily recede under the value-oriented public service reform of the New Labour government (which treated individuals as consumers with choice in the way their public services, including arts organizations, were run), and is set to take new shape since the 2010 Conservative–Liberal Democrat spending review.

florid words – 'refresh', 'revitalise', 'elixir' – and his signature of approval).[30]

The Shakespeare 'brand', then, is not only an impression created by the market, but also has a complex symbolic relationship with that market. Shakespeare's state-supported role in education and theatre makes him at once a symbol of intellectual aspiration, and of 'good for you' cultural democracy; of divorce from the market and profound marketability.[31] We'll see how profitable and effective it can be to exploit the tensions between the realms of culture, commerce and public service. It is these imagined rifts in the identity of 'Shakespeare' that become sources of – even catalysts for – creativity.

BRAND VS. SHAKESPEARE

Of course, the opposition between culture and commerce is difficult to maintain. To separate the two is to revert to a false division of iconic, high culture and grubby commerce that has recurred at least since the late eighteenth century, but that is not, as cultural studies scholar John Frow observed in 1995, 'tenable in the twentieth century', as a wider range of modes of cultural production, and a new array of groups, niches and interests, challenge the stratification of cultural goods by class and status.

High culture is fully absorbed within commodity production. The relation to the market can therefore not be used as a general principle of differentiation between high-cultural and low-cultural products, nor is it any longer possible to employ the traditional value-laden opposition between the disinterested, organic, original, self-governing work of art and the interested, mechanical, formulaic and commercial mass-cultural text. Works of high culture are now produced in exactly the same serial forms as those of low culture: the paperback book, the record or disk, film, radio and television (where there now exist specifically high-cultural channels).[32]

The degree of relationship of a cultural good to the market is no longer the determiner of its status as high or low, art or mass-produced commodity.

Their modes of production are so entwined as to render this a false distinction – and perhaps never more so than in the digital age.[33]

What is intriguing, though, is how compelling this opposition between 'high culture' and 'commodity production' nonetheless remains. This binary was still at work in cultural studies, even as it argued that both were equally worthy of scholarly examination; it is, I would suggest, present in the collocation 'Shakespeare brand'. No matter how entwined these realms might be in actuality, the *perceived* gulf between culture and commodity production, cultural icon and brand, remains potent in the twenty-first century.

Bridging this seemingly vast gulf is an aspiration for many commercial brands, who seek a 'cultural' status for their work.[34] Douglas Holt's *How Brands Become Icons* asks how certain brands, at certain moments, achieve the resonance more naturally associated with iconic cultural figures. Eschewing both older ('mind share', 'emotional') and more recent ('viral') forms of marketing, Holt proposes a model of 'identity branding', in which successful brands, like icons, manage to address the collective anxieties or identity needs of a group or nation at

---

[30] 'Red Bull – Shakespeare', www.tellyads.com/show_movie. php?filename=TA10557, accessed 30 November 2010.

[31] See, for example, the use of this 'for all' quality by a commercial theatre company targeted at schools, Shakespeare 4 Kidz, www.shakespeare4kidz.com/shakespeare-for-all-ages-stages.html.

[32] John Frow, *Cultural Studies and Cultural Value* (Oxford, 1995), p. 27.

[33] See the overlap of cultural and commercial qualities in the products listed in John Wyver's celebration of contemporary culture: www.illuminationsmedia.co.uk/blog/index. cfm?start=1&news_id=872.

[34] See, for example, the suggestion that branders are important 'cultural intermediaries' (Liz Moor, 'Branding Consultants as Cultural Intermediaries', *Sociological Review*, 56 (2008), 408–28); that branding is an ancient cultural practice akin to telling stories and forming identity groups (Elizabeth C. Hirschman, 'Evolutionary Branding', *Psychology and Marketing* (2010), 568–83); and that 'branding represents a cultural process, performed in an interplay between art and business, production and consumption, images and stories, design and communication' (Schroeder and Salzer-Mörling, *Brand Culture*, Preface, p. 3).

a certain time in history. This impossible-sounding task comes with such unlikely edicts as

To become an icon, a brand must not only target the most advantageous contradiction in society, but also perform the right myth, and in the right manner.[35]

Brands are encouraged to engineer for themselves the cultural resonance of icons, whose glittering success is held just out of reach: 'In terms of myth performances, brands can never compete with films, politicians, or musicians. Even the best sixty-second ad (say, Nike's 'Revolution' or Apple's '1984'), can't compete with John Wayne's films, Ronald Reagan's speeches, or Kurt Cobain's songs and concerts' (60). Holt doesn't allow for the possibility that these and other cultural figures from literature, television and film might be just as carefully produced as brands; nor, conversely, that their resonance with particular cultural moments might be equally hit-and-miss. With talk of 'breakthrough performances', brand 'authors' and 'stories' people buy, he aspires to the authorial control, affective punch and perceived cachet that he imagines lie on the other side of the culture/commerce divide.

This aspiration – like the opposite aspiration we can arguably see in the RSC's mixed desire to be 'upmarket' – ironically serves to uphold the distinction between culture and the market. But it is precisely the imagined opposition between these realms that is a source of productive tension, and can be deployed to new creative ends. A 1980s advert for Carling Black Label lager traded very obviously on the perceived high–low gulf between Shakespeare and football (and, by extension, lager) when Hamlet's speech to Yorick's skull descended into a stage kickabout with that iconic prop.[36] The advert tightly juxtaposed Shakespearian speech ('my noble lord Hamlet') and colloquialism ('over 'ere, son, on me 'ead'); cut between Hamlet and Horatio's raucous goal celebrations and the refinement of the inhabitants of the expensive box into which the skull is kicked; and, encapsulating the sense of opposition in one final image, presented a stony bust of Shakespeare wrapped in a football scarf, next to a pint of Carling Black Label.

Almost thirty years later, we might imagine that this perceived opposition of high and low might have lost some of its force, for the reasons Frow outlines above. Nonetheless, the 2010 Red Bull advert still trades, albeit more subtly, off the imagined iconoclasm of Shakespeare's immortal genius being dependent on a mass-produced and anachronistic commercial product. Advertisers are still creatively exploiting the comic sense of transgression of having a cultural icon implicated in a brand.

They play off the perceived opposition of Shakespeare to the market, only to reinsert him into that market for comic – and commercial – gain. The Red Bull advert taps into a long-running comic trope in which Shakespeare's established cultural status is humorously contrasted with the 'realities' of the commercial pressures that shaped his work, and his most famous phrases: visible from a *Blackadder*-based Comic Relief sketch (which sees Shakespeare's crowd-pleasing editor exhorting him to 'trim some of the deadwood' – the soliloquies – out of *Hamlet* because 'it's boring, Bill', and 'it's the ghost that's selling this show at the moment', with Shakespeare reluctantly agreeing to edit down Hamlet's speech to the 'gibberish' of 'To be, or not to be' in order to please 'Joe Public' and get 'bums on seats'[37]) to *Shakespeare in Love* (where Will snatches overheard lines as he desperately scrambles to deliver his play script on time).

As these examples suggest, this perceived tension can be productively deployed not only in advertisements but in larger-scale cultural products, too. *Shakespeare in Love* is an extended exploitation of the perceived incongruity between Shakespeare's iconic status and the reality of irritable writer's block, a vexed personal relationship with his wife, and professional one with Christopher Marlowe (both taken straight from popular knowledge of his life), Hollywood-worthy romance, sex and deceit,

---

[35] Douglas Holt, *How Brands Become Icons: The Principles of Cultural Branding* (Boston, MA, 2004), p. 63.

[36] 'My Noble Lord Hamlet', www.youtube.com/watch?v=OIB3t7xEMX0.

[37] 'Shakespeare sketch: A Small Rewrite', http://www.youtube.com/watch?v=IwbB6B0cQs4.

and a less-than-sublime draft of *Romeo and Ethel the Pirate's Daughter* – before ultimately restoring him to the reassuringly inspired figure who voices the opening lines of *Twelfth Night* as the credits roll. Critics suggest that the makers of the film see themselves 'not as iconoclasts or vulgarians, but as conservers or restorers intent on breaking down the cultural encrustations that have made Shakespeare "highbrow", rarefied, effeminate, and boring'.[38] But that sense of contrast between high and low is carefully retained. The film's press material trades, for example, on the bringing together of the 'high cultural theatrical expertise' of Tom Stoppard with Marc Norman's experience of 'Hollywood blockbusters'.[39] Emma French argues that 'the most successful filmed Shakespeare adaptations are those that effectively blur traditional binaries between high and low, art and commerce, and British heritage and Hollywood popular film in their marketing', in an act of 'hybridisation' that seeks to 'secure the broadest possible audience for the films'.[40] I'd argue, however, that, in their marketing as much as in their content, highly successful film adaptations such as *William Shakespeare's Romeo + Juliet* (which she contends 'challenges the traditional binary between high and low culture' even in its august-meets-vernacular title) and also new, emerging animated products like *Gnomeo and Juliet* ('Shakespeare's legendary tale . . . as you've never seen it before'), are not simply blurring boundaries, but deliberately reasserting them in order creatively to exploit the possibilities of transgression.[41]

In exploring this phenomenon, French's book itself trades off this perceived tension. From *Big-Time Shakespeare* and *The Shakespeare Trade* to the more recent *Selling Shakespeare to Hollywood* and *Marketing the Bard* – and even the title of this article – studies of Shakespeare's relationship with commercial culture can appear to exploit the persistent sense of oxymoronic opposition; Dugas goes so far as to juxtapose the florid font of 'Bard' with the more linear presentation of 'Marketing' on his book's cover. While they might not share the critique of commercialization inherent in books like Herbert Schiller's *Culture, Inc.* (which argues that corporate control of museums,

theatres, performing arts centres and public broadcasting represents 'a broad manipulation of consciousness as well as an insidious form of censorship'), or Debra Silverman's *Selling Culture* (which describes commercially sponsored art exhibits as thoughtlessly displayed assemblages without context), these titles share the same provocative polarity. It is an irony of this field that, in seeking to overturn the false distinction between culture and commerce and, particularly, to avoid critiquing the latter,[42] many academic books nonetheless build on – and even, perhaps, reinforce – that perceived tension.[43] The imagined contrast within 'Shakespeare brand' remains, then, a productive catalyst for academic analysis.

Might this change? In 2010, the Shakespeare 'brand' is constructed not only by the organizations that bear his name and image. New technology, ostensibly at least, gives *individuals* an increased share of control over the image of 'Shakespeare'. Marketers have long known the importance of individuals' self-identification with their brand – or 'how consumers use brands to construct their

---

[38] Michael Anderegg, 'James Dean Meets the Pirate's Daughter: Passion and Parody in *William Shakespeare's Romeo and Juliet* and *Shakespeare in Love*', in Richard Burt and Lynda E. Boose, eds., *Shakespeare, the Movie, II* (London, 2003), pp. 56–71.

[39] French, *Selling Shakespeare*, p. 138.

[40] French, *Selling Shakespeare*, pp. 2, 168.

[41] Suggesting this sense of productive collision, a section on 'the Author' on the film's website says of early modern theatre, 'It was crass. It was business. It was art. And it was genius. Shakespeare had the rhymes. Everyone knew it.' www.romeoandjuliet.com (quoted in French, who refers to this as another blurring of boundaries (*Selling Shakespeare*, p. 114)).

[42] See e.g. French, 'This book contends that a process of assimilation into rather than effacement of high culture in American mainstream popular culture is taking place in the marketing of filmed Shakespeare adaptations' (*Selling Shakespeare*, p. 6).

[43] Russell Jackson's Preface to the book reassures readers that 'By focusing so acutely on the "selling" of Shakespeare films, Emma French is not diverting attention from their artistic value, but drawing attention to an important component of it'; and the back-cover quotations from Melvyn Bragg and John Carey comment on the book's consideration of 'high' and 'low' culture.

self[44] – for selling their car or beauty product. But new technologies for social networking provide visual forums in which individuals can *perform* these acts of self-identification to the wider world, be it through the interest groups ('Am I one of the only people who enjoys reading Shakespeare?'), commercial applications ('Shakespeare Insult Generator') and institutional pages (Atlanta Shakespeare Company, RSC) of Facebook, or the opportunity to mix clips from *Shakespeare in Love* with new soundtracks on YouTube.

The capacity of these online spaces to allow individuals idiosyncratically to collide and combine 'Shakespeare' with other cultural and commercial symbols seems to some highly liberating. It builds on the hope expressed in the twentieth century that mass culture might not be a force for homogenization, but could instead offer a 'rich iconography, a set of symbols, objects and artefacts which can be assembled and reassembled by different groups in a literally limitless number of combinations'.[45] In a challenge to the passivity of consumption, 'Cultural commodities are catalyst, not product; a stage in, not the destination of, cultural affairs.'[46] New technology has reinvigorated a discourse in which people can seize control of brands for their own ends.[47] In such spaces, 'Shakespeare', like other commercial symbols, could function as raw material for new kinds of creative self-expression.

Some critics, though, have always contended that consumers are still controlled by market forces, limited to what is made available to them.[48] A breezier version of this story is found in Rob Walker's *I'm With the Brand*, which describes how, by encouraging individuals to self-identify with a product, viral marketing lets them do the company's marketing work for them.[49] It begs the question of whether consumers are being creative, being duped, or cheerfully, and consciously, colluding in this corporate 'murketing'.[50] The discourse of freedom and creativity might be challenged by the 'hidden puppet-master' that Holt observes behind this seemingly 'authorless' variety of branding; that is, by the larger question of who is in control.

How conservative, then, might these acts of user-generated marketing be when, for all the imagined possibilities of new technology, the catalysis for creativity still often comes from perceived opposition? Walker suggests that the most successful brands in this new branding landscape are those with 'projectibility' – blank and malleable enough to have the priorities of numerous social groups projected on to them. Just as the expressionless cartoon 'Hello Kitty' is adopted both earnestly by children, and ironically by some groups of adults, with astonishing global success, so Red Bull, Walker notes, is *deliberately* indistinct enough to be variously the province of kiteboarders, computer gaming teams, extreme sports players and late-night ravers, and, as a result, leads a $3.7 billion energy drink industry. The cultural figures imagined to rely on Red Bull – including Shakespeare and Isaac Newton – extend this impression of Red Bull's indispensability into intellectual and creative, as well as physical, activity. It is a clichéd

---

44 E.g. Sharon Schembri, Bill Merrilees and Stine Kristiansen, 'Brand Consumption and Narrative of the Self', *Psychology & Marketing*, 27:6 (June 2010), 557–67.

45 Dick Hebdige, quoted in Hewison, *Culture and Consensus*, p. 288.

46 Paul E. Willis, *Common Culture* (Boulder, 1990), p. 129.

47 See e.g. Charles Leadbetter, *We-Think: Mass Innovation Not Mass Production* (London, 2008).

48 See e.g. Herbert Schiller, *Culture Inc.* (Oxford, 1989). John Guillory has argued that this power is not confined to the market, with educational institutions helping to maintain the hegemonic control that confirms the social values of the dominant group (*Cultural Capital: The Problem of Literary Canon Formation* (Chicago, 1993)).

49 Rob Walker, *I'm With The Brand: The Secret Dialogue Between What We Buy and Who We Are* (London, 2008).

50 See also Adam Arvidsson, *Brands: Meaning and Value in Media Culture* (London, 2006), p. 104: 'Internet branding is evolving into a series of techniques that aim to put consumers to work in the production of forms of content that can be sold back to them. The brand becomes the institutional form by means of which capital brings the free labour of the internet back to its fold. In this form, the internet is no longer conceived as a means towards the valorization of an otherwise independent product or service. Rather, it is conceived as an economic space in its own right, an arena for both the production and the consumption of branded content.'

trope of reception studies – and of the routine admiration of Shakespeare – to describe Shakespeare as endlessly adaptable, able to speak to any community; but in the case of the Red Bull advert, it is not so much his projectibility, as the familiar range of associations he brings with him, that is the source of the advert's creativity. For all that the Internet might do to challenge boundaries of high and low, there is a sense that this perceived opposition might continue to be a source of creative tension for some time to come. What changes, with new technology, is the sheer scale on which these tensions can be exploited.

A BRAND TO THE END O'
THE WORLD?

How useful a fiction, then, is 'the Shakespeare brand'? And how far has taking 'brand' seriously brought us? We've seen that the Shakespeare 'brand', while sometimes casually deployed to describe his growing array of commercial manifestations, is in fact potentially shorthand for a highly complex symbolic relationship with the market. The impression of a Shakespeare 'brand', I've suggested, does not pre-exist his commercial use, but is constructed retrospectively by the organizations that appear to deploy it in their own service. Very often, they trade on the impression that 'Shakespeare' is above their commercial concerns. In a volume dedicated to 'Shakespeare as cultural catalyst', this article has argued that it is in the perceived tensions between commerce and culture, selling and public service – rather than in vague notions of universal influence – that Shakespeare's potential for catalysis lies. These categories might appear set to become more blurred as cultural and commercial production and consumption become more closely entwined, and new forms of marketing rapidly reshape the branding landscape (bringing the retrospectively constructed 'Shakespeare' brand closer to other organizations that are increasingly relinquishing control of their image to their consumers). However, it appears that, even in the newest manifestations of 'Shakespeare' in the

digital age, these perceived contrasts are still proving to be a productive tension.

I've suggested in this article that the phrase 'Shakespeare brand' is at best metaphorical. However, reception studies is founded on key metaphors, from the passive image of 'reception' itself to the more politicized sense of seizure, or 'hostile takeover',[51] in 'appropriation'. Julie Sanders has explored the potential of some alternative sources of metaphor – such as, via Genette, the world of horticulture with its images of 'grafting', and of other natural phenomena such as 'filtration' and 'cross-pollination'.[52] With such terms, she seeks to get past the 'linear and reductive' relationship between source and 'secondary, belated' response that some existing metaphors might engender.[53] She eschews linearity with borrowings from musicology (base and improvisation) and science (specifically genetic inheritance and environmental adaptation), fully aware that these are metaphorical images, rather than literal descriptions:

While acknowledging that a volume on the literary processes of adaptation and appropriation can only ever deploy such complex thinking at the level of metaphor and suggestion, nevertheless the Mendel-Darwin synthesis offers a useful way of thinking about the happy combination of influence and creativity, of tradition and the individual talent, and of parental influence and offspring, in appropriative literature, perhaps in all literature.[54]

What emerges from Sanders's call for a more 'dynamic', 'kinetic' and 'diverse' vocabulary with which to talk about adaptation and appropriation is a sense of multiplicity: the ability to talk about at

---

[51] Julie Sanders, *Adaptation and Appropriation* (London, 2006), p. 9.

[52] Sanders, *Adaptation*, pp. 12–13.

[53] She quotes elsewhere from Adrian Poole a list of terms that describes the Victorian reworking of the artistic past: 'borrowing, stealing, appropriating, inheriting, assimilating...being influenced, inspired, dependent, indebted, haunted, possessed...homage, mimicry, travesty, echo, allusion, and intertextuality', p. 3.

[54] Sanders, *Adaptation*, p. 156.

once influence *and* creativity, tradition *and* the individual talent, rather than a mono-directional line of influence or appropriation; this desire is also visible in Christy Desmet's suggestion of a language of mutual 'donation' or dialogue.[55]

As a metaphor, 'brand' holds out the possibility of such doubleness, of looking in both directions at once: seeing Shakespeare as marker and mark; exploited and all-conquering; already meaningful, and made meaningful by his deployment (and thus neither saying entirely that Shakespeare's meaning is already determined, nor that others determine his meaning for him). It is particularly illuminating as a metaphor if it helps us to see, rather than to iron out, productive tensions within his name that can in turn generate what Sanders calls a desirable 'tension of expectation and surprise'[56] in his appropriation. But the danger is that the metaphor grants us permission simply to describe new instances of Shakespeare's presence in the marketplace, without thinking about how 'Shakespeare' functions

there, or analysing the work done in, and with, his name. Furthermore, there is a pressing temptation for English departments to adopt wholeheartedly the notion of 'the Shakespeare brand' as leverage as they compete in what looks set to be an increasingly market-oriented world of higher education; to at once exploit and resist Shakespeare's place in the market in order to guarantee the future of English and the humanities. All metaphors for Shakespeare's reception – including 'brand', and even 'catalyst', problematized elsewhere in this volume – are potentially valuable, provided we acknowledge their limitations, and ask whether they tell us more about us as Shakespeare scholars than they do about Shakespeare.

---

[55] Christy Desmet, 'Paying Attention in Shakespeare Parody: From Tom Stoppard to YouTube', *Shakespeare Survey 61* (Cambridge, 2008), 227–38.

[56] Sanders, *Adaptation*, p. 25.

GLOBAL SHAKESPEARE 2.0
AND THE TASK OF
THE PERFORMANCE ARCHIVE

ALEXANDER HUANG

Crises often usher in great opportunities for innovation. In the face of stiff competition from other forms of entertainment, theatre artists have gone global and digital, taking Shakespeare with them.[1] Hundreds of thousands of Shakespeare-related videos including promotional clips for stage productions – buoyed by a tag cloud – 'live' on the English- and Japanese-language portals of YouTube and other video-sharing and social networking sites around the world.[2] Some of these may be transient, but digital video is a large part of Shakespeare's presence in contemporary world cultures, reconceptualizing the idea of liveness and archive. As digital screens become 'the default interfaces for media access' and data mining, the public can express themselves audiovisually on these sites while shaping the resulting archive.[3]

What are digital video's functions? How can those functions be best facilitated in the field of Shakespeare studies when the disciplinary boundary between text and performance is blurred by virtual performative texts?[4] This article surveys the state of global Shakespeare and analyses the implications of digital video in current and future scholarly and pedagogic practice. While recent scholarship has begun to address Shakespeare's place in the new media and digital culture, it has not fully engaged the digital video archive's impact on the field due in part to a continued interest in new textualities in 'the late age of print'.[5]

VIDEO IN VIRTUAL WORLDS

Online digital video is being tapped as a research and pedagogic resource, a marketing tool, and an art form with a symbiotic relationship with the stage. In fact, video is now the core of virtual environments, websites associated with theatre companies and a small but rich array of scholarly digital archives. Characterized by unique dynamics and challenges, each of these three areas adds a new dimension to global Shakespeare in theory and practice.

---

[1] Portions of this essay have benefited from collaboration with Peter Donaldson whose unfailing helpfulness and generosity as well as his leadership in this field I wish to acknowledge.

[2] Such as South Korea's Daum tvPot and China's Tudou.com and Youku.com.

[3] Pelle Snickars and Patrick Vonderau, 'Introduction', *The YouTube Reader*, ed. Pelle Snickars and Patrick Vonderau (Stockholm, 2009), p. 16; Jens Schröter, 'On the Logic of the Digital Archive', *The YouTube Reader*, p. 341.

[4] W. B. Worthen, 'Performing Shakespeare in Digital Culture', in *The Cambridge Companion to Shakespeare and Popular Culture*, ed. Robert Shaughnessy (Cambridge, 2007), pp. 231–2.

[5] The term was coined by Jay David Bolter, *Writing Space* (Mahwah, 2000), pp. 3–5. Christy Desmet, 'Paying Attention in Shakespeare Parody: From Tom Stoppard to YouTube', *Shakespeare Survey 61* (Cambridge, 2008), pp. 227–8; Richard Burt, 'To E- or Not to E-? Disposing of Schlockspeare in the Age of Digital Media', in Richard Burt, ed., *Shakespeare After Mass Media* (New York, 2002), pp. 1–32; Espen J. Aarseth, *Cybertext: Perspectives on Ergodic Literature* (Baltimore, 1997); Katarzyna Kwapisz Williams, *Deforming Shakespeare: Investigations in Textuality and Digital Media* (Torun, 2009).

These days one can attend a virtual performance of *Hamlet* or a staged reading of *Twelfth Night* on Second Life, a three-dimensional virtual world allowing users to interact online with each other through their personalized avatars. Meanwhile, online quest and role-play games such as *Arden* beckon players to explore first-hand Shakespeare's medieval world or Renaissance Italy.[6] In *Mabinogi Hamlet*, a three-dimensional medieval-themed MMORPG (massive multiplayer online role-play game), one assumes the dual roles of the gamer and the player in the theatrical sense. There is a storyline following the narrative of the Shakespearian tragedy, but the participants are free to reinvent the wheel as they converse with a character named Marlowe who holds the script of *Hamlet*, watch an animation of the ramparts scene, join Hamlet and Horatio on a stealth mission to follow Claudius, and eventually dress up to become Hamlet – letter in hand and joined by Rosencrantz and Guildenstern on a mysterious ship. It takes an average player approximately four hours to finish the quest. Interestingly, the game ends with a curtain call. All the characters and gamers appear on stage to receive applause.[7] Built around sleek visual effects, games such as these are part performance archive and part performance event, combining rehearsed, programmed events and improvisational, contingent actions on and off stage.

As well, many theatre companies have experimented with interactive contents and online videos – live or recorded – to engage existing, future, on-site and off-site audiences before, during and after the productions.[8] Some projects bring globally circulating texts closer to a local audience. When Taiwan's Contemporary Legend Theatre was planning their fourth adaptation of Shakespeare, *The Tempest*, in 2004, the company created a website with rich materials where audiences cast votes for their favourite versions of the adaptation. The company staged the version with the most votes – one that highlighted Taiwan's history as a (post-)colonial island. Other projects focus on bringing local, site-specific performances to a global audience. As the National Theatre Live entered its second season on 14 October 2010,

nearly 200,000 people saw London productions broadcast in high definition to 320 screens in cinemas and theatres in 22 countries. *Hamlet*, directed by Nicholas Hytner with Rory Kinnear in the title role, and *King Lear*, directed by Michael Grandage, were broadcast in high definition to theatre audiences around the world.[9] Understandably, the service is informed by a sense of national pride. Now in its fifth season, *The Met: Live in HD*, the Metropolitan Opera's Emmy award-winning series of digital performance transmissions has appeared in movie theatres in an even longer list of

---

6 *Arden: The World of William Shakespeare*, independent of the renowned Arden Shakespeare editions, is a MMOG (massive multiplayer online game) framed by the narrative of *Richard III*. It is partially funded by the MacArthur Foundation and created by Ted Castronova and his team at Indiana University Bloomington. The newly released *Assassin's Creed II* (Xbox 360 and PlayStation 3), a multimillion-dollar production from Ubisoft makes Renaissance Italy into blockbuster material for a crypto-historical adventure quest game, with Renaissance scholars as consultants. Players can mingle virtually with local residents as they explore highly detailed, 3-D simulations of Florence and Venice in 1477.

7 Developed by NEXON in South Korea, *Mabinogi* has been especially popular in East Asia. It also has a following in North America, Australia and New Zealand. *Mabinogi Hamlet* was released in August 2010.

8 Peter Holland, 'Passing Through: Shakespeare, Theater Companies, and the Internet', in *Shakespeare without Boundaries: Essays in Honor of Dieter Mehl*, ed. Christa Jansohn, Lena Cowen Orlin and Stanley Wells (Newark, 2011), pp. 107–19.

9 Screenings are taking place across the UK, Ireland, the US (including Nassau and Honolulu), Canada, Mexico, South Africa, Australia, New Zealand, Estonia, Finland, Sweden, Poland, Czech Republic, Malta, Germany, Luxembourg, Belgium and the Netherlands. Venues include the Sidney Harman Hall of the Shakespeare Theatre Company in Washington, DC; tickets ($20) are much more affordable than for most live productions of this calibre. Accompanied by majestic music, the promotional video on its website announced that 'for almost fifty years, Britain's National Theatre has been at the heart of theatrical excellence and innovation, then the curtain rose around the world on National Theatre Live – a stunning series of plays captured live in high definition and shown in cinemas worldwide. Now the National Theatre proudly presents a brand new season of the very best of British theatre'. www.nationaltheatre.org.uk/45462/home/national-theatre-live-homepage.html, accessed 15 November 2010.

countries around the world.[10] The video broadcast made stage performances more affordable and increased the production value of the plays for both on-site (privileged) and off-site (mass) audiences. The presence of Shakespeare in contemporary culture owes a great deal to these hybrid forms of entertainment.

As the boundary between traditional notions of live and virtual performances becomes ever more permeable, online scholarly archives, publications and curriculum resources, including such well-established projects as the *Internet Shakespeare Editions*, also evolve to alter the landscape of Shakespeare and performance studies in significant ways.[11] Both online and traditional journals have engaged the Internet in various ways. *Borrowers and Lenders: The Journal of Shakespeare and Appropriation*, an online journal with a global outlook, advocates a hybrid form of publication. It combines multimedia online contents with a style that seems to be 'nostalgic for print'.[12] Readers engage in dialogic reading as they manoeuvre 'between printout and media-rich screen'.[13] In preparation of its recent special issue on new media, *Shakespeare Quarterly* experimented with a hybrid online open-review process and used crowd sourcing to harness the collective wisdom of a self-selected community of scholars.[14] These publications produce permanent documents that cannot be revised. This, of course, contrasts with digital archives, in which revision is always possible and often expected. With institutional backing and public funding, some projects are open access and operate with clearly defined target audiences in mind. *Stagework* (www.stagework.org.uk/) takes teachers, students and theatregoers behind the scenes of productions at the National Theatre and regional theatres in England through rehearsal diaries, short videos of interviews and performance footage with commentary.[15] Targeting a global audience of scholars, educators and students, the MIT Shakespeare Project has expanded to include several video-centric, collaborative archives, including the *Global Shakespeares* (http://globalshakespeares.org/) which contains a global array of videos of live performances from the Arab world to Brazil, and

Hamlet on the Ramparts, a clearing-house of geographically distant visual and textual resources for a single scene (http://shea.mit.edu/ramparts) which recently appeared on a list of editor's picks in the *New York Times*.[16] In the works are online editions of the two-volume *Cambridge World Shakespeare Encyclopedia*, edited by Bruce R. Smith, and the five-volume *Shakespeare Encyclopedia: Life, Works, World, and Legacy*, edited by Patricia Parker. Both promise innovative uses of worldwide audio-visual contents and an emphasis on global Shakespeare, but have yet to decide on a model of operation: fully open-access, commercial solutions,

---

[10] *The Met Live in HD* is available in Argentina, Australia, Austria, Belgium, Brazil, Canada, Chile, Costa Rica, Colombia, Croatia, Czech Republic, Denmark, Estonia, Finland, France, Germany, Hong Kong, Hungary, Iceland, Ireland, Italy, Japan, Latvia, Lithuania, Luxembourg, Malta, Mexico, the Netherlands, New Zealand, Norway, Peru, Poland, Portugal, Puerto Rico, Romania, Slovakia, South Africa, South Korea, Spain, Sweden, Switzerland, the UK and Uruguay, and in national movie theatres, independent venues, schools and museums across the U.S. Prices vary by location. www.metoperafamily.org/metopera/broadcast/hd_events_next.aspx, accessed 15 November 2010.

[11] Located at http://internetshakespeare.uvic.ca. Michael Best, 'The *Internet Shakespeare Editions*: Scholarly Shakespeare on the Web', *Shakespeare*, 4 (2010), 221–33.

[12] Essays are available in the PDF format to be printed out, mimicking the style of print journals. However, online versions of many essays 'quote' film stills and video and audio clips in a manner akin to the way in which texts are quoted for analysis. For example, see Alexander C. Y. Huang, ed., *Asian Shakespeares on Screen: Two Films in Perspective*, special issue of *Borrowers and Lenders: The Journal of Shakespeare and Appropriation*, 4.2 (2009), http://www.borrowers.uga.edu/.

[13] Christy Desmet, 'Appropriation and the Design of an Online Shakespeare Journal', in *Shakespeare in Hollywood, Asia, and Cyberspace*, ed. Alexander C. Y. Huang and Charles S. Ross (West Lafayette, 2009), p. 246.

[14] Katherine Rowe, 'From the Editor: Gentle Numbers', *Shakespeare Quarterly*, 61 (2010), v–vi.

[15] *Stagework* is commissioned and funded by the UK Department for Culture, Media and Sport. For studies of *Stagework*, YouTube Shakespeare, *Arden: The World of William Shakespeare*, and Second Life, see Peter Holland, 'Performing Shakespeare for the Web Community', in *Shakespeare in Hollywood, Asia, and Cyberspace*, ed. Huang and Ross, pp. 252–62; and Desmet, 'Appropriation', pp. 227–38.

[16] http://topics.nytimes.com/topics/reference/timestopics/subjects/h/hamlet/index.html, accessed 2 December 2010.

or a hybrid form. Not all projects are collaborative in nature or embrace the open-access model. As a commercial enterprise launched in October, 2009, *Digital Theatre* (http://digitaltheatre.com/) sells downloadable full videos of stage performances and an iPhone app that tracks theatre productions in the UK, with an emphasis on London. *BardBox* (http://bardbox.wordpress.com/), a syndicated, eclectic collection of videos hosted by commercial services such as YouTube and Vimeo, offers expert commentary on what its sole creator considers 'the best and most interesting of original Shakespeare-related videos', including animations, parodies, recitations, amateur records of stage productions, and student works.[17]

THE RISE OF GLOBAL SHAKESPEARE 2.0

These are signs that the age of Global Shakespeare 2.0 – worldwide performances in digital forms – has arrived. It is an age when archival meanings are co-determined by the locations and digital afterlives of performances.[18] It is an age when Shakespeare has achieved a new level of membership in world literature and on the Internet via diverse channels of exchange, diffusion and dissemination.[19] The term 'global Shakespeare 2.0' is used here to describe a stage in performance theory and practice enabled by digital forms and tools. It is distinct from the hype of what has been called the Web 2.0 in official PR – the brave new, 'democratized' world enabled by the Internet's video and social networking functionalities.

Shakespeare has become a cliché and global Shakespeare a paradox – popularized and commercialized to some, yet decidedly high-brow to others – carrying at once the risk of alienating potential audiences and the promise of rich rewards as a site for artistic innovation. This duality is fuelled by the efficacy of virtual media, video sharing and social networking sites. Defined by remarkable internal divisions and incongruities, Shakespearian performances in our times often embrace

self-referentiality and inter-media citational strategies. Adaptations refer to one another in addition to the Shakespearian pre-text. Baz Luhrmann's 1996 film *William Shakespeare's Romeo + Juliet*, starring Leonardo DiCaprio, is a good example. It brings both the melodramatic and tragic elements of the play into stark relief against modern media fiction and history. Cheah Chee Kong's film *Chicken Rice War* (Singapore, 2000) parodies Hollywood rhetoric and global teen culture. During the audition for a high school production of *Romeo and Juliet* in the film, a young lady challenges her classmate, an aspiring actor: 'What makes you think that you can play Romeo? You don't have the looks, and you can't even speak properly . . . Do you think you look like Leonardo [DiCaprio]?' The two films, along with their undefined Shakespearian sources, engage in the kind of responsive, polyglot, inter-media conversation that makes reading across cultures so compelling today. World literature has come a long way since the time of Johann Wolfgang von Goethe and Christoph Martin Wieland – the latter coining the term *Weltliteratur*. It is now used to refer to the cultural and literary phenomenon driven by globalization rather than a fixed set of texts or canons representing symbolic values of various national cultures. Likewise, global Shakespeare, a phenomenon that began to take shape in the playwright's lifetime, is part of the transnational cultural flow of an ever expanding body of texts that circulate beyond the Elizabethan English culture of origin in various forms of English, in intralingual translation, and in

---

[17] The blog is the brainchild of film historian Luke McKernan who curates the videos and provides basic metadata for each entry.

[18] Cf. Jacques Derrida, *Archive Fever: A Freudian Impression*, trans. Eric Prenowitz (Chicago, 1998), pp. 16–18.

[19] As an institutional and cultural phenomenon, world literature is gaining new momentum, as evidenced by several new initiatives, including the newly founded Institute for World Literature at Harvard University in 2010, directed by David Damrosch, a new anthology of global literary theory in preparation at Routledge, and a rapidly increasing number of undergraduate and graduate courses on global Shakespeare and global literary theory at universities around the world.

intersemiotic transformation.[20] The last category pertains to a broad range of interpretive possibilities, including political readings, theatrical representations of a play, and digital manipulations and archiving – speech into image, verbal signs to non-verbal signs, and subtitling.

There is another side to the story of global Shakespeare. The new historicist and cultural materialist preoccupation with Shakespeare's representation of cultural others since the 1980s has foregrounded the early modern history of globalization in English literature. In the wake of this line of enquiry, the global history of performance has recently been established as an integral part of Shakespearian scholarship and pedagogy.[21] The last two decades have marked the first phase of sustained study of Shakespeare performances in a wider world, and a new wave of English-language scholarship since 2000 has further expanded the idea of global Shakespeare.[22]

The present time is defined by the rise of global Shakespeare 2.0 as new artistic, digital and intellectual paradigms that are moving beyond the celebratory vision of literary universalism. As performance artists challenge fixed notions of tradition, critics are no longer confined by the question of narrowly defined cultural authenticity. Scholars are now seeking answers to how global Shakespeare formulates first-hand experience rooted in different localities.[23] If the first phase of the study of global Shakespeare was defined by the 'ideological investments in the conventions of authenticity' or resonances of the Globe,[24] global Shakespeare 2.0 is shaped by multilocal perspectives enabled by online tools and Shakespeare's 'vernacular applicability' along shifting textual and performative axes.[25] More notable interpretations of Shakespeare's plays are emerging across Europe, North America, Africa, Asia, Latin America and the Middle East, and many performances are being archived, read closely and used as case studies in the classroom. Directors such as Ninagawa Yukio, Sulayman Al-Bassam, Ong Keng Sen and Peter Brook have reached diverse audiences through new strategies to bring together different cultural

contexts and genres even as global Shakespeare continues to be defined by its alterity.

However, it is useful to bear in mind that, encompassing not only non-Anglophone interpretations but also the global circulation of performances in any language, global Shakespeare is not always a rosy undertaking. Rendering *Macbeth* in

---

20 Roman Jakobson, 'On Linguistic Aspects of Translation', in *The Translation Studies Reader*, 2nd edn, ed. Lawrence Venuti (New York, 2004), pp. 138–51.

21 Emily Bartels, 'Shakespeare's "Other" Worlds: The Critical Trek', *Literature Compass*, 5/6 (2008), 1111–38; Carole Levin and John Watkins, *Shakespeare's Foreign Worlds: National and Transnational Identities in the Elizabethan Age* (Ithaca, 2009); Richard Wilson, *Shakespeare in French Theory: King of Shadows* (London, 2009); Eric J. Griffin's *English Renaissance Drama and the Specter of Spain: Ethnopoetics and Empire* (Philadelphia, 2009); Maria Del Sapio Garbero, ed., *Identity, Otherness, and Empire in Shakespeare's Rome* (Aldershot, 2009).

22 Samuel L. Leiter, ed., *Shakespeare Around the Globe: A Guide to Notable Postwar Revivals* (New York, 1986); Gary Taylor, *Reinventing Shakespeare: A Cultural History from the Restoration to the Present* (Oxford, 1991); Dennis Kennedy, ed., *Foreign Shakespeare: Contemporary Performance* (Cambridge, 1993); John Russell Brown, *New Sites for Shakespeare: Theatre, the Audience, and Asia* (London, 1999); Christy Desmet and Robert Sawyer, eds., *Shakespeare and Appropriation* (London, 1999); Ryuta Minami, Ian Carruthers and John Gillies, eds., *Performing Shakespeare in Japan* (Cambridge, 2001); Sonia Massai, ed., *World-Wide Shakespeares: Local Appropriations in Film and Performance* (New York, 2005); Martin Orkin, *Local Shakespeares: Proximations and Power* (London, 2005); Margaret Jane Kidnie, *Shakespeare and the Problem of Adaptation* (London, 2008); Huang and Ross, eds., *Shakespeare in Hollywood, Asia and Cyberspace*.

23 Poonam Trivedi, 'Re-Playing Shakespeare in Asia: An Introduction', *Re-playing Shakespeare in Asia*, ed. Poonam Trivedi and Ryuta Minami (London, 2010), pp. 1–20; Alexander C. Y. Huang, *Chinese Shakespeares: Two Centuries of Cultural Exchange* (New York, 2009).

24 Questions such as 'what is it that endures when [Shakespeare] is deprived of his tongue?' dominated the research in the 1990s (see Kennedy, *Foreign Shakespeare*, p. 17). Michael Billington, 'Was Shakespeare English?', in *Shakespeare: World Views*, ed. Heather Kerr, Robin Eaden and Madge Mitton (Newark, 1996), pp. 15–28; Peter Donaldson, '"All Which It Inherit": Shakespeare, Globes and Global Media', *Shakespeare Survey 60* (Cambridge, 2007), pp. 183–200.

25 Mark Thornton Burnett, 'Writing Shakespeare in the Global Economy', *Shakespeare Survey 58* (Cambridge, 2005), p. 185.

Zulu or touring an Arab adaptation of *Richard III* to London would entail a very different level of cultural prestige from translating Korean playwright Yi Kangbaek into English.[26] Wars, censorship and political ideologies can suppress or encourage particular approaches to selected Shakespearian plays or genres, and the digital enterprise is built upon a volatile relationship among content creators (rights holders), platform providers and funding agencies, as evidenced by Viacom's law suits against YouTube and numerous other cases.

DIGITAL VIDEO AND SHAKESPEARE STUDIES

These cases demonstrate that the Internet is never a neutral, universal platform, but a collective of people and 'institutions shaped by local pressures' to create and conserve cultural value.[27] The field of literary studies has witnessed the so-called 'linguistic turn', 'cultural turn' and, more recently, 'performative turn', each of which is informed by distinct but interconnected philosophical principles. The emergence of new media has been crucial to each transitional period in cultural formations.[28] Though there have been profound changes in the realm of text through what N. Katherine Hayles calls 'media translation', the digital revolution has had an even more profound effect on how we can use images, text, moving image and sound.[29]

The field of Shakespeare in performance stands to gain from archival stability and the repertoire of embodied cultural history. A performance video archive with vetted contents and open-access platform can become both the archive and the repertoire. The digital archive and tools are useful not because they are new but because they are efficient and, in many cases, the only tools to transcend the journalistic mode of research and writing. Just as the arrival of new media technologies – daguerreotype, lithography, typewriter, phonography, cinematography – have reconfigured oral and print cultures, digital video is now transforming the practice and study of the literary and performative arts.

Distinct from analogue media such as photography and film, digital video – as a non-linear, non-sequential medium – can support instant access to any sequence in a performance, as well as the means to reorder and annotate sequences, and to bring them into meaningful conjunction with other videos, texts and image collections. A global archive of Shakespeare as a performed event can play a crucial role in Shakespeare studies by enabling an ever-wider range of interpretive possibilities that activate important aspects of the plays through videos that connect live performances to the concepts of rehearsal and replay. Video recordings have been used in the study of Shakespeare on film and in the theatre for many years, and DVD publication of many commercially released films has made it possible to study the filmtext more closely than in the past, since one can locate and start to play key moments easily, and with some programs one can also bookmark start points for future reference. Reductions in the cost of storage and improvements in video technologies have now made it possible, indeed common, for entire films

---

[26] As Pascale Casanova observes in *The World Republic of Letters* (Cambridge, MA, 2007), world literature consists of a regime of inequality where dominant languages and literatures subjugate minor ones. See also Richard Nichols, ed., *Modern Korean Drama: An Anthology* (New York, 2009) and Kate McLuskie, '*Macbeth / Umabatha*: Global Shakespeare in a Post-Colonial Market', *Shakespeare Survey 52* (Cambridge, 1999), p. 155.

[27] Kate Rumbold, 'From "Access" to "Creativity": Shakespeare Institutions, New Media, and the Language of Cultural Value', *Shakespeare Quarterly*, 61 (2010), 313–37.

[28] This is a point widely recognized in media studies, but it has not received the attention it deserves in literary studies, except for the theorization of the tension between speech and writing. Jacques Derrida, 'Signature Event Context', in *Margins of Philosophy*, trans. Alan Bass (Chicago, 1982), pp. 307–30; David Golumbia, *The Cultural Logic of Computation* (Cambridge, MA, 2009); Jay David Bolter and Richard Grusin, *Remediation: Understanding New Media* (Cambridge, MA, 1999); Friedrich A. Kittler, *Gramophone, Film, Typewriter*, trans. Geoffrey Winthrop-Young and Michael Wutz (Stanford, 1999).

[29] N. Katherine Hayles, *My Mother Was a Computer: Digital Subjects and Literary Texts* (Chicago, 2005), p. 89.

and collections of films to be streamed over the Internet.

Though visual and sonic media have become so large a part of emerging Internet culture, the field of digital humanities lags behind these developments in both theory and practice, and 'remains deeply interested [and invested] in text' or the codex book in both academic and commercial initiatives.[30] In the many new media studies programmes and departments, the emphasis is often on social media, fan culture, video and video games and, in contrast to the digital humanities, too little value is often placed on 'legacy media' and the literature and arts of the past.[31] There is a gap between these emerging fields that a new approach to the study of Shakespeare in performance through online video collections can help to bridge. Shakespeare spans popular and academic interests and his plays are staged throughout the world. Most of the projects discussed in *New Technologies and Renaissance Studies* (2008), including *Records of Early English Drama*, are also oriented towards texts and textual studies. As Michael Greenhalgh and others have written, 'in spite of an increasing number of bright spots, initiatives in the image field have always been more patchy than those involving texts'.[32]

The contrast is even starker in Shakespeare studies: there are many text-based projects, such as online editions.[33] *Shakespeare*, a free iPhone application featuring the complete works of Shakespeare (including *Edward III* and *Sir Thomas More*), offers a new text based on the Globe Edition, First Folio and early quartos.[34] There are electronic versions of other edited texts, digital facsimiles of folios and quartos,[35] and some editorial sites offer clips and partial videos of performances, but even sites particularly focused on performance, such as the International Database of Shakespeare on Film, Television and Radio (bufvc.ac.uk.shakespeare), are not illustrated by visual media, while others include still images or brief video clips.[36] Open-access full video recordings of theatrical productions are still uncommon. Besides MIT's *Global Shakespeares* (launched in August 2010), there are two other projects that also feature online, full-length

performance video resource with different missions and regional emphases. *Asian Shakespeare Intercultural Archive (A/S/I/A)* is an academic project that offers seven full-length streaming videos of recent Chinese, Japanese, Korean and Singaporean productions with English, Chinese and Japanese

---

30 Susan Schreibman, Ray Siemens and John Unsworth, 'The Digital Humanities and Humanities Computing: An Introduction', in *A Companion to Digital Humanities*, ed. Susan Schreibman, Ray Siemens and John Unsworth (Oxford, 2004), pp. xxiii–xxvii, esp. xxiii. See also Williams, *Deforming Shakespeare*; George P. Landow, *Hypertext 3.0: Critical Theory and New Media in an Era of Globalization* (Baltimore, 2006); and Aarseth, *Cybertext: Perspectives on Ergodic Literature*.

31 In his theorization of cinema within the histories of media cultures, Les Manovich defines new media forms through five principles (numerical representation, modularity, automation, variability and transcoding). New media forms are defined in contrast to print, television and other electronic media. Manovich, *The Language of New Media* (Cambridge, 2001), pp. 21–50.

32 Michael Greenhalgh, 'Digital Still Images and Renaissance Studies (with a Short Section on Digital Video)', in *New Technologies and Renaissance Studies*, ed. William Bowen and Raymond G. Siemens (Tempe, 2008), pp. 27–72, esp. 40.

33 Most notably the Internet Shakespeare Editions (internet-shakespeare.uvic.ca).

34 Edited by the PlayShakespeare.com team and co-produced with Readdle, *Shakespeare* is available for free for iPhone users. *Shakespeare Pro* is available for $2.99, and it includes a Shakespeare portrait gallery, a searchable glossary based on David and Ben Crystal's *Shakespeare's Words*, Charles and Mary Lamb's *Tales from Shakespeare*, and other features. *Shakespeare* made it to Apple's 'App Store Pick of the Week' in July 2009 – selected from among the then 65,000 iPhone applications.

35 For instance, the *Perseus Collection: Global Shakespeare* (http://www.perseus.tufts.edu/hopper/collection?collection=Perseus%3Acollection%3AShakespeare_Globe) and *The Shakespeare Quartos Archive* (http://www.folger.edu/pr_preview.cfm?prid=216).

36 Examples include the Stanford *Shakespeare in Asia* site (http://sia.stanford.edu/); Christie Carson, ed., *King Lear* (Cambridge, 2001) CD-ROM; *Global Performing Arts Database* (Cornell University; www.glopad.org/); Royal Shakespeare Company's Education website (www.rsc.org.uk/learning/) includes short clips of current and select past productions; the AHDS-funded Designing Shakespeare contains a text and image database and video interviews conducted by Christie Carson, but does not include videos of live performances (http://www.ahds.ac.uk/performingarts/collections/designing-shakespeare.htm).

subtitles. To view the videos, the user has to create an account and log in. *Digital Theatre* is a commercial enterprise with ten productions and one behind-the-scenes documentary at the time of writing. In partnership with the Royal Shakespeare Company, the Young Vic and other British companies, *Digital Theatre*'s goal is to sell a 'best seat in the house experience'. Launched in October 2009, the company behind the *Digital Theatre* aims to preserve and monetize archival records of live performances: 'British productions that once would have been lost are now being purchased by global audiences.' There are only two Shakespearian productions available, both from the RSC: *The Comedy of Errors* (dir. Paul Hunter) and *As You Like It* (dir. Michael Boyd). It could be said that Shakespeare is a paradoxical presence in the age of YouTube: on the one hand there are Shakespeare videos in abundance on the Web – among them many excerpts from Shakespeare films and many remixes which, for example, alternate sequences from two or more versions of *Romeo and Juliet*, and, on the other hand, there has until now been no substantial collection of videos of Shakespeare theatrical performances designed for scholarly and educational use.

The first decades after the introduction of the Macintosh witnessed the emergence of hypermedia texts, or expanded books, such as the Shakespeare Electronic Archive (SEA). The SEA's *Hamlet* collection links specific lines of text to page images (all variant pages of the First Folio, all copies of Q1 and Q2, and more than 1,200 illustrations) and three complete films.[37] These projects share the expanded book model and a number of them began as stand-alone or modular, plug-in resources, before the advent of the World Wide Web. As newer media gives the 'airy nothing' of Shakespeare in performance a global habitation, an important question to ask is how meanings are formulated, shared and contested, and how we might use the new capacity of the Web to handle large video collections to find a new balance between text and performance. The answers we will get from objects in this multimedia environment that is always in flux depend crucially on the questions

put to them. The encounter between Shakespeare and newer media over the last twenty years has already transformed many of our interpretive and pedagogical practices. Recent advances in network technologies and the growth of social media have brought the field to the cusp of another sea-change.

While one may be limited to digitized texts in a project such as *The Dickinson Electronic Archive* (www.emilydickinson.org/), Shakespeare offers the richest material for negotiating the transition from textual paradigms or the expanded book model to a truly performance-based mode of understanding cultural production and reception. In part this is because Shakespeare is so widely studied, taught and performed throughout the world, but it is also because it has now become possible to bring together a coherent collection of video recordings of complete productions of sufficient depth to create a densely interconnected video environment in which one can move freely from one performance or sequence to others based on the particulars of the performances themselves rather than solely based on their relation to Shakespeare's text, or to the needs of a text-driven understanding of their significance. A video-centred, rather than a text-centred Shakespeare archive has the potential to transform key scholarly and pedagogical practices in the humanities, and to give performance-based study the precision of reference and the depth of access to the basic documentary materials of the field long taken for granted in the domain of textual studies. Of course digital video can never replace live performance, but it can, especially in a globally interconnected online environment, do many things that the performances it records cannot in themselves do. Digitized performances can form new relationships with the local and global, contemporary and even ancient histories of which they are a part.

As stable, accessible, citable video 'texts' they can become common objects for close study in the classroom and citation in scholarship, and they can become a part of the cultural experience of

---

37 http://shea.mit.edu/shakespeare/htdocs/main/index.htm, accessed January 2010.

new, globally distributed and potentially unlimited audiences both now and in the future. Further, wider knowledge of contemporary refashionings of Shakespeare in performance are not only valuable in themselves but can lead us back to Shakespeare's plays with new insight and new paths for interpretation. Works such as Ong Keng Sen's transnational and pan-Asian productions (*Search: Hamlet, Lear, Desdemona*), Kenneth Branagh's *As You Like It* with a strong Japanese motif, and Tim Supple's multilingual *Midsummer Night's Dream* with an Indian and Sri Lankan cast, are generating extraordinary artistic and intellectual energy by recasting gender, racial and social identities. The racial issue disappears by being recast as uneasy familial relations in Japanese interpretations of *Othello*, and it is made hauntingly present through its absence from radically localized, colour-blind Korean performances that seek to redress the wound of Japanese colonization. In the Chinese tradition of performing *The Merchant of Venice* as romantic comedy, the play is often retooled as an adventure of an attractive woman lawyer or an outlandish tale involving a pound of human flesh.[38] This framework has activated elements of the play that, over several centuries of Anglo-European readings, have become obscure to communities that gravitate towards the ethics of conversion as a key site of tension in the narrative.[39] Other examples of reconfigurations of the centre and the periphery abound. These works have led to the transformation of traditions occurring in both directions at once.

Several factors have limited what we expect to be a major transformation in the ways in which Shakespeare on digital video can be used in scholarship and teaching. First, copyright and other intellectual property restrictions have limited the distribution of digital video on the Web. Second, the tools needed to segment and annotate video sequences for study and replay have been lacking until now. The programmability of digital video can highlight theatrical contingencies for analysis.[40] Scholarly study requires precision of reference and provision of the means to make evidence available in excerpts; in the case of text, footnotes and quotation from sources satisfy this

need. In the domain of video, the equivalent functions include the ability to define a video segment precisely, to insert sequences into one's own interpretive construction, which might be a multimedia essay with playable clips in line or as clickable citations, or a set of annotated clips for presentation. *Global Shakespeares*, a non-profit, open-access project, offers some solutions to these issues.

In the domain of text, what Peter Donaldson calls 'a common object' is taken for granted.[41] In text-centric models where other media are present but are adjuncts or expansions of the text, excerpts of texts are cited to draw the attention of a class or readers as evidence to support an argument. The citation can be discussed and referred to as many times as needed in multiple contexts. With well-developed scholarly apparatus and tools such as Google Books one can easily cite digital and codex books as sources. In the domain of performance studies, digital video will be a common object that can be circulated and interpreted by scholars, teachers and students. These replayable clips can become moving image footnotes. Just like texts, a video clip has to be viewed in the context of other films, productions and performance videos of the same play or director, in the context of a worldwide collection of Shakespeare in performance as a whole and in relation to other academic theatrical archives and the expanding user-generated resources available on YouTube and elsewhere.

Currently available digital tools are capable of supporting both the text-centric model and the new model in which image, audio or video collections are the starting place for an

---

[38] Huang, *Chinese Shakespeares*, pp. 69–70 and 115–23.

[39] Janet Adelman, *Blood Relations: Christian and Jew in* The Merchant of Venice (Chicago, 2008).

[40] Manovich, *The Language of New Media*, pp. 47–8; Mark B. N. Hansen, *New Philosophy for New Media* (Cambridge, 2004), pp. 31–2; Matthew G. Kirschenbaum, *Mechanisms: New Media and the Forensic Imagination* (Cambridge, 2008), 3; Yvonne Spielmann, *Video: The Reflexive Medium*, trans. Anja Welle and Stan Jones (Cambridge, 2008), pp. 11 and 112–13.

[41] Peter Donaldson, personal communication, 15 March 2010.

exploration across media.[42] In addition, the global reach and enhanced possibilities for broad participation of the Web have challenged us to rethink the role of the Shakespeare scholar, the place of English-language/Antipodean Shakespeare in a much wider world, as Shakespearian texts, images and videos are remixed and sampled in the new media, and as more Shakespeare performances that originate in other parts of the world appear on the Web, yet remain as much documents of local, national and regional histories of theatre and performance art as they are of Shakespeare plays.

We have come a long way in the three decades since J. L. Styan's *The Shakespeare Revolution*, which imagined a 'new role for stage-centred criticism' that uncovers the original 'Shakespeare experience'.[43] In 1996, before the advent of the multimedia-enhanced Web environment, James Bulman referred to the ways in which the 'technologies of film and video' can transform readers into viewers by making accessible 'performative elements that would have been denied them' in the study of Shakespeare. The access to performance on multiple levels – rehearsal, production, reception – is the first step to engage with the 'multiple material existences' of a single play.[44] Recognizing technology's capacity to assimilate performance to literary text, Douglas Lanier identified the challenge for the field during that time as how to avoid reifying the author-function in performance criticism and 'how *not* to replace the old textuality with a new form of performance textuality which may be "read"'.[45] In our present moment, scholars are still seeking answers to this question, while streaming video, cloud computing and other technologies are offering even more possibilities to make performed events legible and usable as research and pedagogical materials, going beyond video-cassette and DVD technology.[46]

Performances are best studied and taught not as isolated instances of artistic expression but as parts of a dynamic network of forms and meanings. Having instant, unpredictable, cross-genre access to videos presages a new relationship between the embodied performance and spectator. Further, the openness and scope of this network of materials,

valuable in itself, are also an essential first step in any attempt at identifying the most artistically innovative and intellectually interesting productions from each region, and formulating interpretive and historical questions on the basis of an adequate survey of the field.

Recent work has shown an acute awareness of the unfinished business of the earlier 'revolution' of Shakespeare and performance studies. For example, *Shakespeare and Modern Theatre*, edited by Michael Bristol and Kathleen McLuskie, problematizes the relationship between script and theatre, treating the specificities of performance – 'stage behaviours' – not as appendages that give way to the literariness of the Shakespearian script but as agents that participate in defining the play.[47] Dennis Kennedy goes so far as to propose that 'the medium is not the message'; rather, the message 'is in the spectator's presence'.[48]

Indeed, the spectator and performance have recently been recognized as integral components in interpretations of Shakespeare. The second edition of the *Oxford Shakespeare* usefully highlights the performative and collaborative aspects of select texts by rethinking stage directions in the

---

42 Peter Donaldson, 'The Shakespeare Electronic Archive: Tools for On-Line Learning and Scholarship', in *The Internet and the University: Forum 2003*, ed. Maureen E. Devlin, Richard Larson and Joel Myerson (Boulder, 2004), pp. 61–92.

43 J. L. Styan, *The Shakespeare Revolution: Criticism and Performance in the Twentieth Century* (Cambridge, 1977), p. 5; James C. Bulman, 'Introduction: Shakespeare and Performance Theory', in *Shakespeare, Theory, and Performance*, ed. James C. Bulman (London, 1996), p. 1.

44 Bulman, 'Introduction: Shakespeare and Performance Theory', p. 2.

45 Douglas Lanier, 'Drowning the Book: *Prospero's Books* and the Textual Shakespeare', in *Shakespeare, Theory, and Performance*, ed. Bulman, p. 202.

46 The cloud refers to the software that is hosted remotely and that runs once a personal computer connects to the Internet.

47 W. B. Worthen, *Shakespeare and the Force of Modern Performance* (Cambridge, 2003); Michael Bristol and Kathleen McLuskie, eds., *Shakespeare and Modern Theatre* (London, 2001).

48 Dennis Kennedy, *The Spectator and the Spectacle: Audiences in Modernity and Postmodernity* (Cambridge, 2009), p. 4.

context of early theatre practice. In major journals, including *Shakespeare Quarterly*, *Shakespeare Survey*, *Shakespeare* and *Shakespeare Bulletin*, the appearance of regular or annual performance reviews and, occasionally, essays theorizing the relation between performance and Shakespeare criticism signals that performance approaches to the study of Shakespeare are generally acknowledged. One might even say that performance theory has won its battle, since the term performativity has so thoroughly penetrated literary studies that related concepts are regularly evoked in otherwise text-based studies.

However, there remains a gap between theory and practice, and contemporary stage performance of Shakespeare has not been adequately mined for its richness. As Barbara Hodgdon surmises, plays are open sites where 'textual obligation' meet 'performative option'. The field of Shakespeare and performance – as demonstrated by practitioners and critics alike – has embraced a new notion of performance embedded within 'cross-disciplinary allegiances' among theatre, television and digital technologies.[49] As theatre has formed alliances with other media including video, the study of Shakespeare and performance stands to gain from taking advantage of video's capacity to help decouple text and performance in ideological formations and rejoin them as open sites where negotiations of meanings take place.

VIDEO INTERPOLATION: THE CASE OF *HAMLET*

A YouTube session offers useful visual and textual cues for exploration. One can follow the trajectory of a single artist through a career or the history of the staging of a particular work, at each point choosing a path through description, title, tags or simply by the visual content of the automatically generated selection of related videos. While such user-generated video sites themselves offer valuable resources for scholarly enquiry – especially in the early stages of a project – they are notoriously under-annotated and do not provide reliable, systematic metadata. *Global Shakespeares* provides both

a video-driven environment and a more familiar catalogue and filtered search method of moving through the collection, with the option to switch modes at any time.

A new functionality on the MIT *Global Shakespeares* site allows users to include numerous video clips selected and arranged to show not only what happens in filmed Shakespeare, but also how it happens – how meaning is created moment to moment in performance, music and shifting cinematic presentation. In research on Shakespeare in performance as well as in education, especially in assignments requiring close reading of video in conjunction with text, these tools have proved transforming. The *Global Shakespeares* archive utilises MediaThread and VITAL (Video Interactions for Teaching and Learning) media analysis communication platforms developed by Columbia University Center for New Media Teaching and Learning with the classroom environment in mind. One can search a video recording of a Shakespeare performance using the text as an index, to define and save replayable user-defined video segments (virtual clips) and to combine one's own text, Shakespeare's text, or secondary literature and video into multimedia essays or presentations. In addition, one can select and 'import' a video or image from the archive or other websites, such as Flickr and YouTube, for in-depth analysis and annotation. Videos can be clipped and embedded, along with still images if one so chooses, into a multimedia essay or in a shared space for discussion. This kind of communication brings the laser pointer to the essay and encourages deep analysis. Instead of just referencing a video and describing the scene, the writer can embed the exact moment and let the reader view the evidence directly and immediately. Students and professors in co-taught classes that are geographically distant can discuss the particulars of performances remotely using clips made and shared in real time.

---

49 Barbara Hodgdon, 'Introduction: A Kind of History', in *A Companion to Shakespeare and Performance*, ed. Barbara Hodgdon and W. B. Worthen (Oxford, 2005), pp. 4–5.

Such tools make possible precise and copious video illustration, so that an argument or analysis of performed meanings can be shared, extended and critiqued. Even more importantly, having the ability to quickly capture and briefly annotate video sequences can suggest and enable new kinds of discoveries that might not even have been thought of without the tools. Sometimes student work, even in undergraduate subjects, becomes a kind of collaboration with faculty research. A gifted undergraduate at MIT, Mark Seifter, made significant discoveries by very close reading of Michael Almereyda's *Hamlet* that complemented ongoing work by Peter Donaldson on the film's counterpointing of Shakespeare's words with Buddhist and other intertexts from Asian religious traditions. The most notable of these is the contrast between Hamlet's despairing 'to be or not to be' in this film and Vietnamese Buddhist monk Thich Nhat Hanh's discourse on 'interbeing'. Another scene of interest is Claudius's prayer in his limousine. As Claudius is jolted by a nasty and dangerous swerve and laments the failure of his words to reach Heaven, his hand covers the video image of the pilgrimage. These visual citations of Asian religious culture turned out to be significant elements of Almereyda's film. Seifter made several significant finds through minute examination of the film, clip definition and replay in conjunction with Web searches. From the tiny fragment of subtitle visible on the monitor in the backseat of Claudius's limo in Almereyda's *Hamlet*, Seifter was able to identify the film as the German documentary *The Saltmen of Tibet*. Viewing the clip in context, it became clear that the moment was a turning point in the documentary as well as in Almereyda's film – it marked the passage of the salt gatherers into the sacred territory of the salt goddess, just at the moment at which Claudius's attempt at prayer fails. He recognizes his own exclusion from grace. As for the words *Living and Dying* on the book Ophelia reads in *Hamlet*'s footage of her, it first appears to be an alternate title for the renowned *Tibetan Book of the Dead*. However, search among book cover images on the Web revealed that the face on the cover was that of Krishnamurti and the book a

posthumous collection of his thoughts on the same subject – not Tibetan, but still within the orbit of visual allusions to contemporary Asian religious discourses the class was exploring.[50]

The most sustained infusion of Buddhism in the film as released is its use of clips from *Peace is Every Step*, a documentary about Thich Nhat Hanh, leader of the Engaged Buddhism movement. In the context of *Hamlet*, Thich Nhat Hanh's teachings on 'interbeing' answer the brief, repeated video loops of Hamlet reciting the half-line 'to be or not to be' while actively making suicidal gestures – pointing a gun at his head, sticking the barrel in his mouth earlier in the film. As Thich Nhat Hanh continues he is not heard, or not fully heard by Hamlet who is not looking at the screen, but focusing on a hand-held monitor showing his own footage of an erotic encounter with Ophelia.

These key details were elements of design that were not indicated in the published screenplay, and required iterated examination of specific video sequences and the annotations we had made for them in the context of visual evidence from elsewhere in both films and related image materials on the Web. For these works, close reading, the ability to save and revisit clips and annotations, and to weave images and texts into a video-rich analytic framework can alter our understanding.

Other tools offered by the archive frame the object of enquiry to invite particular kinds of intellectual labour. As an archive of Shakespeare as a global, performed event, *Global Shakespeares* connects live performances to the concepts of rehearsal and replay through a federated global search experience. Titles can be located through free search or by using faceted browsing, which allows users to narrow results by selecting one or more choices from lists of Shakespeare play titles, directors, genres, cities and countries. Tags created by researchers, which may or may not be added to

50 Peter Donaldson, 'Hamlet among the Pixelvisionaries: Video Art, Authenticity and Wisdom in Michael Almereyda's Hamlet', in Diana Henderson, ed., *The Blackwell Concise Companion to Shakespeare on Film* (Oxford, 2006), pp. 216–37.

what is publicly available for searching, depending on whether their creator wishes to publish them, help generate search results. The data can be viewed as a table, plotted on a world map with satellite and hybrid map-satellite options, or timeline. Dynamic timelines and maps, used in conjunction with faceted browsing and tagged video, allow users to trace the paths of production and diffusion of touring productions. If 'distant reading' and graphs, as Franco Moretti suggests, can bring about important changes to the study of literature, such tools for visualization are as important for performance studies. For any given period scholars tend to focus on a select group of canonical works and, as a result, they have allowed a narrow slice of history to pass for the total picture.[51] Maps and timelines of the large number of productions can suggest new questions and unexpected relationships, and – especially important for the study of worldwide performance and emerging forms in a global context – counter the biases of metropolitan constructions of the field of study.

CONCLUSION

The archive is hypomnesic. The archive always works, and *a priori*, against itself.   Jacques Derrida[52]

Performance cannot be saved, recorded, documented, or otherwise participate in the circulation of representations of representation.   Peggy Phelan[53]

One of the most thought-provoking moments in *Hamlet* is the ramparts scene. When prompted by his father's ghost to remember him and his words, Hamlet responds by committing the ghost's words to writing: 'Now to my word: / It is "Adieu, adieu, remember me". / I have sworn't' (1.5.111–13). The performance archive is a valuable mnemonic device to preserve ephemeral experiences, but the archiving process will always introduce frictions between embodied (live) and disembodied (recorded) performances. In constructing a privileged relation to our past, the archive as a repository of artefacts and meanings has a dialectical relation to historical knowledge. Jennifer Summit posits that the library

not only contains 'written knowledge' but 'manifests ways of knowing', which is why the archive is central to who we are and what we see.[54]

Part archival record and part performance, digital video can register the theatrical contingency in a manipulable medium (with a rich network of video cross-references) that creates discursive knowledge about Shakespeare as site-specific performed events. The exponential growth of global visual and audio representations of Shakespeare's plays provides a fertile ground to explore a fuller range of multimedia and methods. Archiving the otherwise ephemeral history of performance is an important goal, but even more important are the new research questions such archives enable. If, as Diana Taylor theorized, embodied performances have always 'played a central role in conserving memory and consolidating identities in literate, semiliterate, and digital societies',[55] the digital performance archive complicates how these identities are circulated. Digital video amplifies the kinds of two-way flows and complex repositionings that make Shakespeare so compelling in our time.

In a broader context, these developments might spell the beginning of the end for 'global Shakespeare' as unproductive shorthand. The digital global age and its attendant imagery replay the message of a Eurocentric or North American centred world as a universal on an even grander scale, though often without the heroic narrative of conquest. In an age in which communication is worldwide, instantaneous and image-rich, global Shakespeare can be a site of conflict as well as new artistic and research opportunities. Recognized for its artistic creativity and now established

---

[51] Franco Moretti, *Graphs, Maps, Trees: Abstract Models for a Literary History* (London: Verso, 2005); John Bender and Michael Marrinan, *The Culture of Diagram* (Stanford, 2010).

[52] Derrida, *Archive Fever*, pp. 11–12.

[53] Peggy Phelan, *Unmarked: The Politics of Performance* (London, 1993), p. 146.

[54] Jennifer Summit, *Memory's Library: Medieval Books in Early Modern England* (Chicago, 2008), pp. 1 and 234.

[55] Diana Taylor, *The Archive and the Repertoire: Performing Cultural Memory in the Americas* (Durham, 2003), p. xviii.

as a field of scholarly enquiry, global Shakespeare remains an ostracizing label, categorizing a group of cultural products that can conveniently be cordoned off. Even though Shakespeare's tragedies, comedies and history plays are undeniably intertwined with the history of many theatrical traditions, global Shakespeare does not quite fit comfortably within any discipline. While post-colonial critics commonly privilege works that critique the role of Western hegemony in the historical record of globalization, the meanings of Shakespeare today are not always determined by post-colonial vocabulary or the discourses of globalization. With the dramatically increased availability of primary research material through digital video archives, the field may eventually move towards a mode of enquiry that inherently considers performances in comparative contexts. As the field matures, Shakespeare in performance may no longer require such qualifying adjectives as *Asian*, *European*, *African* or even *global*. Digital video archive can make Shakespeare studies an integral part of public scholarship and the future of humanities as envisioned by Julie Ellison, Kathleen Woodward and others – a new form of 'making knowledge about, for, and with diverse communities', yielding artefacts of public and intellectual value which include low-cost and high-impact digital videos.[56] That is the task of the performance archive.

---

[56] Kathleen Woodward, 'The Future of Humanities – in the Present and in Public', *Daedalus*, 138 (2009), 110–23; *Imagining America: Artists and Scholars in Public Life*, www.imagingamerica.org, accessed 5 April 2011.

AN INTERNATIONAL DATABASE OF SHAKESPEARE ON FILM, TELEVISION AND RADIO

OLWEN TERRIS

In 2005 The Arts and Humanities Research Council granted the British Universities Film & Video Council (BUFVC) funding to establish a three-year research project which would create *An International Database of Shakespeare on Film, Television and Radio* (www.bufvc.ac.uk/Shakespeare).[1] It would employ two full-time researchers and a target was set of 4,000 titles describing films, television programmes and radio broadcasts with Shakespeare-related content. An important proviso was that archival holdings and current distribution and retail information would be cited and updated so that scholars, researchers and students would know where to go to look and to listen. The Database can be searched at no cost and with no registration formalities.

Had the BUFVC bid for money to create a database, for example, of media materials on Jane Austen, Harold Pinter or any one of Shakespeare's contemporaries it may not have been so successful. The name Shakespeare and his association with nation, culture, the national curriculum and civilisation itself has become stronger in post-colonial times. In recent years critical research into Shakespeare and popular culture, particularly by Richard Burt in his edited work *Shakespeares After Shakespeare*, has examined how Shakespeare is both canonized and rejected in the media – how, for example, Shakespeare, and what his work signifies, is used in advertising, popular song, television variety sketches and porn films. Believing Shakespeare the signifier to be as relevant as Shakespeare the author, the Database had to capture and reflect as many of these appropriations as it could.[2]

The Database is international: the research team wanted to nudge users from any lingering belief that only in Britain can Shakespeare be fully experienced and realized and to reveal his global attraction and penetration into other cultures. To reflect this geographical and cultural breadth, television dramas from Poland, films from Hong Kong, radio programmes from Canada, newsfilms from Slovenia, videotapes of stage productions by established and emerging Eastern European directors were researched and documented. The team wanted to embrace Shakespeare spoken in languages other than English and so the researcher will find representations of blank verse spoken in sign language, in Maori, Yoruba, Klingon, Pidgin English, Elizabethan English, rap versions, polari and many other languages and dialects.

Inevitably Shakespeare in Great Britain dominates. Every Shakespeare play broadcast on British television from the 1930s, and the majority of Shakespeare's works broadcast on radio from the 1920s, are documented – the first time, as far as the team is aware, that this has been attempted. The majority of early productions are lost, they were transmitted live and were not or could not

---

[1] As of September 2010 the Database listed 6,930 records: 2,138 radio programmes, 1,529 video recordings (including video recordings of stage performances), 1,852 television programmes, 1,036 films, 697 audio recordings and 154 titles categorized as 'multimedia'. Some titles are classified under more than one category.

[2] Richard Burt, ed., *Shakespeares After Shakespeare: An Encyclopaedia of the Bard in Mass Media and Popular Culture*, 2 vols. (Westport, CN and London, 2007).

be recorded, but it was felt essential to mark their creation and catalogue them fully. Scholars tracing the history of the BBC's schools Shakespeare programming on radio in the 1930s, for example, will discover from the Database in seconds that 47 programmes were broadcast including dramatic readings from Ralph Richardson and Fabia Drake. Similarly, in the first decade of British television (1936–46), a decade which embraced World War II when television broadcasting closed down, there were 34 productions of Shakespeare's plays including readings and dramatized extracts. A remarkable figure – especially considering that from 1998 to 2010 there have been only four 'straight' productions (i.e. productions that used Shakespeare's text) shown on British television, all of them taking their aesthetic from the stage (such as Ian McKellen as Lear and Antony Sher as Macbeth).

These four programmes suggest an emerging pattern in British television of redirecting prestigious stage productions for primetime transmission at Christmas. In 2008 Channel 4 broadcast Trevor Nunn's RSC production of *King Lear* with Ian McKellen in the title role, and on Boxing Day 2009 the BBC screened Gregory Doran's *Hamlet* with David Tennant. The Chichester Festival Theatre's 2007 production of Rupert Goold's *Macbeth* with Patrick Stewart and Kate Fleetwood was restaged and filmed and reached the UK screen in January 2011 (the première was in the United States, broadcast by PBS in October 2010). These transmissions are soon followed by a commercial DVD offering educational and contextual material in the form of interviews with the actors or a short 'the making of' – type documentary. The viewing figures for these productions are unimpressive in broadcasting terms; David Tennant's much heralded *Hamlet* secured 900,000 viewers, many times the total audience for its stage run, but a television rating which can be put into perspective by the fact that a weekday episode of the UK television soap *Coronation Street* regularly secures an audience of around ten million.

Over the past ten years, however, there have been over thirty programmes broadcast on UK television which have used Shakespeare's characters and themes as their inspiration. These appropriations include Andrew Davies's contemporary reworking of *Othello* (2001) with John Othello as the first black Chief Commissioner of the London Metropolitan Police, the 2005 *ShakespeaRe-Told* series in which four more popular plays were rewritten as contemporary dramas, and some 2006 episodes of *Coronation Street* where the death of the character of Mike Baldwin from Alzheimer's disease echoed 'King Lear' in many aspects.

Such allusions and borrowings are a very strong feature of the Database – the researcher can, for example, find comedians reciting Shakespeare in their sketches – Tommy Cooper, Tony Hancock, Jack Benny and Eric Morecambe among many others. Classical Shakespearian actors not being classical offers an interesting reversal – Kenneth Branagh reciting the 'to be or not to be' soliloquy in a Swedish accent while attempting to dance and ski like Abba, or Maurice Evans joining in a skit parodying *Romeo and Juliet* in the radio series *The Edgar Bergen and Charles McCarthy Show* (1947) – Bergen is a ventriloquist, Charles the dummy. It is interesting to see from the Database how often comedians look to Shakespeare for their material – at the same time debunking and canonizing him – as if acquainting and associating yourself with Shakespeare dignifies and elevates the comic status; so the user will find Ken Dodd playing the role of Malvolio, John Cleese as Petruchio and Benny Hill as Bottom.

Media students interested in how and why Shakespeare is used to sell a commodity will find a search on 'advertising' rewarding – for example a commercial for Levi 501 jeans with anti-fit which quotes from *A Midsummer Night's Dream*, or comedienne June Whitfield as Anne Hathaway and Terry-Thomas as Shakespeare in an advertisement for Bird's Eye Cod In Mushroom Sauce (1970). Anne Hathaway prepares the readymade dish secretly in the kitchen and presents it to her husband as homemade saying 'it's as you like it, Will'. If you can fool Shakespeare, the arbiter of taste in every sense, the advert is saying, into believing that false is true, you can fool anybody.

Shakespeare confers authenticity, he sells the real thing.

The relationship between contemporary politics and Shakespeare which the Database can be used to explore is equally informative, for example Senator John Kennedy in 1960 quoting from *King Lear* at a Democratic Convention banquet in Wisconsin in support of his policies:

> I will do such things –
> What they are, yet I know not; but they shall be
> The terrors of the earth.　　　　(2.2. 454–6)

Shakespeare's influence on America's political, civic and cultural life is investigated in the US three-part radio documentary series in 2007, *Shakespeare in American Politics*, while an episode of the UK anthology television arts series, *The South Bank Show*, looks at how *Macbeth*'s themes of tyranny, ambition and power have strong resonances in twentieth- and twenty-first-century politics.

The research team endeavours to explore the archives of as many theatre organizations and broadcasting companies in as many countries as it can, and is of course far more successful when the institution offers an online catalogue of its holdings with comprehensive data and good search strategies. To record every Shakespeare-related work that has been filmed or broadcast throughout the world is an impossible task, and an unachievable ambition given the scale of the AHRC-funded project. We do not, for example, claim that every feature film produced in Spain which alludes to Shakespeare has been discovered and documented. However, what has been achieved in mapping Shakespeare globally is already beginning to reveal interesting relationships between a country's political and cultural history and the popularity and attraction of a particular Shakespeare play. Is it coincidence that the most produced play on Polish television (after *Hamlet*) is *The Taming of the Shrew* with its theme of subjugation? Is a significant pattern emerging when it is discovered that (again after *Hamlet*) *Romeo and Juliet* and the play's concerns with arranged marriage and parental control

provide the narrative structure to so many feature films produced in India and Hong Kong?

Shakespeare as interpreted though dance and music is extremely important to the team, and operas, music, ballet and contemporary dance are documented. The researcher will discover two dance versions of *King Lear*, an opera of *Troilus and Cressida* and a rap version of Mark Antony's funeral oration performed by *Star Trek*'s William Shatner entitled *No Tears for Caesar*. There are fascinating documentaries too – Leonard Bernstein comparing Shakespeare's Iago with Verdi's Iago, choreographer Kenneth MacMillan rehearsing Fonteyn and Nureyev in *Romeo and Juliet*, and the radio programme *Shakespeare and the Brain* in which scientist Quentin Cooper discusses the neurological aspects of language, taking Shakespeare as an example.

Many theatre companies at home and abroad make video recordings of their stage productions, place them in archives, and make them permanently available on-site for research viewing. Interestingly, very few of them (including the Royal Shakespeare Company) advertise this unique research facility to any great extent and the user will frequently have to delve deep into their websites to find information about the service at all. Often these recordings use only a single fixed camera and the technical quality is imperfect but, if a stage production is not restaged for television, as was Richard Eyre's production of *King Lear* with Ian Holm for example, or re-imagined as a film, such as Adrian Noble's *A Midsummer Night's Dream*, it is the only record of how the play looked and sounded and therefore a unique resource. If there were no moving image record of the performance of Antony Sher in Bill Alexander's 1984 production of *Richard III* for example, or Robert Stephens's embittered and melancholic Falstaff in Noble's 1991 production of *Henry IV*, then few would disagree that theatre and performance history would be greatly impoverished. All such recordings at London's National Theatre, the RSC, Shakespeare's Globe theatre in Southwark, Theatre on Film and Tape (TOFT) in New York City, the Stratford Shakespeare Festival in Ontario and within several theatre institutes throughout Europe are documented. The Database was immensely enriched when the RSC took the courageous step of videotaping and archiving all the productions performed as part of the 2006/7 RSC Complete Works Festival – so we have a permanent record of the Munich Theatre's controversial and brutal *Othello* directed by Luk Perceval, Forkbeard Fantasy's *Rough Magyck*, a multimedia take on the supernatural in Shakespeare, and the Tiny Ninja Theatre's *Hamlet*.

The design of the Database was crucial in establishing a structure which would allow researchers to find specific pieces of information quickly and intuitively and facilitate browsing through the generous provision of hyperlinks. We asked ourselves, and theatre practitioners, what do researchers and scholars want to know, what should be recorded? The inevitable answer was everything. Full cast and credits are given – the minor roles and who played them are listed to reveal the less well known fact that Trevor Nunn played First Gentleman in *Cymbeline* in a Marlowe Dramatic Society recording from 1961 and Harold Pinter played Lord Abergavenny in *Henry VIII* in a BBC radio production from 1951. Release, recording and broadcast dates are cited as is information on the period a production was set in, the name of the company performing the work, and where they were performing. Researchers wanted an indication of major articles and references, what text was being used, box office takings, production costs and awards won. Wherever possible this information is provided and for each entry the team tries to incorporate the odd fact which might otherwise not generally be known.

Finding information is time-consuming and absorbing. The research grant made provision for two overseas research trips – one to the United States to work in the Library of Congress and the Folger Shakespeare Library in Washington DC, the Paley Center for Media Studies (formerly the Museum of Television and Radio), and in the Museum of Modern Art and TOFT at the Lincoln Center for Performing Arts in New York City. Archives and broadcast institutions in Germany, Austria and Switzerland were visited, including the Bundesarchiv in Berlin, the Institut für Theaterwissenschaft Bibliothek in Munich and the Österreichischer Rundfunk (ORF), the Austrian public broadcasting station in Vienna. The personal contacts made with archivists in these cities were and remain invaluable. To discover Shakespeare in the archives of countries we were unable to visit (and there are of course many) we are reliant on information gleaned from publicly available web-based catalogues. Without the Web the project would not have taken years longer to accomplish, for it would simply never have happened at all. Unsurprisingly these databases vary enormously in the amount of cataloguing detail given and ease of searching. Many overseas archives have attractive front-end homepages which outline, with an English-language option, their main collections and services. However, once one reaches the catalogue itself the data and search instructions are almost inevitably in the native language and the project team therefore uses dictionaries to conquer Hebrew, Hungarian, Polish and many other languages which we neither speak nor read; recognizing the Slovenian for Peaseblossom and Mustardseed is a challenge.

Within the UK, the BBC Written Archives Centre, the British Library Sound Archive (both essential in gathering complex information on early BBC radio broadcasts), the Birmingham Shakespeare Library (an excellent script collection), the British Film Institute National Library, Shakespeare's Globe theatre, the National Theatre, the RSC, the Shakespeare Centre Library and Archives in Stratford and the Shakespeare Institute were all visited. National filmographies were consulted and weeks were spent just turning pages of early editions of *Radio Times*, the UK television and radio listings magazine. A web-based discussion list was established and members are able to report on films and broadcasts they have recently seen or remembered which incorporated scenes of

Shakespearian interest, or alert us to forthcoming radio plays.[3]

Having decided what scholars might want to know and located the information, the project team's duty remained to help researchers find that information in ways which would reveal unsuspected relationships and provide an historical and cultural context. A database geared mainly to presenting data when the researcher has already formed a strong idea of what they want to find was not the first objective. The user can do this of course and it is a perfectly valid way to interrogate it; if you want to know who wrote the music for a 1960 BBC Third Programme radio broadcast of *Hamlet* with Michael Redgrave in the title role then you can do that, but the team wants to offer more, encouraging users to browse and make sometimes surprising connections. Here are a few examples of how the Database can be searched with, we hope, intuitive search strategies, to further studies of Shakespeare in performance and media studies:

- A set or costume designer can find productions of *Coriolanus*, for example, set in the 1930s, or the Wild West providing the background for *The Taming of the Shrew*.
- An actor's interpretation of the same role through a range of media makes for fascinating study. Kenneth Branagh as Hamlet illustrates this well. In 1988 he was directed in the stage role by Derek Jacobi, and there is a television documentary about the making of this Renaissance Company production. In 1992 BBC Radio 3 broadcast a performance based on this production, this time with Branagh directing himself. In 1993 the V&A National Video Archive of Performance videotaped Adrian Noble's RSC stage production at the Barbican Theatre using three cameras, while the RSC videotaped the same production but a different performance at the Royal Shakespeare Theatre using a single camera; and in 1996 Branagh directed himself again in the 70mm feature film.
- The researcher will find an eclectic range of people talking about Shakespeare – Peter Holland,

comedians Ken Dodd and Lenny Henry, critic Clive James, Akira Kurosawa, John Barton.
- A search by genre will find feature films which incorporate Shakespeare's plots and characters within established cinematic traditions – Shakespeare re-imagined in westerns, horror films and science fiction.
- Shakespeare can be studied through gesture and movement in silent films, mime, animation, masques and dance.
- A keyword search will reveal, for example, productions which have all-male or all-female casts, stagings which employ masks or puppetry or which double roles, open-air productions, colour-blind casting, plays in British or American sign language, Shakespeare plays acted by prisoners, actresses playing Hamlet and so on.

Investigating which Shakespeare plays were filmed or broadcast at significant times can readily be undertaken on the Database. By searching on specific dates the researcher can bring together productions where Shakespeare is evoked to strengthen national identity and bestow cultural validity during public religious festivals, state occasions or anniversaries. Those people interested in how film-makers and broadcasters marked Shakespeare's quatercentenary celebrations in 1964 will discover that over fifty television and radio programmes were broadcast in the UK to commemorate and celebrate the event.

An interest in capturing audience reaction is emerging as students of performance history want to see and hear for themselves how an audience responded to a production and not be overly reliant on critical opinion assembled after the event. It is admittedly difficult for the Database to respond to this demand, but in identifying the many video recordings of stage productions filmed from different angles on several cameras (which can be done easily by choosing the type 'stage

---

[3] Olwen Terris, Eve-Marie Oesterlen and Luke McKernan, eds., *Shakespeare on Film, Television and Radio: The Researcher's Guide* (London, 2009).

recordings'), the researcher is likely to see many shots of the audience as the camera cuts away from the performance space to the auditorium. The sound (or silence) of the audience is there to be studied too. The British Library Sound Archive has made live sound recordings of performances at the RSC and the National Theatre for over fifty years and listening to these recordings is fascinating and frequently surprising. A recording of Donald Sinden as Malvolio in the gulling scene in the RSC's 1969 production of *Twelfth Night* directed by John Barton provides a fine example. The scene illustrates how insights to the play are aided by the sound of audience laughter, intakes of breath and sudden stillness, it shows how highly visual, almost farcical staging can work on the 'blind' audience in the sitting room as Sinden's inventive and manipulative relationship with his stage audience wonderfully and mysteriously works on a different level purely as sound. The Database will give details of how to locate this recording, and point the user to an article in which Sinden talks about how he approached and performed the role.

Browsing is made easy by the generous provision of links which, with a single click, will provide information on related titles. For example, when looking at a record which lists David Tennant in the cast, a click on his name will retrieve a list of all other productions in which he features. Interestingly Tennant can be seen or heard in some fifteen other Shakespeare productions made well before his celebrated 2009 *Hamlet*. Clicking on the name of a theatre company, say the Berliner Ensemble, will take the user to other visual and aural representations of their work. Productions are related one to another: so, for example, looking at the entry for Kurosawa's *Ran*, the researcher will be directed to Chris Marker's documentary film *AK* on the making of that film.

In 2005, the same year that the team began to build an online database documenting Shakespearian performances preserved on nitrate film, shellac recordings and analogue television, along came YouTube. The first video was uploaded by a strange coincidence on 23 April, Shakespeare's birthday. Questions of *how* would we select material, *should*

we be selective, what would be of critical interest, how best to catalogue the videos, rapidly became irrelevant in the face of the thousands and thousands of hits retrieved with a search on the word 'Shakespeare'. Even if we were confident in assessing what is posted legally and what is not (and we are not), the overwhelming numbers continue to defeat us, and expectations concerning the creation, use and distribution of the video content and the ways in which it is commented upon, were rapidly overturned. The vast majority of material on YouTube, as we believe most people acknowledge, is exhaustingly trivial – self-indulgent student jokes, badly lit local amateur dramatics, talentless renditions by thousands of wannabe actors craving their seconds of fame on a digital stage. Yet, and it is a highly significant yet, there is challenging and inventive material on YouTube today, with the unsettling recognition that it may well not be there tomorrow. The website *Bardbox* (bardbox.wordpress.com), developed by Luke McKernan, a former colleague on the project, is a brave attempt to make selections and critical assessments and force these sounds and images into a structure both informative and entertaining. As Luke has written, its 'future significance may lie less in the intentions of the creator and more in who lays claim to the product and chooses to share it with others'.[4]

To complement the Database the BUFVC published *Shakespeare on Film, Television and Radio: the Researcher's Guide*.[5] The book contains essays from scholars on all aspects of Shakespeare in the media – Shakespeare on BBC radio before the war, a history of Shakespeare on British television, Shakespeare on the internet, Shakespeare as manipulated in television commercials. In addition there are bibliographies of Shakespeare on sound and screen, lists of archives, video distributors in Britain and overseas, and guidance on how to cite Shakespeare productions in footnotes and filmographies. One section invited scholars in the field of Shakespeare

---

4 Terris, Oesterlen and McKernan, *Shakespeare on Film*, p. xii.
5 The BUFVC promotes the production, study and use of film and related media in higher education and research.

and media to say which Shakespeare film or broadcast they found most informative or engaging or influential – and, most importantly, why.

The aim of the project was to create a definitive resource which would authoritatively support and extend, and we hope shape, the study of Shakespeare in performance. It remains a conviction that a database should not merely be a finding device but function as a means of analysis and contextualization, a means of provoking debate. We have tried to map audio-visual Shakespeare in its historical, international and cross-media aspects. Through extensive and rigorously compiled data, it becomes possible to draw out national and international histories, patterns of change and responses to circumstances (economic, artistic, political, technological) which we hope will inform Shakespeare studies for many years to come.

'SOUNDS AND SWEET AIRS': MUSIC IN SHAKESPEARIAN PERFORMANCE HISTORY

DAVID LINDLEY

In 1887 an anonymous editorial in *The Stage* observed that:

The more leisurely we reflect upon the diverse effects music has upon the human mind the more certain does it seem that the addition of music to a drama which is intended to touch our stronger sentiments is the very wisest way of enhancing the powers of the drama itself.[1]

The terminology might be distinctly Victorian, but the majority of modern Shakespearian directors also take advantage of the 'enhancing' power of music. In so doing they create a network of reactions and interactions between the familiar text of the play, the values and emphases of their production and the feelings of their audiences. Understanding the nature of those interactions requires attention both to the particular theatrical culture within which the music is generated, and to the wider musical understanding a diverse audience might possess, since music's indeterminate meanings are always constructed in relation to a repertoire of already familiar musical 'languages'. Anahid Kassabian's comments on film music are equally pertinent for the theatre:

any story of identifications with films must take account of engagements between filmgoers and film scores... those engagements are conditioned by filmgoers' relationships to a wide range of musics both within and outside of their filmgoing practices.[2]

In the specific case of song, further complexity is introduced by the multiple interactions between words and music, between the song and the action

of the play, between singer and audience, actor and role. These complex relationships shift and change between one production and another, and more generally between one historical period and another.

So much might easily be agreed; yet it is remarkable that very little has been written about the contribution music makes to Shakespearian performance history. There are important studies of the factual history of what music was performed, who composed it and the physical conditions of its playing, but only very scattered attempts to try to understand the affect and effect of the music either in specific relation to an individual production or more generally in relation to the history of Shakespeare in the theatre.[3] Opera and stage musicals have their own distinct critical literature, but while there is an important and growing body of material on film music, as yet there is very little theoretical or critical discussion of music in what one might call 'straight' drama.

In part the reasons for this neglect are practical. If all performance history is a species of archaeology, then the traces of music in the record are

---

[1] *The Stage*, 16 September 1887, in Russell Jackson, ed., *Victorian Theatre* (London, 1989), p. 204.

[2] Anahid Kassabian, *Hearing Film: Tracking Identifications in Contemporary Hollywood Film Music* (New York, 2001), p. 2.

[3] See, for example, Roger Fiske's monumental *English Theatre Music in the Eighteenth Century*, 2nd edn (Oxford, 1986), and Michael Pisani's compact introduction 'Music for the Theatre: Style and Function in Incidental Music', in Kerry Powell, ed., *The Cambridge Companion to Victorian and Edwardian Theatre* (Cambridge, 2004), pp. 70–92.

particularly fragmentary. Historically, the frequent fires in theatre buildings destroyed many scores. Kemble, for example, responded to the 1808 fire at Covent Garden, lamenting that the theatre

is gone, with all its treasures of every description, and some of which can never be replaced. That library, which contained all those immortal productions of our countrymen, prepared for purposes of representation! That vast collection of Music, composed by the greatest geniuses in that science, – by Handel, Arne, and others; most of it manuscript, in the original score![4]

This might have been one of the most spectacular of losses, but in theatres up and down the country hand-copied scores and parts must frequently have disintegrated through frequent use, been discarded as newer music was supplied, or else have disappeared in flames. In modern times, however, the picture is by no means universally better. The monumental *Shakespeare Music Catalogue* contains a high proportion of ghosts: music that is known about through the survival of theatre programmes, but which has itself disappeared.[5] Even in the best regulated of archives, at the National Theatre or the Royal Shakespeare Company for example – on which much of what follows depends – the musical score is often simply missing. Composers and music directors, sometimes out of principle or for purposes of copyright protection, but also on occasion simply from forgetfulness, fail to deposit scores in the companies' archives. Furthermore, whereas the student of film music can, in the absence of a surviving or accessible score, at the very least listen repeatedly to the music, that luxury is simply not available to the theatre historian when considering productions in the pre-archive video age. Even where such videos exist, the quality of sound reproduction is often so poor that one cannot trust it as an aural record. Finally, the increasing absorption of music into an overall 'sound design' created largely on a computer means that the musical traces of performance vanish with almost unprecedented completeness.

Archival spottiness, however, is not the only inhibition on consideration of music and performance. As Kassabian acutely observes:

Because music has been claimed by an expert discourse, people feel unauthorized to talk about it . . . Most people imagine that they cannot say anything about music, in spite of regular practices of buying, listening to, and often producing music. They imagine this in spite of regular conversations about songs, performers, albums, radio stations, and concerts; about what tapes they use to work out to, walk to, or cook to; about stylistic pedigrees and generic histories, and much more . . . the strong hold of the 'expert discourse ideology' of music has kept a tight lid on the production of studies of film music.[6]

The same is true of conversation about theatre music. This article makes no attempt to produce detailed musical analysis, precisely in order to open up the possibility of rather different kinds of discussion that may be had about the historical shifts in the place of music in Shakespearian performance, and about some of the ways in which instrumental music and song might be considered important to that history.

Music may be neglected in most discussion of Shakespearian performance, but yet it is obvious enough that a musical score may contribute significantly to the success or failure of any particular production. Greg Doran's RSC *As You Like It* of 2000, for example, was much criticized for its design. As Robert Smallwood observes, 'its needlework and tapestry set, designed by Kaffe Fassett, did indeed leave Arden (with its embroidered cushions and magnificent pullovers) looking like a fashion shop rather than a forest'.[7] At least as significant in weighing it down, however, was Django Bates's bass-heavy, percussion-dominated, jazz/rock music, where the singing voice, though miked, was almost obliterated in the density of the accompaniment. Reviewers, like performance historians, often don't refer to the music of a production – but here some of them did, and with universal hostility. Michael Billington, for

[4] James Boaden, *Memoirs of the life of John Philip Kemble, esq*: (London, 1825), p. 459.
[5] Bryan N. S. Gooch and David Thatcher, eds., *A Shakespeare Music Catalogue* (Oxford, 1991).
[6] Kassabian, *Hearing Film*, pp. 9–10.
[7] Robert Smallwood, *Shakespeare at Stratford: As You Like It* (London, 2003), p. 17.

example, found the music 'gratingly inappropriate to the visual style'.[8] The requirement of internal coherence in musical and visual styles that Billington here invokes is deeply embedded in most people's attitude to incidental music. So too is the hierarchy that his comment implies – that the primary job of the music is simply a supportive one. Yet it is possible to argue that music does not simply occupy a secondary role in endorsing dialogue or the visual qualities of the *mise-en-scène*, but that in important respects it may actively condition or even determine the way in which we see the action.

A simple example will make this fundamentally important point. Tim Supple directed *The Comedy of Errors* in 1996 in an RSC touring production which was lauded as transforming the way in which the play might be regarded. It managed to persuade audiences and reviewers alike to see it as much more than the traditionally conceived knockabout farce. Though the comedy was certainly not neglected, the production rendered the disorientations of its plot truly disturbing, and successfully connected its conclusion with the magically restorative world of the late romances. Though, paradoxically, this is the one Shakespeare play with no specification of any musical requirements at all, Adrian Lee's largely improvised score made an essential contribution to the working of the performance. In its combination of Middle Eastern instrumental sounds and a voice chanting Latin words it did not merely *illustrate* by other means the world that the director wished to create, but in the delicate scoring, in the exotic associations of its Middle Eastern musical vocabulary on the one hand, and of the archaic solemnity of Latin chant on the other, it worked significantly to persuade us to listen differently to the play and to see it, as it were, with new ears.

The centrality of the music to this particular staging was in part a product of the way in which the score was generated. The theatre programme informed the audience that 'the music you will hear has been devised with the musicians and composer in constant attendance throughout the rehearsal process'. In a newspaper article the composer suggested to Martin Gordon that the music was improvised because it 'has to fit with the physicality of the scene, which keeps changing as rehearsals develop'. And Gordon notes that 'Supple instructs his actors to regard music as an equal partner – in his hands, music functions not merely as a punctuating or defining device, but as a fundamental part of the process, which can actually drive the physical action.' Supple also believed that the orchestration 'has a very direct appeal to the senses and makes for a very naked and intimate relationship between the performers and the audience'.[9]

There is an ambiguity in this last reported comment. To which 'performers' do the audience have this relationship – the musicians or the actors? The question is highly significant for any account of music in the theatre, and I will return to it in the last section of this article. For the moment, however, it is enough to remark that though the musicians in the gallery of The Other Place were visible to the greater part of the audience, and closely though their music related to particular moments in the play, they were inaudible to the characters within the play. At no point, at least as far as memory and the very imperfect archive video witness, did the actors acknowledge the presence of the musicians or their music, that is until the final curtain-call. For a late twentieth-century audience this poses no problem. We have become entirely comfortable with the notion of music as an accompanying soundtrack, functioning not as part of the action, but non-diegetically, as 'incidental' music. In the near-continuous soundtracks of many films, or in the musical fidgeting that is all too characteristic of televisual drama and documentary, a modern audience has no difficulty in accepting what might seem, on the face of it, the very odd idea that we can hear what those within the world of the play or documentary cannot. Our acceptance of this convention is one of the things that differentiates Shakespearian performance in the last hundred and fifty years or so from its earlier theatrical existence.

Shakespeare does prescribe music as underscoring of dialogue – Sneak's Noise and their music in

---

[8] *The Guardian*, 25 March 2000.

[9] *The Independent*, 3 July 1996.

2 Henry IV are one example, the solitary instrumentalist playing outside Richard II's prison is another – but nowhere is instruction given for music unheard by characters on stage, except when their failure to hear the music is, as it is for Antonio and Sebastian in *The Tempest*, a mark of moral degeneracy, or else in the special case of music accompanying a dumb show. There was, of course, non- or 'extra'-diegetic music in the interludes that were played between the acts at the Blackfriars theatre and its indoor successors in order to allow for the trimming of candles. Marston takes care to prescribe the instrumentation for some of the 'act' music in his plays, which might suggest that he wished to direct and control the effect of such interludes, but it is unlikely either that music was specially composed for every individual play, or that it was ever intended to be anything other than inaudible within the drama's narrative world.[10] The same seems to be true throughout most of the eighteenth century. Music becomes more elaborate, as we shall see shortly, but the fundamental premise remains the same – that there is a conceptual separation between overtures and entr'actes that entertain the audience, and belong therefore to the theatre-as-building, 'framing' the drama, as it were, and the music that is called for within the action of the play.

During the nineteenth century that separation broke down as theatre orchestras grew in size, and their music became more and more pervasive in theatrical representations.[11] 'Incidental' music, a term strictly understood as that which accompanied marches, dances and song, grew to include music 'which accompanies the dialogue and reflects the feeling and emotion of the spoken lines', and derives from the French *mélodrame*.[12] Michael R. Booth writes that:

The orchestra was vitally important as a dramatic element in production. Irving's director, Meredith Ball, wrote music for Lyceum performances, as did specially commissioned composers such as Sullivan. The role of the orchestra's work can best be summed up by a description of its impact in America: 'The continuous music of the Irving plays, now suggesting the emotions of the situation, now intensifying the effects of the

acting, now dominating the scene, now almost unheard in the excitement of the dramatic incident, was unknown. People said of Irving's first productions "Why, they are like grand opera!"'[13]

Booth speculates that its effect:

must have been considerable: [the actor] would need to dominate it, of course, but also to listen to it, to *use* it, to feed off it musically and emotionally, to incorporate its suggestive power into his own voice and his own performance generally.[14]

The increased use of incidental music and underscoring went along with the elaboration of spectacle and the insertion of extra dances and songs which characterised many nineteenth-century Shakespearian productions. Interestingly, it was a practice no more universally applauded at the time than its lineal descendant, the sound-track of cinema and television is now. Kate Terry Gielgud (John's mother), for example, complained of Irving's *Cymbeline*: 'Sad to say I have returned from a Lyceum production disappointed. For one thing, I must confess we sat too near the stage, in the front row of the stalls, and the incidental music at such close quarters was an unmitigated nuisance.'[15] Even the enthusiastic editor of *The Stage* warned that 'A drama overburdened with music drags most fearfully, and disheartens everybody at a first performance.'[16] The anonymous reviewer of Beerbohm Tree's *Tempest* in 1904 fulminated:

at the rare moments when Shakespeare's lines emerge from the prevailing racket, they drag, they limp, they

[10] Martin White disagrees with this generally held view. He writes: 'After experimenting extensively with music, language and action in a range of plays...I am certain that music would have been used...in a manner not dissimilar to the way it was used to accompany action in early cinema and in film scores today': *Renaissance Drama in Action* (London, 1998), p. 154.
[11] See Pisani, 'Music for the Theatre', *passim*.
[12] Pisani, 'Music for the Theatre', p. 71.
[13] Michael R. Booth, *Victorian Spectacular Theatre* (London, 1981), p. 97.
[14] Michael R. Booth, *Theatre in the Victorian Age* (Cambridge, 1991), p. 123.
[15] Muriel St Clare Byrne, ed., *Kate Terry Gielgud: A Victorian Playgoer* (London, 1980), p. 41.
[16] Jackson, *Victorian Theatre*, p. 205.

halt. The actors are so pleased to be heard that they put a false emphasis on every syllable which they utter; and as they always speak to a musical accompaniment, generally slow, it is surprising if they make a single speech intelligible.[17]

Despite such negative comments, it would seem that most nineteenth-century Shakespearian productions used a considerable amount of extra-diagetic music, as well as frequently elaborating on the music actually called for in the action. Such music might be reused from an earlier production, be newly composed, or else assembled from a wide variety of sources.[18] Film, as it inherited its musical practices from the theatre, in its earliest silent years employed the same mixture of musics; during its so-called 'golden age', however, the dominant practice became the composition of fresh, complete scores, a convention itself to be challenged from the 1960s onwards by 'compilation scores', taken from existing music, and often including familiar popular songs.[19] Theatre has in many respects imitated this sequence. Increasingly during the twentieth century fresh scores were demanded, composed by individual musicians for particular productions; more recently, however, especially in film versions of Shakespeare, but also on the stage, directors have used compiled scores in order to generate a particular atmosphere for their production.

One example is the onstage 1930s band called for in David Thacker's 1991 RSC *Two Gentlemen of Verona*. The band played before and during the action, and activated the powerful emotional effect of musical recall. It certainly set the scene and was, in Billington's words, 'appropriate to the visual style' of the director's vision. But, as Peter Holland perceptively observed, it not only drew on a tele-visual language deriving from the popular success of 1980s drama which incorporated popular song, but performed much more ideological work:

Thacker's production was surely about the influence of Denis Potter on Shakespeare. But where in Potter's work the Thirties songs function as a creative disjunction, marking the gap between the sordid and painful action of *Pennies from Heaven* and the language of lyric

sentimental romance, in Thacker's *Two Gentlemen* the songs mediated and reassured, translated the action to a Thirties context in which the characters' obsession with love was validated. The audience needed to have no anxiety; there was no doubt that the disruptions of the action, its sharp pains, could and would be resolved within the terms of the discourse of this romance world.[20]

The key idea here is encapsulated in the term 'mediated'. In various complex ways music enables a mediation between the audience and the text, between its linguistic historical distance and their emotional present.[21] In this production the consistency of the music used in its compilation score suited exactly the period in which it was set. A much more extravagant collection of pieces was put together by Michael Bogdanov in his production of the history plays. Avowedly 'eclectic as the costumes, sometimes commenting on the action, sometimes complementing it', the selection had no internal musical consistency but was built on decidedly random patterns of association, as this extract makes plain:

All the battle scenes echoed to cannon fire and Byrd's *Mass for Four Voices*, emphasizing the religious justification voiced by the participants. Simon Elliott played live accordion music for the French victory at Orleans and Henry VI's Coronation in France was introduced with Mozart's *Coronation Mass*. His wedding to Margaret was celebrated with Handel's *Music for the Royal Fireworks*, various other court scenes in England were

[17] *Blackwood's Magazine*, October 1904, p. 557.

[18] See Pisani, 'Music for the Theatre', pp. 76–7.

[19] The story is, of course, much more complex than can be discussed here. For a comprehensive account of the evolution of film music see Mervyn Cooke, *A History of Film Music* (Cambridge, 2008; corrected edition, 2010). On compilation scores, see Phil Powrie and Robynn Stilwell, eds., *Changing Tunes: The Use of Pre-existing Music in Film* (Aldershot, 2006).

[20] Peter Holland, 'Shakespeare Performances in England, 1990–1', *Shakespeare Survey 45* (Cambridge, 1992), p. 126.

[21] Kenneth Branagh employed the same period music to analogous effect in his 2000 film of *Love's Labour's Lost*. See Ramona Wray, 'The Singing Shakespearean: Kenneth Branagh's *Love's Labour's Lost* and the Politics of Genre', in Pascale Aebischer, Edward J. Esche and Nigel Wheale, eds., *Remaking Shakespeare* (London, 2003).

accompanied by Monteverdi's *Vespers* and Pergolesi's *Stabat Mater*.[22]

This is a theatre director thinking very much in terms that owe a good deal to cinema, but also belong to a postmodern world where the musical references are shorn of any historical particularity.

In both these examples the music, including songs, was almost entirely part of an extra-diegetic soundtrack, but the case of song, which is part of the action of the play, is no less significant in establishing a relationship between action and audience and, historically, the way in which song functions in the theatre has changed at least as much as the incidental music that has so far been the focus of this article.

In Shakespeare's own time it is probable that the majority of the song lyrics in his plays and in others for the adult companies were written to fit existing tunes, or else were lifted from songs already circulating in manuscript or print.[23] For their first audiences, then, the effect might have been something similar to that of the ballads in Gay's *Beggar's Opera*, where the familiarity of the tune, and its associations, formed part of the way the song established its connection with its audience. After the King's Men took over the Blackfriars theatre they were much more likely to seek specially composed settings of the songs, settings which were in the fashionable musical styles of the day. In the Restoration theatre songs were recomposed, and new songs were frequently added, especially to the comedies. There are, however, a number of features of song-setting in the late seventeenth and eighteenth centuries which are markedly different from the characteristic deployment of song in modern production.

In the first place, songs existed very much as set-pieces, designed to show off the vocal abilities of the singer. In 1777, for example, Thomas Linley the younger composed music for *The Tempest* in a revival at Sheridan's Drury Lane theatre.[24] In a new, additional aria, 'O bid your faithful Ariel fly', as well as in his setting of 'Come unto these yellow sands', Linley provided coloratura vocal lines for a young protégée of his father's, Mary Field, making

her stage debut. She must have had a fine technique to manage the runs and flourishes which extend each of these pieces to four minutes in length, and it is obvious that it is her performance as a singer, rather than her skill in creating Ariel as a character, which is intended to appeal to the audience. These songs were entirely new compositions, but for 'Where the bee sucks' Linley retained Arne's 1746 setting, rearranging it, and supplying an extended chorus. This marks the second characteristic of settings of the songs during much of the eighteenth and nineteenth centuries – the tenaciousness with which familiar settings held the stage.

Throughout the eighteenth and nineteenth centuries the songs for both *The Tempest* and *As You Like It*, for example, were most often performed in well-known settings. A 1793 playbill (Illustration 1) is still advertising 'new airs, by the late Mr. Linley', alongside 'Purcell' and 'Arne' (the composer was drowned in a boating accident in 1778 at the age of 22). And then, 50 years later, though there has been an overhaul of the spectacle, the music remains that of Purcell, Linley and Arne (Illustration 2). Persistence is perhaps even more marked in the continuous history of Thomas Arne's 1740 settings of songs in *As You Like It* which were still being used in the Stratford performances of the play in the 1930s – almost 200 years after their composition.

At one level the longevity of these settings is a symptom of the conservatism that derives from Shakespeare's monumental cultural role. During the nineteenth century new music was customary in the theatre for new productions, except in the case of Shakespeare.[25] Here, though new incidental

[22] Michael Bogdanov and Michael Pennington, *The English Shakespeare Company: The Story of 'The Wars of the Roses', 1986–9* (London, 1990), pp. 57, 109.

[23] See Ross Duffin, *Shakespeare's Songbook* (London, 2004) and David Lindley, *Shakespeare and Music* (London, 2006).

[24] The 'storm chorus' in particular, which replaced the overture and possibly Shakespeare's first scene, has been called 'one of the most remarkable achievements in English music'. A recording by The Parley of Instruments, dir. Paul Nicholson, is available on Helios, CDH55256.

[25] See Pisani, 'Music for the Theatre', p. 76.

1. Playbill for *The Tempest*, Theatre Royal, Haymarket, 19 November 1793.

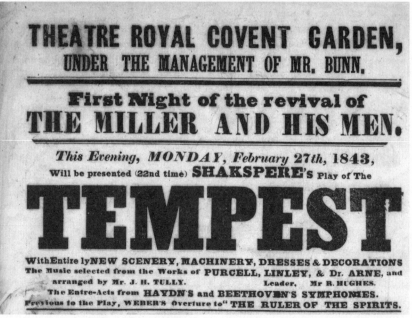

2. Playbill for *The Tempest*, Theatre Royal, Covent Garden, 27 February 1843.

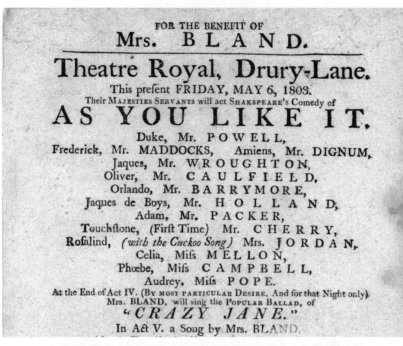

3. Playbill for *As You Like It*, Theatre Royal, Drury Lane, 6 May 1803.

music might be provided, song-settings were slow to be changed. This persistence also testifies to the ways in which repetition and familiarity are so fundamentally a cause and source of pleasure in music. Whether in the obsessive repetition of sing-along *Sound of Music*, or the manufacture of a 'hit' by repeated radio exposure, or just in the warmth of recognition as we play or listen to a familiar piece, this is a basic part of our musical experience, and was clearly understood as part of the appeal to the eighteenth- and nineteenth-century audiences.

In modern performance it would, by contrast, be extremely rare to find old settings of the songs being revived. The difference between contemporary conventions and those of earlier centuries, however, runs deeper than that. Playbills for early nineteenth-century performances of *As You Like It* signal something of the fundamental change in music's place in performance (Illustrations 3, 4). These posters, and many others like them, demonstrate that song was important, not as an indicator of dramatic character, nor for any assistance they

might offer in supporting the increasingly particularized historical settings of the plays, but as a detachable set-piece, part of a varied evening's entertainment which might include comic songs inserted between the acts and other musical diversions. It is only in such a context that the regular, and obviously much-desired introduction of 'The Cuckoo Song' from *Love's Labour's Lost* for Rosalind (or occasionally for Celia) to sing makes any sense at all. This, and other songs were no doubt performed in the same way as Michael Booth indicates actors' points 'were usually taken dead centre, as far downstage as possible, and directed at the audience as much as at another actor'. The *Stratford Herald* reported of the 1879 performance of *As You Like It*, for example, that 'Mr W H Cummings very ably delineated the character of Amiens, and his songs "Under the greenwood tree" and "Blow, blow thou winter wind" – the latter especially – were regarded as distinctive features of the performance, and were loudly encored.' While the option of turning a song into a 'production

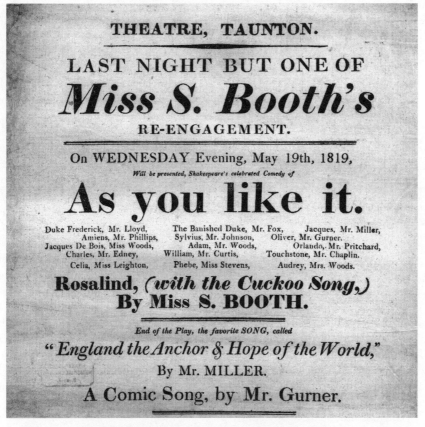

4. Playbill for *As You Like It*, The Theatre, Taunton, 19 May 1819.

number' remains open to the contemporary direc-tor, as we will see, and though a modern Shake-spearian audience might applaud, they certainly would not expect encores.

In contrast to these earlier customs, in the con-temporary theatre specially composed songs are most often accommodated to distinctive features of the production. As with instrumental music it is expected that they will form part of a coherent design. In the 1979 National Theatre *As You Like It*, for example, Elizabethan costume was matched by Harrison Birtwistle's music, which espoused both a pastiche Elizabethan style in its song settings and a rescoring of actual Elizabethan song and instru-mental music for its instrumental bridge-passages. The musical content was sixteenth-century, but the scoring was modern. Stephen Pimlott's 1996

As You Like It did the opposite. It used period instruments – lute and recorder – but Jason Carr's settings were distinctly angular in their vocal line. This accorded with the director's style for the play which combined 'an abstract box set in shin-ing metal . . . and costumes of rigorous Elizabethan exactness even to the faintly absurd puffy behinds of the men's breeches'.[26] Like the production as a whole, the attempt didn't quite come off, not because of its stylistic eclecticism but because the songs were both too obviously difficult for the singer – and almost certainly too alien in style for most of the audience to warm to them.

Both productions did, however, gesture towards a music that in some respects echoed that of the

[26] Smallwood, *Shakespeare at Stratford*, p. 17.

period in which the costumes set the action. More usually, however, directors show a marked indifference to the historical dimension of the musical languages they choose or accept. When Greg Doran directed *Henry VIII* in 1996, the costumes were designed with enormously careful historical accuracy. The setting of 'When Orpheus with his lute' by Jason Carr, however, belonged securely in the world of the stage musical. This disjunction represents a certain continuity with earlier practice, since, as Neighbarger observes,

Even though music historians had already begun to collect and study music from Shakespeare's time and before, there was no recorded attempt to revive any Elizabethan music in the late eighteenth century productions. Paradoxically, in an age that romanticized the idea of the past and claimed to create new music in the spirit of the old, much of the earlier repertoire was criticized for being unsophisticated.[27]

Poel and Arnold Dolmetsch at the end of the nineteenth century made a determined effort to introduce historical instruments and actual or pastiche period music, but it would seem that for most directors and audiences, though music can certainly function to locate a production historically, as we have seen, there is little sense of any consistent need to generate close historical identification. Instead, the effort is much more aimed at matching song-style and the emotional direction of a production. This, however, is not without its problems. Modern directors of *As You Like It*, who, since 1952 at least, have shown a frequent reluctance to give us anything but the glummest, or snowiest, or bleakest representation of Arden in Act 2, have demanded settings of Amiens's lyrics that underline the winter and rough weather, rather than issuing a convincing invitation to 'come hither'. The musical language has often been distinctly discordant and modernist in character. Words and music tug against one another as directorial concept determines the character of the setting. Yet I would argue that it is precisely the ambivalence generated by a music which gives pleasurable expression to sentiments that the surrounding action might undercut that is worth attempting to achieve.

The songs in the play's second half issue different challenges. 'What shall he have that killed the deer' and 'It was a lover and his lass' are each inserted, it would appear, primarily to offer a sense of passing time as the play winds up to its climax. But, characteristically, some modern directors have tried to integrate the songs into the surrounding action. At the National Theatre in 1979, for example, a very detailed dismemberment of the deer during 'What shall he have' fitted with the deployment of real and imaginary folk rituals throughout the production. In Noble's 1985 RSC Jungian version it became a dream sequence for Celia as she lay sleeping on stage, with menacing and aggressive music supplied by Howard Blake.[28] Such attempts bear witness to a directorial anxiety that needs to find thematic justification for these musical set pieces. The desire to integrate is the exact opposite of the eighteenth century's readiness to tolerate the free-standing set piece.

There are, however, productions which are content to accept the narrative disconnectedness of these songs. A highly successful version of 'It was a lover' was that in Cheek by Jowl's production of 1991, revived in 1994/5. Peter Holland had this to say of it:

[it] became what it is obviously intended to be, a show-stopping chorus as Touchstone tried to keep Audrey away from the adult pages, while the four sat and cuddled under a blanket with their eight feet dancing to the tune.

Yet even here there was a specifically musical appropriateness of this set-piece to its particular production. Amiens sang his songs in a falsetto voice throughout, often as the top part in a male-voice chorus. In 'It was a lover' he was in vocal competition with Audrey who essayed ever higher flights into the alto register as her characteristic yodelling was incorporated into the musical

---

[27] Randy L. Neighbarger, *An Outward Show: Music for Shakespeare on the London Stage, 1660–1830* (Westport, CN, 1992), p. 174.

[28] A device that has been imitated in other productions, including that at the West Yorkshire Playhouse in 2010.

setting. In this all-male production the ambivalence of the falsetto singing voice, here deployed both by a 'male' and a 'female' character, suited exactly with Donellan's exploration and subversion of the determining signs of gender.

The significance of the alto voice itself merits a little detour, since it offers a good example of the way in which music can signify in ways other than the direct appeal of its melodic content. For a very long time the male alto voice disappeared from the concert platform (though it has a continuous history in male voice ensembles of various kinds); it re-emerged in the mid-twentieth century particularly in the person of Alfred Deller, and in the context of the early music movement. It was taken up by Benjamin Britten in a number of works, and he chose the alto voice for Oberon in his opera *A Midsummer Night's Dream* in 1960. It is quite probably this opera's haunting music for the fairy king which not only brought the alto voice back into mainstream musical life but also associated it firmly with the other-worldly. It is an association which a number of Ariels have chosen to exploit. Scott Handy, in Adrian Noble's 1998 RSC production, used a falsetto voice in the earlier part of the play, as he sang the songs commanded by Ariel, and only in 'Where the bee sucks' – the first song he, as it were, sings for himself – was his 'natural' baritone voice used. (The same actor uses the same device in the Naxos audio recording of the play – though singing Robert Johnson's seventeenth-century settings, which indicate no such transition.) The pattern was reversed by Julian Bleach in Goold's 2006 RSC production, where the alto voice signalled the spirit's release. One of the most interesting and successful of *Tempest* scores, that by Orlando Gough for James Macdonald's 2000 touring production of the play, followed the same course.

At one level, all of these productions are witnesses to the contemporary desire to psychologise the singing character, and to find a strategy of incorporation and containment of song's centrifugal energies. It is still, however, true that music's affect may reach out to an audience to break through the control at which directors often seem to aim. Simon Russell Beale, the most famous of

reluctant Ariels, in Sam Mendes's 1993 RSC production could not prevent his excellent singing voice registering a quite different emotional possibility from the measured hostility of his service to Prospero. On the other hand, Julian Bleach's hoarse delivery of a deliberately untuneful 'Come unto these yellow sands' in the Arctic *Tempest* of 2006 offered an entirely joyless invitation, at the absolute opposite end of the spectrum from Linley's score, one which would scarcely persuade anyone to go anywhere. This particular setting was an example of the way in which the subordination of the energies of music to directorial design may result, paradoxically, in a Malvolio-like antipathy to musical pleasure.

While some songs, or fragments of songs, are impromptu, and can simply be considered as an expression of the emotional state of the singer who utters them, all performed songs exist in a much more complex relationship to the characters who sing and to their audiences.[29] The performer both is and is not the 'I' of the lyric s/he performs; the song-as-performance is always capable of speaking, as it were, over the heads of the onstage listeners to those sitting in the auditorium. As Mark Booth puts it: 'the singer's words are sung for us in that he says something that is also said somehow in extension *by* us, and we are drawn into the state, the pose, the attitude, the self offered by the song'.[30] A singer not only performs the music of a song, but in significant respects is performed *by* it. The musical setting is not simply contingent upon the words, but remakes them and determines our response to them. Elizabeth Hale Winkler argues that:

although related to the soliloquy in its distinctive manner of presentation, song most often embodies a generalized, rather than an individual, statement. It might be said that while the soliloquy makes the individual subtext explicit, revealing hidden passions and motivations,

[29] For a discussion of these distinctions, see Lindley, *Shakespeare and Music*.
[30] Mark W. Booth, *The Experience of Songs* (New Haven, 1981), p. 15.

the dramatic song reveals the social subtext, expressing communal emotions and thoughts.[31]

If one way of dealing with song in modern production is to attempt to psychologize and individualize it, another – that taken by Paddy Cunneen in the Cheek by Jowl 'It was a lover' and by Orlando Gough throughout his *Tempest* score – is to emphasize a kind of communal voice by setting the songs for vocal ensemble. This actually reflects an older practice, since ensemble settings became fashionable during the late eighteenth and early nineteenth century where, as Leigh Hunt complained:

for one true flight of gaiety and inspiration like Arne's 'Where the Bee Sucks', we have fifty happy pieces of poetry ludicrously contradicted by doleful and pompous music; especially in those solemn personages called Glees, who play into each other's hands as gravely as old ladies at whist.[32]

Nothing, however, could be less doleful than Cunneen and Gough's scores, performed almost entirely by voices, and in the latter case often with a melody line accompanied by rhythmic ostinatos constructed of nonsense syllables. Ariel as singer was simply one among others who created the 'sounds, noises and sweet airs' of Prospero's island, and these sounds were imagined in an entirely contemporary musical language. It accorded, therefore, with the video-projection which created the setting, rather than with the Victorian/Edwardian costuming of the actors. Gough's musical style is actually difficult to pin down. Different listeners have seen in its sound: modernist or 'discordant' harmonies; pop-influenced vocal line; African rhythms and US black street music. It is perhaps that very elusiveness which makes it so appropriate for Prospero's ambivalently magical island. The score provoked varied reactions in reviewers, but it was vital to the affect and effect of the production.

An essential constituent of that effect was that its singers, dressed in black, were visible at the margins of the stage. They acted as stage hands throughout, and in the masque scene became directly involved

in the action: two of them put golden slippers on their hands and mimed at the side of the stage the dance steps that Ferdinand and Miranda were drawn to imitate with increasing enthusiasm. The liminal status of these musicians raises a final issue, the question of the distinctiveness of music in a theatrical context, rather than in cinema or on television. We have seen that there is continuity between the melodrama of Victorian theatre and the sound-track of film. It can be argued, too, that there is considerable similarity in underlying thinking about the place of music across its various dramatic manifestations. So, for example, in her seminal study, Claudia Gorbman suggests that one of the seven principles of film music is that 'it is not meant to be heard consciously. As such it should subordinate itself to dialogue, to visuals.'[33] Her proposition is entirely in line with Peter Brook's statement in 1957, at the time he was assembling his recorded sound for *The Tempest*, that:

It is no longer the ideal to go to an eminent composer...and ask him to write a score to accompany a play...A good incidental score nowadays is more a matter of timbre and tone colour than of harmony or even of rhythm; it has to appeal to a mind which has at least one and three-quarter ears fully occupied with following the dramatic narrative; it is, in fact, quarter-ear music.[34]

Gorbman's first principle: that 'the technical apparatus of non-diegetic music must not be visible' is even more significant for the present argument. It was a notion again anticipated in the nineteenth century, as Rob Dean demonstrates, pointing out that:

during this period it appears that a number of practitioners decided that their attempts at evoking illusory verisimilitude were hampered because the sources which

[31] Elizabeth Hale Winkler, *The Function of Song in Contemporary British Drama* (Newark, 1990), p. 22.
[32] Quoted in Neighbarger, *An Outward Show*, p. 171.
[33] Claudia Gorbman, *Unheard Melodies: Narrative Film Music* (Bloomington, 1987), p. 73.
[34] *Sunday Times*, 22 September 1957.

produced the musical material they employed were visually apparent outside the proscenium arch.[35]

He instances, among other examples, Wagner's hiding of the orchestra pit at Bayreuth. A rather less elaborate arrangement seems to have been entertained by Beerbohm Tree, whose *Tempest* orchestra was 'hidden beneath a mass of vegetables'.[36] The practice continues into recent times – for many years at the RST, for example, musicians were generally concealed behind the stage in the 'Band Box'. Increasingly, as the cost of employing live musicians rises, and as technological development means that computer sound design can take over, theatre music is now perhaps most often generated electronically and experienced through speakers in exactly the same way as it is in the cinema.

Philip Auslander, in his study *Liveness*, discusses the relationship between theatre, cinema and television, between live and what he terms 'mediatized' events, and suggests that:

Initially, mediatized events were modeled on live ones. The subsequent cultural dominance of mediatization has had the ironic result that live events now frequently are modeled on the very mediatized representations that once took the self-same live events as their models.

He concludes that:

since the late 1940s, live theatre has become more and more like television and other mediatized cultural forms. To the extent that live performances now emulate mediatized representations, they have become second-hand recreations of themselves as refracted through mediatization.[37]

His is a rich and complex discussion, to which justice can scarcely be done in brief space. Perhaps, however, the visible presentation of performing musicians is one of the ways in which the theatre resists 'mediatization', or at least offers some complication of the relationship of audience and theatrical performance.

Patrice Pavis, in his primer, *Analyzing Performance*, asserts that: 'The decision to make musical sources visible, or on the other hand to conceal them, has significant repercussions in determining

the nature of dynamic relations between the music and the rest of the mise-en-scène', and a little later continues: 'In Western mise-en-scènes...music's effect is that of accompaniment; it is always indirect, "incidental", and thus judged in terms of the degree to which it serves our understanding of the text and the acting.'[38] I have been arguing that the relationships music establishes are much more varied than the first comment implies, and would suggest that it is precisely the visibility of musicians which plays a significant part in ensuring that the effect may be much more than merely that of 'accompaniment'. Four brief examples of music provided by visible musicians will illustrate something of the range and significance of its importance.

In Supple's *Comedy of Errors*, because the musicians were visible as well as audible to the audience, though not to the play's characters, their music was not simply an accompaniment to the action, but a commentary upon it. In the very simple device of having a drum-beat sound at each of the blows Dromio received, for example, the musicians were positioned exactly as were the audience. They had to be watching in order to time the drum-beats, and we watched alongside them. Their pantomimic response helped us to see this as generically 'comic' violence, and their music as a whole was perceived, at least in part, as a commentary upon the action, not merely an accompaniment to it, a commentary with which the audience participated.

In David Farr's *Winter's Tale* of 2009/10 for the RSC, however, the musicians were much more ambiguously situated. At the beginning of the second part, musicians appeared in costume on the

---

35 Rob Dean, 'From Melodrama to Blockbuster: A Comparative Analysis of Musical Camouflage in Victorian Theatre and Twenty-first-century Film', *Studies in Musical Theatre*, 1 (2007), 140.

36 *Blackwood's Magazine*, October 1904, p. 576.

37 Philip Auslander, *Liveness: Performance in a Mediatized Culture* (London, 1999), pp. 10–11; 158.

38 Patrice Pavis, trans. David Williams, *Analyzing Performance: Theater, Dance, and Film* (Ann Arbor, 2003), pp. 140–1.

stage. They were given a brief snatch of self-introductory dialogue with Autolycus, and then diegetically accompanied him in his songs. So far, so plain; but later in the scene individual instrumentalists from time to time played brief snatches of music to accompany dialogue. The status of this music was not clear. Either we had to perceive the musicians still in the characters in which they had introduced themselves as, and their music, therefore, as their own specific commentary on the action, or else we had, as it were, to imagine that they had retreated from the action, and were performing as the 'theatre band', non-diegetically. Their ambiguous position reflected a rather wider directorial uncertainty about exactly what to do with Bohemian scenes, and the lack of distinction between the musician's diegetic and non-diegetic function was disconcerting rather than enabling. Peter Larsen observes of film music:

when music, images and dialogue are coordinated and appear as a perceptual whole, we automatically expect there to be an underlying intention. We search for a meaning, and we find it – no matter whether the coordination was actually intentional or not.[39]

Here the question of 'whose meaning' the music embodied became unanswerable in the confusion of the musicians' roles.

The presence of the singers in the 2000 *Tempest* was much more positive in its effect, for a number of related reasons. Though they initiated Ferdinand and Miranda's dance, they never spoke or appeared within the action of the play; no attempt was made to give them specific 'characters'. But in this play above all others, where music of strange origin is expressly demanded, an audience could accommodate them easily enough as Ariel's 'corollary'. To give Ariel singing companions within the action has been a not infrequent strategy in production throughout the play's history, but here the visible marginality of the ensemble, and the fact that they functioned as stage hands rather than as 'characters', suited the explicitly metatheatrical questions that the play itself raises. Music belonged to the theatre as much as to the play, from its opening setting of the words 'calm seas, auspicious gales' right

through to its reprise at the end. The singing was virtuoso in quality, with extremely wide ranges demanded, especially of the top soprano, so that we were always aware of its performed presence; it expressly challenged the notion that music should do its work surreptitiously, and that challenge was enforced by the physical visibility of its performers.

The final example is of a non-Shakespearian production, one seen when this article was almost complete, but so apposite to its argument that it merits brief mention. Laurie Sansom's production of Webster's *Duchess of Malfi* at the Northampton Royal & Derngate theatre in 2010 was, musically, at the opposite pole from the visibly non-diegetic musicians of *Comedy of Errors*. Here a group of singers not only sang the music of Gesualdo, but assumed, from time to time, minor speaking roles in the action of the play, and functioned as the singing madmen tormenting the imprisoned Duchess. There were many layers to this boldly imaginative musical device – the fortuitous correspondences of Gesualdo's own career to Webster's play being the least important, if the most publicized. A number of questions might be asked about the nature of the music's effect on audience members for whom unaccompanied Italian seventeenth-century polyphony was not a familiar language, but if it achieved its desired effect it did so precisely because of the ambivalent status of the musicians. As they sang from the margins of the stage, standing behind the bars which framed the set, the music itself became a weapon in the creation of the claustrophobia of Amalfi. The visibility of the singers ensured that we were involved in their music *as* music, as performance; it had therefore the paradoxical effect both of creating powerful emotional reaction in the audience, and yet at the same time, as it framed and stood beside the action, of insisting upon the theatricality of the spectacle we witnessed.

I would argue that in their different ways these four instances of the deployment of visible

---

[39] Peter Larsen, *Film Music* (London, 2005), p. 205.

musicians create complex relationships between audience, music and action, and that the complexity depends precisely on their physical presence. The developing theory of film music offers many insights and suggestions for the historian of theatrical performance – yet it does not quite encompass and explain the ways in which the music that attends theatrical productions is, frequently, a vital element in constituting the interaction between stage and audience, individual and culture, for which the Shakespearian text is catalyst. There is much more work to be done.

USING SHAKESPEARE WITH MEMES, REMIXES AND FANFIC

FRAN TEAGUE

I. USING SHAKESPEARE

The noun 'Shakespeare' has a variety of meanings: it can denote an historical figure, a body of literary texts, a kind of narrative, a style of writing, an historical moment, a literary character and so on. When writers use Shakespeare (in any of those senses), they are doing something that takes a wide variety of forms. They may employ the historical figure in a scholarly work (as in Samuel Schoenbaum's *Shakespeare's Lives*), as an historical figure about whom the writer sometimes speculates (as in Stephen Greenblatt's *Will in the World*), or as a fictional character (as in the film *Shakespeare in Love*). Writers may borrow a phrase in a citation to be profound or, to avoid stuffiness, they may seek a more playful allusion. Writers may employ a setting that is consciously Shakespearian: seventeenth-century London, fifteenth-century Verona, first-century Rome or an atemporal island. Newspaper accounts of suicides, murders and political downfalls can describe these events as Shakespearian. Shakespearian characters people non-Shakespearian plots, while Shakespearian plots undergird non-Shakespearian narratives, whether in *The Sandman* graphic novels or Kurosawa's films. In writing about the way that films use Shakespeare – filmed works and nothing more, no literature, painting, ballet, opera, radio, nor advertisements – Kenneth Rothwell and Annabelle Meltzer developed an elaborate taxonomy that shows the complexity of the whole enterprise. They distinguish among adaptations, modernizations, abridgements, musical and dance versions, travesties, excerpts and documentaries, as well as between motion-pictures and videos. In *Shakespeare and Modern Popular Culture*, Douglas Lanier is careful to include a separate chapter on allusion and citation, as opposed either to homage, adaptation and parody, or to works that invoke the biography and mythology of Shakespeare.[1] Examples proliferate, but the phenomenon itself is undisputed: many works use something that can be labelled as 'Shakespeare'. As Douglas Lanier has remarked after cataloguing all the ways that scholars study Shakespeare adaptations, the field 'has emerged as one of the most robust areas of Shakespearean criticism'.[2] Robert Shaughnessy would agree:

In recent years, the study of the past and present relationships between Shakespeare and popular culture has been transformed: from an occasional, ephemeral, and anecdotal field of research, which, if it registered at all, was generally considered peripheral to the core concerns of scholarship and pedagogy, to one which is making an increasingly significant contribution to our understanding of how Shakespeare's works came into being, and

---

[1] Samuel Schoenbaum, *Shakespeare's Lives* (Oxford, 1991); Stephen Greenblatt, *Will in the World: How Shakespeare Became Shakespeare* (New York, 2004); *Shakespeare in Love*, screenplay by Marc Norman and Tom Stoppard, director John Madden, Miramax (1998). Kenneth Rothwell and Annabelle Meltzer, *Shakespeare on Screen: An International Filmography and Videography* (New York, 1990); Douglas Lanier, *Shakespeare and Modern Popular Culture* (Oxford, 2002) offers chapters on the various forms.

[2] 'Shakespeare and Cultural Studies: An Overview', *Shakespeare*, 2 (2006), 228.

of how and why they continue to exercise the imaginations of readers, theatergoers, viewers, and scholars worldwide.[3]

Yet the study of Shakespeare's use stumbles over certain obstacles.

II. PROBLEMS OF TERMINOLOGY AND TAXONOMY

Scholars have investigated Shakespeare's use under a variety of names: reception study, source study, recycling, appropriation, intertextuality and so on. Each of these names comes with a burden of assumptions about what happens when Shakespeare gets used. 'Source' study suggests that an essentially original source exists like the source of a river, a unique beginning that is fed and increased by other streams. Moreover, there is a sense that finding a source is an action that is somehow complete in itself. The word 'recycled' has ecological overtones, of course, and a sense that the act of re-using is an ethical one, although the recycled work lacks novelty. 'Appropriation' has an etymological link to 'property': creative work is imagined as a form of property that may be seized, appropriated. As Jean Marsden writes:

Associated with abduction, adoption and theft, appropriation's central tenet is the desire for possession. It comprehends both the commandeering of the desired object and the process of making this object one's own, controlling it by possessing it. Appropriation is neither dispassionate nor disinterested; it has connotations of usurpation, of seizure for one's own uses.[4]

In addition, 'appropriate' has another adjectival form that means 'suitable': to say it is 'appropriate' to appropriate Shakespeare may be a claim of class distinction or blurring. Some critics prefer other terms like adaptation (Fischlin and Fortier) or revision (Marianne Novy); the former may come from biology, while the latter simultaneously puns (re-vision) and recalls the work students do. Such embedded assumptions complicate the way that scholars describe using Shakespeare. Even the utilitarian word 'using', the term that I shall employ, comes with preconceptions about how the creative

process happens and whose interest is served (or the nature of the interest).[5]

One term that describes the way in which texts are related is 'intertextuality', but its meaning and usage are unsettled. In 1993, *The Princeton Encyclopedia of Poetry and Poetics* simply defined the term as 'those conditions of textuality which affect and describe the relations between texts', remarking that 'in most respects [it] is synonymous with textuality'. Yet the entry goes on to acknowledge that while traditional literary theory believes that 'a text comes to rest on a prior text which functions as a stable source which is retrieved and made present by a study of allusion, quotation, and reference', developments in literary theory have created a number of problems in understanding such relationships as straightforward. Specifically, in the 1980s, Julia Kristeva chose the term 'intertextuality' to mean the grammar of textuality that underlies such relationships. Other critics, including such influential voices as Barthes and Culler, used the term with greater or lesser elasticity, until Kristeva suggested that the special meaning she had given the term be abandoned.[6]

In two recent essays, Gregory Machacek and Douglas Lanier have both written about the theoretical problems that arise when one considers how a text uses an earlier text. Machacek's essay discusses

---

[3] Robert Shaughnessy, ed., *The Cambridge Companion to Shakespeare and Popular Culture* (Cambridge, 2007), p. 1.

[4] Jean Marsden, *The Appropriation Of Shakespeare: Post-Renaissance Reconstructions of the Works and the Myth* (New York, 1992), p. 1.

[5] Daniel Fischlin and Mark Fortier, *Adaptations of Shakespeare* (New York, 2000); Marianne Novy, *Transforming Shakespeare: Contemporary Women's Re-visions in Literature and Performance* (New York, 1999).

[6] For the developing meanings of 'intertextuality', I've used the definition prepared by Helen Regueiro Elam in *The New Princeton Encyclopedia of Poetry and Poetics*, ed. Alex Preminger, T. V. F. Brogan *et al.* (Princeton, 1993), and Julia Kristeva, 'The Bounded Text', trans. by Thomas Gora, Alice Jardine and Leon S. Roudiez, in *Desire in Language: A Semiotic Approach to Literature and Art*, ed. Roudiez (New York, 1980), pp. 36–63; Kristeva's proposal of 'transposition' in place of 'intertextual' comes in her *Revolution in Poetic Language*, trans. by Margaret Waller (New York, 1984), p. 60.

literary allusion, while Lanier's gives an overview of Shakespeare in popular culture studies. Machacek is rather more concerned with the words critics use to describe allusion, and he shows how terminology can help us do different sorts of reading or hinder us by limiting the questions that we ask of texts. Allusion is a small part of the field that these critics consider, whatever its name, and in that larger field that investigates how one text uses another, terminology and taxonomy remain a problem. To some extent the problem is that distinguishing among various forms or terms requires a certain amount of mind-reading: one must intuit whether the author wished to take over literary property, modify it, mock it to correct it, pay tribute to an earlier work and so forth. Moreover, the effect of the work affects one's understanding of what it is: here again intuition seems to determine whether one reads a work as a commentary on another author, on social conditions, on personal matters, or as a straightforward entertainment. Meaning slips.[7]

Lanier is directly concerned with Shakespeare, and 'reviews the past 15 years of scholarship' about 'the ways in which the works of Shakespeare have been used, plundered, recrafted, and reinflected by generations and cultures not Shakespeare's own'.[8] Like Machacek, who concludes with suggestions for work that might be done, Lanier ends with what he calls 'Prospects', a series of suggestions about what future work might address. Despite the seemingly disparate topics, these essays reach similar conclusions. Both essayists remark on the failure of terminology: that is Machacek's central focus, while Lanier concentrates on the problems in the term 'appropriation'. Lanier also discusses the tensions between historicist and presentist approaches. Both Machacek and Lanier call attention to post-structuralist criticism's concentration on the synchronic and the consequent neglect of the diachronic. (Indeed, Machacek even offers a brief example of how one might integrate the two in a single reading.) Both Machacek and Lanier suggest that academic critics have overlooked an important aspect: the pleasure of reading an allusion fully or the pleasure of an effective use of Shakespeare. They are right: we may ignore past

work because it is inadequately theorized, paying little attention to what that older work could offer, and present studies often fail to engage with the delights of the field.

This article will try a different approach. It begins by making two assumptions with which not everyone will agree. The first assumption is that the terms describing the process of one author using another's work (source, appropriation, derivative, adaptation, allusion, etc.) are all metaphorical, and one could fruitfully discuss the problems with each term, just as Machacek discusses allusion and Lanier appropriation, because − the second assumption − metaphors are by their very nature untidy. I propose we surrender to messiness. Instead of trying to pin metaphors down, like butterflies to be killed and preserved in glass boxes, let them multiply. A particular metaphor has little virtue in itself, for the real power lies in the act of thinking about two works, not in the metaphor chosen to get started. This article will demonstrate that argument using the way that Shakespeare uses other writers, although it suggests some later works that use Shakespeare in the terms of each metaphor. For the purposes of this article, the test metaphors are the meme, the remix and fanfiction.

III. MEMES

Richard Dawkins coined the word 'meme' and it has its origins as a metaphor, not a proven concept: just as living creatures pass on biological information via genes, he argued, humans might pass on cultural information via an analogous mechanism

---

[7] Gregory Machacek's essay, 'Allusion', *PMLA*, 122 (2007), 522–36, is not about a particular author (although Machacek's own interest in Milton is clear) so much as it is about the problems of terminology. On issues of taxonomy, I have been struck by what Tycho (or Jerry Holkins) says on the Penny Arcade site www.penny-arcade.com/2010/5/10/, 10 May 2010: 'That's like any taxonomy I suppose; you start by looking at the creatures around you, attempting to craft broad categories, until one stormy night you're staring into the unblinking eyes of a platypus.'

[8] Lanier, 'Shakespeare and Cultural Studies', p. 228.

called a meme.[9] A meme is a unit of cultural information that replicates itself, virus-like, passing from one human to another; that process is described by the verb 'to meme'. Some memes enjoy more evolutionary success than others, and the concept of the meme helps account for brainworms: the words or tunes that become stuck in our heads. Memes also help explain fads, from Rickrolling, to the Cookie Monster's 'Om nom nom', or the way that the same joke reproduces virally. Moreover, the meme can help account for what performance critic Joseph Roach says about surrogation. The concept of memes, bits of cultural information that humans spread by imitation, with gradual variations, implies that such meming is irresistible, a practice hard-wired into human beings. One cannot demonstrate that such a thing as a meme even exists, but that inability to demonstrate empirically the reality of memes makes the meme an ideal metaphor for this article.

So when might Shakespeare meme? In other words, do units of cultural information replicate themselves in a play, so that he is passing them on without much regard for their aesthetic or intellectual or performance value? Such a meme would have to be sticky, i.e. something picked up by others in the culture. An example, easily anticipated, is the sonnet. Given the immense number of poetic forms, one might reasonably ask why the sonnet spread so quickly across England in the sixteenth century, persisting into the seventeenth. One answer is that the form is a sticky meme, a bit of cultural information that sticks in one's consciousness and insists on replication. Let me add that anyone who has learned to write sonnets finds them hard to resist: they are a complex form, but not too complex and, once a poet controls the form, writing a series of sonnets is tempting. Yet poets may weary of sonnets. Edgar Arlington Robinson, a sonnet writer throughout his career, complained of 'these little sonnet men / Who fashion, in a shrewd mechanic way, / Songs without souls, that flicker for a day, / To vanish in irrevocable light', and it may be worth noting that he wrote fewer sonnets late in his career.[10] If one accepts the sonnet's memetic nature, then sonneteers like Sir

Philip Sidney and William Shakespeare are almost compelled to write in sequences, and the sonnet may even invade their other work.

One arrives at *Romeo and Juliet*, a play that famously uses the sonnet in a dramatic context. The play is also imitative: Shakespeare uses elements both from Sidney's *Astrophel and Stella* and from Arthur Brooke's *Romeus and Juliet*. The former suggests the effectiveness of sonnets for love poetry, of course, as well as suggesting key imagery. The latter offers a plot. As Romeo and Juliet meet at the Capulet ball, they famously generate a sonnet, while bits of sonneteering pop up throughout the play, particularly in Romeo's speeches. Even Mercutio comments (in prose) on the connection between sonneteering and love stories when Romeo appears the next morning:

Now is [Romeo] for the numbers that Petrarch flowed in. Laura to his lady was a kitchen wench – marry, she had a better love to berhyme her – Dido a dowdy, Cleopatra a gypsy, Helen and Hero hildings and harlots, Thisbe a grey eye or so, but not to the purpose.　(2.3.36–41)

So far the notion of meme may be interesting, but it offers nothing new. A puzzle remains, however, when one considers sonnets and *Romeo and Juliet*. The Chorus speaks in sonnets at the beginning of Acts 1 and 2, then vanishes. Unlike Romeo and Juliet, the Chorus uses a poetic form associated with love, but does not speak of love. Instead he first gives the play's argument and then summarizes the action in his second sonnet. One might ask why he uses a sonnet. Memetically, of course, this feature makes perfect sense: the Chorus uses a sonnet because the form is stuck, virally, in the writer's mind. Brooke opens *Romeus and Juliet* with two sonnets, one 'To the Reader' and one giving

---

[9] Most of what I have to say is based on the work of Susan Blackmore, particularly her book *The Meme Machine* (Oxford, 2000). As I mention in my discussion, I found her ideas resonating with those of performance theorist Joseph Roach, especially in his work *Cities of the Dead* (New York, 1996). The website youtube.com has a number of delightful podcasts under the general heading, 'Know Your Meme'.

[10] 'Sonnet' from *The Children of the Night* (New York, 1897), p. 63.

'The Argument'. Shakespeare retained the memory of those sonnets, perhaps because they sound so very different from the rest of the work, written as it is in poulters' measure, and when the dramatist began his own version of the story, he chose to replicate those sonnets.

The first sonnet, giving the argument, is far better than the second, of which Dr Johnson wrote: 'The use of this chorus is not easily discovered. It conduces nothing to the progress of the play, but relates what is already known, or what the next scenes will shew; and relates it without adding the improvement of any moral sentiment'.[11] The dissonance between the Chorus sonnets and the lovers' sonnets may help explain why the Chorus disappears in the rest of the play. The first appearance of the Chorus is retained in all the quartos, but omitted in the First Folio; the Act 2 appearance is omitted in the first (bad) quarto, but occurs in the rest of the quartos and the First Folio. Someone was having second thoughts. If the sonnets are memetic moments, the dramatist or the company or the printer regretted it, perhaps feeling, like Robinson, that the Chorus represented one of 'these little sonnet men / Who fashion, in a shrewd mechanic way, / Songs without souls'. To be sure this notion is speculation, but I would not have noticed that anything existed about which to speculate had I not approached the play while thinking within the metaphor of the meme.

Further, when I glanced at a copy of Joe Calarco's play, *Shakespeare's R&J*, the first thing I noticed is that Calarco uses extra sonnets in his version, but drops the Chorus sonnets: Shakespeare's text yields to the meme. In another use of *Romeo and Juliet*, *West Side Story* transforms the opening sonnet and the lovers' sonnet into dance. The beginning of the show starts with a number entitled 'Prologue', the famous dance-duel between the Jets and Sharks, while the lovers' meeting is a delicate cha-cha that Tony and Maria dance together oblivious to the mambo and swing dancers around them. The lyricism of the sonnet form becomes the dynamic of a dance.

IV. REMIXES AND MASHUPS

My second metaphor is the remix and its cousin the mashup.[12] A remix takes a musical text and remixes it, altering its sound, beat and so on to create a new work that uses the old. A mashup uses more than one work, mixing up disparate tracks to create a collage that is coherent. According to Eduardo Navasse's site remixtheory.net:

Generally speaking, remix culture can be defined as the global activity consisting of the creative and efficient exchange of information made possible by digital technologies that is supported by the practice of cut/copy and paste.

Almost everyone who writes about remix culture points out that this phenomenon is neither new nor limited to music, although the late twentieth-century practice of remixing electronic tracks of music is the origin of the word. If one thinks in terms of remixes and mashups, then, one must think structurally, separating a work into its constituent tracks and then reassembling, distorting, eliminating or emphasizing each one. Obviously if a remix culture considers the way that one writer uses another, then the way that Shakespeare uses other texts and that later writers use Shakespeare can be regarded as remixes and mashups. Branagh's film version of *Henry V*, which cuts and occasionally rearranges the text of Shakespeare's play, is a remix, while *Shakespeare in Love*, citing and combining sonnets, *Romeo and Juliet*, *Twelfth Night* and so on (as well as Webster and possibly *No Bed for Bacon*), is a mashup.

---

[11] Dr Samuel Johnson, *Preface to Shakespeare* (London, 1765), p. 65.

[12] Blackmore cites Beethoven's Fifth as a meme. My attention was first drawn to remix culture and to the mashup by a wonderful programme on Public Radio International's 'To the Best of Our Knowledge' entitled 'Remix Culture'. It is available as a podcast: www.pri.org/arts-entertainment/music/remix-culture-ttbook.html. I also have benefited from reading Lawrence Lessig's *Free Culture*. Finally the remixtheory.net site provides history as well as philosophy about remixing.

While Shakespeare could not download an mp3 file, he could use others' texts in a way that corresponds to the remix and the mashup. One clear-cut instance is the remix of Geoffrey Chaucer's *The Knight's Tale* that Shakespeare and John Fletcher refashion into *The Two Noble Kinsmen*. To the main track of Chaucer's narrative, Shakespeare adds the Jailer's daughter subplot. He also takes the time scheme and condenses it sharply, altering the rhythm. Most of his remixing, however, has less to do with the aesthetic effect than with the dramaturgical: the tournament takes place off stage, while the deities are just suggested and never appear. In all, this remix is a diminution of the Chaucer text, reducing the time that the narrative takes and the spectacle that it affords. Yet when Shakespeare uses Chaucer in this way, remixing and diminishing his tale, he is following Chaucer's own practice, for Chaucer had in turn remixed Boccaccio's *Il Teseida*, a much longer poem in twelve books, reducing it in length and scope.

Of particular interest for this essay is that Shakespeare and Fletcher's remix of *The Knight's Tale* is approximately twenty years later than Shakespeare's mashup of the same work in *A Midsummer Night's Dream*. In that play, the Theseus track combines with other tracks, from traditional fairy lore, from romantic comedy with the young lovers, and from Ovid's tale of 'Pyramus and Thisbe', to become a coherent play. One might imagine such a relatively sophisticated mashup to have come after the more straightforward remix, but to expect the more sophisticated form to follow the simpler results from the error, as O. B. Hardison taught us long ago, of expecting the world of literature to operate like a model of evolutionary development.[13] (To endorse both memes and Hardison's argument is, of course, incongruous. The delightful thing about metaphoric meaning is that it need not be consistent.)

Let me now take the metaphor and consider its implications. If we think of *A Midsummer Night's Dream* as a mashup, then we might consider each of the tracks separately and ask what has happened to them in the new work created from their superimposition on one another. In this instance, I want to concentrate on the Theseus track and how it has been altered to fit it into the mashup. *The Knight's Tale* features grief and death, both linked to warfare and to love: war keeps breaking out, widowed queens seek vengeance, friends duel to the death. When that track occurs in *A Midsummer Night's Dream*, however, the bass line of grief and death is gone. Beyond a brief mention of the war with the Amazons, the lovely speech about the changeling's mother and some lovelorn petulance, the play largely omits death and grief. A similar silencing occurs with the classical deities who populate Chaucer's tale. In Chaucer, the gods take a direct and emotional interest in human affairs: their divine quarrels reflect the squabbles below, but on a grander scale. In the remixed mashup, that track seems to be played at a different speed: it becomes distorted and comic as the Chaucerian gods become the Shakespearian fairies. The power of Venus, Diana and Mars is demonstrated in Chaucer by the extraordinary descriptions of their temples. Their disagreements are adjudicated by Jupiter himself with the aid of the cunning Saturn. But in *A Midsummer Night's Dream*, these gods are replaced by Titania, Oberon and Puck, who exercise power on a much smaller scale.

The discordant tracks that make up *A Midsummer Night's Dream* do fit together quite well, however, and structurally the play is at its best when they interpenetrate, thanks in no small part to the language. When Titania takes Bottom as her lover, when the lovers are changed by Puck, when the whole lot come together in Act 5 to celebrate the marriages, *A Midsummer Night's Dream* succeeds. Yet one could pause for a moment to speculate about why Shakespeare has chosen to use Chaucer's story of Theseus and Hippolyta's wedding to frame his fairy-tale mashup. It does not need this specific couple, after all, since power couples are almost as ubiquitous as mismatched lovers.

---

[13] See O. B. Hardison, *Christian Rite and Christian Drama in the Middle Ages* (Baltimore, 1969), ch. 1, esp. pp. 4–5.

The fairies enter at the close of the play to bless the union of Theseus and Hippolyta. Specifically, Oberon vows to protect the three couples' children:

> And the blots of nature's hand
> Shall not in their issue stand.
> Never mole, hare lip, nor scar,
> Nor mark prodigious such as are
> Despisèd in nativity
> Shall upon their children be.   (5.2.39–44)

We know that the fairy promise is kept for the child of Theseus and Hippolyta. Hippolytus is a beautiful young man, although he never knows his mother, who dies in childbirth. Theseus remarries and his new wife Phaedra finds her stepson so attractive that she attempts to seduce him. Thwarted, she will kill herself and Theseus will intercede with Poseidon to destroy his son, only to realize too late that Hippolytus is innocent. The power of the classical deities is back full force, as is the grief that Shakespeare's play silences. Shakespeare was well aware of Hippolytus's fate, and Harold F. Brooks notes his use of Seneca's *Hippolytus* as a source. Yet in the version of the myth that Shakespeare knew the best, the account in Book xv of *Metamorphoses*, the emphasis is not on the wicked stepmother, but on the way that Hippolytus comes back from death and transforms into a woodland deity who guards a grove in the forest.

[Hippolytus speaks:]   . . . If thou
In talk by hap hast heard of one Hippolytus ere now,
That through his fathers lyght beleefe, and stepdames
     craft was slayne,
It will a woonder seeme to thee, and I shall have much
     payne
To make thee to beleeve the thing. But I am very hee.
[He tells the story of his life, death, and resuscitation by
     Apollo. Cynthia changes his appearance and places
     him in a wood.]
Then Cynthia (lest this gift of hers myght woorke mee
     greater spyght) . . .
Thicke clowds did round about mee cast . . .
For whereas erst Hippolytus hath beene thy name
     (quoth shee)
I will that Virbie afterward thy name for ever bee.

From that tyme foorth within this wood I keepe my
     residence,
As of the meaner Goddes, a God of small significance,
And heere I hyde mee underneathe my sovereine
     Ladyes wing
Obeying humbly to her hest in every kynd of thing.[14]

The classical track that opens and closes the play potentially alters the tone of Shakespeare's mashup. For those who identify Hippolytus, the fairy blessing is simultaneously charming and chilling; for the few who know Ovid's *Metamorphoses* Book xv, the implicit reference to Hippolytus may put Oberon's woodland deity in a new light. While Oberon is clearly not Hippolytus, the similarity in their situations darkens the tone of the work, as well as broadening its scope.

A similar effect comes with the mashup mentioned earlier, *Shakespeare in Love*. The closing moments of that film show Viola walking along a beach after a shipwreck, a clear use of *Twelfth Night*, both the play and the film production by Trevor Nunn. The bittersweet ending when Will and Viola part is mitigated by the final shots of Viola on the beach. Suddenly the world of the film has broadened out to another continent, the anxiety over social class and marriage has vanished, and Viola is striking out on a new adventure.

V. FAN FICTION

Remixes and mashups may be found across the internet, as may fan fiction, but in fan fiction mashups are known as crossovers. The term fan fiction (or fanfic) describes amateur metafictions: a fan (of a book, movie, television show, cartoon or video game) works to learn its 'canon': characters, episodes, *mise-en-scène*. Then the fan writes an extension or modification of that canon: the fanfic can fill in a gap in the text to suggest what might have happened or modify a canonical element to see the outcome (hence the mashup or crossover of two or more canons). While analyses of fanfic often

---

[14] Arthur Golding, trans., *Ovid's Metamorphoses*, ed. Madeleine Forey (Baltimore, 2001), xv: 550–613.

claim its beginning is far in the past, with Homer or Malory, for example, the form really depends on mass culture. As noted media critic Henry Jenkins points out, fan fiction depends on poaching, 'the idea that fans construct their own culture – fan fiction, artwork, costumes, music and videos – from content appropriated from mass media, reshaping it to serve their own needs and interests'. As he writes in his book *Textual Poaching*, 'Fan fiction is a way of the culture repairing the damage done in a system where contemporary myths are owned by corporations instead of owned by the folk.'[15] To consider Shakespeare as someone who writes fanfic, then, is anachronistic, but one may consider a metaphorical enquiry about how Shakespeare is like a fanfic creator when he uses another's work. It seems reasonable to turn to one of his earliest works, for fanfic writers tend to be novices, as well as amateurs. *The Comedy of Errors* is undoubtedly an early work that uses another text, Plautus's *Menaechmi*, as its basis.

Fanfic has its own set of genres, conventions and terminology, and three terms in addition to 'crossover' may apply to *The Comedy of Errors*: Mary Sue tales, het and WAFF. A Mary Sue tale is one with a new character, modelled on the fanfic writer, who is added to the canon, taking part in the adventures of or romantically linked with a canon character. Mary Sue is a mocking name, but the phenomenon is fairly common: fan fiction, after all, permits the writer to enter the wished-for world of a text and imaginatively engage with much-admired characters. Furthermore, the imaginary entrance into a much-loved text is a common fantasy, one in which passionate readers often engage. Het is a shortened form of heterosexual, referring to a romantic or sexual pairing; fanfic is particularly rich in sexual plots, although a fair number are same sex or slash. On American sites, these plots are rated like films. The popular site FanFiction.net, for example, rates tales from K (okay for kids to read) to T (okay for teenagers to read) to M (graphic descriptions). Finally, WAFF is an acronym for warm fuzzy feeling.

When one turns to *The Comedy of Errors*, one finds that Shakespeare has expanded the number of Plautine characters substantially. Instead of one pair of orphaned twins, he provides two pairs, and adds a set of parents. Instead of a wife and courtesan, he offers a wife, a sister, a maid and a courtesan, among others. Among all these added characters in a fanfic, one might look for a Mary Sue, the fan's surrogate. If so, Shakespeare's own history in the early days of his career comes into play: he is away from his family in a city that travellers sometimes found bewildering or mysterious. He presumably considers his family, the wife and children, including twins, that he has left behind in Stratford. He worries about his wife's fidelity or considers his own liberty to sleep with others, or at least that is what happens if the play is a Mary Sue tale. Because the play is het, the fan fiction writer has taken the sexual encounters in Plautus (one that is suggested but unrealized between the native twin and the courtesan and one realized between the visiting twin and the courtesan) and expanded the possibilities, while toning down the rating: now the pairings include the romantic ones between husbands and wives (Antipholus Ephesus and Adriana, Dromio Ephesus and Luce, Aegeon and Emilia), as well as the courtship relationship between Antipholus Syracuse and Luciana, and the implicitly sexual liaisons, all unrealized, between Antipholus Ephesus and the courtesan, Dromio Syracuse and Luce, and Antipholus Syracuse and Adriana). The complexities multiply, but if one has read any fanfic, those extra relationships are exactly what one would expect. In fanfic the writer wants to take a given feature of the canon text and expand on the bits that are most personally exciting. The rating of Plautus would be a T, since the sexual union occurs off stage with no details, while Shakespeare's version is more likely a K. The downgrading of the rating is not unusual either, as some fanfic writers, while enjoying sexual material in the canon world, are themselves squeamish.

Finally, as a fanfic, *The Comedy of Errors* is surprisingly high in WAFF, those warm and fuzzy feelings that some fanfic writers cannot resist. The

---

[15] The first quotation comes from Jenkins's personal website. The second from *Textual Poaching* (New York, 1992).

WAFF alterations particularly interest me because they are connected to the element of crossover in the work. Specifically, when Shakespeare heightens the sentimentality of the ending, he does so by introducing the character of Aegeon in 1.1, who tells a long and complex tale about the family's separation, as well as lamenting his condemnation to death. This scene sets up the play's conclusion: when the sets of twins recognize one another, the husband and wife are reconciled, the young lovers declare their love, and the father and mother reappear. The Plautine text is far less WAFFish, because in it one pair of twins recognize each other, and the husband abandons both wife and mistress to run off with his twin. The disjunction between the cynical Roman and sentimental Renaissance text occurs because, again in fanfic terms, Shakespeare's play is a crossover that incorporates elements from St Paul: the emphasis on relationships between husbands and wives as well as slaves and masters. Moreover, other crossover traces can be seen in the relocation of Plautus's play from Epidamnus to St Paul's Ephesus: Emilia is now the abbess of the Temple of Diana of Ephesus, while Doctor Pinch and his treatment seems to use details from Acts 19, an account of Paul's adventures in Ephesus. The idea of fanfic based on the Book of Acts may seem implausible, but the site FanFiction.net lists nearly 3,000 pieces of fanfic based on the Bible, including 126 that are rated M. While the metaphor of fanfiction is anachronistic, one can enjoy the idea that by using the classics and the Bible, Shakespeare was writing himself into beloved texts, in the same way that the over 1,500 fanfic writers who have posted stories using Shakespeare or the creators of the BBC's *ShakespeaRe-Told* series have written themselves into his plays.

To conclude, terminological arguments are futile if every term represents a metaphor, a way of describing the indescribable. The specific metaphor a scholar chooses shows different things about how a text uses another by focusing attention on different aspects of the text or the creative process. To examine a variety of metaphors may seem belle-lettristic, a return to analyses that do not scrutinize the readerly, the cultural or the textual system, but expanding our metaphors and permitting some messiness does allow us to have greater pleasure in the process. Having pleasure and making a beloved text our own may not be academically respectable, but it is certainly why I got into this field.

'PRETTY MUCH HOW THE INTERNET WORKS'; OR, AIDING AND ABETTING THE DEPROFESSIONALIZATION OF SHAKESPEARE STUDIES

SHARON O'DAIR

Following the thirty-fourth International Shakespeare Conference, held in August 2010 in Stratford-upon-Avon, I assumed I would not be required to think about the talk I gave there until a month or two later, when I hoped to begin revising it.[1] Two days after arriving home, however, I received a kindly email from one Andrew Cowie of the Shakespeare Birthplace Trust in Stratford-upon-Avon, letting me know that my talk 'was being much discussed' at the SBT, including on one of the Trust's sponsored websites, where, he suspected, my talk was being misrepresented.[2] Curious, yet with some trepidation, I went to *Blogging Shakespeare*, 'a digital experiment of the Education Team at the Shakespeare Birthplace Trust'. There I read 'The ISC: A Student's Perspective', which appeared on 17 August 2010, and was written by 'Shakespeare Bookshop', or Matt Kubus, a Ph.D. student at the Shakespeare Institute. The post generated twenty comments in just a few days, including two sibling posts, one entitled, 'Not for an age, but for all time – and all people' at *The American Shakespeare Center's Education Department Blog* and one entitled, 'Asides: Shakespeare and Access: Responding to the ISC Debate', at *The Shakespeare Standard*.[3] The sibling posts generated less commentary, just seven responses to 'Not for an age' and just two to 'Responding to the ISC Debate', but overall, Cowie judged, these were 'a lot of comments'.[4] To my mind, though, twenty-nine comments do not seem many at all and suggest, in a way I hope will resonate through the rest of this article, a disconnect between reality and the bloggers' enthusiasm about democratizing Shakespeare via the internet. As Jeremy observes in 'Responding to the ISC Debate', 'I read recently – I can't remember exactly where – that Ringo Starr and Shakespeare have the same approximate cultural value to the public at large.'[5]

Given my argument in 'Against Internet Triumphalism', I suppose I should not have been surprised discussion of the talk migrated to the Web and, except for the writer of the first post, to those who had not heard it. But I was surprised. What surprised further – much further – was that the blogging and commentary exemplified some of the problems with internet-based cultural democracy identified in my talk. Before proceeding to discuss those problems via the blogging and commentary, as well as the argument I presented at the ISC, I would like to place this article within the topic that governed the 2010 meeting of the ISC. To do

---

[1] The talk was entitled, 'Against Internet Triumphalism.'
[2] Personal email, dated 18 August 2010.
[3] See http://bloggingshakespeare.com/the-isc-a-students-perspective; http://americanshakespearecentereducation.blogspot.com/2010/08/not-just-of-age-but-for-all-time-and.html; and http://theshakespearestandard.com/2010/08/28/asides-shakespeare-and-access/, respectively.
[4] Andrew Cowie, 'Guest Blog from Andrew: Political Shakespeare', *Blogging Shakespeare*, http://bloggingshakespeare.com/page/6, 15 September 2010.
[5] Jeremy [Fiebig], 'Asides: Shakespeare and Access', *The Shakespeare Standard*, http://theshakespearestandard.com/2010/08/28/asides-shakespeare-and-access/, 28 August 2010.

so requires some consideration of the key term in it, 'catalyst'. When Professor Kathleen McLuskie announced two years earlier that this conference would address 'Shakespeare as Cultural Catalyst', she read aloud a slightly different version of this description, which appeared in the 2010 Conference Programme:

Shakespeare played a major part in the early modern cultural transformation we call the Renaissance, and has figured in every major cultural and intercultural transformation since then. The conference will explore ways in which Shakespeare has been a source of energy and inspiration for these changes, whether played out in the theatre, textual study, criticism, or the production of literature and other arts.[6]

McLuskie added a number of explanatory comments, two of which ground my thinking here. Perhaps sensing that this description promotes an overly positive understanding of Shakespeare's role in culture, she added that conference speakers might also explore moments or cultural transformations 'when catalysts go wrong' or go 'too far, too fast.' And, she asked her audience to remember that 'the focus is not with the catalyst itself, but with the two elements it catalyses'. McLuskie, then, suggested that the conference would not focus on Shakespeare *per se*, and she also alluded to the definition of 'catalyst' she favours, for the term is ambiguous, despite the single definition offered by the *OED*: 'a substance which when present in small amounts increases the rate of a chemical reaction or process but which is chemically unchanged by the reaction'.

Other dictionaries show the word's absorption into everyday culture, a fact acknowledged by the *OED*: two of the eight quotations offered by the *OED* to exemplify the word's meaning and usage refer to human agents whom we might well call cultural catalysts. Emphasized in the *OED* selections is the 'unchangingness' or the 'obscurity' of the catalyst, whether chemical or human; in *Mark Lambert's Supper*, for instance, J. I. M. Stewart writes, 'In the intricate chemistry that gives motive-power to the machine he has himself acted as an obscure catalyst.' And Herbert Read observes

that 'Shelley called poets the unacknowledged legislators of the world, and the epithet was well chosen. The catalyst is unchanged, unabsorbed; its activity therefore not acknowledged.' Probably every reader of this article objects to the notion of Shakespeare as unchanging, but I would like to bracket this question in order to assert, for my purpose here, that Shakespeare − or rather, new media or internet Shakespeare − acts as a catalyst in speeding a reaction already taking place between amateurs and professionals in cultural production. What I will argue is that this reaction between amateurs and professionals should be understood as a reaction between, on the one hand, democratized and neo-liberal cultural production and, on the other hand, elite and subsidized cultural production. And I will argue that although the results of this reaction are not yet known − subsequent legal, technological or intellectual developments may blunt the neo-liberal democratization currently taking place − the trajectory of this reaction suggests, overall, a deskilling and a deprofessionalization of our work.

Of course, although I think we all are subject to deprofessionalization, and though my focus here is on Shakespearians housed in English departments, the results of this reaction will be judged differently depending on one's institutional location and one's intellectual or pedagogical commitments; on the larger social stage, too, the changes brought about by democratization, particularly as catalysed by new media and via the internet, are both positive and negative. To date in Shakespeare studies, editors, historicists and performance critics have benefited from digital technology and cultural democratization, while formalists, close readers and those critics who consider themselves writers have not.[7] With respect to pedagogy, the

---

[6] 'Shakespeare as Cultural Catalyst', Thirty-Forth International Shakespeare Conference, Conference Programme, p. 14.

[7] On this point, see, for example, Laurie Osborne, 'SAA Hyperessay on Electronic Shakespearean Criticism', www.colby.edu/personal/l/leosborn/saalong.html. Editorial work and 'arguments which rely on or grow from visual representations of Shakespeare's works', that is, performance

results of this reaction will be judged differently depending upon the conditions under which one teaches – a seminar of fifteen students at an elite undergraduate institution, for example, or a lecture to 250 uninvolved and non-intellectual students at an open admissions university. And it will depend, too, on what one judges the (primary) goal of one's pedagogy to be; is it, say, learning about stage or costume design; learning about Shakespeare's life, works and cultural context; or learning how to craft written criticism about any of the above? Let me emphasize, too, that I am not antediluvian or, worse, Luddite about new media or democratization. Without the post-war democratization of the academy in the United States, I would not have been a speaker at the ISC in the town of Shakespeare's birth and, as far as new media are concerned, I use my fair share. I consider myself among the group of professionals whose interests and passions are not served by the democratization catalysed by new media, but all of my writings, including my dissertation, have been composed on a computer.[8] I have a cell and HDTV; I am one of 500 million worldwide users of Facebook; I buy many of my consumer goods online; and I have a car that is so computerized I did not lift the hood for a year.

Rather than antediluvian, Luddite or anti-democratic, then, I aim to question what seems a too-eager embrace of that which threatens to deskill and deprofessionalize us. I wrote 'Against Internet Triumphalism', as I am writing this revision of it, in order 'to get us to think about what we mean by democracy, neo-liberalism/capitalism, and professionalism – and the relationships among them'.[9] Neither elitism nor democracy is a transparent concept, but each is bandied about as if it were. Elitism is not a synonym for professionalism, and neither democracy nor markets is a synonym for all that is good in the world. Like Thomas Frank, I write to express doubt about our belief 'in the benevolent divinity of technology' and, concomitantly, of markets and entrepreneurship, a set of beliefs that, as Frank describes their operations among professional journalists, 'cancels out our caution [and] forces us to dismiss doubt

as so much simple-minded Luddism'. Such beliefs cause us to 'have trouble grasping that the Internet might not bring only good' to society as a whole and, in particular, that it might not bring much good at all to professors or professional writers.[10] My contention here is that Shakespearians are

---

criticism, benefit from web-based capabilities and production. But Osborne is less certain about the value of web-based production for argumentative, critical prose, which requires a 'linear . . . model . . . of presenting ideas'. Evidence suggests that on the Web, readers' 'willingness to follow from page to page . . . can depend as much on visual appeal as on developing content'.

[8] I am, therefore, part of the 'quiet triumph of the digital in analogue disguise', which Martin Mueller bemoans. For digital enthusiasts, like Mueller, this triumph is not very exciting, because although such scholars 'see that more people can get at more stuff quickly', once they get their stuff, 'they just keep doing what they have always done and simply treat the digital surrogate as if it were another kind of book'. 'Digital Shakespeare, or Towards a Literary Informatics', *Shakespeare*, 4 (2008), p. 304.

[9] See Kubus, 'Student's Perspective', http://bloggingshakespeare.com/the-isc-a-students-perspective. Such questioning is not new, either with respect to markets or democracy. Regarding the latter, Simon During notes in his work-in-progress, entitled 'Compulsory Democracy: Towards a Literary History', that 'Republicans, associationalists, classical liberals, and conservatives have all registered their sense that contemporary democracy needs to be reconstituted. Influential European philosophers [i.e. Badiou, Ranciere, and Derrida] have also been actively engaged in re-theorizing democracy's past, present, and future.' During's goal, it seems, is to recuperate a certain literary conservatism: his book will 'remind us not just that democracy has been imagined (and periodically governed) by a conservatism to which the literary canon is allied, but that, in the epoch of compulsory democracy, conservatism cannot be reduced to the programs of the political right'. Author's typescript, 'Introduction', pp. 1, 10.

[10] Thomas Frank, 'Bright Frenetic Mills', *Harper's*, December 2010, pp. 12, 13. Frank's essay addresses 'so-called content mill[s]' that use freelancers 'to generate articles for about $15 per 300-word item'. The aim of such mills, according to Jeff Jarvis, 'the head of the brand-new Tow-Knight Center for Entrepreneurial Journalism at the City University of New York', is to cut 'content creation into its constituent elements and creat[e] a market for creation to find new efficiencies', p. 13. This is undoubtedly Taylorist. See pp. 93–4, below. For a report from the scene, see Jessanne Collins, 'My Summer on the Content Farm', *The Awl*, November 2010, www.theawl.com/2010/11/my-summer-on-the-content-farm.

doing what professors of journalism are doing, promoting forms of efficiency and profit-making in thinking, writing and pedagogy that are 'toxic to the form of professionalism that J-schools [or English departments, Theatre departments, and universities more broadly] exist to protect'.[11] I ask only that readers not dismiss my doubt 'as so much simple-minded Luddism', thus falling into patterns that, as the responses to 'The ISC: A Student's Perspective' indicate, seem to characterize expression on the internet.

Even though the bloggers and commentators who responded to Kubus's post are not, for the most part, I am guessing, members of the general public, the comments and the sibling blogs demonstrated that internet expression of this sort tends to reinforce rather than challenge pre-existing opinion or conviction. Regardless of the status of the cohort involved – the educated, the uneducated; the wealthy, the poor; the established or the aspiring – such Internet expression leads to polarized debate of an eerily predictable sort, the result of finding oneself again and again in 'echo chambers or information cocoons'.[12] In this case, a group of people echo that 'Shakespeare is for everyone'; that 'professors are elitist'; and that 'everyone's opinion counts'.[13] Furthermore, as Cass Sunstein says of political blogs, 'debate' like this is anarchic, undisciplined and uncontrolled, indulging a 'stunningly diverse range of claims, perspectives, rants, insights, lies, facts, non-facts, sense and nonsense'.[14] As original poster Kubus observed in response to one comment in particular: 'I think my only concern would be the spread of misinformation. I don't think any of the academics at the conference want to keep Shakespeare for the elite (at least I hope not!) . . .'[15]

Happily, Kubus defended all of the 'academics at the conference' from the charge of elitist possessiveness, but he is right to worry about the spread of misinformation on the Internet in the form of such intellectual or political debate. He is right because this is 'how the internet works', as Cass Morris, of the American Shakespeare Center, cheerfully rhapsodizes, in response to a complaint by Jordan about the ethics of 'commenting on an academic paper

that you neither heard nor read'. Morris defends herself, saying,

Well, as I said in my post, I was responding to the blog, not to the paper. I kept names out of it for that very reason, and I made sure it was clear that I wasn't speaking to the paper itself. I don't particularly see anything unethical about that. If I was [sic] going to write an in-depth paper of my own for publication or a conference, there would be a lot more research involved, but since blogs are, by their very nature, less formal, it didn't seem necessary to hunt down the original source. I was just joining the debate, picking up the thread from another blogger – which is pretty much how the Internet works.[16]

How the internet works, then, is that my talk was reduced and, by implication, I was reduced

---

[11] Frank, 'Bright', p. 12.

[12] Cass Sunstein, *Republic.com 2.0* (Princeton, 2007), p. 44. Mathew Hindman's empirical research on digital democracy reveals that most internet 'searches involved citizens searching out news organizations they are already familiar with'. Matthew Hindman, *The Myth of Digital Democracy* (Princeton 2009), p. 71.

[13] Examples include, from Green Thomas on *Blogging Shakespeare*, 'I really don't understand the concept of keeping Shakespeare for the elite and the academics'; from VioletleaR on *Blogging Shakespeare*: 'Shakespeare should not be confined to one sector of society. It is because of a restricted view of the topic which leads the public at large to fear even the discussion of the topic' [sic]; from Garrick Huscared on *Blogging Shakespeare*: 'Shakespeare has been considered out of the grasp of everybody for too long. Dr Owen [sic] is absolutely right to open up things to all people. Let the academics continue in deep thought'; from Annie Maura on *ASC*: 'I completely agree that Shakespeare does and should belong to everyone'; from Cass Morris on *ASC*: 'Everyone's view is interesting'; from Shakespeare BT on *ASC*: 'As a teacher I firmly believe that everyone's opinion has merit. An opinion is after all just that, an opinion, informed by the unique perspective of the person who holds it. It may not be my opinion, it may be informed by a what [sic] I consider a misunderstanding of facts, but it is still of value. At least that's my opinion!' http://bloggingshakespeare.com/the-isc-a-students-perspective; http://americanshakespearecentereducation.blogspot.com/2010/08/not-just-of-age-but-for-all-time-and.html.

[14] Sunstein, *Republic.com*, p. 142.

[15] Kubus, 'Student's Perspective', http://bloggingshakespeare.com/the-isc-a-students-perspective.

[16] Morris, 'Not for an age', http://americanshakespearecentereducation.blogspot.com/2010/08/not-just-of-age-but-for-all-time-and.html.

(even if – or *because* – my name seeped away from the posts), and so too were my colleagues at the ISC reduced, to a sign of extreme positions we do not hold, such as, for example, that we favour 'the concept of keeping Shakespeare for the elite and the academics' or, as another comment put it, that we believe Shakespeare does not and should not 'belong to everyone'.[17] How the internet works is like this: a paper that, according to Kubus's first description, 'developed a vocabulary through which the delegates communicated about their varying opinions of teaching Shakespeare through social networking websites, blogs, e-news articles, and communally-monitored encyclopaedias', quickly became, and in the same post, first, an argument with two sides and then, moments later, a 'debate . . . between . . . two extremes'. One extreme fears the possibility that today 'just about anyone can be a Shakespeare scholar [even those who blog] that David Beckham actually wrote the plays that we all attribute to Shakespeare', and the other extreme eagerly 'foster[s] accessibility to and interaction with Shakespeare's life and times'.[18] Picking up the thread from Kubus, Morris further refined the terms of this debate, concluding that 'I guess what it all sort of comes down to is: Would we rather people talk about Shakespeare and be uninformed and wrong, or would we rather they not talk about Shakespeare at all?' By implication, I am and we are those who would rather that 'uninformed and wrong' persons 'not talk about Shakespeare at all'.[19]

Although others who attended the conference might offer a different judgement, I think Kubus's initial description of my talk is accurate; it 'developed a vocabulary through which the delegates communicated . . . their varying opinions', and even, one suspects, their anxieties, about the implications of the internet and cultural democracy for research and teaching about Shakespeare. And Kubus is right that I 'seemed to be most concerned by the de-professionalisation of the field of Shakespeare studies' in the wake of increasing and, as I have already mentioned, insufficiently theorized understandings of democracy, markets and professionalism.[20] Much discussion followed

my talk that day and throughout the conference but, so far as I know, no one debated or even discussed whether everyone's opinion counts or whether Shakespeare belongs to everyone. No one did, I suspect, because professors know that Shakespeare is like any other topic: politics, the economy, sports, sexuality. People can say whatever they like about these topics, Shakespeare included, without fear of condemnation or, say, flunking. But they cannot do so in every social situation or institution; the university is one such institution where such is not – or at least, *has not been* – the case. Of course, norms have changed about 'what counts' in university classrooms and professional discourse; anyone who came of age in the 1960s or 1970s knows very well how much they have changed, largely as a result of democratization. But pressures to change 'what counts' are being catalysed by, pushed into new territory by, new media or internet Shakespeare, which celebrates 'the cult of the amateur' and 'the wisdom of crowds'.[21] The result is deep(er) confusion among professors and institutions about the role of non-specialists, of new media technology and of standards of evaluation and judgement in Shakespeare studies.

In 2003, Gerald Graff published an influential book, *Clueless in Academe: How Schooling Obscures the Life of the Mind*. Insisting that 'summarizing and making arguments is the name of the game in academia', Graff argues that students will 'do better' when they understand this fact and more importantly when academics, especially English

---

[17] See footnote 13, above.

[18] Kubus, 'Student's Perspective', http://bloggingshakespeare. com/the-isc-a-students-perspective

[19] Morris, 'Not for an age', http://americanshakespearecentereducation.blogspot.com/ 2010/08/not-just-of-age-but-for-all-time-and.html.

[20] Kubus, 'Student's Perspective', http://bloggingshakespeare. com/the-isc-a-students-perspective.

[21] See Andrew Keen, *The Cult of the Amateur: How Blogs, My Space, YouTube, and the Rest of Today's User-generated Media Are Destroying Our Economy, Our Culture, and Our Values* (New York, 2008) and James Surowiecki, *The Wisdom of Crowds: Why the Many Are Smarter Than the Few and How Collective Wisdom Shapes Business, Economies, Societies and Nations* (New York, 2004).

professors, understand that 'a continuum [exists] between the adolescent's declaration that a book or film "sucks" and the published reviewer's critique of it'.[22] Although I would use the word 'relationship' here rather than 'continuum', it is difficult to disagree entirely with this sentiment. In fact, and equally, one could say that a relationship exists between the reductive tendency observed in the Internet debate described above and the, shall we say, normal science Susan Bennett describes and derides in her article, 'The Presence of Shakespeare'. In setting up her analysis of Montana Shakespeare in the Parks, which each summer brings Shakespeare to remote small communities in Montana, eastern Idaho, and northern Wyoming, USA, Bennett says her purpose is not to expand yet again the geographical purview of performance studies of Shakespeare but to interrogate 'how easily predominant assumptions about the presence of Shakespeare are circulated and deployed to account for every kind of performance – irrespective, it turns out, of the actual cultural setting and experience'. Such 'sedimented and normative' assumptions develop, Bennett suggests, partly because our interests are too often with ourselves: in our assessments of Shakespeare production today, 'the local and global (and all points in between) serve a voracious disciplinary appetite for Shakespearean interpretation' rather than as a means to excavate 'the series of practices through which communities create and experience themselves'.[23] Like the debate conducted on the internet, then, our own debate conducted at conferences and in journals can tend towards reductiveness. This point is one Graff would celebrate; being reductive, he claims, or 'translating academic ideas into nonacademic terms is . . . *internal* to successful academic communication itself'.[24]

But while it is easy to see a 'continuum' between popular judgement and professional judgement and between popular debate and professional debate, it is more difficult to say what this means, either theoretically or, especially, in practice. By choosing the word 'continuum', Graff insists that the difference between this 'film "sucks"' and the reviewer's published critique is one of degree not

kind. Graff wishes to minimize difference but difference remains nonetheless and, one is compelled to ask, where on the 'continuum' does difference lie? Where does one draw the line? Or even a couple of lines? The blogger, Morris, quoted above, senses Graff's continuum but identifies significant difference between blogging and writing 'an in-depth paper', which is more 'formal' than a blog post and requires 'a lot more research', including 'hunt[ing] down original sources'. For Morris in this post at least, the form, medium and the context indicate that difference lies in institutional or social location, and in how one behaves in different institutional or social locations. On the blog, Morris plays Graff's adolescent – loose, blowsy, reductive; in the academy, she plays his professional reviewer – tight, marshalling evidence, striving for nuance. Despite her insistence that 'Shakespeare is for everyone', then, Morris acknowledges that different institutional locations require different norms for behaviour: the act of blogging differs from that of 'writing an in-depth paper'. Shakespeare Geek shares this opinion, arguing that blogs make no claim to authority; Shakespearians are not required to pay attention when people promote 'the David Beckham hypothesis' on the internet.[25] What is

---

[22] Gerald Graff, *Clueless in Academe: How Schooling Obscures the Life of the Mind* (New Haven, 2003), pp. 3, 24.

[23] Susan Bennett, 'The Presence of Shakespeare', in *Shakespeare in Stages: New Theatre Histories*, ed. Christine Dymkowski and Christie Carson (Cambridge, 2010), pp. 211–12, 216, 226.

[24] Graff, *Clueless*, p. 11.

[25] But is this true? As Kubus suggests, and as everyone knows, Shakespearians already are teaching with new media and the internet. Perhaps Shakespearians already are engaging the 'David Beckham hypothesis' and doing so sincerely, with kindness. Some readers may scoff, but consider the recent fate of actor David Tennant who, according to Kate Rumbold, was turned into the 'admiring audience' of the videographic efforts of a 15-year-old boy precisely because of the Royal Shakespeare Company's political and economic need, as Rumbold explains it, to foster creativity in all members of the public. Kate Rumbold, 'From "Access" to "Creativity": Shakespeare Institutions, New Media, and the Language of Cultural Value', *Shakespeare Quarterly*, 61 (2010), 326. Shakespearians also face political and economic need, and may find themselves facing similar pressures to become

crucial here in Shakespeare Geek's opinion (or Kubus's or Morris's on this point) is that it echoes political scientist's Matthew Hindman's conclusion about the *undemocratic* force of internet communication: 'it may be easy to speak in cyberspace, but it remains difficult to be heard'. Already, Hindman observes, 'the online public sphere [for political discourse] is . . . a de facto aristocracy', one whose members are 'skilled in the high deliberative arts' and are overwhelming white, male and very well-educated, usually by post-graduate programmes at institutions of high prestige.[26] In different ways, then, Morris and Shakespeare Geek promote with one hand what they take away with another: democratization of our discourse about Shakespeare. This difficulty, if not contradiction, is mirrored in Kubus's, Morris's, and Shakespeare Geek's opinions about the place of blogs in the university classroom. Blogging about Shakespeare seems both to be and not to be an appropriate pedagogical tool; blogging seems both to be and not to be part of scholarship.

And it is mirrored, too, in professional discourse. Consider briefly in this regard Laurie Osborne's 'SAA Hyperessay on Electronic Shakespearean Criticism', posted on her Colby College web page.[27] Osborne's focus is not on pedagogy *per se*, but on the promise and pitfalls of web-based criticism by students and professors. In addition to pitfalls related to technology and the difficult question of the reader's relationship to the text and author, Osborne details the pitfall of evaluation and its relation to expertise. Regarding a non-linear and heavily visual, web-based thesis produced by one of her students, Osborne acknowledges that literary scholars are not trained to evaluate these works and have no expertise in doing so; we have been trained to evaluate writing, not the hyperlinked presentation of verbal, visual and aural ideas. Writing is only part of that task and a minor part at that; an adept presentation of non-linear ideas requires facility with 'programming, spatial relationships, and artistic design'. She recalls her frustration that 'only some [of our] conventional criteria for judging theses apply'[28] and (unsurprisingly, given the attention the student needed to

pay to tasks that are not literary) that the 'method of producing this thesis create[d] distinctive writing problems . . . Other factors – like clear outlines, easy manoeuverability, and useful links – [were] as important as clear writing here.'[29]

With respect to scholarship, consider *Shakespeare Quarterly*'s recent experiment with democratized or open peer review. Before continuing, I should acknowledge, like a newsreader on public television having to report bad news about a corporate sponsor, that I was one of those who became part of *Quarterly*'s 'public phase of external vetting, [which was] open to any reviewer but [especially to] those with relevant expertise'.[30] Guest editor Katherine Rowe's introduction to the issue, entitled 'Gentle Numbers', is consistently positive about the experiment, despite attempts to assuage what I assume she and *Quarterly*'s editorial board considered to be a generally Luddite audience in the readership of *Shakespeare Quarterly*. Crucial for my purpose here is her explanation that changes to *Quarterly*'s usual reviewing practice resulted in a process that 'might best be called a "hybrid" or "partially open" one – in contrast with fully open review models where decision-making authority is distributed across participants'. In a footnote to this assertion, Rowe elaborates upon her meaning: 'As for example, when reader reviews at Amazon.com are ranked

---

the admiring audience of, say, ShullBitter, whose 'Puppeo and Julicat', a bit of doggerel published on FanFiction.net, is 'a retelling of the most beloved romance in English literature, now free of pesky intellectualism! Because cats and dogs make everything better! Public Domain Rocks!' www.fanfiction.net/u/679717/ShullBitter.

26 Matthew Hindman, *The Myth of Digital Democracy* (Princeton, 2009), pp. 142, 139.

27 Laurie Osborne, 'SAA Hyperessay on Electronic Shakespearean Criticism', www.colby.edu/personal/l/leosborn/saalong.html.

28 Osborne, 'Hyperessay'. For example, Osborne writes, 'how can I critique the work's continuity and transitions when the principle is multi-transitional – when, as a reader, I am responsible for how the argument will flow?'

29 Osborne, 'Hyperessay.' The student herself worried 'that the format of writing for the Web might have undermined the clarity of her writing'.

30 Katherine Rowe, 'From the Editor: Gentle Numbers', *Shakespeare Quarterly*, 61 (2010), vi.

by other readers and their responses automatically collected, aggregated, and displayed'.[31] Given the comparison with reviewing at Amazon.com, in which any average Josephine can submit her opinion, her thumbs-up or her rating with stars, the label 'hybrid' or 'partially open' seems overly generous. *Quarterly*'s 'experiment' in democratization not only added a layer of expertise to the process – 'an expert reviewer (the guest editor) joined the initial screening of submissions' – but also resulted in a democratization composed mostly of tenured professors, such as myself. Further, only 'forty-one participants (including the submitters, journal editor, and guest editor)' offered comments in the experiment, which seems a lot until one does the math: subtracting the eight authors and the two editors leaves thirty-one reviewers, which, divided by seven submissions, leaves just under 4.5 reviewers per submission, not considerably more than the two – or is it three? – reviewers *Quarterly* normally uses.[32]

These examples, too, suggest that individuals and institutions are confused about the role of non-specialists, of new media technology, and of standards of evaluation and judgement in Shakespeare studies. The question I posed in 'Against Internet Triumphalism', and that I pose here again, is whether and which institutional, intellectual and commercial interests will eliminate the confusion and with what consequences, particularly for us as professional Shakespearians who, like all professionals, have a vested interest in and a commitment to the public good. With respect to the latter, the ambition of democratizers like the bloggers considered in this article should cause us to pause. So, too, should the ambition of colleagues like Graff, who is explicitly democratic and wants not only to demystify 'the club we [academics] belong to' but also to break up the exclusivity of the club by 'widening our notion of who qualifies as an "intellectual"'.[33] According to Peter Stallybrass, one of the 'most radical aspects' of the digital database is its power to help effect Graff's goal:

Scholarship, as traditionally conceived, has maintained its prestige partly through its privileged relation to the protection and retrieval of scarce resources. Now, however, millions of people who cannot or do not want to go to the archives are accessing them in digital form. And digital information has profoundly undermined an academic elite's control over the circulation of knowledge.[34]

As I have argued elsewhere, in a critique of *Clueless in Academe*, a serious problem with positions like these is that

a profession is by definition exclusive, for without exclusionary practices, the professional organization is unable to protect its members' interests [which include their commitment to public service]. While the composition of the exclusive group can be changed or broken up, the 'bottom line' of a professional group cannot be to break up its exclusivity, for that would be the death of the profession, and those who advocate it would be committing (in another sense) professional suicide.[35]

What should also give us pause – and again with respect to our status as professionals – is what seems to be the ambition of Rowe and *Shakespeare Quarterly* to illuminate *Quarterly*'s 'culture of evaluation' in order to question authority, expertise and standards of judgement: '*Open reviewing brings to front and center the question of who is an expert and how those experts are accredited.*'[36] Rowe does not offer an answer to that question based on the experiment, but I think it significant that she ignores the stark conclusions about our discipline made by sociologist Michèle Lamont, from whose

[31] Rowe, 'Gentle', vi.

[32] Rowe, 'Gentle', v and vi.

[33] Graff, *Clueless*, pp. 24, 25.

[34] Peter Stallybrass, 'Against Thinking', *PMLA*, 122 (2007), 1581.

[35] Sharon O'Dair, 'Clueless about Class in Academe', *symplokē*, 17 (2009), 28. On professionalism, see, for example, Barry Barnes, *The Elements of Social Theory* (Princeton, 1995); Stephen Brint, *In an Age of Experts: The Changing Role of Professionals in Politics and Public Life* (Princeton 1994); Randall Collins, *The Credential Society: An Historical Sociology of Education and Stratification* (New York, 1979); Stanley Fish, *Professional Correctness* (Cambridge, 1995); Raymond Murphy, *Social Closure: The Theory of Monopolization and Exclusion* (Oxford, 1988); and Max Weber *Economy and Society: An Outline of Interpretive Sociology*, vol. 3, ed. Guenther Roth and Claus Wittich (New York, 1968).

[36] Rowe, 'Gentle', vi.

empirical study of peer review panels at five elite foundations she borrows the notion of 'evaluative cultures' and whom she cites in 'Gentle Numbers' to support *Quarterly*'s decision to experiment with its process of peer review. Of the six fields Lamont studied – Philosophy, History, Anthropology, English, Political Science and Economics – only English is experienced by its own practitioners as in the midst of a 'legitimation crisis', the result of a collapse of 'disciplinary consensus regarding the pursuit of knowledge and the associated question of how to define and evaluate excellence'.[37] Of the six fields, only English has shown 'a decline in PhDs granted between 1995 and 2005', a 'demographic decline' Lamont associates with the legitimation crisis and not with, say, a discipline's responsibility to reduce its production of Ph.D.s in response to a tight job market, which might be our reading of the situation.[38] Lamont's findings suggest not only that our legitimation crisis – 'disciplinary broadening and diversification of criteria of evaluation' – is reducing the size of our profession but also reducing the number of grant and fellowship awards we receive; 'literature proposals are less competitive than they once were'.[39] The strong implication of Lamont's analysis is that when a discipline lacks coherence and consensus about quality, the discipline is deprofessionalizing. This disciplinary flabbiness, this lack of discipline, puts 'literary scholars in a vulnerable position when competing on theoretical or historical grounds with scholars whose disciplines [such as Philosophy or History] "own" such terrains'.[40] Literary study is, as one English professor put it, a 'sort of no-man's land or an open field where everybody can be kind of a media expert'.[41] ('Everyone's opinion counts'?)

Established processes of peer review work at these elite foundations because criteria such as meritocracy and democracy, or excellence and diversity, 'do not function as alternative criteria of evaluation, but as additive, complementary factors'. But Lamont is not so naïve or sanguine as to imagine that such integration occurs across the spectrum of higher education in the United States.[42] Rather, with refreshing bluntness, she confirms that 'meritocracy and democracy often operate as antinomic principles'; tension seems irresolvable between a 'democratic mission, the pursuit of knowledge, and market pressures'.[43] Here, Lamont identifies two factors that make the discourse of democratization in the contemporary moment, the moment of the Internet, so confusing but also so dangerous for our profession. First, tensions between merit and democracy, or excellence and diversity, do not exist at elite institutions but do everywhere else (or at least they exist much less noticeably at elite institutions than they do everywhere else) and, second, the market intrudes increasingly into individual and institutional decision-making, in terms of pressures to increase enrolments, to reduce instructional costs, or to develop sources of grant funding, among other goals and requirements.

Regarding the former, since tensions between merit and democracy are muted at elite institutions, democratizing moves there are easy and painless. Indeed, rather than follow Graff and Stallybrass to imply that professionalism is phony, I suggest that most attempts by elite institutions 'to democratize' are phony. As an example, I might turn to the examples of Graff, Rowe or Stallybrass, but let me instead turn to my comments on Kubus's post (and please forgive the informality of my prose, but that is 'how the internet works'). Before I left Stratford,

i picked up the weekly throwaway paper, which featured an article called, i think, 'a bard act to follow.' this paid homage to professor [Stanley] wells, who is retiring from the SBT. the article also noted that 'anyone' can apply to be wells's successor. but will 'anyone' be selected? no. we

---

37 Michèle Lamont, *How Professors Think: Inside the Curious World of Academic Judgment* (Cambridge, 2009), pp. 59, 4. Anthropology, too, has problems in this regard and seems to be following English towards dissensus, recently whether 'to strip the word "science" from a statement of its long-range plan'. Nicholas Wade, 'Anthropology a Science? Statement Deepens a Rift', *New York Times*, 9 December 2010, www.nytimes.com/2010/12/10/science/10anthropology.html.

38 Lamont, *Professors*, pp. 59, 75.

39 Lamont, *Professors*, p. 73.

40 Lamont, *Professors*, p. 73.

41 Lamont, *Professors*, p. 74.

42 Lamont, *Professors*, p. 216.

43 Lamont, *Professors*, pp. 237, 235–6.

all know this. the person selected will be an academic, a theater professional, a museum director, a director of a university, some professional with tons of experience and the ability to fund-raise brilliantly. the person selected certainly won't be an anti-stratfordian and sure won't be an unemployed 20-something, either.[44]

We all know this. And I submit that (phony) democratizing claims like this, which we make often, are not innocuous. They are powerful and powerfully distort our own and the public's understanding of how elite professional institutions like the Trust, the Royal Shakespeare Company or any major university work. For us, I will hypothesize, part of the distortion results from the assumption that the position of institutional power from which we make such democratizing claims is unassailable; its status will not be undermined. I suggested to the blogosphere that my paper at the ISC expressed doubt about that assumption. This article, too, expresses doubt about that assumption.

And this is where the latter comes in, the market or neo-liberalism.[45] In *The Myth of Digital Democracy*, the political scientist Hindman distinguishes between definitions of the word, democracy, between that is, a normative definition – that which is good – and a descriptive definition – that which is. My suspicion is that Shakespearians rely too heavily on a normative definition – Democratization is Always Good! – and ignore or miss the fact that democratization today is effected by a neo-liberalism inimical to our profession. My hypothesis – an admittedly reductive, but, I think, generous one[46] – is that we rely on this normative definition because we assume democratization will be implemented via mechanisms amenable to progressive Left politics. Such democratization I call 'Left democratization,' and in Western democracies in the post-war period, Left democratization in matters cultural gained much strength, notably after 1968. This period might be seen as the apex of Left democratization, enabled through the expansion of elite and subsidized institutions of cultural production, such as arts companies and, especially, universities. The decline and eventual collapse of socialism, both actually existing and theoretical, with its elitist conception of art,

left no counterweight in the larger society to neo-liberalism's market approach to democratization, to what I call 'Right democratization.' In the past two decades, Right democratization has been intensified, first through the dismantling of the welfare state, particularly of government subsidy of arts companies and universities, and second through the efforts of a neo-liberal and global computer industry, the thousands of entrepreneurs, technologists, venture capitalists, programmers and content providers who introduced Web 1.0 and then Web 2.0 technology, that which so many of us now celebrate as democratized or free cultural production, the notion that computer programs allow everyone to do what you do, only better and without the years of work and training.

This history is what makes our current situation, and the catalyst of new media or internet Shakespeare, so compelling for analysis and discussion, for it reveals a contradiction: Shakespearians, and literary scholars more generally, whether young or old, subscribe to the ideology of twentieth-century Left democratization, in which elites lead the masses to good judgement, but in the twenty-first century, actually existing democratization is Right democratization, neo-liberal, capitalist democratization, the kind that celebrates the deskilling of professional art, criticism and pedagogy, all of which is made possible through the imposition (and the embrace?) of the computer algorithm. Right democratization, driven now by algorithms, creates an artistic or cultural environment, such as that on Amazon.com, in which, as Paul Fleming observes, the judgements of 100,000 average Joes can – and do – outweigh the judgements of one Plato.[47]

---

44 Kubus, 'Student's Perspective', http://bloggingshakespeare. com/the-isc-a-students-perspective.

45 On neo-liberalism, see, for example, Zygmunt Bauman, *Does Ethics Have a Chance in a World of Consumers?* (Cambridge, 2008); Zygmunt Bauman, *44 Letters from the Liquid Modern World* (Cambridge, 2010); Richard Sennett, *The Culture of the New Capitalism* (New Haven, 2006).

46 Graff endorses the value of my move here.

47 Paul Fleming, '100,000 Average Joes', *Cabinet*, 15 (2004), 54. See also Paul Fleming, *Exemplarity and Mediocrity: The Art of the Average from Bourgeois Tragedy to Realism* (Stanford, 2009).

Therefore, democratization seems to be neo-liberalism's Trojan horse, a way to undermine further our commitments to what has defined us as a profession, first with regard to expertise, which is the literary, especially the crafts of writing and close reading, and second with regard to our relationship to the market, which, even more than those of other learned professions, has been arm's length, largely non-instrumental or not-for-profit. Indeed, the twenty years between the collapse of socialism and today will, I think, be regarded as a revolutionary moment in our intellectual history, because many of us have consigned or are consigning to the dustbin of history our anti-capitalism, almost two hundred years of wanting, as Michael Bristol once put it, 'to be counted as separate from and oppositional towards the imperatives of the market, commodity exchange, and industrial discipline'.[48] Under the spell of the latest Apple gadget, so nicely designed and so urgently propriety, or under the cover of this wishful but residual Left democratization, or even just because we are bullied into seeking funding wherever it may lie, Shakespearians now embrace those very imperatives: we look to monetize our database websites, seeking businesses to advertise there; we strongly desire to empower the 100,000 average Joes to become writers and scholars, through the promotion of hypertext and the creation of accessible literary databases of enormous scope and power; and we aim to satisfy our 'clients' or 'customers' in the classroom with blogs, tweets and Second Life, not to mention visual literacy or even multiple literacies.

That all of this might not be in either the individual professor's or the profession's best interest is seldom voiced, but I do so here. All of this is made possible through the products of the global and neo-liberal computer industry, in particular the ground of it all, the algorithm's Taylorist instructions, or demands. One may scoff at this assertion, but more than a decade ago, in a prize-winning book, physicist Gene I. Rochlin described the extension of a Taylorist agenda, enabled by powerful algorithms, 'into the world of knowledge-based work'.[49] Desiring to find 'the correct organizational form for any business or activity', computer-enabled Taylorism promotes 'standardization and compliance – at an unprecedented level of detail'.[50] Standardization and compliance require the deskilling of a workforce, in these cases, of a professional workforce: 'what is being replaced, or displaced, is not the direct and tactile involvement of the worker, but tacit knowledge, in the form of expert judgment of the state and condition of operation of the plant, process, activity, or firm, and the range of experiential knowledge that allows flexibility in interpretation of rules and procedures when required'.[51] Today, we might well ask, will Shakespearians become like Rochlin's 'manageroids', professionals who 'look...human and act...human, but hav[e]...no real autonomy or control, and no discretion to evaluate or deviate from the plans and programs of their organization'?[52]

I think the answer is 'yes' – across the profession as a whole, maybe not at elite institutions, but already among those who teach first-year writing – and I suspect this possibility both would and would not surprise Harry Braverman, whose *Labor and Monopoly Capital: The Degradation of Work in the Twentieth Century*, published in 1974, promoted what became known as 'the deskilling hypothesis', the simple idea that modern, scientific production requires the degradation of work, a degradation that results from the separation of doing from thinking and learned skill. Braverman described 'the eclipse of the industrial craftworker', but even in the mid-1990s, it was not just a rhetorical

---

[48] Michael D. Bristol, *Shakespeare's America, America's Shakespeare* (London 1990), p. 35.

[49] Gene I. Rochlin, *Trapped in the Net: The Unintended Consequences of Computerization* (Princeton, 1997), p. 52.

[50] Rochlin, *Trapped*, p. 212. New media theorists Alexander Galloway and Eugene Thacker agree, arguing that algorithms do not deliver 'liberation from the rigid constraints of systems of exchange and production but [are in fact] the very pillars that prop those systems up'. Alexander R. Galloway and Eugene Thacker, *The Exploit: A Theory of Networks* (Minneapolis, 2007), p. 115.

[51] Rochlin, *Trapped*, p. 68.

[52] Rochlin, *Trapped*, pp. 65–6.

flourish when, at the end of an appreciative retrospective review, sociologist Michael Burawoy suggested that Braverman could just as easily have been describing 'the eclipse of the intellectual craftworker'.[53] Today neo-liberalism and state policy offer a striking challenge to 'those who are trying to defend the boundaries of human expertise and integrative judgment in [any organization's] operation'.[54] And they do so because they are doing to white-collar work what they did to blue-collar work: 'draining it of its cognitive elements'.[55] These are 'appropriated from professionals, instantiated in a system or process, and then handed back to a new class of workers – clerks – who replace the professionals'.[56] Teachers' judgements are replaced by those implicit in standardized tests; judges' by those explicit in sentencing formulae; stock traders' by those made instantaneously by algorithmic trading programs.[57] One may scoff, again, and say, 'teachers or stockbrokers are not professors', but just two years ago, in *Critical Inquiry*, Lev Manovich asked these very questions about visual art: 'does the world of social media . . . make professional art irrelevant?' And, 'can professional art survive the extreme democratization of media production and access?'[58] Just this year, at my own institution, three professors of art received a grant totalling $350,000 from the US National Science Foundation to produce a computer-based Art History survey course that requires no professor and in which students do their own crowd-sourced evaluations of their own learning.[59] Next year, in my department, first-year composition will take another step towards automation, operating with the pre-ordained syllabus, which, no doubt, has already occurred elsewhere.

As I put it ten years ago when I tried to justify the ways of workers to Shakespearians, 'capitalism is vulgar', a system in which 'money, regardless of how it is obtained – whether "by sweaty effort or by cheating or perhaps by plain luck", as Peter Berger playfully observes – is what counts in the distribution of privilege, as much as or more so than birth or talent or intelligence'.[60] Do we really mean to suggest that with respect to art, the judgements of 100,000 average Joes, aggregated algorithmically, are equal to those of one Plato? Do we mean to suggest that with respect to art, the judgements of the entrepreneur, let us call him Sergey Brin or Larry Page, who developed that algorithm – and monetized it so very, very handsomely – are equal to those of one Plato? Do we mean to deny the wisdom of Shakespeare's Timon, whom Marx followed in emphasizing the transformative power of gold: 'This yellow slave / Will knit and break religions, bless th'accursed, / Make the hoar leprosy ador'd, place thieves / And give them title, knee and approbation / With senators on the bench.'[61]

I do not think we do. We must confront the complicated meanings of what Fleming calls 'the dilemma of mediocrity in power', a task that has occupied many, including Hegel, de Tocqueville, Mill and Nietzsche.[62] We must voice, and voice strongly, that the coin of the University is not only money and that the market's standard of value – the radical democratization of 'one woman, one vote' – is not appropriate in every social realm: not in art, as Fleming argues;[63] not in the academy,

---

53 Micheal Burawoy, 'Review: A Classic of Its Time', *Contemporary Sociology*, 25 (1996), 299.

54 Rochlin, *Trapped*, p. 10.

55 Matthew B. Crawford, *Shop Class as Soulcraft: An Inquiry into the Value of Work* (New York, 2009), p. 32. See also Richard Sennett, *The Craftsman* (New Haven, 2008).

56 Crawford, *Shop Class*, p. 44. See also Rochlin on the computerization of financial trading and air traffic control.

57 Crawford, *Shop Class*, p. 45.

58 Lev Manovich, 'The Practice of Everyday (Media) Life: From Mass Consumption to Mass Cultural Production?', *Critical Inquiry*, 35 (2009), 329.

59 Professor Brian Evans graciously shared a copy of his grant proposal, 'Pilot: Autonomous Cohorts and Emergent Learning'.

60 Sharon O'Dair, *Class, Critics, and Shakespeare: Bottom Lines on the Culture Wars* (Ann Arbor, 2000), p. 69.

61 William Shakespeare, *Timon of Athens*, ed. Anthony B. Dawson and Gretchen E. Minton (London, 2008), 4.3.34–8.

62 Fleming, *Exemplarity*, p. 166.

63 Explicating Cicero's treatise on orators, Fleming observes, 'in democratic situations in which the majority decides, all that matters is the immediate effect on the greatest number of people. The math is easy: add it up and see who gets the greater approval. In art, opinion is weighted . . . Art . . . resists

as David Kirp argues;[64] and not in (US) politics either, as Sunstein argues.[65] The economist Arthur Okun observed many years ago that 'there is a place for the market, but the market must be kept in its place'.[66] Currently, we are not doing a very good job of keeping the market in its place, and out of ours. Rather, we sometimes invite the market in and much more often acquiesce to those who do. For us to begin to keep the market in its place, however, and to join Fleming, Kirp and Sunstein in suggesting a limit to Right democratization, will require changes to our discourse and behaviour that will be difficult to achieve. At the ISC in Stratford, I was challenged to offer suggestions about how to do so, and I would like to close this article by offering three, all rooted in the foregoing discussion. First, and most important, is to insist that the profession matters, that our legitimation crisis must be solved; second, that all Shakespearians – regardless of the status of their institutions – constitute the profession;[67] and third that those who control the discourse about the profession – professors at elite institutions, as well as the national and international organizations and journals of the profession – must acknowledge the above points and adjust their discourses accordingly. Elites have the power and responsibility to resist Taylorist impositions of the market on behalf of themselves and their fellow professionals who labour in less privileged institutional conditions.

Before the elites can speak, all of us – elite, middling or lowly – must resolve the legitimation crisis, the collapse, as Lamont puts it and as I noted above, of 'disciplinary consensus regarding the pursuit of knowledge and the associated question of how to define and evaluate excellence'.[68] This problem is far bigger than my concern here with the catalysing effects of new media and internet Shakespeare, but these catalysts do provide immediately pressing and germane questions in this regard. Should professional Shakespearians attend in their classrooms or their research to opinions expressed in blogs, for instance, 'the Beckham hypothesis'? Should professional Shakespearians assign and try to evaluate tasks – video mashups of *Romeo and Juliet*, say – for which they have no expertise and in which they

have no training? Should professional Shakespearians ape sociologists to discuss the 1564 fan fictions found on FanFiction.net, many of them written as school assignments?[69] Should professional Shakespearians spend 'twenty minutes to find the torch that [one] needed to hold in order to walk out of the tavern's front door' in the online game, *Arden: The World of William Shakespeare*?[70] I suggest that in answering such questions we keep in mind Lamont's conclusions that the legitimation crisis has resulted in and continues to result in a weakened and weakening profession, in deprofessionalization. And that we keep in mind Espen J. Aarseth's judgement that 'the decision to empower students' or, I would add, the general public, 'by letting them

---

simple majority-rule democracy and requires taste as an educated critical criterion for judgment. The artist only needs an audience of one – if it is the right one, one who knows, a Plato. A lawyer, orator, or politician, on the other hand, must necessarily win over the crowd.' Fleming, *Exemplarity*, p. 22.

64 'Embedded in the very idea of the university', Kirp reminds his readers, 'are values that the market does not honor: the belief in a community of scholars and not a confederacy of self-seekers; in the idea of openness and not ownership; in the professor as a pursuer of truth and not an entrepreneur; in the student as an acolyte whose preferences are to be formed, not a consumer whose preferences are to be satisfied.' David Kirp, *Shakespeare, Einstein, and the Bottom Line: The Marketing of Higher Education* (Cambridge, MA, 2003), p. 7. As noted earlier, Sunstein is exercised very much by this latter and crucial problem: internet technology makes of politics and of civic life an echo chamber, where people hear their own preferences satisfied.

65 Sunstein, *Republic.com*, pp. 33–4.

66 Cited by Kirp, *Marketing*, p. 7.

67 The MLA seems to be moving in this direction. See Sidonie Smith, 'One MLA Serving All Faculty Members', *MLA Newsletter*, 42 (2010), 2–3.

68 Lamont, *Professors*, p. 4.

69 www.fanfiction.net/play/Shakespeare/, accessed 30 November 2010.

70 Peter Holland, 'Performing Shakespeare for the Web Community', in *Shakespeare in Hollywood, Asia, and Cyberspace*, ed. Alexander C.Y. Huang and Charles S. Ross (West Lafayette, 2009), p. 253. In the spring of 2010, in order to watch one act of *Twelfth Night* in Second Life, I registered, selected an avatar, and then spent at least twenty minutes trying to sit down on a bench in Second Life's new Globe.

partake in discussions on equal footing with influential members of an academic field is ultimately not a technological, but a political, ideological decision'.[71] I suggest that the crucial political question now is not democratization of our profession but its strength, indeed its very existence. I hope our answers will suggest that our profession matters, that an assessment of democratization must be made according to descriptive criteria, and that the tension between professionalism and democratization in our institutions is not necessarily to be settled by evacuating the former. 'Consumers are not citizens', Sunstein insists,[72] and I would add that consumers are not students, actors, directors, or professors of Shakespeare, either.

---

[71] Espen J. Aarseth, *Cybertext: Perspectives on Ergodic Literature* (Baltimore, 1997), p. 170.

[72] Sunstein, *Republic.com*, p. 136.

CATALYSING WHAT? HISTORICAL REMEDIATION, THE MUSICAL, AND WHAT OF *LOVE'S LABOUR'S* LASTS

DIANA E. HENDERSON

The words of Mercury are harsh after the songs of Apollo.
                              Love's Labour's Lost, 5.2.913–14

The twenty-first century began with a much anticipated – and, by most measures, disappointing – musical production of *Love's Labour's Lost* on film. Five years later, a much more successful musical adaptation of the play called *The Big Life: The Ska Musical* provided a breakthrough in theatre history, becoming the first 'British black musical' to reach London's commercial West End.[1] This play's recollection of the Windrush immigrants and its integration of ska rhythms with an updated script seemed fresh and transformative; by contrast, most critics and scholars deemed the film musical's use of history nostalgic or superficial, and the deployment of its artistic genre partially successful at best. Nevertheless, a decade on, Kenneth Branagh's film is available on DVD and has gained a more positive overall response from IMDb (Internet Movie Database) respondents, at least, than its early reception might have predicted.[2] Numerous critical articles have examined its nuances and relationship to the Hollywood musical tradition. Meanwhile, Paul Sirett and Paul Joseph's West End hit, despite rave reviews, a BBC Radio adaptation, and even the enduring presence of its opening number on YouTube, has as yet failed to 'cross over' to Broadway or to screen production, and thus to more lasting and international success. It has not gained acknowledgement in recent critical editions of *Love's Labour's Lost*, nor generated discernible scholarly analysis.[3] Beyond merely lamenting the primacy of film/video over 'live' theatre or

decrying the necessity for celebrities in artistic production, what might we say about this turn of events?

In addition to these two musicals based on *Love's Labour's Lost*, the first decade of the twenty-first century has seen a robust critique of earlier versions of 'objective' theatre history and the challenges, both theoretical and pragmatic, of digital media's emergence in helping to shape artistic reception and historical memory.[4] This

---

[1] This label most often referenced *The Big Life*'s (almost entirely) black cast representing a particular form of black British life; the show was also notable in having a black director. For comments on this breakthrough, see Lesley Ferris, '*The Big Life: The Ska Musical*', *Theatre Journal*, 57 (2005), 110–12, and Akin Ojumu, 'Reach for the Ska', *The Observer*, Review Section, p. 7: 18 April 2004. Also www.guardian.co.uk/stage/2004/apr/18/theatre1.

[2] Kenneth Branagh, dir. *Love's Labour's Lost*. Shakespeare Film Company *et al.*, 2000.

[3] By this I mean more searching analysis than the first-round reviews. I am eager to stand corrected, but as yet have not found evidence of attention to *The Big Life* online or in scholarly bibliographies. Fiona Ritchie did review the production ('*The Big Life*, by Paul Sirett', *Borrowers and Lenders: The Journal of Shakespeare and Appropriation*, 1 (2005), 1–5) as did Ferris. I presented two seminar papers on it at Shakespeare conferences in the US and Australia soon after its West End run, discussing collaborative adaptation and gender, respectively. The opening number is available at www.youtube.com/watch?v=YQKVUYvsZ8I with a slightly longer segment at http://vids.myspace.com/index.cfm?fuseaction=vids.individual&videoID=2020482226, last accessed 7 July 2010. Recent print editions of *Love's Labour's Lost* do not mention *The Big Life*.

[4] In addition to two recent volumes I have edited (*A Concise Companion to Shakespeare on Screen* (Oxford, 2006) and

article builds upon awareness of, and indeed participates in, these exciting changes while acknowledging their potential peril for both scholarly self-definitions and some traditional media forms. With the benefit of a few more years of hindsight, I try my best to forego the 'pick or pan' mode which still pervades much scholarly writing despite the combination of journalistic and online criticism making such evaluation increasingly unsatisfying (as well as belated); even in its heyday this mode was seldom particularly helpful for most artists and productions, nor did it often advance the shape of our scholarly agenda. Instead, I consider what we might learn in the medium term through the juxtaposition of these two Shakespeare-related performances, especially regarding their consequentiality as artistic and cultural catalysts, and the way we extrapolate from particular evidence to reach formal or socio-political conclusions. Ultimately, I will argue that the ways we do (and don't) write about these musicals, and the alternative ways we might contextualize them, demonstrate the need for and value of a more thorough historicizing of our own critical practice, not just of the artistic productions we discuss.

* * *

One day the ship dock in London and he went to Piccadilly Circus and watch the big life.
Sam Selvon, *The Lonely Londoners*

In social terms, the ska musical treatment of Shakespeare's comic plot was the more obviously 'catalytic'. Because scripted by Paul Sirett while he was literary manager for the Royal Shakespeare Company, *The Big Life* intimated affiliations with two very different Stratfords: the hub of the Shakespeare industry, and the Theatre Royal Stratford East in London. Stratford East had been made famous by Joan Littlewood's original productions there of *A Taste of Honey* (1958) and *Oh, What a Lovely War!* (1963) – the latter being a particularly pertinent musical to recall as well in evaluating Branagh's film and the genre's possibilities, a topic to which I shall return. Perhaps surprisingly to Shakespearians but appropriate to that theatre's progressive history in representing British racial

and class politics, it was this latter Stratford that had much more to do with this adaptation of *Love's Labour's Lost* coming into existence.[5] Stratford East's proud tradition of community-based performance continued under the leadership of Littlewood's one-time assistant Philip Hedley, whose drama and musical workshops at Stratford East helped train local talents such as Clint Dyer, who made his directorial debut with *The Big Life*, and Paul Joseph, reggae musician and composer of its musical score. Sirett, whose earliest plays were all produced at Stratford East, met Joseph at one of the organization's musical workshops. The Theatre Royal is located in the borough of Newham, which reportedly had the highest percentage of ethnic minorities in Britain (61 per cent) during the years when the play was being developed; Hedley's commitment to this community thus led to Stratford East's inclusion and representation of a diverse theatrical base, and more exceptionally to the hiring of black and Asian directors. At the time of *The Big Life*'s transfer to the West End – literally steps away from Piccadilly Circus – Dyer (whose parents had emigrated from the Caribbean in the fifties) called attention to this progressive distinction from recently heralded 'mainstream' productions of black playwrights' works that had white directors, claiming 'We might not be as starry as a big-name director but surely there must be something we know about the experience that they will never be able to harness.' However, as Akin Ojumu

---

Alternative Shakespeares 3 (London, 2008)), see for example Barbara Hodgdon and Peter Holland, guest editors, 'Watching Ourselves Watching Shakespeare', *Shakespeare Bulletin* 25.3 and 25.4 (2007), with W. B. Worthen with Peter Holland, eds., *Theorizing Practice: Redefining Theatre History* (Basingstoke, 2004) – among many.
[5] Information about *The Big Life*'s production process draws on my correspondence and 24 January 2006 interview with Paul Sirett, as well as the published reviews of the Stratford East and West End productions. See Ferris, Ojumu and Ritchie (notes 1 and 3 above), and Ray Funk, 'Shakespeare Goes Ska on the Windrush', *The Kaiso Newsletter No. 44* (9 May 2004) www.mustrad.org.uk/articles/kaiso44.htm, www.britishtheatreguide.info/reviews/bigliferev.htm, www.stratfordeast.com/big%20life.htm, www.stratfordeast.com/whats_on/The%20Big%20Life.shtml.

immediately added in his *Observer* piece quoting Dyer, 'This is a collaborative effort that involves Sirett and Hedley, both of whom are white, and no one would suggest this musical isn't authentic';[6] indeed, in my own interview with Sirett,[7] he made it clear that he was able to play a major part in this dominantly black group project without challenge from anyone except a very few (white) outsiders.

The production's history thus conjures up and complicates both identity-based racial assumptions and the presumption of a highbrow/lowbrow divide often posited in and about Shakespearian performance. One reason for Sirett's easy involvement would seem to be his breadth of experience and perception: university-educated and RSC-identified, he was also a musician who had played for years in reggae/ska bands, including Bliss. He charts his perception that *Love's Labour's Lost* would lend itself to musical adaptation back to his studies when it was a set text for school exams. In so perceiving, he joins a distinguished line reaching back to Garrick and forward through nineteenth-century opera to Thomas Mann and W. H. Auden and eventually to Branagh.[8] (This also indicates that the heritage and influences informing the Shakespearian musical *per se* are hardly confined to the dominant critical narrative focused on the American Broadway/Hollywood axis, despite its undeniable power – another issue to which I shall return.) At one point Sirett considered a more directly contemporary adaptation with Eastern Europeans in the leading roles, addressing current immigration issues. But because of his realization that some temporal distance could be used to good theatrical effect, as well as his own musical interests and encounters at Stratford East, he instead focused upon the first generation of legal, economically motivated immigration to Britain from its former Caribbean colonies. Again hearkening to the particular location inspiring the show, he cited the analogy with Littlewood's World War I musical that similarly represented important historical events approximately 50 years prior to its performance, managing to combine acid politics (with contemporary overtones) and musical comedy conventions. This is a particularly British stage musical tradition, and worth remembering in our scholarly accounts. At the same time, Sirett credited his work with the RSC as providing practice in deconstructing a Shakespeare play down to its component parts in order then to revivify it for contemporary performance. To my ear, his description precisely echoed Chester Kallman's when he worked with Auden on a *Love's Labour's Lost* libretto for (an apparently unsuccessful) operatic production: 'we stamped Shakespeare to bits and then put it together again'.[9] In his reconstruction, Sirett turned, crucially, to Trinidadian novelist Sam Selvon's *The Lonely Londoners* (1956), from whence he derived not only the post-war socio-political context but also a key scene location (and eventual performance location) and the main title, indicative of the musical's submerged irony: 'One day the ship dock in London and he went to Piccadilly Circus and watch the big life.'[10]

The disillusionment of the Windrush immigrants – gradually becoming 'educated' as to their racial inequality and economic exclusion – provided a counterbalance to both the apparent frivolousness of *Love's Labour's Lost*'s amorous education and the energetic fun of the musical

---

6. Ojumu, 'Reach for the Ska', p. 7.
7. Diana E. Henderson, Interview with Paul Sirett, 24 January 2006, London.
8. On the earlier performance history of the play, see Miriam Gilbert, *Love's Labour's Lost* (Shakespeare in Performance series) (Manchester, 1993).
9. From Kallman's interview with the *New York Times* as cited in John S. Pendergast, *Love's Labour's Lost: A Guide to the Play* (Westport, CT, 2002), p. 161, deriving from Edward Mendelson's edition of *Complete Works of W. H. Auden* (p. 717) – which as well, an anticipation of Kenneth Branagh's stated rationale for his film's (somewhat different) musical genre: 'As Nabokov noted in his journal at the time, Auden believed that "*Love's Labour's Lost* is the only Shakespeare play that will do as an opera. It is structured like an opera and so much of it is already in rhymed verse"' (716). Bate and Rasmussen recently echoed this (and the similar comments of Granville Barker): see note 50.
10. Quoted as part of the epigraph to Paul Sirett and Paul Joseph, *The Big Life: The Ska Musical* (London, 2004), p. 28. (Production opened 17 April 2004 at Stratford East; move to West End 2005; subsequent revival at Stratford East.)

score and comic form; it offered a different structural route to the seriousness Shakespeare inserts
abruptly with Mercade's intrusion (although a version of that concluding *coup de théâtre* also appears in
The Big Life).[11] The other obvious change involved
class: Sirett radically re-imagined Shakespeare's four
studious lords as black men seeking good fortune
in London among the first wave of legal Commonwealth immigrant workers: their pact – for three
years, not one – is somewhat more pragmatically
motivated by the desire for economic and professional advancement. Romantic misfortune still
appears as an initial motive, but in a supporting
role: Bernie (sceptical, like Berowne before him,
of their ability to sustain the prohibitions on 'no
relation with woman' as well as no alcohol, no
cigarettes and weekly fasting) is also reeling from an
on-board breakup with his fiancée Sybil. Because
the lords' motivations are a bit more plausible in
modern 'realistic' terms, their kneejerk misogyny
appears more obviously compensatory and culturally performative, yet also ripe fodder for a dramatic
comeuppance.

More seriously, despite their high hopes these
'lords' soon discover the difficulty of finding a job
or even housing in post-war, racist London, and
thus are forced (by economic rather than the diplomatic 'necessity' of *Love's Labour's Lost*) to share an
East London bed-and-breakfast with 'the ladies':
Sybil, her step-sister Mary, Kathy and Zuleika,
whose absent ex-husband owns the lodging. Close
quarters lead to temptation, and soon the men
are surreptitiously seeking out their singing friend
Admiral – loosely based on the resonantly named
calypso star Lord Kitchener – to attain a romantic song (instead of composing their own sonnets).
Exposure ensues, and the men become allied suitors. But like the visit of the Muscovites in *Love's
Labour's Lost*, their wooing attempt goes awry, as
the women take advantage of low lighting in the
Zanzibar Club to lure the men into misdirecting
their pledges of love. After their temporary humiliation and penitence, the word of death intrudes:
Zuleika's sick father, whom she could not afford
to visit back home in Africa, has passed away, and
only after all the lodgers pool their resources can

she now (too late) return, for his funeral. The journey, coming on the heels of the fantasy Africa
of the Zanzibar Club, recalls another diasporic
back-story for these migrants, a triangulated history as old as the Atlantic slave trade itself: if not
exactly dwarfing the binary hierarchy of colonizer/
colonized or the post-colonial subaltern speaking
back to the imperial centre, which dominates both
critical discourse and the musical's main plot, the
recollection of African origins at least re-places the
Caribbean subjects in another international frame
of kinship, albeit one under the radar of the dominant culture in their new urban 'home'. Again
economic realities shaped by racial inequity create
a social rather than 'natural' change of fortune.

This being a musical, the performance doesn't
end with these more serious undercurrents within
the fiction but – as in Shakespeare's play – with
a song. However, instead of displacing the main
characters' milieu and turning to the natural world
for mixed messages, as Shakespeare does, *The Big
Life*'s finale celebrates a distinctively modern social
world in which Ferdy can fill his time apart being
'good to myself' and join in with all the others to
'never let the love stop!'[12] Here the utopian generic
conventions of the musical finale reinforce the particular importance of composer Joseph's lively score
in providing a tonal counterpoint to the sadder,
more realistic moments within both Shakespeare's
inherited story and Sirett's interpolations.

The spectacle of music and dance also substitutes for much (though not all) of the Shakespearian linguistic fireworks and the comedy provided by its secondary characters: Admiral does
take on some of the flippancy of Costard and
Moth as servants, and Sirett's Reverend inherits
some of Armado's pomposity and hypocrisy in
his ultimately revealed relationship with Jacqueline (the white British descendant of Jaquenetta),

---

[11] Descriptions of the show in performance rely primarily on
my viewing of the West End version in July 2005, sup-
plemented by reviews, comments from Sirett and online
journalism, including Ferris and Funk, both referring to the
Stratford East production.
[12] Sirett and Joseph, *The Big Life*, p. 111.

but these are more akin to gestures than developed narrative variations. This alteration not only befits the show's original performance venue before an audience less disposed to find pleasure in stereotyping ethnic 'others' or lower class fractions but also maintains the fictional world's sympathetic primary focus on black workers. Instead of servants or a Spaniard, the most audacious comedian turns out to be one Mrs Aphrodite, a talkative older spectator who, in the West End production that I saw, held court during scene changes from her dress circle box and imparted her Caribbean-British wisdom to the rest of the theatrical audience. She animatedly opined about the specifics of different West Indian island cultures as well as recalling her own vivid, sometimes salacious experiences. Mediating (indomitably) the temporal and knowledge gap between the fifties Caribbean and twenty-first-century London, she, like the musical numbers, offset the socio-political sadness of a stage fiction in which four young men discover that, in terms of professional advancement, broken dreams are 'the price we pay' for hope.[13]

* * *

I'll make one in a dance or so; or I will play on the tabor to the Worthies, and let them dance the hay.
Dull, in *Love's Labour's Lost* 5.1.146–7

The fortuitous presence of Mrs Aphrodite in particular, as well as *The Big Life*'s use of the musical's generic conventions and a half-century's historical remove, returns us to comparison with Branagh's *Love's Labour's Lost*. For like the insertion of pseudo-historical Pathé-style newsreels in that film as a framing device, this brashly comedic yet very 'real' character in *The Big Life* was not part of the production's original script or conception. In each instance, well along in the process, the creative team perceived a need to provide a bridge for an audience distanced from the world that was represented. Ironically, it was not the wide gap of historical removal from Shakespeare's day that posed the direct challenge, this having been acknowledged from the start and having motivated the temporal relocation of the story from Elizabethan (pseudo-historical) Navarre: rather, it was the seemingly

'small' generational difference of fifty years and the local and formal knowledge of recent history, including artistic and geographical history, that appeared lacking among the audience. Such knowledge was necessary in order to be in on the jokes, and to prevent what Branagh and his producers deemed inappropriately timed laughter during a test audience preview. Whether this laughter in fact resulted from historical distance or ignorance of the conventions of the Hollywood musical – a claim perpetuated by scholars, such as Samuel Crowl, John Pendergast and Russell Jackson, about even the revised released version – remains moot, given the generally recognized shortcomings of Alicia Silverstone's kewpie-doll interpretation of the princess and the mediocre quality of some of the musical and comic sequences. What matters is that the film-makers believed it so, and added the newsreel footage in order to bridge that gap.

Because of its chirpy inclusion of adjectival jocularity, coy maxims and other period phrasing, however, Branagh's voiceover does not sound to a twenty-first-century listener much at all like a 'clever approximation' of Jamesonian 'neutral and reified media speech' (as claimed by Lehmann[14]) – although it certainly aspires to achieve a comparable narrative function (as well as providing humour). Rather than conveying impersonality, the voiceover, as Ramona Wray notes, 'consciously reintroduces and maintains the ironic note earlier entertained by the preview audience' whom Branagh was trying to engage.[15] Thus the

---

[13] Sirett and Joseph, *The Big Life*, p. 85.
[14] Courtney Lehmann, 'Faux Show: Falling into History in Kenneth Branagh's *Love's Labour's Lost*', in *Colorblind Shakespeare: New Perspectives on Race and Performance*, ed. Ayanna Thompson (New York, 2006), pp. 69–88; p. 77.
[15] Ramona Wray, 'The Singing Shakespearean: Kenneth Branagh's *Love's Labour's Lost* and the Politics of Genre', in *Remaking Shakespeare: Performance Across Media, Genres and Cultures*, ed. Pascale Aebischer, Edward J. Esche and Nigel Wheale (Basingstoke, 2003), pp. 151–71; p. 157; this is virtually the same article as 'Nostalgia for Navarre', which Wray published in *Literature/Film Quarterly* the previous year; I cite the later printing.

ultimate effect of the 'Cinetone' news clips was not to reduce but instead *create* another layer of distance between the fiction and the film spectators, with Branagh's chipper voiceover as much a comic stereotype of 1930s British pluck as were the Navarrese lords. The back-and-forth dynamic undermined one's ability to remain immersed (as many period musicals allow) within the conventions of the fantasy plot, and recalled the 'real' world context with amused archness – without fully grappling with the potential tonal incongruity of doing so.

Branagh's interpolations provide a cautionary reminder of the trickiness involved in trying to control audience perceptions, while the scholarly debate about his choices reveals a corollary pressure to match phenomena to the most recent or appealing theoretical frames, as the Lehmann citation above demonstrates. One feels some sympathy in each instance with the desire to please, even when the audience may not appreciate the means chosen. Especially given the financial context and career pressures, one surely understands Branagh's motivation and can appreciate the attempt to make the additional material witty as well as clear, albeit increasing his film's mixed messages about its tonal relationship to Europe's horrific mid-century: in theory the ambiguity might have been emotionally productive, akin to the way the Windrush material gave *The Big Life* a layer of gravitas, or *Oh, What a Lovely War!* carried a contemporary political edge. But the film-maker seemingly did not imagine the effects of the change beyond its local narrative function, or at most a vaguely sentimental sense of loss (of the sort long ago comically exploded by Beyond the Fringe's *Aftermyth of War* skit, for example).

By contrast, *The Big Life*'s Mrs Aphrodite succeeded as a temporal bridge by inhabiting both the fiction's and the audience's location, and speaking very much in the present moment. In the first published text, she existed only as a function: 'At the time of going to print Mrs. Aphrodite's interjections were not finalized'.[16] In fact, Sirett had earlier scripted a female schoolteacher character as a Holofernes substitute – precisely the choice

Branagh's film makes – but in rehearsal director Clint Dyer and Sirett decided that the role was not sufficiently distinct from Kathy, the strait-laced 'good girl' character. As this indicates, Sirett individuated the 'ladies' into temperamentally differentiated characters. Ironically, such attention to actorly distinction was precisely what also motivated Branagh's casting of actors rather than more proficient song-and-dance leads. Yet his closer adherence to Shakespeare's verbal script and Hollywood musical conventions ended up undermining any discernible individuation among the 'lesser' ladies in his film – except for their skin colour, which in turn has provided fodder for scholarly criticism (to be considered later).

While Sirett was consciously considering contrasts in characterization, it was his awareness of audience behaviour – specifically, the theatregoing habits at Stratford East – that led to the particular shape of this new role of Mrs Aphrodite. Audience members there are active and expressive during performances: they will often call out, applaud or talk back during scene changes (a far cry from the conventional audience at the 'other' Stratford, or indeed most West End shows). Anticipating and thematizing that possibility led to the creation of a commentator who talks back with the best of them and encourages (controlled) response. It also makes her provisional – or rather, improvisational – status in the script performative. At first Sirett tried to overlay a whole other layer of mythological allusion derived from her name, relating her maternally to the figure of Eros at Piccadilly Circus – who, *Winter's Tale*-like, comes to life and doubles as Admiral, a mischievous force for love throughout the show. This direct connection with the fiction's fantasy, however, became too forced and distracted from her very different mediating function, which relied on her proximity to the audience and the freedom of improvisational comedy. Choices were made and some textual witticism pruned. Arguably, in Branagh's film, it is

---

[16] Sirett and Joseph, *The Big Life*, p. 27. When I last communicated with Sirett, there were to be some changes pending in the second edition; this I have not been able to locate.

by contrast the attempt to maintain multiple but uncoordinated functions – plot explanation mixing with a different generic type of comedy mixing with gestures at the historically 'real' – that prevents the added newsreels from succeeding in quite the way he wished.[17] Of course, the challenge of predicting a film's effect on multiple, diverse audiences widely distributed in locale is also far more difficult than is adapting a script to fit a particular city or a known audience, reminding us of an advantage to staying local, and theatrically rooted, when attempting a complex generic remediation, even in this screen-dominated era. And conversely, the smooth fit with that local context may in part explain *The Big Life*'s remaining unproduced on screen or abroad: its very success in finding an improvisatory solution may have made it harder for producers to imagine how the show would readjust or transcend the particular performance context in an equally lively manner.

* * *

Enter blackamoors with music; the boy Mote with a
speech; the King and his lords, disguised . . .
Love's Labour's Lost, 5.2.156.2–3

Knowledge of *The Big Life* and this consideration of audience throw into relief several critical shibboleths about Branagh's film as well. One concerns the twenty-first-century amenability of the musical form *per se*. While it is certainly true that many teenagers will not be familiar with thirties Hollywood musicals, as Crowl (and Pendergast after him) emphasizes in accounting for the film's limited box office success, many who know and love those musicals were likewise not swept away by Branagh's version. By contrast, audiences both familiar and unfamiliar with ska music enjoyed *The Big Life*'s insertion of musical numbers into an historical moment comparably distant and potentially even less familiar to many than Hollywood and World War II would be. Of course, this observation is based on a theatrical run, albeit extending to two very different London locales with quite different audience norms. Nor would I deny that there were compromises and conventions in *The Big Life* off-putting to some even in those venues, including its

heteronormativity (to cite one complaint I heard from a scholarly attendee). Its potential for greater mass appeal cannot be fully tested in the absence of a film version: some might argue that the musical's energy relied in great part on its 'liveness', a position my emphasis on Mrs Aphrodite in the previous paragraphs could support.

Nonetheless, musical films such as *Saturday Night Fever*, *Strictly Ballroom* and even (arguably but more comparably) *Moulin Rouge* show how the impression of performance's physical energy can be captured on film, and one can imagine redeploying from other sub-genres any number of cinematic effects that have successfully created adrenaline rushes or the illusions of intimacy and engagement. Furthermore, given the success of more recent Broadway stage-to-film musicals such as *Chicago* and *Mamma Mia!* (hardly confined to their original target audiences, one age group, or prior fans, nor attributable to superior technical performances), the specific reasons for *Love's Labour's Lost*'s comparative failure do not seem quite so self-apparent or attributable to allusive awareness or genre. But they *may* recall the need to maintain a strong core vision as well as a sense of one's core audience, a vision that, even if it does not please everyone, conveys a sense of sticking to a coherent set of priorities. In inserting the Cinetone clips Branagh stepped away from an immersive musical experience, and away from the 'let's put on a show' attitude conveyed by his accompanying documentary trailer; that and his production notes emphasize his song-and-dance 'boot camp' and a company spirit

---

[17] Branagh's formal addition likewise leads, circuitously, back to the historical source for *The Big Life*'s opening sequence. By a suggestive and haunting coincidence, the real-life Pathé film of the Windrush arrival – at Tilbury, of all places – features a little *a cappella* ditty from the actual 'king of calypso' Lord Kitchener about 'London, this the place for me' – after first presenting Ingrid Bergman and Alfred Hitchcock's Heathrow arrival 'from Hollywood' to make a 'British film'. The hierarchies and assumptions within these Pathé clips strangely anticipate the reception contrast between the Windrush and Hollywood-themed musicals discussed here. Available at www.britishpathe.com/record.php?id=27376, last accessed 8 November 2010.

hearkening back to the fresh naïveté of the Mickey Rooney/Judy Garland version of the musical genre (which Crowl also notes, aptly referring to 'what might be called the Andy Hardy strain in his production aesthetic').[18] *Love's Labour's Lost* as released (especially on DVD) thus seems to pull in several directions at once, blurring its audience (which audience?) appeal.[19] By contrast, even if one does not find Branagh's *Much Ado* personally satisfying, for example, one cannot deny it had its tone, audience and priorities fairly clearly established, and attained the commercial success to which it aspired.

Nevertheless, Russell Jackson, like Crowl, shifts much of the responsibility for *Love's Labour*'s problems away from the director and onto the form of the Shakespearian musical itself. Jackson cites the contrast between Mercade's entrance and the 'integration' model of the musical which creates an idealized community, as embodied in the 'There's No Business Like Show Business' number: 'The difficulty here is not so much that of the director's editorial choices in the final cut of his film as a mismatch between the customary syntax of movie musicals and the structure of the Shakespearean comedy.'[20] Again, *The Big Life* hints otherwise: at least on stage (and it is worth emphasizing that many of the 'fairy-tale' film musicals being invoked here, via Rick Altman's theorizing, began on stage) the musical is more capacious than this implies and can incorporate precisely these two impulses from *Love's Labour's Lost*: integration *and* the abrupt recognition of 'real world' sorrow. Film musicals involving Stanley Donen (*On the Town, Damn Yankees!*) and Bob Fosse (*Cabaret, All That Jazz*) – the former a producer of Branagh's film, the latter alluded to through the choreography of 'Let's Face the Music and Dance' – certainly rely on an awareness of human costs and suffering just beyond the fantasy, and sometimes within it. Jackson obviously knows this and acknowledges the 'shades of Bob Fosse' in 'Let's Face the Music and Dance', yet regards Branagh's shift to this other key (substituting for instead of including the text's Muscovite masque) as likewise a 'structural' problem.[21] Nevertheless, precisely the same substitution of a club scene for the masque works in *The Big Life*, as does

the mixing of tonalities within the musical form. Jackson's own account of the director's allusion to the scene as taking place at the 'CopacaBranagh' (wince-producing as it is) implies some such awareness of a tonal shift. It also calls attention to the way in which, if one wishes to apply Altman's categories, Branagh's film participates not only in the 'fairy-tale' but also the 'show business' model of the musical. His *Love's Labour's Lost* is in fact more capacious (and inconsistent) a pastiche than reiterated association with the debonair Astaire allows: through its eventual choreographic allusions to Fosse, the musical mimics the development in Shakespeare's play towards – but not quite to – sexual fulfilment, as well as foreshadowing *Love's Labour's Lost*'s jarring shift of tone. 'There may be trouble ahead', as the song goes.

* * *

What ish my nation?   *Henry V*, 3.2.66

A related strain in the scholarship asserts that this musical's difficulties are attributable to nationalism, be the presumption that the form is

---

[18] Samuel Crowl, *Shakespeare at the Cineplex: The Kenneth Branagh Era* (Athens, OH, 2003), p. 41.

[19] Even if Branagh's bootcamp did not produce all the results wished, it is a salutary reminder of the work involved within the Hollywood system, and the importance especially of the Arthur Fried unit at MGM. Branagh regularly makes the actorly process a priority, which helps artists achieve new skills (as distinct from just deploring inabilities and lack): how did you ever get to the world of *42nd Street* unless you took risks with the understudies, or in this case ingénues like Alicia Silverstone?

[20] Russell Jackson, 'Filming Shakespeare's Comedies: Reflections on *Love's Labour's Lost*', in *Shakespearean Performance: New Studies*, ed. Frank Occhiogrosso (Madison, NJ, 2008), 62–73: pp. 70–1. Anna K. Nardo, 'Playing with Shakespeare's Play: Branagh's *Love's Labour's Lost*', *Shakespeare Survey 61* (Cambridge, 2008), pp. 13–22 argues quite the converse, finding Branagh's 'meta-musical' choices consonant with the Shakespearian play. Jackson's generally helpful and characteristically modest account of his unique perspective on Branagh's film was published well after his involvement in the film-making and the release of the other musicals mentioned above. He, like Lehmann, draws on the categorization of musicals in Rick Altman's *The American Film Musical* (Bloomington, IN, 1987).

[21] Jackson, 'Filming Shakespeare's Comedies', p. 69.

inherently American or that Branagh's work is self-consciously positioned in relation to Britain's imperial decline. Crowl, for example, counters the late playwright Wendy Wasserstein's comment that *Love's Labour's Lost*'s production numbers are 'performed with an arched eyebrow' by asserting that the 'problem lies more, I think, in the very American nature of the movie musical. It is not a genre that travels well.'[22] One can begin by noting obvious counter-examples: Lerner and Loewe's *My Fair Lady* and *Gigi* immediately spring to mind, as do the more thoroughly French vehicles for Maurice Chevalier in his younger days (Ah yes, I remember them well!). This leads one to query, secondly, how the nationality of a musical is determined: by its director, its production company, its originary location of performance, its fictional location, its cast, and/or . . . ? The usual problems that arise when scholars overlook the collaborative process recur here. Finally, and embracing these first two points, the premise is rooted in the very same Amero-centric tradition that obscures both cross-medial influence and the more historically fluid history and composition of the film musical.

These issues are worth further consideration because they extend well beyond discussion of Branagh's film. My main concern is with overhasty generalizations or critical assumptions that prevent us from helpfully describing where and why artistic productions succeed or fail; some of these misdiagnoses, if attended to, could discourage other artists and producers from pursuing certain possibilities – such as a film of *The Big Life*, or another Shakespearian film musical, to name two. (If our criticism is not consequential in this domain, we might wish to consider whether our methods are contributing to its irrelevance, and whether our use of scholarly tools truly illuminates the artworks of putative interest.) The critics under scrutiny here have been invoked precisely because their work is in specific ways quite valuable and yet illustrative of a wider problem. More still needs to be said about media differences (which Jackson addresses) and varieties of pastiche, about historically informed remediation, and about the general overreliance on just a few canonical descriptions of the musical form

(especially Rick Altman's excellent work) as genre theory.

In Branagh's case, the film obviously hearkens back to Hollywood's heyday, but as Crowl notes it also gestures at 'vaudeville and Broadway'[23] – and, I would add, well beyond and across the Atlantic. The inclusion of the song 'The Way You Look Tonight', sung by Branagh production regulars Geraldine MacEwan and Richard Briers, provides an intertextual allusion to another of his ensemble films, *Peter's Friends*; there the song is anchored (beautifully) by Imelda Staunton and Hugh Laurie, with Stephen Fry and Emma Thompson's presence recalling layers of British comic performance tradition and Branagh's own marriage, by the year 2000 themselves occasions for somewhat wistful recollection if not nostalgia.[24] Building on Ramona Wray's attention to *Love's Labour's Lost*'s inclusion of 'personal history' as well as the 'heyday of British television – the experimental dramas of Dennis Potter' in the choice of 'Let's Face the Music and Dance',[25] I demur from her political conclusion and would instead contend that such British referentiality does something other than locate (or lock) Branagh within an historically linear sequence: it evokes a multiplicity of performances that defy singular location, either in time or space – an aesthetic consistent with Branagh's casting attempts to create an international Shakespeare, and with Shakespeare's own use of comic setting. It encourages us to think more playfully about time as well, to realize that the act of reprising old standards need not be indicative of nostalgia, decline or rivalry (personal or national) but of artistic participation: for Branagh growing up (as for me), the songs in his musical were always already 'retro' and aesthetically rather than historically situated; the act of enjoying them might evoke nostalgia for our parents' generation but not our own. Turning back to

---

[22] Crowl, *Shakespeare at the Cineplex*, p. 40.

[23] Crowl, *Shakespeare at the Cineplex*, p. 46.

[24] The song as performed in *Peter's Friends* is available on YouTube at www.youtube.com/watch?v=2W6JKXYxIUQ (last accessed 29 November 2010).

[25] Wray, 'The Singing Shakespearean', pp. 155–9.

the issue of pastiche with this (and Stanley Donen's production credit) in mind, the use of old songs in *Singin' in the Rain* seems more akin generically than does the politically charged model of Potter's *Pennies from Heaven* or Littlewood's *Oh, What a Lovely War!* And if so, Branagh's musical is indeed more 'American' than it is British, at least if we think of the cross-medial British tradition as well.

My primary point, however, is that such nation-based labels do not capture the fluidity, layering and interpretive challenges of actual artistic practice *and* post-colonial late capitalism. Exclusive emphasis on the 'special relationship' between the United States and Great Britain, or the tension therein, has an increasingly limited value in twenty-first-century media studies and critique: if it is not exactly replicating the binary hierarchicalism it purports to expose within artworks, it certainly feels a bit dated – to precisely the era represented in the two musicals that are my focus – and thus impedes the perception of more complicated global exchanges and transnational artistic flows. Like the steady invocation of Altman's theories of the musical genre based on the American model (and dominant as that Broadway/Hollywood-derived model might have appeared during the late twentieth century), it obscures other traditions – the kinds that recently have been labelled (inelegantly but conveniently) 'glocal' – as well as emergent possibilities.[26] This has consequences both for our understanding of the musical genre and the adequacy of our cultural studies interpretations.

The most sophisticated (and characteristically intelligent) version of such nation-based reading may be Katherine Eggert's 'Sure Can Sing and Dance', which argues that Branagh's film is 'post-postcolonial.' She rightly observes that *Love's Labour's Lost* contains a broader range of specifically pseudo-British allusions (the *Mary Poppins* tea party on the ceiling in the 'Cheek to Cheek' number, for example) rather than just thirties Hollywood models, in several instances the American version of a cited fiction having outstripped the British source in popularity. These and other specific insights contribute to the value of her

article. Nevertheless, they are made primarily in the service of an overarching cultural studies argument that regards the entire film (and Trevor Nunn's *Twelfth Night*) as an anxiously British reaction to the 'American Shakespeare-on-film hegemony'.[27] This bold interpretation derives in part from an historical reading of the Astor Place riots, which occurred at a time when the United States occupied the 'subaltern' cultural position vis-à-vis Great Britain. Nicely synthesizing post-colonial insights and recent work on popular Shakespeare, Eggert regards the outcome of those nineteenth-century protests as a victory for American Shakespeare 'which substitutes style for substance, emotion for language, and bodies for text', and combines this with the assertion that now 'critics generally agree that Shakespeare without Shakespeare, stripped as much as possible of Shakespearean language and translated into American

---

[26] Wray has played a role in calling attention to these other dynamics, especially the Irish dimension of Branagh's work, and I do not mean to imply that she or the other scholars discussed here are blind to the more complicated landscape. What I *would* posit is that our current argumentative models too infrequently capture those nuances when coming to political conclusions, and that the pressure to produce memorable critical 'interventions' may be displacing or trumping attention to the fine particularities unearthed by their scholarship.

Dennis Kennedy in 'Confessions of an Encyclopedist' similarly argues that such works must 'look overtly at the convoluted ways that national notions of theater are challenged by the post-colonial, by the internationalizing of commerce and culture, by diaspora, immigration, race, or global television' (in Worthen with Holland, *Theorizing Practice*, p. 35). For examples of musical theatre further afield and back in time: see, for example, Andrew Lamb's discussion of the seventeenth-century origins of zarzuela (named after Philip IV's hunting lodge outside Madrid) and of nineteenth-century *genero chico*, including Ruperto Chapí's *Las bravías* (1896), loosely based on *The Taming of the Shrew* (Lamb, *150 Years of Popular Musical Theater* (New Haven, 2000), pp. 242–4).

[27] Katherine Eggert, 'Sure Can Sing and Dance: Minstrelsy, the Star System, and the Post-postcoloniality of Kenneth Branagh's *Love's Labour's Lost* and Trevor Nunn's *Twelfth Night*', in *Shakespeare, The Movie, II*, ed. Richard Burt and Lynda E. Boose (London, 2003), 72–96; p. 75.

popular idiom, has triumphed'.[28] This leads her to conclude that Nunn's and Branagh's

films in fact allegorize an anxiety about the relation between the British and American film industries, an anxiety that consists of the blend of attitudes toward Hollywood I mentioned above – nostalgia, mockery, and affection. This blend is accomplished through . . . several kinds of filmmaking techniques . . . including homages to Hollywood; references to the career of previous Shakespeare-film directors; racial- and ethnic-minority casting; and the use of music and dance. Together, these techniques model the relation between British and American Shakespeare as a postcolonialist relation – just as it was in 1850, except that now the British Shakespeare actor risks occupying the position of the minstrel.[29]

Ingenious in its own terms, the neatness of this formulation hints that the argumentative thrust remains focused on the defining relationship between nations, not on potential variety or particular artistic choices. In itself, the shifting power relations between nations acted out through artworks provides fertile territory for analysis. Nevertheless, the priorities here do not lead the critic to seek out genuinely new ways in which the artworks might be rethinking Shakespeare, or even to explore intertextual complexities that might trump nationality within these contemporary films; rather, they are regarded as historically constrained acts of (nationally inverted) repetition compulsion. Among other things, this requires Eggert to claim that '[a]s the Donen lineage would suggest, *Love's Labour Lost* is also notably spectacular rather than text-centered',[30] perpetuating that hoary dichotomy even though one can just as easily find in Donen a witty pastiche-centred aesthetic that involves both the visual and verbal, as I have suggested above. Eggert similarly misses or at least under-represents Branagh's attention to lyrics and lyricism, including his concluding voiceover of lines from Berowne's famous 'Promethean fire' speech, which supplements his enactment during 4.3 of the relationship of poetic metre to dance rhythm. Instead, national (and speculatively personal) anxiety crowns all.

Looking back at *The Big Life* as an instance of a contemporary British musical might help move the conversation forward fruitfully at this point, both by bracketing the United States and by complicating the tendency to make specific productions stand in for an entire nation's imaginary at one historical moment. The stage musical clearly reminds us that there is no one undivided British subject position, and never was; that the inclusion of 'racial- and ethnic-minority casting' of specifically black *British* actors at the turn of the twenty-first century represents an actual (and long overdue) gesture not so much towards 'cool Britannia' as a reconceived Commonwealth; and that, for all the anxiety produced by and the spectral generic presence of the United States, that 'special relationship' is not the only or sometimes even the dominant mental model for British artists.

These considerations in mind, let us attend further to the particularity of genre and the mediascape, before returning, in conclusion, to the socially significant questions of race and gender. Katherine Rowe has suggested the limitations for those studying screen Shakespeares of a film studies model that isolates the medium,[31] and to her concerns I would add its inadequacy in describing the experience of contemporary actors, who move frequently and often fluidly between the different performance media. Especially in Britain, moving between film-making, television and theatre can become part of a successful artist's daily life. In Branagh's case, it is worth recalling that within a year of his film musical's release, he was directing the stage production of *The Play What I Wrote*, a tribute to the British television comedy duo Morecambe and Wise that hearkened back to the team's origins in British variety (and radio, film, etc.): among their most famous skits was a parodic duplication of Gene Kelly's 'Singin' in the

---

28 Eggert, 'Sure Can Sing and Dance', p. 74.
29 Eggert, 'Sure Can Sing and Dance', p. 76.
30 Eggert, 'Sure Can Sing and Dance', p. 75.
31 Katherine Rowe, 'Medium-Specificity and Other Critical Scripts for Screen Shakespeare', in *Alternative Shakespeares 3*, ed. Diana E. Henderson (London, 2008), 34–53.

Rain' dance – *sans* rain, except as dumped on the unfortunate viewing policeman.[32] A decade before (while Branagh was planning his *Much Ado*, and within five years of his leaving the company), the RSC had produced a highly regarded *Two Gentlemen of Verona* directed by David Thacker, set in the 1930s and using Tin Pan Alley songs (including ones by Berlin, Gershwin and Porter) between scenes; 'making the whole production a kind of pastiche of 1930s musicals', Tetsuo Kishi notes, 'the context of the old-fashioned musical clashed against and transformed the context of the Shakespeare play'.[33] These serve as indicators of the way Branagh's local, contemporary artistic world was saturated with reworkings of musical standards (to which one may again add the Dennis Potter television shows cited by Wray, and Woody Allen's *Everyone Says I Love You* (1996) as cited by Jackson, produced a year before Branagh starred in the same director's *Celebrity*). In such a mediascape, locating 'the' meaning of the musical as nostalgic or solely a US Hollywood signifier seems far too reductive.[34] After all, as Gerald Bordman's history of the American stage musical itself recalls, the integrated musical really started with Gilbert and Sullivan, and by the 1980s Broadway was again awash in British imports.[35]

Put more positively, the kinships and possibilities of the musical genre, both on film and stage, are less prescribed than the nation-based narratives tend to imply. Without discounting the validity of much important work on the American musical tradition's involvement with US national identity – about which both Altman and Fran Teague have much to offer – Shakespeare's high/lowbrow appeal over the centuries and the complexity of that popularity[36] have allowed his performance history to prefigure some kinds of transnational, cosmopolitan exchanges that are one silver lining of post-colonial globalization. Teague remarks that she excluded film from her study of *Shakespeare and the American Popular Stage* because 'I came to believe that Shakespearean films have been international from their outset.'[37] One might say that when adding music's 'universal language' to such films – even ones as laden with particular allusions

and historical moments as is *Love's Labour's Lost* – that observation becomes all the truer. And supplementing Teague, I would assert that the twenty-first-century stage is beginning to look much more international as well.

A TALE OF TWO ISLANDS, AND MORE . . .

The Big Life illustrates that no nation is an island – singular – in this brave new world. It also reveals how the United States can participate in that global landscape as a spectral presence only: not through its assumption of the British imperial mantle, but rather via Broadway precedents for staging a Caribbean musical and Caribbean-inflected Shakespeare. For while *The Big Life* became (with wonderful irony, given its story) the first 'homegrown' black British musical to reach the West End, *Once on This Island*, based on Rosa Guy's novel *My Love, My Love* and set in the French Antilles, preceded it there in September 1994 (after its 1990 off-Broadway and Broadway runs and its 1994 Birmingham Rep première). Although its songs were composed by the well-known (white) American team of Lynn Ahrens and Stephen Flaherty,

---

32 See www.youtube.com/watch?v=03GqaQkhuYw; last accessed 27 November 2010.

33 Tetsuo Kishi, 'Shakespeare and the Musical', in *Shakespeare and the Twentieth Century*, ed. Jonathan Bate, Jill L. Levenson and Dieter Mehl (Newark, DE, 1998), 157–67; p. 165.

34 Thus I part company when, for example, Wray claims that *Love's Labour's Lost* 'unwittingly sets up a disjunction between genre and nation: its implicitly patriotic and nostalgically "British" sensibility runs against the grain of its generic aspirations' (p. 154). Nardo, though more focused on defending Branagh's specific choices, notes the temporal playfulness and hybridization of his musical in her conclusion (p. 22).

35 Gerald Bordman, *American Musical Theatre: A Chronicle*, 2nd edn (Oxford, 1992).

36 See for instance my 'From Popular Entertainment to Literature', in *The Cambridge Companion to Shakespeare and Popular Culture*, ed. Robert Shaughnessy (Cambridge, 2007), pp. 6–25, on the trickiness of locating his works, and an implicit critique of the enduring heavy reliance on Lawrence Levine's (nevertheless valuable) book.

37 Frances Teague, *Shakespeare and the American Popular Stage* (Cambridge, 2006), p. 3.

the British black casting for that 1994 production would have seemed, for most audience members, to have broken down the colour barrier; it went on to win the Olivier Award for Best New Musical. However, *Once on This Island* remains a folk fable set in a traditional culture, far removed from the offstage realities of multi-ethnic Britain or the onstage fusion of those two worlds that *The Big Life* represents. Nor does it anticipate the ska musical's fusion of canonical British storytelling with black history.

The Shakespearian dimension of *The Big Life* has a different potential pre-history or at least a partial precedent, in a *Two Gentlemen of Verona* far different from the RSC's 1930s-style production – this one being the 1971 Joseph Papp-produced musical with book and lyrics by John Guare (the former with director Mel Shapiro) and music by Galt Mac-Dermot (of *Hair* fame). It transferred from the New York Public Theatre's summer Shakespeare in the Park to Broadway, winning the 1972 Tony for Best Musical by infamously beating out Stephen Sondheim's *Follies* (just to mention, at last, another offstage giant of the genre who has repeatedly demonstrated the musical's witty capaciousness). To the point here is the musical *Two Gents'* transposition of Shakespeare's Verona to Milan movement into a Caribbean to Manhattan trip – allowing the magnificently non-colour-blind 'racial- and ethnic-minority' casting of a young Raul Julia and Clifton Davis in the leads. Like *The Big Life*, the live energy and breakthrough authenticity of *Two Gentlemen of Verona*'s multi-ethnic cast appears to have been a key element to the production's success (although Bordman regards its reliance on vocal amplification as a sign of the 'lamentable state of musical production and talent': 'Singing in "live" Broadway shows was rarely fully "live" anymore').[38] Its West End production in 1973 imported the Broadway director and choreographer, but starred British actors Derek Griffiths and Benny Lee. Perhaps these productions account in part for *The Big Life* not having appeared to some quite as new and remarkable when it made its West End breakthrough, despite its unique refusal to exoticize or simply romanticize its Caribbean roots.

In fitting both of the twenty-first-century musicals based on *Love's Labour's Lost* into a larger set of traditions – Shakespearian, variety and musical – my hope is to reinforce an important role for performance history within cultural studies analyses, one which adds depth to both our appreciation and critique of specific artistic productions. This is especially true of performances that invoke history – in ways that we might theoretically or intuitively question. What turns out to work (or not) is a stubbornly hard knot to untie, especially for artists at the casting and performing phases: it may be easy for us to hypothesize retrospectively, but often our scholarly accounts seem less illuminating about the works themselves than about our own current moment in critical discourse. Keeping scholarship and art in productive rather than lop-sided dialogue remains challenging.

Of urgent import in both domains is the vexed category of 'race'. Attention to *The Big Life* again may provide a fruitful route to a wider discussion about issues of race in modern Shakespeare production. There have been several attempts to 'read against the grain' of the general practice of putatively colour-blind casting, and certainly this is one way to reveal unintended consequences and cultural blindspots regarding race when updating Shakespeare. We can hope it is no longer acceptable merely to remark in passing, as John Pendergast did in 2002, that 'surprising casting choices' in staging *Love's Labour's Lost* have included 'a black actress, Josette Simon, as Rosaline, and in Kenneth Branagh's film version, Carmen Ejogo played Maria. There is some textual support for the former choice . . .'[39] Nevertheless, the critical pressure to find something to expose can lead to counterclaims of overreading or wilful misapprehension:

---

38 Bordman, *American Musical Theatre*, p. 674. He also recalls 'initial resistance from the patrons, who resented a $15 top [price ticket] for much the same show that had been given free months earlier'; these two comments put together reveal major changes within mainstream musical theatre during the past 40 years, and play against any unhistoricized contrast of film vs. theatre as media.

39 Pendergast, *Love's Labour's Lost: A Guide*, p. 141.

in the case of *Love's Labour's Lost*, when Courtney Lehmann attributes to a standard British pronunciation a racist subtext – 'Maria (pronounced "Mariah" to give the name a "black" inflection)' – I fear we have entered the domain of critical self-parody.[40]

Furthermore, such reading provides fodder for others to argue, as does Richard Burt with typical rhetorical flair, that cultural criticism has worked itself into a 'color bind' where one is damned whatever the artistic choice made.[41] Burt's own use of evidence may be somewhat suspect, particularly when he cavalierly dehistoricizes and despecifies the scholarly examples to which he alludes, but this does not entirely undo the pertinence of his broader point. Lehmann's account of Adrian Lester's dancing (as Dumaine) unfortunately fits his bill: she interprets a fairly standard dance move as distinctively constituting Branagh's subconscious presentation of 'Dumaine's predatory sexuality', yet when Lester dances a solo with grace and understated flair it is attributed to Branagh's white containment. If Branagh doesn't include 'Diga Diga Doo' – and one ponders why on earth he would, given his self-conscious narrative-based substitution of Tin Pan Alley wit for Elizabethan lyricism – he is charged with effacing the black origins of musical theatre, yet if he includes a British mixed race (half Scottish, half Nigerian) actress as part of a cross-racial couple, she is presumed to raise spectres of racist stereotypes.[42] Thus when, in the lead-up to Dumaine's dance, his white fellow-lord (thinking he is alone) gauchely accompanies his few introductory bars of 'I've Got a Crush on You' with repeated pelvic thrusts – inducing a cringe from the hidden Berowne/Branagh as well as ourselves – Lehmann claims: 'The only explanation for Longueville's behavior, then, is a racial one, as if the hypersexuality historically ascribed to the black female has rubbed off on him in his first dance with Maria.'[43]

To the contrary, this is hardly the 'only' explanation if one attends to the musical number as the film's correlate to *Love's Labour's Lost*'s 4.3 sequence in which Dumaine's more 'natural' poem upstages

the Prince and Longaville's sophistical sonnets; the tacky writhing during the lead-in performatively reinforces the musical pleasure that comes with Dumaine's entrance and the resolution into the song's main verse. Providing further counterevidence, the filmed sequence (like the textual) makes no visual gesture whatsoever at specific reference to the ladies (that lack of referentiality indeed constitutes the core of the lords' comic problem, as poets as well as wooers), so there is only the critic's desire to discern a contradictory racial subtext grounding her 'as if' speculation.

I elaborate my disagreements with this particular dimension of Lehmann's article because her comments have currency in Shakespeare studies and the point is consequential. Her often insightful analysis – more precise in spotting choreographic allusions than most Shakespearians, for example – makes these passages, and her jarring invocation of Emmett Till within an article on Branagh's film, all the more lamentable. Nevertheless, I do not wish to personalize the critique; rather, one again senses here the pressure of our own critical moment, the need to produce a reading that fits the dominant discursive expectations *and* the desire for criticism to play a positive political role – or at least to sound progressive.

Even when rhetoric substitutes for logical suasion, such readings may still have a catalytic effect in the classroom, allowing for lively debates and attention to topics that in a broader context do indeed have major cultural consequences. In

---

40 Lehmann, 'Faux Show', p. 80.
41 Richard Burt, 'Civic ShakesPR: Middlebrow Multiculturalism, White Television, and the Color Bind', in Thompson, ed., *Colorblind Shakespeare*, pp. 157–85.
42 Lehmann also proclaims that Branagh's is the only 'English' dance pairing among the four couples, though clearly she is aware of his being Northern Irish by birth (p. 77). Whose race, and whose nation counts? The complexities of the Commonwealth thematized in *The Big Life* may only be traces in the casting of Branagh's film, but they would seem to matter if one is going to highlight race as a term of analysis. Reducing everything to black and white seems dated on either side of the twenty-first-century Atlantic.
43 Lehmann, 'Faux Show', p. 81.

addition, they may encourage scholars to return to the film and look again, more carefully, as I was forced to do. Were Branagh (or more likely, Branagh via input from Jackson as his textual consultant) to attend to such critique, however, I wonder at its use value or productiveness, either in encouraging him to risk non-traditional casting in future or in turning to scholars for input. After all, it was that preview audience that disrupted his original design; arguably too much self-consciousness leads to weaker artistic products. Artists repeatedly say so to scholars, and scholars repeatedly discount their perspective as avoidance of the scholars' own priorities and emphases.

But perhaps the 'damned if you do, damned if you don't' antinomy, like this ongoing professional debate, is inevitable given the social category under discussion, in which case it is not enough simply to recognize the pattern. Race, writes David Nirenberg,

demands a history, both because it is a subject both urgent and vast and because its own logic is so closely akin to that of the disciplines (etymology, genealogy, history) with which we study the persistence of humanity in time. For those same reasons, any history of race will be at best limited, strategic, and polemical and at worst a reproduction of racial logic itself. In either case, histories of race are best read . . . not as prescriptive but as provocations to comparison. There is energy to be drawn from the collision of such polemics with our own particles of history, and new elements of both past and present to be found in the wreckage.[44]

The question is how you *use* the antinomy, to provoke or be complacent – and how to decide which stance is which. Regarded thus, there is something true within the falsity of Lehmann's analysis, when she concludes that Branagh's film 'ultimately moves away from sexualized, racial othering towards simply sexual othering'.[45] In fact, I'd say it was so all along, the very absence of gendered variety among the ladies prompting critical attention to race as the only remaining visible form of differentiation. As others have noticed, the decision to emphasize ensemble dance numbers and

identify the ladies by dress colour undermines their individuation, despite the director's interest in casting actors (vs. singer-dancers). If the film tends to evacuate non-trivial, non-visual differences among the women, no wonder that race (or at least colour) stands out. But this allows race to be a provocation as well – for us to notice a departure from the normative whiteness of World War II film history and fairy-tale musicals. And in including black British actors among the aristocrats, Branagh does at least update (if only obliquely) that world, not through layered historicism but through retrospective fantasy.

Into that world now emerges a new strain of British musical with *The Big Life*. Blind neither to race nor gender differences, it accordingly makes space for changes from Shakespeare's script that befit the times. Rather than the ladies (from France) coming to the lords' territory (Navarre), the men are now collectively the new kids in London town, coming to the women's 'home' – albeit one they do not own, in a city that marginalizes them as well. The whole question of territory, of being at home, is seriously at stake. Music, language and allusion become the means by which the men and women together try to re-create home, and thus function as something more fundamental than in *Love's Labour's Lost*: they are, but are not merely, fashion, decoration or amusement. In the book as well as songs, Sirett provides fun with word sounds, and the women and men get parallel scenes in which to mock or play in song and language. One of the most amusing numbers ('London Song') makes fun of British place names and mannerisms. By substituting song-buying for sonneteering, Sirett adds another Cyrano-like function for Admiral and shows the men easily outwitted. But this difference also reinforces

<hr />

44 David Nirenberg, 'Race and the Middle Ages: The Case of Spain and Its Jews', in *Re-Reading the Black Legend: The Discourses of Religious and Racial Difference in the Renaissance Empires*, ed. Margaret R. Greer, Walter D. Mignolo and Maureen Quilligan (Chicago, 2007), 71–87; pp. 86–7.

45 Lehmann, 'Faux Show', p. 86.

a change in emphasis between Shakespeare's object of mockery and *The Big Life*'s: whereas the Navarrese lords fail in being amateurish and clichéd rather than original in their own linguistic compositions (a dynamic Branagh's Tin Pan Alley pastiche aptly updates), here the song signifies the Caribbean community and the value of romance itself as something holding the displaced immigrants together.

Throughout, the men are more vulnerable to being abused by the marketplace, and less adept at manipulation and deceit: unlike the Muscovites, they come to the Zanzibar Club without a disguise. The changes from Shakespeare's play diminish the potency of their superficial misogyny, as does the more equalized experience and desirousness of the women and men. Although the women follow their fictional French ancestors in demanding the men wait a year (right down to Sybil telling Bernie 'to spend all your spare time doing volunteer work in a hospital'[46]), in private the women immediately express doubt whether they are 'going to keep them waiting a year?' and decide to respond the very next day:

Sybil. Tomorrow?
Zuleika. Sure that's not too soon?
Mary. I don't think I can hold out much longer.
Zuleika. Truth be told – me neither.[47]

Although the women have a much longer record of past ill-treatment and reasons to distrust the opposite sex in this version of the story, it is now death and only death that can (or implicitly should) delay sexual satisfaction for men and women alike. And these particular men no longer have to be cured of their scoffing superiority: having exposed the irrationality of his earlier jealousy, Sybil is sending Bernie to the hospital simply to have him do good works.

As in Branagh's film, one of the most obvious changes from Shakespeare in *The Big Life* is the erasure of evident hierarchy among the four 'lords': Ferdy's desire to be a university professor is presented in song as equivalent to Bernie's plans to practise engineering and Lennie's to repair cars. Nevertheless, academicians might appreciate the royal traces of a philosopher-king and the narrative trajectory emphasizing his 'fall' most vividly, a thoughtless white professor and the humiliation inflicted by his racist secretary dragging Ferdy down to a job in an asbestos factory (whose dangers we recognize, but he does not). A contrarian could contend that the absence of anything other than a conventional 'good liberal' politics is the weakness of *The Big Life*. In fact, an early draft included one of the men being beaten to death, but the creative team wisely decided that was too much of a tone shift; the Stratford East audience appreciated the mixture of elegiac remembrance but especially enjoyed the strength, energy and celebration of a culture not overwhelmed by adversity. Ultimately, *The Big Life* illuminated the crossover appeal of a popular musical collaboration with Shakespeare, realizing its potential for present-tense community building that is neither simply nostalgic nor anti-historicist – though it certainly has been thoroughly commercialized. Within this context, the distance of fifty years from the fictionalized events allowed one to enjoy the changes they have brought – among them, the opportunity to create a Shakespearian musical comedy out of that difference, without effacing the history of race.

* * *

You, that way; we this way.
Love's Labour's Lost, 5.2.914

To what ends do we wish to put our powerful tools of analysis, contextualization and critique? At the local level, after reading Lehmann (and Wray and Eggert), we come away with a richer sense of the problems in Branagh's film. But will we help create an audience interested in watching, much less producing, future Shakespeare musicals – and is that part of our job? Do we prefer a 'simulacrum of the theatrical experience', as Bill Carroll puts it,[48] even if film's attempts to replicate what some

---

46 Sirett and Joseph, *The Big Life*, p. 105.
47 Sirett and Joseph, *The Big Life*, p. 107.
48 William Shakespeare, *Love's Labour's Lost*, ed. William C. Carroll (Cambridge, 2009), p. 50.

see as a residual medium are often found wanting, and even though we seem not to notice as a collective when someone attempts a far less nostalgic version of an updated *Love's Labour's Lost* on stage, as *The Big Life* does – though at the cost of foregoing altogether the Shakespearian verse Carroll desires to hear?[49] The absence of the verse text seems to have led to *The Big Life*'s exclusion from all the performance histories within recent editions of Shakespeare's comedy: even the RSC-sponsored 2008 edition of *Love's Labour's Lost* makes no mention of the Windrush musical (despite Sirett's one-time RSC connection), while calling attention to earlier musical attempts and analogues as well as more recent stage productions.[50] Is it that Shakespearians, alert to what's on at the National, Globe or RSC, are not so comfortable with the overtly commercial West End? Although Lehmann suggests that historically 'in its transition from the more rarified venue of theatre to the mass medium of cinema, the fairy tale musical moved increasingly far from its beginnings in Ruritania' and became a place of more cultural 'tensions',[51] in this instance it seems that theatre has recaptured the catalytic edge, the performative clash, and become the far less rarified location as a result.[52] Yet we as Shakespearians seem more engaged with Branagh's perceived lapses and indeed performative of our own nostalgia, pining for the film that might have been. Since we can no longer go 'to Piccadilly Circus and watch the big life' – or at least *The Big Life* – ourselves, perhaps putting it in the canon of Shakespearian performance history and into dialogue with Branagh's film will suggest the multiplicity of frames of reference and debate

available to us today, catalysing some productive – and productively forward-looking – clashes of our own.

---

[49] 'There are in fact some fine moments in the production, which has its defenders, but Branagh's unwillingness to take the play on its own terms [which is correlated with fewer lines from Shakespeare] . . . led far away from any simulacrum of the theatrical experience. It is likely that more people have viewed the Branagh musical than the combined audience for all previous theatre productions of *Love's Labour's Lost* since 1595, an unfortunate result, especially considering the play's theatrical resuscitation since Guthrie and Brook' (*Love's Labour's Lost*, ed. Carroll, p. 50). If the theatrical experience also departs radically from the Shakespearian text, as *The Big Life* does, would this defence of theatre also disappear? And when Broadway prices to see Al Pacino in *The Merchant of Venice* during the 2010 holiday peak season top $400 per ticket, are the comparative shortcomings of any Shakespeare film the right object of our distress?

[50] 'This is the Shakespeare play that almost reminds us of a Mozart comic opera. It has a kind of musical structure, with all sorts of symmetries and counterpoints. A nineteenth-century production once combined it with the music of *Così fan tutte* (which also has paired lovers and Muscovite disguises). And in Thomas Mann's great novel *Dr. Faustus*, it is the play that the composer Leverkühn is turning into an opera. To approach it in a quasi-musical way, structurally, perhaps helps draw attention away from all the recondite language, the Elizabethan in-jokes' (William Shakespeare, *Love's Labour's Lost* (Royal Shakespeare Company edition), ed. Jonathan Bate and Eric Rasmussen (New York, 2008), pp. 150–1). The edition refers to the 2008 RSC production starring David Tennant, but not to the 2004–5 musical.

[51] Lehmann, 'Faux Show', p. 74.

[52] Audience behaviours in the West End were atypical, according to Sirett and other accounts: this included the frequent assumption by first-time theatregoers that they should enter via the Stage Door (unless this was a more than usually cunning plan); the audiences were certainly more ethnically varied and participatory than is the norm there.

KABUKI *TWELFTH NIGHT* AND KYOGEN *RICHARD III*: SHAKESPEARE AS A CULTURAL CATALYST

SHOICHIRO KAWAI

'East is East, and West is West, and never the twain shall meet', wrote Rudyard Kipling in 1892, at a time when Japan was not yet familiar with Shakespeare. Shakespeare's work began to be introduced to Japan in this period, one in which 'Japanese contemporary theatre' was identified with Kabuki. Inevitably, when a Shakespeare play was first successfully translated into Japanese by Shoyo Tsubouchi in 1884, it was in the Kabuki style, under the Kabuki-like title, *The Strange Tale of Caesar: The Sword of Freedom and the Echo of its Sharp Blade*.[1] This version captured the public's fancy so much that many translators followed suit. Robun Kanagaki, the first Japanese to publish a section of a Shakespeare play (*Hamlet*) in translation (in 1875), adapted *Hamlet* in a Kabuki style in 1886. Keizou Kawashima, the first Japanese to translate an entire Shakespeare play, *Julius Caesar*, in 1883, adapted *Romeo and Juliet* in 1886, also in a Kabuki style. The first of Shakespeare's plays to be performed in Japan was a Kabuki adaptation of the trial scene from *The Merchant of Venice*, renamed after Issa Kobayashi's haiku, *Money is Everything in This World, No Matter Which Cherry Blossoms are in Bloom* (*Sakuradoki Zenino Yononaka*), performed in Osaka on 16 May 1885. It was and continues to be a common practice in Kabuki to perform only one scene from a long play.[2]

Thus, the reception of Shakespeare's plays began through adaptations and it took some time until Shakespeare's plays were properly translated without Japanizing characters' names. Hamlet and Ophelia were first given their names in the 1907 production of *Hamlet*.[3] Japan has since assimilated Shakespeare's work and the Shakespeare of the West has become an integral part of the East. As is shown by Akira Kurosawa's films *Throne of Blood* (1957) and *Ran* (1985), which are prime examples of Japanese Shakespeares, Shakespeare has functioned as a cultural icon to adapt and appropriate. So many variations currently exist in Japan that one may, in effect, choose one's own Shakespeare.[4] From *manga* Shakespeare to rock'n'roll Shakespeare, we have witnessed abundant appropriations and adaptations that prove the ways in which Shakespeare can be cooked and served on any cultural plate.[5]

---

[1] I owe the translation of this title to Robert Tierney's paper, 'The Sword of Freedom and People's Rights Movement', read at the 48th Conference of the Shakespeare Society of Japan on 3 October 2009. For a detailed analysis of this 'translation', see Tetsuo Kishi, 'When Suicide Becomes an Act of Honour: *Julius Caesar* and *Hamlet* in Late Nineteenth-Century Japan', *Shakespeare Survey 54* (Cambridge, 2001), pp. 108–14.

[2] For further information on the early reception of Shakespeare in Japan, see also Yasunari Takahashi, '*Hamlet* and the Anxiety of Modern Japan', *Shakespeare Survey 48* (Cambridge, 1995), pp. 99–111; James R. Brandon, 'Shakespeare in Kabuki', in Minami Ryuta, Ian Carruthers and John Gillies, eds., *Performing Shakespeare in Japan* (Cambridge, 2001), pp. 33–53; and Harue Tsutsumi, 'Kabuki Encounters the East: Morita Kan'ya's Shintomi-za Productions, 1878–79' (Ph.D. Dissertation, Indiana University, 2004).

[3] See Toshio Kawatake, *Hamlets in Japan* (Tokyo, 1972). A production of *The Strange Tale of Caesar* in 1901 might be the earliest example of a play's use of the original names of the characters.

[4] See my 'More Japanized, Casual and Transgender Shakespeares', *Shakespeare Survey 62* (Cambridge, 2009), pp. 261–72.

[5] For *manga* Shakespeare, see Ryuta Minami, 'Shakespeare for Japanese popular culture: Shojo Manga, Takarazuka and

Nevertheless, the case is in fact quite different in the very genre where Shakespeare was first adapted, Kabuki. In the early twentieth century Kabuki adaptations soon grew out of fashion, and Kabuki actors began to perform Shakespeare in a Western rather than Kabuki style. In fact, in the twentieth century, there were no Kabuki adaptations until 1991. Recently, Shakespeare has turned from a cultural icon into a cultural catalyst, from being transformed to transforming. Borrowing material from Shakespeare used to be novel and stimulating enough on its own and Shakespeare used to be exploited and transformed. But now Kabuki and Kyogen would rather explore than exploit Shakespeare and they do so by transforming themselves. In order to substantiate this point, before I turn to Kyogen, let me first examine how Shakespeare has been working as a cultural catalyst in Kabuki.

SHAKESPEARE AND KABUKI

Although *shinpa* (the 'new school' of Japanese theatre) played a major role in receiving Western theatre, Shakespeare was readily received in Kabuki as well, because, as Toshio Kawatake has pointed out, both share a certain 'baroque' grandeur, as well as other qualities.[6] Kabuki, which originated in 1603, established a tradition of performance that exclusively used male actors, just as Elizabethan theatre did, and some Kabuki plays even have plot resonances with Shakespeare's plays. In *Birthday Picture of Buddha* (*Shaka Nyorai Tanjoe*, 1695), written by Monzaemon Chikamatsu (aka the 'Japanese Shakespeare'), the protagonist inadvertently kills a lord's pigeon and is ordered to cut off his own flesh in the exact amount of the bird's weight. Just as in *The Merchant of Venice*, the play argues that it is impossible to cut out the precise weight of flesh. Hanji Chikamatsu's *Mount Imo and Mount Se: An Exemplary Tale of Womanly Virtue* (*Imoseyama Onnna Teikin*, 1771) contains a story about the star-crossed lovers of 'two households, both alike in dignity' and at odds, whose love is consummated in death. Nanboku Tsuruya's *The Puzzle of Tangled Love Resolved* (*Kokorono Nazo Toketa Iroito*, 1810) portrays a girl who is forced to marry a man she does not love,

and who drinks a potion that makes her appear to be dead, only to be saved by her true lover. Naturally, Kabuki actors were intrigued by Shakespeare's plays. At first, Shakespeare was adapted in a Kabuki style, but in 1912 Koshiro Matsumoto VII (1870–1949) played Falstaff in a Western-style production of *The Merry Wives in Windsor*, in a cast that included actresses.[7] After that, however, Kabuki actors dropped the Kabuki acting style in Shakespeare performances; surprisingly, until 1991, almost no Kabuki adaptations were seen in Japan.

From the beginning of the twentieth century, Kabuki actors attempted to approach Shakespeare without a Japanizing filter. Sounosuke Sawamura, a twenty-one-year-old Kabuki actor, performed scenes from *Julius Caesar* in English in 1907. A second young Kabuki actor, Sadanji Ichikawa II (1880–1940) dedicated eight months during 1906–1907 to touring and watching theatrical performances in Europe, never once going sightseeing but devoting himself solely to theatre. He attended acting school in London and even interviewed Sarah Bernhardt. After returning to Japan, he co-founded the epoch-making Théâtre Libre with the Western-style director Osanai Kaoru (1881–1928) in 1909 and began to produce the work of Ibsen, Chekhov, Gorki and others. Their successful production of *Othello* in 1925, with Koshiro VII as Othello, Sadanji himself as Iago, and the extremely good-looking female impersonator Shouchou Ichikawa II as Desdemona, was perhaps Japan's first truly Western-style production of

---

Twelfth Night', in Dennis Kennedy and Yong Li Lan, eds., *Shakespeare in Asia: Contemporary Performance* (Cambridge, 2010), pp. 109–31. For rock'n'roll Shakespeare, see Yukari Yoshihara, 'Popular Shakespeare in Japan', *Shakespeare Survey 60* (Cambridge, 2007), pp. 130–40. For recent Shakespeare representations, see also Alexander C. Y. Huang and Charles S. Ross, eds., *Shakespeare in Hollywood, Asia, and Cyberspace* (Indiana, 2009).

[6] Toshio Kawatake, *Hikaku Engekigaku* (Tokyo, 1967), pp. 201–2.

[7] This was the Japanese première production of *The Merry Wives*. For information on early Kabuki-Shakespeare productions, see Shigetoshi Kawatake, 'Shakespeare Productions in Japan', in *Shakespeare Studies* (Tokyo, 1949), pp. 205–57.

Shakespeare; an English observer commented that it was no different from productions in London and New York.[8] The Kabuki style was completely dropped in Shakespeare productions in 1960, when Koshiro Matsumoto VIII (1910–82) played Othello alongside modern actors and actresses under the direction of the influential playwright and critic, Aritsune Fukuda (1912–94), who translated the play into modern colloquial Japanese. Since then, modern-style Shakespeare productions have become the norm, with or without Kabuki actors. Thus, Japan's première production of *Richard III* starred Kanzaburo Nakamura XVII in 1964, while Tamasaburo Bando V's Lady Macbeth in 1976 was the first instance of a Kabuki female impersonator acting in Western costume. Kabuki actors were so versatile that Koshiro VIII's son, Koshiro Matsumoto IX (1942–), was able not only to play all of the protagonists of the major Shakespearian tragedies but also to star in musicals such as *Man of La Mancha* on Broadway and *The King and I* in London's West End, both in English.[9] In 1987, his son, Somegoro Ichikawa VII, played Hamlet at the age of fourteen, the youngest Hamlet ever in Japan.[10]

Thus in 1991, when the Japan Society planned to produce Kabuki, Kyogen and Bunraku adaptations of Shakespeare for its centennial anniversary at the Tokyo Globe, and on the occasion of the World Shakespeare Congress held in Tokyo, they could find no contemporary adaptations and had to turn to earlier ones. For Kabuki, they resurrected the oldest Hamlet adaptation in Japan, written in 1886 and never performed, although perhaps not without good reason. Transformed into a straightforward revenge tragedy, it is as much 'translated' as Bottom is in *A Midsummer Night's Dream* (3.1.113). In it, Hamlet does not suffer inwardly at all. Hamlet and Ophelia's scenes, including the nunnery scene, were cut because the two roles were played by the same actor. Moreover, Hamlet is not poisoned at the end; he commits *hara-kiri* after killing Claudius. In this Kabuki adaptation, Shakespeare was erased. Disappointed that Kabuki had not directly confronted Shakespeare's text, James Brandon expressed his desire 'to see

contemporary Kabuki actors bring their superb art to bear on Shakespeare's own text, something that has not happened in our lifetime'.[11]

This did happen in the twenty-first century, with Yukio Ninagawa's Kabuki version of *Twelfth Night*. Named *NINAGAWA Twelfth Night*, the production premièred in 2005, and was revived in 2007, and again in London and Tokyo in 2009. This was not only the first Kabuki adaptation that had appeared since 1936,[12] but also the first to represent Shakespeare properly in the mode of Kabuki while still remaining close to Shakespeare's text. The entire project was planned by the young Kabuki star, Kikunosuke Onoe V (1977–), who had had experience of performing Western roles, for example as Orestes in Ninagawa's 2000 production of *The Greeks*.

Kikunosuke confided to me in a private conversation his wish to refresh Kabuki by confronting Shakespeare's text properly, and asked me which play he should choose. I suggested to him that, because he is able to play both male and female roles, he should decide on either *Twelfth Night*, in which he could play both Viola and Sebastian, or *As You Like It*, in which he could play Rosalind. There was a tacit understanding between us that in performing Viola and Sebastian he could

---

8 *Pace* James R. Brandon, who writes, 'from 1925 until 1960, no Kabuki actor appeared in any play by Shakespeare' ('Shakespeare in Kabuki', p. 45), there were many examples to the contrary: *The Merchant of Venice* was performed by Sadanji and Ennosuke Ichikawa in 1933, by Jusaburo Bando in 1948, by Ennosuke in 1948, and by Kikugoro's company in 1957; Zenshin-za produced *The Merchant of Venice* in 1947 and 1948, *Much Ado about Nothing* (Japan's première) in 1948, *A Midsummer Night's Dream* in 1949, and *Romeo and Juliet* in 1950.

9 Koshiro IX starred in John David's *Hamlet* (1972), Ninagawa's *Romeo and Juliet* (1974), *King Lear* (1975), *Othello* (1975), Giles Brook's *King Lear* (1993) and David Levaux's *Macbeth* (1996).

10 Koshiro IX's daughter Takako Matsu played Ophelia in Ninagawa's first London production of *Hamlet* in 1998, and Lady Macbeth in Kankuro Kudo's rock'n'roll *Metal Macbeth* in 2006.

11 Brandon, 'Shakespeare in Kabuki', p. 51.

12 Goro Soganoya adapted *The Merry Wives* into *A Mouse in a Trap* in 1936.

employ Kabuki's conventional device of the quick change, in which an actor playing the male protagonist turns into a lady in a fraction of a second. Alternatively, he could simply act out both femininity and masculinity while playing Rosalind-as-Ganymede with no costume change. In deciding upon *Twelfth Night*, he not only employed the conventional quick change to play the two roles – Viola and Sebastian – but also played both the masculine and feminine Cesario, betraying 'his' true identity as a woman, as he might have done in playing Rosalind.[13] The task of preparing a Japanese script for the production was assigned to a professional Kabuki scriptwriter. Fortunately, the scriptwriter followed Yushi Odashima's translation faithfully, simply translating Odashima's work into the language of Kabuki and arranging the sequences so that Kikugoro VII (Kikunosuke's father and the leader of the company) could play both Feste and Malvolio. Although Kabuki actors deliver their lines much more slowly than ordinary Japanese, the scriptwriter did not account for length and tempo in the script, and the première production ran as long as four and a half hours (including two intervals). Before it was brought to London, it had to be cut to a more or less ordinary running time of three and a half hours (including one interval). Nonetheless, its original length shows how faithful the script was to the original. Moreover, Kikunosuke took great care in adapting *Twelfth Night* to a Kabuki context, costuming Olivia in the same red kimono with golden embroidery as Princess Yaegaki's in *Twenty-four Models of Japanese Filial Piety* (*Honcho Niju Shiko*). Both Olivia and Yaegaki are high-born ladies who dare to express their passionate love to an unknown young man, a lookalike of their future husband. Likewise, Kikunosuke made *Twelfth Night* and Kabuki confront one another by costuming Sebastian in the same red kimono and purple *kamishimo* (the samurai's formal clothing) as those of Yaegaki's fiancé Katsuyori, whose mirror image Minosuke she comes across and falls in love with. The paralleling of Olivia with Yaegaki and of Cesario/Sebastian with Minosuke/Katsuyori worked beautifully, while doing no harm to Shakespeare's text.

The subplot was richly portrayed as well. Kamejiro Ichikawa II, whose witty Maria entertained the audience tremendously, wore eyeliner to make Maria look sharp and clever, played tricks with a fan to show her frivolity, and even crawled on the floor to get a laugh, all of which he would never do in an ordinary Kabuki production. This deviated from ordinary Kabuki productions to the extent that it was Shakespeare's *Twelfth Night* as conceived by modern Kabuki actors. Thus Shakespeare functioned as a cultural catalyst to transform Kabuki.

SHAKESPEARE AND KYOGEN

Kyogen theatre, which depicts humour in the everyday life of common people in a feudal society, is the comic counterpart to Noh, with a history that dates back more than 600 years. Its style is far more natural than the formalistic Noh and much simpler than the stagey Kabuki. Kyogen is a drama of mimicry, with the colloquial language of the Edo period, performed on an empty Noh stage with very few props. There are some 260 extant Kyogen plays, most of which are comical or farcical short pieces with running times of approximately 15 to 40 minutes. Their brevity characteristically marks the difference between Kyogen and other genres of theatre; Kyogenizing Shakespeare, then, necessarily involves simplification. On the other hand, Kyogen and Shakespeare share many similarities, as has been succinctly pointed out by Yasunari Takahashi.[14] One of the striking resemblances is found in their theatrical space. Kyogen is traditionally performed on the Noh stage, which was originally open-air but has been housed inside theatre buildings since 1868. Like Shakespeare's, it was an open-air thrust stage, covered with a pavilion-like roof that was supported by two pillars at the front

---

13 The characters' names are Japanized in the adaptation, but here I use the original names for the sake of simplicity. The same is true for other Japanized productions discussed in this article.

14 Yasunari Takahashi, 'Kyogenising Shakespeare/ Shakespeareanising Kyogen', in Takashi Sasayama, J. R. Mulryne and Margaret Shewring, eds., *Shakespeare and the Japanese Stage* (Cambridge, 1998), pp. 214–25.

of the stage. Both the Noh and Shakespeare's stage use no curtain, sets or lighting effects, demanding the audience's imagination for the location of each scene.

The first Kyogen adaptation of a Shakespeare play was of *The Taming of the Shrew* in 1952. Tohkuro Miyake IX, the Kyogen actor, created short sequences based on the main plot: the father prevents his shrewish daughter from harassing her younger sister, after which a would-be bridegroom appears and miraculously tames the shrew. In the end, he reveals his identity as a horse trainer, which is supposed to serve as a punch line. One may hesitate to call it a Kyogen version of *The Shrew*, for in it the richness of the original play is lost, but certainly Shakespeare is being consumed here as a cultural icon.

The second Kyogen adaptation of Shakespeare's play to take place in Japan was Yasunari Takahashi's *The Braggart Samurai*, based on *The Merry Wives of Windsor*. It was written especially for Mansaku Nomura, the distinguished Kyogen performer, to play Falstaff at the Tokyo Globe on the occasion of the World Shakespeare Congress in 1991.[15] Takahashi also found simplification inevitable in Kyogenization. He cut the whole subplot of the wooing of Anne, and erased Mistress Quickly and other subsidiary characters while turning Pistol and Nym into Kyogen's conventional servant figures, Taro-kaja and Jiro-kaja. The adaptation focuses on how Mistress Ford and Mistress Page deceive the lecherous and greedy fat Falstaff and the jealous Master Ford. Such simplification clearly indicates that this adaptation is an appropriation of Shakespeare. It is a Kyogen play with materials borrowed from Shakespeare, rather than a Shakespeare play expressed in the mode of Kyogen.[16]

Takahashi's next Kyogen adaptation, however, emphasized Shakespeare more than Kyogen. *The Kyogen of Errors*, adapted from *The Comedy of Errors*, premièred in Tokyo in 2001 and was performed at Shakespeare's Globe in London in the same year. It follows exactly the same dramatic sequences as the original play, and no characters are lost except the courtesan. It takes about one hour and forty-five minutes to perform, close to the running time of

The Comedy of Errors. What is most striking about the play is that its tempo is as fast as the original, which is unthinkable in the typically slow-paced Kyogen style. Yukio Ishida, playing the Antipholus twins, moved so quickly backstage, particularly in the sequence between Acts 2 and 3, that it appeared to the audience that the Ishida playing Antipholus of Syracuse, who had just left the stage, could not be the same Ishida playing Antipholus of Ephesus, who then emerged from a different entrance almost immediately. At the same time, the director, Mansai Nomura (Mansaku's son), guided the audience so that they wouldn't be lost in the confusion: he made it a rule that whenever people of different nationalities met on stage, one or the other should wear masks. In this way, the audience could enjoy the dramatic irony caused by mistaken identities. Masks also offered a sense of strangeness that made the identity of the wearer unclear. Because identity is established in relation with others, when surrounded by masked people it is easy to lose confidence that one knows who one's self really is. Masks, then, express this sense of lost identity, which is one of the important themes of the play. *The Kyogen of Errors* has hence become an excellent rendition of *The Comedy of Errors* in a Kyogen style; here Shakespeare functioned as a cultural catalyst to revamp Kyogen.

Mansai Nomura, the renowned Kyogen actor, played not only Taro-kaja in Takahashi's two adaptations, but many other major roles as well, including King Oedipus in Ninagawa's productions in Tokyo and Athens. He played a role in Kurosawa's *Ran* at the age of eighteen; Hamlet, at the age of twenty-four in Moriaki Watanabe's 1990 production; and Ariel in Robert Lepage's 1993 production of *The Tempest*. He is now a key

---

[15] The script of *The Braggart Samurai* is printed in *Shakespeare and the Japanese Stage*, pp. 214–40.

[16] The same thing can be said for the first Bunraku adaptation of Shakespeare's play, *The Tempest: Arashi Nochi Hare* (*Sunshine After the Storm*), written in 1991, first performed in 1992 and revived in 2009. The first Bunraku production of Shakespeare, *Hamlet* in 1956, was not an adaptation but simply a puppet theatre of *Hamlet*, with the characters' names and plot left unchanged.

figure in the meeting of Kyogen and Shakespeare. Comparable to Sadanji II, the leading figure in the early-twentieth-century classical theatre, Mansai also studied in England for a year in 1994–1995 and became a leading figure in the early-twenty-first-century classical theatre, acting as the artistic director of the Setagaya Public Theatre since 2002. He also starred in Jonathan Kent's 2003 production of *Hamlet*, which toured to London.

For Mansai, I adapted Shakespeare's *Richard III* into a Japanese play called *The Country Stealer*, which premièred in Tokyo in 2007 and was revived in 2009. While preparing the draft for this play, I first planned to superimpose *Richard III* on a Japanese historical setting. At the close of *Richard III*, Richmond unites the two houses of Lancaster and York and terminates the Wars of the Roses, the war of red and white. There was also a famous war of red and white in Japan, fought during 1180–1185 between the Heike clan (represented by red banners) and the Genji clan (represented by white). As in English history, the white side triumphed, after which the Genji leader, Yoritomo Minamoto, founded the Kamakura Shogunate and became the first shogun to govern Japan in 1192. Just as Richard gains the crown by seeking the downfall of his elder brothers, so Yoritomo feared his younger brother Yoshitsune, who possessed remarkable military prowess. The Japanese people are quite familiar with the story of Yoshitsune and his confidant, Benkei, a Buckingham-like, trustworthy character. I went as far as preparing a provisional script of an adaptation of Richard III-as-Yoshitsune, but Mansai wished to play a Richard who diverged as little as possible from Shakespeare's original. Accordingly, I discarded the plan, and tried to rearrange my own translation of *Richard III* in a Kyogen style. Being faithful to the original text, however, works against the simplification that Kyogen requires. In order to follow Shakespeare's text, we therefore decided not to stick to a Kyogen framework, and the result, *The Country Stealer*, is thus an adaptation that diverges from the Kyogen style. Somewhat similar to *NINAGAWA Twelfth Night*, it took nearly three hours to perform at its première and was shortened for the revival. We limited the number of Kyogen performers to three, the roles of Richard, Buckingham and Catesby, the three conspirators who victimize the other characters played by ordinary actors.

I told Mansai that Richard in the first half of the play seems to be under the influence of the Vice figure in medieval morality plays, and that the Vice may be comparable to Kyogen's stock character, Taro-kaja, the mischievous servant figure who often contrives a trick to satisfy his desires. Arguably, Taro-kaja *is* a merry and good-humoured Vice, scheming and manoeuvring to his advantage and, to the pleasure of the audience, enjoying outwitting the others. Like clever and tricky slaves in Roman comedies, Taro-kaja is witty enough to be the play's trickster, either to help or deceive his master. Richard III, who can 'seem a saint when most [he] play[s] the devil' (1.3.336), resembles Ambidexter the Vice in Thomas Preston's *Cambises*, who boasts of his protean versatility and suddenly lapses into laughter in the middle of crying. That is exactly what Mansai did, pretending to weep and then bursting into laughter, while delivering Richard's line: 'Clarence, whom I indeed have cast in darkness, / I do beweep to many simple gulls' (1.3.325–6).

Laughter is an important dramatic element in the first three acts of the play, in which the audience may enjoy Richard's jovial ingeniousness. We got many good laughs from the audience, especially in the last scene of Act 3, where Richard, directed by Buckingham, feigned piety so that the citizens might choose him their king, even while declining the citizens' offer of the crown. Ishida Yukio, who played Buckingham, spoke directly to the audience as if they were the citizens, feigned frustration at Richard's incessant denials, finally stepped down to the audience, crying, 'Come, citizens. 'Swounds! I'll entreat no more' (3.7.209), and asked the audiences to leave the theatre, which of course, they didn't. At that moment, Mansai, playing Richard, admitted that he was persuaded to be their king by the audience-as-citizens, who clung to their seats.[17]

---

[17] See also my article in *Shakespeare Survey 62*, p. 266.

Richard acts not only as the Vice to entertain the audience but also a murderous villain whose soul is to be questioned. In order to dramatize Richard's self-reflective interiority, we created a new character, his shadow, to represent his inner thoughts. Richard first refers to his own shadow as a reflection of his deformity (1.1.26), but after having successfully wooed Lady Anne, he refers to it as a favourable self-image (1.2.250). In our production, as soon as Mansai-as-Richard voiced his will to see his own shadow along the way, a mime performer slid down to his feet and imitated his movement like a shadow lying on the floor. Eventually the shadow stood up, emerging from the ground as Richard's confident and malicious *Doppelgänger*. Because the word 'shadow' is also referred to in the play as 'a ghost' (1.4.53; 5.5.170) and 'an insubstantial being' (4.4.83; 5.5.169), the *Doppelgänger* carried those connotations and acted like the god of death. Echoing Macbeth's line, 'Life's but a walking shadow', this shadow ominously walked about the stage with a Noh mask in hand; whenever he placed it on the face of a victim, it signified death.

Richard's self-reflective soliloquy immediately after his nightmare in the last act marks one of the most significant dramatic moments of the play. Richard admits that his soul is terrified: 'shadows tonight / Have struck more terror to the soul of Richard / Than can the substance of ten thousand soldiers' (5.5.170–2). The 'shadows' – or the ghosts of those he killed – are not simply the apparitions of the dead, but agonizing psyches directly encroaching on his spirit. It was crucial, therefore, that we stage that nightmarish ghost scene as convincingly and threateningly as possible; hence, we turned to the psychic power that Noh masks are supposed to possess. In the scene before the ghost scene, where Richmond and Richard go to sleep in their tents, we had sleeping soldiers sitting across the stage. They gradually stood up, one after another, and turned around to show their masked faces,

signifying death. We had a professional Noh mask-maker create a dozen special Noh masks for this purpose, producing an extraordinarily frightening effect in the dim light. Again, in the scene where Richard is killed, the dead soldiers lying in the battlefield rose up wearing their masks and swarmed over Richard. Just as the Ghosts of Prince Edward and York say, 'Let us be lead within thy bosom, Richard, / And weigh thee down to ruin, shame, and death' (5.5.101–2), so the ghosts gathered round him and weighed him down, and, while Richmond brandished his sword against him, the shadow appeared out of nowhere and placed a 'Buaku' villain's mask on him. Through this sequence, we established an association between this special mask and Richard's soul. The association was important to our production's connection between the spiritual world of the play and our mundane world: its framework was based on that of *Mugen-Noh*, the genre of dream play in Noh theatre in which a traveller typically visits an historical site and meets a ghost who narrates his or her story. In our production, the traveller was a woman in modern dress. She entered the Noh stage and picked up a Noh mask, thereby inviting the dream of *Richard III* to unfold. She then entered the dream to play all of its female roles. When the play was complete, she stood alone on the Noh stage, put down the Buaku mask and exited. Thus, by resorting to both Kyogen and Noh techniques, we represented the inscrutable psychic entities underlying *Richard III*.

Cultures differ historically as well as geographically. The history of the Japanese theatre, dating back to the medieval era, may help us overcome cultural differences. In the poem quoted at the beginning of this article, Kipling also writes, 'there is neither East nor West, Border, nor Breed, nor Birth'. Indeed, Shakespeare as a cultural catalyst overrides the border, revitalizing Kabuki and Kyogen, despite their differences in breed and birth.

THE *SONNETS* AS AN OPEN-SOURCE INITIATIVE

JULIE SANDERS

It is nothing new to state that Shakespeare's *Sonnets* have enjoyed a diverse set of attentions, reworkings and responses from the moment of their first circulation in the late sixteenth century. As Paul Edmondson and Stanley Wells have previously remarked, the *Sonnets* are '[h]yper-productive of new meanings, in wildly different contexts', noting in turn how these fourteen-line miniature dramas continue to inspire 'an inexhaustible catalogue of praise and modification'.[1] Michael Schoenfeldt makes a similar claim when he observes that 'the Sonnets have frequently functioned as a mirror in which cultures reveal their own critical presuppositions'.[2] The most recent of these interventions is poet Don Paterson's personal commentary on these sequenced poems, a composite and engaging melding of his own critical and creative talents.[3]

Adaptation studies has long since familiarized itself with the critical rhetoric of cultural context and with the idea that texts adapt themselves to speak to and find purchase in alternative times, spaces and places. It would be natural enough, then, and not without critical interest, to offer a survey of the rich history of reception that Shakespeare's *Sonnets* have enjoyed, from ad hoc literary adaptations by seventeenth-century manuscript compilers to the more overt responses and reconfigurations of John Milton through to Oscar Wilde to Anthony Burgess, and from musical and artistic responses as diverse as Igor Stravinsky and Benjamin Britten to Rufus Wainwright; such a survey might also encompass visual culture in the work of artists as juxtaposed as Sidney Nolan and Eric Gill.[4]

What this particular essay seeks to do, however, is argue that the *Sonnets* constitute and in effect have

[1] Paul Edmondson and Stanley Wells, *Shakespeare's Sonnets* (Oxford, 2004), p. 176.
[2] Michael Schoenfeldt, 'The Sonnets', in *The Cambridge Companion to Shakespeare's Poems*, ed. Patrick Cheney (Cambridge, 2007), pp. 125–43.
[3] Don Paterson, *Reading Shakespeare's Sonnets: A New Commentary* (London, 2010). See also Paterson's article on the composition process of his commentary, 'Shakespeare's Sonnets', in *The Guardian*, 16 October 2010, where he uses the phrase 'cultural cipher' to refer to the Shakespearian sonnet sequence; as well as Neil Corcoran's *Shakespeare and the Modern Poet* (Cambridge, 2010) for an erudite account of the blend of critical and creative writings in many modern and postmodern poetic oeuvres including those of T. S. Eliot, W. H. Auden, W. B. Yeats and Ted Hughes; I would argue that Paterson's intervention follows in this long line of creative and critical poetic commentaries on Shakespeare and not least the *Sonnets*.
[4] Milton's Sonnet 'On Shakespeare' (1630), consciously echoes the 'Shakespearian' form of three quatrains and a couplet, though its preference for rhyming couplets rather than interleaved quatrains also strikes an innovative note. Wilde published 'The Portrait of Mr W H' in 1889; and Burgess's novel *Nothing Like the Sun*, ostensibly a fictional biography of Shakespeare, which takes its title from Sonnet 130, was published in 1964. Stravinsky set Sonnet 8 to music, Britten set Sonnet 43 as part of a larger work that is discussed in the next section of the article, as is the series of settings produced by Rufus Wainwright for the Berliner Ensemble's *Sonette* production in 2009 directed by Robert Wilson. Eric Gill published *All the Love Poems of Shakespeare* with a series of textually inspired engravings in 1947; Sidney Nolan's sequence of remarkable portraits based on particular sonnets produced in the 1960s was encouraged by his friend Britten. These images can be seen at www.sidneynolantrust.org/gallery/Shakespeare'ssonnets.php, last accessed 9 October 10.

always constituted an 'open source initiative' and to interrogate the reasons for this claim. This availability for reinterpretation and commentary dates from the moment of the *Sonnets'* first composition and circulation. The *Sonnets'* status as artistic product has inspired and encouraged innovative uses by numerous reading publics. Is there, then, something intrinsic to the form and function of sonnet sequences in early modern culture that lent itself in particular ways to the kinds of re-visioning and 're-mediations' that we are perhaps more accustomed to thinking about in response to contemporary literary, aesthetic and cultural forms?[5]

In posing these questions, I am driven by a genuine desire to advance the disciplinary sub-field of adaptation studies, at least as it currently operates in relation to the Shakespearian canon. In striving for the latter objective, I aim consciously to build on important new emphases within current early modern scholarship, not least research relating to material book culture, the 'sociology of the text', and the history of reception as exemplified by recent ideas about miscellanies and the 'gathered text'.[6] The social, collaborative and group context for understanding textual adaptation in the form of manuscript variations, the acts of gathering and collection required both by manuscript culture and by the act of producing print anthologies or collections, feeds off and is enlivened by parallel areas of development and debate in early modern scholarship. These include current thinking around social networks and family and household contexts as well as repertory studies' wider engagement with notions of collaboration and literary 'co-activity' in the early modern theatrical worlds, amateur and professional, provincial and metropolitan, through which Shakespeare moved.[7]

The aim of this article is, however, twofold. As well as seeking to enliven and enrich adaptation studies' approaches to the particular and peculiar brand of 'Shakespeare' by encouraging these kinds of encounters with current early modern scholarship, my intention in opening a wider debate around composition, craft and creativity, using the early modern moment as the springboard for those discussions, is to enable adaptation studies to benefit from fresh interdisciplinary engagements. To that end, ideas and theories of creativity and reception stemming from linguistics, from educational theory, and from present interests in new media and technologies, emerging not least out of business studies as well as from within the more familiar domains of literary criticism and performance studies, will be deployed and applied to a discussion of the accretive history of the *Sonnets*. In this way, the rich collaborational contexts for the early modern period, already briefly sketched but unpacked further later in this article, find correlates and consonances in contemporary debate about the 'democratic space' of the Internet where 'user-makers' are the norm and where notions of the 'creative commons' and freedom of expression among its constituent citizenship proliferate. In particular, Christine Harold's notions of 'Ourspace' and the possibilities and potential of 'user-generated content', a response in part to concerns about corporate control of imaginative space, are invoked and explored alongside modern

---

5 For a fuller explication of this phrase and its particular application in a new media context, see Jay David Bolt and Richard Grusin, *Remediation: Understanding New Media* (Cambridge, MA, 1999).

6 In my use of the term 'gathered text' in this way, I would like to acknowledge the influence of ongoing research by Rebecca Bullard and her colleagues at the University of Reading on the culture of miscellanies.

7 I have been most influenced in this thinking by the work of Lucy Munro, *Children of the Queen's Revels: A Jacobean Theatre Repertory* (Cambridge, 2005), and Gordon Mc-Mullan (see for example his discussion in 'What Is a Late Play?', in *The Cambridge Companion to Shakespeare's Last Plays*, ed. Catherine Alexander (Cambridge, 2009), pp. 5–27 (esp. pp. 20–1). The context of family and household production is discussed in Chapter 4 of my *The Cultural Geography of Early Modern Drama, 1620–1650* (Cambridge, 2011). On literary co-activity, see also Suzanne Gossett's introduction to her edition of Francis Beaumont and John Fletcher's *Philaster* (London, 2009), esp. p. 8; she herself acknowledges this discussion is a response to ideas raised in James P. Bednarz, 'Between Collaboration and Rivalry: Dekker and Marston's Coactive Drama', *Ben Jonson Journal*, 10 (2003), 209–34. On cultural creativity in an early modern context, see Elisabeth Salter's ground-breaking study, *Cultural Creativity in the Early English Renaissance: Popular Culture in Town and Country* (Basingstoke, 2006).

theories of 'craft' culture.[8] Here also sociology as a relevant discipline comes into play. The work of Richard Sennett in particular, not least his recent arguments in favour of a new idea of the craft workshop or 'atelier' as a means to understand contemporary phenomena such as open-sourcing and cloud or crowd technologies, proves a key driver for the ideas around adaptation (and Shakespeare) as a cultural force that are presented.[9]

This self-consciously eclectic evidence base will, I hope, contribute to fresh ways of thinking about and accounting for the accretive and adaptive history of Shakespeare's *Sonnets*. This study of adapted sonnets is less concerned with the 'when' or even 'why' of those acts of adaptation (though all these have at various times engaged and intrigued me) than with the way in which those acts of creativity become themselves a means of registering the cultural shifts and changes in which Shakespeare has played a central and often a shaping role.

I. MUSICAL SONNETS

Rufus Wainwright is one contemporary musical artist who has had a pronounced relationship with the *Sonnets* as raw material for his musical settings as well as using them as a springboard for interdisciplinary artistic collaborations. An early example of this engagement is the setting for piano and voice of Sonnet 29, 'When in disgrace with fortune and men's eyes' that Wainwright contributed to a special recording coordinated by Michael Kamen in 2002, called *When Love Speaks* and with proceeds going to RADA. The resulting work was a combination of spoken versions of the sonnets performed by recognizable actors, many of them with a background working for the Royal Shakespeare Company – Alan Rickman, Juliet Stevenson, Michael Maloney and others – and musical settings provided by an eclectic grouping including Bryan Ferry, Annie Lennox, Keb' Mo' and Ladysmith Black Mambazo. The ostensible 'fidelity' of Wainwright's approach in this first example of sonnet adaptation is notable. His 'lyrics' are the lines of the sonnet sung straight with no refrains or interpolations; the fourteen-line unit is simply maintained

and observed in the setting, although in a manner typical of Wainwright's interpretative verbal style he plays on and against the expected rhythms of the iambic pentameter in his delivery of individual phrases.

This initial Wainwright venture into the inspirational realm of the *Sonnets* was subsequently the prompt and stimulus for a far larger multimedia collaboration with the Berliner Ensemble and avant-garde director Robert Wilson in 2009. Twenty-five sonnet settings were commissioned from Wainwright for the purposes of a full-scale dramatic production, *Shakespeares Sonette*. This was initially performed in Berlin but later travelled to the Spoleto Festival in Italy. Recordings deriving from this project were included on Wainwright's recent collection *All Days are Nights: Songs for Lulu* (2010: Sonnets 43, 20 and 10 feature there) but there are also a host of striking video clips available at the time of writing on YouTube which are in many respects a better indication of the nature of these sonnet adaptations since they are presented through the medium of embodied performance.[10]

The production's cast combined cabaret artistes such as Georgette Dee alongside well-known German actors.[11] The Ensemble performed the sonnets through the realization of a series of related characters, performed marionette-style and with white

---

8 Christine Harold, *Ourspace: Resisting the Corporate Control of Culture* (Minneapolis, 2007), p. xviii. I am indebted to Sujata Iyengar for this reference provided as part of discussions at the 'Shakespeare Brand' seminar at the International Shakespeare Conference in Stratford-upon-Avon, August 2010. My thanks are also due to all the participants in that seminar and in particular to its convenor Susan Bennett for inspiration with regard to this article and related thinking.

9 See in particular Sennett's *The Craftsman* (Harmondsworth, 2009) and also a work inspired by some of Sennett's arguments, Matthew B. Crawford's *The Case for Working with Your Hands* (London and New York, 2010).

10 A news report for DWTV's Arts 21 programme notes for example the 'extravagant synthesis' represented by the production and its combination of talents and influences. In the same report, Wainwright himself acknowledges the influence of Schubert and the Ensemble's own self-conscious nods to the Brecht-Weill legacy are noted.

11 For cast details, see www/changeperformingarts.it/Wilson/shakespeare.html, accessed 17 October 2010.

'masked' faces inspired by those figures which are frequently read into the Shakespeare sequence as embodied (and disembodied) presences – a fair youth, a dark lady, an Elizabethan Queen – as well as, for want of a better term, Shakespearian character types: fools and fairies, for example. Gender crossings and complex power dynamics lay at the heart of these representations and Shakespeare himself appeared as an ageing, almost spectral figure on stage, alluding in the process to the themes of age and mortality omnipresent in the poems themselves. Sonnet 29 was rather different in the production when compared to the recorded version on *When Love Speaks*, not least in terms of the conscious movement away from any position of perceived fidelity to the originating sonnet form. The opening line in performance was repeated across a number of different characters' vocalizations, producing a more expansive and indeed communal effect to the contained sonnet rendition of the RADA project. Wainwright's work itself can be seen in this example being adapted and reconfigured by the collaborative theatrical process. Registering the effect of the Berliner Ensemble on the Wainwright composition, and by a complex process of filtration on the Shakespearian 'source texts', provides an important template for the kinds of creative processes I am seeking to limn and account for in this article.

It is, of course, nothing new as such to set sonnets to music; we have manuscript collections extant from as early as the 1620s that exhibit this tendency, demonstrating and evidencing a vibrant afterlife in an alternative medium of the poetic texts themselves.[12] One particularly fine instance of the *Sonnets* in a musical setting is Benjamin Britten's closing section of his *Nocturne* Opus 60, a setting of Shakespeare's Sonnet 43 'When most I wink, then do mine eyes best see' written initially for the exquisite tenor voice of Britten's life-partner Peter Pears and subsequently recorded by major vocal artists such as Ian Bostridge in fresh artistic collaborations.[13] In these kinds of collaborational and adaptational partnerships we begin to locate the inherent suitability of Shakespearian texts, plays and poems for ongoing, evolutionary adaptation

of this kind as well as the provision of space for group engagement in the act of adaptation that the widespread familiarity with his work appears to encourage.[14]

In a similar vein, as part of the Royal Shakespeare Company's Complete Works Festival at Stratford-upon-Avon in 2007, composer Gavin Bryars (who had previously set sonnets by Petrarch and Scottish poet Edwin Morgan to music) worked with Opera North to create *Nothing Like the Sun*. This musical enterprise involved eight musicians from the Opera North ensemble and two voices, the soprano Anna Maria Friman and the tenor John Potter, as well as the creative input of actor and performance artist Gavin Friday.[15] In addition the multimedia sequence (live performance was juxtaposed with screened images throughout) included compositional contributions from Anthony and the Johnsons and Natalie Merchant. As with *Shakespeares Sonette*, in performance *Nothing Like the Sun* was a striking mix of classical concert, art installation (simultaneous film screenings are often integral to Bryars's work), and recital readings by RSC performers like Nina Sosanya. The complicated relationship between voice, text, instrument and body in this co-created staging was a challenge to more mainstream Stratford audiences, but as with the previous examples the emphasis was on the co-creation of meaning both on the part of the performative ensemble and spectator-auditors. What I want to stress, however, in the deliberate counterpointing of contemporary and early modern

---

12 See Edmondson and Wells, *Shakespeare's Sonnets*, p. 117.

13 Bostridge, for example, recorded the Britten settings with the Berliner Philharmoniker conducted by Sir Simon Rattle. As with the Wainwright-Wilson-Berliner Ensemble triad it is difficult to determine where creativity and input begin and end. Britten also set John Donne's Holy Sonnets to music in 1945; see Bryan N. S. Gooch, 'Britten and Donne: *Holy Sonnets* Set to Music', *Early Modern Literary Studies*, Special Issue 7 (2001), 13.1–16 http://purl.oclc.org/emls/si-07/gooch.htm.

14 Cf. Linda Hutcheon, *A Theory of Adaptation* (London and New York, 2006).

15 Gavin Bryars, 'The Perfect Form', *The Guardian*, 24 February 2007; see www.guardian.co.uk/books/2007/feb/24/classicalmusicandopera.music, accessed 9 October 2010.

examples in this discussion is that this sense of co-activity and co-production is *not* a postmodern invention but is intrinsic to the way in which the *Sonnets* were first envisaged, produced and understood.

2. GATHERED TEXTS AND PERFORMATIVE EXAMPLES

Jeffrey Todd Knight's wonderful research on the 'gathered text' that is the Shakespearian sonnets in print makes the highly persuasive case that when thinking about the *Sonnets* we need to think about 'processes of assembly and reassembly'. For Todd Knight this takes place primarily within a book history context, but, as I hope to indicate, this notion of user-generated context proves equally applicable to YouTube and database Shakespeares as to seventeenth-century codex versions.[16] We need, then, when historicizing the reception of the *Sonnets* to think about the collectors and the readers of these texts as much as their assumed 'producer' in the sense of the author or even the publisher. In turn, I wish to expand or, perhaps more accurately, redirect those terms and think about them afresh in the context of contemporary adaptation studies. If we think about adaptational reworkings and responses as themselves processes of assembly and reassembly, as 're'-gathering the text as it were, we release new understandings of the cultural creativity and, not least, a fuller understanding of the group dynamic at play in these collaborational acts.[17] The kinds of adaptational productions I am gesturing towards in this article can be understood as simply a (post)modern version of the kinds of 'composite volumes', text-reader interactions, and the fluid and dynamic relationships they entail, that Todd Knight explores in his instructive and persuasive research.[18] I am interested, then, in the methodology of the adaptations and appropriations provided as the facilitating examples in this argument. Their methods and their performative contexts shed interesting light on the idea of Shakespeare as a cultural catalyst that is examined in other ways in this volume but also furnishes me with a way forward when thinking about

adaptation studies as future practice, form and field. To that end, I am consciously gathering together a series of informing paradigms – from information technologies, from performance studies, from cognitive linguistics and from creativity theory more generally – in order to proffer less a series of close readings than, as already noted, suggestive frameworks. I would attest that the general idea is more widely applicable and could be performed separate from the primary material presented here. The main criterion at play in my choice of adaptations is to provide working examples of collaborative practice undertaken in response to the *Sonnets*. Understandably, perhaps, many of these come from the creative industries, which are inherently collaborational institutional spaces in themselves.

From musical theatre, I now turn more explicitly to drama as a mode and form. The rise to prominence of physical theatre groups in the recent history of British theatre, encompassing as that umbrella term does the work of groups as diverse as DV8, Frantic Assembly, Shared Experience, Kneehigh and Punchdrunk, has had a particular impact within the sphere of Shakespearian adaptation and in ways that make manifest the collaborative and accretive nature of adaptation that I am arguing for as an essential aspect of the form here.[19] The *Sonnets* have, perhaps unsurprisingly, figured in this body of work, as well as in more conventional scripted theatre, as a particular and fertile site of adaptation. *L.O.V.E* was a 1992 production conceived of and performed by radical Welsh physical theatre group Volcano (and also controversially revived in 2003 for a British Council tour of

---

16 Jeffrey Todd Knight, 'Making Shakespeare's Books: Assembly and Intertextuality in the Archives', *Shakespeare Quarterly*, 60 (2009), 304–40 (p. 305). On contemporary creativities in a new media context, see David Buckingham and Rebekah Willett, eds., *Video Cultures: Media Technology and Everyday Creativity* (Basingstoke, 2009).

17 Cf. Elizabeth A. Mannix, Margaret A. Neale and Jack A. Gonzano, eds., *Creativity in Groups* (Bingley, 2009).

18 Todd Knight, 'Making Shakespeare's Books', p. 313.

19 For complementary analysis of the relationship between physical theatre and Shakespeare, see Douglas M. Lanier's 'Post-textual Shakespeare' in this volume (pp. 145–63).

Georgia, Armenia and Azerbaijan). The production was described on the original poster as 'Based on Shakespeare's *Sonnets*'.[20] 'Based on' as a phrase in itself suggests diversion and digression as well as influence, and the production certainly lived up to this billing. The piece featured three performers, two men and a woman, embroiled in a heady love triangle. Their struggles and engagements were played out on stage through the medium of dance. As with the Berliner Ensemble's *Shakespeares Sonette*, we can see in this performance triad a conscious nod to the sub-biographical figures traditionally associated with the Shakespearian sequence: the speaker of the sonnets, the fair youth and the dark lady. This production was entirely clear that it assumed from the outset a deep sexual entanglement between this trio. The show was choreographed by Nigel Charnock, best known as a member of DV8. There is a separate argument to be made, perhaps, about the *Sonnets* and their particular relationship with dance forms; those 4–4–4–2, or 8–6, and 4–4–3–3 structures have been mapped forwards and backwards into and out of dance measures from Shakespeare's time onwards. But I am interested in thinking about Volcano and Charnock as co-producers not only of meaning in this production through the physical act of dance but also as creators of 'text'.

In pre-show interviews Charnock was transparent about his determined resistance to any notion of 'fidelity' to his source material: 'for all the breadth and intensity of emotion explored, nothing actually happens. We needed to create a narrative, so I spent many nights with the sonnets spread out on my bedroom floor, scrubbing out lines and adding different ones together, making Shakespeare say what I wanted him to say.'[21] We might regard this as yet another version of the 'gathered (or regathered) text'. In 'making Shakespeare say what I wanted him to say' Charnock ensured that the Shakespearian was not the only 'voice' in this production; the performers moved to recordings by Shirley Bassey of 'The Look of Love' and George Harrison's gorgeous song 'Something' amongst other musical undertows. We witness in several of these examples adaptations filtered through other

adaptations, layering upon layering as a quite self-conscious act that deliberately resists easy lines of influence and ownership of the material being presented in the performative moment.

The Volcano production was framed by Sonnet 147: 'My love is as a fever, longing still . . . ', which set the tone for the heightened emotional atmosphere of the performance. There is not space or time here to do justice to the entire piece so in the context of this argument I wish to highlight in particular – as did many reviewers at the time – the striking and suggestive interpretation that the performance offered of Sonnet 129, 'The expense of spirit in a waste of shame'. Kate Bassett, writing in *The Times* was struck by the correlation that was made between 'the drum-beat of electronic rock and the angry rhythms of sonnet 129' and David Adams in *The Guardian* observed 'the repetition of the assertion that lust is "perjured, murderous, bloody, full of blame, savage, extreme, rude, cruel, not to trust"; the words rhythmically chanted as they [the dancers] catch, swing, and ritualistically attack one another'.[22] There is much reflection in the reviews and in interviews with Charnock that the company were in this production seeking to 'shake out' new meanings from the *Sonnets*, but there is also a sense of the re-performance of ideas familiar from a more private reading experience taking place, now utterly reshaped and reconfigured by the performative, group context.[23]

---

[20] There is a very useful archive of reviews and related material available on the company's own website at www.volcanotheatre.co.uk, accessed 10 October 2010.

[21] See www.volcanotheatre.co.uk/290/past-productions/love.html for an archive of this material including reviews and video recording of moments of the production, accessed 10 October 2010.

[22] See www.volcanotheatre.co.uk/lovereviews.htm, accessed 10 October 2010.

[23] Many will recognize elements of RSC voice training techniques in this physicalizing of Sonnet 129: in workshop techniques used by Cicely Berry and Andrew Wade groups of actors are encouraged to share the vocalization and with a bit of luck eventually the physicalization of the poem: reading up to a point of punctuation but then passing it on; shouting it on; pushing it on; learning what it is to voice these poems aloud, to make them pieces of muscular performance

There are, of course, many other theatre company engagements, amateur and professional, with the *Sonnets* that I could have explored in this context: Shared Experience's 1991 *Sweet Sessions* directed by Nancy Meckler is just one. It is worth noting at this point the kinds of theatre companies being drawn to work of this nature in terms of Shakespearian adaptation; they are ones like Volcano or Shared Experience, or indeed DV8, with a company ethos, an ensemble approach, and with established co-creative working methods. This in itself says a lot for me about why the *Sonnets* function as a particular, and sometimes peculiar, site of fertile adaptational work. *Sweet Sessions* included a central female figure who was a doctoral student working on the *Sonnets*. She was witnessed on stage attempting to index the poems' imagery; the figures of the Dark Lady and the Young Man appeared to her and sought to challenge the basis of her academic knowledge.[24]

A similar staging of the site of academic encounter with the text and its possibilities and resistances featured in one of the seven one-act plays that formed the commissioned 1998 North American collection: *Love's Fire*. That particular contribution, *The General of Hot Desire*, was authored by John Guare (best known for *Six Degrees of Separation*) and was inspired by Sonnets 153 and 154, a paired grouping on Cupid. The play commences with a couple reading the two sonnets and then what we see is a stage scene littered with various editions of the *Sonnets* and also (much to the disdain of one of the characters) a copy of *Cliffs Notes*. The Signet, Pelican and Cambridge editions are all name-checked and at one point someone produces Helen Vendler's *The Art of Shakespeare's Sonnets*, a now seminal work of literary criticism published in 1997, the very year when these plays were commissioned and first performed. The preciseness of the deployment of this textual signifier on stage – as if a footnote is rendered into dialogue – is striking:

Erika. *The Art of Shakespeare's Sonnets*, Belknap/ Harvard. Published 1997. Helen Vendler is the expert![25]

There is lots of wrangling over meanings and over the ways to rework Shakespeare in a modern performative idiom in the course of this single act drama; one memorable line remarks:

Harriet. You're making it a musical about Cupid in a bathtub.

Other plays in the *Love's Fire* collection involve music and dance, picking up on the resonances noted earlier between the *Sonnets* and these parallel art-forms: Ntozake Shange's *Hydraulics Phat Like Mean* responds to Sonnet 128's musical thematics and had an original jazz score by Chico Freeman in performance; *Angels in America* author Tony Kushner continued age-old play with the ambiguous sexualities of the *Sonnets* in his *Terminating . . . or Ambivalence*; composer Philip Glass (himself a respondent to Shakespeare in musical contexts) became a curious kind of Godot figure ever awaited at a snobbish, back-biting East Hampton drinks party (Sonnet 94 was the inspiration there – 'They that have pow'r to hurt and will do none'); and there is a striking three-way dialogue in Eric Bogosian's *Bitter Sauce* (inspired by Sonnet 118 – and it's worth noting perhaps that in each case the sonnets that were the inspiration for the play were read aloud in full as part of the performance) about love and betrayal that picks up on central themes and ideas that flow across the Shakespearian sequence. What Guare's play in particular physicalized on stage for me is the kind of cross-temporal, cross-cultural making and remaking of the *Sonnets* that I am arguing has been key to their creative identity from the early modern

and the meanings this produces, the transformations this can effect.
24 Details courtesy of Edmondson and Wells, *Shakespeare's Sonnets*, p. 170.
25 John Guare, *The General of Hot Desire in Love's Fire: Seven New Plays inspired by Seven Shakespearian Sonnets* introduced by Mark Lamos (New York, 1998), p. 99. Interestingly, in accounting for his 'New Commentary' on the *Sonnets*, poet Don Paterson also runs through the editorial commentary to which he has had recourse as well as the tense relationship he had with Vendler's study throughout the process, on more than one occasion repairing the book having thrown it in anger against a wall (*Shakespeare's Sonnets*).

period onwards. We also register, in ways deeply satisfying for an academic audience, how literary criticism has been part and parcel of the creative communities co-producing the *Sonnets* in different moments and media. There is, then, a more sustained argument to be held in which an historicist account of the *Sonnets'* role in cultural production and the creative industries across time could be detailed.

I am conscious that the picture I am painting in this article is one full of positives in that I seek to demonstrate the potential for endless creativity and even 'play' in the *Sonnets* and their availability for interpretation. As the introduction hinted, I would even go so far as to invoke recent work in the fields of management theory and sociology on the potentials for democracy and citizenship-building in a number of the models I am myself deploying and appropriating here.[26] In her recent Writers and their Work book on *Macbeth* Kathleen McLuskie has made an equally trenchant case for the flip-side of thinking about creativity in response to Shakespeare and its place on the adaptational spectrum or cline, wondering if some of the works we end up discussing and thinking about ultimately have much to do with Shakespeare at all.[27] I am certainly not claiming that the operation of adaptation is always democratizing, nor am I suggesting that such responses are value-free or that our own critical judgements must be suspended in the process of recognizing their concomitant potentialities.[28] But I do think that to move adaptation studies, particularly in the Shakespearian scholarship context, onto the next level we need to acknowledge what we might learn, and indeed embrace, from cognate domains: from business studies, game theory, performance studies, new sociological thinking on open-source initiatives and crowd-sourcing, and from a return to ideas of craft and the space of the artisanal workshop as most recently espoused by Sennett. If the biographical tendency in literary critical responses to the *Sonnets* has been much remarked upon, I would argue that there is also something in adaptations and responses, even to the *Sonnets*, that moves beyond direct identification with 'Shakespeare' and is far more about remaking,

reshaping, and re-crafting. Once again, the collaborational context is key: these are joint productions, within and across cultures and times.

3. OPEN-SOURCE MODELLING: CREATIVITIES AND CRAFTS

There is a growing field of studies in literary linguistics at the moment around ideas and practices of multi-modality but it focuses on a world that is actually highly familiar to the Shakespearian scholarly community and especially those who work on adaptation and appropriation. I could have drawn my facilitating examples for this article from a range of genres and mediums; thus far I have invoked music, song, dance and performance, but there is also film (for example, Derek Jarman's 1985 *The Angelic Conversation* with music by Coil and Benjamin Britten and readings by Judi Dench of the *Sonnets* set against slow moving photographic images suggestive of the 'landscape' of desire), and fine art more generally. Translation is another form that I would seek to interpret and comprehend from within a collaborational, co-active and co-productive framework, one which lends itself to the kinds of opening up to ideas deriving from the open-source initiatives to which I now want to turn more explicitly. As Elisabeth Salter has noted: 'It needs to be understood that for both an act of translation and an act of appropriation, the meaning of the resulting "text" remains flexible,

---

[26] See, for example, Chris Bilton, *Management and Creativity: From Creative Industries to Creative Management* (Oxford, 2007), and Barbara A. Misztal, *Intellectuals and the Public Good: Creativity and Civil Courage* (Cambridge, 2007).

[27] Kathleen McLuskie, *Macbeth*, Writers and their Work (Plymouth, 2009), p. 135.

[28] For an important corrective to my self-acknowledged positivism, I would urge readers to the scholarship of Sharon O'Dair. See, in particular, in addition to her contribution to this volume, her *Class, Critics and Shakespeare: Bottom Lines on the Culture Wars* (Michigan, 2006) and her forthcoming study, *Elitist Equality: Class Paradoxes in the Profession of English*. I am grateful to Sharon for her robust comments on my ideas and for an ongoing and utterly stimulating dialogue on these topics.

and available for "cultural creativity"'.[29] The *Sonnets* have an in-built flexibility which is maintained throughout the long history of their reception and their recontextualization in the form of new creative works and critical commentary. Their 'readers' are always, in this version of events and cultural process, 'makers', translators and interpreters of the poems' meanings and their cultural resonance. I deliberately gestured towards performance studies as a disciplinary field in the early sections of this article because I think that there are intriguing synergies between the open-source movements as they are defined within information technology circles and the work and practices pioneered by Augusto Boal and his Theatre of the Oppressed, which saw the 'spect-actor', as he termed the viewer-receiver in a theatrical context, as an equal collaborator and indeed 'maker' in the production.[30]

There is, then, an intriguing interdisciplinary connection to be made here, as we move more and more in the present age of academia and research practice into the realm of digital humanities, between different disciplinary lexicons and methodologies which have alternate provenance in fields as diverse as computing science and performance, and from attention to which adaptation studies will surely benefit. I am particularly interested in the open-source initiative (or OSI) stemming from computing science, programming communities and information technologies, as a model for Shakespearian adaptation studies and its own evolving ways of working. On its site OSI defines itself in the following terms, as: 'a development method for software that harnesses the power of distributed peer review and transparency of process'.[31] The OSI as a collective is about greater flexibility and access to new ideas and to that end has pitted itself against mainstream corporate practice by articulating the self-professed aim of putting 'an end to the predatory vendor lock-in'. My point would be that all these free remakings of Shakespeare on YouTube and elsewhere are part of a related 'crowd-sourcing phenomenon' and are similarly resistant to the placing of controls or limits on cultural capital, not least the 'Shakespeare Brand'. In a related manner, Shakespearian

scholars and performers are engaged in gathering data across multiple channels: web, email, text messaging, multimedia messaging, Twitter, books, theatre, dance, creative writing. Adaptation studies may enable new ways of bringing these sometimes oppositional communities into greater contact and dialogue with one another. For this reason, it is the OSI model of participatory design which I am partly locking onto in this article (and the role of the Wiki site as a place for people to lodge, download and find out about the vast range of possibilities for the *Sonnets* is just one striking example of the kinds of dialogues around creativity and cultural production that might take place). I am deeply influenced in doing so by Sennett's recent work on craft and craftsmanship and not least his invocation of the Linux OSI programming community in the context of his influential book, *The Craftsman*, where he states that: 'People who participate in "open-source" computer software, particularly in the Linux operating system are craftsmen'.[32] Sennett sees the OSI as a community of sorts, then, and 'the Linux system [as] . . . a public craft'.[33] Adapted and re-mediated Shakespeares on the Web, on YouTube or elsewhere, represent, I would posit, a suggestive analogue to Sennett's account of the Linux programming initiative: 'The underlying software kernel is Linux code [and] is available to anyone, it can be employed and adapted by anyone; people donate time to improve

---

[29] Salter, *Cultural Creativity*, p. 38.

[30] Augusto Boal, *Theatre of the Oppressed* (London, 2008 [1979]). For a more detailed study of Boal's work, see Frances Babbage, *Augusto Boal* (London, 2004). For related ideas, see also Stuart Hampton Reeves, '"Done Like a Frenchman": *Henry VI*, the Tyranny of the Audience and Spect-Actorial Adaptations', *Multicultural Shakespeare*, 4 (2007), 73–87. Cf. Margaret Healy and Thomas Healy's recent essay collection *Renaissance Transformation: The Making of English Writing (1500–1650)* (Edinburgh, 2009), which, with its focus on 'making' and collaboration in an early modern context, provides another important early modern parallel to the ideas of contemporary creativity presented here.

[31] www.opensource.org, accessed 17 October 2010.

[32] Sennett, *The Craftsman*, p. 24.

[33] Sennett, *The Craftsman*, p. 24.

it.'[34] If I substituted 'Shakespeare' for 'Linux' in this quotation, surely it would still make some sense to scholars of adaptation as describing a particularly active and creative audience of (often volunteer) makers and crafters. The key to Linux for Sennett is that it is continuously evolving and never finished and this would seem equally applicable to the Shakespearian context and the accretive history of the *Sonnets* that I am attempting to limn here.[35] Sennett also writes eloquently of the ideal space of the workshop or atelier and it occurs to me that we could think about 'Shakespeare' as a laboratory or workshop in this regard and see some of our practice as being about new methods and modes of working, but also new ways of deriving pleasure from this raw material of the Shakespearian canon.

Sennett's notion of domain shifts and the ways in which craft practice gets stretched out over time chimes with recent linguistic work in the realm of creativity, not least the pioneering scholarship of Ronald Carter.[36] Engagement with work in these cognate spheres of linguistics and sociology offers us as Shakespeare scholars a useful and, dare I say, positive sense of the ongoing interaction with the canon or 'repertoire' that we constantly grapple with at the heart of the adaptation debate.[37] It is helpful, I think, to talk in terms of Shakespearian adaptations as 'dynamic repairs' of the 'repertoire', as Sennett does of adaptations and updates more generally in *The Craftsman*.[38] Interventions, sometimes playful, sometimes critical, sometimes both in parallel, are explored by Sennett in a range of fields and domains; and he places genuine emphasis in his arguments on the importance of experience, of improvisation and of play, as well as noting the importance of anticipation and revision in crafting.[39] Craft is creative, then; and adaptation is craft. We are attending in all of these observations to a heightened consciousness in our own cultural moment of the power of the network and of collaborative co-production: this reflects, as already noted, moves in early modern scholarship and repertory studies more generally when thinking about Shakespeare and contemporaries; but it is also, for me, a way of thinking about and analysing modern and post-modern modes of creativities in relation to Shakespeare and the canon.

In his study of the inherent creativity of everyday discourse, Ronald Carter argues that repetition can in itself be a creative act and suggests that 'creativity [can] be at the same time both an exceptional and an ubiquitous phenomenon'.[40] This finds immediate consonance with Salter's observation that it is a strange mix of the 'mundane' and the 'exceptional' that seems most conducive to acts of cultural creativity.[41] The tangled discussion of 'value' and 'worth' that seems to cluster around debates about Shakespeare remediated in the popular cultural context may be worth re-examining from this perspective. Carter suggests that there are rules and criteria in all of these relationships even when the creative and adaptational responses appear to take place in the most free-form and unstructured ways: 'creativity must not go too far, and must not deviate too far from accepted norms. The creative artist or thinker [or indeed open-source programmer?]

---

[34] Sennett, *The Craftsman*, p. 24. See also Katherine Rowe's stimulating 'Shakespeare and Media History', in Margreta de Grazia and Stanley Wells, eds., *The Cambridge Companion to Shakespeare* (Cambridge, 2010), pp. 302–24, which shares, in its exploration of the power and potential of remediations, many of the central tenets of this article. 'Over the past decades', Rowe claims, 'changes both within and outside the field of Shakespeare studies have reframed the phenomenon of adaptation as the normative way that Shakespeare's works have been transmitted' (p. 304).

[35] Sennett, *The Craftsman*, p. 26.

[36] Ronald Carter, *Language and Creativity: The Art of Common Talk* (London and New York, 2004).

[37] Sennett, *The Craftsman*, p. 126. 'Repertoire' is Jonathan Bate's preferred term in his recent *English Literature: A Short Introduction* (Oxford, 2010) and is particularly instructive when applied to a largely dramatic oeuvre such as Shakespeare's.

[38] Sennett, *The Craftsman*, p. 194.

[39] Sennett, *The Craftsman*, p. 269. See also Pat Kane's review which picks up on the theme of play: 'Play and Craft: Review of Richard Sennett's *The Craftsman*', *Scottish Review of Books*, 4 (2008), reproduced in full in *The Play Ethic: Exploring the Power and Potential of Play in Web/Tech Organisations and Pop Culture* www.theplayethic.com/2008/05/play-and-craft.html, accessed 17 October 2010.

[40] Carter, *Language and Creativity*, pp. 3, 10.

[41] Salter, *Cultural Creativity*, p. 47.

must respect though not necessarily conform to the norms, the canons or the received views which operate at any one time within the communities which respond to or are affected by the creative output.'[42] For Carter, invention builds on existing knowledge; it is not solely promulgated by the individual genius but is consciously made. Non-Western models of creativity, he argues, offer one crucial corrective but Carter also recognizes considerable interdisciplinary potential in the application of systems perspectives. He alludes, in particular, to the work of psychologists in terms that seem remarkably similar to those in which performance studies specialists referred to participatory practice in the wake of Boal: 'What we call creativity is a phenomenon that is constructed through an interaction between producers and audience.'[43] Creativity is seen as essentially dialogic; in a productive sense this takes us back to the dramaturgic form of those duets and dialogues in the *Love's Fire* collection; or, indeed, full circle to the shared aesthetic of the performance co-productions with which I began this article. Mastery of a domain is argued for by many of the theorists I have cited here as essential to creativity; is that why we keep making the case for teaching Shakespeare but also increasingly for teaching Shakespeare in a creative and receptive (and, dare I suggest, adaptational and transformative?) context?[44]

CONCLUSION

In thinking through the theories of craft and creativity promulgated by Sennett, Carter, Salter, Harold and others, but also the moves of the open-source initiative more generally, I am trying to think about ways that adaptation studies, and Shakespearian studies in particular, might and, perhaps, *should* respond to new ideas and thinking about the power of the network; about the potential for creativity and play in all of these spheres and also for dynamic work and good citizenship. To that end, a quotation included as an epigraph in Carter's *Language and Creativity* has haunted my consciousness as I wrote this article: it derives from a work of sociology on the ways in which young people

remake the world around them, its objects, spaces, and texts. It acknowledges the play and 'extraordinary creativity' inherent in these actions but also the 'desperate work in their play'.

We are thinking of the extraordinary creativity of the multitude of ways in which young people use, humanize, decorate, and invest with meanings their common and immediate life space and social practice – personal styles and choice of clothes, selective and active use of music, television, magazines, decoration of bedrooms; the rituals of romance and subcultural styles; the style, banter and drama of friendship groups, music-making and dance. There is work, even desperate work in their play.[45]

This notion of 'desperate work' is one that is entirely applicable to the world of 'Shakespeare studies' today, beset as it is by cuts to higher education funding and state-supported art in the wake of the global financial crisis. But the notion too of the endless reinventions and attendant riches of youth culture is equally relevant to the 'Shakespeare' we currently find being adapted and remediated in all kinds of personal spaces, both material and virtual. This context of common culture and creative space (and its humanizing possibilities) is something in which, I believe, Shakespeare's *Sonnets* prove both the most exciting and the most robust of raw

---

42 Carter, *Language and Creativity*, p. 40.
43 Carter, *Language and Creativity*, p. 30. See, for example, Mihaly Csikszentmihalyi, 'Implications of a Systems Perspective for the Study of Creativity', in R. J. Sternberg, ed., *Handbook of Creativity* (Cambridge, 1999), pp. 313–35; p. 313.
44 Teaching contexts are themselves rich raw material for Shakespeare adaptation. Numerous UK and US lesson plans involve the remaking of Shakespearian sonnets. A mediated example of this practice which will be familiar to many appears in the 1999 film *10 Things I Hate About You* directed by Gil Junger and itself a loose adaptation of *The Taming of the Shrew*. There we witness Julia Stiles as Kat Stratford re-winning Heath Ledger/Patrick Verona's love through her sonnet homework, performed through a mist of adolescent tears at the front of the classroom.
45 P. Willis *et al.*, *Common Culture: Symbolic Work at Play in the Everyday Cultures of the Young* (Buckingham, 1990); cited in Carter, *Language and Creativity*, p. 1.

materials, partly because they have as a form always been open to reinterpretation and remaking.

Catalyst and cipher; craft and creativity: it might be argued that I am falsely utopian in the account I offer here of the potential for creativity and for play in the myriad (monitored and unmonitored, facilitated and free-form) responses to Shakespeare that can be found in mediums and contexts as diverse as the school classroom, on YouTube, in graphic novels or on fan-sites, in academic monographs and on the commercial stage, shuffled on an iPod or as part of a Google mashup. These are all, I would maintain, 'Shakespeares' and it remains for us as attentive scholars and teachers to attend to the cultural contexts that not only make them possible but which are in part created and fostered by them. Even more so, these are all sources and resources of 'pleasure'. To say that is not to decry the value of serious and rigorous study of Shakespeare and the early modern context; it is, however, to suggest that in allowing for the pleasure found in one domain, we might find a valuable point of entry by which to introduce the user-makers of these remediated Shakespeares to the cultural creativities and open-source initiatives of the past.

'A STAGE OF THE MIND': *HAMLET* ON POST-WAR BRITISH RADIO

SUSANNE GREENHALGH

Writing in July 1949, after a week of 'Hamlet mania' on the BBC's Third Programme, the radio drama critic of *The Listener* was led to wonder whether 'Hamlet, as social and psychic portent, has come home to roost in our day and age'.[1] He was responding not only to the quirks of one programme's scheduling, but to the way in which *Hamlet* had come to be widely acknowledged, as a *Times* editorial put it, as 'the Play of Plays' in Britain in the years during and immediately after World War II.

Played 'cut' or played 'whole', played in the corrupt text of the First Quarto, played with scenes transferred or with its archaisms cruelly modernized, its hold on the public imagination is seemingly unshakeable. It remains the one English classic which the modern man is confident he would recognize and enjoy in whatever outlandish convention it was played.[2]

What is significant here is the emphasis on the reordering of the play, whether by 'scenes transferred' or 'outlandish convention', together with the confidence that, such is its intrinsic and enduring modernity, some essence of *Hamlet* will survive to be recognized and enjoyed by a contemporary mass audience.

If *Hamlet* was now to be viewed as a site of infinite adaptation, a modernist text in process rather than inviolable holy writ, the medium of radio had played a significant role in this new conceptualization. When sound broadcasting first developed across the world in the 1920s, it was regarded primarily as a means to relay and comment on events, performances and subject matter produced by pre-existing cultural institutions such as theatre, publishing and the cinema. However, radio practitioners almost immediately began to explore the possibilities for original sound-based art forms and genres, in ways that often aligned it with modernist ethics and aesthetics.[3] Radio held out the promise of a new type of drama, no longer tied to the history and conventions of theatre but capable of evolving its own styles of fluid, intimate dramaturgy and internalized modes of performance to create a 'stage of the mind'.[4] Shakespeare's appeal to an audience's 'imaginary forces' in the opening Chorus speech of *Henry V* was often invoked as an analogy to support radio's claim to make 'better pictures' than theatre. However, there are also specific obstacles that radio adaptation must overcome, notably the need to find aural equivalents, such as sound effects or narration, for visual aspects of the original play, and the avoidance of too many characters in a scene, since radio has only a few means of focalizing a speaker compared with the resources of theatre, film and television. Both of these potential problems, together with the assumption that

---

[1] Philip Hope-Wallace, 'Touching the Lord Hamlet', *The Listener*, 7 July 1949, 395.

[2] 'The Play of Plays' (anonymous editorial), *The Times*, 7 January 1949, 5.

[3] On BBC radio as a modernist medium see Todd Avery, *Radio Modernism: Literature, Ethics and the BBC, 1922–1938* (Aldershot and Burlington, 2006) and Angela Frattarola, 'The Modernist "Microphone Play": Listening in the Dark to the BBC', *Modern Drama*, 52 (2009), 449–68.

[4] Herbert Read, 'Sotto Voce – A Plea for Intimacy', *BBC Quarterly*, 4 (1949), 5.

listeners can only hold concentration for set periods of time, mean that most radio productions of Shakespeare have been radically cut or rearranged, while a variety of techniques such as distance from the microphone, use of echo chambers, multiple studios and 'radiophonic' sound effects have been employed to clarify, reinterpret and intensify the aural experience of the plays. In short, radio has been arguably the most adaptive of mediums, one in which the listener subjectively creates the *Hamlet* that she hears.

Marjorie Garber has recently added the 'volatile period of the thirties' to that of World War I as important moments in the scholarly and cultural investigation of *Hamlet*.[5] She draws attention in particular to the inter-war and wartime 'context of spies, counter-espionage, code-breaking, learned textual scholars' in which the play was reread and reinterpreted. If *Hamlet* came to be perceived as a type of fascinating Enigma machine, wartime experience of the mental and emotional cost paid by those forced to take arms perhaps further sharpened its post-war relevance. A *Hamlet*-focused 'culture of adaptation' continued in Britain in the late 1940s, discernible also in theatre and academe, but most visible and distinctive in the work produced by the BBC's recently inaugurated Third Programme. While this post-war 'culture' produced a number of reinterpretations and reinventions of the play itself, in the form both of performances and talks by scholars and writers, its most striking feature was the body of *Hamlet*-derived works produced as radio features, an innovative and uniquely radiogenic genre which was already associated with artistic quality and originality. The play inspired a range of programming which was used to hold a mirror up to the new Programme's institutional, intellectual and artistic development and ambitions, in ways, as I have argued elsewhere, that characterized the BBC's relationship with Shakespeare from its earliest days.[6] The authors and producers of the Third (who were often one and the same) took this process still further. Their use of, and interest in, *Hamlet*, was not simply interpretative but doubly adaptive, since the play was typically used as a source of new writing. By embracing the

emergent intellectual awareness and acceptance of an endlessly rewritable and extendable *Hamlet*, the Third's programme-makers created a model of, and justification for, their own experimental but intrinsically elitist cultural agenda and its productions.[7]

'C' FOR CULTURE: THE THIRD PROGRAMME

The BBC had had a 'good war' in many respects. Its news coverage and varied entertainment programming had come to be broadly recognized as a national lifeline in stormy times, but it was also open to the charge that its embrace of wartime austerity measures had damaged the quality and cultural reach of its content, subsumed to the political demands of the time. In 1939 the pre-war National and Regional services had been combined into the 'mixed programming' Home Service, and the Forces Programme (General Forces Programme after America entered the war) was introduced, providing mainly popular music and light entertainment, and quickly becoming mainstream

---

5 'A Tale of Three *Hamlets* or Repetition and Revenge', *Shakespeare Quarterly*, 61 (2010), 28–55; p. 45.
6 Susanne Greenhalgh, 'Shakespeare Overheard: Performances, Adaptations and Citations on Radio', in Robert Shaughnessy, ed., *The Cambridge Companion to Shakespeare and Popular Culture* (Cambridge, 2006), pp. 175–98.
7 Other *Hamlet*-related Third programmes in these years included the Closet Scene (3.4) performed in English and French with Alec Guinness and Jean-Louis Barrault as Hamlet (23 March 1947), and an extended version of this programme, augmented by a performance in Spanish, in which Augustin Sire played the Prince (11 July 1947). There were readings of translations by Salvador de Madariaga and Wilhelm von Schlegel ('The Original and the Translation', 20 and 23 March 1947), as well as a number of talks by writers and academics such as Ormerod Greenwood, T. S. Gregory, André Gide, C. V. Wedgwood, Henry Reed and John Bamborough. The opening of 1949 saw a one-act version of the Scylla and Charybdis sequence from James Joyce's *The Second-Best Bed: A Usyless Discussion on Hamlet or Hamnet* (1 January 1949). This had been part of planning for a full-scale dramatization of *Ulysses* which never got made. In 1950 there was a feature exploring the meaning of Ophelia's words 'They say the owl was a baker's daughter' (4.5), in the setting of a university Senior Common Room (25 April 1950).

listening. Planning for the post-war period focused on reorganizing and augmenting the BBC's provision by creating a third Programme, code-named 'C' for Culture, which would provide for those who desired more sustaining fare. As a *Times* leader noted,

[t]he B.B.C. have given some ground for complaint that, from the beginning of the war, they allowed their policy to be guided by an unnecessarily low estimate of the public taste – a taste that they themselves in earlier years did decisive work to educate . . . a return to the high standards of initiative and responsibility which marked the first stages of the B.B.C.'s career – had to be attempted . . . The institution of 'programme C' can be made an occasion of all-round revival, and, with concerted and tactful handling of the three programmes as an inter-related scheme, it should be possible to stimulate an appetite that will not be satisfied in any field with anything short of the best.[8]

The new Programme would occupy a modest proportion of the available broadcasting hours, transmitting only between the hours of 6.00 and 11.50 p.m. It would contain no news coverage but encourage thoughtful and informed journalistic discussions and talks. It would have a flexible schedule, allowing it to produce long, virtually uncut, plays, operas or concerts. More use of improved recording technologies would decrease previous BBC emphasis on live broadcasts and thus improve broadcast quality through effective editing. It would have a deliberately internationalist outlook, as part of a commitment to peaceful post-war foreign relations. Most importantly of all, the Programme would be conceived of and developed as a minority service (its daily audience in practice generally totalling around 2 million), unashamedly concentrated on artistic and intellectual matters. As the BBC's Director-General, William Hayley, wrote in the *Radio Times* introduction to the new Programme, it was intended for the 'alert and receptive listener . . . willing to first of all make an effort in selection and then to meet the performer half-way by giving his whole attention to what is being broadcast'. It would demand 'a breadth of sympathy, a readiness to try new things',[9] and an audience which would enjoy itself

'without crutches . . . and satisfy its desire for knowledge without a primer'.[10] Thus the Third opened on 29 September 1946 with a schedule that included a satirical feature programme called 'How to Listen' (complete with some mock-Shakespearian lines), and a performance of Bach's Goldberg Variations.[11]

The immediate post-war period was one of great economic and material hardship for Britain. In early 1947 a severe winter combined with fuel shortages led to widespread power cuts and energy rationing, and the Third – evidently judged an expendable luxury – was ordered off air for two weeks by the government. A few months later, however, *The Times* concluded optimistically that the service had indeed confirmed 'the existence of a great and largely unsatisfied appetite for culture in almost all its forms' and 'the programme itself had combined high seriousness with adventure', proving that radio was 'an invention that ought to be as important for thought and education as the discovery of printing'.[12]

The Third's most innovative and distinctive radio genre was the Feature, a blend of documentary and literary writing, which had reached maturity during the war years, when it had been co-opted for propaganda as well as artistic purposes. Frequently the creation of author-producers, the Feature was

---

8 'C for Culture' (anonymous editorial), *The Times*, 20 September 1946, 5.

9 William Hayley, 'Breaking New Ground in Radio', *Supplement to the Radio Times*, 26 November 1946, i.

10 George R. Barnes, 'Breaking New Ground', i.

11 See www.bbc.co.uk/radio3/classical/thirdprogramme/gallery/gallery.shtml?1 for a PDF of the *Radio Times* for the Third's opening week, and www.bbc.co.uk/radio3/classical/thirdprogramme/introduction.shtml for a recording of the Director General's Introductory Talk describing the rationale for the new Programme and its programming policy. As part of its 60th anniversary celebrations in 2006 the BBC also broadcast a revised version of the original 'How to Listen' programme (Radio 4, 29 September 2006). The 'How to' programmes were written by Stephen Potter, a former university lecturer and critic, often in collaboration with Joyce Grenfell, and included 'How to Appreciate Shakespeare' (Third, 20 April 1947).

12 'Advance on the Air' (anonymous editorial), *The Times*, 7 April 1947, 5.

increasingly regarded as 'a new hybrid art form specific to radio, which would be most able simultaneously and harmoniously to fulfil the three requirements of the BBC Charter',[13] to inform, educate and entertain. At its most serious and experimental such programming aspired to create what has been called 'the Great Music of audio': a montage of 'Ordinary talk of ordinary people; poetry; prose fiction; folk-song; historical documents; natural sound; "art music"; radiophonic sound; the reflection and analysis of the learned; drama; the expertise of actors, instrumentalists, singers; radiophonically treated speech. All these things can be orchestrated to create a "new sound" which is something more than all its components taken separately.'[14] For one of its most devoted adherents, the modernist poet, novelist and radio producer Rayner Heppenstall, the Feature was not only 'the womb of radio' but a 'vast and uncharted territory' in which lay 'all the remaining possibilities of creative broadcasting'.[15] Whereas the Drama Department, under the direction of John Gielgud's brother, Val, had concentrated mainly on the adaptation of stage-plays, especially the classics, the Features Department devoted itself to new writing and experiment with genre, especially the blending of factual content with innovative form. Its work also drew on, and was often accompanied by, critical or scholarly apparatus in the form of talks by academics, their involvement as writers or consultants on programmes, and articles on the programmes by the producers or writers in publications such as Radio Times or The Listener. In this sense BBC staff members were clearly an increasingly influential part of the class of professional readers and rewriters examined by André Lefevere: simultaneously patrons, providers and consumers in the process of literary translation, and thus important manipulators of literary fame and audience expectation.[16]

HAMLETS FOR THE 'CIVILIZED EAR'

The cluster of Hamlet features on the Third must also be viewed in relation to the broader ways in which the play and its associations circulated in contemporary Britain, confirmation of its canonicity, adaptability and topicality. These in turn might be the subject of radio news coverage or discussion by arts review programmes. The accumulation of varied stage versions starring some of the leading actors of the day played an important part in creating the broader cultural context in which this work emerged; as did the growing body of semi-popular, publicly debated and theatrically influential critical works on the play, such as John Dover Wilson's What Happens in Hamlet and Ernest Jones's Hamlet and Oedipus.[17] In 1942 Sadler's Wells had premièred Robert Helpmann's one-act ballet version in which he also danced the prince. The long list of stage Hamlets includes several other wartime performances, notably in 1944 when Helpmann played the role for the Old Vic Company, John Byron starred at the Memorial Theatre, Stratford-upon-Avon, and John Gielgud essayed it for the fourth time at the Haymarket, an acclaimed performance which featured briefly in Humphrey Jennings's documentary A Diary for Timothy, made for the Crown Film Unit in 1945, and in turn influenced the production Gielgud toured to military bases in the Far East at the end of the war. In America the British-born actor Maurice Evans created and starred in a two-hour 'GI' version for military audiences which later played on Broadway. In 1945 Alec Clunes took the role at the Arts Theatre, and Donald Wolfit starred in a touring production, while in 1948 Helpmann and Paul Scofield alternated the role at Stratford-upon-Avon, joined

[13] Kate Whitehead, The Third Programme: A Literary History (Oxford, 1989), p. 111.

[14] Michael Mason, The Listener, 18 November 1971, quoted in David Hendy, Life on Air: A History of Radio 4 (Oxford, 2007), pp. 64–5.

[15] Rayner Heppenstall, ed., Imaginary Conversations: Eight Scripts of the Broadcasts in the Third Programme (London, 1948), p. 11.

[16] André Lefevere, Translation, Rewriting and the Manipulation of Literary Fame (London, 1992).

[17] John Dover Wilson, What Happens in 'Hamlet' (Cambridge, 1935; 2nd edn, 1937; 3rd edn, 1951), Ernest Jones, Hamlet and Oedipus (New York and London, 1949).

by Robert Eddison (Bristol Old Vic Company), Jean-Louis Barrault (Edinburgh Festival) and the Oxford University Players, who presented a 'political' version of the First Quarto *Hamlet*, directed by a young Kenneth Tynan. On radio, even during the war years, when much of BBC drama production was relocated outside London (and after a false start when Shakespeare and other classics were considered too 'serious' for the times) there was a fairly regular flow of abbreviated Shakespeare broadcasts, in which *Hamlet* featured, including a 1940 production starring John Gielgud, Celia Johnson and Emlyn Williams; and a series of half-hour programmes called 'Shakespeare's Characters' for the General Forces Service, 1944–5, adapted by Herbert Farjeon. Once the war ended two major productions followed in quick succession. Howard Rose directed the Canadian actor Barry Morse in a *World Theatre* production for the Home Service in April 1946. On screen the newly reopened television service provided the first visual broadcast of the play a year later, produced in two parts by the veteran George More O'Ferrall and directed by Basil Adams, with John Byron reprising his Stratford role as the prince (BBC, 7 and 14 December 1947) in an interpretation that emphasized the religious aspects of the play.

Another vital ingredient was Laurence Olivier's film of the play, which had its royal première on 6 May 1948, and dominated news coverage for months before and after its release, especially following its success in America and five awards, including Best Film, in the 1949 Academy Awards. Several of the radio spin-offs produced by the Third Programme in these years deliberately engaged with, challenged or elaborated on the implications of Olivier's film, especially its psychologizing interpretation, which, as Julie Sanders points out, is a central reason for the play's status in the twentieth-century literary canon, as an 'exploration of a mind in crisis',[18] together with the possibilities or dangers represented by the film's mass media representation of Shakespeare. In so doing these spin-offs not only responded to the play's focus on the necessity and cost of violent action in ways suited to a post-war society but also became expressions of

the internal conflicts and public debate concerning the nature and size of audience for the new cultural formation that was the Third Programme. While these *Hamlet* retellings implicitly mounted a defence of the BBC's cultural agenda regarding the new Programme, as well as asserting the play's relevance to the cultural moment, they also hinted at fissures that would lead eventually to the Third's slow transition from a speech-centred station to its current focus, as Radio 3, on classical music.

The return of television broadcasting after wartime closure did not yet pose any threat to radio's primacy but the newer medium was attracting increased public interest, however small its actual audience, and there was a felt need to answer with flagship radio productions. On Boxing Day 1948 John Gielgud starred once again in a three and a half hour production adapted by M. R. Ridley, a transmission which proved so popular that it was repeated by public demand on New Year's Eve.[19] All the *Hamlet*-related programmes on the Third in the next few years would in some sense be in dialogue with this 'entirety' production. Broadcast at the end of the year which had seen the release of Olivier's film, the radio version's austere, subtle, yet also glintingly witty and densely textured rendering of the play could also be viewed as a deliberate answer to the artistic and institutional 'butchery' represented by both the celluloid and televisual *Hamlets*.[20]

To come to the Third Programme *Hamlet* was like hearing Bertrand Russell after a week of Christmas card mottoes; and how pleasant at the end of a year marked by vulgarizations of the great play to find a performance which was, in the cardinal respect, aristocratic.[21]

---

[18] Julie Sanders, *Adaptation and Appropriation* (London, 2006), p. 54. See also Richard Halpern, *Shakespeare among the Moderns* (Ithaca, 1997).

[19] There is a recording of the live broadcast on CD from Naxos NA341712, and a transcript is available in the Shakespeare Collection of the Birmingham Public Library.

[20] Philip Hope-Wallace, 'First Steps in Butchery', *The Listener*, 13 May 1948, 795.

[21] Philip Hope-Wallace, 'Uncle, Uncle!', *The Listener*, 30 December 1948, 1024.

Whereas Olivier's film aroused controversy through the extent of its cuts and textual modifications, Ridley's scholarly adaptation limited itself to the tweaking of obscure references (the 'little eyases' went), and the removal or replacement of words to clarify meaning. Occasional internal trimming of some speeches was more than balanced by additions from the Second Quarto, such as the 'How all occasions do inform against me' soliloquy. An 'austerity' product of a war-worn, still rationed society, the radio play's edgy, morally troubled atmosphere arguably reflected the after-effects of battle and the emerging realities of cold-war politics in a way that Olivier and his text consultant Alan Dent deliberately excluded from their film by omitting Fortinbras and other political scenes, turning the Prince into an introspective Freudian case-study of a man who could not make up his mind in a *mise-en-scène* designed to evoke the labyrinthine workings of the unconscious. Having corresponded acerbically with Alan Dent in the *Times* letter pages about the film's cuts, and referred disparagingly to the film in his radio reviews in *The Listener*, Philip Hope-Wallace was prompted to identify as a 'cardinal problem of our time' the need 'to determine how far you are entitled to adulterate the caviare to make it palatable to the million'.[22] He thus gave voice to the institutional dilemma which confronted the Third from its postwar launch: should it proceed on the assumption that 'the Third Programme listeners know their "Hamlet" well enough to need announcer's asides as little as musicians need to be told "now back to the minor"', or accept that 'for the honour of radio as an art' it needed to assist audiences in peace-time as well as war, by simplifying, cutting, adding explanatory narrative, in short providing 'crutches' for an audience of novice, but aspiring, Shakespearian listeners?[23] The Hope-Wallace/Dent correspondence prompted a *Times* editorial on the pros and cons of cutting, and the desirability (or otherwise) of film adaptations of Shakespeare, concluding 'we are invited to believe that there is no way of commending the major plays of SHAKESPEARE to the millions except by thus shocking civilized ears'.[24] The battle lines had been drawn:

how far could the other mass medium, radio, find a way to deliver *Hamlet* (standing in for any great classic) to a mass audience, in ways that probed the limits of adaptation and innovation but did not attract condemnation as a distortion or dissolution of the original?[25]

Although broadcasting for only six hours a day, the Third required plenty of content, in the form of talks, discussion programmes, drama and features, and, like the burlesques and parodies of the commercial theatre, it inevitably fed off the public awareness of *Hamlet* that characterized these years. While its terms of address remained overtly highbrow, the Programme was also liable to occasional bouts of cultural subversion which inevitably involved it with more popular cultural modes, particularly film and detective fiction. Indeed, in some respects the Third's interest in *Hamlet* could be considered a form of serious-minded Shakespeare 'fan fiction'. Douglas Lanier's list of the modes to be found in modern versions of this genre is

22 Hope-Wallace, 'First Steps in Butchery', 795.
23 Philip Hope-Wallace, 'Sea of Troubles', *The Listener*, 6 May 1948, 756.
24 'Alas, Poor Hamlet!' (anonymous editorial), *The Times*, 12 May 1948, 5. The Leader writer concluded that 'the Shakespearian can only echo the compliment addressed by the Greek scholar to MR. POPE: "A very pretty film, Sir Laurence, but you must not call it Shakespeare".'
25 All these versions of the play – especially Olivier's film – inevitably produced a spate of spin-offs, skits, burlesques and pastiches, which themselves testify to the familiarity with the play and its adaptations at the time, and which reached a peak in 1948. That year saw a comedy review, 'Green Room Rag' at the Saville Theatre in June which featured a 'conversation between Hamlet and Henry V' that 'rendered very ludicrously the possible feelings of the chief Shakespearian gentlemen yet to reach the screen'; a musical, *The Kid from Stratford*, about the discovery of a musical comedy written by Shakespeare while he was recovering from an illness, starred the diminutive comedian Arthur Askey in a scene that caricatured Hamlet. See 'The Theatres', *The Times*, 27 September, 1948, 6. At the Palladium there was a Christmas confection for children, based on Richmal Crompton's *Just William* book series, which featured preparations for a charity performance of *Hamlet* (December 1948). Even the compilers of the *Times* crossword responded to the *Hamlet* buzz by regularly including clues which demanded detailed knowledge of the play.

therefore helpful in categorizing the different types of spin-offs to be found in the Third's *Hamlet* programming. Lanier identifies six modes in all: *extrapolations* build from 'events mentioned but not developed in the "master narrative"' to fill in 'gaps of motive or event', or extend the plot line or motive in a new narrative direction; *interpolations* dovetail new material with the plot of the source; *remotivations* leave plot or situation unchanged but alter the characters' motives; *revisions* take the original characters and situation but change the plot; *reorientations* turn the viewpoint of the narrative in a new direction, similar to what Julie Sanders calls *transfocalization*;[26] and *hybrid narratives* combine narrative elements or characters from two or more Shakespearian sources.[27] This last category also points to another significant aspect of the Third's reworkings of *Hamlet* – the employment of hybrid writing genres and the ways in which writing itself is reflected on in several of the pieces.

It is no accident therefore that several of the *Hamlet* spin-offs were produced for a series grounded in genre experimentation. *Imaginary Conversations*, initiated by the novelist Eric Linklater, was a fluid and indeed novelistic radio format, in which historical characters engaged in debate in ways that illuminated the ideas or literary achievement for which they were known. Based on William Savage Landor's dialogues (which Heppenstall termed 'the first historical feature-scripts'[28]), this 'minor *genre*'[29] was dismissed as 'literary whimsy' by some, while others pointed out its similarity to earlier works such as Maurice Morgann's *Essay on the Dramatic Character of Sir John Falstaff* (1777).[30] It had 'no fixed convention', but was designed to 'convey the thinking and emotions of their chosen subjects and to present them through their living voice'.[31] The series was developed further by Heppenstall, who deliberately commissioned writers who were not playwrights. Though the scripts had clear dramatic features they were not considered plays: indeed Heppenstall labelled them as 'tales' in the second collection of published scripts he edited. In the first full year of the Third's existence he commissioned the novelist

and critic G. W. Stonier to explore the reasons for Ophelia's madness as part of a 'Shakespeare birthday week' season (24 April 1947), a broadcast preceded by Herbert Read's 'extrapolation' *Thieves of Mercy* (20 April), which explored what might have happened to Hamlet while captured by pirates, to portray a thinking man's transformation into a fighter – an experience no doubt familiar to many of its recently demobbed audience. The piece, which Read referred to as a play,[32] was spoken by a Reader (Cecil Trouncer) and the characters of Hamlet (Cyril Cusack) and the Pirate Captain (John Laurie), but remained within the bounds of the genre as originally envisaged. Heppenstall described it as 'a talk illustrated by two fragments of dialogue',[33] and the Reader's lines could just as well have formed the basis for one of the frequent speculative talks by critics on similar subjects. The transition into the 'reconstruction' of the missing scene is deliberately ironic, even parodic.

But how proceed? Would you, dear Listener, take seriously a scene which Shakespeare should have written, in words to match his own? Our vanity is not so enormous. We might, of course, attempt a period sea-piece, something in this manner...

[*There is a melodramatic burst of music from Tschaikovsky's* [sic] *"Hamlet" Overture. Out of this emerge sounds of sea-wash, creaking yards, gunfire, the crash of two ships grappling, wild shouts and the clatter of cutlasses.*][34]

As the Reader comments, this is a 'radio version of Ercles' vein', unsuited to a Third Programme

---

26 Sanders, *Adaptation and Appropriation*, pp. 48–9.
27 Douglas Lanier, *Shakespeare and Modern Popular Culture* (Oxford, 2002), p. 83.
28 Heppenstall, *Imaginary Conversations*, p. 14.
29 Heppenstall, *Imaginary Conversations*, p. 15.
30 See Michael Innes, 'Discoveries in Shakespeare', *Radio Times*, 27 March 1953, 8.
31 Douglas Cleverdon, 'The Art of Radio in Britain', unpublished monograph for UNESCO, cited in Ian Rodger, *Radio Drama* (London, 1982), p. 81.
32 Herbert Read, *Thieves of Mercy*, in Heppenstall, *Imaginary Conversations*, p. 100.
33 Read, *Thieves of Mercy*, in Heppenstall, *Imaginary Conversations*, p. 98.
34 Read, in Heppenstall, *Imaginary Conversations*, p. 102.

Hamlet, since the 'mythical hero of our modern consciousness, might well speak in our own language, and use words and handle concepts which would be strange to Shakespeare's ear'.[35] The concepts Hamlet comes to handle in the rest of the 'featurette' (its running time was thirty minutes) amount to existentialism, culminating in his seizing on the Captain's man-of-action philosophy, as expressed in the line, 'To do or not to do, that is the only question' as a means of putting conscience aside to become 'bloody-minded'[36] and take on the task of revenge. As the Reader concludes, with a wry acknowledgement of wartime demands and their aftermath, 'the most merciful gift would have been the gift of a free mind, which is not a mind free of responsibilities, but a mind ruled by them, and freely active in their discharge'.[37]

Stonier's portrayal of an Ophelia slipping away into madness in a soundscape of endless corridors and spiral staircases was much closer to drama, taking the 'Conversation' format in a new direction and becoming 'almost a self-contained play',[38] one which drew on cinematic rather than theatrical or philosophical models and, unlike Read's piece, probed a feminine 'mind in crisis'. In Lanier's terms it is a blend of extrapolation and refocalization, imagining scenes absent from the play which might account for Ophelia's madness and suicide. While the musical references and sound effects in *Thieves of Mercy* were used ironically, in *Ophelia* they were part of an attempt to create an aural equivalent for the female psychological disturbance portrayed in certain films of the period, such as Alfred Hitchcock's thriller *The Spiral Staircase* (1946) and, of course, Olivier's *Hamlet*, which Stonier's work preceded. It had an elaborate musical score by Elizabeth Lutyens (who later composed music for several Hammer Horror films), and featured 'an almost intolerably high-pitched chord'[39] played alternately on violins and organ as leitmotif for Ophelia's state of mind. It aimed at an 'atmospheric' effect,[40] which created a vertiginous Elsinore that echoed Ophelia's fall into madness through sound and dialogue alone: 'round and round, round and round, tenebrously, like a sweep's brat in a chimney: shall we never reach starlight?'[41] Thus Ophelia follows Hamlet as he drags the body of Polonius to the attic up a spiral staircase in the dark, and the moment when her touch identifies her father's corpse becomes one of almost Gothic terror. In the central scene, before escaping from her room to find him, she is discovered writing her own account of Shakespeare's play-scene, in a letter to her brother Laertes, her monologue interrupted from time to time by the sounds of the search for Hamlet getting closer: 'How can I write it? But I must, I must.'[42] The act of writing thus becomes identified with Ophelia's struggle to keep sane and ultimately to be in control of her own story. The sequence of knockings, and the search of her room during which a music stand is broken, also seem designed as deliberately 'filmic' touches, echoing thriller sequences of wartime police raids and heightening the sense of a world ruled by masculine brutality. In the end this is no feminist re-visioning, however. Ophelia remains a victim, in awe of the domineering men who make use of her or ignore her, and Horatio's concluding speech describes a moment in which she might have spoken further but instead continues to her watery death, which is evoked in terms that recall paintings by Pre-Raphaelite artists. Stonier's spin-off ultimately remains bound within the limits of the play, and ends at the point of Ophelia's disappearance, but it has the power to change the perspective from which Shakespeare's *Hamlet* is seen, not least by its citation of popular filmic elements. Effectively it does not simply 'fill in gaps of motive or event' but *reorientates* the play by foregrounding Ophelia's, rather than Hamlet's, psychological state. As one listener reportedly wrote, 'henceforward she would always

35 Read, in Heppenstall, *Imaginary Conversations*, p. 103.
36 Read, in Heppenstall, *Imaginary Conversations*, p. 109.
37 Read, in Heppenstall, *Imaginary Conversations*, p. 110.
38 G. W. Stonier, *Ophelia*, in Heppenstall, *Imaginary Conversations*, p. 110.
39 Heppenstall, 'Producer's Note', in Heppenstall, *Imaginary Conversations*, p. 112.
40 Heppenstall, 'Producer's Note', p. 113.
41 Stonier, in Heppenstall, *Imaginary Conversations*, p. 126.
42 Stonier, in Heppenstall, *Imaginary Conversations*, p. 120.

feel that Shakespeare's *Hamlet* contained these scenes'.[43]

The following year there were several more *Hamlet*-related broadcasts, notably *The Hawk and the Handsaw* (19 November 1948) for the second series of *Imaginary Conversations*, directed by Heppenstall and written by the academic J. I. M. Stewart under his crime-writer pseudonym, Michael Innes.[44] This put Hamlet in the psychiatrist's chair to confront him with some of the fashionable psychoanalytically tinged critical interpretations current at the time and popularized in Olivier's film. Ruby Cohn, presumably taking her cue from the title of the edited collection in which it was published, *Three Tales of Hamlet*, classifies it as 'fiction', and considers that, along with Heppenstall's drama *The Fool's Saga* and Innes's talk *The Mysterious Affair at Elsinore*, it trivializes the myth of Hamlet. Cohn does not appreciate the different ways in which each inflects the Feature genre, and is content to label them 'slight' in comparison to the 'offshoots' created by Joyce and other modernists, since they appear to have no political motivation.[45] It is true that Heppenstall classes them as 'entertainments' but, as he also makes clear, the two dramatic pieces were given 'extremely complicated' productions with large casts and orchestra, and contained 'really stratified' narratives.[46] Taken together with Innes's 'interlude', they constitute a striking intervention into the contemporary cultural politics of both Shakespearian interpretation and broadcast adaptation. *The Hawk and the Handsaw* is a *hybrid narrative*, since it takes the Doctor from *Macbeth* to Elsinore, forty years after the events of Shakespeare's play, and turns him into a 'Freud-cum-Jones' psychoanalyst.[47] Fortinbras is king, and Horatio appears to have taken on Polonius's job, but has not yet finished the 'chronicle' in which he will carry out his promise to tell Hamlet's story, which could stir political unrest. In the meantime the Players have arrived with Shakespeare's version, snatches of which drift up to the Doctor as he recalls his previous visit, and the consultations he had with the young prince, narrated as flashbacks. The unsurprising outcome of the analysis is a Renaissance version of the Freudian Oedipal

story as the root of Hamlet's melancholy. Hamlet's discovery of an affair between his father and the girl with whom he was childishly in love triggered off a transference of his own guilty desire for his mother and consequent hatred towards his father so that he 'saw' the murder he secretly wished to commit, his fantasy fed textually by the book *The Murder of Gonzago*, given him as a distraction from his grief. As Graham Holderness recognizes, Innes's play is thus a revisionist enterprise, which, with deliberate irony, sets out 'both to elucidate the play's mysteries and to foreground the contemporary hermeneutic context of the 1940s', especially with regard to the influence of Freudian theory.[48] Indeed Hope-Wallace considered 'the effort to create a mock-Shakespearean ambience' unnecessary since the 'new "characters" were really only interesting as mouthpieces for the theory'.[49] Innes's script certainly does not attempt the melodramatic power of Stonier's *Ophelia*. Like Read's appropriation of modish philosophy in *Thieves of Mercy*, it takes a seemingly playful approach to psychoanalytic criticism of the play, including, by implication, Stewart's own scholarly work, informed as it was by his study of psychoanalysis in Vienna as a young man.[50] However, a mood of almost Orwellian cynicism about politics is also discernible in the play's complex structure of flashbacks and constant

---

43 Heppenstall, 'Producer's Note', p. 113.
44 Heppenstall had briefly been a student of Stewart's at Leeds University. Graham Holderness discusses the play in some detail in 'Visions and Revisions: *Hamlet*', in *Textual Shakespeare: Writing and the Word* (Hatfield, 2003), pp. 178–212, but attributes authorship to Heppenstall, who directed it. The published edition makes it clear the script was Innes's. See Rayner Heppenstall and Michael Innes, *Three Tales of Hamlet* (London, 1950).
45 Ruby Cohn, *Modern Shakespeare Offshoots* (Princeton, 1976), p. 180.
46 Rayner Heppenstall, 'Dialogues of the Dead', *Radio Times*, 4 February 1949, 7.
47 J. I. M. Stewart, *Myself and Michael Innes* (London, 1987), p. 133.
48 Holderness, 'Visions and Revisions', p. 187.
49 'Suppression', *The Listener*, 25 November 1948, 819.
50 See Michael Innes, 'The Hawk and the Handsaw', *Radio Times*, 19 November 1948, 7.

juxtaposition of different retellings of the *Hamlet* story, turning it into a self-conscious reflection on the very processes and consequences of adapting and appropriating Shakespeare through the medium of radio by a writer and critic who would go on to create a body of such 'critical conversations'.[51]

Innes's *The Mysterious Affair at Elsinore: a New Investigation* (26 June) was part of the summer *Hamlet* season in 1949, broadcast as a reading by Innes himself. Although published as a 'tale' it is both a variant on the *Imaginary Conversations* format, and an ironic version of the standard Third Programme academic talk, and presents, only to discount, the case for various explanations of the events of the play and the identity of the real murderer of King Hamlet. The solution gradually becomes obvious – Fortinbras did it. Like the other *Hamlet* pieces it contains a strong element of self-reflection on the act of writing itself, this time in the vein of donnish humour about academic exegesis. Cohn appears to miss the point when she identifies the speaker as a 'solicitor'.[52] Actually, the self-presentation is that of a don-cum-detective – exactly the role fulfilled by Innes himself as academic and mystery writer. As no recording survives of any of these scripts it is impossible to know how self-mocking Innes's delivery actually was – Hope-Wallace detected 'ponderous jocularity'[53] – but it had presumably benefited from its previous presentation to the Oxford University English Society.

The final new *Hamlet* work that summer was by Heppenstall himself, apparently inspired by Innes's engagement with contemporary readings of *Hamlet* and the elaborate production given to *The Hawk and the Handsaw*. It was a version, however, not of Shakespeare's play, but of the European sources upon which he supposedly drew, and so implicitly offered itself as an imagined, newly discovered *Hamlet* Ur-Play. *The Fool's Saga – Hamlet in Scandinavia* was broadcast the day after Innes's *jeu d'esprit* (27 June) while a repeat of the Gielgud production heightened the 'Hamlet fever'. It is an historical epic, which dramatizes the Nordic story of Amleth, Prince of Denmark, as told by Saxo Grammaticus in about AD 1200, which, in a translation by François de Belleforest in his *Histoires Tragiques* (1570), may have been known to Shakespeare.[54] In this version there are four women in Amleth's life: his mother, who has conspired with her brother-in-law to kill her husband but later helps Amleth revenge, the Queen of the Picts and the Princess of the Britons, each of whom he marries, and an Ophelia figure, Thora. Although each has her own motives concerning Amleth, they also form a kind of matriarchal chorus, after his death summing up his life through their relationship with him, in counterpoint to the verdict of his soldiers who eulogize him as a warrior and leader. The script is complicated, with many shifts of location and time, from Scotland, to Denmark, to Britain, and speeches written and delivered in the appropriate dialect and accent. Although Amleth is

---

[51] *The Hawk and the Handsaw* was given a new production on the Third, with Paul Scofield as Hamlet (20 July 1951, repeated 28 March, 1959). Innes went on to write a number of other Shakespeare spin-offs for radio, including 'The Road to Dunsinane' (Third, 15 November 1950), 'Discovery of the Bermudas' (Third, 29 October 1959) and a four-part series called 'Discoveries in Shakespeare', also produced by Heppenstall. These 'dramatic episodes' (Innes, 'Discoveries', p. 8) were largely concerned with critics of Shakespeare, and consisted of 'A Visitor to Dorset Garden' (2 and 3 April 1953) which featured the characters of John Dryden, Thomas Rymer, Thomas Betterton and Charles d'Avenant [sic] at a rehearsal of *Macbeth*; 'Nemesis at Wycombe Abbey' (27 and 29 April 1953), which presented a debate between Samuel Johnson and Maurice Morgann; 'A Smack of Hamlet' (21 and 23 May 1953, repeated 28 November 1953), which dealt with Coleridge's Shakespeare lectures; and 'The Trial of Ancient Iago' (22 and 24 June 1953), which arraigned the villain of *Othello* before a court of 'critics and representative figures of various ages'. His play *The Danish Tragedy* (5 March 1958) was an attempt at recreating the possible Ur-play by Thomas Kyd, on which *Hamlet* may have been based. Stewart's autobiography, *Myself and Michael Innes* (London, 1987), pp. 138–55, contains the script for what he terms a 'featurette' entitled 'Mr. W.H.' set in Venice. This was apparently originally broadcast in 1952 under the title 'Fools of Time' and repeated as 'To Mr. W.H. All Happiness', 19 November 1958.

[52] Cohn, *Modern Shakespeare Offshoots*, p. 180.

[53] 'Touching the Lord Hamlet', *The Listener*, 7 July 1949, 39.

[54] See the Introduction to the Arden Shakespeare Third Series *Hamlet*, edited by Ann Thompson and Neil Taylor (London, 2006), for a helpful discussion of these sources.

thematically at the centre of the play the action primarily deals with the reactions of others to him and what he does, emphasizing that 'A man is worthier than a word, but the word endures.'[55] Heppenstall revises and remotivates Hamlet's story through the early sources rather than contemporary influences such as those of Dover Wilson or Ernest Jones, whose reading of the play he set out deliberately to challenge.[56] In particular, the feature highlights the processes of saga-making: how the story of Amleth is interpreted and retold, both through the different versions of his womenfolk, and, most importantly, through the characters of the three poets, who represent each of the three peoples of the British Isles – the goddess-worshipping Celts, the Romanized, semi-Christian Britons and the invading pagan Danes. The play begins and ends with the Ollave (John Laurie) interpreting runes on a shield which tell first the story of the murder of Amleth's father and, finally, Amleth's own story. In another scene the three poets watch a battle and attempt to record it, each in the conventions of his particular craft and language. *The Fool's Saga*, then, like several of the other features, foregrounds the acts of writing and retelling the story of Amleth/Hamlet, and does so in ways that remind its audience that this is a history of war, invasion and cultural change as well as psychological turmoil.

These *Hamlet*-based radio works form a temporal and interpretative 'cluster' of adaptations, in a broader culture particularly hospitable to the idea of appropriations and derivations from the play. As such they provide an intriguing multiple example of adaptation as 'its own palimpsestic thing'.[57] As Margaret Jane Kidnie points out, however, if the 'critic's goal is . . . accordingly, to trace a potential web of relations in which connected instances participate', this still leaves the question of 'how one arrives at a perception of the adapted work and its adaptations'.[58] In the case of the Third Programme *Hamlet* spin-offs, the different works are linked not only by their context of commissioning and production, but by their scheduling in association with other related programmes from different genres, such as talks and performances of the play as short scenes or in its entirety. In particular the

broadcasting 'flow' of *Hamlet* variants was anchored – one might say, legitimated – by the original and repeat broadcasts of the Richmond/Gielgud production in 1948 and in the summer of 1949, which appeared – however deceptively – to provide an inherently stable and authoritative version of the play when set against the problems raised by Olivier's much more explicitly cross-media and adaptive film. As well as being the creations, in most cases, of one producer, several of the broadcasts were also linked intertextually by casting (for which Heppenstall was also responsible), which further de-familiarized the play through the use of non-standard English accents. The Irish actor, Cyril Cusack, played Hamlet in both the Stonier and Read *Conversations* (and would go on to play Stephen Dedalus in the *Hamlet* excerpt from *Ulysses* the following year). The Scottish actor John Laurie (who also acted in all three of Olivier's films) was the Pirate Captain in *Thieves of Mercy*, and played the Doctor in *The Hawk and the Handsaw* and the Ollave in *The Fool's Saga*. Despite the lack of surviving recordings, I suggest that these auditory connections and echoes between the different programmes might have further accentuated the habitual Third Programme listener's sense of their interrelationships, and thus might have contributed to an acceptance and enjoyment both of the deconstructive playfulness which characterized the spin-offs themselves and the intellectual and thematic links which could be made between them. The Third Programme's schedule of *Hamlet* broadcasts in the late 1940s created a 'continuum of adaptations',[59] some accepted as versions of the play, others undeniably new works in close relation to it, others offering what might be considered 'speculative alternatives', whether in the idiom of film melodrama, detective fiction, psychoanalysis

---

[55] Heppenstall and Innes, *Three Tales*, p. 188.

[56] Heppenstall and Innes, *Three Tales*, pp. 8–9.

[57] Linda Hutcheon, *A Theory of Adaptation* (London, 2006), p. 9.

[58] Margaret Jane Kidnie, *Shakespeare and the Problem of Adaptation* (London, 2009), p. 4.

[59] Hutcheon, *A Theory of Adaptation*, pp. 170–2.

or matriarchal rewriting of history. In the context of the parallel appearance of Olivier's film they also constituted an example of what Kidnie has called 'border skirmishes', signalling a form of cultural politics.

Arguments about whether or not forms of corruption or adaptation are taking place are a sign of how different sides are competing for the power to define, for the moment, the cultural construction that will 'count' or be valued as authentic – and the more canonical the work, the more hotly disputed is the debate about its authentic instances.[60]

As Whitehead has argued, 'the Third Programme's existence was riven by a series of incompatibilities, contradictions, and paradoxes, which had to lead to its eventual fragmentation and demise'.[61] The same could be said of its appropriation of *Hamlet*. The Third was created to achieve two ultimately unstable cultural objectives, to innovate and to maintain literary and artistic heritage. The BBC's Listener Research Report in February 1947 already found that there was dissatisfaction with its emphasis on 'unfamiliar works at the expense of the classics'.[62] Along with its preservation of the play's authority and canonical status through reverent adaptation, the Third's *Hamlet* spin-offs provided a critical and artistic space in which to innovate around the concept of what was – and was not – a classic, to develop further its hybrid, radio-specific genres, and to reflect on the very processes of rewriting old works and creating new ones. When the Third first came on air Hope-Wallace had called for 'experiments, the new verse dramas, the specially written entertainments in radio form, not reproductions of the stage classics. There should be great scope for adaptations of a far richer and truer kind than is possible in the cramped Home and Light.'[63] For a brief period his hopes were realized in *Hamlet*, but by the mid-1950s this Coleridge-style fixation with the play had run its course and discussion at the Third centred on the pros and cons of staging a new production of the play or repeating the Gielgud version once again.[64] While there would be recurrent cycles of Shakespeare programming in the years to come, to date no one work has ever dominated the airwaves in the way that *Hamlet* did in the late 1940s in Britain, when, it seems, the play was indeed the thing to catch the post-war consciousness, if not the conscience, of the Third's broadcasters and their imagined – and perhaps actual – audience of 'alert and receptive listeners'.

---

[60] Kidnie, *Shakespeare and the Problem of Adaptation*, p. 31.
[61] Whitehead, *Third Programme*, p. 2.
[62] Cited in Whitehead, *Third Programme*, p. 57.
[63] 'Anxious Enquiry', *The Listener*, 3 October 1946, 452.
[64] Humphrey Carpenter, *The Envy of the World: Fifty Years of the Third Programme and Radio 3 1946–1996* (London, 1996), p. 207.

POST-TEXTUAL SHAKESPEARE

DOUGLAS M. LANIER

No tongue, all eyes! Be silent.

(The Tempest, 4.1.59)

In 2007, a curious billboard appeared in London advertising the move from Waterloo to St Pancras stations for the London hub of the Eurorail train to Paris. Above the logo 'London is changing' was featured the image of a skeleton kneeling on a stage, holding in his bony hand the fully fleshed head of a man who looked back at the skeleton's skull with astonishment. In 2004 and 2005, a poster campaign in Swiss cities advertised the Espace 2 channel of Radio Suisse Romande with the image of two teens kissing in a subway train filled with inattentive passengers, accompanied by the simple, one-word caption, 'Shakespeare.' These advertisements provoke a deceptively simple question: is this Shakespeare? In what sense Shakespeare? To ask the question 'is this Shakespeare?' is to ponder the nature of the boundaries that extend around the designation 'Shakespearian', laden though that designation is with cultural power and value. Like lines on a map, those boundaries may have the illusion of permanence at a given moment, but in reality they are always in flux, constantly being renegotiated in response to a variety of cultural forces. Here I will be discussing a particular kind of limit case that poses a challenge to one of the founding principles of Shakespeare studies. My claim, in a nutshell, is that both popular culture and avant-garde performance have transgressed and redrawn the boundary of what can constitute 'Shakespeare' with ever-greater insistence in the last twenty years, and that they have done so in response to a newly powerful cultural dominant in the late twentieth and early twenty-first century. Though I will eventually turn to two noteworthy recent performances of Shakespeare, I begin with examples from advertising because advertising stands at the intersection of popular culture and avant-garde aesthetics, amplifying (and thus making visible) ideological and representational strategies it borrows from elsewhere. Though the aims of the ads and the performances are quite different, what they reveal are the traces of processes at work in popular and performance culture more generally. I hope to suggest how, under the pressure of mass mediatization, contemporary Shakespeare may be undergoing something of a paradigm shift that raises foundational questions about how we, as Shakespearian professionals, conceptualize the 'essential' or 'authentic' Shakespeare and situate his cultural value.

The challenge posed by these ads is that there is not a single word from Shakespeare's text in either example, despite the fact that they depend for their effect on being identified as 'Shakespearian'. Like so much of contemporary advertising, these examples are driven almost entirely by arresting images. What text there is has been pared to the absolute minimum and the sales information has been squeezed to the edges of the frame. If we compare these ads to Shakespeare-themed ads from earlier periods, we immediately recognize a very different ratio of visual image to word. An ad for Ridge's Baby Food from 1885, for example, also uses Shakespeare to reinforce its message, but Shakespearian authority is vested in its three textual citations – 'What say these young ones' (*King John*, 2.1.522), 'It be wholesome food' (*The Taming of the Shrew*, 4.3.16), and 'The food that to him . . . is . . . luscious' (*Othello*, 1.3.347) – rather than the image of mother and nurse feeding a happy child.[1] This ad would not be recognized as Shakespearian at all were it not for for quotations from Shakespeare's text. A remarkable ad for Olin Industries from 1945 features an image of post-war ruins, amidst which we see a fallen bust of Shakespeare and a thriving flower; the prominently featured citation, 'out of this nettle, danger, we pluck this flower, safety' (*I Henry IV*, 2.4.9), summarizes the ad's message – post-war Europe provides Olin with lucrative manufacturing opportunities – as a Shakespearian aphorism.[2] In the earlier examples, invoking Shakespeare in service of sales seems to *require* the presence of Shakespeare's text. But in the contemporary examples with which I began this article, insofar as we are willing to grant that they are Shakespearian, the Shakespearian meaning and authority they invoke is decidedly *post-textual*, independent of Shakespeare's words.

That is not to say that the contemporary ads are post-textual in the same way. In the case of the Eurostar ad,[3] our identification of it as Shakespearian turns on a visual commonplace, Hamlet holding Yorick's skull, one of a small set of iconic images that signal 'Shakespeare' to the viewer – Romeo at Juliet's balcony, Julius Caesar in a toga, the Droeshout engraving in the First Folio, to name a few. However, this image is not merely of Hamlet, but of an outdated mode of performing *Hamlet* – behind the skeleton are painted flats in Romantic style; there is a hint of proscenium staging; the skeleton's gesture is formal and declamatory; the human head in the skeleton's grasp has the windswept look and passionate expression of a Romantic portrait. These visual articulations of the Hamlet commonplace make 'Shakespeare' into an icon of old-fashionedness against which the Eurostar can define itself as contemporary, cosmopolitan, cool. For those viewers who might remember the passage from which this is taken – 'where be your gibes now?' – Hamlet's meditation on the irony of Yorick's now faded triumph

is turned into modernity's meditation on Shakespeare's once glorious cultural position, his having now wasted away to a skeleton chatting to a disembodied, no doubt overly intellectual head. But, and this is the crucial point, the ad doesn't assume we remember this passage. Its horizon of recognition is visual, not textual. Simple though it may be, the image depends upon our picking up visual subtleties to understand it – it is simple, but not simplistic. The ad for Espace 2 is more elliptical, by design.[4] In fact, the connection to Shakespeare is prompted only by the caption. Is the association with Shakespeare as poet of eternal love? Is the ethnic difference between the Middle-Eastern man and white European woman evocative of the kind of cultural divide that separates Romeo and Juliet? Are we meant to link the particular shade of blue that dominates the ad with the shade of blue that suffuses the pool scene in Baz Luhrmann's *Romeo + Juliet* where the lovers share their first kiss? Is the fluorescent lighting meant to be reminiscent of the fluorescent-light crosses

---

[1] *The Illustrated Sporting and Dramatic News*, 12 December 1885, p. 323. It is noteworthy that the ad explicitly identifies each textual citation by source play, act and scene.

[2] *Life Magazine*, 10 September 1945, p. 115. This ad identifies the textual citation only by source play (listed just as *Henry IV*), and it adds the name 'Shakespeare', as if in recognition of the target reader's potential doubt about its author.

[3] This ad was part of a campaign in late 2007 designed by LEG SA, based in Paris. Each ad in the campaign took a traditional image of British culture and gave it a visual twist from contemporary British culture: replacing a grenadier guard outside St James's Palace, for example, was the character Po from the children's show *Teletubbies* (produced in the UK); on the front of a £55 note is the grinning face of Mr Bean, Rowan Atkinson's screwball character from the popular television show *Mr Bean*.

[4] This ad is part of a campaign designed by the Swiss firm Rive Gauche Communications for Espace 2, dating from 2004. Other ads in the campaign followed the pattern of a single 'cultural' name accompanied by an initially cryptic image that depended on the viewer's parsing the allusion. A picture of hazelnuts, nutcracker and a glass of wine, for example, bore the label 'Tchaikovsky'; a shot of a digital clock reading '23.59' was labelled 'Monk' (an allusion to Theolonious Monk's song 'Round Midnight'); and a close-up of a worker wiping his grimy hands with a rag had the caption 'Sartre' (an allusion to his play *Dirty Hands*).

in the final scene of Luhrmann's film? The cryptic caption 'Shakespeare' prompts us to analyse the image for cues and rifle through our archive of Shakespearian visual references to make sense of it. That process requires little substantial recourse to the Shakespeare text. And once we've parsed the image, the ad's message comes into view: it demonstrates the contemporaneity and universality of high culture, what Espace 2 calls 'la vie côté culture', in particular its relevance to a hip youth market. Our very ability to make sense of the cryptic connection between Shakespeare and this image of lovers identifies our appropriateness as Espace 2 listeners, or so the ad seems to say: we have sufficient high cultural literacy to recognize the general resonances of 'Shakespeare' but also sufficient pop cultural literacy to recall specific images from Luhrmann's *Romeo + Juliet*. And since we, not the ad, make the connection explicit, we are flattered by our own capacity to read the allusive link – and, by implication, this is the kind of savvy listener who is 'cultural' and tunes into Espace 2. Both ads trade on Shakespeare's cultural capital, but that cultural capital is located primarily in our ability to recognize Shakespeare as image, not Shakespeare as text; the primary frame of reference is visual, not literary, culture. This is post-textual Shakespeare.

In one sense, post-textual Shakespeare is nothing new. The dumb show and theatrical dance were features of the early modern stage, manifest in Shakespeare's work in the dumb shows in Hamlet's *Mousetrap*, *Macbeth* and *Pericles*, and the dance sequences in *A Midsummer Night's Dream* and *The Tempest*. The Boydell Shakespeare Gallery at the end of the eighteenth century capitalized upon the nascent trend of Shakespeare painting, shifting the focus from capturing actors performing Shakespeare to converting Shakespearian characters and narratives themselves into visual images. The nineteenth century, besides being the heyday of the Shakespeare illustration, saw other attempts to convert Shakespeare to non-textual form – dance in the form of Shakespeare ballet,[5] and music in the form of symphonic programme music.[6] And the first two and a half decades of the twentieth century generated a robust tradition of silent

Shakespeare on film.[7] What distinguishes these wordless Shakespeares from contemporary post-textual Shakespeare are several factors. First, these earlier examples are not so closely linked with the prevailing media for Shakespeare in their day. That is, earlier non-textual Shakespeares tended to be alternatives to print and stage Shakespeares, not substitutes for them. By contrast, contemporary post-textual Shakespeare is intimately linked with the unprecedented dominance of mass media and the ways in which those media have shifted the dominant modalities of communication away from text. There is also an historical dimension of cultural politics at work here. In the nineteenth century the Shakespearian text was elevated to the status of secular scripture; late in the century there emerged a class of hermeneutic professionals devoted to methodical study of an 'authentic' Shakespearian text they sought to establish, professionals who displaced the heretofore amateur and journalistic critical tradition which had focused primarily on biographical criticism and

---

5 Examples include *Antony and Cleopatra* (as *Antoine et Cléopâtre*, first adapted 1761); *The Tempest* (first adapted 1774); *Macbeth* (first adapted 1785); *Hamlet* (first adapted 1788); *Othello* (first adapted 1818); and *A Midsummer Night's Dream* (first adapted 1855). *Romeo and Juliet* is, by far, the Shakespeare play most often adapted to ballet form; it was first adapted in 1811. Adaptation of Shakespeare to ballet form has remained popular throughout the twentieth century, particularly when accompanied by orchestral suites written on Shakespearian themes.

6 Examples include Beethoven's *Coriolan* (1801); Mendelssohn's *A Midsummer Night's Dream Overture* (1826, revised 1842); Berlioz's *Ouverture de la Tempête* (1830, later incorporated into *Lélio ou Le Retour à la vie*), *Roméo et Juliette* (1839), and *Marche funèbre pour la dernière scène d'Hamlet* (1844); Liszt's *Hamlet* (1858), Tchaikovsky's *Romeo and Juliet Fantasy Overture* (1869), *The Tempest* (1873) and *Hamlet* (1888); Richard Strauss's *Macbeth* (1888); and Elgar's *Falstaff* (1913). This genre retained its popularity in the twentieth century.

7 I have excluded one seemingly obvious item on this list, sign-language Shakespeare, because sign-language is indeed a language, though in performance signing shares qualities with physical theatre. For a cogent discussion of sign-language Shakespeare and its relationship to some of the issues raised in this article, see Peter Novak, "'Where Lies Your Text?': *Twelfth Night* in American Sign Language Translation', *Shakespeare Survey 61* (Cambridge, 2008), 74–90.

debates about Shakespearian performances. By situating themselves as keepers of the historical text, these Shakespearian professionals, who would soon become central to the establishment of English as an academic discipline, drove a wedge between popular culture and textual Shakespeare. Though Shakespeare's value as a cultural icon continued to be recognized across the cultural divide of highbrow and lowbrow, his language was to become a sticking point, too tied to academic professionals and too archaic and intellectualized to be easily assimilable to pop culture, except as the object of parody. Indeed, for much of the twentieth century Shakespeare's text served primarily as a foil against which pop culture could define itself as modern, democratic, immediate and fun. And yet, because Shakespeare remained a potent cultural icon, twentieth-century popular culture is also marked by repeated efforts to loosen the ties between Shakespeare and the words he wrote, in an effort to recover Shakespeare's cultural authority for wider popular appropriation.

Two primary cultural drives underlie Shakespeare's contemporary post-textualization. One is what W. J. T. Mitchell has called 'the pictorial turn' in late twentieth-century culture, a decisive shift in the relative ratios of image and word in the dominant media of our day.[8] Those media – advertising, film, television, the Internet – offer more information visually and with greater visual density; new technologies allow greater control over the content of images than ever before, and we are expected to process images at greater speeds. This visual information we now routinely process from media depends upon, and at the same time escalates, a heightened visual literacy which has become a crucial part of postmodern experience. In the nineties, Shakespeare film sought to develop strategies through which Shakespeare might be recast more definitively in visual terms, the language subordinated if not eliminated entirely. To illustrate, we might compare Olivier's and Branagh's handling of the 'idol ceremony' speech in their films of *Henry V*. Olivier's visuals – the king blank-faced by the campfire as dawn breaks over his shoulder – are subordinated to the spoken text, which is

delivered in voiceover. Turn off the soundtrack, and one would be hard-pressed to work out what is happening. Branagh's performance is just as low-key, but as he walks through the camp the images behind him – a cart piled with flags, shields and battle regalia, a humble soldier asleep in another cart – convey the contrast between the empty accoutrements of royalty with the peaceful rest of the commoner and thereby shift the ratio of image and word in the direction of image. The doubled prologue of Baz Luhrmann's *Romeo + Juliet* explicitly thematizes this change. At first the play's prologue is delivered to us as if on a television newscast in which the announcer's words trump the banal (and initially small) image, but then we are unexpectedly pulled into the film's postmodern mediaverse where the very same prologue is redelivered to us in hypervisual terms. Each phrase of the prologue is converted before our eyes into visuals, the words themselves becoming images which accelerate beyond our ability to read them, the entire sequence acclimatizing the viewer to the accelerated speed and hyperallusive

---

[8] See W. J. T. Mitchell, *Picture Theory: Essays on Verbal and Visual Representation* (Chicago, 1995), pp. 1–23 (the phrase 'pictorial turn' first appears on page 11). Though Mitchell acknowledges the pictorial turn in modern media, he stresses the continuing interplay between word and image in contemporary culture rather than some final triumph of image over word. In his most recent work, Mitchell has insisted upon the mixed nature of all media: see his 'There are No Visual Media', *Journal of Visual Culture*, 4 (2005), 257–66. Nevertheless, the rise of 'visual culture' as a discipline within the academy testifies to contemporary culture's emphasis on the image. For an introduction to issues in visual culture, see Nicholas Mirzoeff, *The Visual Culture Reader* (London, 2002, 2nd edn); Marita Sturken and Lisa Cartwright, *Practices of Looking: An Introduction to Visual Culture* (Oxford, 2007, 2nd edn); and Stanley Elkins, *Visual Studies: A Sceptical Introduction* (London, 2003). Jonathan Crary's *Techniques of the Observer: On Vision and Modernity in the Nineteenth Century* (Cambridge, MA, 1992) stresses that contemporary visual culture (and the anxieties which attend it) has its origins in nineteenth-century developments in media and performance technology. Crary's discussion accords in many ways with Richard W. Schoch's overview of nineteenth-century scenography in 'Pictorial Shakespeare', in Stanley Wells and Sarah Stanton, eds., *The Cambridge Companion to Shakespeare on Stage* (Cambridge, 2002), pp. 58–75.

visual flow of the film that follows. The nineties generated several cinematic strategies – Branagh's illustrational style, Luhrmann's hypervisual style, Julie Taymor's postmodern arthouse style, Hoffman and Radford's heritage film style – but all worked to tilt the sensory balance in the direction of image and away from Shakespeare's language. By the time we get to the end of the decade, Shakespeare on film seemed increasingly able to do without his language entirely, as a number of teen modernizations seemed to illustrate. To put this in business parlance, once rendered in post-textual form, Shakespeare was able to become fully 'cross-platform content'.

The other main impetus behind Shakespeare's recent post-textualization is globalization. As Arjun Appadurai notes, globalization tends to favour free transnational flows of people, money, goods and technologies.[9] That which impedes those flows risks being eliminated, marginalized or transmuted into more fluid form. So it is with Shakespeare: his work is a valuable resource, but because of its textual form, it has limited cross-cultural fungibility. Though translation is one means for engaging the problem, it ultimately arrives at the very problem it seeks to remedy – linguistic boundaries. Non-textual forms – physical movement, music and especially image – would seem to offer much freer cross-cultural communication. In short, images travel well and, in Shakespeare's case, visual media would seem more commensurate with his putative universality. This point was made long ago by Georges Méliès's 1907 silent film *Le Rêve de Shakespeare* (aka *Shakespeare Writing Julius Caesar*).[10] The plot is simple: frustrated by writer's block as he tries to compose a script, Shakespeare settles into a daydream at his desk. Behind him, in one of Méliès's trick optical shots, appears an elaborate version of the assassination of Julius Caesar, clearly the vision Shakespeare sees in his mind's eye. The scene then returns to Shakespeare's study, where Shakespeare dances merrily about and, in imitation of what he has imagined, he stabs a loaf of bread with glee. The film's final image is a cross-fade from the living Shakespeare, with arms confidently folded, to a bust of Shakespeare,

surrounded by the flags of many nations. Méliès is claiming that Shakespeare is a film-maker *avant la lettre*, that is, the source and power of his work springs ultimately from visual images, not words. (It's no accident that Méliès the film-maker himself plays Shakespeare.) It is because Shakespeare's imagination is fundamentally cinematic, grounded in the 'universal' vocabulary of silent images, that, Méliès suggests, his status as a cultural icon can be international. The blockage that the writing Shakespeare suffers at the start of the film is thus as much cultural as it is personal, and shifting from text to image allows Shakespeare to move past it. *Shakespeare Writing Julius Caesar* touts the power and global reach of its own silent medium, and it maintains that the power of Shakespeare, the 'universal' poet, accords with – or ought to accord with – that medium's non-textual nature. With this film of Shakespeare's daydream, Méliès announces the cultural dream that would be pursued by popular culture and mass media throughout the twentieth century, one that has been crucial to Shakespeare's accelerated globalization in image and film in the past twenty years.

Some caveats here. First and obviously, all non-textual modes of expression include points of reference and expressive elements which situate them locally. The claim that images and movement are legible across all cultures has been a persistent

---

9 Arjun Appadurai, 'Disjuncture and Difference in the Global Cultural Economy', in *Modernity at Large: Cultural Dimensions of Globalization* (Minnesota, 1996), pp. 27–47.
10 This film is lost, but Robert Hamilton Ball prints the entirety of the scenario (as well as a surviving photo) and briefly discusses it in *Shakespeare on Silent Film: A Strange Eventful History* (London, 1968), pp. 35–6. See also Judith Buchanan, *Shakespeare on Silent Film: An Excellent Dumb Discourse* (Cambridge, 2009), p. 119. Buchanan stresses that Méliès's vision of an international, 'universal' bard was at odds with the more self-consciously nationalistic and corporate appropriations of Shakespeare by other silent film producers, most notably Vitagraph. Though Buchanan's point is quite correct, it nevertheless seems noteworthy that the competition between Vitagraph and other film producers over appropriation of Shakespeare was energized at least in part by the potential of Shakespeare on silent film to circulate internationally more freely than, say, theatrical performances.

problem for intercultural performance and has opened it up to charges of exoticism, incoherence or colonial appropriation.[11] Nevertheless, in an age of the Internet and digital media the accelerated global circulation of what were once local visual cultures has demonstrably lessened the gap between local knowledge and cross-cultural consumption in a way not matched by textual culture. One might think, for example, of how the visual vocabularies of Japanese *manga* or Bollywood cinema have become a familiar part of a globalized image culture in the past twenty years. A second related issue involves the problem of mistaking the cultural dominance of certain visual vocabularies – the styles and reference points of Western mass media, for example – as evidence of their 'universality' rather than their dominance being a function of power relations between competing media at the present moment. A third caveat returns us once again to advertising and the relationship of post-textual Shakespeare to circulations and transformations of global capital, both economic and symbolic. So long as Shakespeare's cultural authority is located in his language, capacity for cross-cultural appropriation of that authority, I have been arguing, has been seen as fraught with limitations. But if Shakespeare can be refigured as post-textual, a matter of images not words, the considerable cultural capital he represents can become more freely fungible, capable of much wider use in the marketplace. Shakespeare's cultural capital, in short, follows the logic of global capital in an age of mass media. This helps us to understand the symbiotic relationship between the cinematizing of Shakespeare in the nineties and the concomitant accelerated circulation of Shakespeare in global culture at century's end (though, of course, the latter is multiply determined). If the project of resituating Shakespeare on film involved making Shakespeare predominantly visual and loosening his long-standing relationship to text, that process also contributed to the general sense that Shakespeare, recast in this way, might circulate freely – or at least more freely – across cultural borders.

I've been suggesting that post-textual Shakespeare has been the province of mass media and popular culture, but two recent theatrical productions suggest that it is also becoming a stage phenomenon. I want briefly to examine the work of two companies that have staged performances of Shakespeare without words, the Synetic Theater, based in Washington DC, and Punchdrunk, based in London, in particular Synetic Theater's 2010 production of *Othello*, and Punchdrunk's *Sleep No More*, its production of *Macbeth*, first staged in 2003 and revived in 2009. These provocative productions seek to align Shakespeare with what has come to be called 'physical theatre', a mode of performance that has come to prominence in the last two decades. Physical theatre is a hybrid of many different performance practices – mime, clowning, dance, gymnastics, street performance, site-specific theatre and performance art.[12] At the heart of its many forms, however, are two concerns, bodily performance and the highlighting of physical presence. As the term 'physical theatre' implies, emphasis falls strongly, often exclusively, on bodily movement and visuals rather than on words to convey content. The key touchstone here is of course Antonin Artaud, with his call for a primordial, pre-verbal theatre that affects spectators viscerally.[13]

---

[11] A cogent overview of these issues can be found in W. B. Worthen, 'Shakespearean Geographies', in *Shakespeare and the Force of Modern Performance* (Cambridge, 2003), pp. 117–68, esp. pp. 123–34. See also Patrice Pavis, 'Introduction: Toward a Theory of Interculturalism in Theatre?', in *The Intercultural Performance Reader*, ed. Patrice Pavis (London, 1996), pp. 1–21.

[12] For introductions to this highly varied mode of performance, see Simon Murray and John Keefe, *Physical Theatres: A Critical Introduction* (London, 2007), and Josephine Machon, *(Syn)aesthetics: Redefining Visceral Performance* (Basingstoke, 2009). According to Murray and Keefe, the term 'physical theatre' was first applied to the work of the company DV8 in 1986. Examples of DV8's productions can be found on two DVDs, *DV8: The Cost of Living* (Digital Classics, 2006) and *DV8: Physical Theatre* (Arthaus, 2007).

[13] See *The Theatre and Its Double*, trans. Mary Caroline Richards (New York, 1994), which contains the essay 'No More Masterpieces'. Artaud's first manifesto for a theatre of cruelty succinctly lays out its aims: 'instead of continuing to rely upon texts considered definitive and sacred, it is essential to put an end to the subjugation of the theater to the text, and to recover the notion of a kind of unique

Physical theatre both rejects the primacy of language and self-consciously foregrounds the power of its physical presence. Conjoining Shakespeare and physical theatre is by no means obvious or inevitable, particularly if we recall Artaud's battle cry, 'no more masterpieces'. To make that link is fundamentally to recast Shakespeare's relationship to stage performance and text and thus to recast what constitutes the 'essence' of the Shakespearian. In the Shakespeare productions of Punchdrunk and the Synetic Theater, there is a productive tension between mass-mediated popular culture and Artaudian physical theatre that surfaces at several levels – in the productions' performance techniques, in the sorts of cultural references they put into play, in the particular quality of experience they seek to give their audiences. Though it is clearly not these companies' intent, their emphasis on the bodily and the visual brings their approach to Shakespeare into affiliation with popular post-textualization of Shakespeare. This conjunction of cultural contexts is, it seems to me, crucial for understanding how these companies reconceptualize Shakespeare and why these performances have been popular with audiences.

SYNETIC THEATER'S *OTHELLO*

Synetic Theater[14] has been producing wordless Shakespeare performances since 2002, when it premièred *Hamlet . . . the rest is silence*. Since then, it has produced adaptations of *Macbeth*, *Romeo and Juliet*, *A Midsummer Night's Dream*, *Antony and Cleopatra* and *Othello*, with a *King Lear* its most recent Shakespeare production, as well as other 'classic' tales with wide cultural currency. The company is the brainchild of director Paata Tsikurishvili and his wife and choreographer Irina, both of whom trained in Soviet Georgia with Amiran Shalikashvili, director of the Georgian State Pantomime Theatre.[15] The influence of their background in avant-garde theatre, film and ballet is readily apparent in Synetic's productions. Also noteworthy is the Tsikurishvilis' status as Georgian emigrés in Germany and then the United States. In interview[16] Paata Tsikurishvili has remarked that

having first come to know Shakespeare through translations into his native tongue, he regarded Shakespeare as a Georgian author, but he and his wife's immigration to the West necessitated their cultivating a performance style for Shakespeare legible across cultural and linguistic borders. Paata Tsikurishvili locates Shakespeare's essence in narrative and the emotional states of his characters, elements he regards as transcultural, and so Synetic productions tend to have a strong, linear storyline somewhat unusual for physical theatre. This also explains why the company has preferred Shakespearian tragedy, for Shakespeare's word-driven comedy, observes Paata, is so culturally specific that it is difficult to physicalize. Non-balletic dance and mime are the central components of Synetic's stage vocabulary, combined with original, through-composed music, and often stylized set design and costuming. Abstraction in the production design helps assure that most characters read as types rather than individuals, though in the case of *Othello* by using different degrees of stylization and naturalism for various characters, the company helps manage the audience's empathy with the tale's protagonists. Many Synetic productions of Shakespeare share a narrative arc, opening with some form of trauma associated with escape, exile and dislocation. We first see Romeo and Juliet trapped in a prisonhouse of gears from which they try unsuccessfully to break free; *Midsummer* opens with

language half-way between gesture and thought' (89). Though it has been highly influential on contemporary theatrical practice, Artaud's stress upon bodily presence and its relationship to primal or direct, unrepresented experience has come in for criticism. See, for example, Jacques Derrida, 'The Theatre of Cruelty and the Closure of Representation', in *Writing and Difference*, trans. Alan Bass (Chicago, 1978), pp. 232–50, and Philip Auslander, *Liveness: Performance in a Mediatized Culture* (London, 1999).

14 The term 'synetic', the company's own creation, combines 'kinetic' and 'synthetic', stressing both the basis of the company's productions in bodily movement and its desire to bring together a variety of performance arts into a single, distinctive, synaesthetic whole.

15 Additional biographical information is available at www.synetictheater.org/aboutus/mission/html.

16 Conducted by phone, 30 July 2010.

the birth of the Indian boy and death of his mother; the initial image of *Antony and Cleopatra* is of the struggle for power between Cleopatra and Ptolemy, presented as a literal scramble up the staircase of an Egyptian temple where there awaits a writhing snake-like dancer, symbol of Egypt's seductive power. *Othello* opens with a double trauma, reflecting the sense that the play has double protagonists. The production begins with Iago centre-stage in dappled light resembling a net, vacillating between laughter and regret; this image is also the play's final tableau. Othello first appears as one of a group of slaves tormented by Turkish captors. As one of the slaves, a black woman, dies from being beaten, she gives Othello the handkerchief he will eventually give to Desdemona, prompting Othello to lead a rebellion and ally himself with the Venetians. The final moments of Synetic productions often recall the opening traumas; there the protagonist comes tragically to recognize how fully that moment has shaped his or her psychology or the events of the narrative. *Antony and Cleopatra*, for example, ends where it began, on the stairs of the Egyptian temple, and *Othello* too has a circular structure. Haunting many of Synetic's Shakespeare productions, and particularly its *Othello*, are issues of exile and cultural dislocation, notable themes given the transcultural ambitions of the performance style.

Synetic's *Othello* is exemplary of the company's approach to Shakespeare. The set is composed of triangles, appropriately enough, which evoke shards of broken glass. The score by Konstantine Lortkipanidze, composer for many of the company's productions, underscores and intensifies the emotional tenor of the scenes, serving as a kind of continuous soundtrack for the action. Colour-coding helps those unfamiliar with the narrative to keep the characters straight, but it also works to type the characters: the Turks are in brightly coloured flowing robes with masked faces, the Venetians in black and white stylized Renaissance costumes, Roderigo distinguished from the others by his sickly yellow hat and gloves and flower. More individualized are Othello and Desdemona – Desdemona appears all in white and Othello, once he joins the Venetians, is all in black. Othello and

Desdemona are also set apart in their bodily style. The Venetian court often functions as a single synchronized ensemble, whereas Othello and Desdemona move more independently and naturalistically. Although Othello's revolt from slavery would seem to announce race as a central concern, in fact the black and white costuming of Othello and Desdemona rarely reads in terms of racial difference, at least until the final scenes. It's remarkable that race figures so little in Othello's relationship to Venice. When Iago mimes telling Brabanzio that 'an old black ram is tupping your white ewe', the image is presented to us as pantomime comedy, not to be taken seriously; both ram and ewe are played by white actors. Brabanzio's confrontation with Othello early on is the one, very brief instance where Othello's moorishness is at issue. Otherwise, the production focuses far more on sexuality and gender, particularly so in the production's approach to Iago. Like the other Venetians, he is dressed in black and white, but his face is ghoulishly whited-up and his hair punkishly spiked, as if he were both clown and demon. Red accents in his hair and costume indicate buried sexual passion, a point made considerably clearer by the fact that Emilia and Bianca, both openly erotic in this production, are also in red. When Othello is welcomed to Venice and chooses Cassio as his companion, Iago lapses into a frenzy, but it is Othello's love for Desdemona that utterly unhinges him and sets his plotting in motion. This Iago is plagued by pornographic visions. Repeatedly he imagines his lusty wife in Othello's embrace, despite the fact that in Iago's and Emilia's erotic *pas de deux* over Desdemona's lost handkerchief, her sexual attention is directed entirely towards him. For Iago, Desdemona represents both an ideal of erotic purity Othello has stolen from him and a perverse object of lust he seeks to defile. This becomes amply clear when Iago comforts Desdemona after Othello has publicly humiliated her and then grotesquely tries to steal a kiss. With his plotting Iago seeks to project his own contradictory erotic fantasies and jealousy onto Othello.

A key challenge for physical storytelling is how to reveal the interiority of character, particularly when that interiority is at odds with outward appearances, and it is here that Synetic's *Othello* focuses much of its attention and marks an advance over its previous Shakespeare productions. After Othello makes his first romantic connection with Desdemona, Iago is given a solo scene before a mirror – what amounts to a physical soliloquy. Overcome with rage and grief, he smashes through the mirror and becomes three different characters (two men, one woman), all marked with Iago's distinctive red accents. Thereafter, the three act as a conspiratorial unit, the original Iago often playing 'honest' Iago while the other two Iagos help with his schemes, offer him encouragement and provide him an onstage audience. This approach gives us a bodily analogue for Iago's self-regarding, fractured ego; the fact that his mirror-self splits into male and female suggests that Iago is unable to navigate a crisis of gendered subjectivity and desire. The oversize triangles which dominate the set design, vaguely reminiscent of shards of glass, remind us constantly of Iago's shattered ego-ideal that dominates every aspect of the narrative. A second mirror-soliloquy later on adds to our understanding of his psyche. After the three Iagos watch Othello and Desdemona consummate their relationship, the trio stands again before the shattered mirror. This time the Iagos pull Othello, then Cassio, through the mirror frame into their world, and they play out their fantasies of revenge and control by manipulating Othello and Cassio's movements, miming pulling strings as if the two were puppets. One might expect the third figure in this sequence to be Desdemona, but who next appears is Emilia, dressed seductively in red and eluding Iago's grasp. She and Othello immediately fall into a passionate dance, while the trio of Iagos mime being trapped behind the mirror, forced to watch Iago's perverse projections until lovelorn Roderigo arrives to break the spell. Fractured by fantasies of his own male grandeur and fears of women's erotic independence, Iago undertakes to project his own psychological crisis onto Othello.

That projection becomes quite literal, for a second innovation in this production is its use of mini-camera/projectors, the Iagos' weapon of choice.

The Iagos record Cassio's encounters with Desdemona and Bianca, then project fragmented close-ups of them onto the set for Othello to see.[17] This technique of showing the spectator the pornographic couplings Othello imagines has become *de rigueur* in *Othello* films of the nineties, of course, but on the stage those projections function rather differently. Though Iago's links to the mirror and the screen suggest a Lacanian scenario, perhaps more interesting here is how film, as technique and as ideological force, is pitted against the world of the stage. Within the fiction, Iago becomes a cinematic adapter, but his films are engines of bodily fragmentation and fetishization, qualities which violate the sort of physical presence and integrity that stage performance affords. Increasingly, the images Iago projects are close-ups of body parts, distorted, magnified, perversely edited. What is more, the Iagos project those images around the stage, so that the images become quite literally the environment, physical and psychological, within which Othello must move. The invasion of projected image into performance space is exploited with great ingenuity. At one point, Othello finds himself pressed between triangles on which are projected Desdemona and Cassio, which he fights to keep apart while preventing himself from being crushed. At another point, Iago holds up a giant version of Desdemona's handkerchief which becomes a screen on which he projects images, while Othello, writhing in anguish, appears as a shadow behind. These projections enervate Othello. Once he enters Iago's world of the shattered yet wrap-around mirror/screen, he becomes trapped in an environment of denarrativized images which feed his fears and fantasies. Iago's moment of triumph comes when Othello picks up the handkerchief that Cassio leaves behind. Pressing it to his face, Othello then places it over his head. This gesture foreshadows his

---

[17] Iago's deployment of modern recording technology in his deception of Othello is not new. In the film adaptation *All Night Long* (1962, dir. Basil Dearden), the Iago figure Johnny Cousin uses a tape recorder, a hidden microphone and some clever editing to awaken the jealousy of Aurelius Rex, the Othello figure.

death, signifies discomfort with his own blackness, and obliterates his identity with what has become one of Iago's screens. Eventually even Desdemona's own white dress also becomes a screen for projected images, now from Othello's imagination, and she is murdered, becoming a saintly martyr in death, raised on a cross at the back of the stage.

In the play's final scene, Emilia steals Iago's projector and reveals its images to the onstage crowd who have gathered in Othello's chamber. Here Othello finally recognizes the device's power and his deception. The projector then becomes a weapon with which Emilia, Iago and Othello are stabbed, though when Iago first uses the projector to murder Emilia, it is difficult at first for the spectator to work out just what has happened – notably, having functioned cinematically within the production, the projector doesn't move easily back into the realm of stage illusion where it can function metaphorically. In one of the most fascinating and revealing stage images of the production, after wounding Iago and wresting the handkerchief from him, Othello once again places the white handkerchief over his head and then briefly projects images onto it before killing himself with the projector. Here race and erotic projection briefly converge, for Othello comes to recognize how becoming a screen for Iago's fantasies drew him into racial self-hatred. But what actually emerges here most strongly is not the issue of racial identity at all but the psychological power of the cinematic image, its ability to fragment or dwarf otherwise integral bodies and grotesquely distort or magnify desire, its capacity to overwhelm and invade the psyches of spectators. What emerges, in short, is an allegory of the tension between physical theatre and mediatized culture, a tension which the production, with its combination of live action and state-of-the-art video technology, participates in as much as it comments upon. If Shakespeare's *Othello* is a play about the power of storytelling, Synetic's production of *Othello* addresses competing modalities of non-verbal storytelling in a contemporary context, pitting the physical body and the theatrical against screen images and the videographic. And the final fates of Othello and Iago offer

rather different, though in the last analysis both tragic, assessments of the effects of mediatization. In Othello's case, as he dies he uses the handkerchief to cover his self-inflicted wound. Besides stressing the link between Othello's self-destruction and the screen the handkerchief has become, this gesture also returns us to the moment where Othello first receives the handkerchief from the wounded slave and, spurred on by her death, demonstrates his larger-than-life prowess as a fighter (and physical actor) in the slave rebellion. The lament is not so much for Desdemona as for Othello's own heroic potential. Indeed, it is tempting to read this exiled hero's death-by-projection in terms of the effects of Western mass media on non-Western cultures, an issue about which one might expect the Tsikurishvilis to be particularly sensitive. But Othello's death is not the whole story. Fittingly for a production so dominated by Iago's psychology, the final tableau features two of the three Iagos dying in the original Iago's arms, in a perverse *pieta*. It is as if these alter-Iagos are what Othello has fatally wounded when he stabs Iago with the projector in the final scene, and their deaths serve for Iago a sacrificial, redemptive function, allowing for his psychological reintegration, the exorcism of his projective demons. Indeed, as the lights fade he stares at the audience with, for the first time in the performance, an expression of grotesquely ecstatic joy. But as his face recedes into the darkness, we see his barely perceptible features slip into pain, as if in ever-so-fleeting recognition of the tragedy he has brought on others and on himself.

PUNCHDRUNK'S *SLEEP NO MORE*

Punchdrunk has taken a very different approach in its four post-textual Shakespeare productions, *A Midsummer Night's Dream* (2002), *The Tempest* (2003), *The Firebird Ball* (their *Romeo and Juliet*, 2005), and *Sleep No More* (their *Macbeth*, 2003 and 2009). Punchdrunk's approach to performance stresses immersion and interaction, combining elements of installation art, video gameplay, historical re-enactment, Grand Guignol- and theme parks with more conventional elements of physical theatre like mime, dance and music.[18] Director/designers Felix Barrett and Maxine Doyle locate their productions in vacant buildings in which they create elaborate environments through which audiences freely wander. Setting thereby becomes in many ways the dominant 'character'. Even so, Punchdrunk productions are not site-specific in the strictest sense,[19] for they don't engage the specific history of the site; the audience's awareness of the building's former use adds semiotic 'texture', but that texture tends to be one element among many. Some of the spaces in the environment are installations in which mysterious collections of objects evoke a mood, hint at past events, or function as metaphors; these meticulously composed spaces present spectators with far more materials than they can possibly process. Scattered elsewhere throughout the site are live performances, fragments of narrative; in the case of *Sleep No More*, those performances were wordless, though recognizably from *Macbeth*. To follow a narrative thread, one must follow a performer as he or she pursues a character's path through the overarching story and the building. Indeed, one must take on faith that there *is* an overarching story, for it is physically impossible to see all of the performances going on throughout the site. This means that one's spectatorial choices profoundly shape one's experience of the production; since one is experiencing elements of the production in non-sequential order and often in fragments, one is constantly struggling to make sense of what one happens to encounter.[20] Our growing awareness of an overwhelming excess of meaning and the necessary incompleteness of our experience is in fact an essential element in the production. Even so, built into the work's structure is a moment where all the actors, with spectators following them, converge in one space so that we can all witness a key event. Barrett and Doyle have spoken of this element as a 'crescendo', a sequence in which the events and resonances of the work culminate in a single, memorable dramatic image.[21] Besides providing an intimation of narrative climax and a focus for the performance's metaphorical associations, the 'crescendo'

conveys the sense that there is some larger narrative we have all been in the midst of, though it remains just out of grasp. Adding to the synaesthetic quality of the experience is the use of music, sound, dramatic lighting, even touch and smell. The final scene of *Sleep No More*, for example, was performed in a dark, foggy room crowded with bristly pines and heavy with the scent of evergreen, with a musical score that conveyed a sense of oceanic ebb and flow as well as growing menace. Punchdrunk productions, in short, create

---

[18] Discussions of Punchdrunk's aesthetic can be found in Felix Barrett and Maxine Doyle of Punchdrunk, 'In the Prae-sens of Body and Space – The (Syn)aesthetics of Site-Sympathetic Work', in Machon, *(Syn)aesthetics*, pp. 89–99; 'Felix Barrett in Discussion with Josephine Machon' and 'Maxine Doyle in Discussion with Josephine Machon', in *BST Journal*, 7, posted at http://people.brunel.ac.uk/bst/vol0701/home.html (under 'Perspectives'); and a lecture by Colin Nightingale, Punchdrunk's Creative Producer, in PSFK's Good Ideas Salon, January 2009, posted at www.psfk.com/2009/03/good-ideas-in-storytelling-from-good-ideas-london.html.

[19] According to Josephine Machon (*(Syn)aesthetics*, p. 203), Felix Barrett prefers the term 'site-sympathetic' to describe the relationship in Punchdrunk productions between performance and venue. Properly speaking, a 'site-specific' performance could be performed only within a particular space, for the specific venue is essential to its meaning and character. Punchdrunk productions, by contrast, 'respond sensually' to their performance spaces, using their qualities as important ingredients or resources but perhaps not as crucial ones. *Sleep No More*, for example, premièred in London at the Beaufoy Building in Kennington in 2003; it then played in Boston in 2009–10 at the Lincoln School in Brookline. Both buildings were abandoned schools; the fact that they were spaces formerly inhabited by children is significant to the show's themes.

[20] Maxine Doyle comments that 'it's great for us when people say that they feel like they were the only person having that experience and it felt like the first and only time that event happened in that way, when in actual fact it's happened hundreds of times over the course of a run' (Machon, *(Syn)aesthetics*, p. 96). That is, it is the contingent nature of the audience's experience, the sense that one has accidentally happened upon an event or meaningful detail in the site that others are missing, that contributes a special spontaneity and intensity to Punchdrunk productions. It also gives them considerable replay value, for a second experience of a Punchdrunk performance would by its nature almost certainly be different from one's first.

[21] Machon, *(Syn)aesthetics*, p. 96.

mysterious alternative worlds designed to stimulate pre-rational forms of cognition: tactile contact, instinctive response, imaginative association, fantasy. The entrance to the performance space for *Sleep No More* in Boston – an almost entirely unlit, claustrophobic passageway – suggests a maze without landmarks, precisely the kind of experience we are about to have, but more metaphorically it calls to mind a birth canal, as if we were returning to a more primal perceptual mode.

Macbeth is a fortuitous choice for Punchdrunk, for the play explores the psychological space between waking and dream. *Sleep No More* seeks to recover that uncanny imaginative state from a text now overly familiar to most viewers. Much of the *Macbeth* narrative is in fact performed (in fact, some scenes are performed more than once), but the audience's experience of it is fragmented and out of sequence. What emerges far more strongly than story are associative links that build as one explores the site. Felix Barrett says of Shakespeare's texts, 'I respond to the poetry, they're poetic texts.'[22] Maxine Doyle explains the matter in this way:

[Barrett]'s concept became about space and form rather than content. He felt dissatisfied by the way that the dialogue worked in spaces. He felt that it killed the magic and mystery of the event, that the images that he created were more evocative than the words. So that's why he sought out a choreographer to work with because he felt that physical language would work better. And then we made a wordless Macbeth . . . For me the text exists in the unseen words, it exists in the relationship and the exchange and the situations that the texts create. I think that's what's really powerful for me. Looking at Shakespeare, for example, the characters are so rich and the situations are so clear so that it's actually really easy to strip it down to its essence.[23]

The focus of Punchdrunk's approach to Shakespeare is not story, that narrative content which appeals most to the rational intellect, but rather the metaphorical richness of Shakespeare's writing, which, so Barrett and Doyle claim, engages more visceral and emotional registers of audience response. It is as if Shakespeare's dialogue and narrative serves merely as a vehicle for the kaleidoscopic welter of images his writing puts into play,

images which in their engagement with so many senses and sheer density seek to transcend language and rational thought and which trace their origin to primal registers of emotional and imaginative experience. Doyle's concept of the 'unseen words' refers to those elemental qualities that lie behind and give power to those utterances at the surface of the received Shakespearian text. To get at those otherwise unseen essences, it is necessary to pare away Shakespearian dialogue from the performance of Shakespeare, lest one become fixated on the narrative or ideational content of the play. Rather, if theatre is to offer an *experience* rather than just a re-presentation of those qualities, it must communicate the essence of Shakespeare (or any other classical text) through an intense, semiotically rich, non-linear, interactive event which above all engages its audience through bodily perception. To be sure, this conception of the Shakespearian script participates in a long history of performance theory which values the ineffable and distrusts the textual, stretching from Lamb's comments about the unperformability of *King Lear* to Artaud's call for a theatre of cruelty to method acting's valuing of subtext over text. What distinguishes Punchdrunk's approach from forebears and predecessors is, first, its perhaps somewhat surprising commitment to classical repertoire and, second, its sheer daring, its willingness to take this re-conceptualization of Shakespeare performance to its logical (certainly not the right word) conclusion.

As the title *Sleep No More* implies, Punchdrunk's aim with its performance of *Macbeth* is to convey viscerally the inchoate sense of menace, doom, guilt and bodily violation that comes to haunt Macbeth and wife by providing a physical experience of the dreamlike space between waking and sleep, that state in which rationality is suspended, one's capacity for imaginative association and bodily perception is heightened and one's experience of reality seems disturbingly fluid and uncanny. Arguably it is

---

[22] Machon, *(Syn)aesthetics*, p. 96.
[23] 'Felix Barrett in Discussion with Josephine Machon', *BST Journal*.

this nightmarish state of mind that comes to dominate Shakespeare's play, as it becomes increasingly difficult to distinguish where Macbeth's psychological world ends and exterior reality begins. At the same time, however, this state of mind is enormously productive of potent images and deeply resonant webs of association, as if Macbeth's poetic imagination were awakened and freed from rational constraint by his sleeplessness. To create an experience of this menacing dreamspace, explains Barrett, 'we've lifted the quintessential images' and created from them 'an alternative physical and visual text of the play',[24] in the process vastly multiplying the images' resonances. The site is filled, for example, with evocations of children we never directly see. One scene involves Macduff taking leave of his very pregnant wife; their home is figured as a Victorian doll's house. In one dark hallway is a starkly lit baby carriage, in which are wrapped two packages, suggestive of the children Lady Macbeth may or may not have had and perhaps of the murdered children of the play, as if ensconced in tiny coffins recast as 'gifts'. In another area is an exhibit which combines a defiled shrine of the Virgin Mary with a collection of children's shoes, the latter suggestive of the Holocaust. These and other evocations of children resonate with the abandoned schools within which performances of *Sleep No More* have taken place, spaces once inhabited by children and still heavy with their memory. Another group of elements concerns blood. Both Macbeth and Lady Macbeth bathe after Duncan's murder as spectators look on, and the tub they use becomes stained with blood. Elsewhere there is a room filled with tubs and medical equipment reminiscent of a primitive laboratory or taxidermist's – in the only tub filled with water swims a huge leech. Babies and blood come together with forbidden desire and blasphemy in a terrifying scene in the basement. There, in uncomfortably close proximity to the audience, the witches perform an orgiastic dance amidst strobes, blazingly intense red lighting and deafening music, conjuring a horned, blood-covered demon who presents them with a tiny bloody babe. This cluster of associations – blood, desire, blasphemy – surfaces again in the climactic banquet scene. In a perverse version of the Last Supper, the Scottish court enjoys a gluttonous banquet which slowly morphs into grotesque kissing and groping, until a bloody Banquo rises to terrify Macbeth, and he and Lady Macbeth separate the banqueters, among whom is Duncan himself. The slow-motion movements of the actors gives the scene a dreamlike and cinematic quality, but the aching pace also conveys psychological time as the guilt-ridden Macbeth experiences it in this scene. Soon afterward, the trees of Birnam Wood begin to move, and a darkly clad dancer leads Macbeth to the centre of the room, where he is hanged before our eyes – the climax of the performance. To add to the spectator's instinctive sense of irrational unease, throughout the venue are scattered references to folk superstitions, including items like mirrors, peacock feathers, hair, playing cards and salt.[25]

These images are set against a production design which often harkens to upper-class life in the twenties and thirties, an era in which aristocratic refinement still held sway but where upper-class political power had significantly eroded, a combination which invited decadence. Most of the principals of the cast are costumed in vintage formal wear, at least in the public spaces. On the lower floor of the building in the Boston performance are several rooms which resemble an ageing resort hotel with shabby-genteel furnishings; elsewhere is an elaborately detailed woman's boudoir of the same period. In the ballroom before the banquet is staged, couples in evening attire waltz to scratchy recordings of jazz tunes as a cryptic drama plays out between some of the characters.

---

[24] Joan Anderman, 'Mystery Theater: British Troupe Punch-drunk Teams with the ART to Explode Theatergoers' Expectations', *Boston Globe*, 4 October 2009, posted at www.boston.com/ae/theater_arts/articles/2009/10/04/sleep_no_more_allows_audience_members_to_pick_their_own_show/.

[25] These and other allusions to superstitions woven into the performance are catalogued in assistant director Paul Stacey's programme notes, 'Very Superstitious', posted at www.americanrepertorytheater.org/files/SNM%20program%2013_0.pdf.

The strangely impassive aloofness of the dancers becomes more and more troubling as the scene progressed, as if they had become caught up in a decadent demi-monde of their own. Indeed, here the production seems obliquely reminiscent of elements from Stanley Kubrick's *The Shining*, a similar ageing resort haunted by images of its upper-class, murderous former occupants. The mannered and clearly faded elegance of this aristocratic milieu is in sharp contrast with the near-mad, irrational passions that we see on display in some of the private rooms. Macbeth and Lady Macbeth's bedchambers are relatively intimate in scale, forcing us close to the couple in their bed and bath, and the scenes they perform there suggest the intensity of the passions they share. Those who take the time to explore the Macbeths' domestic space discover in Lady Macbeth's effects letters which reveal her passionate relationship with Macbeth. When Lady Macbeth is overtaken by guilt, she quite literally begins to climb the bedroom walls and furniture in a frantic sequence of movements that conveys very effectively the interiorized claustrophobia of her guilt. The veneer of elegance in the performance's public spaces only serves to magnify the transgressive quality of the lust for power and blood that drives the action and the principals' guilt behind the scenes. Indeed, the contrast between superficial 'civilization' and the power of irrational states of mind accord with Barrett and Doyle's fascination with primal modes of cognition in their theorizing about Punchdrunk productions.

Even so, describing the production in this way risks making it seem a more coherent and rational experience than it is. For one thing, the associative links are more oblique and yet more powerful than I can convey here. What symbolic sense this world has we must make ourselves, using what we can remember of *Macbeth* as a guide, and yet the links we make have considerable depth because the site is so over-saturated with detail. What Barrett and Doyle are offering is a physical and visual analogue for the semantic plenitude of Shakespeare's poetry – an experiential poem. Moreover, the associations extend well beyond *Macbeth* to resonant images from visual culture at large. In addition to

Holocaust and Catholic iconography, the production evokes images from the myth of Icarus, Hammer Horror films, and Gothic romance, to name a few. The subplot of the production is taken from Hitchcock's *Rebecca*, with Mrs de Winter wandering through the building searching for her husband (who in this version is Duncan), all the while intimidated by Mrs Danvers. Besides being appropriate to the *Sleep No More*'s production design, Hitchcock's film shares with *Macbeth* a prevailing Gothic mood, as well as a number of specific themes – murder and guilt, isolation and secrecy, obsession and fear, the tension between aristocratic elegance and irrational passion, the haunting of the present by the past – and narrative motifs – phantom children, returning corpses, closed doors, the guilty tyrannical male, the witchy. But an equally important point of convergence with *Macbeth* is simply the uncanny, dreamlike quality of Hitchcock's visuals which drive the film's narrative. Indeed, *Rebecca* announces its concern with dream and memory with its famous opening line, 'Last night I dreamt I went to Manderley again', and much of its protagonist Mrs de Winter's experience in the film, particularly in Manderley, plays like some Gothic nightmare. Both *Macbeth* and *Rebecca* exemplify the kind of aesthetic content and intense yet ambiguous tone that *Sleep No More* seeks to explore, and they are also 'classics' which provide knowledgeable audience members with touchstones by which they can orient themselves as they try to make sense of the *Sleep No More* environment.

Like *Macbeth* (and *Rebecca*), *Sleep No More* addresses memory and perception. Not only does *Sleep No More* require us to remember the fragments we have seen in order to piece them into some idiosyncratic imaginative whole, it also reminds us how our experience of *Macbeth* has become inseparable from what Geoffrey O'Brien has called 'the phantom empire' of images that occupy the modern cultural imaginary, many of which descend from Shakespeare's play.[26] That is, the performance traces forward and backward the

---

[26] Geoffrey O'Brien, *The Phantom Empire: Movies in the Mind of the 20th Century* (New York, 1995).

play's thematic and visual genealogy, addressing not just how *Macbeth* itself is semiotically over-saturated but also how culture at large is over-saturated with *Macbeth*. Central to *Sleep No More*'s effect is its oceanic quality, the sense of being confronted with a semiotic space so detailed, vast and complex that it overwhelms our attempts to grasp it rationally. Although the production has a specific tone and thematic shape, its edges, as it were, seem to extend outward to the semiological horizon. Contributing to this sense of being adrift is the production's menacing soundtrack, which plays continuously throughout the performance. Though different themes play in different areas, the musical structure is predominantly one of ebb and flow, with rising volume and tension followed by release, over and over again. And because much of the soundtrack is lifted from Hitchcock films and cleverly reprocessed, the music seems tantalizingly familiar yet not quite identifiable, just out of reach of recognition. One last element of the production contributes to the kind of theatrical experience *Sleep No More* offers – the fact that spectators must wear white carnival masks and are forbidden to speak throughout the performance. The aim of this practice, claim the producers, is to make audiences feel more anonymous and thus less self-conscious about being so close to the players and more adventurous in exploring the performance space.[27] The carnival masks can't help but evoke associations with the ominous voyeurs of Stanley Kubrick's film *Eyes Wide Shut*, but given the performance environment's resemblance to a large-scale haunted house, the masks serve primarily to make the spectators into anonymous contemporary ghosts. This leads to an unsettling reversal of spectator and performance. Rather than we as spectators situated in present reality watching a theatrical re-presentation of the past created for our benefit, we become unreal traces from another time which haunt the real-time, bodily-present performance world before us, a performance which never acknowledges our existence and seemingly doesn't demand our presence in order to be performed. We become ghosts in the vast, Deleuzian semiotic machine that *Macbeth* has become, struggling

to make sense of a world just outside our comprehension. The scramble of white-masked spectators to follow characters through dark hallways reminds us that the site, like Shakespeare's play, is haunted by our own voyeuristic fascination with horror and guilt and our scramble for significational mastery.

BUT IS IT SHAKESPEARE?

As limit cases for the performance of Shakespeare, the Synetic Theater's *Othello* and Punchdrunk's *Sleep No More* raise anew some of the foundational questions of performance criticism: what is the relationship of the Shakespearian text to performance? If these works do not perform the Shakespearian text, are they really Shakespeare performances and, if they are, *how* are they Shakespearian? What cultural forces and pressures are at work in the wordless form of these performances, and how (if at all) do they redraw the possibilities of what might be designated

---

[27] Despite Punchdrunk's emphasis on immersion and interaction, the performance does place limits on where spectators can go and how they can engage with the performers. Some doors in the *Sleep No More* environment are locked or blocked off, suggesting, perhaps unintentionally, that there are areas out of sight where materials are displayed or performances are taking place; the inaccessible spaces, that is, may add to the sense that as spectators we are experiencing only part of a much larger whole. (The truth is that those areas no doubt serve as offstage areas for the actors or passageways which allow them to move unseen from one performance space to another.) Those spectators who take off their masks or who speak are reminded of the rules by minders dressed in black who discreetly monitor the audience's behaviour. Though in theory there is nothing to prevent spectators from physically engaging with the actors directly, in practice audiences tend quickly to adopt the position of voyeurs situated at a distance from the live performances, craning in only when the action the actor is performing is small-scale. Sometimes the actors push spectators aside as they move from one scene to another, but otherwise there is little contact between audience and performer. However, Julie Lipkin of the *Cape Cod Times* reports in her review how a teenager's picking up billiard balls from a pool table led to an extended interaction between actor and spectator; see Lipkin, 'Dream Team', *Cape Cod Times*, 14 November 2009, accessed on Lexis-Nexis, 10 November 2010.

'Shakespeare'? One might even ask, in what sense do these performances really leave the Shakespearian text behind? Both companies, their directors claim, begin their production processes with close engagement with the Shakespearian text, though they proceed with markedly different assumptions and aims. Paul Stacey, assistant director for *Sleep No More*, goes so far in his programme notes as to claim that 'Every line of Shakespeare's *Macbeth* is embedded in the multiple languages – sound, light, design, and dance – of *Sleep No More*.'[28] As the performances evolve, however, Shakespeare's words are pared away as they are translated into visual, physical, musical and even architectural forms. Thinking of this process in terms of 'translation' (and of performance as, in Stacey's phrase, 'multiple languages') might prompt us to consider its relationship with linguistic translation. With translation of Shakespeare, we have become accustomed to thinking in terms of equivalence, approximation, analogy and creative reinvention as means by which a translator might bridge the gap between Shakespeare's language and the target language. Indeed, we have become increasingly comfortable with translations that do not aim for word-for-word, image-for-image, even speech-for-speech fidelity. Is intermedial translation of Shakespeare, then, to be regarded as any different in kind from linguistic translation? As I've been suggesting, it is different at least in one way: it requires its practitioners explicitly to posit an essential Shakespeare of which Shakespeare's language is only a contingent textual manifestation. In the case of the Synetic Theater, that essential Shakespeare is to be located in the narrative and the characters' psychology, not the particular words the characters speak; in the case of Punchdrunk, it is located in particular primal feeling-states of guilt, fatedness and abjection which one experiences instinctually and bodily rather than rationally through Shakespeare's story and imagery, feeling-states which cannot be simply reduced to the text. All directors do this kind of positing of an essential Shakespeare, cutting, rearranging or rewriting passages they regard as extraneous to what they posit is a play's essential core. Paring away *all* of Shakespeare's text

simply radicalizes the implications of that very routine performance process.

These wordless performances also raise the question of how audiences understand these performances. Do they recognize them as Shakespearian and, if so, how? In what sense 'Shakespearian'? Do these performances require or trade upon the audience's prior knowledge of the Shakespearian text? To put this another way, does the audience – or more precisely, the 'ideal spectator' – supply from memory the Shakespearian text that the performance excises? I saw the Synetic *Othello* with a companion who did not know the story, and she was able to follow the action readily and in detail. (Of course, one might object that the general shape of the *Othello* narrative is familiar enough from its diffusion in popular culture; whether that generalized pre-text is specifically Shakespearian would be a matter for some debate.) One measure of the Synetic Theater's skill, I would argue, is that one need not know the text or story beforehand, though perhaps certain moments – say, the allusion to the black ram and white ewe – are enriched by one's recognition of the reference. Whether or not Synetic's skills would be sufficient to perform a play narratively more complex and less familiar to audiences, say *Timon of Athens* or *Cymbeline*, would be interesting to test. The issue of reception is even more complex in the case of *Sleep No More*, where the narrative line is far less clear and the Shakespearian content less readily recognizable. Reviewers regularly remarked on the issue; Lyn Gardner, writing for *The Guardian*, notes that 'you will need more than a passing knowledge of [*Macbeth*] to make the connections' to *Sleep no More*, but goes on to say, 'I suspect that the experience is sufficiently novel that, even if you had never heard of the play, you would take a puzzled

---

[28] Stacey, 'Very Superstitious'. Despite this claim, it seems very unlikely that even a well-seasoned *Macbeth* scholar would be able to identify where all of the lines are physically embedded in the sprawling production, particularly since it is impossible – by design! – to see the whole performance. In other words, the status of the Shakespearian text's (partial/absent) presence in the production needs to be carefully theorized.

pleasure in the evening.'[29] Even the title, *Sleep No More*, seems to mark some distance from its Shakespearian source and perhaps refuses the label of being in some way properly 'Shakespearian'. A full discussion of reception would require examination of promotional materials, programmes and reviews, as well as audience surveys and their analysis, all well outside the scope of this article. But it is worth observing that the Synetic Theater and Punchdrunk have by and large preferred to work with 'classic' texts. On the one hand, it might be said that classical texts provide the requisite depth of narrative, characterization and imagery needed to support two hours of physical performance.[30] On the other hand, undoubtedly some level of prior audience familiarity with the work is helpful in making the productions comprehensible and, equally important, commercially appealing. For Felix Barrett, the value of using classic texts is that they provide audiences with known cultural landmarks with which to orient themselves:

The reason why we use these great classics is, for a start the audience need a hook because the conventions take some getting used to. In order to empower the audience they need to feel that is a puzzle, a conundrum that they can grasp. They need to be able to piece together the history. That's why we never write a piece from scratch, there has to be that awakening, where it clicks for each individual.[31]

The crucial question becomes, then, what level or sort of prior familiarity with Shakespeare is needed for these wordless performances to 'click'? Is the familiarity one with the Shakespearian text *per se*, or does that familiarity spring from other sources? Though for the performers these productions may begin with the Shakespearian text, from the audience's perspective these performances actively refuse Shakespeare's long-standing association with text, and they depend upon a prior knowledge (if they depend on it at all) that is itself independent of close familiarity with the Shakespearian text. This is why I characterize these productions as instances of 'post-textual Shakespeare', for their relationship to the Shakespearian text is supplemental in the deconstructive sense, radically complicating that text's status as a locus for the 'essential' Shakespeare.

This discussion raises a third issue, one of the disciplinary authority to which Shakespeare scholars have traditionally laid claim. The founding gesture of professional Shakespeare study more than a century ago was to reject Victorian biographicalism and focus instead on establishing 'authentic' texts, texts which genuine scholars were obligated to establish and explicate with rigour and which, some performance practitioners aver, even provide detailed guides to their own performance. The equation of the 'essential' or 'authentic' Shakespeare with the Shakespearian text has become so routine that it has the force of common sense for Shakespearian professionals – I mean, what else would you study or appeal to? The growing reach of post-textual Shakespeare offers us an opportunity to reappraise the authority of the Shakespearian text, to trace how and why Shakespeare has migrated across various media and how those migrations relate to dominant and emergent social formations, to think more rigorously about where scholars, performers and the culture at large locate the 'essential' or 'real' Shakespeare and how and why they do so. Given the post-textualization of contemporary culture, it is time for Shakespearians to parse carefully and perhaps to reconsider their devotion to text. Shakespeare is not just any text but *the* text, one of our culture's secular scriptures, and so in the case of Synetic's *Othello* and Punchdrunk's *Sleep No More*, 'doing' Shakespeare wordlessly makes a powerful case that even his power springs from an elemental quality outside or before language, precisely the conviction that underlies the practices of physical theatre. Beyond their sheer virtuosity, what makes these productions fascinating and provocative is the way, by

---

[29] 'Review: *Sleep No More*', *The Guardian*, 17 December 2003, p. 26.

[30] Felix Barrett states that 'the reason why we've used Shakespeare so much is because those descriptions, there's so much in there, so many moments, installations are described within the text it's just a matter of unpicking' (*(Syn)aesthetics*, p. 96).

[31] 'Felix Barrett in discussion with Josephine Machon', *BST Journal*.

their very claim to be 'doing' Shakespeare without words, they complicate long-standing assumptions about what is essentially Shakespearian, and thus complicate our assumptions about where Shakespeare's cultural value lies. Equally interesting is how these performances conceptualize and contextualize the putative universality of Shakespeare within contemporary mediatized culture, something Punchdrunk does with considerable agility.

These performances may be dumb (in the sense of wordless), but they are not dumbed-down or ineloquent, and judging from the crowds I saw at both shows, they speak, so to speak, to contemporary audiences. But are they Shakespeare? To ask this question is to contemplate our own disciplinary assumptions and to confront fully the conditions of Shakespeare's afterlife in an increasingly post-textual world.

I AM WHAT I AM NOT: IDENTIFYING WITH THE OTHER IN *OTHELLO*

STEPHEN COHEN

The relationship between tragedy and race in the critical history of *Othello* has been nearly as fraught as that between the play's romantic protagonists, and for many of the same reasons. The play's earliest critic, Thomas Rymer, found the black Othello so improbable a tragic hero and his relationship with Desdemona so inappropriate as to render the play incapable of producing the requisite tragic effect.[1] Later critics like Coleridge, endeavouring to defend Shakespeare's reputation and the play's status as tragedy, often did so by denying Othello's blackness in order to preserve his plausibility as tragic hero and romantic lead.[2] By the mid-twentieth century, most critics had come to accept both Othello as black and *Othello* as tragedy, and turned to consideration of what sort of tragedy, and tragic hero, the play offered. Those who read it as the tragedy of a noble hero and a great love destroyed by a treacherous villain often did so not by denying but by downplaying Othello's race and emphasizing instead the universality of his feelings and responses, while those who stressed the hero's own culpability in his downfall frequently did so in terms that evoked his 'barbarous' origins and the consequent incommensurability of his marriage. With the increased cultural and critical attention to ideologies of race in the 1960s and 1970s came the now commonplace argument that *Othello* is a tragedy not of race but of racism, exposing and condemning not Othello's race-based inadequacies but rather Iago's destructive use of racial stereotypes and prejudices. This pointed refutation of racial essentialism was often supported by an appeal to universalism, arguing that racist processes of differentiation function, for psychological, political or economic reasons, to obscure a common humanity that the play finally affirms.

In recent years, however, tragedy and race have suffered a separation, if not a divorce, in *Othello* criticism: while in keeping with the historicist and materialist turns in early modern studies, much has been learned about the historical circumstances and cultural data that inform the play's racial imaginary, little has been said about the role of tragic form in its ideological or affective use of those materials. In the argument that follows I seek to redress

---

[1] Quoting Iago's 'Ay, there's the point' speech on the unnaturalness of Othello's marriage (3.3.233–43), Rymer observes, 'The Poet here is certainly in the right, and by consequence the foundation of the Play must be concluded to be Monstrous; And the constitution, all over, to be *most rank, Foul disproportion, thoughts unnatural*. Which instead of moving pity, or any passion Tragical and Reasonable, can produce nothing but horror and aversion, and what is odious and grievous to an Audience' (*A Short View of Tragedy: Its Original, Excellency, and Corruption* (London, 1693), pp. 120–1).

[2] Echoing Rymer, Coleridge claimed that 'it would be something monstrous to conceive this beautiful Venetian girl falling in love with a veritable negro. It would argue a disproportionateness, a want of balance, in Desdemona, which Shakespeare does not appear to have in the least contemplated.' Instead, 'Othello must not be conceived as a negro but as a high and chivalrous Moorish chief.' From, respectively, Coleridge's *Literary Remains* and *Table Talk*, quoted in Edward Pechter, ed., *Othello: A Norton Critical Edition* (New York, 2004), pp. 231, 232. On the intersection of race and genre in early *Othello* criticism see Kim F. Hall, '*Othello* and the Problem of Blackness', in *A Companion to Shakespeare's Works Volume I: The Tragedies*, ed. Richard Dutton and Jean E. Howard (Malden, MA, 2003), pp. 357–74.

this lack by demonstrating the reciprocal roles of racial ideology in the complexity of *Othello*'s formal structure and of formal expectations in the play's depiction of racial otherness. The key to this reciprocity is the concept of identification. Central to early modern and subsequent understandings of both genre and race, identification structures the play's activation as well as its thematization of tragic affect and racial ideology: *Othello*'s formal and racial enticements and anxieties come to a head in an audience's ability – or inability – to identify with its characters. As the play's critical history suggests, however, the results of this dynamic are not universal, but depend upon the reader/viewer's critical and ideological positions. In examining the origins and history of the play's identificatory dynamic, I aim neither to recapture originary meaning nor to correct a history of misreadings, but to reunite race and tragedy in an *Othello* that speaks to our own critical and cultural circumstances.

Though more often associated with late eighteenth-century and Romantic aesthetics, identification was a critical component of early modern dramatic theory. For the period's theorists, the essence of theatre's power lay in its ability to evoke empathetic identification in the service of ethical mimesis: to induce its audience to put themselves into the position of, or see themselves as, its characters, whose virtues and vices they would be moved to imitate or avoid. Essential to the efficacy of this mechanism was the regulatory function of genre: by locating conventional character types in familiar narrative trajectories, genres helped guide an audience's reaction to its identificatory impulse. Defences of drama typically enumerate the major genres' particular effects, with, for example, the glory accruing to the epic hero enticing us to emulate his virtues, or the mockery of comedy teaching us to eschew the foolishness and villainy of its clowns and scoundrels.[3] This connection between genre and the social efficacy of identification was especially significant to the early modern understanding of tragedy. From Aristotle the period's theorists drew the importance of the appropriate tragic emotions, the production of

which required identification: if we are to feel pity and fear at the hero's downfall, we must be able to see ourselves in him.[4] On the foundation of this emotional response, early modern writers built the genre's ethical impact: Thomas Heywood explains that 'If we present a Tragedy, we include the fatall and abortive ends of such as commit notorious murders . . . to terrifie men from the like abhorred practices.'[5] This interdependence of identificatory, affective and didactic effect is exemplified by one of the period's favourite instances of tragic power, the malefactor who sees his own offences represented on stage and is moved to repentance or confession.[6] If we are tempted to discount the simplistic ethical efficacies of early modern genre theory as the wishful thinking of literary apologists, we would be mistaken to discard at the same time the importance placed upon identification as the key to dramatic effect.[7]

---

[3] For two representative accounts of the correlation between genres and their identification-based social effects, see Philip Sidney, *An Apology for Poetry* (1595), ed. Forrest G. Robinson (Indianapolis, 1970), pp. 41–50, and Thomas Heywood, *An Apology for Actors* (London, 1612), F3–F4.

[4] '[P]ity is occasioned by undeserved misfortune, and fear by that of one like ourselves', in Aristotle, *Poetics* 1453a5, trans. Ingram Bywater, in *The Rhetoric and Poetics of Aristotle* (New York, 1984), p. 238. On the role of Aristotle in early modern genre theory, see Daniel Javitch, 'The Emergence of Poetic Genre Theory in the Sixteenth Century', *Modern Language Quarterly*, 59 (1998), 139–69.

[5] Heywood, *Apology for Actors*, F3. Cf. Sidney, who in addition to the aversive identificatory power of 'high and excellent tragedy . . . that maketh kings fear to be tyrants, and tyrants manifest their tyrannical humors' describes a broader tragic affective efficacy 'that with stirring the affects of admiration and commiseration teacheth the uncertainty of this world, and upon how weak foundations gilden roofs are builded' (*Apology for Poetry*, p. 45).

[6] Sidney tells the story of 'the abominable tyrant Alexander Pheraeus' who fled weeping from a tragedy (*Apology for Poetry*, p. 46), an episode reminiscent of Shakespeare's use of the same notion of tragedy in *Hamlet*'s 'Mousetrap' plot. Heywood, *Apology for Actors*, G1–G2, recounts similar stories concerning domestic rather than political crimes.

[7] For two nuanced discussions of the importance of empathetic identification in early modern tragedy, see Heather James, 'Dido's Ear: Tragedy and the Politics of Response', *Shakespeare Quarterly*, 52 (2001), 360–82, and Katherine

The affective and ideological functions of identification are equally significant to the early modern understanding of race. As fluid and overdetermined as the period's conceptualization of race was, it was consistently grounded in two opposed models of difference. In the first, difference is fundamental and ineradicable: the 'other' is associated with the sub-, semi-, or inhuman, with monsters and devils, and is defined and understood by opposition or exclusion, as the 'not us'. In the second, difference, however formidable, is underlain by a fundamental likeness, at least *in potentia*: otherness is rooted in the inessential or malleable, and the racial or cultural other is, or can become, if not 'us' then at least acceptably 'like us'. G. K. Hunter describes a version of this dichotomy and its relevance to *Othello*, locating it in early modern theories of blackness derived from classical and religious discourses. The dominant understanding associated blackness with 'the ugly and the frightening . . . the devil and his children, the wicked and the infidel'; and *Moor*, however vaguely defined and multiply understood in geographical, religious or racial terms, was, '[l]ike *Barbarian* and *Gentile* . . . a word for "people not like us", so signalled by colour'.[8] Against this view of absolute otherness, however, stood a belief in an essential spiritual equality underlying superficial difference: the 'doctrine of the Evangelists that faith could wash away the stains of sin', and 'that all men are within the scope of the Christian ministry'.[9] As our understanding of the variety and complexity of early modern intercultural encounters has expanded and evolved, critics have located this same fundamental dichotomy in other aspects of the period's epistemology of difference, from the geographical (the cunning, wilfully evil Asian or North African vs. the noble, or at least tractable, New World savage) to the religious (the stubbornly anti-Christian Muslim or Jew vs. the pre-Christian pagan ripe for conversion).[10] In each case, the distinction is between an exclusionary and an assimilative understanding of difference: between an 'other' that is essentially and irredeemably alien, and one that is potentially assimilable to the Christian, European or English norm – between an Ethiope

that could not, and one that could, be washed white.

As important to the interaction of race and genre in *Othello* as their mutual foundation in the power of identification is the differential function of identification in each. Dramatic theory is based on the identification of self with other: audiences see themselves as, or like, the characters on stage, whose characteristics they then emulate or repudiate. The identification implicit in the assimilative version of cultural difference, however, is that of other with self, seeing the racial, religious or national other as at least potentially like oneself, and thus capable of increased likeness through conversion or absorption. When the English thought about the reversibility of this vector of intercultural influence, it was not with the optimism of theatre's ethic of self-improvement but with anxiety. Recent criticism has challenged the proto-colonialist model of early seventeenth-century English intercultural contact by noting the equivocal position of the English

---

Rowe, 'Minds in Company: Shakespearean Tragic Emotions', in Dutton and Howard, eds., *A Companion to Shakespeare's Works Volume I*, pp. 47–72.

8 G. K. Hunter, 'Othello and Colour Prejudice', *Proceedings of the British Academy*, 53 (1967), 139–63; pp. 142, 147.

9 Hunter, 'Othello and Colour Prejudice', pp. 152, 153.

10 For the former, see Ania Loomba, 'Shakespeare and Cultural Difference', in *Alternative Shakespeares Volume 2*, ed. Terence Hawkes (London, 1996), pp. 164–91; for the latter, Julia Reinhard Lupton, '*Othello* Circumcised: Shakespeare and the Pauline Discourse of Nations', *Representations*, 57 (1997), 73–89. Edward Berry, 'Othello's Alienation', *Studies in English Literature*, 30 (1990), 315–33, links the two perspectives to the two Spanish views of the 'Indians' of the Americas: either as inhuman and thus fit for enslavement and slaughter, or as potential subjects for Christian conversion. The same distinction may be seen in the period's two chief theories of the origin of blackness: geographical, produced by the heat of the southern sun (and thus superficial, allowing for a potential sameness 'under the skin'), and spiritual, a result of Cham's disobedience to Noah (and thus a sign of a more fundamental, interior difference); see Karen Newman, '"And wash the Ethiop white": Femininity and the Monstrous in *Othello*', in *Shakespeare Reproduced*, ed. Jean Howard and Marion O'Connor (London, 1987), pp. 143–62; esp. pp. 145–8.

nation in its own eyes, at once vulnerable and powerful, threatened as well as threatening. The perceived vulnerability was manifest not only in the threat of military conquest, but also in the fear of conversion or adulteration, of Englishmen 'turning Turk' in foreign lands or of foreign workers and fashions infiltrating and corrupting England.[11] If the assimilative model of difference enables the culturally and politically hegemonic aspirations of imperialism, its understanding of the boundaries of difference as permeable rather than absolute adumbrates in turn the vulnerability of English personal and national identity to the seductive power of identification that the exclusionary model's refusal of identification seeks to deny or forestall.

Given this suggestive overlap between dramatic and racial theories of identification, it is unfortunate that the two are rarely brought into dialogue, especially in the criticism of a play as dramatically compelling and racially charged as *Othello*. Critics who examine *Othello*'s exploitation of the formal mechanisms and affective consequences of identification have for the most part ignored the complicating role of race in encouraging or discouraging identificatory relationships between characters and audience, while those who explore the play's ideologies of race and difference neglect the empathetic implications of the dramatic means by which those ideologies are deployed.[12] By attending to both the dramatic and ideological functions of identification, the reading that follows attempts to both explain and remedy this critical blind spot: first by demonstrating how *Othello*'s interweaving of formal expectations and racial presuppositions creates an identificatory complex whose affective and ideological temptations long structured, and now frustrate, critical response; and then by taking up the resultant opportunity to reconsider the role of identification in our responses to both tragedy and racial difference.

It is a commonplace of *Othello* criticism that the play begins by introducing, in effect, two Othellos. The first, described in 1.1 by Iago, Roderigo and Brabanzio, is depicted as prideful, stubborn and foolish, a thief, an animal, a sorcerer and a devil. The second, presented in 1.2 by Othello himself, appears calm, well-spoken, noble and judicious, a leader who commands the respect of his men. As Hunter and other race-critics have noted, these two Othellos correspond to the period's two chief notions of race, the former exploiting negative stereotypes of blackness to emphasize the Moor's difference while the latter underlines the General's linguistic, personal and professional integration into Venetian society.[13] *Othello* does not, however, simply present these cultural data; it incorporates them into its formal affective mechanisms. Susan Snyder and others have noted the relationship between the play's first act and the structure of Shakespearian romantic comedy: the first three scenes present a comedy in miniature, with impeded lovers, an opposed parent and rival suitor, flight from parental authority, and a concluding public revelation and approbation of the united lovers.[14] The same climactic confrontation in 1.3 that provides comedic closure also appears to adjudicate between the play's racial theories: the Duke sanctions Othello and Desdemona's match by endorsing an assimilative understanding of blackness, telling Brabanzio, 'If

---

[11] On 'turning Turk', see Daniel J. Vitkus, 'Turning Turk in *Othello*: The Conversion and Damnation of the Moor', *Shakespeare Quarterly*, 48 (1997), 145–76. Loomba discusses the anxieties surrounding the potential bidirectionality of intercultural influence, arguing that stories of exotic foreigners assimilating to European Christianity functioned to offset fears of the assimilation of Englishmen to alien cultures: see 'Shakespeare and Cultural Difference', p. 187 and *Shakespeare, Race, and Colonialism* (Oxford, 2002), pp. 18–19, 73.

[12] An important exception is Edward Pechter, *'Othello' and Interpretive Traditions* (Iowa City, 1999).

[13] Hunter, 'Othello and Colour Prejudice', pp. 148–52; cf. Eldred Jones, *Othello's Countrymen: The African in English Renaissance Drama* (London, 1965), pp. 86–109.

[14] Susan Snyder, *The Comic Matrix of Shakespeare's Tragedies* (Princeton, 1979), pp. 70–90. See also Leslie A. Fiedler, *The Stranger in Shakespeare* (New York, 1972) and Carol Thomas Neely, 'Women and Men in *Othello*: "What should such a fool / Do with so good a woman?"', in *The Woman's Part: Feminist Criticism of Shakespeare*, ed. Carolyn Ruth Swift Lenz, Gayle Greene and Carol Thomas Neely (Urbana, 1980), pp. 211–39.

virtue no delighted beauty lack, / Your son-in-law is far more fair than black' (289–90). Here formal and racial identificatory impulses work in tandem, as the desire to identify with the romantic-comedy hero reinforces – and is reinforced by – the Duke's description of an Othello whose virtuous interiority, despite his outward appearance, renders him as 'fair' as the play's normatively white audience.

Yet as the remainder of 1.3 makes clear, the Duke's ruling provides neither formal nor ideological closure, and these twin irresolutions are likewise intertwined. Rather than concluding when the lovers exit, the scene continues with the conversation between Iago and Roderigo. Iago suggests – to the audience as well as Roderigo – that, contrary to the conventions of romantic comedy, the lovers' publicly sanctioned marriage is not the end of the story, and he does so by invoking a milder but no less pointed version of the exclusionary racial rhetoric of 1.1. Using language freighted with violence, sensuality and exoticism ('violent commencement' (343–4), 'luscious as locusts' (348)), he insists that the relationship cannot last because of the insurmountable racial and cultural difference between the two: 'These Moors are changeable in their wills', he tells Roderigo, and Desdemona will, when 'sated with his body', realize the impossibility of her union with 'an erring barbarian' and turn elsewhere for satisfaction (346, 350, 354). The threat of cuckoldry that haunts romantic comedy becomes explicitly plausible here because of the continuing plausibility of Othello's fundamental racial alterity.

Iago's reinstatement of racial difference not only reopens the formal closure of the play's comedic trajectory, however; it also bifurcates that trajectory into two potential comedic structures that correspond to the play's two theories of blackness and their identificatory foundations. The first is an extension of the romantic comedy already described, in which Othello and Desdemona must overcome the continuing obstacle represented by Iago and the frustrated rival suitor Roderigo. This version of comedy depends upon the Duke's assimilative understanding of blackness to make the union not only plausible but acceptable, and it

invites the (male) audience's identification with Othello as he pursues the marital happiness towards which such plots move. The second comedic plot is that offered by Iago to Roderigo, in which Othello is not protagonist but obstacle, the absurdly inappropriate lover who appears to have triumphed but whose victory will be undone by the young hero – Roderigo – and his clever assistant. Iago's projection evokes less the pattern of Shakespearian 'festive' romantic comedy than the satirical 'cuckold comedy', along with related plot and character archetypes from other familiar comic traditions: critics have, for example, identified Iago with New Comedy's witty servant and the *commedia dell'arte* Harlequin, and Othello with both the *senex* and the *miles gloriosus*.[15] As Iago's persuasion of Roderigo makes clear, this version of comedy relies upon an exclusionary understanding of blackness and the consequent absurdity of a successful relationship between Othello and Desdemona. It invites us to identify not primarily with Othello but with Iago, whose generic status as the knowing, controlling trickster-figure at the centre of satiric comedy is reinforced by the formal and rhetorical devices which from the play's first lines position him as the locus of knowledge and subversive power.[16] As Act 1 comes to a close, the audience's anticipatory response to the act's comedic cues at once guides and is guided by their relationship to the play's

---

[15] On *Othello* as cuckold comedy, see Russ McDonald, 'Othello, Thorello, and the Problem of the Foolish Hero', *Shakespeare Quarterly*, 30 (1979), 51–67; on satiric comedy, Pamela Allen Brown, '*Othello* Italicised: Xenophobia and the Erosion of Tragedy', in *Shakespeare, Italy and Intertextuality*, ed. Michele Marrapodi (Manchester, 2004), pp. 145–57; on New Comedy, Frances Teague, '*Othello* and New Comedy', *Comparative Drama*, 20 (1986), 54–64; on *commedia*, Barbara Heliodora C. Mendonça, '*Othello*: A Tragedy Built on a Comic Structure', *Shakespeare Survey 21* (Cambridge, 1968), pp. 31–8.

[16] On the various ways that Iago invites our identification, see Hugh Macrae Richmond, 'The Audience's Role in *Othello*', in '*Othello*': *New Critical Essays*, ed. Philip C. Kolin (New York, 2002), pp. 89–101; Lynda E. Boose, '"Let it be Hid": The Pornographic Aesthetic of Shakespeare's *Othello*', in *Othello*, ed. Lena Cowen Orlin (Basingstoke, 2004), pp. 22–48; and Pechter, '*Othello*' and Interpretive Traditions.

juxtaposed racial ideologies. The linchpin of this connection between genre and ideology is the play's evocation of the possibility – or impossibility – of different sites of identification.

Othello is, of course, not a comedy, though its racially charged use of comedic conventions continues to inflect our response to the play's action well beyond the voyage to Cyprus. It is only at the conclusion of the 'seduction' scene in 3.3, when Iago's plot to dupe and humiliate his victims is transformed into something much bloodier, that the play's genre is definitively transformed as well. By this point, however, the play's dual alignments of dramatic form and racial ideology have so coloured audience response that out of comedy emerges not one but two tragedies, each formally linked to one of the precedent comedies and each predicated upon the correspondent understanding of racial difference and its identificatory implications. They may be designated the tragedy of jealousy and the tragedy of race.

The tragedy of jealousy locates the root of the play's tragedy in the jealousy to which Iago incites Othello; it bears what might be described as a relationship of opposition to the romantic comedy from which it emerges, as the projected happy ending of comedy heightens the tragic destruction of Othello and Desdemona's love. Like its comedic correlate, the tragedy of jealousy is premised on an assimilative racial ideology which discounts Othello's superficial racial difference and allows the audience to see him as 'like us', an identification which in concert with tragedy's formal identificatory imperative permits us in turn to see ourselves in him, admiring his nobility, pitying his downfall and fearing that we too might fall prey to jealousy. Our identification invites us to take Othello at his own estimation as 'one that loved not wisely but too well' (5.2.353), a good man who, while not blameless, was victimized by the 'demi-devil' Iago.

If *Othello* as tragedy of jealousy invites us to empathize with its hero as victim, the tragedy of race, while not denying Iago's role in Othello's downfall, focuses on the Moor's own culpability – a culpability based less on the universal susceptibility to jealousy than on the racially specific characteristics associated by the play and its culture with Othello and blackness: gullibility, violence, superstition and a susceptibility to sexual jealousy that we are invited to view not as potentially our own but as a weakness of the racial other. This version of Othello's tragedy is premised on an exclusionary ideology of race and, like the satiric comedy from which it emerges, it neither presumes nor encourages a primary identification with its protagonist. We may (or may not) sympathize with Othello, but our tragic empathy is rendered problematic by race-based deficiencies that make him more pathetic than pitiable and by increasingly horrific deeds that render him more a figure to be feared than one whose fate we fear to share. This effect is enhanced by the play's proffering of an alternative site of identification in Iago, who invites us to share his perspective by assuming the familiar Shakespearian meta-role of onstage dramatist, his frequent soliloquies making us his audience and inviting our complicity in his machinations. Nor is this invitation ideologically innocent: Iago speaks, as Edward Pechter and others have noted, not only to but also for 'us', bringing his rhetoric of complicity and intimacy to bear upon a discourse of proverbial wisdom and common knowledge that functions to normalize his divisive understanding of race.[17] By alienating us from the play's protagonist, the tragedy of race produces a very different sort of tragedy, less a reversal than an extension of its satirical comedic correlate, one that replaces affective impact with emotional ambivalence and ironic commentary, akin less to *Romeo and Juliet* than to *Troilus and Cressida*.[18]

The affective appeal and ideological power of these two readings are evidenced by their persistence: they remain, in one form or another, the twin poles of the play's modern critical history. If *Othello*'s first critics struggled to reconcile the play's genre and its protagonist's race, twentieth-century criticism responded to the presence of

---

[17] Pechter, *'Othello' and Interpretive Traditions*, pp. 75–105.
[18] Cf. Pechter, *'Othello' and Interpretive Traditions*, pp. 28–9.

a black tragic hero and its affective demands by dividing, in effect, into two camps, which Carol Thomas Neely has characterized as 'Othello critics' and 'Iago critics'.[19] Othello critics respond to tragedy's formal imperative to identify with its protagonist by means of an assimilative understanding of race, acknowledging Othello's blackness while denying or eliding its relevance in favour of a universalizing reading of his plight. They see him as he sees himself: as a true lover and a noble warrior brought low less by his own faults than by a fiendish adversary – a fate to which any of us might prove vulnerable. Iago critics, while rarely acknowledging an identificatory relationship with Iago or his exclusionary view of racial difference, nonetheless manifest the characteristics of both: whether with Iago's scornful glee or the genteel regret of the Venetian aristocrats, they acknowledge Othello's virtues but focus on his flaws, often in explicitly racial or implicitly racialized language that emphasizes not their universality but their particularity. This emphasis on difference mitigates, when it does not eliminate, the identificatory response at the heart of tragic affect.

The critic most responsible for the twentieth-century image of the heroic Othello destroyed by his scheming subordinate is A. C. Bradley, in his immensely influential *Shakespearean Tragedy*. Bradley repudiates nineteenth-century efforts to deny Othello's blackness only to reject the relevance of race to Othello's character by dismissing as 'hopelessly un-Shakespearean' a concern with historical or cultural specificity: *Othello* is not in its essence a portrait of a Moor because Shakespeare was not interested in Moors but in human character.[20] For Bradley, Othello's race is most significant when it is least significant: his blackness functions chiefly to stir our admiration of Desdemona's ability to overlook it, 'follow[ing] her soul until her senses took part with it'.[21] This deracializing of Othello is essential not only to Desdemona's affection but to Bradley's as well. Othello, he declares, is Shakespeare's most sympathetic tragic hero – 'he stirs, I believe, in most readers a passion of mingled love and pity which they feel for no other hero in Shakespeare' – and he defends

this claim against those who emphasize Othello's culpability by insisting not merely on his nobility but on his universality: '*any* man situated as Othello was would have been disturbed by Iago's communications'.[22] For Bradley, our ability to see Othello as a tragic hero depends upon our ability to identify with him, to see ourselves as him; and to do so requires the effacing of racial difference so that we may see him as us.

This sublimation of race in the service of an empathetic identification that subsumes difference within an implicitly white, western, male 'universality' is perhaps the characteristic gesture of *Othello* criticism in the first two-thirds of the twentieth century, equally at home in formal and historical scholarship. The former typically displaces the historically specific significance of race as a social issue in favour of a symbolic or formal function that allows for its generalization, as in Kenneth Burke's claim in his paradigmatic formalist reading of the play, that 'the role of Othello as "Moor" draws for its effects upon the sense of the "black man" [or 'principle of self-doubt'] in every lover'.[23] The latter either denies the historical and/or diegetic existence of early modern racial prejudice[24] or acknowledges its presence only to

---

[19] Neely, 'Women and Men', p. 211. On early criticism of the play, see notes 1 and 2 above. If Rymer and Coleridge come to very different conclusions – the one that *Othello* fails to produce the requisite tragic emotional response, the other that Othello is not a 'negro' – they seem to share a common grounding in an exclusionary ideology of race that prevents them from identifying with a black tragic hero.

[20] A. C. Bradley, *Shakespearean Tragedy* (1904; 3rd edn, Basingstoke, 1992), pp. 170, 159.

[21] Bradley, *Shakespearean Tragedy*, p. 173.

[22] Bradley, *Shakespearean Tragedy*, pp. 163, 165.

[23] Kenneth Burke, '*Othello*: An Essay to Illustrate a Method', *Hudson Review*, 4 (1951), 165–203; p. 182. See also Fiedler: 'for Shakespeare "black" does not primarily describe an ethnic distinction... but a difference in hue – and temperament – distinguishing from one another even what we would identify as members of the same white race'; Othello's blackness 'is, in short, primarily symbolic' (*Stranger*, pp. 171–3).

[24] Responding to Paul Robeson's claim that the play was about the plight of minorities, Robert Withington claims that neither the Venetians in the play nor the Elizabethans in its audience saw Othello through the lens of race. Instead, he argues,

declare its ultimate irrelevance to Shakespeare's dramatic intentions. While Othello responds to Iago's racially motivated manipulation with 'the credulity of a negro', writes K. W. Evans, if his play is to be a tragedy, 'The dramatist's only solution was to persuade his audience to transcend the old familiar stock response to Moors, unite with Othello in a common humanity, and so attain that degree of identification with the play's hero without which tragic effects are impossible.'[25]

Certainly the best-known anti-Bradleyan or 'Iago critic' is F. R. Leavis, primarily for the Iago-like relish with which he attacks Bradley's description of Othello as noble hero/victim. Bradley's portrait of the heroic Moor destroyed by Iago's machinations is the result, Leavis argues, of a critical (over)identification with Othello: 'to see the play through Othello's eyes rather than Shakespeare's'.[26] To do so is to assign a diabolical agency to Iago that the play cannot support while ignoring Othello's own culpability. While Leavis makes explicit reference to race only once, many of the terms in which he describes Othello's faults – 'sensual possessiveness', 'obtuse and brutal egotism', 'ferocious stupidity' – echo the racial stereotypes of both Shakespeare's and Leavis's time.[27] Other critics make plainer the connection between Othello's flaws and his race, and the resultant attenuation or disruption of tragic identification and affect. For Mark Van Doren, the play is still a tragedy capable of producing the requisite effects, but while 'there is the pity of it . . . there is also the terror' – terror not *for* Othello, but *of* him.[28] Othello is a great man but his nobility is a fragile shell that ultimately fails to contain the racially freighted darker side that brings about his downfall: 'The jungle in Othello is ever the enemy to his garden. The ordered rows of his princely manner are in constant danger of being overwhelmed by a wild-beast growth, savage in its strength and monstrous in its form.'[29] This reading of Othello's tragedy as his failure to restrain the savage other lurking within him haunts much of the anti-Bradleyan strain of criticism as it struggles, with varying degrees of success, to reconcile Othello's race with his status as tragic hero.[30]

The cultural developments of the 1960s and 1970s and their effect on the academy fundamentally changed our understanding of *Othello*, making it more difficult either to declare Othello's race to be immaterial or to present racist stereotypes as objective racial data. At the same time, as criticism became more politically self-aware, critics' own identificatory responses to the play became less unconscious than self-conscious ideological interventions. Nonetheless, race-oriented criticism of *Othello* remained bifurcated by the same two theories of difference and their identificatory premises and consequences. On one side were those who continued to see in the play a tragedy of race, with Othello's blackness the source of the flaws that precipitate his destruction. Unlike their predecessors, however, these critics neither explicitly nor tacitly sanctioned the racist stereotypes that underlie such an understanding, but instead condemned the play for its endorsement

---

the play is about jealousy, which 'is easily comprehended at all times. And who is not susceptible to innuendo?': 'Shakespeare and Race Prejudice', *University of Colorado Studies*, 2 (1945), 172–84; p. 175.

[25] K. W. Evans, 'The Racial Factor in *Othello*', *Shakespeare Studies*, 5 (1969), 124–40; pp. 130–1.

[26] F. R. Leavis, 'Diabolic Intellect and the Noble Hero: or The Sentimentalist's Othello', in *The Common Pursuit* (New York, 1952), p. 152. Given his insight into the identificatory complex of the Othello critic, it is ironic that Leavis fails to recognize the affiliations of his own perspective with Iago's. On Leavis and Iago, see Pechter, *'Othello' and Interpretive Traditions*, pp. 28–9, as well as Christopher Norris, 'Poststructuralist Shakespeare: Text and Ideology', in *Alternative Shakespeares*, ed. John Drakakis (London, 1985), pp. 47–66, who notes that in its deployment of cynical realism against naïve idealism, Leavis's critique of Bradley replicates Iago's destruction of Othello (pp. 59–60).

[27] Leavis, 'Diabolic Intellect', pp. 145–7. Like many Iago critics, Leavis sees Othello's race in the context of his marriage, noting that Othello's 'colour, whether or not "colour-feeling" existed among the Elizabethans, we are certainly to take as emphasizing the disparity of the match' (142).

[28] Mark Van Doren, *Shakespeare* (New York, 1939), p. 225.

[29] Van Doren, *Shakespeare*, p. 235.

[30] In his Introduction to the Oxford Shakespeare *Othello* (Oxford, 2006), Michael Neill traces this reading from A. W. Schlegel through Leavis to Laurence Olivier's famous 1964 performance (p. 117).

of those stereotypes – an endorsement they often associated with the perspective of Iago, repudiating the play's invitation to identify with him.[31] On the other side were those who saw the play as a tragedy not of race but of racism. In these readings the precipitating cause of the tragedy is not the flaws inherent in Othello's blackness but the Venetian racism exploited by Iago, a racism that the play does not endorse but rather exposes and refutes. While the critical politics of the tragedy of race reading focus on condemning *Othello*'s perceived exclusionary racial ideology, those of the tragedy of racism are often committed to endorsing the play's assimilative or universalizing understanding of race: if Othello is partially culpable in his own destruction, these readings argue, the fault lies not in his race but in his common humanity. In one of the earliest such readings, Eldred Jones details the deployment of racial stereotypes in *Othello* only to argue that they are ultimately discredited by Othello himself: 'Othello emerges', he argues, 'not as another manifestation of a type, but as a distinct individual who typified by his fall, not the weaknesses of Moors, but the weaknesses of human nature.'[32]

If the differences both between and within the two categories of interpretation I have outlined here – the exclusionary 'Iago reading' and the assimilative/universalizing 'Othello reading' – indicate the role of readers' critical and ideological commitments in their reaction to the text, the persistence of the basic dichotomous response itself suggests the power of the play's identificatory complex. Yet generations of contradictory critical efforts have demonstrated nothing so much as the inadequacies of both positions, especially as their mutually exclusive identificatory constructs buckle under the pressure of the play's tragic climax. The diminishing frequency of Iago's soliloquies, the attenuation of his control over the other characters, and the steadily increasing scope of his villainy – from gulling Roderigo, Cassio and Othello, to plotting and encouraging murder, to killing Roderigo and Emilia – render continued identification with him increasingly difficult. That same villainy, coupled with his repeated

association towards the end of the play with devils, animals and foreigners ('demi-devil' (5.2.307); 'Spartan dog' (371)), also undermines Iago's divisive racial ideology – not, however, by 'whitening' Othello but by 'blackening' Iago. For at the same time, the second half of the play persistently underlines Othello's racial otherness, associating him with the exoticism, witchcraft and violence that the Duke's adjudication in 1.3 sought to deny, climaxing in the racially charged murder of Desdemona and Othello's consequent 'be-devilling' by Emilia ('O, the more angel she, and you the blacker devil!' (5.2.140)). Concurrently, we are dramatically estranged from Othello by the increasing distance between his knowledge and ours and the increasing narrative and emotional importance of that distance, culminating in our mounting horror at what we know to be his erroneous justifications as he prepares to kill Desdemona. The cumulative effect problematizes our ability to see him as a tragic Everyman, as fundamentally 'like us'.

---

[31] The availability of this sort of reading, and the complexity of its identificatory politics, has been enhanced by another academic consequence of the cultural changes alluded to above: the diversification of the professoriate. See, for example, the essays in *Othello: New Essays by Black Writers*, ed. Mythili Kaul (Washington, DC, 1997), especially S. E. Ogude, 'Literature and Racism: The Example of *Othello*', pp. 151–66; and Jacqueline Y. McLendon, '"A Round Unvarnished Tale": (Mis)Reading *Othello* or African American Strategies of Dissent', pp. 121–37. See also Jyotsna Singh on the different identificatory responses of European and African readers to the play's racism, in 'Othello's Identity, Postcolonial Theory and Contemporary African Rewritings of *Othello*', in Orlin, ed., *Othello*, pp. 171–89.

[32] Jones, *Othello's Countrymen*, p. 40; see Hunter, 'Othello and Colour Prejudice', for a similar argument. A more recent example is Martin Orkin, 'Othello and the "plain face" of Racism', *Shakespeare Quarterly*, 38 (1987), 166–88 which reads the play as at once exposing the pernicious effects of Iago's racism and revealing Othello's fallible judgement to be not a racially based failing but 'a human problem' to which we are all susceptible (p. 176). On the universalizing tendencies of such anti-racist readings, see Berry, 'Othello's Alienation', p. 316. For an anti-racist reading that avoids humanist essentialism see Hugh Grady, '*Othello* and the Dialectic of Enlightenment: Instrumental Reason, Will, and Subjectivity', in *Shakespeare's Universal Wolf* (Oxford, 1996), pp. 95–136; esp. pp. 130–4.

The exclusionary and assimilative responses' endurance in the face of mitigating evidence may be attributable to the cultural weight and emotional resonance of the ideological positions they support. Of late, however, these positions have become increasingly problematic: while the racist underpinnings of the tragedy of race and its exclusionary theory of difference have been abundantly clear for some time, recent post-colonial and other non-Eurocentric criticism has emphasized the difficulties with an assimilative view of race that would subsume all difference within a white, Western, Christian vision of 'universality'.[33] Not only does it elide or erase the very difference it purports to embrace, but, as the normative tenor of much 'Othello criticism' suggests, the assimilative gesture paradoxically but necessarily entails an understanding of the universalized category ('man', 'human', 'us') that implies, and relies upon, a demonized non-normative category for those who do not share our 'universal' values: witness the Othello critics' demonization (or pathologization) of Iago, whose monstrosity demonstrates and defines Othello's humanity.

This combination of textual irresolution and ideological dissatisfaction emerging from the exclusionary and assimilative readings of the play has produced a critical impasse that has contributed to the virtual abandonment of the effort to bring together tragic affect and racial ideology in understanding *Othello*'s politics of identification.[34] Recent formalist work on the play, while shifting its focus from genre to the use of theatrical technique and rhetorical form in the manipulation of empathy, has eschewed the role of race in the play's empathetic dynamic.[35] At the same time, race-oriented historical criticism of *Othello* has turned not inward to the racial politics of literary form but outward to interdiscursive analysis, exploring the play's evocation of a variety of historical figures, cultures, discourses and intertexts. While this important work has expanded our understanding of the concepts of race, religion and nationality that undergird the play's construction, it rarely addresses *Othello*'s tragic properties or the role of those properties in shaping the play's

representation of, and the audience's response to, this cultural data.

What follows, then, is an attempt to address this impasse, reintegrating tragedy and race in *Othello* in a reading of the play's identificatory politics that offers an alternative to the exclusionary/assimilative binary and its ideological limitations. *Othello*, we have seen, not only utilizes but also thematizes the power of empathetic identification in racial politics, metadramatically rehearsing our own identificatory quandary in that of the characters. In both the exclusionary and assimilative readings, we respond to Othello as the Venetians do, as a (potential) object of identification: either refusing that identification, or ignoring difference in order to see him as 'like us', so that we may then see ourselves as 'like him'. The play's depiction of identificatory dynamics, however, allows for a third perspective on its protagonist, viewing Othello as neither excluded nor assimilated object of Venetian identification but as a subject negotiating his own identificatory relationship with a racial and cultural other.[36] His struggle to do so and its role in his destruction

---

33 E.g. Berry, 'Othello's Alienation', esp. pp. 315–19. See also Ania Loomba, 'Sexuality and Racial Difference', in *Critical Essays on Shakespeare's Othello*, ed. Anthony Gerard Barthelemy (New York, 1994), pp. 162–86; esp. p. 165, on the implicit racism of ignoring Othello's race.

34 Neill, *Othello*, pp. 121–3 notes an unresolved tension in a number of late twentieth-century critics who find evidence for both racist and universalizing anti-racist readings. He quotes Virginia Mason Vaughan, *Othello: A Contextual History* (Cambridge, 1994): 'I think this play is racist, and I think it is not. But . . . if I insist on resolving the contradiction, I will forge only lies and distortions' (p. 70). Critics who have noted and explored this tension between 'Othello' and 'Iago' readings include Berry, 'Othello's Alienation', Grady, 'Othello and the Dialectic of Enlightenment' and Pechter, 'Othello' and Interpretive Traditions.

35 See, for example, Richmond, 'The Audience's Role', and Kent Cartwright, *Shakespearean Tragedy and Its Double: The Rhythms of Audience Response* (University Park, PA, 1991), pp. 139–79.

36 Critics generally see Othello as a victim of sexual or racial projection (usually on the part of Iago) rather than an agent of identification; see, for example, Janet Adelman, 'Iago's Alter Ego: Race as Projection in *Othello*', *Shakespeare Quarterly*, 48 (1997), 125–44, and Stephen Greenblatt,

allow us to recast the play as a tragedy not of race or jealousy but of identification. The nature of that struggle, and the resultant complexity of our own identificatory relationship to him – at once like and unlike us, subject and other – proffer a third model of identification that critiques the deficiencies of the other two, and in so doing speaks less to nineteenth- and twentieth-century racist and universalist ideologies than to our own increasingly decentred global situation.

Discussions of Othello's self-conception in Act 1 have typically aligned themselves with either the assimilative or the exclusionary theory of race, arguing for either an Othello who sees (or wishes to see) himself as an assimilated Venetian, or one who – whether proudly, unhappily or unconsciously – sees himself as an outsider. Focusing on the same set of justificatory self-descriptions (1.2.17–28, 1.3.76–94 and 1.3.127–69), these arguments emphasize either Othello's eloquent – if perhaps anxious – command of Venetian military and social mores, or his recourse to 'outlandish' references and descriptions, not least of his own origins and adventures. I would propose, however, that Othello's assertion of his own heritage and accomplishments not in the face of but in the terms of Venetian norms – 'I fetch my life and being / From men of royal siege, and my demerits / May speak unbonneted to as proud a fortune / As this that I have reached' (1.2.21–4) – suggests a third option: an empathetic identification with another culture which does not require the surrender or abjection of one's own. His description to the Senate of his 'traveller's history', the attractions and dangers of its exotic content couched in both the rhetorical distinctiveness of the 'Othello music' and the familiarity of the European travel narrative, bespeaks a sense of identity in dialogue with others that it need neither reject nor negate, at once indicating and inviting empathy for the other *as* other, rather than as a version of oneself.

It is an invitation that would seem to have been accepted, given Othello's description of Desdemona's response to his story, phrased at once in the languages of cultural difference and affective response: 'She swore in faith 'twas strange, 'twas passing strange, / 'Twas pitiful, 'twas wondrous pitiful' (1.3.159–60). In Othello's understanding, Desdemona seems to have been able to empathize with his story even while acknowledging its cultural distance from her. Its power was such, he says, as to have overcome her reluctance and forged an emulative identification with Othello's otherness that is sublimated into attraction (and linguistically indistinguishable from it, in his multivalent phrasing): 'She wished she had not heard it, yet she wished, / That heaven had made her such a man' (161–2). It is with this narrative-driven 'witchcraft' of intercultural, rather than assimilative, identification that Othello answers Brabanzio's accusations and the assumption of absolute racial difference that underlies them. In doing so, moreover, he offers the same identificatory model to us as well, as a counter to Iago's exclusionary ideology of race. And while Othello is the abjected object of the construction of racial (non-)relations dominated by Iago's subjectivity, he is at once subject and object of his own intercultural mode of identification, modelling the empathetic response he invites from both on- and offstage audiences even as he insists upon his own otherness.

The fragility of this complex relationship is, however, immediately underscored. When Desdemona enters, her 'witnessing' of Othello's version of their bond is at best equivocal, seeming less to accept than to efface racial and cultural difference. Her first speech, defending the legitimacy of the marriage, compares her own marital duty to her mother's and in so doing equates Othello and Brabanzio, assimilating the former within Venetian cultural norms:

> But here's my husband,
> And so much duty as my mother showed
> To you, preferring you before her father,
> So much I challenge that I may profess
> Due to the Moor my lord. (1.3.184–8)

'The Improvisation of Power', in *Renaissance Self-Fashioning* (Chicago, 1980), pp. 222–54. Critics who do address Othello's identificatory agency tend to emphasize his failed efforts to assimilate within Venetian culture (e.g. Berry, 'Othello's Alienation').

This erasure of difference further resonates in Desdemona's ambiguous description of her attraction to Othello:

> My heart's subdued
> Even to the very quality of my lord.
> I saw Othello's visage in his mind,
> And to his honours and his valiant parts
> Did I my soul and fortunes consecrate . . .
>
> (1.3.250–4)

Even if line 252 is taken not as an effacement of Othello's appearance ('I saw not Othello's face but his inner self') but as an assertion of empathy ('I saw Othello as he sees himself'), the following lines' echo of Othello's description of Desdemona's attraction to his adventures and accomplishments notably lacks the earlier account's pointed acknowledgement and acceptance of 'strangeness'. This absence and its destabilizing effect on Othello's delicate identificatory balance is underlined by his defensively assimilative response, which in endorsing Desdemona's request to accompany him to Cyprus vigorously disavows any erotic motivation on his part – a denial which distances him from the sexual desire that his adversaries have associated with blackness, emphasizing instead the primacy of his role as defender of Venice.[37]

The first act's most explicit invocation of an assimilative model of racial ideology is of course the Duke's final consolatory speech to Brabanzio, which minimizes Othello's difference by privileging an interior, normative whiteness (and in so doing may lend force to a similar reading of Desdemona's earlier reference to Othello's 'visage'): 'If virtue no delighted beauty lack, / Your son-in-law is far more fair than black' (1.3.289–90). Positioned as it is, this assimilative gesture would seem to supplant both Brabanzio's and Othello's very different understandings of racial difference and its impact on empathetic response. Yet if the Duke's couplet strives for the formal power of closure and the rhetorical force of conclusive judgement, it is undercut by Brabanzio's own exit rhyme: 'Look to her, Moor, if thou hast eyes to see. / She has deceived her father, and may thee' (292–3). His mordant recasting of Desdemona's equation

of Othello and himself – here not as honoured husbands but as victims of female duplicity – complicates the Duke's facile inclusiveness, intimating that the assimilative denial of difference may be as threatening to Othello as the exclusionary racism with which Iago closes the first act – and, in its demonization of Desdemona, no less dependent on an abjected other, a 'them' which defines, by opposition, the normative 'us'.[38]

This same dynamic of assimilation and abjection is evoked in Act 2 by Othello's reaction to the brawl that disrupts the dual celebration of his marriage and the destruction of the Turkish fleet. Arriving to quell the disturbance, he asserts a common European Christian identity that relies on, even as it is threatened by, an other with whom identification is both absurd and self-destructive: 'Are we turned Turks, and to ourselves do that / Which heaven hath forbid the Ottomites? / For Christian shame, put by this barbarous brawl' (2.3.163–5). If Othello evinces even here a susceptibility to the dichotomous Venetian identificatory model, it is in keeping with the play's gradual shifting of generic ground that the tragic logic of this model does not take hold until Act 3 scene 3 when Iago succeeds in substituting for the ideal of Othello's intercultural relationships with his wife and adopted city a degrading assimilative identification with Venetian patriarchy and the violently exclusionary abjection of Desdemona that it entails. Yet if Iago is thus the agent of Othello's destruction, Othello remains the subject rather than the object of this identificatory struggle, and it is from his perspective that we witness its consequences.

---

37 Cf. Newman, '"And wash the Ethiop white"', pp. 131–2.
38 Brabanzio's challenge may also return our attention to the 'if' that qualifies the Duke's equation of virtue and beauty/fairness/whiteness, activating beneath the Duke's definitiveness a linguistic complexity and subtextual fecundity that at once underlines the equation's conditional application to Othello (*does* his virtue ensure his assimilable whiteness?) and presages both the tainting of Desdemona (as Iago shatters the link between her fairness and her virtue) and the relationship's tragic trajectory (as the virtuous Othello comes to lose or 'lack' both Desdemona's 'delighted beauty' and his own virtue).

When Othello rejects Iago's initial insinuations about Cassio and jealousy, he does so in terms that reiterate his confidence in a relationship founded on the recognition and acceptance of difference – 'Nor from mine own weak merits will I draw / The smallest fear or doubt of her revolt, / For she had eyes and chose me' (3.3.191–3) – even as his ocular emphasis prompts our unease as we recall the earlier ambiguity surrounding what Desdemona does indeed see when she looks at her husband. Seizing upon Othello's implicit acknowledgement of his otherness, Iago's response –

> I know our country disposition well.
> In Venice they do let God see the pranks
> They dare not show their husbands; their best
>   conscience
> Is not to leave't undone, but keep't unknown.
>
> (205–8)

– counters with an identificatory Hobson's choice that excludes Othello's intercultural middle ground: he can either remain outside the Venetian community (as the implicit 'you' in opposition to Iago's 'I') at the cost of an unbearable insecurity, or join 'our' community at the price of sexual humiliation by an abjected 'they'. When Othello indicates a desire to hear more, Iago leaps into the opening provided by Brabanzio in 1.3, tempting Othello with identification with the Venetian magnifico while reframing as deception what Othello understood as Desdemona's empathetic reaction to his otherness: 'She did deceive her father, marrying you, / And when she seemed to shake and fear your looks / She loved them most' (210–12). When Othello cannot but agree, Iago presses his advantage, rhetorically transferring the taint of witchcraft at the heart of Act 1's exclusionary version of race from Othello to Desdemona: 'Why, go to, then. / She that so young could give out such a seeming, / To seel her father's eyes up close as oak, / He thought 'twas witchcraft!' (212–15). The pivotal speech in Iago's persuasion (233–43) secures his hold on Othello by reintroducing Act 1's negative understanding of blackness but, if the explicit object of that understanding is Othello, its implicit object as well as its subject is

Desdemona. Iago recasts what Othello believes to be her act of interracial identification first as monstrous perversion ('Foh, one may smell in such a will most rank, / Foul disproportions, thoughts unnatural!' (237–8)) and then as a temporary erring from an exclusionary norm ('Her will, recoiling to her better judgement, / May fall to match you with her country forms / And happily repent' (241–3)). Desdemona thus becomes, in Iago's paradoxical but emotionally powerful construction, both unnatural monster and racial exclusionist. Both positions serve as evidence of her betrayal of Othello – a betrayal not simply of marital fidelity, but of the interracial empathy that he believed bound them – and do so in such a way as to invite Othello to despise not his own otherness but Desdemona's.

It is precisely this reaction that is reflected in Othello's mid-scene soliloquy, in which the acknowledgement of his race and its potential role in her betrayal – 'haply for I am black' (267) – triggers not self-loathing but the abjection of Desdemona: 'I am abused, and my relief / Must be to loathe her' (271–2). As the bestializing metaphor through which he imagines his rejection of her suggests ('If I do prove her haggard . . .' (264–7)), Othello has begun to see Desdemona from across a divide unbridgeable by empathetic identification.[39] Moreover, as the second half of his soliloquy suggests, this exclusionary abjection is closely linked to Othello's assimilative identification with the play's normative community of white, male aristocratic Venetians, which functions as both cause of and compensation for Desdemona's alienation. Switching from 'I' to 'we', Othello generalizes his situation to place himself in the company of married men ('O curse of marriage'), great men (''tis the plague of great ones'), and finally all men: ''Tis

---

[39] In doing so he highlights the gender as well as the racial difference between them, invoking the hierarchical assumptions of the former that had, at least in part, been palliated by the identificatory dynamic of the latter (as, for example, when Othello speaks of Desdemona as a 'warrior' like himself). On the complex relationship between racial and gender difference in *Othello*, towards which this article can only gesture, see Loomba, 'Sexuality and Racial Difference', and Newman, '"And wash the Ethiop white"'.

destiny unshunnable, like death. / Even then this forkèd plague is fated to us / When we do quicken' (272, 277, 279–81).[40] In doing so he effaces the difference whose recognition had earlier served as warrant for Desdemona's affection ('For she had eyes and chose me') in favour of a likeness that degrades even as it reassures.

Othello's bond with Desdemona is not, moreover, his only relationship affected by this self-destructive assimilation within the Venetian community of cuckolds: for if Desdemona is the object of Othello's jealousy, Cassio is its rival subject, and his relationship with Othello is likewise transformed by Iago's manipulation of identification. The mutual regard of Othello and Cassio is reflected in the lieutenant's role not only as confidant but as participant in Othello's wooing of Desdemona: 'When I have spoke of you dispraisingly [he] / Hath ta'en your part' (3.3.73–4), she reminds him, and the reminder seems instrumental in Othello's promise to consider Cassio's reinstatement. It also, however, provides an opening for Iago's insinuations – 'Did Michael Cassio, when you wooed my lady, / Know of your love?' (96–7) – which, through the logic of his replacement of identification-with-difference with the assimilative uniformity of universal cuckoldry, transform the empathy required to take another's part into a desire to supplant that other. Jealousy, in the play's identificatory dynamic, is the inversion of empathy, replacing emulation with competition, and reciprocal affection with violent retaliation: 'They laugh that wins', says Othello as he witnesses what he believes to be Cassio's triumphant narration of his displacing of Othello in Desdemona's affection and bed; 'I see that nose of yours, but not that dog I shall throw it to!' (4.1.121, 139–40).[41] And while Iago focuses Othello's attention on Cassio, Othello's generalizing fantasy – 'I had been happy if the general camp, / Pioneers and all, had tasted her sweet body, / So I had nothing known' (3.3.350–2) – suggests that his jealousy is as much structural as personal: the erasure of difference required by Othello's Venetian assimilation creates equivalences that render each man both a fellow cuckold and a potential cuckolder. The more one fears cuckoldry, the more comfort one takes in the fraternity of victimhood; yet the more one empathizes with the cuckolded, the more one dreads one's own betrayal: this reciprocal reinforcement creates an emotional spiral that adds credence to both the rapidity and persistence of Othello's jealousy.[42]

The perversion of empathetic identification that alienates Desdemona and vilifies Cassio culminates in 3.3 with the supplanting of both wife and lieutenant by Iago, Othello's new confidant and his sponsor in the community of Venetian cuckolds. In the scene's climactic mock marriage, whose murderous vows mark the play's formal commitment to tragedy, Iago pledges to 'give up / The execution of his wit, hands, heart / To wronged Othello's service' (468–70) and is rewarded with the lieutenancy. That Iago roots his vow of faithful service in 'remorse' (471), or pity, for Othello's suffering underlines both the parallel with and the perversion of the bond between Othello and Desdemona. From this point, though Othello continues to struggle with his feelings for Desdemona, their nature is altered. The collapse of his original understanding of their relationship is only enhanced – by, for example, her horrified reaction to the story of the handkerchief's exotic origins and her rejection of the proffered identification with its previous owner, Othello's mother (3.4.55–75). In the absence of that understanding, the ornaments of aristocratic Venetian womanhood that once complemented her virtue – ''Tis not to make me jealous / To say my wife is fair, feeds

---

[40] Pechter notes Othello's pronoun shift, as well as the source of his sense of the commonality of cuckoldry in Iago's Venetian 'common knowledge' ('Othello' and Interpretive Traditions, pp. 104–5).

[41] This logic, significantly, is not Othello's alone: it underlies not only Iago's desire to retaliate for his suspicion that Othello has slept with Emilia by being 'evened with him, wife for wife' (2.1.298), but also Emilia's argument that women should imitate their husbands' infidelities: 'Then let them use us well, else let them know / The ills we do, their ills instruct us so' (4.3.101–2).

[42] This dynamic is further reflected as Othello prepares to kill Desdemona, telling himself that 'she must die, else she'll betray more men' (5.2.6): Othello's cuckolders become, in turn, fellow cuckolds, whose cause he here takes up.

well, loves company, / Is free of speech, sings, plays, and dances well / . . . / For she had eyes and chose me' (3.3.187–93) – instead exacerbate her deception:

Othello. A fine woman, a fair woman, a sweet woman.
Iago. Nay, you must forget that.
. . . .
Othello. Hang her, I do but say what she is – so delicate with her needle, an admirable musician. O, she will sing the savageness out of a bear! Of so high and plenteous wit and invention.
Iago. She's the worse for all this.
Othello. O, a thousand, a thousand times!

(4.1.174–88)

As a result, Othello's attraction to Desdemona narrows to an objectifying physical desire: planning her murder, he tells Iago, 'I'll not expostulate with her, lest her body and beauty unprovide my mind again' (4.1.199–201). It is just this sort of physical attraction that Iago posits early in the play as the only plausible explanation for a relationship 'betwixt an erring barbarian and a super-subtle Venetian' (1.3.354–5) which, he assumes, cannot possibly be based on a sustained interracial empathy.

It is this mutually reinforcing complex of failed identification-with-otherness and debasing normative assimilation that Othello brings to the murder of Desdemona. He enters the bedchamber prompted by what he believes to be a reciprocally empathetic bond with Iago: 'O brave Iago, honest and just, / That hast such noble sense of thy friend's wrong', he says in response to what he takes to be Iago's killing of Cassio, 'Thou teachest me' (5.1.32–4). His state is not a reversion to a purportedly essential savagery, but a profound self-alienation born from the collapse of his original sense of self-and-other: torn between sensual attraction ('O balmy breath, that dost almost persuade / Justice to break her sword!' (5.2.16–17)) and a (self-)destructive sense of obligation to the Venetian fraternity of cuckolds ('Yet she must die, else she'll betray more men' (6)), he retreats to an abstract sense of 'justice' devoid of mitigating empathy. If he cannot fully resist pity, it is, he

insists, not empathetically human but punitively divine: 'This sorrow's heavenly, / It strikes where it doth love' (21–2). When Desdemona wakes, his concern for her soul while disregarding her life – and his righteous anger when she resists his plan – darkly parodies the logic of conversion that underlay the European assimilative response to New World encounters with the native other, with Othello as both victim and now subaltern agent of its annihilation of difference. Ultimately, however, as her denials 'stone' his heart, turning sacrifice to murder as he ignores her pleas for time to pray, Othello's killing of Desdemona demonstrates the dehumanizing consequences of an exclusionary logic that refuses to recognize the self in the unassimilable other.

Read in this way, the tragic power of *Othello*'s emotional climax provides affective evidence for the inadequacies of both the assimilative and the exclusionary understandings of difference. If the 'othering' of Desdemona and its deadly consequences underline the dangers of the exclusionary refusal of empathy, their connection to Othello's disastrous identification with Venetian patriarchy reveals the failings of an assimilative model whose 'universalizing' ideology is not so much inclusive as homogenizing, unwilling to accommodate difference beyond its normative bounds. In this sense, the play's diegetic exploration of empathetic identification is in accord with the lessons of its bifurcated critical history. If that history is based on Othello's role as the object of an identificatory struggle, however, with critics either identifying with a universalized Othello or failing to do so in the face of his unassimilable otherness, the foregoing reading locates Othello as the subject of such a struggle, pursuing or rejecting various modes of identification with the play's other characters. In doing so, it both expands and complicates our potential identificatory response to the play. For if our horror at Othello's treatment of Desdemona may induce us to question his status as noble tragic hero, by inviting us to question the exclusionary ideology which motivates that treatment, the play challenges our willingness to apply it to Othello himself. We may, that is to say, deplore Othello's actions, but we cannot disavow our identificatory connection to him without committing an act of affective violence not unlike his own. Conversely, while the play's unease with the assimilative response to difference may speak to anxieties about the threat of contamination or adulteration through the absorption or emulation of foreign cultures, Othello's status as the subject rather than object of this anxiety – it is he, not Venice, who is degraded and destroyed by his assimilation – invites us to understand the danger of assimilation from the perspective of the outsider rather than the dominant culture. In doing so the play challenges us to empathize with Othello as identifying subject without ignoring or eliding his status as other.

It is, then, through the problematizing of identification that we are at last invited to identify, however partially and uncomfortably, with Othello. Whether based on an assimilative or exclusionary response to difference, the failure of Othello's identificatory efforts in the second half of the play both produces and reflects our difficulty responding to him in either mode. Yet if *Othello* is finally neither the universal tragedy of a heroic Everyman nor the cautionary tale of a barbarian reverted to savagery, the play does offer a third tragic path, and a third identificatory model, that point the way beyond contradiction and negation. The answer lies in Othello's final long speech. As elusive as it is important, the speech has served as the capstone of any number of disparate interpretations, having been read as everything from the triumphant recovery of Othello's noble nature to the confirmation of his savage alterity to the demonstration of his irreconcilable cultural fragmentation. Seen in terms of the foregoing discussion, however, Othello's valediction marks the return not only of the rhetorical eloquence that characterized his introductory self-descriptive speeches, but of their particular content as well, the hybridization of self and other that marked his mode of identification-with-difference. Yet while he begins, as he did earlier, by asserting his connection to Venice ('I have done the state some service' (5.2.348; cf. 1.2.18)), the other with which he primarily identifies here is not Venice but the exotic and abjected alien:

he is '[l]ike the base Indian', his tears like gum from 'Arabian trees' (356, 359). That this identification does not fully constitute identity, however, is suggested by Othello's choice of figure: not the geographic metonymy of a 'traveller's history' but instead simile, a rhetorical form of identification-with-difference whose 'like' recognizes similarity without asserting sameness. This gesture prepares the way for Othello's final self-accounting:

> in Aleppo once,
> Where a malignant and a turbaned Turk
> Beat a Venetian and traduced the state,
> I took by th' throat the circumcisèd dog
> And smote him thus. (361–5)

If Othello's fear and scorn at the thought of turning Turk in Act 2 anticipated his tragic division between assimilation and exclusion, his return to the figure of the Turk here suggests a very different relationship to otherness, an ability to identify not only with the dominant Venetians but with the despised 'enemy Ottoman' as well, to recognize the other as other yet acknowledge one's likeness to it.

Yet if Othello's final identification with difference echoes that with which he began the play, the two are nonetheless as different as comedy and tragedy. Othello's initial understanding of his relationships with Desdemona and Venice bespoke a desire to bring together the best of self and other, to recognize and emulate the good in the other (nobility, military prowess, virtue, love) without denying or destroying difference – a gesture in keeping with, even as it pushes the ideological boundaries of, the celebratory unions of the comedic ethos. His deathbed identification, however, is not with good but with ill – the malign violence of the Turks as well as the cruelly retaliative 'justice' of the Venetians – and is tragic in both consequence and moral implication. Yet as Othello's self-destructive attempt to extirpate that malignancy suggests, this tragedy is in its socio-ethical effect not the early modern tragedy of repudiation, which teaches us how not to behave, but rather the simpler yet more challenging – and more timely – tragedy of recognition and identification, which insists that we empathize with that which we would abject, denying neither its monstrosity nor its kinship with ourselves.[43] To do so requires that we recognize not merely our own monstrosity, real or potential, but also its – and our – potential status as the object of an 'other' subjectivity.

Like the play's other tragic readings, this version of *Othello*'s tragedy evokes, through its depiction and production of empathetic identification, an ideology of difference: one that demands that we neither reject the other as inhuman nor re-imagine it as a version of ourselves, but rather that we empathize with the other *as* other, no matter how disturbing or frightening. Read in this way, *Othello* leaves a contemporary audience not without a point of identification but with a challenge: to identify neither with Iago and his rhetoric of racial exclusion nor with a deracinated, 'universalized'

Othello, but with a Moor whom we recognize – and in whom we recognize ourselves – not despite, but because of, his otherness. In an early modern England poised between fear of foreign incursion and its own colonial enterprise, such a recognition may have been difficult; in an imperialist England or an exceptionalist America, much more so. In a post-colonial world at the end of the 'American century', however, this Othello may be one that we must learn to recognize.

---

43 Cf. Terry Eagleton, *Sweet Violence: The Idea of the Tragic* (Malden, MA, 2003) on a version of tragedy that 'involves coming to pity what we fear, finding our own selves reflected in the abhorrent and abominable . . . If we are to escape the sealed circuit of the self, or the equally windless enclosure of self and other, we have to have sympathy for the other precisely as monstrous' (165).

DESDEMONA'S BOOK, LOST AND FOUND

ROSHNI MOONEERAM

Cultures, or what are known as cultures, do not mix. They encounter each another, mingle, modify each other, reconfigure each other. They cultivate one another; they irrigate or drain each other; they work over and plough through each other, or graft one onto the other. (Jean-Luc Nancy)[1]

The alternative to separatism is border thinking, the recognition and transformation of the hegemonic imaginary from the perspectives of people in subaltern positions. Border thinking then becomes a 'tool' of the project of critical cosmopolitanism. (Walter Mignolo)[2]

INTRODUCTION

Natasha Distiller, in her article 'Shakespeare and the Coconut: Close Encounters in Post-apartheid South Africa', argues that Shakespeare continues to be deployed within a framework reliant on 'a particular display of English literariness understood to exist in a binary relation to a putative Africanness'.[3] Whereas the persistent applicability of the trope of the coconut to the image of Shakespeare is an indication of ongoing hierarchies of social and economic power in the South African context, I explore an alternative way of engaging (with) Shakespeare off the East coast of Africa in the post-colonial context of Mauritius where a putative Africanness is a creolized one. Uninhabited until the end of the sixteenth century, Mauritius underwent several waves of colonization which brought together European settlers, slaves from various parts of the African mainland,

Madagascar, India and indentured labourers from various parts of India and China.[4] A Creole language developed in the seventeenth/eighteenth century on the sugar cane plantations during French settlement, partly drawing from the French dialects spoken at that time and based on a different grammatical system, arguably influenced by an African substrate.[5] This lingua franca has by now also acquired a vocabulary drawing from several of the Asian languages spoken in Mauritius and increasingly from English and remains the main spoken language. It is within this context of creolization, which already indicates a practice of border crossing, that I

---

[1] Jean-Luc Nancy, *Being Singular Plural* (California, 2000), p. 151.

[2] Walter Mignolo, *Local Histories/Global Designs: Coloniality, Subaltern Knowledges, and Border Thinking* (New Jersey, 2000), p. 174.

[3] Natasha Distiller, 'Shakespeare and the Coconuts: Close Encounters in Post-apartheid South Africa', *Shakespeare Survey 62* (Cambridge, 2009), pp. 211–21; p. 212.

[4] After being a Portuguese, Dutch, French and British colony, Mauritius has been independent since 1968 and a republic since 1992.

[5] The genesis of Mauritian Creole remains highly disputed between linguists such as Robert Chaudenson, who maintain the overarching influence of dialect-influenced French, and Philip Baker, who advocates an African substrate. Megan Vaughan, in *Creating the Creole Island, Slavery in Eighteenth-Century Mauritius* (Durham, NC and London, 2005), argues that 'To put it at its simplest, the linguists' debate is about who made the language – the slaves or their masters, the Africans or the French' (p. 206).

consider the appropriation of *Othello* by Dev Virahsawmy, linguist, political activist, creative writer and translator who writes exclusively in the local language, Creole. Whereas Shakespeare accessed in English in his traditional associations of Britishness and tradition survives, just about, through an elitist English-medium education system inherited from colonial days in Mauritius, it is as Virahsawmy's Shakespeare deployed to complex multivalent ends that the Bard thrives. If fathoming out the various points where a catalysis may lie in the complex two-way traffic between the source text and Virahsawmy's appropriation were not complex enough, Dev Virahsawmy also moves away, in *Prezidan Otelo*, from the post-colonial writing back project, itself constrained by the problematic binaries of colonial thinking. In an attempt at charting diffuse and manifold catalyses, which, by definition, operate in the untidy framework that Nancy ascribes to culture, I look at the dynamics of branding in Virahsawmy's works and the development of his theory of Creole cosmopolitics.[6]

The significance of a brand or author's name, as Lanier argues, 'is not controlled by a single marketer or critic but rather emerges from myriad interactions between producers, consumers, and various cultural intermediaries and contexts'.[7] Indeed, the branding of Shakespeare, far from being stable, changes in relation to the historical conditions and social practices of the respective communities in which the Bard is appropriated. Virahsawmy's renderings of Shakespeare in the vernacular are a main form of praxis through which he seeks to exert some influence as organic intellectual and culture activist.[8] His translation of Shakespeare as well as other world literary giants forms part of his cosmopolitan project of building bridges across literary cultures and making canonical texts accessible to a local audience in the vernacular.[9] I have argued elsewhere that over the past thirty years Virahsawmy has self-consciously used Shakespeare (in translations, adaptations and original plays peopled with Shakespearian characters) for the purposes of linguistic legitimization and nation-building.[10] One of the ways in which Shakespeare

has acted as cultural catalyst has been in Virahsawmy's linguistic project within the framework of post-colonial creolistics,[11] an engaged form of linguistic activism which aims to validate citizenship and the rights of Creole speakers who constitute the majority of the Mauritian population (80 per cent).[12] By way of making a transition from my previous investigations into language standardization through Shakespeare to Virahsawmy's literary self-fashioning and development of a theory of Creole cosmopolitics,[13] I will explore, after a brief synopsis of the play, a telling sociolinguistic item in *Prezidan Otelo* (2003).

Prezidan Otelo

Virahsawmy's play opens on Christmas eve on a tropical island to the lyrics of a subversive rendition of *Jingle Bells*, whereby far from riding on a sleigh, in anticipation of an exciting event, everyone is in a race to get richer quicker in a world on the brink of an ecological disaster and where any faith

---

6   Françoise Lionnet, 'Matière à photographie: cosmopolitique et modernité créoles à l'Ile Maurice', *French Forum*, 34 (2009), 75–99, borrows the term cosmopolitics from Bruce Robbins and Pheng Cheah, eds., *Cosmopolitics: Thinking and Feeling beyond the Nation* (Minneapolis, 1998).

7   Doug Lanier, 'Shakespeare: Myth and Biographical Fiction', in Robert Shaughnessy, ed., *The Cambridge Companion to Shakespeare and Popular Culture* (Cambridge, 2007), p. 93.

8   Virahsawmy describes himself as an organic intellectual in the Gramscian sense in 'La poésie mauricienne d'expression créole (CM) et la "culture de la langue"', in Daniel Baggioni and Carpanin Marimoutou, eds., *Formes-Sens/Identités* (St Denis, 1989), pp. 77–104.

9   Virahsawmy has translated, amongst others, works by Molière, Hugo, Arnold, Blake, the Grimm brothers and the Indian epic *Mahabharata*. All his works can be accessed from his website, http://boukiebanane.orange.mu.

10 Roshni Mooneeram, *From Creole to Standard: Shakespeare, Language and Literature in a Postcolonial Context* (Amsterdam and New York, 2009).

11 I borrow this term from Michel Degraff. Although Virahsawmy does not himself use this term, Degraff's uses of Gramsci are germane. See 'Linguists' Most Dangerous Myth: The Fallacy of Creole Exceptionalism', *Language in Society*, 34 (2005), 533–91.

12 From the 2000 Mauritius Population Census.

13 Virahsawmy does not himself use this term.

in the human or magical has been 'locked up' by merchant bankers. The chorus repeats the dispiriting line: 'Bonom Nwel finn pase' (Father Christmas has been/is past), three times ending on the final line 'Bonom Nwel finn tase' (Father Christmas has got stuck). The protagonist, Otelo, is the President of this country, with Yago as his Prime Minister and Desdemona as Vice-Prime Minister and also a personal friend to the President. Otelo is married to his gay partner and they have adopted two children. Yago, jealous of Otelo and of the friendship between the latter and Desdemona in particular, sets about to destroy her, though, as in Shakespeare's play, his malignity remains mostly motiveless. The handkerchief is replaced by one of Khalil Gibran's books of poetry with a handwritten inscription by Otelo given by the latter to Desdemona to seal their friendship. Yago distorts Otelo's homosexuality into paedophilia and engineers a series of events which results in the death of Desdemona's son and triggers Otelo's belief that Desdemona has betrayed his trust through the symbol of the discarded gift. A feminist sense of agency is very much at work in Virahsawmy's rewriting as it is across much of his creative and philosophical writing.[14] His Desdemona is not one who admires Othello for the dangers he has passed and who in turn is loved by him for her pity but is an empowered, politically active woman, one who has successfully fought for national independence and for women's rights. An unambiguous Emilia here sets the record right over the missing book and there is reconciliation between the two friends, Otelo and Desdemona, at the end. Virahsawmy's vocal Emilia, far from being reduced to 'nothing, but to please [Yago's] fantasy' (3.3.303), articulates with confidence her distrust in and defiance of Yago, confronting him with his obsessive view of women as sexual slaves. She plays a crucial role in the denouement which forestalls the destruction of Desdemona's political integrity. Virahsawmy thwarts expectations of a victimized black Othello as much as he circumvents a demonical Yago who, in *Toufann*, his irreverent rewriting of *The Tempest*, already had a voice against this enduring perception, and does so again here.[15]

THE POLITICS OF LANGUAGE

Dammarro and Kaspalto, two characters who made their first appearance in *Toufann*, inspired by Trinculo and Stephano from *The Tempest*, are still the junkie and the alcoholic they were then, homeless, directionless, jobless and penniless. The politics of language choice and language use in Dammarro and Kaspalto's idiolects, which is key to *Toufann*,[16] remains a preoccupation of Virahsawmy's in *Prezidan Otelo*. Dammarro reflects, in this latter play, on his manipulative strategy of code-switching in addressing a local crowd at a political meeting:

Dammarro. Pa bizen dir, mo ti tap mo daway pou gagn toupe. Mo koz angle mo dir twa. Enn filwar koze sorti al kraz dan zorey kouma vag lor brizan . . .
Kaspalto. Angle? Dimoun ti konpran?
Dammarro. Pa kone. Pa enportan, mo kwar. Enn mo mam dan klib mas ti vinn felisit mwa. To'nn gagn lizour, mo dimann li. Pa tro me mo stil ti enpresionan. Kikfwa mo ti bizen fer politik. (1.6)
[*Dammarro.* Obviously, I hit back a few for Dutch courage. I spoke English, would you believe. A string of words surfaced pounding the ear like waves against the reef . . .
Kaspalto. English? Did people understand?
Dammarro. No idea. It's not important, I don't think. One of my pot-smoking mates came to congratulate me. Did you get it, I asked. Not really but I was still impressed. Maybe I should have done politics.]

This revealing sociolinguistic commentary is a reminder of the status of English in Mauritius as an official language, used exclusively and perhaps misused by a politically manipulative elite.[17] It also

---

[14] *Ziliet ek so Romeo* (2001), for example, draws from Shakespeare's *Romeo and Juliet* as much as it is a retelling of the expulsion of Adam and Eve from Eden from a feminist perspective.
[15] *Toufann* translated into English by Nisha and Michael Walling (London, 2004).
[16] See Roshni Mooneeram, 'Language Politics in Dev Virahsawmy's Postcolonial Rewriting of *The Tempest*', *Journal of Commonwealth Literature*, 46 (2006), 67–81.
[17] English occupies an anomalous position in Mauritius. Although it had been a British colony from 1810 to 1968 and English has retained an (unofficial) official status since

suggests Virahsawmy's awareness of translation as a manipulative activity. Educated in the UK, previously a university lecturer in English studies, and self-aware of his membership in an elite group, Virahsawmy thus reinstates cultural democratization as the driving force behind his Creole Shakespeare project. While it is true that, on one hand, the power that the Shakespeare brand enjoys from its historical associations is being exploited to legitimize his cultural explorations, on the other, it is used critically and its use is negotiated amidst the conflicting ideologies that it represents within Virahsawmy's own framework of post-colonial creolistics. The seemingly contradictory sets of relations that surround Shakespeare in its indissolubility from the English language can be further articulated through Neville Alexander's distinction between the dominance and the hegemony of English.[18] While dominance results from historical power and is, therefore, subject to change in relation to changes in the global balance of political powers, hegemony is much more subject to the intervention of agents who are mobilized to counteract the discursive structures which accompany and support the dominance of a particular language. To extend this linguistic framework to Shakespeare, one can argue that whilst Virahsawmy acknowledges the dominance of Shakespeare in both global and local terms, he also demonstrates his own agency in renegotiating the terms by which Shakespeare is perceived and deployed.

Dammarro's and Kaspalto's disgruntlement at the end of *Prezidan Otelo*, to which I will come back, is a reminder of their threat of a similar riot at the end of *Toufann*. With names which are constructed from linguistic and cultural resources recognizable to a local audience[19] and appearing across a number of Virahsawmy's plays, these two characters can be said to be developing as props to the latter's art. Virahsawmy not only self-consciously inscribes his own position and ideology into *Prezidan Otelo* but engages actively in literary self-fashioning. There is increasing evidence in Virahsawmy's growing corpus of translations and adaptations of Shakespeare, in his citations of Shakespeare in otherwise original plays,[20] in the

intertextual threads he weaves across these texts and in the many instances of self-reference, that he fashions his own iconicity through Shakespeare, that the latter, in fact, has been re-branded as *his* trademark.

TOWARDS CREOLE COSMOPOLITICS

Françoise Lionnet cogently argues that if 'cosmopolitan' evokes a certain elite culture of travel and sophistication that can readily be contrasted with nationalism and parochialism, creolization, whether cultural or linguistic, on the other hand, tends to remain a devalued and misunderstood phenomenon, in large part because of its association with slavery.[21] She calls for a *rapprochement* between cosmopolitanism and creolization which she terms 'Creole cosmopolitics'. Cosmopolitics, she argues, in the sense given to it by Robbins, is applicable to the complex identity relations in Mauritius for ethnic groups who have at once attachments to distant ancestral cultures and one of national belonging. Quoting Robbins and Cheah, 'Instead of an ideal of detachment, actually existing cosmopolitanism is a reality of (re-)attachment, multiple attachment, or attachment at a distance', Lionnet argues that it is precisely this sense of multiple belonging that

---

then, according to the 2000 Population Census English is the language usually spoken at home by 0.2% of the population.

[18] Neville Alexander, 'Creating the Conditions for a Counter-hegemony Strategy: African Languages in the Twenty-first Century', in Salikoko Mufwene and Cécile Vigouroux, eds., *Globalization and Language Vitality: Perspectives from Africa* (London/New York, 2008), pp. 255–71.

[19] Kaspalto in Creole literally means to break free of one's coat and, by extension, to have a drink. It is also the name of a cheaply available wine. Dammarro is from a popular Hindustani song and means to have a spliff.

[20] *Sir Toby* (1998) and *Dr Hamlet* (2000), for example.

[21] Bruce Robbins and Pheng Cheah, *Cosmopolitics: Thinking and Feeling beyond the Nation* (1998), p. 3, in Françoise Lionnet and Thomas Pear, 'Mauritius in/and Global Culture: Politics, Literature, Visual Arts', *International Journal of Francophone Studies*, 14, Special issue, 'Between Words and Images: The Culture of Mauritius' (2010), 1–31; p. 8.

characterizes the creoleness of contemporary Mauritian identity and society. I would like to extend this framework by arguing that Virahsawmy practices a form of Creole cosmopolitics which builds on the existing practices of creolization in Mauritius, highlighting these as a stepping stone to embracing a wider cosmopolitanism by connecting with cultures beyond those that inform the main ethnic groups from Europe, Africa, South Asia and China. In *Prezidan Otelo* Virahsawmy works beyond the confines of colonial difference to embracing complex layers of conversations characterised, to draw from Nancy, by relations of irrigation, modification, reconfiguration and grafting, as links are forged between Shakespeare and Gibran and Mauritianness in the articulation of a Creole identity.

BRANDING GIBRAN

In this section I focus on Virahsawmy's rendition of what is, arguably, the most fetishized object in Shakespeare's play, the handkerchief, and propose a reading of his considered choice of object against the multifaceted significance of the handkerchief. The inclusion of Gibran seems to be testimony to the fact that great literature exists independently and beyond Shakespeare and occidental literature. The fact that the 'book of poetry' is not specified corroborates the point that Virahsawmy is deploying Gibran as another brand, albeit of less significance than Shakespeare, but nonetheless one which questions Britain's status as exporter of cultural products and which, in his rewriting, plays a pivotal role. The links between identity and art which bring significance to the handkerchief help to contextualize the thrust of Virahsawmy's re-branding. In *Othello*, the handkerchief takes on an almost metaphysical status epitomizing European fascination and fear of racial and sexual difference and anxieties about miscegenation.[22] It denotes, argues Virginia Mason Vaughan, 'Othello's exotic otherness, his orientalism, his alienation from Christian values and hence Venetian culture'.[23] Passed on to him by his mother, the handkerchief also provides a powerful connection to art through identity. Indeed, the highly charged symbolism ascribed to the handkerchief suggests that the connection that people feel to cultural objects that are identified as theirs, because they were produced within a world of meaning created by their ancestors, is particularly strong. More insidiously, the handkerchief becomes the symbolic transfer of loyalties from one patriarchal generation to another. The handkerchief, possessing magical powers which kept his father bound to his mother, represents to Othello a male fear of the power of women from whom it is important to break away. When the handkerchief is lost Othello's reaction betrays how both the fear and hatred of his wife are related to his feelings about his parents. Betrayed by Desdemona, just like his father was by his mother, he can only retaliate.

Virahsawmy's choice of a book of poetry by Gibran highlights, in contrast, a connection which is neglected in discussions of cultural patrimony, the connection not through difference but despite difference. We can, Virahsawmy maintains, respond to art that is not ours. The choice of Gibran suggests the supposition that all cultures have enough overlap in their vocabulary of values to begin a conversation. Appiah's view of conversations, literal and metaphorical is helpful here: 'Conversations across boundaries of identity – whether national, religious or something else – begin with the sort of imaginative engagement you get when you read a novel or watch a movie or attend to a work of art that speaks from some place other than your own.'[24] Gibran also emphasizes the different premises on which Otelo and Desdemona's relationship is based. Their relationship is clearly already one of friendship both within and beyond their mutually supportive professional

---

[22] See, for example, Karen Newman, '"And wash the Ethiop white": Femininity and the Monstrous in Othello', in Jean E. Howard and Marion O'Connor, eds., *Shakespeare Reproduced: The Text in History and Ideology* (London, 1987).

[23] Virginia Mason Vaughan, *Othello: A Contextual History* (1994), quoted in Martin Orkin, *Local Shakespeares: Proximations and Power* (London, 2005), p. 30.

[24] Kwame Anthony Appiah, *Cosmopolitanism, Ethics in a World of Strangers* (New York, 2007), p. 84.

roles, but the book emphasizes the point that this relationship, far from being governed by realpolitik or opportunism, is based on values that transcend those of political power and material gain. Whereas the marriage, sealed by the handkerchief in Shakespeare, is an enslavement of the man against his better judgement, here it is an engagement with the experience and ideas of others that binds the friendship between Otelo and Desdemona. The book, linked to neither ancestry nor a coercive form of magic, is empowering rather than blindly binding, allowing space for connections through choice and through the power of an art that belongs to neither of them.

The contradictions of de-branding Shakespeare and bringing in Gibran while still exploiting the former is particularly resourceful in relation to Virahsawmy's cosmopolitan vision. One of Virahsawmy's concerns about a small nation with no pre-colonial past and with diasporic links from three continents, Europe, Africa and Asia, going back three centuries is the question of how far back one must go for the sake of cultural authenticity. While Shakespeare's Othello, through his attachment to the handkerchief, grants the past 'more epistemological authority than it deserves',[25] Virahsawmy chooses a poet who is almost contemporary, from a part of the world that is different from any of the ancestral homes for ethnic groups in Mauritius, and who is himself borne across. Virahsawmy thus reinforces his stance against 'conceptions of allegiance that presuppose consistency and uncritical enthusiasm'.[26] His Otelo's ability to theorize a version of the past that does not pivot on atavistic attachments is key to ensuring that the play does not unfold into inevitable tragedy. Gibran's book becomes a symbol of a cosmopolitan vision which emphasizes multiple or flexible attachments to more than one nation or community. While the creolization that has already been in place in Mauritius is a successful reminder that cultures are made of continuities and changes and that the identity of a society can survive and thrive in uncharted directions through these changes, Virahsawmy maintains a sense of vigilance in relation to the complacency that underlines discourses of

harmonious multiculturalism. In *Toufann*, he had already warned against a tyrannical Prospero of Indian descent, wielding political power and advocating his belief in 'pure blood'.

CRITICAL COSMOPOLITANISM

As Virahsawmy moves away from the insular and self-admiring rhetoric of the post-colonial nation towards the construction of a critical cosmopolitan vision, Shakespeare mobilizes the imagination for political and ethical tasks beyond nation-building. Through Yago's sexual othering of Otelo as the devil, homophobia is compared to racism which, in a previous sugar colony, has a particularly monstrous and persistent resonance. Shakespeare is deployed to undermine a commitment to values that Virahsawmy's target readership might have settled into. Yago's distortion of Otelo's sexual orientation into perversion is loquacious, 'enn pervers, enn pedofil pe diriz mo pei' (a perv, a paedophile is ruling my country), 'sa mons la' (that monster), whose aim is to pass a law which would give him 'pouvwar fer masak ar zanfan, fer pedofili vinn legal' (the power to molest children, legalise paedophilia), 'Bizen anpes sa bouro la viol ek tortir nou zanfan' (We must stop this murderer from torturing our children) (1.4). Otelo's gay marriage, adoption of children and creation of an alternative family whilst in a position of leadership is as much a blow to the values of contemporary Mauritius as Shakespeare's Othello's marriage would have represented a threat of pollution to an Elizabethan audience. By conflating anxieties over race and those around homophobia, Virahsawmy rearticulates the main qualities of the cultural power of Shakespeare in its association with Britishness and tradition, using, instead, Shakespeare as a means by which his contemporary target culture can read its own biases.

---

[25] Linda Charnes, 'Shakespeare and Belief in the Future', in Hugh Grady and Terence Hawkes, eds., *Presentist Shakespeare* (London, 2006), pp. 64–78; p. 76.

[26] Rebecca Walkewitz, *Cosmopolitan Style: Modernism beyond the Nation* (New York, 2006), p. 9.

The parallels between Shakespeare's Othello, a stranger from a mysterious other world that lies beyond a Renaissance audience's reach or comprehension and the treatment of homosexuality in a contemporary Mauritian context are effective. Although homosexuality was pivotal to *Toufann*, it remained 'a sanitised form of homosexuality',[27] that which could not be defined. It was as a result of an accident which insinuated impotence that Ferdjinan refused a heterosexual identity with Prospero's daughter, choosing instead an androgynous half-robot, Aryel, as partner. Whereas Ferdjinan's homosexuality was problematically conflated with a lack (of sexuality) and associated with the other-worldliness of a robot, Virahsawmy treats homosexuality much more assertively in *Prezidan Otelo* and does so in interaction with both his previous work, *Toufann*, and Shakespeare's *Othello*. While Shakespeare's Othello recognizes, despises and destroys the Moor in himself, or rather what Venice makes of the Moor in him, Virahsawmy's Otelo never once succumbs to Yago's deformed image of his homosexuality. The stigmatization of homosexuality in *Prezidan Otelo* does not get internalized to turn upon itself in self-loathing and, ultimately, self-destruction. By the same token Virahsawmy's story is not a self-fulfilling prophecy of the black President killing off the black slave within him. Although race is only hinted at and never specified, blackness would be very much present in the audience's mind. Otelo's blackness, the (white) elephant in the room, is an appropriate reminder that race relations in Mauritius remain tense, underpinned by the unarticulated shame of slavery.

The fact that it is Otelo's hand-written dedication which brings value to this gift takes on further levels of significance. It is not the writing of others which defines his relationship with Desdemona, but his own. Otelo's inscription is already a sign that he has the ability to write a new script about his own life, one that would not be determined by his past or past incarnations. What is at work in Virahsawmy's *Prezidan Otelo* is precisely a sophisticated example of what Mignolo describes as one of the tasks of critical cosmopolitanism, that is the clearing up of the encumbrances of the past, the Renaissance and Enlightenment prejudices that surrounded the concepts of race and manhood and which remain as persistent as other forms of marginalization in contemporary times.[28]

The ending, however, does not provide comic relief to what could have been a tragedy. Far from offering a blueprint of a future and ideal plural society from a single point of view, Virahsawmy offers instead a practice of diversality. He eschews definitions of national cohesion by valuing the triviality of diversion and focusing on Dammaro and Kaspalto's tricks and ruses. At the end of the play when Yago's ploy is laid bare and Desdemona and Otelo are reconciled, Dammarro and Kaspalto step out of the frame of the play and threaten a mini-riot as a sign of protest against the play's title, *Prezidan Otelo*, which they maintain obliterates any of the work they have done to get the action going. Because they cannot decide whether this very play should be named Dammarro and Kaspalto or Kaspalto and Dammarro, in fact, it is suggested that they retain the original title. It is then Yago's time to complain that no one proposes to name the play after him. Unlike Shakespeare's Iago who swears to keep mum:

Demand me nothing. What you know, you know.
From this time forth I never will speak word.

(5.2.309–10)

Virahsawmy's Yago remains vocal:

Zot temwen zot tou! Mari discrimination! Person pa propose pou apel sinema la Yago. Enn lemon ipokrit, mo dir zot. Pa kwar zot pa kone. Zot tou bien kone. San mwa zot pa ekziste. Orevwar. Nou pou rezwenn. Marke, garde. (*Prezidan Otelo*, 5.2)

---

27 Chantal Zabus, *Tempests after Shakespeare* (New York, 2002), p. 242.

28 Walter Mignolo, 'The Many Faces of Cosmo-polis: Border Thinking and Critical Cosmopolitanism', *Public Culture*, 12 (2000), 721–48.

[You are all witnesses here! This is abject discrimination! No one proposes to call the show Iago. What a hypocritical world. Don't pretend you don't know. You all know only too well. Without me you don't exist. Farewell. We will meet again. Mark my words.]

This ending also proposes a sense of fallibilism which is fundamental to both rewriting as a genre and to Virahsawmy's cosmopolitan revisioning, 'the sense that our knowledge is imperfect, provisional, subject to revision in the face of the new evidence'.[29] Far from projecting an elitist, aesthetic, harmoniously 'easy' cosmopolitan view, he works more along the lines of Mignolo's critical cosmopolitan values, endorsing a sense of constant alertness. The quarrelling voices from Shakespeare and elsewhere serve to debunk the 'postcard' and exoticized view of Mauritian culture, reinscribing instead several layers of competing agency.

There is resonance in *Prezidan Otelo* of Mignolo's call for a cosmopolitanism which emerges from historical locations of the colonial difference and which would not hide the coloniality of power from which different cultures came into being in the first place. Virahsawmy neither hides Otelo's blackness nor makes it irrelevant. But since Shakespeare is no longer confined to the obvious medium through which to write back to the centre, he becomes the catalyst for a wider transformative project which brings into a multi-layered conversation a number of silenced and marginalized voices, from that of homosexuals, to women, to Yago. What we witness is not a triumphant Otelo over a defeated Yago but rather a blurring of the boundaries between the hegemonic and the subaltern both within Shakespeare's *Othello* and Virahsawmy's rewriting, in a striking example of what Mignolo calls 'border thinking' or 'border epistemology'.

CONCLUSION

I have argued that Shakespeare, in the Mauritian context, functions as a catalyst in the transformation of the cultural institutions of the local vernacular, literature and social values, and in the development of Virahsawmy's theory of cosmopolitanism. The many levels of resonance between the sociolinguistic context in which Shakespeare was writing, his creative use of language, his attempts to take genres away from the previously exclusively courtly literary precedent to a more urban audience, have all been enabling to Virahsawmy's own projects. As Shakespeare is relocated in constantly shifting and increasingly uncharted environments, within Virahsawmy's literary career, the deployment of the Bard becomes increasingly unpredictable and the ways in which he acts as a catalyst multifaceted. In the context of Mauritius, the name of Shakespeare and Virahsawmy are now indissoluble and as Virahsawmy gets bolder in his adaptations of Shakespeare, the latter serves to buttress the former's literary brand. In commenting on the impact of allusions on the restructuring of literary traditions, Erickson's reflection is particularly pertinent, 'We might think of allusions as tiny microcosms of canon formation in which localized explorations ultimately have larger cumulative repercussions.'[30] Shakespeare, in his function as a potent catalyst in the Mauritian context, has had, in turn, his established associations rearticulated. This process, at a geopolitical level, steers the signification of Shakespeare in an African context away from the trope of the coconut, just as, at a disciplinary level, it steers Shakespeare in adaptation away from the tired binaries of post-colonial theories.

---

[29] Appiah, *Cosmopolitanism: Ethics in a World of Strangers*, p. 144.
[30] Peter Erickson, *Citing Shakespeare: The Reinterpretation of Race in Contemporary Literature and Art* (Basingstoke, 2007), p. 8.

NON-CATALYST AND MARGINAL SHAKESPEARES IN THE NINETEENTH-CENTURY REVIVAL OF CATALAN-SPEAKING CULTURES

JESÚS TRONCH-PÉREZ

My contribution to this volume on Shakespeare as a 'cultural catalyst' will take this term in the broad sense of an agent speeding up a reaction, without implying that the agent remains unchanged in the process, and will consider one type of 'cultural reaction', that of writers of a minority (or 'minorized') language that seek to restore its social use and literary prestige.[1] The language I will refer to is Catalan and the specific 'reaction' is the revivalist movement known as *la Renaixença* ('rebirth' or 'renascence'), initiated in the 1830s in the Spanish regions of Catalonia and Valencia, and later in the Balearic Islands and in the French region of Roussillon.

After exploring whether Shakespeare was a catalyst in, and in what ways Shakespeare's works contributed to, the revitalization of Catalan-speaking cultures in Spain in the nineteenth century, I will show that, contrary to the preconceived idea that translations and adaptations of Shakespeare infuse social and literary prestige in the minorized culture, most of the early Shakespeares in Catalan constitute marginal forms of literary and theatrical use that bespeak other kinds of contributions to the recovery of cultural identity or simply disregard such an aim.

After a fifteenth-century Golden Age, especially due to Valencian authors such as Ausias March and Joanot Martorell, Catalan began its literary decline when the cultural elite forsook it in favour of Spanish, the language of the dominant political institutions, although Catalan continued to be deployed in administrative and most public uses. After the War of Succession in the early eighteenth century, the diglossic situation worsened as the new Bourbon monarchy imposed the law and customs – including the language – of Castile in those kingdoms of the Crown of Aragon (including Valencia, Majorca and the Principality of Catalonia) that had supported its Habsburg opponent. Removed from the administration and education, Catalan remained the low-prestige language for domestic purposes and some popular and peripheral literary uses. In the 1830s, partly influenced by Romanticism, the earliest voices vindicating the use of Catalan for literary and social purposes began to be published and initiated the *Renaixença*, akin to the Felibritge movement for Occitan and the *Rexurdimento* for Galician (the latter initiated in 1864).[2]

It is easy to hypothesize that appropriations of Shakespeare in a minorized language are part of a strategy for survival or invigoration of its declining culture. Translations, theatre productions or literary or theatrical uses of Shakespeare seek to transfer the prestige associated with the renowned classic author to the subordinated language and its culture.

---

[1] This article is part of the Research Project FFI2008-01969/FILO 'Shakespeare's Presence in Spain in the Framework of his Reception in the Rest of Europe', financed by the Ministerio de Ciencia e Innovación.

[2] Or at a later date, Kristlik Selskip foar Fryske Tael en Skriftennisse (Christian Society for the Frisian Language and Literature), created in 1908, and Jongfryske Mienskip (Community of Young Frisians), created in 1918.

For instance, Jules Cubaynes, an Occitan translator of Shakespeare, stated in 1955 that a language provided with translations of the classics was a language that had reached maturity and that should be taken seriously.[3] Similarly, and more recently, Mauritian writer and cultural activist Dev Virahsawmy has been rewriting Shakespeare in Mauritian Creole 'for the purposes of linguistic legitimisation, nation-building, linguistic and literary self-fashioning' within his struggle 'to debunk the persistent colonial discourses that position the vernacular in a position of deficiency'.[4]

In the case of Catalan, telling confirmation of this hypothesis can be found from 1898. Arthur Masriera's preface to his *Hamlet*,[5] the first full translation of a Shakespeare play into this language, explains how his rendering was commissioned as part of theatre director Adrià Gual's project to dignify Catalan theatre. He refers to Shakespeare in bardolatrous terms as 'the prince of playwrights' and 'the colossus of Theatre'. Buffery remarks that Masriera's translation was 'driven by the desire to facilitate the Catalan language and the Catalan stage with a monument enjoyed for years in all other European languages'.[6] By 1938, another significant Catalan translator of Shakespeare, Cèsar August Jordana, was pointing out that the tradition of good translations into Catalan demonstrated a desire to enrich 'a new and still weak culture', but still a desire that other cultures could even envy.[7]

This span of forty years between 1898 and 1938 almost coincides with the consolidation of the revivalist impetus in the form of *Modernisme* and *Noucentisme* (although Catalan did not have official status yet). Shakespeare was, together with Ibsen and Wagner, the most important foreign author to be translated into Catalan in the early twentieth century.[8] As scholars Par and Esquerra noted,[9] in the short span of four years between 1907 and 1911, seventeen translations of Shakespeare were published in the affordable pocket-size volumes of the series 'Biblioteca Popular dels Grans Mestres' [Popular Library of Great Masters]. It is with respect to the Catalan-speaking book market in this period that Shakespeare may be confidently said to

be a catalyst. However, it remains to be ascertained whether a 'Shakespeare catalysis' was happening in Catalan theatre and literature in general. This, however, is not my concern in this article. My analysis of the presumed catalytic role of Shakespeare will focus on the early Shakespeare manifestations in Catalan up to 1898. I take this date as *terminus ad quem* since it coincides with the first full translation of Shakespeare, the above-mentioned *Hamlet* rendered by Masriera,[10] and more or less coincides with the end of the *Renaixença*.

---

[3] 'una Lenga pervesida de sas traduccions classicas es una Lenga arribada a sa majoritat e que deu èstre presa al seriòs', in his article 'Utilitat d'una traduccion occitana de las majas òbras classicas grecas e latinas' *Oc*, 297 (1990), 25–34; esp. p. 28 (first printed in *Oc*, 197 [1955]).

[4] Roshni Mooneeram, 'Desdemona's Book, Lost and Found: Cosmopolitanism and Branding in *Prezidan Otelo*' presented at the seminar 'Deploying the Shakespeare Brand' at the 34th International Shakespeare Conference, 10 August 2010. See also her *From Creole to Standard: Shakespeare, Language and Literature in a Postcolonial Context* (Amsterdam, 2009).

[5] Arthur Masriera, trans. *Hamlet, Príncep de Dinamarca* (Barcelona, 1898).

[6] Helena Buffery, 'El parany del ratolí' *Journal of Catalan Studies*, 1 (1997). www.uoc.edu/jocs/1/translation/translation. html, n.p.

[7] Cèsar August Jordana, 'L'art de traduir', *Revista de Catalunya*, 15 (1938), 357, reprinted in Dídac Pujol, *Traduir Shakespeare: Les reflexions dels traductors catalans* (2007), p. 119.

[8] Enric Gallén, 'El teatre', in *Historia de la literatura catalana*, ed. J. Molas *et al.* (Barcelona, 1986), vol. VIII, pp. 379–448; esp. p. 385.

[9] Alfonso Par, *Shakespeare en la literatura española* (Madrid, 1935), vol. II, pp. 114–17, 211–43; esp. p. 214; and Ramon Esquerra, *Shakespeare a Catalunya* (Barcelona, 1937), p. 130. Other sources on Shakespeare in Catalan are María Isabel Iglesias, 'Shakespeare en Catalán,' *Filología Moderna*, 15–16 (1964), 227–34; Xavier Fàbregas, 'Notes introductòries a les traduccions catalanes de Shakespeare', in *Estudis de llengua i literatura oferst a R. Aramon i Serra en el seu setanté aniversari. Miscel·lània Aramon i Serra vol. 1* (Barcelona, 1979), pp. 181–204; Pujol, *Traduir*; and the recent monograph by Helena Buffery, *Shakespeare in Catalan: Translating Imperialism* (Cardiff, 2007).

[10] The earliest unadapted Shakespeare on stage was Adrià Gual's production of *Twelfth Night* (*Las festa dels reis* in the Catalan translation by C. Capdevila) in January 1904 with the theatre company Teatre Íntim (Intimate Theatre), which he founded in 1898 and with which he hoped to renovate and dignify Catalan theatre. See Buffery, *Shakespeare*, pp. 30–4, and Juan

From a survey of the early Catalan Shakespeares,[11] one could draw a map divided into three basic areas: a predominant line of theatrical parodies and their publications for a popular audience starting in 1873; Víctor Balaguer's reworking of Shakespearian themes for more 'serious' or highbrow addressees from 1876; and partial translations of *Hamlet*, sometimes included in critical appraisals.

By 1873, Shakespeare had been known for over a century in Spain (in Spanish),[12] and the bilingual citizens of the Catalan-speaking territories would already have an image of Shakespeare as one of the greatest literary or dramatic geniuses, an idea mainly generated by the praise endowed on the English bard by critics who, as in most European countries, championed him as the main advocate of their prevailing Romantic aesthetics. Yet those bilingual citizens would have had little chance to get to know Shakespeare's plays relatively unmediated in print or on the stage. It was in the 1870s when the first attempts were made to publish Shakespeare's complete works in Spanish,[13] very likely spurred by the success of Italian companies led by Adelaida Ristori, Tomaso Salvini, and especially Ernesto Rossi, performing in the main Spanish capitals since 1857. As the prominent Spanish Shakespearian scholar Alfonso Par observed,[14] these companies greatly contributed to increasing the presence of Shakespeare in Spain, and, more interestingly, they 'discovered' Shakespeare on the stage for the Spaniards since they offered theatregoers, for the first time, 'unadapted' (although cut) versions of *Othello, Hamlet, Macbeth, Romeo and Juliet* (as well as adaptations of the latter and of *The Merchant of Venice*). Before the Italians, only citizens of Madrid and Barcelona could have enjoyed Ducis-derived versions of *Othello* or of its parodies (as detailed later) and of *King John*, and a translation of Casimir Delavigne's *The Sons of Edward*, and much less frequently a recasting of *Romeo and Juliet* based on Le Tourneur's French translation and a rewriting of *Richard III*.[15] Surely Par would have agreed that Rossi's and other Italian companies' Shakespearian seasons were a real catalysis in the popularization of Shakespeare in Spain,

since a good number of translations and stage adaptations began to appear from that time.

After this contextualizing of the early Shakespearean manifestations in Catalan within the reception of Shakespeare in Spain, it should be first pointed out that all the Catalan-speaking Shakespeares come from Catalonia, not from Valencia, the Balearic Islands or the Roussillon. The absence of Shakespeare in the cultural reaction of Valencian, Balearic and Roussillonese authors correlates with the fact that the *Renaixença* movement was comparatively weak in these regions in relation to that of Catalonia.[16]

In terms of their catalytic contribution to Catalan culture, the partial translations of *Hamlet*[17]

F. Cerdà, 'Shakespeare and the Renovation of Spanish Theatrical Culture (1898–1936)', Ph.D. dissertation, University of Murcia, 2010, pp. 92–125.

[11] A survey of evidence taken from Alfonso Par, *Representaciones shakespearianas en España*, (Madrid, vol. I in 1936, vol. II in 1940), from sources in n. 9, and from library catalogues, digital archives and bibliographies.

[12] He was first mentioned in 1764 in a defence of Spanish national theatre; the earliest theatre production was a *Hamlet* adaptation, staged in 1772, based on J. F. Ducis's 'imitation'; and the earliest full translation, *Hamlet* again, by playwright Moratín in 1798 (Par, *Shakespeare*, I, pp. 74, 78–86, 113–17).

[13] A compilation of translations by different authors in Francisco Nacente, ed., *Los grandes dramas de Shakespeare* (1870–1?), and two attempts of direct and verse translations of Shakespeare's complete plays by Jaime Clark (1873–4?) and Guillermo Macpherson (1873–97).

[14] Par, *Shakespeare*, II, pp. 39–40, 63; and *Representaciones*, vol. II, pp. 86–7.

[15] Par, *Representaciones*, vol. I, pp. 26–31, 39–41, 77–8, 153–6, 177–8, 184–5.

[16] As I pointed out in 'Translating Shakespeare in Sociolinguistic Conflicts' (lecture delivered at the 8th ESRA conference in Pisa, November 2009), translated Shakespeare can be taken as an index for the vitality of a minorized language.

[17] F. [Josep Franquesa y Gomis], 'Hamlet. Acte tercer – Escena primera' [translation of 3.1], *La Ilustració Catalana*, I (30 August 1880), pp. 43–6; Eduart Tamaro, 'Hamlet y Ofelia' [one-paragraph introduction to the translation and to illustration by J. Narváez], *La Ilustració Catalana*, I (30 August 1880), p. 43; Ovidi de Llanza, trans. 'Hamlet, Monólech', *L'Avens*, 32 (15 June 1884), p. 322; and Celestino Barallat y Falguera, *Shakespeare y Moratín ante la fosa y traducción catalana de un cuadro de Shakespeare: memoria leída en la Real Academia*

can only be assessed unfavourably. They constitute three fragments (from 3.1 and 5.1) of only one
play, although certainly one of Shakespeare's most
canonical titles. As early experiments in translating Shakespeare into Catalan, they were indeed
sporadic and relatively marginal. Although two of
them were published in two literary and artistic journals in Catalan, they only reached a limited learned readership of already convinced Cata-
lanists. The two other areas of the map of early
Shakespeares are theatre productions of deriva-
tives, which support Cuccu's statement that the
spoken word and the image (rather than the
written word) opened the way for the introduction of Shakespeare in Catalonia.[18] Yet, it
should be remembered that most of those theatrical adaptations were also printed and often
reprinted.

The case of Víctor Balaguer (1824–1901) needs
to be examined closely. An author in both Spanish and Catalan and a prominent politician in
nineteenth-century Spain, Balaguer is one of the
significant figures of the *Renaixença*, although more
as a poet and enthusiast than as a dramatist. At the
age of fourteen, he started to write Romantic dramas in Spanish. His *Julieta y Romeo* (whose heroine, he claimed, was neither Shakespeare's, Soulié's
nor Rojas's)[19] had a single, unsuccessful performance in the Teatro Principal of Barcelona in
1849.[20] Towards the late 1850s he started to write
in Catalan and contributed to the restoration of
the medieval poetry contest known as *Jocs Florals*
in Barcelona in 1859, a key cultural institution of
the *Renaixença*.[21] In the 1860s Balaguer befriended
Italian actor Ernesto Rossi in one of his Spanish
tours, an acquaintance that apparently drove Balaguer back to Shakespearian themes.[22] In his 1876
collection *Tragedies*, he published *Coriolà* [*Coriolanus*] (crediting Plutarch and not Shakespeare as
his source) and *La sombra de Cèsar* [*Caesar's Shadow*],
among other Romantic-inspired short tragedies
dramatizing historical characters such as Hannibal,
Nero or Columbus.[23] However, the Shakespeare-
related plays did not reach the stage and only *Coriolanus* was performed, but in a Spanish translation,
not in Catalan.[24]

In 1878 Balaguer turned back to the star-crossed
lovers of Verona with the tragedy *Les esposalles
de la morta* [*The Betrothal of the Dead Maiden*],[25]
first performed in the following year at the Principal, a theatre of the aristocracy and wealthy middle class (with a predominant repertoire of social
or moral bourgeois comedy, a type of Spanish
operetta called zarzuela, eighteenth-century Spanish drama and French bourgeois comedy).[26] This
earned him the honour, as Par puts it, of being
the first playwright to provide Catalan with a play
indirectly related to Shakespeare.[27] *Les esposalles de
la morta* was often revived on the stage and in
reprints,[28] and was even translated into Spanish
and into Swedish.[29] Balaguer reduced the cast to

de Buenas Letras, celebrada el 1 de diciembre de 1890 (Barcelona,
1896).

[18] Marina Cuccu, '*Les esposalles de la morta*: Víctor Balaguer i
el mite de Romeu i Julieta', in *El segle romàntic*, ed. M. Jorba
et al. (Vilanova i la Geltrú, 1997), pp. 441–53; esp. p. 441.

[19] In the epilogue to *Julieta y Romeo: tragedia en tres actos*
(Barcelona, 1849). Frédéric Soulié's *Romeo et Juliette* was published in 1838. Balaguer's play was reprinted as *Los amantes
de Verona* [*The lovers of Verona*] in the collection *Junto al hogar*
in 1853.

[20] Par, *Representaciones*, vol. I, pp. 222–6.

[21] The *Jocs Florals* were restored in Valencia in 1879.

[22] Cuccu, '*Les esposalles*', p. 443.

[23] Víctor Balaguer, '*Coriolà*', '*La sombra de Cèsar*', in *Trajedias*
(Barcelona, 1876).

[24] At the Teatro Novedades in Barcelona 1–3 September 1877
(Par, *Representaciones*, vol. II, p. 113). Xavier Fàbregas mentions performances of the Spanish version in Madrid and
Havana without providing a date ('Àngel Guimerà i el teatre
del seu temps' in *Historia de la literatura catalana*, ed. Martí
de Riquer *et al.* [Barcelona, 1988], VII, pp. 543–604; esp. p.
566).

[25] Víctor Balaguer, '*Las esposallas de la morta*', *Revista Catalana
de Literatura, Ciencia i Arts* (Nov. 1878), reprinted as *Las
esposallas de la morta: tragedia* (Barcelona, 1878).

[26] Carme Morell, *El teatre de Serafí Pitarra* (Barcelona, 1995),
pp. 163–5. I wish to thank Enric Gallén, Manuel Jorba and
Miquel Gibert for their clarifications of the history of Catalan theatre.

[27] Par, *Representaciones*, vol. II, p. 118.

[28] On the stage, in 1881, 1888 and 1896 (Par, *Representaciones*,
vol. II, pp. 118–20, 124, 136 and 146); reprinted in 1879 (two
editions – one in the collection *Novas Tragedias*), 1882, 1893,
1894, 1911 and 1918.

[29] Cuccu, '*Les esposalles*', p. 450.

Romeu, Julieta, Capuletti (Julieta's father), Conrad d'Arles (equivalent to Paris) and Fra Llorenç, and structured the plot in three scenes, beginning roughly at the Shakespearian Act 2 scene 5, and showing, among other divergences, Romeo's off-stage killing of Julieta's brother and Julieta's waking up before Romeu dies.[30] Using mostly decasyllables in alternating rhymed patterns and unrhymed stretches, Balaguer resorted to medieval expressions and archaisms and rejected popular forms, as other 'highbrow' writers of the *Renaixença* did. Generally, the play's Romantic imagery has been positively praised.[31]

In the context of the history of Catalan-speaking theatre, Balaguer's short tragedies constitute one of the earliest attempts at the genre, contributing to what historians define as the 'learned' or 'highbrow' trend of Catalan theatre that sought to provide the language with literary dignity in contrast to the popular trend best represented by the one-act plays called *sainets*, which employed plain language and domestic themes and characters.[32] The former attempted to show that Catalan was appropriate for 'serious' drama, while 'popular' playwrights disregarded considerations of literary prestige. In this respect, it should be stressed, as Buffery notes, that with Balaguer's *Les esposalles de la morta* 'Shakespeare is credited with being the source for one of the earliest incursions into serious theatre in Catalan in this period.'[33] For Cuccu, the play 'had the effect of a detonator within Catalan highbrow theatre' and sought to raise its status to 'the level of Schillerian tragedy'.[34] Fàbregas points out that with this short tragedy Balaguer aimed at bringing Catalan theatre in line with the European tradition through the use of the well-established myth of the star-crossed lovers.[35]

At the same time, the motif of a Juliet coming back to life correlates with the notion of 'la Morta-Viva' (literally 'the dead-and-alive'), used at that time to allude to the precarious situation of Catalan, a 'dead' language that needed to be reborn or revived.[36] In the final scene, Romeo employs these key words when he draws the shroud covering Juliet in the family mausoleum:

¿Com estàs tan *hermosa*, morta mia?...
Me sembles viva...[37]
[How can you be so beautiful, when dead?...
You seem to be alive...]

All these observations may well lead one to argue that Shakespeare was appropriated by Balaguer in order to infuse prestige not only into the language but also into Catalan theatre, and particularly tragedy. However, as Buffery points out, Balaguer did not publicize his play by using the name of Shakespeare,[38] and in his final assessment Fàbregas considers that Balaguer's attempt to provide Catalan theatre with a firm structure for tragedy was unsuccessful.[39] Theatre historian Francesc Curet devotes one page to Víctor Balaguer and only mentions *Les esposalles de la morta* as an example of a 'normal' tragedy in contrast to Balaguer's previous 'synthetic' and plotless tragedies.[40] The plays of Àngel Guimerà, the playwright who 'created' Catalan tragedy, have only been connected to Shakespeare in terms of their elevated thought

---

[30] As in early sources of Shakespeare and later adaptations by Thomas Otway (1679), Theophilus Cibber (1740) and David Garrick (1748).

[31] Fàbregas, 'Guimerà', p. 564; Xavier Fàbregas, ed., *Víctor Balaguer: Les esposalles de la Morta; Raig de lluna* (Barcelona, 1968), p. 13.

[32] Antoni Carbonell *et al.*, *Literatura catalana* (Barcelona, 1979), pp. 324–8; Fàbregas, 'Guimerà'; Gallén, 'El teatre'.

[33] *Shakespeare*, pp. 26–7. See also Fàbregas, *Balaguer*, p. 9.

[34] Cuccu, 'Les esposalles', pp. 443–4 ('va tenir l'efecte d'un detonador dins el tetre català culte', 'el nivell de la tragèdia schilleriana').

[35] Fàbregas, *Balaguer*, p. 11.

[36] See *Los fills de la Morta-Viva* [*The Offspring of the Dead-and-Alive*] (Valencia, 1879), a compilation edited by Constantí Llombart, a prominent figure of the Valencian *Renaixença*, and dedicated to Víctor Balaguer. Llombart defines his work as part of the 'honorable enterprise of restoring and bringing its primitive splendor back to our mother tongue' (p. xxi).

[37] Quoted from Fàbregas, ed., *Víctor Balaguer*, p. 41.

[38] *Shakespeare*, p. 27. Buffery warns that Balaguer might have deliberately omitted Shakespeare because he wanted to offer 'an alternative, Catalan version rather than one based on the authoritative intentionality of the Bard', and therefore to prioritize the 'Catalanness' of his play (p. 27).

[39] 'Guimerà', p. 564.

[40] *Historia del teatre català* (Barcelona, 1967), p. 198.

and the expressiveness of their words, phrases and images.[41]

Balaguer's *Romeo*-based piece was soon paralleled by two adaptations in Spanish[42] and a burlesque in Catalan, all of them performed at the Barcelona Odeón theatre. This was a popular, second-rate playhouse that, together with the Romea theatre, created its own Catalan-speaking sections and staged most of the bilingual and Catalan-only plays in the period.[43] The burlesque was Josep Maria Codolosa's *Les ventalles de la porta* [literally *The shutters of the door*], staged and printed in 1881.[44] Parody was a common genre in Catalan theatre at that time, especially after the roaring success in 1864 of a parody of an historical drama that boosted the dramatic output in the language and its social appreciation.[45] The title *Les ventalles de la porta*, a phonic rhyming distortion of the title of Balaguer's tragedy (as was also conventional in parodies),[46] clearly announces Codolosa's parodic strategy. Written in a 'Catalan that everyone understands', as the title page stresses, his verse mocks Balaguer's 'serious' language, deliberately placing the text in the popular tradition of Catalan theatre that reacted against and mocked the archaisms of learned poets such as Balaguer and those rewarded at the *Jocs Florals*. As in the numerous *sainets*, Codolosa's play takes place in a down-to-earth setting, a shoemaker's shop. This reduction of the 'grand dimensions' of Shakespeare's tragedy 'to the petty and the ridiculous scale of ordinary, everyday life' is also characteristic of Shakespearian travesties in England and in Austria, as Draudt has shown,[47] as is the lowering of the social class of the characters and the trivialization of the issues. Just as Westmacott's Othello, the Moor of Fleet Street, is a street-sweeper, and Kringsteiner's Othello is a servant of a wealthy Viennese gentleman,[48] Codolosa's 'Romeo' (Mateu) and 'Juliet' (Pauleta) are the children of two rival shoemakers; and Shakespeare's 'nightingale' and 'lark' (3.5.2–7) are turned into the jangling of a she-donkey's bell and the bleat of neighbouring goats. All in all, Codolosa's travesty continued a tradition of parodying conventions of Romantic drama, particularly the lovers' suicide.[49] He wrote a few more

satiric plays and poems but they were insignificant in terms of their contribution to Catalan literature.

Before Balaguer's Catalan version of *Romeo and Juliet* and its travesty appeared, two parodies of *Othello* had been performed: *Otello o il moro di Valenzia* by Abelardo Coma, first produced in 1873 and then published the following year; and an anonymous *Otello o il moro de magnesia* performed in 1877.[50] *Othello* had been a successful title on the Spanish stage since 1802, when the renowned actor Isidoro Máiquez impersonated the moor of Venice in a

---

41 Curet, *Història*, p. 233 (also quoting earlier comments by José María Pereda, *Nubes de estío* (Madrid, 1981)).

42 Jaime Piquet's five-act melodramatic pieces, *Julieta y Romeo* and *La venganza de Romeo* [*Romeo's revenge*], first performed in 1878, even before Balaguer's tragedy was staged (Par, *Representaciones*, vol. II, pp. 114–15 and 101). Piquet had already written plays in Catalan but he turned to Spanish in order to capitalize on the popularity of the myth.

43 Morell, *Serafí Pitarra*, pp. 163–5.

44 Par, *Representaciones*, vol. II, pp. 123–4. Josep Maria Codolosa, *Las ventallas de la porta: (parodia de Las esposalles de la morta): sabaterada en dos cuadros escrita en vers y en català del que tothom enten* (Barcelona, 1881).

45 Morell, *Serafí Pitarra*, pp. 166–83; Carbonell, *Literatura catalana*, pp. 329–30; Curet, *Historia*, pp. 123–35. The parody is *L'esquetlla de la torratxa*, by Frederic Soler, one of the prominent playwrights in Catalan.

46 Morell, *Serafí Pitarra*, p. 250.

47 Manfred Draudt, '"Committing Outrage against the Bard": Nineteenth-Century Travesties of Shakespeare in England and Austria', *Modern Language Review*, 88 (1993), 102–9; esp. p. 109. See also Richard W. Schoch, *Not Shakespeare: Bardolatry and Burlesque in the Nineteenth Century* (Cambridge, 2002).

48 Draudt, 'Committing', p. 103.

49 Morell, *Serafí Pitarra*, p. 239. The fact that the production was sponsored by the Academia de la Llengua Catalana (Catalan Language Academy) and dedicated to Catalanist societies (Par, *Representaciones*, vol. II, p. 123), may suggest that a Shakespeare-related play, however indirectly, was a deliberate contribution to the revivalist movement, but the production simply seemed to celebrate the first session of the Academy the previous day, a project that soon came to an end for lack of agreement on spelling rules.

50 Par, *Representaciones*, vol. II, pp. 104–6 and 111. Abelardo Coma, *Otello il moro di Valenzia: parodia scrita in versi. Música di Francisco di P. Sanchez Gabanyach* (Barcelona, 1874). No text of the second piece has been found. Par wonders if it is Coma's parody with a new title (vol. II, p. 111).

version of Jean-François Ducis's adaptation written by J. M. Carnerero (under the pseudonym of Teodoro Lacalle or de la Calle).[51] To this should be added Rossini's opera since 1821 and Carnerero's parody *El caliche* (and other parodies with similar title) from perhaps 1823 to 1844.[52] The Ducis-derived *Othello* dominated the Spanish Shakespeare productions until the 1830s, but interest in the play was revived in the 1860s with successive tours of Italian companies, especially Prosperi's (in 1862), Rossi's (1866, 1868, 1875), and Salvini's (1869). In the wake of these performances, a new *Othello* in Spanish, adapted by Francisco Luis de Retés in 1868, regained the play's hold on the Spanish stage for years to come.[53]

By September 1873, when Abelardo Coma's *Otello, il moro di Valenzia* was performed at the Teatro Tivoli, Barcelona theatregoers must have been so well-versed in versions of *Othello* in Spanish and Italian that the parodic force of Coma's rehandling of the story was warranted. As was also common in parodies (even in British and Austrian travesties[54]), Coma's burlesque contained three songs, composed by Sánchez Gavanyach, that allowed the comic tenor Federico Fuentes y Coll to show off his skills. Besides, the songs and the fact that the prose dialogue was written in a Catalanized Italian or Italianized Catalan placed Coma's travesty in line with parodies of the socially exclusive operas performed at the Liceo. Although Par deplored this piece, he acknowledged its popularity on the stage and in print with three editions (in 1874, 1896 and 1902), as well as noting that it had the 'sad privilege' of being the first Catalan text related to Shakespeare and the first Shakespeare-related production stemming from the *Renaixença*.[55]

Coma's one-act travesty focuses the action on Shakespeare's last scene. The list of roles introduced Otello as a 'moro infurismato' (an 'infuriated moor'), Iago, as 'pillo redomato' ('arrant rascal') and Casio as 'pollo pelato' ('lit. plucked chicken; fig. a guy with no money, or rude guy', as Afonso and Salvador translate).[56] Emblematic of the cheapening of the story is the fact, as Par points out,[57] that the dagger with which Otello kills his wife, Iago and himself is made of puff-pastry,

whose handle Otello himself eats up before he dies. The domestication of the setting to 'Valenzia' is quite irrelevant, other than being in line with the phonetic distortion of the name Venezia (as in a lost one-act play in Spanish performed four years earlier)[58] and with the downgrading distortion of the plot. The dialogue includes colloquial idioms (such as '¿Non vol caldo? cuatri tassa' [You asked for broth, you got four bowls], p. 7) whose Italianization would prompt immediate comic effect, and humorous wordplay and incidents that deflate the tragic expectations of the situation.[59] Far from using Shakespeare for endowing the incipient Catalan *Renaixença* with prestige,

[51] See José Luis Cano, *Historia y poesía* (Barcelona, 1992), pp. 20–1. The attribution to J. M. Carnerero is largely overlooked in the literature on this 1802 *Othello*. For the general reception of *Othello* in Spain, see Angeles Serrano Ripoll, *Las traducciones de Shakespeare en España: el ejemplo de* Othello (Miami, 1988); for a close study of these early *Othellos* in Spanish, see Keith Gregor, 'From Tragedy to *Sainete*: *Othello* on the Early Nineteenth-century Spanish Stage', in *Shakespeare and Spain*, vol. 13 of *Shakespeare Yearbook*, ed. J. M. González and H. Klein (2002), pp. 322–41; and Clara Calvo, 'De-foreignising Shakespeare: *Otelo* in Romantic Spain', in *Spanish Studies in Shakespeare and His Contemporaries*, ed. José Manuel González Fernández de Sevilla (Newark, DE, 2006), pp. 117–29.

[52] See Par, *Representaciones*, vol. 1, pp. 77–80, 110, 163, 177, 215; and Calvo, 'De-foreignising', pp. 124–7.

[53] *Otelo, el moro de Venecia*, first performed in Barcelona in 1868, and published in Madrid that year as a *Drama trágico en cuatro actos, en verso, escrito con presencia de la obra de W. Shakespeare, por D. Francisco Luis de Retés*.

[54] Draudt, 'Committing', p. 105.

[55] *Representaciones*, I, pp. 104–7 and 163–4; Par, *Shakespeare*, II, p. 116.

[56] Maria João da Rocha Afonso and Mercedes Salvador Bello, 'Portuguese and Spanish Burlesques of Shakespeare's Plays: From the 18th Century to Our Days', *I Congreso Internacional de Estudios Anglo-Portugueses*, 5 (Lisboa, 2001), 570–9.

[57] *Representaciones*, vol. II, p. 105.

[58] Par states that *El nuevo Otelo, o el moro de Valencia* shown in December 1869 at the Olimpo cannot be Coma's parody (*Representaciones*, vol. II, p. 96).

[59] See for instance, when Desdemona's 'Caro . . .' ['Dear . . .'] is interrupted by Otello's 'Caro ni baratto' ['Neither dear nor cheap'] (p. 9), or when Desdemona interrupts Otello with 'Aspérate cui un instante . . . / tenesti una can bianca' ['Wait a minute . . . / you have a white hair'] (p. 8).

as Balaguer did, this parody was simply used in order to provide easy comic entertainment, without any literary ambition, for popular audiences and for commercial purposes, capitalizing on the vogue of Italian actors and of *Othello* in more 'serious' venues.

The formula of parodying the success of Italian companies with a travesty of *Othello* in a garbled mixture of Italian and Catalan was repeated in 1883 by Antonio Ferrer y Codina and Alfredo Pallardó in their *Otel-lo o il moro di Sarrià*, also performed at the Teatro Tivoli in late January and early February and again in April.[60] Par states that this parody resulted from a conversation the two authors had after a performance by Rossi.[61] The text was published that year as *Otel-lo o il moro di . . .* , leaving a blank space to be filled by the place of performance. Sarrià was a municipality near Barcelona (now a district of the capital of Catalonia) and apparently there was an earlier performance in Badalona, since its inhabitants are mentioned in the dialogue. As in Coma's burlesque, this one-act *Otel-lo* 'pick[s] up on the carnivalesque *charivari* aspects' of Shakespeare's play,[62] focusing on its last episodes, but contains notable divergences: Yoneta (the Shakespearian Emilia) arranges a secret love encounter with hunch-backed Sebastianello for that night; her uncle Yago is in love with Desdémona and dupes Otel-lo into believing that Sebastianello has cuckolded him during his absence; Otel-lo waits for Sebastianello in the dark, makes him believe he is his enamoured and allows him to kiss his hand before he strangles him. Emblematic moments of the parodic devices are Otel-lo's soliloquy in scene XI juxtaposing the high language reminiscent of Othello's 'Farewell' speech at 3.3.350–60 and the low style of 'Io que con ella, ristaba me contenti que un gosso ab un os' ['And I was happier with her than a dog with its bone']; and Otel-lo's offstage killing of his wife: the stage direction calls for 'great shouting to represent the slaughter of a pig' and on entering the stage Otel-lo dismisses the fact with a colloquial 'Se ha acabatto la arrosso' ['that's all there is to it'].

Ferrer and Pallardó's Otel-lo is a rich general who owns a luxurious palace, 'larger than the

Vatican', on the outskirts of the Catalan town of Badalona, and who 'Comanda lis suavos di Cárlos setto' ['is in command of Charles VII's Zouaves'], as Desdémona says.[63] This reference to the Zouaves anticipates the exotic Moorishness of Otel-lo: the Zouaves were infantry soldiers, originally in the French army, whose Algerian origin was noticeable in their conspicuous Oriental uniform. Moreover, the fact that Desdémona refers to 'Charles II's Zouaves' invites us to a two-paragraph excursion into contemporary political resonances. 'Cárlos setto' refers to the self-proclaimed 'King Charles VII', the third Carlist contender to the Spanish throne in the dynastic and military conflict initiated after the death of Ferdinand VII in 1833 between his daughter, who was crowned Queen Isabella II, and his brother Don Carlos de Borbón y Parma. In political terms, Carlism was a conservative movement opposed to the liberalism of supporters of Queen Isabella II, defending traditional values of monarchism, Catholicism, and the restoration of the customary laws suppressed by the centralism of the first Bourbon king in the early eighteenth century and continued by the nineteenth-century constitutionalist liberals.

By turning Otel-lo into a Carlist general of 'Charles VII', Ferrer and Pallardó located the action in the relatively recent Carlist War (1872–6) during the turbulent years comprising the deposition of Isabella II in 1868, the brief reign of Amadeus I of Savoy, the short-lived Republic and the effective restoration of the Bourbon Alfonso XII in 1875. The Carlist army in Catalonia was commanded by the brother of the pretender 'Carlos VII', Don Alfonso Carlos, who had been lieutenant of the Pontifical Zouaves in the 1860s and had brought a regiment of Zouaves as a personal

---

[60] Par, *Representaciones*, vol. II, pp. 127–9. N. N. [Antonio Ferrer y Codina, and Alfredo Pallardó], *Otel-lo o il moro di . . . parodia en un acto y en prosa italiana macarrónica* (Barcelona, 1884).

[61] Par, *Shakespeare*, II, p. 116.

[62] Buffery, *Shakespeare*, p. 26.

[63] Ferrer and Pallardó, *Otel-lo*, p. 7.

guard and as shock troops.[64] By the time Ferrer and Pallardó's parody was staged in 1883, Carlism had been defeated militarily (in 1876) and politically reduced to a weak and fragmented option for devout Catholics and anti-liberals of all classes, both of whom were mainly from rural areas of southern and inland Catalonia. It is likely that Catalan spectators and readers of this burlesque would associate Ferrer and Pallardó's Otel-lo with Don Alfonso Carlos – or perhaps with the rash and fierce Carlist commader Francisco Savalls, who was also an officer in the Papal Zouaves.[65] There is scarce evidence to infer the authors' and their audiences' political leaning, but the general farcical treatment of the story and its protagonist and a brief comment from Desdémona's protégée disapproving of Otel-lo's Carlism[66] lead to the hypothesis that this 'Shakespearian' hero is a parody of Don Alfonso Carlos or of another Carlist military leader and that the burlesque is a jab at their ideology, which found support in reactionary sectors of all classes but mainly in rural areas (in Catalonia, in the south and inland districts). Those unsympathetic to the Carlist cause would much more enjoy a burlesque play in which a Carlist general is the object of derision, especially when Otel-lo ridiculously first enters the stage with big earrings, a turban and a coloured umbrella.[67] The town of Sarrià and its voluntary militia led by Josep Martí, 'el Xich de les Barraquetes', was notorious in the defence of the parliamentary Republic against Carlist forces and particularly in January 1874 against the governmental army that had dissolved the parliament in Madrid. A Carlist Otel-lo being 'the moor of Sarrià' would indeed add greater edge to its mockery.

As with Codolosa's Romeo-related burlesque, our understanding of the social repercussions of this parody of Othello is enhanced when situated within the dynamics of the theatre system in Barcelona and nearby towns. On analysing performances since 1873, a pattern emerges in which serious and burlesque Othellos reply to one another in their respective playhouses. For instance, in 1874 the renowned actor Rafael Calvo staged Retés's Spanish version of Othello in January at the Teatro

Principal, and came back to this playhouse in the summer (although with no Shakespeare): soon the Tivoli replied with Coma's parody on 29 July and 9 August, followed by another 'serious' Othello at the Teatro Español on 30 August.[68] To this pattern, one could add the sociolinguistic dimension, inasmuch as the 'serious' Shakespeare is staged in the dominant language (Spanish, and also in Italian) while the subordinated language (Catalan) is used for undistinguished, parodic distortions which, in turn, distort the language into a 'macaronic' Italian. As Buffery notes, the parodies were not even 'marketed as Catalan-language versions'.[69] Thus, rather than promoting the social and artistic legitimization of Catalan, Shakespeare is associated with low-prestige theatrical uses and therefore with a conservative role that maintains the low status of the language.

Hamlet must also have been the object of mockery in the anonymous two-act parody Hamletto, principe of Val-licarca, performed at the Romea theatre on 12 February 1883.[70] Unfortunately the text is lost, but it is likely that the parody followed the Othello examples discussed above: the title suggests

---

[64] María de las Nieves de Braganza y Borbón, *Mis memorias sobre nuestra campaña en Cataluña en 1872 y 1873* (Madrid, 1934); V. Garmendia, *La segunda guerra carlista (1872–1876)* (Madrid, 1976).

[65] Josep Fontana, *Historia de España: La época del liberalismo* (Barcelona, 2007), pp. 379–80.

[66] When Desdémona answers that Otel-lo commands the zouaves of Charles VII, her protégée utters 'Y ha gustos qui merexen palis' ['Some tastes deserve a good bashing'] (p. 7).

[67] Ferrer and Pallardó, *Otel-lo*, p. 8.

[68] Simlarly, 1883 also saw four later productions of Retés's Spanish adaptaton of *Othello* in the Barcelona playhouses of Romea, Novedades and Olimpo, and the following year brought Rossi's fourth seasonal visit with *Otello* at the Principal in March and at the Buen Retiro in June, to which *Otel-lo o il moro de Sarrià* responded at the Jovellanos in December (Par, *Representaciones*, vol. II, pp. 128–31).

[69] *Shakespeare*, p. 26.

[70] Par, *Representaciones*, vol. II, p. 127; *La Vanguardia* (3 Feb. 1883), p. 863, which announces that the production is for the benefit of actor Federico Fuentes, and defines the parody as written in Italian and consisting of two acts and seven scenes.

the use of Italianized Catalan and the domestication of the location to Vallcarca, a neighbourhood of Barcelona. As far as records tell, this *Hamletto* was only performed once, a lack of success that is also characteristic of *Hamlet* in early and mid-nineteenth-century Spain. It might have capitalized on a certain popularity of the tragedy initiated by Rossi's performances of the play (in 1866, 1868 and 1874), followed by Carlos Coello's 'imitation' in Spanish *El príncipe Hamlet* (performed in Barcelona in 1873 and 1879)[71] and by the Italian *Amletos* played by Ceresa (1880) and by Emmanuel (1880 and 1882). After 1883, serious *Hamlet*-related shows continued on the Barcelona stages, both with Italian companies and with Coello's Spanish adaptation,[72] but the prince of Denmark did not find a parodic echo again, as had been the case with the moor of Venice.

Although I have set 1898 as the *terminus ad quem* date of my survey, it is worth adding a brief comment on another deviant version of *Hamlet* in Catalan, staged that year.[73] It is a three-act *Hàmlet* 'translated and adapted to the Catholic stage' by the priest and bilingual writer Gaietà Soler (under the penname of Angel Guerra). The adapted action dispenses with female characters, and only counts on Hamlet, the Ghost, Claudius, Polonius, Horatio and Marcellus. Some of Gertrude's speeches or lines are assigned to Claudius or to Polonius, and Claudius even replaces Gertrude in the equivalent 'closet scene', the penultimate scene in Soler's piece, where Hamlet faces his enemy only to finally forgive him at the Ghost's request. Following the Ducisian tradition, in the last scene the prince convinces the rebellious mob seeking Claudius's head of his mercy towards his uncle and is offered the crown, which he accepts with gratitude. Thus Soler's *Hàmlet* becomes a story of the overthrow of a fratricidal tyrant and punishment of the plotting councillor at the hands of a hero that ultimately stands as an example of magnanimity and Christian forgiveness induced by an 'otherworldly' paternal figure. Interestingly, the dialogue is written in verse (combining octosyllables and decasyllables) in contrast to the prose of the *Othello* parodies; and the text of the play-within-the-play is

in Spanish (heavily indebted to Moratín's version), seemingly reflecting the diglossic situation of Catalan: the 'everyday' speech of the characters is in a rather literary Catalan while the public function of a serious play is in Spanish.

The revivalist movement of *La Renaixença* did not use Shakespeare as a brand that would confer prestige to the language until the close of the century (with Masriera's full translation in 1898). With the exception of Balaguer's *Romeo and Juliet*, Catalan-speaking spectators did not hear in their native language either *Othello*, *Hamlet* or any Shakespearian comic protagonist. It is only in the work of Víctor Balaguer that one can find a conscious attempt to draw on Shakespeare as cultural catalyst in order to enhance the literature of a minority language; but even so, Balaguer's catalysis is restricted to the generic promotion of tragedy and his overall contribution is in its own way marginal. Although *The Betrothal of the Dead Maiden* was successful both on stage and in print, within the context of Catalan theatre Balaguer's use of Shakespeare (which Balaguer never justified) remained unique and rather ineffective. The dominant mode in which Shakespeare was introduced in Catalan-speaking cultures was through popular burlesques rather than through the higher cultural forms with which Shakespeare is often associated. These burlesques were fully integrated into the theatrical tradition and participated in the tensions of the theatrical system in Catalonia, though not in Valencia, the Balearic Islands and the Roussillon. Both Balaguer and the parodies were stimulated by the popularity of Shakespeare created by the Italian companies performing in Barcelona since the 1860s. While Balaguer used some Shakespeare themes for his purpose of dignifying Catalan as a theatre language, the theatrical parodies of *Othello* and *Hamlet* were written in an Italianized Catalan or a 'macaronic' Italian that contested such

---

[71] Par, *Representaciones*, vol. II, pp. 100 and 104.
[72] Par, *Representaciones*, vol. II, pp. 122–46.
[73] Par, *Representaciones*, vol. II, pp. 148–9. A. G. [Gaietà Soler], *Hamlet. Drama en tres actes y en vers* (Barcelona, 1898).

appropriation, while Codolosa's *Romeo*-related parody in the 'Catalan that everyone understands' took part in the rejection and mockery of the literary Catalan that authors such as Balaguer were seeking to recover and improve.

In a minorized culture, forms of public artistic expression are predominantly marginal and aimed at the less-educated, so it should come as no surprise that early uses of a cultural icon such as Shakespeare took these forms. Indeed, the parodies appropriated Shakespeare's aura and popularity, but with a view to provide entertainment to the lower and middle classes without artistic aspirations associated with high culture. This reflects a cultural positioning different from the prestige-seeking agenda of Balaguer's isolated and relatively ineffectual Shakespeare-related plays and of the translations and theatre productions that would become common from 1898. Although to a greater or lesser degree the early Catalan Shakespeares, however irreverent and marginal, made their own particular contribution to the popularization of Shakespeare in Spain, one can only conclude that they do not constitute a catalyst for the revival of Catalan-speaking culture in the nineteenth century.

SHAKESPEARE, MÁCHA AND CZECH ROMANTIC HISTORICISM

MARTIN PROCHÁZKA

This article is an attempt to examine, in Ton Hoenselaars's words, one of the 'countless traces... of foreign cultural and ideological encounters with [Shakespeare's] histories', focusing on the capacity of *Henry IV, Part 2* 'to mediate in non-English processes of national formation and preservation'.[1] Despite detailed attention paid to one of these traces, the influence of *Henry IV, Part 2* on the dramatic fragments of the leading Czech Romantic Karel Hynek Mácha (1810–36), my objective is more general: to study the potential of Shakespeare's histories to transform historical awareness[2] in the context of the early nineteenth-century European Romantic nationalist movements. Specifically, I am interested in the way Mácha's use of *Henry IV, Part 2* in his project of historical dramas facilitated an important change in his understanding of Czech history: a shift from perceiving it as a predetermined 'providential' narrative[3] of national emancipation[4] to a more 'realistic' 'concern with history as processes and the inner necessities of historical change'.[5] As the exploration of Mácha's reading and transformation of *Henry IV, Part 2* will show, this change of historical awareness challenged not only the simplistic and utopian perception of Czech political identity but also the early nineteenth-century position of Shakespeare as a supreme literary and dramatic authority.

It is no surprise that the productions or translations of the histories did not appear in the period of early Czech appropriation of Shakespeare (1782–1807),[6] when tragedies (*Macbeth*, *King Lear*) and comedies (*The Merchant of Venice*) were mainly seen as educational tools facilitating the spread of literacy. In 1792, the preface to a Czech translation of a German adaptation of *King Lear* pointed out the meaning of theatre for the education of the people, and amplified Friedrich Schiller's argument in favour of the communal nature of theatre and its role as a seedbed for the people's cultural growth.[7]

---

1 Ton Hoenselaars, 'Shakespeare's History Plays in Britain and Abroad', in *Shakespeare's History Plays: Performance, Translation and Adaptation in Britain and Abroad*, ed. Ton Hoenselaars (Cambridge, 2004), p. 17.

2 For a detailed analysis of the links between national and historical awareness, see Miroslav Hroch, *Social Preconditions of National Revival in Europe: A Comparative Analysis of the Social Composition of Patriotic Groups*, trans. by Ben Fowkes (New York, 2000), pp. 11–12.

3 On the 'providential' concept of history and European and US nationalisms, see Anthony D. Smith, *Nationalism: Theory, Ideology, History* (Oxford, 2001), pp. 42, 156.

4 The 'providential' approach of Czech nationalists to history can be illustrated by a poem by the Catholic priest, František Vacek Kamenický (1806–69). The text makes a direct analogy between national emancipation and resurrection: 'O Lord, kindle a new life in the people buried alive, so that we may rise again according to your Gospel!' Quoted in Vladimír Macura, *Znamení zrodu* [*The Sign of Birth*] (Prague, 1983), p. 92 (unless expressly stated, all translations from Czech are by the author). The Czech version of 'providential' history is not widely different from the US versions, see Mark A. Beliles and Stephen K. McDowell, *America's Providential History* (Charlottesville, 1989).

5 Ronald R. Macdonald, 'Uneasy Lies: Language and History in Shakespeare's Lancastrian Tetralogy', *Shakespeare Quarterly*, 35 (1984), 23.

6 My periodization follows that in Pavel Drábek's extensive *Habilitationsschrift*, *České pokusy o Shakespeara* [*Czech Attempts at Shakespeare*] (Brno, 2010).

7 Martin Procházka, 'Shakespeare and Czech Resistance', in Heather Kerr, Robin Eaden and Madge Mitton, eds., *Shakespeare: World Views* (Newark and London, 1996), p. 51.

As a matter of fact, Shakespeare's histories suited the ideological demands of Austrian feudal absolutism even less than his tragedies or comedies.[8] The regime tended to use drama as a means of peaceful political and social consolidation and the plays dealing with civil wars were simply not desirable. Moreover, there is evidence that Shakespeare's histories were perceived as culturally too remote to be understood by contemporary German or Austrian audiences.[9] Although in 1828 *Henry IV, Part 1* enjoyed in Vienna some popularity based on the scenes with Falstaff, the attempt to produce *Part 2* was unsuccessful, chiefly because 'the comical scenes could not make up for the lack of interest in the political action'.[10] Finally, in late 1830, the production of both parts of *Henry IV* was suppressed by the Austrian authorities.[11]

Later nineteenth-century Czech political initiatives, namely the project of the National Theatre launched in 1848 as a peaceful protest against the Emperor's prohibition of the re-establishment of the Czech Parliament, did not refer to any specific dramatic tradition, let alone to Shakespeare's histories. Rather, they emphasized theatre as an institutional framework in which Shakespeare could be constructed as a 'representative man'[12] as well as a universal value standard. The first attempt at a political use of Shakespeare's historical play occurred only in 1916: in the production of both parts of *Henry IV* during the Shakespeare festival at the National Theatre, which articulated the problem of the Czech royal succession after the liberation from Austrian rule.[13]

Although the importance of Shakespeare for historical poetry and drama was generally recognized and emphasized in the period of the Czech national emancipation,[14] historical dramas modelled on Shakespeare are very rare. The usually mentioned *Soběslav* (1826) by Václav Kliment Klicpera (1792–1859) is more influenced by contemporary German *Ritterdrama* or *Schicksaltragödie* (fate tragedy).[15] And the dramatic poem *Čestmír* (1835) by Josef Kajetán Tyl (1808–56), described as an attempt to reach 'the sphere of Shakespeare's and Schiller's art', is closer to Byronic revolt against 'the icy, rotten souls relishing their dust' than to

8 Contemporary Czech drama, mostly adaptations of the works of Austrian or Prussian playwrights, responded to the threat of peasant rebellions (the most significant one was suppressed in 1775) and later to the French revolution by emphasizing the necessity of restoring traditional feudal bonds and reorienting the allegiance of the subjects from local feudal landlords directly to the Emperor. Shakespeare's plays, which problematized feudal allegiance, could not be used for this purpose. On political issues connected with the early Czech adaptation of *Macbeth*, see Procházka, 'Shakespeare and Czech Resistance', pp. 46–8. Significantly, this adaptation followed a German one made by a clerk of the Czech Office of Censorship, Franz Joseph Fischer (Drábek, *České pokusy o Shakespeara*, p. 79).

9 See Heinrich Laube, *Das Burgtheater: Ein Beitrag zur deutschen Theater-Geschichte* (Leipzig, 1868), p. 51. After staging both parts of *Henry IV*, Friedrich Ludwig Schröder (1744–1816), a leading actor of the late eighteenth and early nineteenth century, remarked that the production 'will be repeated . . . in the hope that the manners so widely different from ours, will be understood' (all translations from German are mine). Although *Henry IV, Part 1* and *Part 2* were produced by the Viennese Burgtheater in 1816 (Laube, *Das Burgtheater*, p. 107), there is evidence that in the Czech lands the Austrian authorities' fear of alien ideological and cultural influences precluded staging and publishing of any plays by Shakespeare. See Drábek, *České pokusy o Shakespeara*, pp. 103ff.

10 Eduard Castle, 'Schreyvogel, Joseph', in *Allgemeine Deutsche Biographie*, vol. 54, published by the Historische Kommission bei der Bayerischen Akademie der Wissenschaften (Munich, 1908), p. 210.

11 Both plays were staged by Joseph Schreyvogel (1768–1832), a dramatist and director known, among others, for his sympathies for the French Revolution. In 1830, the plays were merged into one and staged again (the last performance took place on 14 December 1830). However, they were soon labelled as 'unenjoyable tragedies' and suppressed by a Czech aristocrat, the High Chamberlain and the President of the Austrian Academy of Fine Arts, Johann Rudolf Czernin of Chudenitz (1757–1845). See Eugen Kilian, 'Schreyvogels Shakespeare-Bearbeitungen', *Jahrbuch der Shakespeare-Gesellschaft*, 39 (1903), 98. One can only speculate whether the suppression was not partially motivated by the revolutionary events of 1830.

12 Michael Bristol, *Shakespeare's America, America's Shakespeare* (London, 1990), pp. 123ff.

13 Procházka, 'Shakespeare and Czech Resistance', pp. 50–6.

14 'Would that the time would soon come giving rise to a dramatic poet who, like Shakespeare in England of yore, could paint with bold strokes the heroes of our ancient age.' Josef Krasoslav Chmelenský, 'Divadelní zprávy' ['Theatre News'], *Česká včela* [*Czech Bee*], 1.48 (1834), 383.

15 Cf. Jan Hyvnar, 'Klicperovy neúspěšné pokusy o tragédii' ['*Klicpera's Abortive Attempts at a Tragedy*']

the tragic conflict of *King Lear* translated and produced by Tyl in the same year as *Čestmír*.[16] Unlike Klicpera's and Tyl's dramatic attempts, the fragments of historical plays by Karel Hynek Mácha, can be read as the first actual response to Shakespeare's histories in the Czech lands.

Mácha's fragments[17] are an attempt to revise the accepted early nationalist representation of history as a predestined spiritual process taking place in 'eternity' with a single central aim: the increase of the consciousness of the Czech culture, language and political rights, suppressed by the Habsburgs after the insurgency of the Czech estates in 1618–20. The nationalist idea of the purpose of Czech history was most eloquently expressed by a historian Slavomír Tomíček (1806–66) in his scathing review of the best Czech Romantic poem, Mácha's verse tale *May* (1836):

We defy this and suchlike Hegelianism that holds that there is no purpose in eternity . . . These philosophers, while placing themselves outside eternity, forget to think of themselves and their fellow beings as the inhabitants of eternity . . . where the Life of the Spirit is constantly entering diverse forms of being and causing them to be more or less aware of themselves. Now this self-awareness gradually increases, and increase it must, in accordance with Nature's laws.[18]

According to Tomíček and his fellow-nationalists, Czech history was a providential process manifesting itself in spiritualized Nature, identical with 'eternity'. The main purpose of this process was the increase of national consciousness caused by a metaphysical power: the spiritual essence of the universe, similar to the 'Absolute Spirit' of the German philosopher G. W. F. Hegel. Hegel's conservative disciples, called 'the orthodox Hegelians', have connected this 'Absolute Spirit' with 'the people's (or the nation's) spirit' (*Volksgeist*):

The *Volk* itself is a personality. The *Volksgeist* itself is an individual who does not harm the individualities of those who constitute it. Inasmuch as the *Volksgeist* is no empty and false concept, its individual elements [*Glieder*] are annihilated and restored [*aufgehoben*] in it.[19]

Although Hegel's philosophy was publicly repudiated by the Czech nationalists (the main reason

was its prohibition by the Austrian government), it became a strong incentive for the creation of

---

Divadelní revue [*Theatre Review*], 1 (28 February 2005), www.divadlo.cz/art/clanek.asp?id=7482, accessed 20 May 2010.

16 Felix Vodička, ed., *Dějiny české literatury* II [*A History of Czech Literature* II] (Prague, 1960), p. 407. However, other historical plays by Tyl, namely *Slepý mládenec* [*The Blind Youth*] (1836) and *Brunsvik* (1843), can be read as attempts to come to terms with *King Lear*. These plays emphasize national unity and traditional values, and suppress the dark moments and cruel horrors of Shakespeare's tragedy. In *Čestmír* the main hero's sacrifice establishes national unity and historical optimism. In *Slepý mládenec*, the blinding of the protagonist is represented as a sacrifice, healing the criminal hero and bestowing prophetic and saintly gifts on him, so that he is able to help his dying father and dishonoured former lover. This optimistic resolution of the conflict resembling both plots of *King Lear* is brought about by the supreme authority of divine love as well as by the wisdom of the people, whose spokesperson, the servant Záruba, is partially modelled on Kent. Finally, in *Brunsvik*, the old king's madness is redeemed by the compassion of common people uniting the nation and leading it to the war against foreign oppressors.

17 My reading of Karel Hynek Mácha's dramatic fragments uses the following critical editions: *Spisy* I: *Básně a dramatické zlomky* [*Complete Writings* I: *Poems and Dramatic Fragments*], ed. Karel Janský (Prague, 1959) and *Spisy* III: *Literární zápisníky, deníky, dopisy* [*Complete Writings* III: *Literary Notebooks, Diaries, Letters*], ed. Karel Dvořák, Karel Janský and Rudolf Skřeček (Prague, 1972).

18 Jan Slavomír Tomíček, 'Československá literatura' ['Czechoslovak Literature'], *Česká včela* [*Czech Bee*], 3.22 (31 May 1836): 182.

19 Carl Friedrich Göschel, 'Friedrich Richter: Die neue Unsterblichkeitslehre . . .' ['The New Doctrine of Immortality . . .'], *Jahrbücher für die wissenschaftliche Kritik*, 17 (January 1834), 134. According to Jon Bartley Stewart, 'Göschel was convinced that Hegel's philosophy was consistent with Christianity and one could find in his texts clear evidence of a theory of immortality in accordance with Christian doctrine': Jon Bartley Stewart, ed., *Johan Ludvig Heiberg: Philosopher, Littérateur, Dramaturge and Political Thinker* (Copenhagen, 2008), p. 105. This was very important for Czech nationalists, who were eager to embrace Hegel's philosophy of history but wary to express their sympathies in public. On the one hand, the connection of Mácha with 'Hegelianism' emphasized the subversive, anti-nationalist and anti-regime features of his poetry. On the other hand, it associated Mácha with left-wing Hegelians (*Junghegelianer*), attacked in Göschel's review and criticized also by conservative Czech nationalists.

nationalist ideology founded on the notion of the *Volk* as a collective personality and for the Romantic interpretations of Czech history.

Mácha's dramatic fragments outline a notion of history that differs from the Hegelian speculations of Czech nationalists or their forgeries of medieval manuscripts, which were supposed to prove the ancient origins of Czech literature as well as the presence of the chief medieval cultural values in nineteenth-century Czech national emancipation.[20] In Mácha's fragments of historical dramas, the main agents of Czech history are struggling feudal leaders, confused about the issues of sovereignty and prioritizing particular power interests. The amassed momentum of local conflicts produces the major disaster of the Battle of White Mountain in 1620, which led to a forfeiture of political autonomy and a near loss of national identity and significantly determines the course of early modern Czech and European history. In his Romantic primordialism,[21] Mácha traces the origins of this cataclysm to the turmoil of the late reign of Wenceslas IV (1378–1419) which led to the religious Hussite wars and, also, in the manner pioneered by Chateaubriand and his Czech follower Josef Linda (1789/92–1834), to the early conflict between paganism and Christianity.

While Mácha's historical fiction (a planned tetralogy of historical novels out of which only the first volume *Křivoklad* was published in 1834) was to focus on the events heralding the Reformation wars, his dramatic fragments evolved from an early attempt to capture the events before the Battle of the White Mountain (*Král Fridrich* [*King Frederick*] written in 1832) to a sombre panorama of early Czech history and its two major moments: the murder of St Wenceslas, the patron saint of Bohemia, and the feudal wars in the tenth and eleventh centuries.

The events of early Czech history are represented in three fragments, *Boleslav. Truchlohra o jednom jednání* [*Boleslav: A Tragedy in One Act*], *Bratrovrah aneb Václav a Boleslav* [*The Fratricide, or Wenceslas and Boleslav*], both dealing with the murder of St Wenceslas by his brother Boleslav in

929, and in the tragedy entitled *Bratři* [*The Brothers*]. The last-mentioned text is Mácha's most extensive outline of a five-act drama, representing the conflict between the early eleventh-century princes Jaromír and Oldřich, members of the ruling family of the Přemyslids. All these texts and Mácha's research materials are found in a notebook called *Poznamenání* (Notes), which can be dated after 2 August 1832.

Whereas the fragments dealing with the murder of St Wenceslas are based on hagiographic material (the plot of the play is modelled on the St Wenceslas legend), the last outline of the play called *The Brothers* shows serious effort to come to terms with Shakespeare's histories and tragedies, using them as models for the composition of poetry (especially for the lyrical imagery of dramatic monologues) and for the representation of history.

Like Elizabethan and Jacobean dramatists, Mácha uses historical narratives in the form of chronicles and older plays. The *Brothers* fragment derives from a German drama, *Jaromir und Udalrich, Herzoge von Böhmen* [*Jaromír and Oldřich: The Dukes of Bohemia*] written by a Prague antiquarian and historian, Wolfgang Adolf Gerle (1781–1846), and performed in 1827.[22] Both Mácha and Gerle refer to a very popular sixteenth-century account of Czech history, the chronicle by Václav Hájek of Libočany (d. 1553).

---

[20] On the forged medieval *Manuscript of Dvůr Králové* (Rukopis královédvorský, 1817) and *Manuscript of Zelená Hora* (Rukopis zelenohorský, 1818), see Martin Procházka, 'Romantic Revivals: Cultural Translations, Universalism, and Nationalism', in Susan Bassnett and Martin Procházka, eds., *Cultural Learning: Language Learning, Selected Papers from the Second International British Studies Conference* (Prague, 1997), pp. 75–89, and 'From Romantic Folklorism to Children's Adventure Fiction: Walter Scott in Czech Culture', in Murray Pittock, ed., *The Reception of Sir Walter Scott in Europe* (London, 2006), p. 176. See also James Porter, 'Literary, Political and Artistic Resonances of *Ossian* in the Czech National Revival', in Howard Gaskill, ed., *The Reception of Ossian in Europe* (London, 2004), pp. 209–21.

[21] The term is discussed e.g. by Anthony D. Smith, *The Nation in History: Historiographical Debates about Ethnicity and Nationalism* (Cambridge, 2000), pp. 5–26.

[22] Mácha, *Spisy III*, pp. 372–4.

Gerle's play is centred on the theme of feudal struggle for power motivated by the inordinate desires and passions of the protagonists from the princely house of the Přemyslids and by the disastrous efforts of the rival clan, the Vršovci, to usurp the throne. In contrast to Gerle's piece, which is close to *Schicksaltragödie*, Mácha's play recasts the main nationalist theme – the political and cultural conflict between the German and the Czech population of Bohemia – into a familiar pattern of the feudal struggle for inheritance.

As Mácha's notes and outlines of individual scenes show, he was chiefly interested in the contemporary moral and political implications of the sombre story, especially in the futility of the nationalist nostalgia for the invented glorious Czech past called figuratively the 'tearful Ossianic longing for the nebulous'.[23] In this respect, Mácha's dramatic fragments can be seen as an antithesis to the sacred book of the Czech nationalists, the allegedly medieval, forged *Rukopis královédvorský* [*The Manuscript of Dvůr Králové*, 1817], where Prince Oldřich is glorified as a liberator of Prague from the Polish invaders.

The tragic conflict of the *Brothers* fragment is concerned with the crisis of legitimate feudal power, which opens the door to civil wars and causes moral degradation of Czech rulers and nobility. Their fall can be redeemed only by a prince who has stayed apart from the wars and thus become 'the worthiest to rule' the country.[24]

Mácha uses Shakespeare's tragedies and histories as a means of emancipation from Gerle's and Hájek's traditional renderings of national historical narratives. Initially, he attempts to model *The Brothers* on *King Lear* and meditates changing the character of Vyhoň Dub in Gerle's play into a Kent-like figure, refusing obedience to Prince Boleslav and criticizing his disastrous policy which had caused the division of the Czech state.[25]

In the further stage of composition Mácha evidently becomes aware of the unsuitability of *King Lear* for his aims. The important theme, described by Mácha as the 'Main Idea' of the *Brothers* fragment, namely the restoration of historical continuity and feudal lineage through the moral

integrity of the hero,[26] finds no correspondence in Shakespeare's tragedy. Contrary to the major emphasis of *King Lear* on the violence of the act of division, breaking of human bonds, decline of royal authority and resulting atrocities committed by wilful individuals, Mácha stresses the futility of the power struggle within and between feudal families.

The theme of strife for feudal power between the Czech clans brought Mácha closer to Shakespeare's histories. As some of his *Zápisník* (Notebook) entries show, he concentrated on

---

[23] 'Eine ossianische weinerliche Sehnsucht nach dem Nebelhaften. – Mit kalten Armen umhalst ihn die eiserne Jungfrau (Nemesis), bis er zusammenbricht, eine Riesenleiche mitten unter den Trümmern des Baues, der mit ihm stürzt (Brat[ři]. Jarom[ír])' (Mácha, *Spisy* III, p. 36). Here, Mácha may refer to the forged medieval documents *Manuscript of Dvůr Králové* and *Manuscript of Zelená Hora* and point to the shaky nature of the nationalist historical invention: the 'gigantic corpse under the ruins of the building' may refer to the collective body of the nation which had based its identity on an invented ancient past and was destroyed by the 'Nemesis' of historical necessity. However, other interpretations, referring directly to Mácha's interest in contemporary drama, are also possible. The passage was excerpted from a review in *Blätter für literarische Unterhaltung* (Magazine for Literary Entertainment) discussing a trilogy of historical dramas, *Alexis* (1832) by a German playwright and novelist Karl Leberecht Immermann (1796–1840). The trilogy describes an abortive rebellion of Alexei, a son of Peter the Great, against his father's attempts to modernize the Russian empire. Mácha's excerpt may also imply that the poet was interested in Immermann's treatment of the father–son conflict, which, according to the reviewer, was 'no struggle between the old and the new but the clash between fervent activity of a creative genius and indolent enthusiasm of baffled will' (Willibald Alexis [Georg Wilhelm Heinrich Häring], 'Alexis: Eine Trilogie von Karl Immermann', *Blätter für literarische Unterhaltung*, 9 December 1832: 1446). Mácha was interested in the theme of the modernization of the feudal state, a problematic issue in the ideology of contemporary Czech nationalism that was split between the nostalgia for old feudal institutions and the attempts to modernize Czech society in political and economic ways. However, he saw the conflict between the old and the new in a Romantic way as an encounter between creativity and unproductive enthusiasm.

[24] Mácha, *Spisy* I, p. 257.

[25] Mácha, *Spisy* III, p. 16: 'Vyhoň Dub, as Kent in Shakespeare's tragedy *Lear* . . . firmly speaks against Oldřich.'

[26] Mácha, *Spisy* I, p. 257.

several scenes from *Henry IV, Part 2*, especially on the King's meditation in 3.1.44–74 ('O God, that one might read the book of fate, / And see the revolution of the times')[27] and, possibly, on the dialogue between the King and his son, who has taken his crown away in 4.3.[28]

Although Mácha's excerpts from *Henry IV, Part 2* are rather scanty, his reading of Shakespeare can be reconstructed on the basis of thematic analogies as well as performative features of dramatic utterances. As in Shakespeare, Mácha is not preoccupied with mere 'deceitful appearances . . . but with the sources of illusion in the recesses of personal life, in the distorted imagination'. This preoccupation leads him 'to a profound searching of something that, opposed to appearance and in spite of time and death, may be welcomed as reality'.[29] In Mácha's case, however, this is no mere 'preoccupation with mutability' and the figure of *tempus edax rerum*,[30] but with the self-delusions of his protagonists. Among them, the most distinct is Herouš, Mácha's analogue of Hotspur, a young hero from the rival feudal clan, who already imagines himself as a ruler of the whole country and fails to notice that his vision 'is a mere dream and will sink with [him] / Into the grave'.[31] Like Hotspur, who is '[f]latt'ring himself with project of a power / Much smaller than the smallest of his thoughts,' and resolved to lead 'with great imagination / Proper to madmen . . . his powers to death' (1.3.29–32), Herouš is 'lifted by [his] fancy / To the highest pinnacle of hope', where he abandons 'the actual for a dream'.[32]

Mácha's treatment of historical conflict is highly ironic, he reminds us of Hal who realizes that '[t]o speak effectively in the new world created by the usurpation requires the exploitation of all the figurative resources of language, of irony, of understatement, of wary hyperbole and deft paronomasia'.[33] Some of these are also prominent speech figures in *The Brothers* but their importance grows in later work by Mácha, especially the historical novel *Křivoklad* where the circular, hopeless nature of the conflict is symbolized by the metalepsis combined with hyperbole and meiosis, referring to the two protagonists: 'King Hangman! Hangman

King!'[34] Although Mácha's dramatic fragments and historical fiction do not contain evidence of

---

[27] Mácha's exerpts are from A.W. Schlegel's translation *King Heinrich. Zweiter Teil* (Vienna, 1825). However, Mácha also tried to read Shakespeare in the original, for in his *Deník z roku 1835 (verze A)* [*Diary of 1835, Version A*] he mentions returning a copy of 'Shakespeare in English' to his friend Antonín Strobach.

[28] The editors of Mácha's *Spisy III* have pointed out that Oldřich's speech from 'a Scene from Act II' may refer to 4.3 of *2 Henry IV*. Although the textual evidence is scanty, the complex irony of Scene 4.3.161–7 where Prince Harry mistakes his father's sleep for death ('a sleep / That from this golden rigol hath divorced / So many English kings' 4.3.166–8) is developed elsewhere in Mácha's fragment.

[29] L. C. Knights, 'Time's Subjects: The Sonnets and *King Henry IV, Part II*', in *Some Shakespearean Themes, and an Approach to 'Hamlet'* (Stanford, 1965), p. 41.

[30] Mácha's concept of time was more reflexive than Shakespeare's, influenced by the proto-existentialist features of Romanticism, Baroque religious poetry and anticipating Bergson's *durée*. In his chief lyrical epic poem *May* he expresses the nature of time in a string of catachretic metaphors of the transience of individual consciousness, lapse of historical time as well as of the discontinuity of time in general:

> The last indignant thoughts of the defeated dead,
> Their unremembered names, the clamour of old fights,
> The worn-out northern lights, after their gleam is fled,
> The untuned harp, whose strings distil no more delights,
> The deeds of time gone by, quenched starlight overhead,
> . . .
> As the smoke of burnt-out fires, as the shatter'd bell's chime,
> Are the dead years of the dead, their beautiful childhood time.
>
> (Karel Hynek Mácha, *May*, trans. Edith Pargeter (Prague, 1965), p. 61)

Despite his reflective lyricism, Mácha valued, as his excerpt from *Henry IV, Part 2* demonstrates, Shakespeare's 'concrete' understanding of time as 'history in all men's lives' (3.1.75). This is also evident in his numerous excerpts from Walter Scott's novels (see Procházka, 'From Romantic Folklorism to Children's Adventure Fiction', pp. 185–8).

[31] Mácha, *Spisy I*, p. 263.

[32] Mácha, *Spisy I*, p. 265.

[33] Macdonald, 'Uneasy Lies', p. 33.

[34] Mácha, *Spisy II*, 24. The historical irony implied in this cluster of rhetorical figures is that the Hangman is a descendant of the first Czech royal house of the Přemyslids, while King Wenceslas IV was called Hangman because of his cruelty displayed, for instance, during the torture of St John

mastering 'new languages'[35] typical of Hal, there is ample evidence of his experiments with the colloquial idiom of different classes of Czech society in his tales (especially 'Marinka', 1835) and Notebook fragments.

Although one could search for further analogies between *Henry IV, Part 2* and Mácha's fragmentary historical drama, there is a crucial difference concerning the representation of the supreme political authority. It has been frequently emphasized that this authority undergoes deep transformation in Shakespeare's play. As James Calderwood pointed out

Shakespeare begins *Henry IV*, with a fallen language whose lack of inherent truth is emblemized in the lie. But as his soliloquy indicates, Hal is prepared to use the lie rather than wilt before it as Richard did. After all, he who uses Falstaff must by definition use the lie. But also, by creating from the false image of the wastrel prince a true symbol of English kingship, *Hal will incorporate the lie into a constructive political program*, a drama of skillful offence 'redeeming time when men least think [he] will' (1.2.240). And that is Shakespeare's artistic goal as well – to wrest truth from a language devoid of divine or natural authority, to shape from the unseemly material of the lie an authentic order and meaning.[36]

In Mácha's allusions to *Henry IV, Part 2* there is no evidence that the Czech Romantic was aware of this transformation of language and authority.[37] Unsurprisingly, Mácha ignores Falstaff and his exchanges with Hal. It can be conjectured that he understood them (fully in keeping with many nineteenth-century interpretations of Falstaff) as a mere condescension to vulgar taste.[38] Although in Mácha's later work, ironic representation of royal authority can be found, its irony, as in the above discussed case of *Křivoklad*, is tragic and lacks the features of humour and the carnivalesque typical of the scenes with Falstaff and related characters. And the pragmatic aspects of political discourse, unredeemed by religious virtues and values, are not developed in *The Brothers*, pervaded as it is by satire of the political idealism of Czech nationalists.

Although in both parts of *Henry IV* royal authority seems to lose its divine origin and power, it is still connected with an important traditional economic, moral and political paradigm of *mancipatio*, the acceptance of values and authority as a *gift* from some higher political, metaphysical or ideological agency.[39] This paradigm both connects and differentiates Shakespeare's and Mácha's representations of kingship. In *Henry IV, Part 2* the act of *mancipatio* legitimizing Prince Harry's ascension is phrased in lines echoing the older play (*The Famous Victories of Henry the Fifth*),[40] thus marking the renewal of the traditional feudal value pattern:

---

of Nepomuk. Mácha used this technique against the frequent idealization of the feudal past among the Czech nationalists.

35 See Macdonald, 'Uneasy Lies', p. 33, and Steven Mullaney, 'The Rehearsal of Cultures', *The Place of the Stage: License, Play and Power in Elizabethan England* (Chicago, 1988), pp. 76–80.

36 James L. Calderwood, *Metadrama in Shakespeare's Henriad* (Berkeley, 1979), pp. 52–3 (emphasis added).

37 Reflecting critically on approaches like Calderwood's, one becomes aware of the problematic nature of the notion of 'fallen language', which presupposes the existence of a kind of paradisal condition of 'innocent language' and thus necessarily reproduces a familiar paradigm of sacred history. Disregarding the problem of 'fallen language' or 'lie' in Shakespeare's play, Mácha may fall short of doing justice to the pervasive pragmatism of modern politics but he, at the same time, seems to deconstruct more efficiently a different political discourse based on the idealism of nationalist ideology, finding expression in the notion of the 'timeless totality of language' (Procházka, 'Romantic Revivals', p. 83). For the deconstruction of the 'fall' of language in the Old Testament story of the Ten Commandments see Jacques Derrida, 'Edmond Jabès and the Question of the Book', *Writing and Difference*, trans. Alan Bass (Chicago, 1978), pp. 64–78.

38 The exception is a short parodical passage from *Henry IV, Part 2*, 3.2.33–45, where Justice Shallow preaches to Silence about the certainty of death: 'Death, as the Psalmist saith, is certain to all; all shall die' and then resumes: 'How a good yoke of bullocks at Stamford fair?' (cf. Mácha, *Spisy* III, p. 125). The passage is quoted in A. W. Schlegel's translation (see above). Even here, however, there is a serious theme, the inevitability of death, central for Mácha's mature work.

39 See Marcel Mauss's discussion of the gift as a feature of a different value system to that based on the rational value exchange typical of political economy (*The Gift*, trans. D.W. Hall (New York, 1990), pp. 50–1).

40 William Shakespeare, *The Second Part of King Henry IV*, ed. Giorgio Melchiori (Cambridge, 1989), pp. 166n and 234.

'To thee it [the crown] shall descend with better quiet, / Better opinion, better confirmation' (4.3.316–17). Unlike in *2 Henry IV*, in Mácha's dramatic fragment the *mancipatio* becomes impossible due to the continuing deadly strife between the two sons of the ruler. The only power which could legitimize the new monarch would have to come directly from 'eternity'.

However, Mácha, who in his major poem called *Máj* (*May*, 1836) identified eternity with nothingness,[41] had serious problems in constructing this providential agency. Evidently, the traditional topology linking – in a single symbolic place, the chamber called Jerusalem where Henry IV expires[42] – the immutable divine order of the universe with the forgiveness granted by divine mercy, no longer worked in the pre-1848 Europe recently shattered by the revolutionary events of 1830. It is quite likely that in these circumstances, Mácha was prompted to read the final scenes of the play ironically and, surprisingly, to understand 'the book of fate' speech of the old king (3.1.44–78) as an *emancipatory* act. The problem of his reading, which found the origin of the legitimizing power in an abstractly conceived historical necessity (mentioned by Henry IV and called by Warwick 'a history in all men's lives' (3.1.75)), was that neither the inherent notion of historical change ('the revolution of the times') nor 'chance's mocks / And changes' (3.1.50–1) could *morally* justify the ascension of the new ruler. Therefore, in contrast to Shakespeare's play, the ascension of Břetislav was not represented directly in terms of feudal lineage but in a utopian way.

This way differs from the utopian tendencies in early nationalist writings because it does not project popular desires and current ideological strategies on historical material. Mácha's utopian gesture consists in supplanting the randomness of historical events by the ethical concept of *justice as historical necessity* ('Nemesis') establishing the new *telos* of national existence.[43] Here one may speculate about the influence of Canto IV of Byron's *Childe Harold's Pilgrimage* where the figure of Nemesis is used to establish a link between the speaker's individual life and universal history.

In his grappling with Shakespeare, as well as feudal and nationalist traditions, Mácha articulated his resistance to the nationalist versions of *mancipatio*, or the bestowal of authority accomplished under the vigilant eyes of the police and censorship of the Metternich regime. According to the Czech revivalists, the national cause, as the outcome of God's gift of language, was safely removed from the realm of history and politics to the divine sphere and incorporated in the providential agenda.

Another and directly related aspect of Mácha's use of Shakespeare can be defined – in relation to Jerome McGann's notion of 'Romantic ideology'[44] – as an individual aesthetic gesture whose political implications are inherent in the clash between the artist's need of self-assertion and the 'public', moral and ideological determinants of his situation. Moreover, it can also be stated in terms of *mancipatio*: great works of literature may be understood 'as unasked for and perhaps unwanted obligations' and 'an offer we cannot refuse'. The individual dimension of this relationship consists in the struggle of artists to escape 'from the ministerial relationship to their predecessors and to achieve a magisterial position'.[45] However, to rise to this

---

[41] In Mácha's chief poetic work, *May*, the universe, synonymous with eternity, is 'mere nothingness – for ever' (Mácha, *May*, p. 32). This state of the universe is epitomized by an oxymoron 'fallen dwelling of eternity' (65) which also relates to the authority of ancient history and language.

[42] The analogues of this model, or *topos*, in Mácha's work are symbolic images of ancestral halls. In one of them, in the verse-tale fragment *Mnich* [*The Monk*], the ancestral hall is identified with a tomb dominated with a crucifix, where the figure of Christ has a face covered with black veil signifying death (Mácha, *Spisy I*, p. 171).

[43] On the problem of this position see e.g. Jacques Derrida, *The Spectres of Marx*, trans. Peggy Kamuf (London, 1994), p. 27: 'And what if disadjustment were on the contrary the condition of justice?' See also my chapter 'From 'Affirmative Culture' to the 'Condition of Justice': A Reading of a Czech Post-Communist *Hamlet*', in *Arbeit am Gedächtnis*, ed. Michael Frank and Gabriele Rippl (München, 2007), pp. 409–22.

[44] Jerome J. McGann, *The Romantic Ideology* (Chicago, 1983).

[45] Bristol, *Shakespeare's America: America's Shakespeare*, p. 41. Bristol draws on Harold Bloom's *Poetry and Repression* (New Haven, 1976).

position involves redefining the whole political agenda and is virtually impossible without subscription to socially acceptable values and ideology, which Mácha was unwilling to do. As a result, Mácha's emancipatory use of Shakespeare is in fact contained within the general ideological articulation of *mancipatio*, in terms of justice, responsibility and moral authority.

AN IRISH CATALYSIS: W. B. YEATS AND THE USES OF SHAKESPEARE

ANDREW MURPHY

In April 1901, W. B. Yeats was in Stratford-upon-Avon, staying at the Shakespeare Hotel, watching the Benson company perform the history plays in sequence, and reading criticism of the plays at the library of the Shakespeare Memorial Theatre. 'I do not', he wrote to Augusta Gregory, 'even stop for Afternoon tea.'[1] This period of Shakespearian immersion resulted in two magazine articles, published in the *Speaker*, then subsequently reprinted as a single piece, under the title 'At Stratford-on-Avon', in the collection *Ideas of Good and Evil* (1903). In his letter to Gregory, Yeats observed that 'The more I read the worse does the Shakespeare criticism become. And Dowden is about the climax of it.'[2] The 'Dowden' referred to here was, of course, fellow Irishman Edward Dowden, Professor of English at Trinity College Dublin from 1867 until his death in 1913, author of the highly successful *Shakspere: A Critical Study of his Mind and Art*, and inaugural general editor of the Arden Shakespeare.

Yeats and Dowden had a complex relationship. The professor had been an undergraduate at Trinity with Yeats's father, the painter John Butler Yeats, and they remained lifelong friends.[3] Dowden offered much encouragement to the younger Yeats in the early days of his writing career, helping to convince the Dublin publishing firm of Sealy, Bryers and Walker to produce a pamphlet version of the poet's *Mosada* in 1886, and helping also to solicit subscriptions for the publication.[4] When *The Wanderings of Oisin* was published in 1889, Dowden wrote to Yeats:

It gave me great pleasure to get your volume of poems, & to get it from yourself, & see it a fact accomplished, & last to read it from cover to cover. I do not think there is a page in it which has not its own beauty, & there is also a kind of unity in the whole book...A great many were already familiar to me, & I think it is a good sign of your quality that I remembered them so well.[5]

Yeats was initially overawed by the cultured Trinity don, with, as the poet puts it, his 'orderly, prosperous house where all was in good taste, where poetry was rightly valued', but in time he became disenchanted with the professor, eventually coming to see in Dowden the incarnation of everything he most hated about Victorian Dublin

---

[1]   Letter from Yeats to Augusta Gregory, 25 April 1901, in John Kelly and Ronald Schuhard, eds., *The Collected Letters of W. B. Yeats*, vol. 3 1901–1904 (Oxford, 1994), p. 62.

[2]   Yeats, *Collected Letters*, p. 61.

[3]   After Dowden's death, when W. B. Yeats was trying to prevent his sisters from publishing a volume of the professor's poetry at the family's Cuala Press, his father wrote to him: 'I would ask you, indeed beg of you, to remember that [Dowden] not only was a very old friend, but the best of friends', Letter from J. B. Yeats to W. B. Yeats, 11 December 1913, in Joseph Hone, ed., *J. B. Yeats: Letters to his Son W. B. Yeats and Others 1869–1922* (New York, 1946), p. 168.

[4]   See R. F. Foster, *W. B. Yeats: A Life*, vol. 1: *The Apprentice Mage 1865–1914* (Oxford, 1998), pp. 38–9.

[5]   Letter from Dowden to W. B. Yeats, 17 January 1889, in Richard J. Finneran, George Mills Harper and William M. Murphy, with Alan B. Himber, eds., *Letters to W. B. Yeats*, 2 vols. (New York, 1977), vol. 1, p. 4.

society.[6] In advance of the appearance of the *Reveries* volume of his *Autobiographies*, he wrote to his father: 'the book is a history of the revolt, which perhaps unconsciously you taught me, against certain Victorian ideals. Dowden is the image of those ideals and has to stand for the whole structure in Dublin, Lord Chancellors and all the rest.'[7]

What particularly divided Yeats and Dowden was politics and, more specifically, the politics of culture. Yeats became a political and cultural nationalist under the tutelage of the Fenian activist John O'Leary; Dowden, by contrast, was a Liberal Unionist, part of that group of Liberals who broke with the party in the wake of Gladstone's first attempt, in 1886, to introduce Home Rule for Ireland. For Yeats, nationalism was an enabling force, which released him into creativity as he sought to drive forward an Irish national literary project. In 'What is "Popular Poetry"?' he writes that Nature

wanted a few verses from me, and because it would not have seemed worth while taking so much trouble to see my books lie on a few drawing-room tables, she filled my head with thoughts of making a whole literature, and plucked me out of the Dublin art schools . . . and sent me into a library to read bad translations from the Irish, and at last down into Connacht to sit by turf fires.[8]

His early prose work is often shot through with insistent nationalist sloganeering, as the following quotes from a series of articles published in the American newspapers the Boston *Pilot* and the *Providence Sunday Journal* in the late 1880s indicate:

Creative work has always a fatherland

Ireland is the true subject for the Irish

There is no great literature without nationality, no great nationality without literature

One can only reach out to the universe with a gloved hand – that glove is one's nation, the only thing one knows even a little of.[9]

For Yeats, at this early point in his career, nationality is paramount and it is the engine that drives culture.

In an article published in the *Fortnightly Review* at the time when Yeats was expressing these views, Dowden took exactly the opposite line to the poet, rejecting the notion that national identity must always be the wellspring of culture. The primary task of the writer, in Dowden's view, should not be the production of work that always springs from native concerns, but, rather, the creation of well-crafted work, whether informed by national concerns or not. Any national significance should only ever be, for Dowden, a secondary and not a primary effect in the work. Thus, he observes:

Let an Irish . . . writer[10] show that he can be patient, exact, just, enlightened, and he will have done better service for Ireland, whether he treats of Irish themes or not, than if he wore shamrocks in all his buttonholes and had his mouth for ever filled with the glories of Brian the Brave.[11]

The sharp satiric edge to Dowden's comments here is undoubtedly a function of the fact that he was,

---

6 W. B. Yeats, *Reveries Over Childhood and Youth*, in Richard J. Finneran and George Mills Harper, gen. eds., *The Collected Works of W. B. Yeats*; William H. O'Donnell and Douglas N. Archibald, eds., vol. 3, *Autobiographies* (New York, 1999), p. 94.

7 Letter from W. B. Yeats to J. B. Yeats, *c.* November/December 1915, in Allan Wade, ed., *The Letters of W. B. Yeats* (London, 1954), pp. 602–3.

8 'What is "Popular Poetry"?', in Finneran and Harper, gen. eds., *Collected Works*: George Bornstein and Richard J. Finneran, eds., vol. 4, *Early Essays* (New York, 2007), p. 8.

9 All quotations from Finneran and Harper, gen. eds., *Collected Works*: George Bornstein and Hugh Witemeyer, eds., vol. 7, *Letters to the New Island* (New York, 1989), pp. 12, 21, 30, 78.

10 In the original this reads 'an Irish prose writer', but Dowden's fundamental point applies, for him, to writing more generally.

11 Edward Dowden, 'Hopes and Fears for Literature', *Fortnightly Review*, 45 (1889), 176–7. 'Brian the Brave' is a reference to Brian Boru, the eleventh-century High King of Ireland.

by this time, increasingly becoming an active public campaigner for the anti-Home Rule movement, so the essay as a whole is characterized by a tendency to slide from the measured tones of the study towards the robust rhetoric of the platform. Yeats, of course, found Dowden's comments in the essay deeply offensive and, in 1895, he engineered a public challenge to the professor's views of the Irish literary movement in the correspondence pages of the Dublin *Daily Express*, observing in a letter to his father at the time: 'The contraversy [sic] has I think done good. Dowden has certainly got the worst of it.'[12] Dowden's response to Yeats's attack was simply to repeat the substance of his *Fortnightly Review* comments in a letter of his own to the *Express* and to reproduce the *Fortnightly* essay in its entirety in his collection *New Studies in Literature*, published later in the same year.[13]

It was six years after this public clash that Yeats visited Stratford. Having challenged Dowden publicly on the issue of Irish literature, he would now take the fight to the professor in his own – Shakespearian – territory.[14] Dowden's *Shakspere: A Critical Study of His Mind and Art* and Yeats's Stratford essay serve nicely, between them, to map the broad range of differences that separated the two men. First of all, there is the question of what constitutes literary interpretation for each of them. Dowden was, in effect, the 'first Shakespearian', in the modern sense of being the first scholar to spend his entire working life as a university academic, teaching English literature and writing about and editing the works of Shakespeare (among other writers). His career is emblematic of the increasing professionalization of literary studies from the middle decades of the nineteenth century onwards. It comes as no surprise, then, to find him declaring, in the 'Preface' to *Mind and Art* that 'I believe that Shakspere is not to be approached on any side through dilettantism.'[15] 'Dilettantism' was, for Dowden, the mark of the ill-informed, belles-lettristic amateur.[16] By contrast with Dowden, who held an undergraduate degree and a doctorate from Trinity, Yeats had broken with family tradition by not attending the Dublin

college, admitting in *Reveries* that he had felt that 'neither my classics nor my mathematics were good

---

[12] Letter from W. B. Yeats to J. B. Yeats, *c.* 1 February 1895, in Kelly, gen. ed., *Collected Letters*: John Kelly and Eric Domville, eds., vol. 1, *1865–1895* (Oxford, 1994), p. 436. The context here was a public lecture in Dublin celebrating the work of the Irish poet Samuel Ferguson. In one of his very first published essays, Yeats had, in 1886, taken Dowden to task for failing to offer public praise of Ferguson's work, observing: 'It is a question whether the most distinguished of our critics, Professor Dowden, would not only have more consulted the interests of his country, but more also, in the long run, his own dignity and reputation . . . if he had devoted some of those elaborate pages which he has spent on the much bewritten George Eliot, to a man like [Ferguson]' – 'The Poetry of Sir Samuel Ferguson', in John P. Frayne, ed., *Uncollected Prose by W. B. Yeats*, 2 vols, vol. 1, *First Reviews and Articles 1886–1896* (London, 1970), pp. 88–9.

[13] For Dowden's letter, see *Daily Express*, 22 January 1895, p. 5, under the heading 'LITERATURE IN IRELAND'. On the extended dispute between Yeats and Dowden in this period see, in particular, Phillip L. Marcus, *Yeats and the Beginning of the Irish Renaissance* (Ithaca, 1970), pp. 108–20, and Foster, *Apprentice Mage*, pp. 145–8.

[14] The most thoroughgoing account of the influence of Shakespeare and other Renaissance writers on Yeats's own writing is provided in Wayne K. Chapman, *Yeats and English Renaissance Literature* (Basingstoke, 1991). See also Rupin W. Desai's still enormously valuable *Yeats's Shakespeare* (Evanston, 1971).

[15] Edward Dowden, *Shakspere: A Critical Study of His Mind and Art* (London, 1875), p. vi. Subsequent references are incorporated parenthetically into the text.

[16] Dowden was particularly opposed to an older form of 'belles-lettristic' criticism, which he regarded as being overly concerned with considerations of literary style, rather than with the analysis of content. His views on the matter are most clearly expressed in an 1887 exchange of letters with Macmillans, concerning a volume he was contracted to contribute to the publishers' 'History of English Literature' series. George Saintsbury was the author of the *Elizabethan Literature* volume in the sequence and, when that book appeared, Dowden wrote to Macmillans, withdrawing from the project, on the grounds that there was no possibility that his own work could ever be compatible with Saintsbury's. By contrast with his fellow critic, Dowden observed: 'I should never criticise style apart from the thoughts + feelings conveyed by the style, nor say that the matter or substance of a book is of little consequence to the student of literature . . . I may say that anything I should write would be actively opposed in ideas + in method to what Mr Saintsbury has written. While . . . I recognise M^r

enough for any examination'.[17] In one early article, he writes about a sense of gloom that descended on him, as he sat in the National Library in Dublin and realized that he was surrounded by people who were engaged not in reading or thought as an end in itself, but rather were studying in preparation for exams of one sort or another. 'I can remember', he writes, 'sitting there . . . looking with scorn at those bowed heads and busy eyes.' By contrast with these other readers, Yeats himself sits in the library, 'listening', he tells us, 'to my own mind as if to the sounds in a sea shell'.[18]

For Yeats (with Trinity specifically in his mind), the 'academic class is always a little dead and deadening' and, in 'The Body of the Father Christian Rosencrux' (1895), he writes that 'I cannot get it out of my mind that this age of criticism is about to pass, and an age of imagination, of emotion, of moods, of revelation, about to come in its place.'[19] His dismissive attitude to formalized, directed scholarship finds an echo in the Stratford essay. Despite, as we have seen, having told Gregory that he was working concentratedly day after day, in writing his article he affects an attitude of studied casualness: 'I have *turned over* many books in the library at Stratford-on-Avon', he writes, and, again, 'I cannot claim any minute knowledge of these books.'[20] There is, we might say, an element of critical *sprezzatura* at play here, which may signal a deliberate attempt to set up a strong contrast between himself and the Trinity professor.[21]

This critical distinction between the determined professional and the intuitive interpreter in fact also colours the two men's views of the biographical Shakespeare. At the time when he was working on *Mind and Art*, Dowden wrote to Elizabeth Dickinson West (a former student who would become his second wife), observing: 'I instinctively, in self-defence, put some of myself into Shakespeare.'[22] It is a revealing comment. Dowden's father was a Presbyterian linen draper from Cork city and T. W. Lyster (librarian at the National Library in Dublin) observed of Dowden that 'He inherited from his father a steadfast accuracy in financial affairs, as in all other matters in life' and that

'That was no small thing in a man of letters.'[23] What is striking about Dowden's vision of Shakespeare in *Mind and Art* is the extent to which

---

Saintsbury's wide reading + good taste, I fear that at the present time when there is something like a struggle between scholarship + dilettantism, his book, in consequence of his method, will tell rather in favour of dilettantism than of real study', Letter from Dowden to Mr [George?] Macmillan, dated 1 November 1887, British Library Add MS 55029/37.

17 *Autobiographies*, p. 90. Yeats and his circle maintained a deep dislike of Trinity, seeing it as a bastion of Anglocentric Unionism. Yeats observed of the college that she 'desires to be English . . . she has set herself against the national genius, and taught her children to imitate alien styles and choose out alien themes', W. B. Yeats, *A Book of Irish Verse Selected from Modern Writers* (London, 1895), p. xxv. John Eglinton claimed that Augusta Gregory had explained why she had sent her son to Oxford rather than Trinity by observing 'Oxford, you know, is much nearer Ireland than Trinity College!' – John Eglinton, *Irish Literary Portraits* (London, 1935), p. 6. For Yeats's most sustained attack on the college, see 'Dublin Scholasticism and Trinity College', in Frayne, ed., *Uncollected Prose*, vol. 1, pp. 231–4.

18 *Letters to the New Island*, p. 4.

19 'The Academic Class and the Agrarian Revolution', in John P. Frayne and Colton Johnson, eds., W. B. Yeats, *Uncollected Prose*, 2 vols., *Reviews, Articles and Other Miscellaneous Prose 1897–1939* (London, 1975), vol. 2, p. 150; 'The Body of the Father Christian Rosencrux' in *Early Essays*, p. 144.

20 'At Stratford-on-Avon', in *Early Essays*, p. 78 (emphasis added). Subsequent references to the essay are incorporated parenthetically into the text.

21 In a rather nice phrase, Peter Ure has observed that Yeats 'enjoyed . . . his little bout of coughing in ink as a fake Shakespeare scholar', 'W. B. Yeats and the Shakespearian Moment', in C. J. Rawson, ed., *Yeats and Anglo-Irish Literature: Critical Essays by Peter Ure* (Liverpool, 1974), p. 205.

22 Dowden to Elizabeth Dickinson West, 16 June 1874, in [Elizabeth Dickinson Dowden, ed.], *Fragments from Old Letters E.D. to E.D.W. 1869–1892* (London, 1914), 2 vols., vol. 1, p. 99.

23 'The Late Professor Dowden, Lecture by Mr. T. W. Lister', *Irish Times*, 18 November 1913, p. 7. Dowden retained a financial interest in the family business and, in a letter to Elizabeth West of 23 February 1883, he wrote: 'Learning is all very fine, but give me linen! I believe I make a very good draper. I shall be happy to receive the favour of any orders and shall execute them with attention and punctuality – Terms cash' (*Fragments*, vol. 1, p. 157). Dowden oddly anticipates Joyce's parody of him in *Ulysses* here: 'William Shakespeare and Company, limited. For terms apply: E. Dowden, Highfield house', James Joyce, *Ulysses* (Harmondsworth, 1971), p. 204.

he stresses the importance of the playwright's commercial dealings. '[A]ll through his life', Dowden writes, 'we observe in Shakspere a sufficient recognition of external fact, external claims, and obligations. Hence worldly prosperity could not be a matter which would ever seem unimportant to Shakspere' (33). And again:

The Shakspere invariably bright, gentle, and genial is the Shakspere of a myth. The man actually discoverable behind the plays was a man . . . of strenuous will, and whose highest self pronounced in favour of sanity. Therefore he resolved that he would set to rights his material life, and he did so. (383)

Yeats felt that this centralizing of the material aspects of Shakespeare's life informed Dowden's interpretation of Shakespeare's work as well. The poet focused in particular on the way in which Dowden and other academic critics viewed Henry V and Richard II as a contrasting pair of characters. In his book Dowden valorized Henry V by setting up a comparison with a number of Shakespeare's other kings, including Richard. Henry, he writes,

is the king who will not fail. He will not fail as the saintly Henry VI failed, nor as Richard II failed, a hectic, self-indulgent nature, a mockery king of pageantry, and sentiment, and rhetoric; nor will he only partially succeed by prudential devices, and stratagems, and crimes, like his father, 'great Bolingbroke'. The success of Henry V will be sound throughout, and it will be complete. (74–5)

Peter Ure has noted that 'In Yeats's Stratford essay Pater is brought in to redress the balance upset by Professor Dowden.'[24] Pater's 1889 essay on 'Shakespeare's English Kings' presents Richard as 'the most sweet-tongued' of all of Shakespeare's kings, conceiving him as 'an exquisite poet . . . able to see all things poetically, to give a poetic turn to his conduct of them, and refreshing with his golden language the tritest aspects of that ironic contrast between the pretensions of a king and the actual necessities of his destiny'.[25] Yeats follows Pater in his positive portrait of Richard, observing:

I cannot believe that Shakespeare looked on [him] with any but sympathetic eyes, understanding indeed how ill-fitted he was to be king, at a certain moment of history, but understanding that he was lovable and full of capricious fancy . . . He saw indeed, as I think, in Richard II the defeat that awaits all, whether they be artist or saint, who find themselves where men ask of them a rough energy and have nothing to give but some contemplative virtue, whether lyrical fantasy, or sweetness of temper, or dreamy dignity, or love of God, or love of His creatures. (79)

Yeats, then, sees Richard's failure as having an elemental positive charge to it and, like Pater, he celebrates what he takes to be Richard's aesthetic sensibility. By championing Henry in preference to Richard, contemporary critics (with Dowden at their head), had become, in Yeats's view, simply 'vulgar worshipper[s] of success' (p. 78) and, indeed, in his The Trembling of the Veil, he would later write of Dowden that he 'turned Shakespeare into a British Benthamite'.[26]

Yeats's account of Dowden's criticism, while undoubtedly accurate up to a point, is also, however, rather reductive. In the case specifically of Henry V, Dowden's interpretation is considerably more nuanced than the poet allows. Dowden does see Shakespeare as presenting Henry as an ideal figure, but only, in fact, in a specific context: 'He must certainly,' Dowden writes, 'be regarded as Shakspere's ideal of manhood *in the sphere of practical achievement*, – the hero, and central figure therefore of the history plays' (210, emphasis added). What Yeats fails to register in his essay, however, is that, elsewhere in his analysis, Dowden locates Henry

---

[24] Ure, 'Shakespearian Moment', p. 207. As William M. Murphy points out in *Prodigal Father: The Life of John Butler Yeats (1839–1922)* (Ithaca, 1978), the poet's interpretation of the relationship between Richard and Henry also very closely mirrors the views of his father (see pp. 97–100). In *On the Boiler* (Dublin: Cuala Press, [1938]) Yeats observes that, from his father, he learned 'to set certain passages in Shakespeare above all else in literature' (p. 14).

[25] Walter Pater, 'Shakespeare's English Kings', in *Appreciations with an Essay on Style* (New York, 1903; Kessinger rpt), p. 201.

[26] *Autobiographies*, p. 193.

in a broader context, where the values of practical achievement have far less purchase. Thus, he writes:

in the tragedies, Shakspere has flung himself abroad upon the dim sea which moans around our little solid sphere of the known. Such easy and pious answers to the riddles of the world as constituted the working faith of a Henry V belong to a smaller and safer world of thought, feeling, and action; not to this. (225–6)

Dowden's valorizing of Henry thus extends only to the specific sphere of the history plays and he recognizes that, in the greater scheme of things, practical values can only ever have a limited application.

Dowden's biographical reading of Shakespeare is also more complex than Yeats indicates. Certainly, the Shakespeare presented by Dowden as a commercially minded pragmatist can at times sound perilously similar to John Dover Wilson's memorable description of the Stratford bust of the poet as resembling a 'self-satisfied pork butcher' (or, perhaps, a smug Cork linen draper). But Dowden in fact offers a greater argument in *Mind and Art* which suggests that Shakespeare cultivated the pragmatic side of his character not so much as an end in itself, but rather specifically in order that it might serve as a counterweight against two potentially excessive (and self-destructive) drives rooted deep in his own make-up: drives which Dowden identifies as the Romeo obsession and the Hamlet obsession. The former involved 'abandonment to passion' and the latter 'abandonment to brooding thought' (47). For Dowden, both these drives *and* Shakespeare's commercialist instinct were held in a tense, creative balance throughout the playwright's life. His overall sense of the dynamic operating within Shakespeare's personality is nicely caught in a comment Dowden made in a letter written to Elizabeth West just as he was beginning work on *Mind and Art*. Shakespeare, he observes, 'had his outer sphere of metaphysic and self abandonment *and that was his truest self*; but he had his inner sphere of practicality and self-restraint'.[27] This may well seem like a rather crude psychological model to us in our own (post-Freudian) times but it does

at least indicate that Yeats's accusation that Dowden had turned Shakespeare into a British Benthamite is not entirely accurate.[28]

There are broader issues at stake between Dowden and Yeats than simply the question of how one reads particular Shakespearian characters, or how one conceives of the psychological narrative of Shakespeare's own life. Yeats and Dowden held radically different conceptions of Renaissance culture and this had implications for their respective wider visions of culture more generally. Shakespeare's work was centrally important to Yeats. In 1937, just two years before his death, thinking about the writers that he most valued, he wrote: 'I owe my soul to Shakespeare, to Spenser and to Blake, perhaps to William Morris.'[29] But Yeats saw Shakespeare (and to a lesser extent Spenser) as being oddly located in relation to his own early modern historical moment.[30] In *The Trembling of the*

---

[27] Dowden to Elizabeth West, January 1874, in *Fragments*, vol. 1, p. 83; italics in original. There is a sense in which this, more complex, model can also be mapped as easily on to Dowden as it can on to Shakespeare. On 26 September 1870, John Todhunter wrote to him: 'You are by nature impulsive + almost chivalrous, but you have studiously subjected your heart to the guidance of your head, making your life a life of calculation + weighing of consequences + hence it is that "a real enthusiasm in passing through you becomes mingled with unreality" which means simply that you have not yet got out of hell – you have not got eternal life', Edward Dowden Papers, Trinity College Dublin, TCD MS3147–54a/66.

[28] Dowden, in any case, would not have seen himself as a Benthamite. In a letter of 15 November 1873 to Elizabeth West he writes: 'I am certainly at present not a Utilitarian, *i.e.* I do not positively believe in the doctrine . . . Whenever I did look into the matter, it seemed to me that in mere point of argument the Utilitarian side was not always the stronger, and that they strained and perverted facts (if others invented facts)', *Fragments*, vol. 2, p. 39.

[29] 'Introduction', in Finneran and Harper, gen. eds., *Collected Works*: William H. O'Donnell, ed., vol. 5, *Later Essays* (New York and London, 1944), p. 211.

[30] For Yeats, the *Faerie Queene* was connected back positively to the medieval poetic tradition, but Spenser's layering of allegory on to the narrative had the effect of fastening it fatally to Spenser's own era. He writes of the poet: 'He wrote of knights and ladies, wild creatures imagined by the aristocratic poets of the twelfth century, and perhaps chiefly by English

Veil Yeats contends that, up through the medieval period, 'Europe shared one mind and heart, until both mind and heart began to break into fragments a little before Shakespeare's time.'[31] For Yeats, the Renaissance is associated with the rise of personality – or individualism – at the expense of community identity, and also with the increasing dominance of reason over the imagination.[32] This, in Yeats's view, is a fatal development, as he explains in an 1897 essay on William Blake:

The reason . . . binds us to mortality because it binds us to the senses, and divides us from each other by showing us our clashing interests; but imagination divides us from mortality by the immortality of beauty, and binds us to each other by opening the secret doors of all hearts.[33]

The process of fragmentation that Yeats sees happening in the Renaissance, prompted partly by the rise of reason, was, in his view, accelerated by the emergence of mercantilism and of Puritanism, both of which he sees as fostering a narrow materialism and as also anticipating the utilitarianism of his own time. In an essay on Edmund Spenser, written in the year following 'At Stratford-on-Avon', Yeats writes of a 'new Anglo-Saxon nation that was arising amid Puritan sermons and Marprelate pamphlets', a nation characterized by the 'earnestness and logic and the timidity and reserve of a counting-house'.[34] The early modern period is thus, for Yeats, just that: an early version of the commercialist world of his own era, that world obsessed with, as Matthew Arnold had it, 'Doors that open, windows that shut, locks that turn, razors that shave, coats that wear, watches that go'; this was a world that Yeats emphatically rejected.[35]

Rupin W. Desai has noted, in *Yeats's Shakespeare*, that Yeats thought of Shakespeare 'as one born out of due time who exemplified in his best work the attitudes of a past era'.[36] In his Stratford essay, Yeats thus figures Shakespeare (and some of his fellow poets) as sitting outside of the developments that most characterized the Renaissance, celebrating the fire of medieval culture, just at the point when it was starting to die back into its own embers:

The courtly and saintly ideals of the Middle Ages were fading, and the practical ideals of the modern age had begun to threaten the unuseful dome of the sky; Merry England was fading, and yet it was not so faded that the poets could not watch the procession of the world with that untroubled sympathy for men as they are, as apart from all they do and seem, which is the substance of tragic irony. (79–80)

The Renaissance represents, for Yeats, not a 'rebirth', but, in some ways, a form of cultural death. Or, to the extent that anything is being born in the period, it amounts simply to an anticipation of that rough beast Yeats would later imagine slouching towards Bethlehem.

In direct contrast to Yeats, Dowden saw Shakespeare as being a man not *out of* his time, but, precisely, *of* his time. Early in *Mind and Art* he declares: 'we know something of the Elizabethan period,

---

poets who had still the French tongue; but he fastened them with allegorical nails to a big barn-door of common sense, of merely practical virtue', 'Edmund Spenser' in *Early Essays*, p. 265.

[31] *Autobiographies*, p. 165. As Tom McAlindon has made clear, Yeats's view of the Renaissance here is influenced by William Morris's medievalism: 'While Morris conceded that the Renaissance constituted in many ways "the period of greatest life and hope that Europe had known till then", "a blaze of glory", the greatest achievements of the period were, he contended, "the fruit of the old, not the seed of the new order of things". For him the Renaissance was the end of the Middle Ages and so was misnamed; and his awareness of the terrible disintegration which the period heralded compelled him to look upon it with anger and dismay', 'Yeats and the English Renaissance', *PMLA*, 82 (1967), p. 158.

[32] On personality, see Yeats's comment, in *The Trembling of the Veil*: 'Somewhere about 1450, though later in some parts of Europe by a hundred years or so, and in some earlier, men attained to personality in great numbers' (*Autobiographies*, p. 227).

[33] 'William Blake and the Imagination', *Early Essays*, p. 85.

[34] *Early Essays*, p. 263. In 'Pages from a Diary in 1930', Yeats offers a pithily compacted history of early modern imperialist mercantilism: 'The capture of a Spanish treasure ship in the time of Elizabeth made England a capitalist nation', *Explorations* (London, 1962), p. 334.

[35] Matthew Arnold, *The Works of Matthew Arnold*, 15 vols., *On the Study of Celtic Literature* (London, 1903), vol. 5, p. 92.

[36] Desai, *Yeats's Shakespeare*, pp. 57–8.

and we know that Shakspere was a man who pros-
pered in that period. In that special environment
Shakspere throve; he put forth his blossoms and
bore fruit' (8). Dowden's view of the relationship
between the medieval world and the world of the
Renaissance is also a mirror image of the interpretation advanced by Yeats. In a striking contrast, he
observes: 'Sir John Mandeville brought back stories
from obscure valleys communicating with hell, and
haunted by homicidal demons, Raleigh brought
back the tobacco plant and the potato' (12). For
Yeats, of course, this would simply have smacked
of yet more Benthamite utilitarianism. But Dowden's broader interpretation of the Renaissance was
that the period had a positive valence, rooted precisely in the expansion of knowledge of all kinds
and, indeed, in a reformation project which he
saw as displacing a retrogressive Catholicism. Thus,
Dowden writes: 'in the Renascence and Reformation period, instead of substituting supernatural
powers, and persons, and events for the natural
facts of the world, men recurred to those facts,
and found in them inspiration and sustenance for
heart, and intellect, and conscience' (11–12). And,
for Dowden, it is precisely from this sustenance
that Renaissance literature springs. For Yeats, then,
Shakespeare and his fellows celebrate a civilization
on the point of being, we might say, thrown upon a
filthy early modern tide. For Dowden, by contrast,
it is precisely the emergence of a kind of modernity
that enables a new and more vibrant form of culture
to evolve – a culture that, in his view, is positively
continuous with his own. In brief: Yeats's Shakespeare looks ruefully backwards; Dowden's looks
positively forwards.

But there is a further – and rather surprising –
element to the narrative of cultural decline that
Yeats advances in the Stratford essay, an element
that, in fact, includes Shakespeare, rather than setting him aside as an anachronous figure within
his own period. Thinking about the sequence of
Shakespeare's history plays (which he had been
attending during his stay in Stratford) Yeats begins
to speculate as to how national history might have
come to serve as a greater source of inspiration for
English writers.[37] 'Had there been no Renaissance

and no Italian influence to bring in the stories of
other lands,' he observes,

English history would, it may be, have become as important to the English imagination as the Greek myths to
the Greek imagination; and many plays by many poets
would have woven it into a single story whose contours,
vast as those of Greek myth, would have made living
men and women seem like swallows building their nests
under the architrave of some Temple of the Giants.

For Yeats, here, the influx of narratives from other
cultures during the Renaissance has the effect of
inhibiting a full rendering of English history into
mythology – a mythology that, had it been allowed
to develop, could have served as a primary set of
source materials for English writers. The Renaissance, then, is, in Yeats's view, erosive of English
culture, not just because of the emergence of Puritanism and a form of proto-utilitarianism within
the period but also because the particular *cultural
process* that characterized the Renaissance – the
exposure of English writers to texts from other cultures – is, for Yeats, destructive of a truly national
literature. In the absence of this foreign influx,
Yeats argues, 'English literature, because it would
have grown out of itself, might have had the simplicity and unity of Greek literature', but this was
not to be, and Yeats concludes that 'I can never get
it out of my head that no man, even though he
be Shakespeare, can write perfectly when his web
is woven of threads that have been spun in many
lands' (82 – all quotations in this paragraph).[38]

---

[37] F. C. McGrath has registered the influence of Walter Pater
here again, noting that Pater and Yeats 'both comment on
the unity of the English history plays and speculate on the
hypothetical possibilities of a completed cycle of English histories, had Shakespeare chosen to complete such a venture',
'Paterian Aesthetics in Yeats' Drama', *Comparative Drama*, 13
(1979), p. 36.

[38] Neil Corcoran offers an interesting reading of this assertion
which (partly, at least) runs contrary to my own analysis here,
observing that the passage 'is better read not as a bizarre reservation about Shakespeare, whose extravagantly combinatory
eclecticism has so frequently been considered the essential
impulsion to, and the entire ground of, his creativity, but
as a prompt that Yeats is giving himself about the kind of
Antaeus-like rootedness in the mythology of Ireland which

Yeats's rather arresting claims here resonate, of course, with the views he expressed about Irish literature in his essays of the late 1880s: 'there is no great literature without nationality', 'one can only reach out to the universe with a gloved hand – that glove is one's nation'. For Yeats, the English Renaissance represents something like a breaking of the compact between culture and the nation, in the wake of the adulteration of national narratives by foreign influences. In drawing the essay to a close, Yeats turns, in fact, specifically to Ireland in his final paragraph. Shakespeare was, as we have seen, a man out of his time for Yeats, a man out of sympathy with the society that was developing around him. Somewhat oddly, Yeats proposes at the conclusion of his essay that 'The people of Stratford-on-Avon have remembered little about [Shakespeare], and invented no legend to his glory' (82). The point of this curious assertion, however, is that it sets Yeats up to make a comparison which enables him to move from Stratford to Ireland: by contrast with what Yeats presents as Stratford's neglect of Shakespeare, 'The poor Gaelic rhymer', he writes, 'leaves a nobler memory among his neighbours, who will talk of angels standing like flames about his death-bed, and of voices speaking out of bramble-bushes that he may have the wisdom of the world' (83). So the native, Irish-language poet, by contrast with Shakespeare, is, on the one hand, more appreciated by (and more connected to) his community and, on the other hand, is also more directly connected with the natural and spiritual worlds.[39] Yeats's move here makes clear, I would argue, that he fashions the English Renaissance in the way that he does in order that it may serve as a negative analogue for the Ireland of his own time; in writing about the Renaissance Yeats is always also writing about Ireland.

In the same year that he wrote his Stratford essay (1901), Yeats also contributed a 'Postscript' to a collection of essays entitled *Ideals in Ireland*, edited by Augusta Gregory. In this piece he asserts:

I think that our Irish movements have always interested me in part because I see in them the quarrel of two traditions of life, one old and noble, one new and ignoble, one undying because it satisfies our conscience though it seem dying, and one about to die because it is hateful to our conscience though it seem triumphant throughout the world.[40]

The 'two traditions of life' identified here are, of course, the Irish and the English, and Denis Donoghue has noted that, for Yeats, 'Ireland was a nation to the extent of its cultural difference from England.'[41] Tracking back through Yeats's vision of the Renaissance in the Stratford essay in the light of this, we find that much of what he criticizes as negative in the period can be seen as having, in Yeats's view, a direct positive analogue in the Ireland of his own time. To take, for example, Yeats's proposition that the influx of continental texts to England had the effect of impeding the growth of a form of national history that might have served as a mythology that English writers could have drawn on as a rich source of inspiration: this narrative of English cultural failure can be set in parallel with an equivalent narrative of Irish success. In the latter decades of the nineteenth century Celtic mythology was popularized in the translations and adaptations of writers such as Standish O'Grady and Augusta Gregory.[42] It is worth noting here that some of O'Grady's narratives were published specifically under the title *History of Ireland*, emblematizing, in its own way, the fluid relationship between history and myth that Yeats indicates in his Stratford essay.[43] These texts had, of course, precisely the sort of enabling impact

---

sustains an immense amount of his own work', *Shakespeare and the Modern Poet* (Cambridge, 2010), p. 37.

[39] There is, of course, a certain irony here in the fact that Yeats himself could not speak Irish.

[40] W. B. Yeats, 'A Postscript', in Augusta Gregory, ed., *Ideals in Ireland* (London, 1901), p. 105.

[41] Denis Donoghue, 'Ireland: Race, Nation, State', *Yeats Annual*, 14 (2001), p. 17.

[42] In an introductory note to Gregory's *Cuchulain of Muirthemne*, Yeats observes: 'When she has added her translations from other cycles, she will have given Ireland its *Mabinogion*, its *Morte d'Arthur*, its *Nibelungenlied*' (*Explorations*, p. 4).

[43] Standish O'Grady, *History of Ireland: The Heroic Period* (London, 1878–80), 2 vols.

on Irish writing that Yeats imagines a mythologized English national history might have had in
the Renaissance: literary works based on the stories of mythological figures such as Cú Chulainn,
Oisín, Deirdre, Gráinne and Méabh proliferated
from the closing decades of the nineteenth century
onwards (and, indeed, Yeats's own work is densely
populated with these figures).[44]

I have also suggested that Yeats registers a kind
of proto-utilitarianism in the Renaissance which
anticipates the worst materialist aspects of his own
era. Again, the poet saw a strong contrast here
between England and Ireland, as he consistently
imagined Ireland as a kind of determinedly anti-
materialist realm.[45] This idealism was, of course,
ultimately placed under severe strain by Yeats's disillusionment with those who 'fumbled in a greasy
till', but, for the Yeats of the very beginning of the
twentieth century at least, it was still a live notion.
In a lecture delivered just a few years after he wrote
his Stratford essay, for example, Yeats contended
that

Ireland will always be in the main an agricultural country. Industries we may have, but we will not have, as
England has, a very rich class nor whole districts black-
ened with smoke like what they call in England their
'Black Country' . . . Wherever men have tried to imagine a perfect life, they have imagined a place where men
plow and sow and reap, not a place where there are great
wheels turning and great chimneys vomiting smoke.[46]

And it is not just industrialism that Ireland has
been spared. Where, for Dowden, the Renaissance represented a period of positive discovery
and the advancement of knowledge, for Yeats, the
triumph of science was achieved at the expense
of human connectedness and spirituality – as he
later put it: 'Descartes, Locke, and Newton took
away the world and gave us its excrement instead.'[47]
Again, Ireland provides a point of contrast, as Yeats
observes in an essay published in 1905: 'The scientific movement is ebbing a little everywhere, and
here in Ireland it has never been in flood at all.'[48]
Again, where Yeats sees Puritanism as a pernicious force in early modern England, he presents
Ireland as a territory that is largely free from

the influence of radical Protestantism. This is, of
course, potentially a tricky issue for Yeats, being,
himself, of Protestant stock.[49] But he squares this
particular doctrinal circle by idealizing a form of
peculiarly Irish Christian belief, which he sees as
still being inflected by the pagan systems that it
displaced.[50] Thus Yeats observes that 'Behind all

---

44 For Yeats, mythology also had a *living reality* in the Ireland
of his time, particularly outside the urban centres: 'There
is no place in Ireland where they will not point to some
mountain where Grania slept beside her lover, or where the
misshapen Fomor were routed, or to some waters where the
Sacred Hazel once grew and fattened the Salmon of Wisdom
with its crimson nuts', 'The Tribes of Danu', in Frayne and
Johnson, *Uncollected Prose*, vol. 2, p. 56.

45 The 'anti-materialist' reading of Ireland is, of course, both
common and enduring. In a speech delivered in New York
in 1905, Douglas Hyde described Ireland as 'an ancient
nation whose half-deserted streets resound ever less and less
to the roar of traffic, whose mills are silent, whose factories
are fallen, whose very fields are studded with ruined gables –
memories of the past; and yet, around that nation, morality
of life, purity of sentiment, unswerving devotion to faith,
and to fatherland, and to language, have shed a halo in the
eyes of Europe that is all its own' – Douglas Hyde, 'The
Gaelic Revival', in Breandán Ó Conaire, ed., *Language, Lore
and Lyrics: Essays and Lectures* (Dublin, 1986), p. 180.

46 Richard Londraville, ed., 'Four Lectures by W. B. Yeats,
1902–4', *Yeats Annual*, 8 (1991), pp. 113–14.

47 'Pages from a Diary in 1930', in *Explorations*, p. 325.

48 *Samhain*, 1905, *Explorations*, p. 197.

49 One might also point out, of course, that Ireland was
emphatically not free of radical Protestantism, most notably
in the northeasternmost corner of the island. Ironically, in
fact, radical Protestantism can be said to be central to the
founding moment of Irish nationalism – the emergence of
the United Irishman movement of the closing years of the
eighteenth century.

50 Yeats was not unique in this. John Hutchinson, in *The
Dynamics of Cultural Nationalism: The Gaelic Revival and
the Creation of the Irish Nation State* (London, 1987) points
out that Celticist scholars earlier in the nineteenth century,
working under the umbrella of the Royal Irish Academy,
'identified the golden age in the period of primitive Christianity cherished by Protestant and Catholic alike, one which
combined a natural piety with a devotion to the arts and
crafts' (p. 87). There is also, again, a link back to Pater
here. In his 'Introduction' to Pater's *The Renaissance* (Oxford,
1986), Adam Phillips notes that 'The Christianity of Pater's
Renaissance men is always being fortunately undermined by
paganism, by the Hellenic ideal of harmonious perfection,
by an enlightened sensuality' (p. ix).

Irish history hangs a great tapestry, even Christianity had to accept it and be itself pictured there.
Nobody looking at its dim folds can say where
Christianity begins and Druidism ends.'[51] Or, as he
put it more simply in an essay on fairies in *The Celtic
Twilight*: in Ireland 'The Catholic religion likes to
keep on good terms with its neighbours.'[52] The
value of the Druidical substructure of Irish Christianity connects religion in Ireland with Yeats's
interest in occult forms of belief.[53] For Yeats,
Ireland remains, in his own time, a kind of liminal space, where the line between this world and
the next is shimmering and imprecise: 'In Ireland
this world and the other are not widely sundered;
sometimes, indeed, it seems almost as if our earthly
chattels were no more than the shadows of things
beyond.'[54] In summary, then, Ireland is, finally,
everything that England is not; modern Ireland is
everything that early modern England is not, and
while the English Renaissance may – at least in
some senses, for Yeats – have been a failure, the
Irish Revival can be a success precisely because it is
unencumbered by the disadvantages that Yeats sees
as blighting the culture of Shakespeare's time.

In a characteristic formulation, Yeats writes, in
1904, that 'Everything calls up its contrary.'[55]
Viewed within the greater context of his career, the
Stratford essay can be seen as the high watermark
of a certain kind of narrowly nationalist cultural
thinking. Just months after he wrote the essay, Yeats
began mapping out his ideas for the Irish national
theatre in a series of articles published in *Samhain*.
The position adopted in 'At Stratford-on-Avon' is
immediately modified in these essays and then, in
time, effectively reversed.[56] To begin with, Yeats
makes clear that he is not so much opposed to foreign influence in and of itself, but rather that, in an
Irish context, he specifically opposes the excessive
influence specifically of *English* literature. The new
theatrical movement should, he asserts, 'do its best
to give Ireland a hardy and shapely national character by opening the doors to the four winds of the
world, instead of leaving the door that is towards
the east wind open alone'. And he specifically
identifies Shakespeare as a central element in this

problem: 'At the moment, Shakespeare being the
only great dramatist known to Irish writers has
made them cast their work too much on the
English model.'[57] Yeats urges Irish writers to turn

---

[51] 'Introduction', *Later Essays*, p. 207.
[52] 'A Remonstrance with Scotsmen for Having Soured the
Disposition of their Ghosts and Faeries', *The Celtic Twilight*,
in *Mythologies* (London, 1989), p. 108.
[53] Yeats's account of his first encounter with the Theosophist
Madame Blavatsky is interesting in this regard, as he associates her with the Irish peasantry, a touchstone of authenticity for him: 'I found Madame Blavatsky in a little house
at Norwood, with but, as she said, three followers left –
the Society of Psychical Research had just reported on her
Indian phenomena – and as one of the three followers sat in
an outer room to keep out undesirable visitors, I was kept
a long time kicking my heels. Presently I was admitted and
found an old woman in a plain loose dark dress: a sort of old
Irish peasant woman with an air of humour and audacious
power', *Autobiographies*, p. 153.
[54] 'Tales from the Twilight' in *Uncollected Prose*, vol. 1, p. 172.
The trope of the imprecise boundary between the immediate material world and the world of spirits and ghosts is
insistently repeated in Yeats's prose fiction. On the peculiarly
intense connections between Anglo-Irish Protestantism and
the occult in this period see Foster, *Apprentice Mage*, pp. 50–
1, and also Foster's 'Protestant Magic: W. B. Yeats and the
Spell of Irish History,' *Proceedings of the British Academy*, 75
(1989), 243–66.
[55] *Samhain*, 1904, in *Explorations*, p. 147.
[56] The reversal registered here may perhaps stem in part from
Yeats's disillusionment, as he attempted to take the national
theatre project forward, with the level of resistance he
met, particularly in the Irish popular press (most notably
William Martin Murphy's *Independent*, D. P. Moran's *Leader*
and Arthur Griffiths's *United Irishman*). Marjorie Howes has
also tracked the emergence at precisely this time of a larger-
scale shift in Yeats's thinking, connected with issues of gender association: the 'gendered construction of Celticism's
political and aesthetic shortcomings was sponsored not least
of all by Yeats himself, who consistently coded his move
away from Celticism as a transition from feminine to masculine and more truly national art', Marjorie Howes, *Yeats's
Nations: Gender, Class, and Irishness* (Cambridge, 1996),
p. 17.
[57] There is, of course, a certain irony here, in that, as Desai
indicates in considerable detail in *Yeats's Shakespeare*, Yeats's
own plays are very heavily indebted to his close reading of
Shakespeare. Desai argues very interestingly in relation to
Yeats's spirit guide, Leo Africanus, that 'Yeats does not seem
to have remained enamored of his obscure guide for long.
There are indications in his later writings that Shakespeare
took Africanus' place, and that Yeats came to regard him as

from English – and, particularly, Shakespearian – models, but, in the process, to embrace the literature of other European countries: 'It is no great labour to know the best dramatic literature, for there is very little of it. We Irish must know it all, for we have, I think, far greater need of the severe discipline of French and Scandinavian drama than of Shakespeare's luxuriance.'[58] By 1903, the stark declarations of the early *Pilot* and *Providence Sunday Journal* essays are beginning to be reversed, as Yeats now declares that 'One can serve one's country alone out of the abundance of one's heart, and it is labour enough to be certain one is right, without having to be certain that one's thought is expedient also.'[59] In the following year he asserts that 'A writer is not less National because he shows the influence of other countries and of the great writers of the world. No nation, since the beginning of history, has ever drawn all its life out of itself.'[60]

There is a certain irony in the fact that the movement away from the most rigorous forms of cultural nationalism that we witness occurring in Yeats's later thinking serves, in fact, to bring him closer to the position that Dowden had mapped out in the *Fortnightly Review* essay the young Yeats had found so objectionable. In that article, Dowden asserted that 'No folly can be greater than that of fancying that we shall strengthen our literary position by living exclusively in our own ideas, and showing ourselves inhospitable to the best ideas of other lands.' In a striking formulation, Dowden had neatly declared that '[t]he shock of strangeness is inspiriting' – a formulation the later Yeats would surely have endorsed.[61]

There is a further irony to be registered here too: when the greater part of Ireland did finally gain independence in 1922, the new state embarked upon a cultural policy which, in many respects, can be seen as, effectively, the application, in an especially rigorous form, of the nationalist cultural

programme that the young Yeats had vigorously espoused, as the Free State cut the country off more and more from outside influences. Between 1930 and 1939, for instance, the Irish state banned some 70 per cent of the books reviewed in the *Times Literary Supplement* and, in 1942, the writer Seán Ó Faoláin observed of Ireland that 'Life is so isolated now that it is no longer being pollinated by germinating ideas windborne from anywhere.'[62] Yeats, of course, was profoundly disillusioned by these developments and actively fought against the emerging conservative, obscurantist ideology of the new state during his time as a member of the Irish Senate (1922–8).[63] I would suggest in conclusion that, had the newly independent country been more willing to embrace what Yeats's Shakespearian adversary styled the inspiriting shock of strangeness, it is possible that the poet might have found a more congenial home there.[64]

---

his daimon' (112). On Leo Africanus, see Foster, *Apprentice Mage*, pp. 462–6.

[58] *Samhain*, 1901, in *Explorations*, pp. 76, 78, 80.

[59] *Samhain*, 1903, in *Explorations*, p. 103.

[60] *Samhain*, 1904, in *Explorations*, p. 157. In 1925, in 'The Child and the State', Yeats declared again that 'all things should begin with the nation and with the genius of the nation', but this was in the context of a now heavily revised (and determinedly Anglo-Irish) conception of the nation, rooted in the anti-materialist philosophy of Berkeley and the conservative politics of Burke, Frayne and Johnson, *Uncollected Prose*, vol. 2, p. 458.

[61] Dowden, 'Hopes', p. 176 (both quotations).

[62] See Paul Bew, *Ireland: The Politics of Enmity 1789–2006* (Oxford, 2007), p. 482; Seán Ó Faoláin, *An Irish Journey*, quoted in Terence Brown, *Ireland: A Social and Cultural History, 1922–2002* (London, 2004), p. 163.

[63] See Donald R. Pearce, ed., *The Senate Speeches of W. B. Yeats* (Bloomington, 1960) – especially the materials on divorce and censorship.

[64] My thanks to George Bornstein for his feedback on a draft of this article. Thanks also to Terence Brown, Nicholas Grene and Christina Hunt Mahony for discussing the relations between Dowden and Yeats with me.

FRANÇOIS-VICTOR HUGO AND THE LIMITS OF CULTURAL CATALYSIS

RUTH MORSE

What was it that made Shakespeare such a catalyst in continental European culture and theatre? The default position is that we already know: we know the stories of neoclassical curiosity and romantic inspiration, of Shakespeare wild-child genius, the exotic import contributing to secular nation-formation through a large-scale vernacular text. Naturally, all the scholarly editorial work was done in England, first in the Folio of 1623, and then, steadily, if not without acrimony, by a sequence of editors from Rowe, through Pope to consolidation in the Johnson-Steevens received edition.[1] On the continent, particularly in central Europe, that text, those texts, provided a repertoire on which cultural and political theatrical inspiration as well as nationally unifying written linguistic standards could be erected. In France, they ordered these things differently: beginning from universalist arguments about classical correctness (which Johnson himself acknowledged and questioned), the received story is one of resistance, domestication and absorption.

From the earliest moment, so runs the tale, Voltaire called attention to Shakespeare, corrected and improved; people listened, and continued to attend to Shakespeare even after Voltaire changed his mind.[2] It remains an *idée reçue* in French opinion that the history of what counts in French reception of Shakespeare turns on Voltaire's definition of the importance of correctness, forgetting that the Thunderer would have had no need to fulminate had he been winning – something Voltaire's detractors were not slow to notice. The trouble is that this story is only just right enough to convince. It is not the whole story; it is a polemic which owes its life to Voltaire's supporters, as well as to the creation of a loyal opposition – not to Shakespeare, but to an anti-anti-Shakespeare. Elevating the position advocated by late Voltaire guarantees a hegemonic authoritarianism which gave the Romantic proponents of a kind of anti-anti-Shakespeare a banner and rallying cry. As often within a politics of cultural reaction, 'Exotic' or 'Oppositional Shakespeare' proposed a default position of its own: revolutionary, anti-authoritarian (State, Church, Academy) and popular. So France created, partly following the arguments of Pope and Johnson, a philosophically idealist binary and, as with all binaries, the first term hardened the second with the necessary exclusion of third terms or other possibilities.[3] One way of addressing the problem

---

[1] In the period of primary export, the long eighteenth century, it was of course too early for the idea that an editorial role had been played by copyists such as Ralph Crane, or friends who compiled the Folio, or the printers who produced it.

[2] The history is explored by T. R. Lounsbury, *Shakespeare and Voltaire* (New York, 1968 [1902]). There is a more recent popular narrative which preserves the traditional account in John Pemble, *Shakespeare Goes to Paris: How the Bard Conquered France* (Hambledon, 2005). See also Michèle Willems, 'Voltaire', in Roger Paulin, ed., *Continuum Great Shakespeareans 3* (London and New York, 2010), pp. 5–43, see esp. pp. 41–3.

[3] The first major inspiration, in French words and structures, was, of course, Ducis. John Golder's pioneering work has shown how and why, but also suggested that Ducis built

is called 'Ducis', author of the first great continental stage successes, whose adaptations had multiple advantages, not least by inspiring disdain, thus spurring on other translators or adapters to do better. Or, at least, better about what they saw, or thought they saw, or wanted to see.[4] Universalist arguments depend upon what appear to be the axioms of reality; the difficulties of attacking fundamental assumptions need not be underlined. Not incidentally, the extent to which many arguments about Shakespeare, like similar arguments about 'romance', contribute to the prestige of 'nations' has only in recent decades come under scrutiny.

Two further received ideas have resisted redefinition. First, there is the assertion that 'Shakespeare' in translation cannot be Shakespeare, an all-too-insistent, still-too-familiar, demand for singularity (a rather large singularity) as well as 'authenticity', as if we could dig our way back to one 'real thing', to accuracy in a degree that we now understand was beyond anyone's reach, because the question is so misplaced. The history of the 'Early Music' movements offers a useful parallel. A second, more recent assertion claims a Shakespearian Common Era, a seismic catalysis in a series of those metaphorically tectonic shifts which define the modern. That these assumptions, too, subtend various forms of nationalist and linguistic prestige invites examination.

This article focuses on one aspect of these complex and stubborn questions, opening outwards from the French experience of Shakespeare, or 'not Shakespeare', since my subject must appear, at first glance, to be a translation, merely. A preliminary clarification is important: the Hugo concerned is *not* the great novelist and poet, that monster Victor-Marie Hugo, but his second son, the radical journalist François-Victor (1828–73), also known as Victor Hugo, whom I shall distinguish from his father in the French style as Hugo *fils*. Long assumed, within France, to be merely a translator, a window upon the real Shakespeare, Hugo was something extraordinary. His edition and translation, made after advanced textual study,

and directly from the quartos and folios, of an *Oeuvres Complètes de W. Shakespeare* (containing the plays, poems, Shakespeare's will, and three volumes of apocrypha) forms one of the most important transmissions of Shakespeare ever made; outside the German sphere of influence, the most important. I shall offer an overview, beginning upbeat, but ending with a more sombre reflection in part on missed opportunities. First, then, as M. Michelin has it, *un peu d'histoire*; second, a look in some detail at Hugo *fils* and Verdi, to suggest the importance of Hugo's work; third, to sketch a larger argument about semantic choices in a particular linguistic moment; and in conclusion to reflect on this most important worldwide intermediary for cultural catalysis, on its achievements and on its failure.

I. AN HISTORICAL PREAMBLE

First, there is no question but that François-Victor Hugo's *translations* (that is, the plays in close-equivalent French prose) have had extraordinary staying power: they are still sold in ostensibly revised editions (not much revised, in my experience of comparison). They remain the cheapest source of paperback Shakespeare in France; they also remain the cheapest source of play-scripts, which – since they are long out of copyright – can be stropped, chopped and dropped without constraint or complaint from author, translator or publisher. The first Pléïade Shakespeare of the

---

upon the earlier example of La Place: John Golder, *Shakespeare for the Age of Reason: The Earliest Stage Adaptations of Jean-François Ducis 1769–1792* (Oxford, 1992); Ruth Morse, 'The Age of Exploration: Pierre-Antoine de La Place (1707–93) as Shakespeare-archaeologist', in Roger Paulin, ed., *Shakespeare in Eighteenth-Century Europe* (Göttingen, 2007), pp. 215–30, repr. in *Shakespeare, les français, les France*, ed. Ruth Morse, Cahiers Charles V No. 45 (2008); John Golder, 'Voltaire, Ducis et le Néo-Classicisme Révolutionnaire: de *Zaïre* à *Othello*,' in *Shakespeare, les français, les France*, ed. Morse, pp. 139–60.

4   Golder, *Shakespeare for the Age of Reason*; and his essay, 'Voltaire, Ducis, et le néo-classicisme révolutionnaire'.

mid-twentieth century still contained many of them alongside, among others, Gide's *Hamlet*.[5] In the 1960s, as part of French celebrations for the four hundredth anniversary of Shakespeare's birth, Gallimard commissioned J. B. Fort to produce what purported to be the complete Hugo translation, but was nothing of the sort – even for a trade edition a shocking travesty of scholarly editing which entirely misrepresented its subject.[6] As an indication of the prestige of the project, Gallimard produced a large-format multi-volume deluxe edition as well as a three-volume set intended for students and scholars: *Shakespeare, Théâtre Complet: Traduction de François-Victor Hugo*. It is, however, not difficult to see how this high-handed and incompetent re-edition should have come about.

Except for purposes of criticism – often competitive – translators tend to be invisible, a window, for the obvious reason that we treat translations as instrumental.[7] And for that reason, there is no study of Hugo's translations, no bibliographical listing, no attentive analysis.[8] Evidence is anecdotal: informal surveys reveal that every French colleague I asked has read one or more of them, often at school, and that many other non-French non-anglophones preferred them to what was available in their own vernacular; my survey further suggests a wide-spread view that although they're – of course – very old-fashioned now, they've lasted because they're, well, not bad. In the theatre, naturally, text-revision is part of the cutting and re-arranging necessary to performance. Derrida was among many who treated Hugo *fils* with some deference, as a competent, acceptable translator, but it is a deference characteristic of spot-checked agreement with a modern reader's or translator's own ideas.[9] That is, the great thing about a translation is that you do not need to treat its decisions with respect. Shakespeare-in-translation, too, can be improved without reference to the translator's ideas or methods. The idea that translators might have consistency in method and procedure is relatively recent, and it is to that observation that I now turn.

2. THE EDITION 1859–1865

François-Victor Hugo's claims upon our attention begin with his basic competence but reach far further, not least because the question of transmission entails a larger question of what is transmitted. He was the first translator of Shakespeare into French whose English was adequate to the task; who had studied the scholarship available at the time, both in Paris and in the British Museum; for whom Shakespeare's originality was not a handicap of incorrectness; who was, perhaps consequently, the first editor of Shakespeare to understand that he wrote in scenes and not in Acts; who challenged the Folio arrangement; and who presented the plays accordingly, with a comprehensive sense of how Shakespeare borrows from himself, returns

---

[5] It is hard to overestimate the prestige of this long series of editions, which confer honour upon their subjects as well as those who compile them. Handsome hardbacks, printed on India paper (called 'papier Bible' in French), with ribbon markers, they constitute a library of world classics and guarantee the publisher, Garnier, a position of cultural arbiter. The quality of the editions varies.

[6] Both versions of the edition have long been out of print (Gallimard, Paris, 1961–4). The editor, J. B. Fort, was a scholar and himself a translator of Shakespeare. He reproduced the translations and a very few of the notes in a purported chronological order of composition, with the traditional act and scene divisions, and with an error- and prejudice-riddled introduction of his own, including observations such as the insistence that anything good in the translations must have been the work of the more famous father.

[7] Frances Vernor Guille's French doctorate barely discusses the Shakespeare translation at all and, when it does, it focuses on the public life and the son's role in his father's work. See her *François-Victor Hugo et son oeuvre* (Paris, 1950).

[8] What looks like a comprehensive bibliographical listing of translations into French is in fact a compilation of holdings in Paris libraries and archives: M. Horn-Monval, *Les Traductions françaises de Shakespeare, à l'occasion du 4e centenaire de sa naissance, 1564–1964* (Paris, 1963).

[9] Jacques Derrida, 'What Is a "Relevant" Translation?', trans. Lawrence Venuti, *Critical Inquiry*, 27 (2001), 174–200. The original text of the essay was an address to the professional Translators' Association. 'Qu'est-ce qu'une traduction 'relevante'?', in *Quinzièmes Assises de la Traduction Littéraire (Arles 1998)* (Arles, 1999), pp. 21–48, repr. in Marie-Louise Mallet and Ginette Michaud, eds., *L'Herne* (Paris, 2004), pp. 561–74.

to previous themes, plots and characters. The texts he translated were thus unlike previous editions or translations, which accepted British scholarship and its 'received text'. Having made his editorial decisions, he then translated Shakespeare's words, including slang, dialect and improprieties, daringly, under the shadow of French public decorum: what you can't say, you can't say, and you can't direct actors to perform it either.[10] What he transmitted differed in every way from earlier editions in any language. Finally, the idea that he never intended his work to be performed is only that, another received idea.

The charming tale of how this edition came to be is oft told, but always follows the father's anecdote. Not only was Victor Hugo France's greatest poet of the age, and therefore a living national treasure, he was socially and politically radical enough to be dangerous to Napoleon III. In 1852 he was exiled to Jersey, then from 1855 to 1870 to Guernsey, sometimes officially and sometimes voluntarily – vociferously – constrained, loudly refusing to live under the Second Empire. Despite eighteen years of exile, his English remained exiguous.[11] For his sons, who accompanied him into exile, he had previously bankrolled an anti-clerical, anti-monarchic radical paper opposed to Napoleon III and France's institutionally conservative Church, busily consolidating its post-Revolution comeback. The two journalist sons, Charles and François-Victor, edited – and largely wrote – an anti-government publication which the government suppressed when they advocated unacceptable legislation. Both sons were by turns writer, reporter and occasional political prisoner, Charles for advocating the abolition of the death penalty, François-Victor for proposing an amnesty to allow all political exiles to return home. At his early death, François-Victor merited an obituary in the *New York Times* for his political courage, not for his literary achievement.[12] The hundreds, perhaps thousands, who lined the streets, were silently demonstrating their support of Hugo and his family, but above all their opposition to the government.

As Hugo himself tells the story, François-Victor willingly followed his father to the Channel Islands where they each proposed a project: the father said he would contemplate the ocean; the son that he would translate Shakespeare.[13] The joke is that Hugo was called *l'homme océan*, so contemporaries also understand 'self-contemplation'. Less charmingly, Hugo-*père* was a monster of egotism and control, and tied his children to his purse strings: neither son was allowed a profession or a marriage and neither had any independence, although their father's wealth was extraordinary. Even the wife left behind in Paris (the long-term mistress was housed separately on the island) to oversee business had to account for every sou to her husband. And so did the sons. François-Victor, who had a grounding in contemporary English at his mother's instancing, set to this daunting life's work, and it began to appear seven years later, in 1859, intended for use both as an 'accompaniment' and as a 'replacement' translation, for the study, the drawing room, and, eventually, the stage.[14] The first edition asserted its bilingual utility with dashes in the

---

[10] As discussed by Ton Hoenselaars, 'Shakespeare for "the People": François-Victor Hugo Translates *Henry V*', *Documenta*, 13 (1995), 243–52. All early continental Shakespearians worry about suitability for representation; the limiting case is obscenity, and, as with the first edition of the *OED*, obscenities were habitually censored in print as well as on stage. The use of the commonplace 'mouchoir' in high tragedy was too low, too indecorous, for early nineteenth-century theatregoers, and ruined Vigny's attempt to represent *Othello*.

[11] I rely upon the brilliant and ground-breaking biography by Graham Robb, *Victor Hugo* (New York, 1998 [1997]). Robb offers some amusing evidence of his incompetence, e.g. p. 324. François-Victor plays only a minor role in this book, but Robb's research reveals much that has hitherto been unknown or dismissed.

[12] 17 January 1874, as part of an overseas correspondent's 'Parisian Gossip' column dated December 1879.

[13] This is from the opening of Hugo's *William Shakespeare* (Brussels and Paris, 1864) and constantly reprinted since. This book began as a general introduction to the edition of Hugo-*fils*, but outgrew its role. There is a short essay at the end of vol. xv. See Robb, *Victor Hugo*, pp. 399–401.

[14] These terms distinguish translations meant for bilingual reading from those intended to stand alone, without reference

midst of prose sentences to mark the position of the original verse line-breaks.[15] The second printing took them out, but this so-called 'second edition' was made up of mixed sheets – announcing that a first edition was sold out was a family publicity ploy.

It is important to avoid proceeding as if the translations were the whole thing. They were not. They are preceded by long introductions; accompanied by annotation and commentary; and followed by appendices with source extracts. Unfortunately, the original edition in fifteen volumes (plus, soon, three volumes of Apocrypha) struck upon the rock of publisher recalcitrance: the public seems to have found the edition strange as well as expensive. So, second, the soon-established habit of reproducing the plays stripped of their paratexts travestied Hugo's project. I shall return to the limits of Hugo's catalytic effect below.

Hugo revealed his ambitions with the first volume, which for the first time juxtaposed two texts of *Hamlet* (the 1603 and 1604 Quartos), rather than the amalgamation that was traditional. The next three volumes offered 'Tyrants', 'Fairies' and the first group of two groups of 'The Jealous' (*Les Jaloux* here means specifically 'the jealous men'). The two early editions, or perhaps early print-runs, follow this revolutionary rearrangement by related subject (listed in the appendix below), which not only called into question the Folio order of the plays, but offered thematic connections which radically redirected attention to themes and schemes and assimilated Shakespeare's interests to concerns familiar to post-romantic revolutionaries. As a critic, Hugo-*fils* was early to see how Shakespeare recycled his own material, making himself his great source. The new arrangement failed to convince, and was soon abandoned, but so many volumes had been printed that they continued to circulate.

This is the place to reveal that, having persuaded the General Editors of the Continuum *Great Shakespeareans* series that Hugo ought to be included, I discovered how difficult it was to find the books, even in great British or American libraries, whose policies in the mid-nineteenth century would have given no reason to buy relatively obscure translations. Repeated searches on the internet unearthed a number of individual volumes, in varying conditions; only after examining them am I able to offer the early generalizations here about their printing history. Additionally, colleagues on the continent and in the US generously aided and abetted the hunt. In fact, when I began working on this project I was able to buy uncut volumes from as early as 1859, some of which used mixed plates from left-over sheets (that is, with *and* without the dashes to indicate line-breaks). As so often, it is not possible to know exactly what state a volume represents merely from entries in catalogues – or even from looking at the book before cutting all the pages. This goes some way to explaining how the edition in effect disappeared and was forgotten, as the increasingly truncated representation, without Hugo's apparatus, was republished without question for over a hundred years.

This is also the place to record that, at least in France, resistance to Hugo's most startling idea that Shakespeare thought in scenes rather than acts, which was part of what failed to convince his public to buy the edition, continues to this day. Even the best essay on Hugo's translation finds it inconceivable that Shakespeare should not have understood that plays are divided into five acts.[16] Gallimard

---

to the original; I developed the implications of this divide in *Truth and Convention in the Middle Ages: Rhetoric, Reality, and Representation* (Cambridge, 1991; 2005).

[15] It is the self-styled second edition which the Bibliothèque Nationale makes available without comment on its website; I have worked from my own copies.

[16] Marie-Claire Pasquier, 'François-Victor Hugo traducteur de Shakespeare', in *13ème Assises de la Traduction Litteraire (Arles 1996)* (Paris, 1997), pp. 93–112. Mme Pasquier acknowledges a correction by Jean-Michel Déprats in a footnote, but records it as a belief among Anglo-Saxon scholars. It appears to be impossible to conceive of a great author ignorant or unpersuaded of the truth of five-act structure. Very little has been written about Hugo, and what there is tends to be derivative and inaccurate, e.g. Nicole Mallet, 'Hugo, père et fils, Shakespeare et la traduction', in *TTR*, 6 (1993), 113–130.

continually reprint just the translations in a variety of paperback imprints, without editorial comment. Fortunately, perhaps, their ostensibly complete edition has been out of print for many years.

So there is a curious contradiction at the outset: a reader able to read Hugo's edition as Hugo intended it to be read is offered a quite different Shakespeare from Hugo's translations alone. If, then, one only read the translations, although they were good and reliable, that was all they were. You could not divine Hugo's linguistic strategy, his polemic or his originality as a scholar. As time passed, the patina of age made Hugo's French old-fashioned and inspired new translators to do better. Given the history of publishing in France, it seems to me impossible that anyone reading Shakespeare in French in the last 150 years could have avoided reading Shakespeare in the words of François-Victor Hugo at some point, and possibly at every point. Editions of Hugo's translations not only erased Hugo's paratexts, but totally erased his original organization and presentation. They offer a special case for discussions of cultural catalysis because not only are they not Shakespeare, they are not Hugo-*fils* either. The edition makes no sense – or it does not make the sense Hugo meant it to mean – as a series of independent volumes of the translations. For if the Hugo translations alone appear to stimulate re-examination of Shakespeare, they open interpretation in ways unanticipated and, to a remarkable extent, the opposite of what Hugo intended.

3. THE EXAMPLE OF OTHELLO

Verdi's encounter with Hugo's Shakespeare offers a counter-example to the tale of woe I have been describing. His engagement with Shakespeare began early. Though he grew up on approximating Italian and French translations, which often improved and censored their originals, he seems to have acquired new ones, including Hugo's, promptly. In addition to Verdi's three completed Shakespeare operas, there was a fourth, which occupied him on and off for many years; but he never began to set his projected *Re Lear*. To give some sense of the role played by Hugo's translation and paratext, let us consider two moments from Verdi's engagement with Shakespeare. Verdi and his librettists had access to previous French translations, Pierre Le Tourneur's (1776–83), and those which followed, periodically, ostensibly, replaced – but actually lightly updated – by a series of men of letters who could not possibly have translated from the English (including Dumas and Guizot). Despite traditional scholarly reports to the contrary, Le Tourneur sought systematically to correct and improve his original. Verdi, who was in his mid-forties when Hugo's work began to appear, was typical in his beliefs: he believed in 'authenticity', he believed in fidelity to Shakespeare and he believed that he had achieved it in his own proudly Italian variety of music drama, even if some of what he achieved also immortalized Davenant.[17] By contrast to the young Wagner's *Das Liebesverbot* (1834) with its light comedy interpretation of *Measure for Measure*, Verdi set Shakespeare. His circumstances required him to find authenticity by combining an extraordinary degree of verbal compression with a musical language which offers complex simultaneity, a multiplicity we recognize as Shakespearian. Far from a box-ticking catalogue bound by word, by sense or by scene-by-scene equivalence, Verdi's Shakespeare grappled with Shakespeare's core. Grappling with the core meant 'character', and 'character' meant 'decision under pressure'. The first of Verdi's three completed Shakespeare operas was his *Macbeth* of 1847. Despite working with a translation we would not, today, have much time for, he heard Macbeth's inner turmoil and scored it; he dared give the unusual instruction to the diva to make Lady Macbeth sound ugly, an instruction difficult to follow.

There is a gulf between *Macbeth* and *Otello*. Verdi always made his own synopses, which his librettists set in constant communication with the master.[18]

---

[17] David R. B. Kimbell, *The Young Verdi and Shakespeare*, in *Proceedings of the Royal Musical Association* (1974), pp. 59–73.
[18] See Philip Gosset, 'The Hot and the Cold: Verdi Writes to Antonio Somma about *Re Lear*', in *Variations on the Canon: Essays on Music from Bach to Boulez in Honor of Charles Rosen*

The *Macbeth* libretto, using Verdi's synopsis, was the work of Francesco Maria Piave (1810–76), using a recent Italian translation by Carlo Rusconi (*c.* 1839). The Italian production was a success, though Verdi's rewritten version, for Paris in 1865, was not. In France, French translation outranked Italian representation of Shakespeare, and Verdi's was multiply 'not-Shakespeare'. Responding to accusations that he understood nothing of the play, nothing of Shakespeare, he wrote (in a much-quoted letter of 1865) that Shakespeare had been his bedside book for many years. It was, of course, never Shakespeare that sat by his bedside table, but a succession of Italian adaptations and increasingly improved translations, then Hugo. Verdi's testimony, in this moment of disappointment, reminds us for how long many, even most, readers assumed that style, including translation, was transparent – that window again. George Orwell insisted upon something like this, but good prose is never like a window: we can look at it as well as through it, and the writer or translator has always tinted the glass. After *Macbeth* Verdi began thinking about a *Lear*, using a new translation by Giulio Carcano, but *Il Re Lear* remained a series of sketches.

Then there is Hugo. Verdi's supralinguistic compression of Shakespeare's characters only increases as he struggles with *Iago* (1887), his working title for the new opera which became *Otello*. Verdi found melodic equivalents for the terrible moment of seduction when Othello abandons his own style to begin singing in Iago's, creating what Wilson Knight might have needed to call the Iago music, rather than the Othello music.[19] Arrigo Boito, his librettist, read English, as did Verdi's long-time companion, Giuseppina Strepponi, and all of them were at ease in French. James Hepokoski has shown how influential upon the libretto was François-Victor Hugo.[20] Othello appears in Hugo's volume v, 'Les Jaloux 2'. In the Verdi archives Hepokoski found three copies of François-Victor Hugo's translation, annotated in Boito's hand, and Hepokoski quotes Hugo at length – necessarily, however, in English translation – to show how far Hugo is the key to Verdi's Iago, particularly to Iago's motivation.[21]

More can be derived from considering Hugo's whole volume: of the five murderous enraged men collected in 'Les Jaloux', Hugo juxtaposes *Cymbeline*'s Posthumus and Othello, uniting two falsely accused wives. In context, with Hugo's introductions, the play looks quite different: it has the anti-monarchism, the anti-clericalism and the bedrock denial of a beneficent deity characteristic of the radical translator. This is a compressed paraphrase of Hugo's peroration:

This is the most painful, the most heart-breaking of all Shakespeare's endings. In the poet's other plays, the action explains the unavoidable bloody conclusion. It is conceivable that Hamlet dies: he killed Ophelia's father. It is still conceivable that Romeo dies: he killed Juliet's cousin. It is understandable that Lear succumbs: his curse killed his own daughter! It is legitimate that Macbeth falls: he killed Banquo, he killed Lady Macduff! But what did Othello do to die this cruel death? What did Desdemona do! What made them deserve to be carried off to the tomb? Their consciences were clear: they never committed, even foolishly, an evil deed; they were free of remorse as of blame. They were good, honest and loyal. How did they incur this punishment? They commited no misdeed ['faute' NB Hugo is preparing his own dramatic ending: this word runs from error through offence to sin].

They did! They did commit an offence, the primordial offence, the offence which is earlier even than Cain's offence. They were guilty, like the first and the last of us, of the original offence. They were begotten on this earth. They were born already damned in a world where happiness is forbidden to those most worthy, where all joys exact the price of sorrows, where laughter produces tears, in a world where good has evil as its necessary punishment, where love has jealousy as its other side; where genius has envy as its shadow. They were born in

on His Eightieth Birthday, ed. Robert Curry, David Gable and Robert L. Marshall (Rochester, NY, 2008).

[19] 'The Othello Music', in *The Wheel of Fire: Interpretations of Shakespearean Tragedy* (Oxford, 1960 [1930]). Hugo *fils* is at pains to repudiate Schlegel's powerful interpretation, and succeeds.

[20] James A. Hepokoski, *Giuseppe Verdi, Otello* (Cambridge, 1987).

[21] Hepokoski, *Giuseppe Verdi*, p. 182.

a world where social injustice amplifies natural imperfection, where virtue is only a licence for one to be tested, service guarantees ingratitude, heroism only designates one for martyrdom, in a world where bad faith triumphs over good, where any Socrates drinks hemlock, any Brutus commits suicide, where any Dante is exiled, where Tiberius reigns. Yes, Othello and Desdemona suffered because they were born. Both were tortured to expiate humanity's crime. Let those who are tempted to find that expiation too hard, refrain from hating the poet, faithful historian of life. The true author of this conclusion is not Shakespeare. It is God.[22]

Here I want only to refer to three questions: the range of the acceptable in period decorum; the limits of translator understanding; and the magic of adaptive risk. Because, if one only has the translation, it looks as if Verdi followed an idea of Desdemona familiar in the period – as a sweet and naïve creature; if you have the paratext you can see that while Hugo sees abjection in Desdemona's Act 4 (as we call it) reactions to Othello, that is not all he sees. Hugo's Introduction emphasizes how much Othello suffers in obeying honour over love, and Hugo conjures up Othello's crime of passion with some striking wordplay, as Verdi repeats the melody of 'un baccio', and the words of Hugo's introduction, finding a musical equivalent for Hugo's desire-suffused depiction of ambivalence. The tenor can convey this if he can act and does not succumb to sentimentality.

Jamais Othello n'a plus aimé sa femme qu'au moment où il va l'assassiner. Jamais elle ne lui a paru plus belle, plus séduisante, plus désirable, plus irrésistible! Jamais elle ne lui a causé, plus qu'en ce moment, les éblouissements des sens... Un baiser, un baiser encore, un de plus, et ce sera le dernier! (80)... Il enlève l'oreiller nuptial, cet oreiller où, hier encore, reposaient deux têtes adorées, et il en fait un étouffoir. Il arrache les draps de noce, ces draps tièdes encore de la première nuit, et il en fait une garotte. Il saisit tout le mobilier de l'amour, et il en fait l'appareil de la mort (81).

[Never has Othello loved his wife more than in this moment when he is about to murder her. Never has she seemed more beautiful, more seductive, more desirable, more irresistible! Never before, never more than in this moment, has she so dazzled his every sense... He lifts the bridal pillow, that pillow where two adored heads still rested yesterday, and uses it as an *étouffoir*. He tears off the wedding sheets, these sheets still warm from the first night, and makes a garrotte from them. He seizes all the furnishings of love and transforms them into the machinery of death.]

'Etouffoir' can mean 'an airless room', corresponding to English 'stifling', but it is a technical term from the contemporary piano pedal, creating a shocking pun by making the pillow the mechanism which stops the music of the keys. And then Emilia and the *anagnorisis*. I've said 'the tenor *can*' because many do not; as with the sopranos of *Macbeth*, there is often rejection of the composer's tough-minded decisions. Zeffirelli's *Otello* reinstates poetic justice by killing Iago; Verdi's own Iago escapes.

Translators' daring is the magic of what they do, but Hugo has in mind something else, something so politically and intellectually bold that one wonders how he escaped more time in prison. Hugo was a radical, and a free thinker, and he conveyed his ideas across Europe – if readers acquired an early edition. The muffled piano key is not the end of his introduction. Hugo asks what can have made the lovers guilty, what invited their tragedy, and he answers with a complex peroration about the guilt of having been born into an unjust world where good invites evil, where iniquitous societies exaggerate human imperfection, where ill will triumphs over good. His last sentence asserts that the true author of the play's tragic end is not Shakespeare, but God. These are fighting words, and it is to words that I want now to turn.

4. THE SEMANTIC MOMENT

The example I have just given has implications which have to do with arguments at certain times and in certain places, questions of moment; how they attract attention, stamping their hollow feet

---

[22] My paraphrase. The text is easily available at http://gallica.bnf.fr/ark:/12148/bpt6k200691q.image.f80. pagination.langEN. *Les Jaloux II*, pp. 82–4.

and demanding an answer, within agreed presuppositions. In the mid-century moment, Hugo was the right man in the right spot, not just because the Romantic battle over Shakespeare had powerful leverage, but because the politics of mid-century, with the institutional crises of monarch, constitution and Church made Shakespeare a powerful stick with which to beat autocracies; that is, not just a stick with which to beat supposedly sterile academicism. Supposedly sterile academicism is always a sign of a greater malaise. From outside a culture, Shakespeare offers one of the world's most powerful examples of external legitimation. Hugo punctuated his introductions with clarion calls to political freedom and to freedom of thought. As we might now say, the paratext thunders. It is not Shakespeare, but it spoke to believers in liberty and independence and free nations all over Europe. Like much Romantic polemic, it cast itself as addressing theatre characterized as backward-looking or trivial. Verdi found Hugo a reinforcement of the multiplicity he achieved both in *Otello* and in his last opera, *Falstaff*, which I cannot discuss here. We cannot always be as certain as we are here of the existence of what otherwise remain ghostly chain lines of intermediaries between an English edition or version of Shakespeare – or not-Shakespeare – and a new translation or adaptation.

Thus far I have made some striking claims about Hugo as a scholar and critic. Let me now turn to the close work of the translations. How revolutionary are they at the micro level? Given the moment of the French language in the middle of the nineteenth century, not just in terms of rhetorical presuppositions about decorum but in terms of available vocabulary, my first impression was that Hugo was imbricated in French Catholic language of transcendence, sacral kingship, sacrifice and so forth. I expected that the implications of this might take us back to Shakespeare's English to think more carefully about semantic change in his time, too, and how hard it sometimes is to be exact about shades of meaning – as it is in the slides among meanings – in the example from *Othello*. This is hardly the moment to expand on this assertion, but Shakespeare's own usage varies, sometimes

according to status, sometimes by archaizing speech suited to an old-fashioned or rustic character. The more closely I study Hugo, the more impressive I find his variations. These disappear when someone like Derrida simply substitutes a word he prefers, wiping away a speck from the window. At this point in my research I am clear that Hugo does find, despite the limitations of French conceptual terminology, a non-Catholic field of reference in the world of classical antiquity.[23]

The first of the two volumes of '*Les Jaloux*' contains *The Winter's Tale*. In Sicily, where an oracle pronounces and where in the last, reuniting, scene (Hugo's XIII) 'Il est nécessaire que vous appeliez à vous toute votre foi' ('you must call upon all your faith' rather than 'it is required/ you do awake your faith'), Hugo is *less* implicated in the language of Christian belief than is Shakespeare. Hugo is more matter of fact: 'nouvelles surprises' for 'more amazement' and 'stupéfaction' for 'marvel'; Hermione is 'délivrée', delivered, rather than redeemed; her actions are 'innocentes' rather than 'holy'; her gaze upon Polixenes was 'pur' not Shakespeare's 'holy'. Only when the dead queen speaks to ask the gods' blessings upon her daughter do Hugo's choices approach Shakespeare's, though he has 'urnes' rather than 'vials'.

Later editions suppressed all his textual work as a farrago, like his ridiculous idea that a great playwright did not think in acts. This was not a ridiculous criticism. Received ideas are remarkably tenacious. In every age we are sensitive to the loyalty readers continue to ascribe to received translation, that is, what we're used to in the reading and hearing of important texts, with their ferociously defended vocabulary, even in secular texts. Then, of course, there is sensitivity to register, something hard to acquire, hard to teach, hard to translate. Hugo's translations are also, now, harder for audiences to understand than the vibrant work of, say, Jean-Michel Déprats or the estrangement effect of the director Stuart Seide, who makes his own translations, helping French theatres to achieve what

---

23 I have discussed this in 'Reflections in Shakespeare Translation', *Yearbook of English Studies*, 36 (2006), 79–89.

Verdi described as the true end of his work: to fill the house.

I offer these contradictory attitudes as a reminder of the range of contemporary received ideas, easily assimilated to the contrast between the more educated and readerly, versus the less instructed but supposedly more tenaciously prejudiced. For Shakespeare as cultural catalyst, progressive, even revolutionary, I am afraid that the reply to the question of whether subsequent readers or directors were, like Verdi, catalysed by Hugo's subtle decisions is that they had no opportunity, because Hugo's editorial and critical work was entirely lost.

CONCLUSION

After an early and controversial success, Hugo's *translations* went on to dominate francophone engagement with Shakespeare. Editions after the first two appeared in a variety of forms which preserved only his thoughtful, accurate prose. New introductions were written in ignorance of the originals. It is these truncated editions which have become known over most of the francophone world, as well as that world which prefers to make its own translations from French rather than directly from English.[24] Hugo's prose, which by now has just enough archaism to offer an appropriate historical distance, is a very good not-Shakespeare, and holds the stage. Some might say, too much so.

Readers who had the good fortune to obtain an early multi-volume edition were sometimes, like Verdi, offered stimulating innovations in many directions, something it really is no exaggeration to call revolutionary. But the edition did not survive the threefold shock of Hugo's revolutionary introduction; his original rearrangements by theme which so convincingly called traditional genre categories into question; and his brilliant insistence that Shakespeare thought in scenes rather than in acts, the first great editorial breakthrough to come from outside the British Isles. Resistance – not just publishers' resistance – stimulated conservative outcry and the suppression of his paratextual triumph. Rather like other conservative backlashes,

readers' resistance to something ignorantly perceived as inauthentic, editorially and socially radical led to the failure of the edition. But the failure of the edition did not extend to the failure of the translations.

Verdi and Boito took full advantage of Hugo's *Jaloux* as they did of *Les Joyeuses Épouses de Windsor*. But later readers and writers were not so fortunate. Hugo's transforming work was itself undone, de-metamorphosed, into something more familiar, increasingly less an inspiration against academicism, and apparently more safe than Hugo's brilliant secularizing choices intended it to be. Cocooned in new introductions, of sometimes remarkable conservatism, throughout the twentieth century by editors who treated Hugo as a mere window, it was returned to the acceptable, the received text, the traditional ideas of the Bard and his works. When we think of Shakespeare as a cultural catalyst, we think of catalysis as forward-looking progress, but it need not be. Hugo's translation was a lost opportunity, remade into presentations not progressive at all. I began by calling this article 'not Shakespeare', but the limits, the suppression, even, of what might have been a catalytic moment, makes me call it, with a difference, 'not Hugo' either.[25]

Appendix

Publication history of *Oeuvres Complètes de W. Shakespeare*, 15 volumes (Paris: Pagnerre,

---

24 I am grateful to Prof. Pavel Drábek, who was in the audience at Stratford when I gave the first version of this paper, for bringing the Czech translator, Bohumil Štěpánek (1902–85), to my attention. Between us we were able to ascertain that Štěpánek, more comfortable in French than in Early Modern English, used Hugo's translations in the course of the 1920s as accompaniment translations to assist his own work. I was able to consult a thesis by his student, Miss Seibertová, written in English, for details. There must be many more such examples, but they will only come to light by accident, as translators who use translations as cribs are loath to announce the fact.

25 For generous reading, thanks are due to Profs. A. E. B. Coldiron, Stefan Collini and Philip Gossett. It is a pleasure to acknowledge the generous listening of the scholars gathered at Stratford in 2010 and to thank the committee of the ISC for catalysing me to test these ideas.

1859–66), François-Victor Hugo (1828–73), editor and translator

1859
  Les Deux Hamlet [Quarto 1603, Quarto 1604]
  Les Féeries
    Le Songe d'une Nuit d'été, La Tempête
  Les Tyrans
    Le Roi Jean, Richard III, Macbeth [Hugo's alternative title was *Le Talion* (p. 57)]
  Les Jaloux I
    Troylus et Cressida, Beaucoup de Bruit pour rien, Le Conte d'Hiver
1860
  Les Jaloux II
    Cymbeline, Othello
  Les Comédies d'amour
    La Sauvage apprivoisée [now more usually *La Mégere apprivoisée*], *Tout est bien qui finit bien, Peines d'amour perdues*
  Les Amants Tragiques
    Antoine et Cléopâtre, Roméo et Juliette
1861
  Les Amis
    Les Deux Gentilshommes de Vérone, Le Marchand de Venise, Comme il vous plaira
  La Famille
    Coriolan, Le Roi Lear
1862
  La Société
    Mesure pour Mesure, Timon d'Athènes, Jules César

1863
  La Patrie I
    Richard II, Henry IV (première partie), Henry IV (deuxième partie)
  La Patrie II
    Henry V, Henry VI (première partie)
  La Patrie III
    Henry VI (deuxième partie), Henry VI (troisième partie), Henry VIII
1864
  Les Farces
    Joyeuses Épouses de Windsor [now usually *Les Joyeuses Commères de Windsor*]
    La Comédie des erreurs, Le Soir des rois
1865
  Sonnets (reprinted, orig. 1857), *Poèmes*, Testament
  This volume also contains an 'afterword', by Victor Hugo (not to be confused with his book, *William Shakespeare*)
1866
  Les Apocryphes
    Titus Andronicus, Une Tragédie dans l'Yorkshire, Les Deux Nobles Parents
    Péricles, Edouard III, Arden de Feversham
    La Tragédie de Locrine, Le Fils aîné du Roi Brutus; La Vie et la Mort de Thomas Lord Cromwell; Le Prodigue de Londres; La Puritaine ou la Veuve de Watling Street

'YOU TAUGHT ME LANGUAGE':
SHAKESPEARE IN INDIA

POONAM TRIVEDI

If one were to name the most significant and abiding legacy of the British Empire in India it would not be parliamentary democracy, nor cricket, but the English language. Though, at a generous estimate, only 8 per cent of the people can read and write English even now, the impact of its introduction since the early nineteenth century has been incalculable. Because with the English language came not just its literature and Shakespeare but, for better or worse, the whole intellectual tradition of the West, interaction with which has had a far-reaching effect on Indian society and culture. Yet, if catalysis is the introduction of a foreign element to precipitate a transformative change or development, it was neither English nor Western thought, but colonialism which produced a paradigm shift. In the cultural history of modern India, it is colonialism which has been the main cause of cataclysmic change and since English language and literature, with Shakespeare at its centre, came in its wake, their role and impact are intertwined and tainted with that of colonialism.

This relationship of over four hundred years between India and Britain has been an evolving one: from one of mercantile trade, to territorial expansionism, to imperial domination, to equity in a 'commonwealth of nations,' to today a tentative reinventing towards a more meaningful sharing and exchange as voiced by the British Prime Minister, David Cameron, on 30 July 2010, during his first visit to India, in his wish to see more British students enrolling for study in India! The fortunes of English literature and Shakespeare in India have also undergone similar shifts. This India–Britain

relation, politically fraught and socially and intellectually contested, has been copiously written about, and dissected too. One need not recapitulate these debates – most are well known. This article will narrow down to some key moments which have been bypassed in the more socio-political debates to focus on the linguistic and literary impact of colonialism with Shakespeare as its centre, its repercussions on the theatre and on the pedagogic and literary-critical sphere. In short, a look at the literary, performative and critical languages we were 'taught' or imbibed through colonialism.

The Empire brought and taught us the English language but not without a struggle for space in the Indian subcontinent. Portuguese was the dominant language of maritime trade in the fifteenth and sixteenth centuries and the English traders who arrived in India in the early seventeenth century had to conduct business in Portuguese. Today, more than sixty years after independence, shorn of the taint of colonialism, English is perceived as a language of opportunity; everyone wants to learn it. It is in fact 'homed' in India – the constitution and the census name it as one of the 'Indian' languages, i.e. those spoken in India.[1] The teaching of English in India which had begun early in the eighteenth century as part of missionary activity came into its own with the opening of Hindu College in Calcutta in 1817. This head-start in learning English has today given us an edge over other Asian countries in the establishment of the BPO (business

---

[1] For figures regarding languages in India see Census of India http://www.censusindia.gov.in.

process outsourcing) industry, which is a somewhat double-edged validation of the teaching and circulation of English that serves to produce only 'cyber-coolies'.[2] The fact that political and economic hegemonies control the flow and exchange of languages and literatures is further borne out by an often forgotten fact that at the very first official encounter between India and England, when Sir Thomas Roe, James I's ambassador, visited the Mughal court in 1615 to petition for trading rights, no mention was made of English literature or Shakespeare. Shakespeare was not yet an exportable commodity and the Mughal Emperor, Jahangir, though steeped in Persian learning, evinced little curiosity about this foreign language and literature. As a matter of fact, Jahangir's court records and memoirs make no allusion to the English Ambassador, while we learn from Roe's own account that he suffered the humiliation of having his gifts returned. As Peter Stallybrass has concluded, 'England was too marginal to count'.[3] The differences not just of economics but also of world views were simply too vast at that moment: 'We were indifferent to Shakespeare in the early phases of our connection with England', observes R. K. Dasgupta, 'not only because the East India Company men were too commercial, we too were a little too spiritual.'[4] It is not surprising therefore that the diary of the first Bengali to visit England, Mirza Sheikh I'teshamuddin, an educated courtier, in 1767, does not mention Shakespeare in his chapter on theatre and entertainment despite being impressed with the orderliness of the playhouses,[5] and even though by now Dr Johnson's edition of Shakespeare had been published and Garrick was preparing to hold his jubilee celebrating Shakespeare in 1769.

The turning point came with the successive victories of the English at the battle of Plassey in 1757, the defeat of the Marathas at Panipat in 1761 and in the Anglo-Maratha wars between 1775 and 1782, all of which firmly established English supremacy over most of India. Increasing trade and political dominance created a need for greater linguistic exchanges: the College of Fort William was set up in 1800 for the officials of the East India Company to learn Indian languages and then in 1817, the first college for Indians, Hindu College in Calcutta, to imbibe not just English, but a broader Western education. However, it was Macaulay's Minute on Education in 1835 which officially mandated the use of English for administration and for instruction in government-funded schools. Hence, within less than a decade, in 1844, Lord Hardinge, the then Governor-General, passed a resolution assuring preference in selection for public office to Indians who had distinguished themselves in European Literature. Colonial coercion is to be found in the promotion of English language and literature right from the beginning and it affected the Indian reception of this literature and Shakespeare. If we turn to China and Japan, similar Asian societies with ancient traditions of their own indigenous literature, and compare their initial reception of English and Shakespeare about half a century later, we find that it was taken up voluntarily, on their own terms and not through direct political imposition. Contrary to the Indian experience, Shakespeare was part of a felt need to modernize and engage with the West as an antidote to the threat of colonization by the West. Hence the Chinese and Japanese engagement with Shakespeare was and has continued to be freer, more localized and answerable to their immediate needs. For example, in both these countries the very first Shakespeare translations were adaptations of *The Merchant of Venice* (1913 and 1885) which

---

[2] Phrase coined by Harish Trivedi, 'Letters to the Editor', *Times Literary Supplement*, 27 June 2003, in response to an article by Susan Sontag, 'The World as India: Translation as a Passport within the Community of Literature', *TLS*, 13 June 2003.

[3] Peter Stallybrass, 'Marginal England: The View from Aleppo', in *Centre or Margin: Revision of the English Renaissance in Honor of Leeds Barroll*, ed. Lena Cowen Orlin (Cranbury, 2006), p. 35.

[4] R. K. Dasgupta 'Shakespeare in Bengali Literature', in *East-West Literary Relations* (Calcutta, 1995), p. 82.

[5] Mirza Sheikh I'teshamuddin, *The Wonders of Vilayet: Being a Memoir, originally in Persian, of a Visit to France and Britain in 1765*, translated by Kaiser Haq (Leeds, 2002), see chapter 7 'London Entertainments'. The journal begins by recapping events of 1765 after which Mirza sets sail in 1766 and reaches London *c.* 1767.

correlated the money issues of the play with the growing political challenge of the new Western monetary systems at the end of the nineteenth century.[6] In India, on the other hand, it was *The Comedy of Errors* which attracted the earliest translations (1865 Gujarati; 1866 Malayalam; 1875, 1877 Marathi etc.) because it was seen to be similar to a Sanskrit play and, in a gesture of self-assertion, it was even retitled after it – *Bhrantivilasa* – in the Sanskrit (1877), Bengali (1884) and Kannada (1911) versions. As critic and playwright G. P. Deshpande has put it, 'we discovered in Shakespeare an icon, not a contemporary . . . because we were required to take a look at the marvel of our colonial masters, we had to view it from below. The net result was that we were denied a realistic view of the Bard . . . Our relationship with English theatre was not natural. We had to look up at it with our necks raised!'[7]

However, colonial hegemony and mimicry does not quite suffice to account for the enthusiasm that was displayed by Indians both in Calcutta and Bombay for reading and performing Shakespeare right from the beginning. Even before Macaulay's Education Act of 1835, teachers at Hindu College, particularly a Capt. D. L. Richardson, had enthused the young with his electrifying readings of Shakespeare. Students were also given lessons in elocution and, soon enough, recitations, readings, performances of scenes and then full plays became part of the regular school calendar. 1822 is the date of the first recorded performance of scenes from Shakespeare by students in English and 1840 of the first full play in Calcutta,[8] and 1861 in Bombay. Shakespeare performance became an annual feature and Shakespeare Societies and Dramatic Clubs were set up in colleges for this express purpose: e.g. the Parsi Elphinstone Dramatic Society and the Elphinstone College Shakespeare Society, both in Bombay, in 1861 and 1864. The Parsi Elphinstone Dramatic Society began with a performance of *The Taming of the Shrew* and the Elphinstone College Society continued the enthusiasm for Shakespeare with *Two Gentlemen of Verona* in 1865, *Othello* and *Twelfth Night* in 1866, *Shrew* 1867 and *Merchant* 1873 all performed in English.[9] St Stephens College at Delhi initiated weekly readings of

Shakespeare in 1894, which developed into the Falstaff Club in 1899, and then led to the establishment of the St Stephens College Shakespeare Society in 1924 which continues to hold an unbroken record of an annual production of Shakespeare till today.[10] This enthusiasm for amateur performance spilled outside the schools too: in 1831, the first private Bengali theatre, Prasanna Kumar's Hindu Theatre, built on the Western proscenium model in Calcutta, opened with scenes from *Julius Caesar* and a Sanskrit play in English translation.

This teaching, elocution and performance of Shakespeare was of course central to the curriculum designed to create pliable colonial subjects, who in Macaulay's words would become 'a class of persons Indian in blood and colour, but English in taste, in opinion, in morals, in intellect'.[11] But why was this elocution and playing taken up with such zest by the Indians? How did it add to the economic and social advantage for the growing middle class? And why did Shakespeare alone among the other canonical authors in the syllabus like Bacon, Milton, Richardson, Johnson, Addison and Goldsmith attract this inordinate attention? The increasing shift from language instruction to what Linda Colley has called 'a more unalloyed state sponsorship of Shakespeare [towards] the end of the

---

[6] See Ruru Li, *Shashibiya: Staging Shakespeare in China* (Hong Kong, 2003) and Yukari Yoshihara, 'Japan as "half-civilised": An Early Japanese Adaptation of Shakespeare's *The Merchant of Venice* and Japan's Construction of its National Image in the Late Nineteenth Century', in *Performing Shakespeare in Japan*, ed. Minami Ryuta, Ian Carruthers and John Gillies (Cambridge, 2001).

[7] G. P. Deshpande, *Dialectics of Defeat: The Problems of Culture in Postcolonial India* (Calcutta, 2006), pp. 89–90.

[8] For the performance of Shakespeare in Calcutta, see *Shakespeare on the Calcutta Stage: A Checklist*, ed. Ananda Lal and Sukanta Chaudhuri (Calcutta, 2001).

[9] For the performance of Shakespeare in Bombay, see Kumudini Mehta, 'English Drama on the Bombay Stage in the Late Eighteenth and the Nineteenth Century', Ph.D. diss., University of Bombay, 1960.

[10] For the activities of the St Stephen's College Shakespeare Society see issues of the college magazine, the *Stephanian*.

[11] 'Indian Education: Minute of the 2nd of February 1835', in *Macaulay: Prose and Poetry*, ed. G. M. Young (London, 1967), p. 729.

nineteenth century',[12] seen for example in the institution of a 'Shakespeare day' celebrated throughout the colonies on 23 April, may be one factor. Within a hundred years elite Indians had not only mastered the language but were also in thrall to its central figure, Shakespeare. As recounted by R. J. Minney in an article in the *Empire Review* of May 1925, 'English to [the Indian] means little more than Shakespeare . . . The Indian, able to read and write English, is as ardent an admirer of Shakespeare as the greatest Shakespearean in England. To him Shakespeare is a god.' He also points out that 'the Indian possesses an inordinate love for reciting Shakespeare'. Among the educated, it manifested a predilection to quote from Shakespeare in everyday life. As Minney further notes : 'in India Shakespeare coloured headlines and reports of the police court' and 'Indian judges sent their fellow-countrymen to death with consoling quotations from the plays of Shakespeare.' 'Indian public speakers' too, he recalls, 'would pause suddenly, and, raising the pitch a little, break out into a recitation of some passage from a play of Shakespeare, the words of which were in keeping with the sentiments of the speaker.'[13] Thirty years later, actor-manager Norman Marshall would recount the unnerving experience of many a visiting theatre company who found that quite a few persons in their audience, especially in the university towns, 'know entire plays by heart' and were quick to prompt a hesitant Shakespearian actor![14]

This veneration for Shakespeare may be accounted for by colonial conditioning, but this 'craze for elocuting', 'speaking out' and /or 'speaking with' and performing and embodying Shakespeare's words needs further investigation. We need to step back and look at the whole phenomenon of public speech and amateur theatre from the perspective of performance theory. For while the study of Shakespeare was an imperial imposition, the performance was not. As a matter of fact, Shakespeare was being performed for Europeans, and witnessed by elite Indians at the Calcutta Theatre (1775–1808) several decades before the institutionalized teaching of English literature begins. For the Empire brought and 'taught' us not just the English

language but also introduced us, even more irrevocably, to Western performative languages. Modern Indian theatre has developed by the wholesale adoption of western staging conventions, like the box stage, illusionism and realism in opposition to indigenous staging practices of open-air theatres, non-illusionism and stylization. It also gave us amateur theatre, a process of role playing, impersonation and being which was radical because performance in traditional theatre in India had been governed by caste and social custom. Amateur Western theatre gave a new liberationist freedom 'to be'; anyone and everyone could live in new and different personas, become and embody an 'other'. Cultural historians in India have argued that this new-found enthusiasm for literature and the arts in the nineteenth century – Indian music, particularly, underwent resurgence – compensated for the loss of political power. Many Indian intellectuals were also convinced that they could get at the secret of the English political successes through a mastery of their literature. I would add amateur theatre, elocuting, quoting – and performance has been theorized by Judith Butler as 'citationality' – as another means of coping with and even resisting imperial domination. An amateur theatre movement developed by the late nineteenth and early twentieth centuries not just among English-educated Indians but among the vernacular speakers too. And the social space that it provided, the clubbing together of like-minded people, generated a font not just of entertainment or leisure, but also a space for fermenting and enacting social awareness and reform. Needless to add that Shakespeare was always a mainstay of the amateur performances.

We need to recall that the nineteenth century, before modes of electronic communication came into being, was the great age of public speaking,

---

[12] Linda Colley, 'Shakespeare and the Limits of National Culture,' Hayes Robinson Lecture Series No. 2 (Egham, Surrey, 1999), p. 19.

[13] R. J. Minney, 'Shakespeare in India', *Empire Review*, 292 (May 1925), 534–5.

[14] Norman Marshall, 'Shakespeare Abroad', in *Talking of Shakespeare*, ed. John Garrett (London, 1954), p. 103.

an art which was honed in elocution classes. The elocutionary movement was defining a medium of persuasion and power. Public speaking was recognized not only as a creative force, but also one of hegemonic control. It was used to solidify and perpetuate power relations as well as valorize a certain decorum of speech, gesture, class, gender and colour. For Indians, impelled by colonial hegemony, there was an obvious practical necessity to opt for the study of English (though it was only the middle class which did it, the Hindu and Muslim aristocracy keeping their distance). The middle class took up the recitation and performance of Shakespeare not so much out of complicity with colonial processes but more to wrest that creative force which is built into the performative from under hegemonic control. The impersonation of English speech and manners, even though on stage, was subversive for many, as evidenced by the hostile notices which appeared in the Anglo-Indian press. When Prasanna Kumar's Hindu Theatre opened in 1831 with scenes from *Julius Caesar*, under the direction of H. H. Wilson, Sanskrit scholar and Company servant, the newspaper *East Indian* wrote:

We hear that the performances are to be in the English language. Who advised this strange proceeding we know not, but it is surely worth reconsidering. What can be worse than to have the best dramatic compositions in the English language murdered outright, night after night, foreign manners misrepresented and instead of holding the mirror up to nature caricaturing everything human? We recommend our Hindu patriots and philanthropists to instruct their countrymen by means of school [education] and when they are fitted to appreciate the dramatic compositions of refined nations, it will be quite time enough [sic] to erect theatre...A theatre among the Hindus with the degree of knowledge they at present possess will be like building a palace in the wastes. (*Asiatic Journal*, January–April 1832)

Mimeticism produces equivalence, and through performance Indians were perceived to be measuring up to the master. Dwight Conquergood's analogy of the eighteenth- and nineteenth-century elocutionary movement with the enclosure acts of the sixteenth and seventeenth centuries,

particularly apt in this context, further illuminates the Indian situation. He points out that 'elocution expressed in another key the body-discipline imposed on the bourgeoisie...a verbal counterpart, in the domain of speech, of the enclosure acts that confiscated the open commons' from the poor for the privileged. But he reminds us that 'the spoken word dimension of elocution provided for "spillage" from the enclosed written word that the unlettered poor swept up and made their own'. Hence, 'the spillage of elocution' could be swept up, appropriated and made one's own for changing audiences and contexts; the creative force of elocution as performance could be harnessed for 'subaltern needs'[15] despite the hegemonic control. The Indians' 'inordinate love' for reciting Shakespeare makes more sense now.

Another larger creativity was unleashed in the translation of Shakespeare in Indian languages in print and on stage from 1852 onwards. Like performance, translation too was not mandated by the state but, nevertheless, every language cut its dramatic teeth as it were with Shakespeare in translation. The earliest translations were broad adaptations, appropriations in fact, mainly for performance, tailoring the play to suit local tastes. In the second phase, beginning towards the end of the nineteenth century, more faithful translations aiming to capture the metaphoric and imagistic richness of the language were attempted. While there was a decided decline in the number of translations during the intensification of the nationalist movement from the 1920s, pointing to the ubiquitous 'political unconscious' in the Indian engagement with Shakespeare, post independence, after 1947, there has been a steady growth of scholarly translations by eminent writers in many languages. Alongside this, playwrights/directors have also asserted a post-colonial freedom to cut up and play around with the once sacrosanct text of Shakespeare. While there is as yet no consolidated bibliography of all translations and the Complete Works

---

[15] Dwight Conquergood, 'Rethinking Elocution: The Trope of the Talking Book and Other Figures of Speech', *Text and Performance Quarterly*, 20 (2000), 329.

as a whole have been published in only four languages – Bengali, Marathi, Malayalam and Kannada, it can be asserted that all the major twenty-two Indian languages have translated most of the plays and poems, and many in several versions. The story of the impact and influence of these Shakespeare translations on the literary and performative culture of each of these major, and some minor, languages, has been investigated sporadically and would need more than a whole book to recount in each case. However, it is readily acknowledged that an indirect Shakespearian influence on the dramatic and even fictional output of every language is to be found – in the crafting of the structure of the plays, in characterization, speech and genre, particularly the tragic. Yet, this large-scale engagement with Shakespeare should not be seen as obsequious mimicry or a passive acceptance of the foreign. The Indian system of literary theory and interpretation, the *Rasa sidhanta*, based on an aesthetic abstraction and embodiment of human emotions, which had been the primary force shaping indigenous literary sensibilities, facilitated Indian readers to enter into the poetic intricacies and the psychological realism of the Shakespearian oeuvre. 'The Indian mentality has a curious craving for poetry',[16] R. J. Minney observed, and several Indian writers, including Rabindranath Tagore, have referred to the turbulence of emotion, the 'frenzied fury of passion'[17] animating Shakespearian characters, as its most arresting feature. As Indian critic R. K. Dasgupta has put it with reference to the Indian response to Western literature, 'we discovered the difference and yet acknowledged its greatness'.[18]

Further, not only did Shakespeare in translation feed the urgent need for intellectual stimulus, it also simultaneously provided a means of resistance. Since a draconian Dramatic Performances Act had been passed in 1876 to proscribe the growing criticism of the colonial regime on stage, seemingly faithful translations worked in subversive turns of phrase or dialogue to have their say. An 1882 Hindi translation by Munshi Ratan Chand of *The Comedy of Errors*, a copy of which is to be found in the Shakespeare Centre Library, interpolates

'Hindustan' in place of England to invert the satirical hierarchy of countries discovered by Dromio of Syracuse in the globe-like kitchen maid whom he has accosted. Thus, India instead of England stands 'in her face for just as Hindustan is the best of all countries, so was her face the best part of her person'. Further, in the ensuing sexual cartography, the translator demotes England to take the place of the Netherlands, the last and the lowest in Shakespeare's list: 'this was such a tiny country that exceedingly hard as I looked, I could find it nowhere. It must be hidden among those parts of the body I didn't look at.'[19]

The Parsi Theatre, the first commercial theatre of modern theatre of India which became hugely popular all over the subcontinent during the years 1860–1920, performed another kind of appropriative subversion. It borrowed all the performative languages and conventions of nineteenth-century Western theatre and plundered the Shakespearian canon, translating, adapting and collating to reproduce the plays in a hybrid mode of realism with melodrama, spectacle, special effects, music and dance. More than twenty-five plays of Shakespeare were performed in this extravagant style by its touring companies all across the country. The value of the Parsi theatre, as testified by C. J. Sisson, lay in the fact that it popularized the plays of Shakespeare, as 'living, dynamic forces'[20] amongst an audience cutting across all classes. Given that this plagiarized Shakespeare – very often the debt was not acknowledged – coincided with the aggressive propagation of English education, its bold and cavalier appropriations in the vernacular can, further, be seen as acts of cultural resistance, 'upstaging' at the popular level the dictates of the empire. The Parsi theatre also constitutes a crucial link between

---

[16] R. J. Minney, 'Shakespeare in India', p. 534.

[17] Rabindranath Tagore, 'The Message of the Forest', in *The English Writings of Rabindranath Tagore*, Vol. 2: *A Miscellany* ed. S. K. Das (New Delhi, 1996), p. 388.

[18] R. K. Dasgupta, 'Shakespeare in Bengali Literature', p. 90.

[19] Munshi Ratan Chand, *Bhramjalak Natak* [Drama of a Web of Confusion] (Lucknow, 1882), pp. 39–40.

[20] C. J. Sisson, *Shakespeare in India: Popular Adaptations on the Bombay Stage* (London, 1926), p. 19.

the Amateur Dramatic Clubs of Bombay which sprang up in the 1860s and the beginnings of the Indian film industry. Many theatre companies were headed by the Parsis whose dramatic talents had been honed in these ADCs; they rewrote and performed versions of Shakespeare for the Parsi companies and, then, with the coming of the cinema, transferred their talents to it. For example, the first Indian *Hamlet* on screen, *Khoon ka Khoon* (1935) by Sohrab Modi began as a stage play.

Another kind of dialogue with Indian traditions was initiated with the indigenization of Shakespeare in the Indian folk theatre forms. While it is the recent Kathakali *Lear* (1990s) which has given this tradition a visibility in critical discourse, this practice began as early as the 1860s with *As You Like It* being adapted into the Yakshagana. Questions have been raised about the cultural value of such experiments where tragic waste was sought to be reconciled to the largely harmonizing ideals of Indian literature. There is of course a renewed validation of the folk theatrical form when faced with the challenge of fusing the Western logocentric logic of a Shakespearian play into eastern performative conventions. However, some of the more ambitious of such productions did achieve a rapprochement of philosophic perspectives. In B. V. Karanth's *Barnam Vana* (1979), the first such thoroughgoing indigenization of *Macbeth*, Birnam Wood became a forest (*vana*)-like web of illusions, a *maya-jaal* out of Vedantic philosophy – a 'labyrinthine jungle of ambition' – which ensnares him, and which was actualized on stage by the dappled lighting effect of the branches of an actual tree which formed the backdrop of the open-air stage. This forest/web was represented as preventing Macbeth from expressing his *dharma* or inner essence of 'human kindness'.[21] In Lokendra Arambam's *Stage of Blood* (1997), Meitai tribal beliefs were invoked to stage *Macbeth* as a parable of disharmony between human and environmental forces. Here the stage – representing the human domain – literally floated on a lake under a bare sky, water and sky providing a cosmic reflection on the vanity of human discord.[22] A 2007 adaptation of *A Midsummer Night's Dream*, Chetan Datar's *Jungal*

Mein Mangal (Love in a Jungle) in the tamasha form took a post-colonial perspective on the Indian boy, reversing him into a spoilt-brat expatriate from America, a 'Bush-baal' (boy from George Bush's land), handling whom creates a rift between Oberon and Titania.[23] Many such productions may be cited, but it is more than evident that a Shakespeare which began as central to a curriculum which was being promoted to undermine the Indian literatures and central to a theatre which was marginalizing the indigenous, was eventually not only facilitating the folk forms, but was also in itself being extended by them and acquiring a new range of meanings. Shakespeare by now was subverting the very roles which had been designed for him.

The third and perhaps most radically transformative 'language' that was taught and came to us via the Empire and English studies was the critical reading practice of Shakespeare and all literature. The entire Western literary intellectual apparatus – from the bibliographic to the textual, to the imagistic and generic readings – were imported effecting a complete change from the parameters of indigenous interpretative methods. Though colonial education inculcated a reverential assimilative attitude and not a critical interrogative one, some Indians, Smarajit Dutt and Ranjee Shahani[24] for example, did offer critiques of Shakespeare from

---

21 For a longer account of this production, see my 'Folk Shakespeare', in *India's Shakespeare: Translation, Interpretation and Performance*, ed. Poonam Trivedi and Dennis Bartholomeusz (Newark, 2005).

22 For a longer discussion see my '"Tis the bloody business which informs thus . . . ": Local Politics and Performative Praxis, *Macbeth* in India', in *World-Wide Shakespeare: Local Appropriations in Film and Performance*, ed. Sonia Massai (London, 2005), pp. 47–54.

23 For a detailed discussion see my 'Shakespeare and the Indian Image(nary): Embodiment in Versions of *A Midsummer Night's Dream*', in *Replaying Shakespeare in Asia*, ed. Poonam Trivedi and Minami Ryuta (New York, 2010), pp. 54–75.

24 Smarajit Dutt published three books: *Shakespeare's* Macbeth: *An Oriental Study* (Calcutta, 1921), *Shakespeare's Othello: An Oriental Study* (Calcutta, 1923) and *Shakespeare's Hamlet: An Oriental Study* (Calcutta, 1928) and Ranjee G. Shahani, *Shakespeare Through Eastern Eyes* (London, 1932).

the comparative perspective of Sanskrit poetics and found him lacking in the philosophical depths that the Indian literary canon was used to.

Today, with the critical theory revolution and particularly with the development of post-colonial theory, the post-colonies have found a voice and space in which to examine the matrices within which their particular induction into English studies is embedded. However, a curious double demand is being placed on the Indian teacher of English, especially of Shakespeare, from the Western academy, with an insistent valorizing of only post-colonial readings. Paradoxically, the classroom teaching of transmitting and putting in circulation the exponential proliferation of mainstream criticism is derided as 'derivative' and not valued as a necessary professionalism.[25] The post-colonial teacher/critic is made to walk a tightrope – walking west, but looking east. She must follow the agenda set by the Western academy: for example hammer out racism in every instance of an *Othello* performance,[26] even though racism or colour-discrimination amongst a predominantly coloured people like Indians may take other more complex and intricate forms. *Othello*, as I have argued elsewhere, is the most frequently performed tragedy in India, not because Indian critics and audiences are blind to the racism and see it only as a domestic tragedy of sexual jealousy but because, on the contrary, they exude a subliminal sympathy and identity with Othello – something which is corroborated in Alan Wilkie's account of performing in India (1913), when he notes that Indian audiences were apt to weep 'openly and unashamed' during performances of Othello 'whose colour doubtless added to their sympathies'.[27] Post-colonial interventions in Shakespeare studies are the order of the day, but if not more acutely localized and contextualized they tend to fall into the danger of replicating the growing neo-colonial discourse of the West. For instance, it is apt to be forgotten that Indians were habitually referred to as 'niggers' by the English during the colonial period,[28] and discoursing the experience of such victimhood of just a generation ago might be a bit more problematic and require more finesse than researching racism

towards Moors or Africans from the safer distance of the Western academy.

It has also been argued that the post-colonial reader of Shakespeare has to 'repress' his alienation from the text and that appreciation is subscribing to the 'myth of the universal bard' complicit with colonial impositions. While there are no fixed, permanent and unchanging patterns of a seamless transmission of a universal meaning, all historicization needs to recreate some 'universal hooks', i.e. consensual meanings, for new generations of readers to lock into a text. Stage performance even more so, functioning on the principle of imitating/copying forms of action and behaviour, trades in the 'universal' creating forms of recognizability and identification, without which theatre, particularly the replaying of Shakespeare, would lose its audience. As I have been arguing, the induction of Shakespeare in India is part of what has been described as the 'political thrust and parry'[29] of colonialism. While the impositional thrusts have been variously documented, the deflections and parrying by the Indians have not. Gauri Viswanathan has done stellar work in revealing the political and ideological machinations behind the construction of English studies as a subject especially designed for the colonies.[30] What has been missing is the understanding of the agency – limited, circumstantial, opportunistic or even subversive – which was exercised by the Indians

---

[25] Jyotsna Singh, 'Different Shakespeares: The Bard in Colonial and Postcolonial India', *Theatre Journal*, 41 (1989), 458.

[26] Ania Loomba, 'Local-manufacture Made-in-India Othello Fellows: Issues of Race, Hybridity and Location in Postcolonial Shakespeares', in *Postcolonial Shakespeares*, ed. Ania Loomba and Martin Orkin (New York, 1998).

[27] Richard Foulkes, *Performing Shakespeare in the Age of Empire* (Cambridge, 2002), p. 151.

[28] See '"Haply, for I am black": the Colour of Indian Revisions of *Othello*', in my forthcoming book, *Performance and Post-coloniality: Indian Theatre and Shakespeare*.

[29] Harish Trivedi, 'Shakespeare in India: Colonial Contexts', in *Colonial Transactions: English Literature in India* (Manchester, 1995), p. 15.

[30] Gauri Viswanathan, *Masks of Conquest: Literary Study and British Rule in India* (London, 1990).

in response and which is essential to complete the picture of this literary, cultural, dialectical and dialogic transaction.

Three years ago a private arts foundation in Chennai (Madras) instituted an annual 'Hamara [our] Shakespeare Festival' for the express purpose of creating a space for Indian languages and theatres to renew their engagement with Shakespeare. Several full plays, redactions and adaptations have been performed to great approbation. In July 2010 a verse translation of forty-two sonnets, including some from the plays, entitled *Sach ke Moti* (Pearls of Truth) was published in Punjabi.[31] In an India where Shakespeare is no longer a component of compulsory school English, and where education shows a decline of interest in the humanities, are events like the 'Hamara Shakespeare' theatre festival and a new translation of the sonnets to be considered a nostalgic colonial throwback, post-colonial appropriations or an expression of the 'profit' of the languages that were taught via Shakespeare?

---

[31] K. B. S. Sodhi, *Sach ke Moti* [*Pearls of Truth*] (Ludhiana, 2010).

THERE IS SOME SOUL OF GOOD:
AN ACTION-CENTRED APPROACH TO
TEACHING SHAKESPEARE IN SCHOOLS

JONOTHAN NEELANDS AND JACQUI O'HANLON

I really look forward to doing Shakespeare when I come to school . . . Instead of just writing what happens in the play, like conversations between characters, we actually live it and we try to feel how the characters must feel. I think that is a good way of learning.

(ten-year-old girl from a school in Rotherham in the RSC Learning and Performance Network)

IM ANFANG WAR DIE TAT[1]

This article offers an account of the theory, practice and relevance of the Royal Shakespeare Company's recent work with schools in England and the implications that this might have for creating a foundation for internationalizing a pedagogy for teaching and learning Shakespeare based in the practices of the ensemble and the rehearsal room. We argue that there is something distinctive about this approach that takes the artistry and critical engagement of its pedagogy beyond the conventional uses of 'active methods' in the teaching of Shakespeare. It begins with a commitment to the idea that engagement with Shakespeare and his plays should be a cultural as well as a curriculum entitlement for children of all ages and abilities.

This double entitlement to Shakespeare is grounded in the desire to establish purpose and rewards in learning that may lead, by choice, to other life-long and life-wide outcomes, in particular giving a broader range of children and young people the choice of Shakespeare, now and in later life, as a source of pleasure and as a reference point for understanding the complexities of their own and other lives. 'Life-wide' is used here as a reminder that school-level education must be about more than pursuing narrow measures of academic success in qualifications. As A. C. Grayling puts it, 'education is for the person and not just the employee' and 'the outcome of education should be the continuing desire and ability to learn and to benefit from what one learns'.[2]

There is also, in the combining of cultural and classroom entitlements, a recognition that Shakespeare's artistry with language, in particular, can appear to be a formidable obstacle in the pursuit of intellectual and aesthetic rewards for young people who may be more used to the immediate pleasures of popular culture. Shakespeare makes intellectual demands on audiences as well as on performers and directors. The guiding academic principle for curriculum entitlement is that modes of learning should be an authentic re-creation of the real work done by actors, directors, audiences and critics.[3] This approach expects students to engage with the technicalities and artistry of the language as in all 'real work' with Shakespeare.[4] This in turn has

---

[1] 'In the beginning was the deed': Johann Wolfgang Von Goethe, *Faust* (New York, 2000), line 1237 (p. 34).

[2] A. C. Grayling, 'Liberating Learning, Liberal Education', in Patrick Derham and Michael Worton, eds., *Liberating Learning* (Buckingham, 2010), pp. 10, 9.

[3] The empirical evidence to support the formation of the RSC's 'authentic achievement' pedagogical position is taken from Fred Newmann and Associates, *Authentic Achievement: Restructuring Schools for Intellectual Quality* (San Francisco, 1996).

[4] In the RSC approach there is always work with text. We do not use adaptations. However, the text is often extensively edited to make it more accessible to different ages and abilities.

required the development of a range of sophisticated teaching strategies to help students come to know Shakespeare's language through visceral, active and carefully staged workshop experiences.

One distinctive feature of this approach is the planning of workshops as 'journeys' in which students feel the authentic theatre experience of progressing towards deeper and more challenging felt-engagement with the textual, theatrical and intellectual elements of the play. For instance, a two-hour workshop on *Hamlet* with young people who have no prior knowledge or experience of the play might begin with physical exercises that encourage thinking about narrative themes, characters and settings. What kind of a story will this be? What kind of a world? Where is the text leading us? These initial exercises bridge from the mythic narrative elements of the play towards Shakespearian complexities. They are also designed to be accessible and non-threatening activities to gain the class's confidence and trust.

Nurturing this trust is a necessity because this is a participatory theatre workshop or lesson in which all present are assumed to be 'players' as well as spectators. It is a direct rather than directed form of drama that requires social and artistic acting together in order to create imagined worlds and events. Acting in these circumstances requires the public expression of feelings and sensitivities.

The class walks the space and makes statues, on cue, of *the only son of a king, the ghost, the assassin, an avenger of a great wrong, the daughter of the king's advisor, the second husband, the castle of secrets.* Then, in groups, they make quick and instinctive tableaux to represent spying, romance, madness, unrequited love and a funeral that becomes a wedding. Fragments of text are now added so that groups can reinvent their tableaux with the text included and spoken. The spying group, for example, are given:

> At such a time I'll loose my daughter to him.
> Be you and I behind an arras then.
> Mark the encounter.   (2.2.164–6)

Extensive discussion is encouraged around this and the other fragments of text and their relationship to the image made as a response and frame for the text. What does it mean to 'loose your daughter to him'? What kind of a father 'looses' his daughter on a young man? And then watches with another? Does the daughter know? What reasons might the father have for doing this? Who might the other character be? Why does she do it? Does the young man know? How will he feel? What kind of a world is it where fathers treat their daughters so?

In response to these questions, volunteers are invited physically to place a hand on characters in the tableaux and speak their innermost thoughts in role, to find and demonstrate empathy and personal connections across time and genre. This *thought-tracking* exercise allows students to explore the dramatic convention of inner speech made public. The exercise also establishes the conventions of a theatre in which participants can move fluidly between acting and commenting, between their own realities and the imagined reality of the play world of Elsinore.

Later, each student gives another a 'guided tour' of Elsinore, either in role as a guard with a new recruit or as a servant inducting a new employee. The partners are blind and the tour guides can use language of their own and from the text, as a camera to bring the castle alive in the imagination of the partner. The *castle of secrets* is reinvented once more by the whole class and now invited to whisper its secrets.

An oral storytelling of the back story is given by the teacher in which the class physically represents not only characters but also settings and ideas as the spoken narrative unfolds. There is a conscious 'heightening' of the funeral becoming a wedding, to emphasize Hamlet's point of view:

Prince Hamlet had never felt so alone. He was devastated by his father's death, and angry with his mother. Were all women as fickle? Would Ophelia behave like that? Could he trust any woman now? He clenched his fists, and cried, 'Frailty, thy name is woman! O God! A beast would have mourned longer!' He blamed his mother for being weak and marrying again so soon. But he knew

---

For examples of edited text and the RSC's workshop exercises for young people, see *The RSC Shakespeare Toolkit for Teachers* (London, 2010).

that there was nothing he could do, 'But break, my heart, for I must hold my tongue!'

The class discusses why Hamlet must hold his tongue and where he might go in the castle to be alone now and to reflect on what has happened. A volunteer Hamlet is given the choice from the possibilities generated in the class and the space in the circle now comes to be collectively imagined as whatever 'place' the actor has decided upon – the orchard or a crypt for instance. Volunteers physically model Hamlet at this moment in this place by sculpting the 'actor', considering how the body speaks differently according to its 'body English' as James Moffett described it,[5] testing alternatives to find the right *gestus* for this appalling moment of realization.

Again the 'actor' makes a choice from those offered. The class writes its own words and phrases of personal response to Hamlet's predicament on torn sheets of paper and place them on, near, around the 'actor'. The effect is of an installation of actor and found poetry littered in and around 'Hamlet' who is locked in a gestic sculpture. The class speaks the strewn words chorally as witnesses of the moment depicted in the installation.

The class is invited to consider who might be observing Hamlet at this moment. Where would they be in the space – how near, how far? On this occasion, volunteers enter as Gertrude, Ophelia, Polonius and Claudius. They are asked to decide on a given cue whether they are more likely to move towards or away from Hamlet. The actions are executed and the class are invited to *thought-track* characters to try and explain why they might have moved as they did.

Finally, the class works on 'O that this too too solid flesh would melt'. An edited version of the soliloquy is fragmented and distributed around the group. It is spoken as the class moves across the circle, passing on their cue to the next speaker; it is spoken as the class walks randomly around the space; it is spoken as they reform into a circle. Finally, the figure of Hamlet is reinstated amongst the 'litter' of the sheets of responses used earlier.

Each member of the class 'returns' their fragment to Hamlet by physically giving it to him as they speak – hugging, holding, pointing, stroking, hiding, back turned. The workshop finishes when all are in a tight sculptured formation around Hamlet and the soliloquy is complete again – the chaos of the exercise is returned to the order of the poem. Conceptually and experientially, this is a long journey from statues of handsome princes.

The pedagogic emphasis in the RSC approach on the authentic work of theatre, the quality of relationships and the importance of experience, has its beginnings in the social constructivist line from John Dewey and Lev Vygotski through Jerome Bruner, Margaret Donaldson and Maxine Greene amongst others.[6] But in its stress on interpretative choices, discovery, risk and struggle the model perhaps owes most to John Dewey's proposal for an experience-based, real-world problem-solving paradigm for teaching and learning:

First, that the pupil have a genuine situation of experience . . . secondly, that a genuine problem develop within this situation as a stimulus to thought; third, that he possess the information and make the observations needed to deal with it; fourth, that suggested solutions occur to him which he shall be responsible for developing in an orderly way; fifth, that he have the opportunity and occasion to test his ideas by application, to make their meaning clear and to discover for himself their validity.[7]

In this context, the 'situation of experience' is the challenge of actively engaging with Shakespeare's texts as actors and directors do by becoming immersed in the practical problems of how to make social and personal sense of the language and translate the 'script' into action of different kinds. The genuine problem is the practical and

---

[5] James Moffett 'Informal Classroom Drama', *English in Australia*, 108 (1994), pp. 63–78.

[6] For instance, Jerome Bruner, *Towards a Theory of Instruction* (Cambridge, MA, 1976), Maxine Greene, *The Dialectic of Freedom* (New York, 1988), Lev Vygotski, *Mind in Society: The Development of Higher Psychological Processes* (Cambridge, MA, 1978).

[7] John Dewey, *Democracy and Education* (New York, 1916; repr Teddington, 2007), p. 167.

intellectual enquiry of students into how action might be arrived at, an enquiry that is based both on a shared understanding of the language and on shared observation in our own worlds of the events and behaviour depicted in the text. The solutions are the range of interpretative choices that students make as 'actors' in rehearsal, testing each one against their collective understandings of the meanings in the text and their own sense of the 'drama' of humanity. And it is in the 'doing' of these choices and their critical reflections on them that students come to understand their relevance and accuracy.

It is significant in the context of the discussion on ensemble-based theatre-making and teaching that follows that the quotation above comes from Dewey's *Democracy and Education* and that it is acting-centred and based in meaningful experiences. It suggests a different pedagogic relationship between teachers and learners, in which the expectation is that students will co-construct learning and be encouraged to negotiate their learning journeys with the teacher as facilitator rather than as the omniscient source of legitimate knowledge. A similar relationship between director and company characterizes ensemble theatre-making, as we shall argue, and the British Drama in Education tradition, with its emphasis on process, student autonomy and improvised action, that also contributes to the current RSC model of learning.[8]

Dewey placed an explicit emphasis on the potency of action: that we learn best by making and doing; that we change our worlds through our doing and we are active in forging our destinies. The RSC approach focuses on participation by young people as both actors and social commentators in the discovery of Shakespeare's scripts. The learning is based on critical enquiry, social interpretation and exploration of choices, carefully traced back to text and context. It is also based in the processes of acting to learn: using the intellectual and practical resources of classical theatre-making to construct practical and embodied knowledge of the plays rather than to receive and store stock responses; acting on the plays as well as acting within them.

CONNECTING WITH SHAKESPEARE

Following extensive consultation the RSC launched its *Stand up for Shakespeare* manifesto (SUFS) online in March 2008.[9] SUFS reflected a growing concern amongst cultural organizations like the RSC, teachers, academics and policymakers that one unintended outcome of the compulsory National Shakespeare test, introduced in England in 1991, was to narrow and reduce the quality and range of Shakespeare teaching, learning and performance in schools. In effect the Shakespeare SAT (Standard Attainment Test) was a test of generic reading comprehension and the ability to present an argument in continuous prose.

The National Curriculum for English for 11- to 14-year-olds includes the entitlement for all students to study 'at least one play by Shakespeare', the only writer nominated for statutory inclusion. However, critics of the test argued that, in practice, students would often study only the set scenes rather than a whole play, and that this study was likely to be entirely textual and often based on the line-by-line analysis of the text as literature rather than as a script for performance. Rather than encouraging students to develop a life-long interest and engagement in Shakespeare, the 'teaching to the test' approach was more likely to alienate young people from the plays and make it less likely that they would connect with them in later years. There was an additional concern that the focus on readership and the literary in the study of Shakespeare was not helping young people to see and experience the plays as theatre. In fact, for most, exposure

---

[8] This tradition places an emphasis on negotiated learning, teacher as facilitator rather than as instructor and the use of questioning and higher-order thinking skills in enacted and embodied fictional situations that refer in content to real world issues and dilemmas. See, for instance, Jonothan Neelands, *Making Sense of Drama* (London, 1984); Dorothy Heathcote and Gavin Bolton, *Drama as Learning: Dorothy Heathcote's Mantle of the Expert Approach to Education* (London, 1996); and for a critique of the liberal education tradition in Drama in Education see, for instance, David Hornbrook, *Education as Dramatic Art* (Brighton, 1989).

[9] RSC – Stand up for Shakespeare www.rsc.org.uk/education/sufs.aspx, accessed 19 October 2010.

to the plays was often in the form of electronic versions like the *Animated Tales* and films rather than through live performance.

The SUFS manifesto proposed three key tenets to underpin the teaching and learning of Shakespeare in schools: *Do it on Your Feet*; *See it Live*; *Start it Earlier*.

Taken together these principles represent a significant challenge to the status quo of teaching and learning Shakespeare in schools and colleges in England at least.

Young people are up on their feet, moving around, saying the text aloud, exploring the feelings and ideas that emerge. There is a focus on physical and emotional responses, as well as intellectual responses to the text. Active approaches are used to inform and test critical analysis. Pupils investigate a range of interpretive choices in the text and negotiate these with their teacher. Drama techniques are used to explore language, meaning, character and motivation. Understanding of the play is assessed through a combination of creative oral and written responses. (SUFS)

The stress on 'active, exploratory and problem-solving methods' suggests that students are being encouraged and given the open space to make their own connections, discoveries and journeys. These social constructivist methods require sophisticated pedagogic skills from teachers in addition to high levels of subject knowledge. They require teachers who are confident at managing group work in open spaces, who are skilled at questioning and scaffolding as well as personalizing learning, who are concerned with the emotional, cultural and social as well as academic development of learners. In this sense, the SUFS is as much about raising the quality of the instructional objectives for teaching and learning as it is about raising the profile of Shakespeare as a dramatist.

This wider ambition does not necessarily mean that there is a crude instrumentalism at work in which Shakespeare becomes a 'means' to social and behavioural outcomes rather than an 'end' in itself. The claim here is that the best practices of the ensemble rehearsal room mirror the best practices of a collaborative and participatory Shakespeare classroom and that how Shakespeare is realized theatrically and learned in the classroom is important in shaping our relationship to the plays, as students, audiences and creators of theatre.

TOWARDS A REHEARSAL-ROOM PEDAGOGY FOR SCHOOLS

The turn towards engagement and authentic experience rather than contemplative study, or 'teaching to the test', is a shift away from the teaching of Shakespeare at school level as a specialized form of readership training and necessary preparation for exams and entry into University English departments – which few students aspire to or achieve – towards the nurturing of the skills and learning required to engage with Shakespeare culturally as a life resource available to all who may choose it. To predicate the pedagogy of Shakespeare in schools on the trajectories of a few students may exclude others whose needs may be more immediate, different and requiring an alternative pedagogy. However, this emergent RSC pedagogy struggles constantly to find an appropriate balance between vernacular and scholarly modes of engagement. The stress on experience and access is tempered by the desire to give all students the intellectual tools and the socio-historical knowledge that might feed an enhanced enjoyment of Shakespeare.

This pedagogic turn towards the experience rather than the subject of Shakespeare is closely tied to the idea of giving all children and young people the means of access to the 'transcendent thrill' of the 'sixth sense of art' which, as the former UK Minister for Culture, Tessa Jowell, explains,

is not just a pleasurable hinterland for the public, a fall back after the important things – work and paying tax – are done. It is at the heart of what it means to be a fully developed human being.[10]

Those of us who come to enjoy and live with Shakespeare, both as complex cultural activity but

---

[10] Tessa Jowell, *Government and the Value of Culture* (London, 2004), p. 2.

also as part of our broader cultural life of shared references, stories and explanations of human nature, do so because we were shown how to share in their 'fullness'. This route into the complexities of Shakespeare for some young people comes from a home and school education that prizes engagement and knowledge of powerful forms of culture like Shakespeare. Pierre Bourdieu in his study of the social hierarchization of taste concluded that

cultural needs are the product of upbringing and education...preferences in literature, painting or music are closely linked to educational level...and social origin...To the socially recognised hierarchy of the arts corresponds a social hierarchy of the consumers.[11]

The challenge then for a cultural organization such as the RSC is to develop an educational programme which engages with children and young people who are unlikely to have Shakespeare as part of their cultural birthright and for whom school may be the only opportunity they are given to discover the potential 'fullness' that Shakespeare offers. In the absence of a personally meaningful and authentic introduction to Shakespeare, many young people come to fear and resent his apparent difficulties and 'irrelevances'.

One young man told us that 'Shakespeare speaks for posh people, not for kids in Coventry' – where and how did he learn this? From school? From home? From both? How might he be led to reclaim Shakespeare as the birthright of the disadvantaged and oppressed in the long line that might include Thomas Cooper and the Chartists, Rabindranath Tagore and the birth of democratic freedom in India, and Nelson Mandela and his fellow ANC inmates on Robben Island. A survey, commissioned by the RSC, of attitudes to and engagement with Shakespeare amongst 1,500 fifteen-year-olds, showed that less than 20 per cent of them agreed that his plays are relevant to events in the modern world or that they can help us to understand ourselves and others better. Almost half of the respondents considered Shakespeare boring and difficult.[12]

However, the survey also showed that students who read aloud and acted out scenes from the plays and who covered Shakespeare in Drama as well as English classes had more positive attitudes and more willingness to engage. This was also true for those who had performed or seen live performances. The most critical finding was that an individual teacher can make all the difference. The differences in attitudes and engagement between students were four times greater within a school than between schools. A passionate, skilful, confident, knowledgeable teacher who blends literary study with performance and other drama approaches can positively transform students' attitudes to Shakespeare.

DEFINED BY ENSEMBLE

For this reason the RSC's education resources have been focused on teachers rather than students. By working in sustained relationships with teachers on the kinds of authentic and practical work done by actors, directors and others, the RSC expect to impact on the life chances of a greater number of students than would be achieved by offering learning opportunities directly to them. A recent and influential policy study of the characteristics of the world's top performing educational systems concluded that the only effective means of improving the quality and outcomes of learning for the young is to improve the quality of teaching.[13] The most substantial RSC educational initiative has been the creation of a Learning and Performance Network (LPN) as 'the vehicle through which the RSC can place itself at the centre of the educational

---

[11] Pierre Bourdieu, *Distinction: A Social Critique of the Judgement of Taste* (Cambridge, MA, 1984), p. ii.

[12] Steve Strand and Sheila Galloway, *Attitudes to Shakespeare Among Year 10 Students: Report to the RSC on the Learning and Performance Network Baseline Survey 2007/08* (Warwick, 2009), p. x.

[13] This report by the Director of Standards for the New Labour administration was used to shape a new national MA in Teaching and Learning as a required qualification for new teachers: Michael Barber and M. Mourshed, *How the World's Best Education Systems Come Out on Top* (London, 2007).

debate into the efficacy of a different, more holistic approach to the teaching of Shakespeare and other literature'.[14]

Since 2006, the LPN has engaged 400 'hard to reach' schools in three-year programmes of sustainable professional development accredited by the University of Warwick. The RSC has increasingly focused its resources on building long-term relationships with a small number of schools. These schools may be geographically remote from Stratford-upon-Avon, or in areas of significant urban disadvantage. They are all in the public system. A significant minority of these schools have twice the national average of eligible students having free school meals, students with special educational needs and students from an ethnic minority group, at 13 per cent, 8 per cent and 24 per cent respectively. Before the LPN intervention the teachers often lacked confidence in key areas of competence, for instance, in basic knowledge of the plays, using drama and theatre techniques in their English classrooms, or even allowing students to speak Shakespeare aloud. They also tended to lack confidence in key pedagogical skills associated with the RSC approach such as the use of sophisticated questioning skills, group work and setting tasks that encourage higher-order thinking.[15] The external evaluation of the RSC's Learning and Performance Network programme in 2010 concluded that

Without exception the key teachers in core schools significantly changed their teaching practices not only in relation to the teaching of Shakespeare but also in relation to work with other texts and in the use of dramatic processes per se.[16]

Successful classroom Shakespeare encourages students to work in pairs or in groups, taking and sharing responsibility. A distinctive claim of the RSC's pedagogical project is that it foregrounds this idea of a 'co-operative, shared activity' in educational, artistic and societal dimensions. The approach requires and encourages children and young people to learn, imagine, create and coexist socially in the context of the Shakespeare workshop.

The ideal of 'ensemble' has become a useful bridging metaphor for the work of the RSC's company of actors, the organization and its model for teaching and learning Shakespeare. Artistic Director Michael Boyd has referred to it as a 'guiding star' for the RSC.[17] The LPN is a long-term commitment in which participating teachers are encouraged to see themselves as belonging to a 'community of practice' in Jean Lavé's and Etienne Wenger's sense.[18] The training element engages them in the very same ensemble and rehearsal-room practices that they will then model in their own classrooms.

The development of this teaching and learning model coincided with the reclaiming of the ensemble tradition at the RSC:

At the heart of our work lies the principle of ensemble. We believe that dynamic, distinctive theatre is made by working together with trust and mutual respect – that the whole is greater than the sum of its parts.[19]

There is a potent set of social ideas in this mix – participation, collaboration, trust and mutual respect. Are these necessary to the making of Shakespeare's theatre and to teaching and learning Shakespeare in schools? The RSC draws on the practices of early modern theatre and on the traditions of training and mutuality of the legendary ensemble companies of Central and

---

[14] www.rsc.org.uk/learningandperformancenetwork.

[15] Teachers in the LPN were asked to assess their confidence in these and other key areas of practice before and following working with the RSC. In the areas cited there were statistically significant shifts in confidence. See Jonothan Neelands, Geoff Lindsay and Sheila Galloway, *Stand up for Shakespeare The Royal Shakespeare Company Learning & Performance Network: Research for the Training and Development Agency for Schools* (University of Warwick, 2009).

[16] Pat Thomson, Chris Hall, Anton Franks and Ken Jones, *Interim Report to Creativity, Culture and Education: The Learning and Performance Network* (Nottingham, 2010), p. 13.

[17] Robert Hewison, John Holden and Samuel Jones, *All Together: A Creative Approach to Organisational Change* (London, 2010), p. 48.

[18] Jean Lavé and Etienne Wenger, *Situated Learning: Legitimate Peripheral Participation* (Cambridge, 1991).

[19] www.rsc.org.uk/about-us/ensemble/, accessed 15 October 2010.

Eastern Europe including the Berliner, the Maly and Gardzienice, as well as its own legacy from Peter Hall and Michel St Denis. More recently, Michael Boyd sought to capture the dynamic and promise of ensemble-based theatre making in an article for *The Stage* (2 April 2009):

At the heart of our developing practice at the RSC, there's a set of values and behaviours which we have found are both required and enabled by ensemble working . . .

Cooperation: the intense, unobstructed traffic between artists at play and the surrender of the self to a connection with others, even while making demands on ourselves. *Altruism*: the moral imagination and the social perception to realise that the whole is greater than the sum of its parts. The stronger help the weaker, rather than choreographing the weak to make the strong look good. *Trust*: the ability to be appallingly honest and to experiment without fear. *Empathy*: caring for others with a forensic curiosity that constantly seeks new ways of being together and creating together. *Imagination*: keeping ideas in the mind long enough to allow them to emerge from the alchemy of the imagination and not the factory of the will. *Compassion*: engaging with the world and each other, knowing there may be mutual pain in doing so. *Tolerance*: accommodating difference and allowing mistakes. *Forgiveness*: allowing and recovering from big and potentially damaging mistakes. *Humility*: the expert who has nothing to learn has no need for creativity, because the answer is already known. *Magnanimity*: the courage to give away ideas and love, with no thought of transaction or an exchange in return. *Rapport*: the magic language between individuals in tune with each other. *Patience*: this is only really possible over years. Art can be forced like rhubarb, but it tends to bend in the wind. *Rigour*: dancers and musicians take life-long daily training for granted, and theatre could do with catching up.

But why should these values and behaviours be essential to the teaching and learning of Shakespeare in classrooms and to the professional development of teachers? The quality of relationships and the necessity of risk and trust are common to an ensemble-based theatre company like the RSC, and to all physically and emotionally engaged forms of drama work in school. Geoffrey Streatfeild, who was in the RSC 2007–9 Histories Ensemble, described the ensemble in terms very similar to those made for other forms of drama and theatre education:

Our ever growing trust enables us to experiment, improvise and rework on the floor with an astonishing freedom and confidence. This ensemble is a secure environment without ever being a comfort zone. All of us are continually challenging ourselves and being inspired by those around us to reach new levels in all aspects of our work.[20]

The making of relationships in drama in the classroom or studio and in the professional ensemble often requires the taking of extraordinary risks for all involved. The teacher/director is taking risks in seeking a shift in the normative power relations within the class/company and between the class/company and the teacher/director and even by moving back the desks in both cases, or by exploring the choices rather than dictating/directing them. Young people/actors must make themselves vulnerable and visible in order to participate and must know that there is protection and mutual respect for difference from within the group to match the personal and social challenges of taking a part in the action. The ambition for the LPN was to provide the intellectual and practical resources and opportunities and experiences which have allowed teachers and learners to aspire to ensemble-based learning and to model a rehearsal-room pedagogy that matched the three core aspirations of the RSC as a cultural organization: 'connect with Shakespeare; be defined by ensemble; be engaged with the world'.

On this basis, it is possible to speak of a rehearsal room pedagogy – a regularised means of working towards a deepening understanding of the possibilities of text-based performance. A rehearsal room pedagogy requires the enactment of exercises designed to produce intellectual exploration, creative experiment and mutual understanding and respect. It also has at its heart *the interpretation of a text* on which all those in the rehearsal room are expected to work, discuss, brainstorm, explore and try out/act out.[21]

---

[20] Geoffrey Streatfeild, Histories Ensemble 2007–9, cited in RSC Histories Cycle Programme Notes, 2007.

[21] Pat Thomson, Chris Hall, Anton Franks and Ken Jones, *The Learning Performance Network: An Education Programme of the*

BE ENGAGED WITH THE WORLD

The important loop here is back to the idea of theatre as part of our larger social conversation. As Boyd suggests, the 'guiding star' of the ensemble, though it might be more easily achieved in the rehearsal room or classroom than at the level of society, is an ideal of how we might live together in fairness and justice. Both the idea of 'democratizing' engagement with Shakespeare and the necessity of action for shaping a participatory society argue for experiencing Shakespeare's plays in schools, and beyond, as scripts primarily for action, rather than as texts to be contemplated. There is resonance here with the claim, most recently made by Martha Nussbaum, that the humanities and the arts in any case develop the inner and social resources and abilities needed to live a 'full' life of mutual respect and equitable distribution of resources:

> . . . the ability to think critically; the ability to transcend local loyalties and to approach world problems as a 'citizen of the world' and, finally, the ability to imagine sympathetically the predicament of another person.[22]

And, of course, isn't there also the sense that Shakespeare's plays, when understood, help us to do all three? Isn't that an important gift to the young – learning how to engage with and understand his dramatic work as a provocation and reference point for reflecting and acting on our private and public worlds, and developing the humanizing instincts of universalism and compassion? Tagore, who translated *Macbeth* into Bengali when aged fifteen, reminds us that 'we may become powerful by knowledge, but we attain fullness by sympathy'.[23]

Within Western modernist aesthetics there is a long tradition of ascribing personal and social transformations to drama and other kinds of 'artistic' experiences. From Shakespeare to Ibsen to Brecht to Boal, Brook and Bond one can trace a faith in the idea that, through artistic transformations of the stage, society itself can be changed. Within this modernist perspective we have become used, as Raymond Williams put it, to 'the general idea that some relation must exist between social and artistic

change'.[24] At the heart of the RSC project there is critical hope in the power of collective human agency to make a difference to the world. Children and young people are encouraged through practical discovery and skilful questioning to make their own 'interpretive choices', as actors, about how to play Shakespeare's language. They learn that his texts are provisional and open to interpretation and that they can 'change' the playing of the play through their choices. There is here the hope that they may also learn that they can make interpretative choices in the wider world as well, including choices about who they might become or how the world might be re-imagined.

The lived experience of the ensemble-based rehearsal room and classroom reflects Nussbaum's abilities learnt from the arts and humanities and, in turn, the plays of Shakespeare offer the 'mirrors' for critical personal and social reflection. There are connections to be made both between the myriad ideas of acting/behaving in the plays themselves and in the acting/behaving in their making and learning, as Rex Gibson recognized:

Students' imaginative habitation of a play, taking parts, speaking the language, and directly experiencing characters' dilemmas, aids empathetic identification, develops awareness of moral, social and political issues, and sharpens insight into the complexity of human relationships.[25]

He stresses action and the active but, of course, part of the authentic work of the ensemble, in both the rehearsal room and the classroom, is to study the text closely and together and know and apply its conventions.

But, in emphasizing to young and emergent audiences the social significance of Shakespeare's

---

Royal Shakespeare Company (Newcastle-upon-Tyne, 2010), p. 13.

22 Martha Nussbaum, *Not for Profit: Why Democracy Needs the Humanities* (Princeton, 2010), p. 7.

23 Rabindranath Tagore, *Personality* (London, 1917), pp. 116–17.

24 Raymond Williams, *The Long Revolution* (London, 1961), p. 246.

25 Rex Gibson, 'Narrative Approaches to Shakespeare: Active Storytelling in Schools', *Shakespeare Survey* 53 (Cambridge, 2000), p. 161.

plays and the means of making them, are we in danger of reducing his work to a springboard into citizenship education? Are we resisting the 'treasures' that will only emerge with the kind of literary training that is associated with study at university level? The RSC, of course, is a theatre company. It makes sense for them, in terms of their identity and core business, to foreground the metatheatrical dimensions of Shakespeare's theatre and its continuing influence on the shaping of contemporary drama.

There is, in any case, a chaos in the performance of Shakespeare that eludes the fixity of literary meanings and multiplies interpretations for scholarly contemplation. Shakespeare in performance defies orderly and contained study of the authorial achievements of a single mind because it is socially made and sensuously received and because its semiotics are multiple, simultaneous and transient. This is even more the case in the intentional jouissance of the ensemble in the rehearsal room which is designed to find 'contemporary' relevance and fresh ways of seeing and knowing the plays. On the first day of rehearsals for *A Midsummer Night's Dream* in 1970, Brook told his actors that the truth 'has to be found by each actor' and that the play would 'yield its secrets, if each individual relates himself to the play'.[26] And in his response to the eventual performance, John Russell Brown famously remarked that: 'The director, with his actors to help him, discovered something which is not in the text at all.'[27]

To contradict Jaques, we are not 'merely players'; we are all social and/or artistic actors driven by events in the world to shape new social and artistic ideas and responses. No one is personal. We are all social and sociable, acting together in and on the world as well as on the stage.

Cornelius Castoriadis argues that the germ of democracy that was fermented in fifth-century Athens was based on the idea that a polity could continually reinvent itself and the ways in which people lived together, by engaging the public imagination, leading to political action founded on the principles of equity, fairness and necessary participation. For Castoriadis, the theatre of Athens was essential to the formation of an autonomous, self-regulating democracy and was a reminder of the imaginary nature of social life and the possibility of social transformations on the scale of the artistic transformations of the stage.[28] This connection between the plays of Shakespeare, the social space of his theatre and ours is critical, of course, in any discussion of its creative potential for young people facing an uncertain future.

Nussbaum argues that that the citizen requires more than fact and logic to be wise:

> The third ability of the citizen . . . is what we can call the narrative imagination. This means the ability to think what it might be like to be in the shoes of a person different from oneself, to be an intelligent reader of that person's story and to understand the emotions and wishes and desires that someone so placed might have.[29]

The classical actor and the learner in an ensemble-based classroom develop their own and others' narrative imaginations through the processes of 'becoming' Shakespeare's characters in language and deed. Acting requires from both an embodiment and manifestation of the subtle *aporiai* and complex, ambidextrous, multifaceted natures of Shakespeare's characters in whose shoes they stand. They can find empathy through the language and its action on us. They can play with the differences within and between themselves. They embody and play within intellectual positions which are different from their own. In so doing they discover how to see the world from different points of view; to see 'some soul of good in things evil'.

At the heart of all forms of theatre and particularly Shakespeare's dramatic imagination is the

---

26 Albert Hunt and Geoffrey Reeves, *Directors in Perspective: Peter Brook* (Cambridge, 1995) p. 142.

27 John Russell Brown, 'Free Shakespeare', *Shakespeare Survey* 24 (Cambridge, 1971), p. 134.

28 For Castoriadis, tragedy was a necessary political device rather than an art in the same sense as dance and music. See Cornelius Castoriadis, 'The Greek *Polis* and the Creation of Democracy (1983)' in Derek Curtis, ed., *The Castoriadis Reader* (Oxford, 1997).

29 Nussbaum, *Not for Profit*, pp. 95–6.

behaviour of the actor – one who acts. The centrality of human action to theatre is what defines its claim to be a creative art. As *Hamlet* reminds us, ideas that form in the imagination are only given substance when they become material actions. Aristotle defined an action as an intentional behaviour guided by phronesis (practical wisdom) which affects the world around us. Mirroring this Aristotelean sense of informed and intentional action, John Hope Mason defines creativity as 'acting in or on the world in new and significant ways'.[30] This definition foregrounds the capacity for human agency to change the world by working in and on it; acting to make a difference. In the context of the Shakespeare workshop, students discover how to flex their imaginations and develop their own powers of agency within the structures of language, character, setting and plot. In so doing both the students and the plays are changed – re-created.

In the *Fall of Public Man*, Richard Sennett[31] charts the demise of the idea and expectation that we are all social actors, performing within the polity of the public sphere. He argues that during the nineteenth century, and particularly after the failed European revolutions of 1848, public man withdrew from public life into the intimacies of the private and personal, mirrored in a growing fear and awe of 'performers' and performing artists and those who dared to act in public. The idea of the actor and acting became reserved, for the 'unreal' world of the stage and was associated with artificial and fake responses, compared with the authenticity of an interior life of reaction, contemplation and thought.

Many of us are still wary of doing 'drama' or being made to 'act' because of self-consciousness and a sense that 'acting' is at best foolish and at worst deceptive. In a survey of English finalists at Warwick, one remarked that she did not want to take a performance option for her Shakespeare module because, 'I was wary of practical seminars distracting from a focus on the core issues of the text. Didn't want thespianism to get in the way of discussion of the play.'

And yet we consider 'performance data' and expect the minutes of our meetings to include 'action points' which will require others to act. In the smallness of these worlds we are still able to recognize the need and responsibility for us to act in significant ways in order to create new ways of doing things or to make what we do more ethical, efficient and effective. But when we turn to the wider public sphere we seem to lose confidence in the idea of ourselves as actors whose actions can make a difference to the world we share.

Sennett and Castoriadis describe an historical trajectory away from *participation* to *representation* in the life of the society; a loss of faith in the creative potential of society to act together to change the ways in which we live and with the natural world on which we depend. By insisting on its principles of connecting with Shakespeare's plays, being defined by ensemble and being engaged with the world, the RSC approach to teaching and learning Shakespeare emphasizes engaged, reflexive, critical acting in both social and artistic senses. The capacity of young people for action and for 'fullness' through complex cultural activity is nurtured by being given access to the necessary intellectual and practical resources. It is a model for how cultural learning might engage them in the 'achievement' that Nussbaum captures:

It is all too easy to see another person as just a body – which we might then think we can use for our own ends, bad or good. It is an achievement to see a soul in that body, and this achievement is supported by poetry and the arts, which ask us to wonder about the inner world of that shape we see – and, too, to wonder about ourselves and our own depths.[32]

---

[30] John Hope Mason, *The Value of Creativity: The Origins and Emergence of a Modern Belief* (Aldershot, 2005), p. 232.
[31] Richard Sennett, *The Fall of Public Man* (New York, 1992).
[32] Nussbaum, *Not for Profit*, p. 102.

THE ROYAL SHAKESPEARE COMPANY AS 'CULTURAL CHEMIST'

SARAH OLIVE

As other articles in this volume suggest, the extent to which Shakespeare is a true catalyst, a substance that is chemically unaltered by the reaction that it initiates or speeds up, is a concept that deserves critiquing. Jonathan Bate, for instance, argues that Shakespeare is a 'catalytic converter'.[1] This article seeks to expand the critique, problematizing the possibility that Shakespeare is a cultural catalyst. Narratives of Shakespeare as a cultural catalyst involve him unilaterally conferring kudos onto individuals, corporations and other organizations that associate themselves with his person, life and works, or acting as a spur to further creativity and greatness. However, I will demonstrate that Shakespeare *is* altered by the interaction between his works, institutions and audiences. Furthermore, this article examines the way in which the phrase, 'Shakespeare as cultural catalyst', fails to acknowledge that not all reactions are naturally occurring, unaided by human intervention. It contends that the phrase attributes Shakespeare – a body of literary works or a long-dead playwright, poet and person (to name but a few of the labels ascribed to him) – with agency while obscuring the power of those who act on him. These agents include editors, directors, conservators, teachers and the institutions to which they belong, as well as independent scholars, Shakespeare enthusiasts and bloggers. I argue that these organizations and individuals, like chemists, *facilitate* reactions, or processes, around Shakespeare by bringing together the necessary ingredients. These might include Shakespeare and readers, Shakespeare and students, as well as Shakespeare and tourists, among others.

Furthermore, the phrase neglects the different subjectivities, contexts, objectives and assumptions of those contributing to the catalytic process.

In *Cultural Selection*, Gary Taylor argues that an author such as Shakespeare cannot survive, let alone continue to *dominate* vast areas such as English education, without the help of what he terms a 'survivor': 'Culture is not what was done but what is passed on. Culture therefore depends not only upon the maker who stimulates but upon the survivor who remembers, preserves, and transmits the stimulus.'[2] If it is envisioned at all in Taylor's conception, the catalytic role is shared between the work's author and a survivor or survivors. Like many successful 'makers', Shakespeare has had multiple survivors or carriers who have promulgated his value – early examples include Heminges and Condell, editors of the Folio, as well as contributors to the volume, such as Jonson. In turn, they recruited new guardians of Shakespeare's value through their readers, through inspiring other editors, other eulogizers, and so the cycle continues. This is necessary, explains Taylor, 'Because the dying of human carriers never ceases, the need to pass on memories to new carriers never ends.'[3]

Given this naturally high turnover of advocates, it could be argued that institutions rather than individuals offer a greater security or stability ensuring Shakespeare's ongoing influence. Indeed, Terry

---

[1] Jonathan Bate, 'Catalytic Converter', International Shakespeare Conference (Stratford-upon-Avon, 2010).
[2] Gary Taylor, *Cultural Selection* (New York, 1996), p. 89.
[3] Taylor, *Cultural Selection*, p. 8.

Eagleton has argued that Shakespeare is brought to life as a construct of institutions rather than as an authorial source.[4] They include libraries like the Folger; places of study, such as the Shakespeare Institute; heritage organizations, for example, the Shakespeare Birthplace Trust; dedicated Shakespeare theatres along the lines of the Royal Shakespeare Theatre and the Globe; regular Shakespeare festivals, for instance, Ontario; as well as conference committees, like that of the Shakespeare Association of America. These organizations offer a strong degree of continuity, in terms of the size and focus of their operations, even as they evolve from time to time. For instance, Shakespeare remains at the core of these organizations whether they vary their purpose from conservation to providing access, from engaging a domestic audience to an international one.

To reinvest the discussion of Shakespeare as a cultural catalyst with a sense of institutional agency, this article looks at the RSC's role as a cultural chemist, through its provision for schools. It draws particularly on the second Regional Schools Celebration and the Young People's *Comedy of Errors* staged in 2009, supplementing observation with analysis of printed material including programmes. It suggests that the RSC can be understood as wittingly combining various elements (play-texts, theatrical spaces, people, the company's ethos) to set in action, observe and reflect on processes around a pseudo-catalytic ingredient, Shakespeare. These processes include staging plays or educating teachers and students. As a consequence of these activities Shakespeare, not truly catalytic, is altered, his value reconstituted as the value of RSC ethos and pedagogy. A similar metaphor for the RSC has been previously deployed in Richard Wilson's article 'NATO's Pharmacy: Shakespeare by Prescription'.[5] I have been inspired by Wilson's use of pharmaceutical imagery but also, to some extent, by the substance of his argument: for example, his assertion of the hidden prescriptiveness that underlies progressive pedagogies used by the RSC in their teacher training.[6]

I have anticipated the criticism that this article sets up yet another metaphor despite the fact that, as the eponymous heroine of *Educating Rita* cautions her professor (in a play commissioned by the RSC), 'any analogy breaks down eventually' (2.1).[7] The risk is even greater when using terms from outside one's own field of knowledge. In countering such objections, although the idea of institutions as cultural chemists may not endure, it fits the purpose of this article. It allows me to critique and delimit the use of the term 'cultural catalyst' by highlighting the changes Shakespeare undergoes through contact with such organizations and the agency of those involved in what is, after all, a cultural rather than scientific process.[8] Although it is not my primary concern, I have also found it impossible to ignore the potential for critiquing the institution itself which a notion of the RSC as cultural chemist facilitates. Thus throughout this article, I pause to show contradictions or gaps in RSC education's self-fashioning. I conclude by considering the organization's interrelation with another institution and agent in shaping Shakespeare – government.

That the values of the RSC are made, by the company, to stand in for the value of Shakespeare, in a way which changes what constitutes Shakespeare for students and teachers, is demonstrable through an analysis of events such as the Regional Schools Celebration. I contend that this value shift is represented through the use of the discourse of professional theatre, including an emphasis on ensemble work and the actor's journey; within that, the development and sharing of a discourse for Shakespeare which equates to a shaping of

---

4 Terry Eagleton, 'Afterword' in Graham Holderness, ed., *The Shakespeare Myth* (Manchester, 1988), p. 205.

5 Richard Wilson, 'NATO's Pharmacy: Shakespeare by Prescription', in John Joughin, ed., *Shakespeare and National Culture* (Manchester, 1997), pp. 58–80.

6 Wilson, 'NATO's Pharmacy', pp. 62–3.

7 Willy Russell, *Educating Rita*, ed. Suzy Graham-Adriani (Harlow, 1991), p. 53.

8 'Cultural' in the modern sense of 'a process of human development' rather than the 'tending of natural growth'. See Raymond Williams, *Keywords: A Vocabulary of Culture and Society* (London, 1983), p. 87.

him in collective memory; slippages in discourse concerning terms such as 'text' and 'production'; and the promotion of Shakespeare done actively and outside the classroom as the supreme experience (both in terms of educational and personal development potential). Before addressing these elements directly, I will briefly outline the event itself.

THE REGIONAL SCHOOLS CELEBRATION AND THE YOUNG PEOPLE'S *COMEDY OF ERRORS*: SETTING THE SCENE

The Regional Schools Celebration, held at the Courtyard Theatre in Stratford-upon-Avon over two days in June 2009, was the culmination of the RSC Learning and Performance Network's interaction in that year with state schools nationwide. The network involves the RSC forming three-year partnerships with schools, many of which are situated in areas of economic and social deprivation. A key feature of the programme is that a smaller group of schools act as 'hub schools', sharing their knowledge and experience with a larger group of local schools to explore 'Shakespeare's work through performance'.[9] Teaching staff involved are drawn variously from English, Drama and the arts more widely. For the Regional Schools Celebration, each of the eleven regions the schools fell into was assigned a Shakespeare play. Schools within the same region divided the play between them: for example, looking at different scenes or themes or characters to produce twenty-minute performances. In addition to teachers' input, each school worked with an RSC practitioner before showcasing their work at a regional festival.

I attended the enthusiastic and enjoyable performances on 16 June, when six schools from Cumbria, Yorkshire, Cheshire and Surrey performed their 'responses' to *Much Ado About Nothing*, *The Tempest*, *The Winter's Tale*, *The Comedy of Errors*, *King Lear* and *Macbeth* on stage at the Courtyard. The responses constituted cut down versions of the plays or specific scenes. Shakespeare's language

was variously foregrounded or subdued depending on the age of the students: older students worked with lines directly from the plays while younger ones worked with varying combinations of 'edited Shakespeare text, negotiated adaptation and complete improvisation' as well as reordering and modern paraphrase.[10] Three of the performing schools were primary (or junior) schools and three of them secondary schools, so the performers ranged in age from 6 to 16 plus. Their audience consisted of the classes' fellow students and teachers, parents, RSC governors and some members of the general public.

While waiting for the performances to begin, images of the school groups and news clippings covering their work were projected onto the stage, provoking cheers from their students. There was no interval in the two hours' running time, which included a welcome and a summing up by the writer, broadcaster and comedian Hardeep Singh Kohli, who also presented certificates after the performances. There was also a warm-up for the participants and audience taken from rehearsal-room exercises designed to engage the actor's 'three tools' of body, voice and brain. This was run by the Masters of Ceremony Ann Ogbomo (an RSC actor and graduate of the Teaching Shakespeare programme jointly run by the RSC and the University of Warwick) and Steve Marmion (who has worked with the RSC as an Assistant Director). Ogbomo and Marmion's role included 'interviewing' a teacher and group of students from each school on stage before their performance as well as soliciting and fielding feedback from the audience after each production. Thus, without discussing the performances individually (a task beyond the scope of this article), an intertwining of education and entertainment was evident throughout, from the figures of the presenters to the content of the event.

The Young People's Shakespeare *Comedy of Errors* was a seventy-five-minute production of the

---

9 RSC, 'Regional Schools Celebration' (Stratford-upon-Avon, 2009), p. 2.
10 RSC, 'Regional Schools Celebration', p. 3.

play specially adapted by the RSC, in collaboration with the theatre company Told by an Idiot, to engage school audiences. The production adopted much of that company's ethos to generate an 'experience' that would be universally accessible to primary and secondary school children: 'Through collaborative writing, anarchic physicality and a playful but rigorous approach to text, the company is committed to creating a genuinely spontaneous experience for the audience. Using a wealth of imagery and a rich theatrical language, we aim to tell universal stories that are accessible to all.'[11] In this sense, the production represents Shakespeare *for* not *by* young people, something about which the title 'Young People's Shakespeare' is ambiguous. It premièred in schools in the West Midlands, followed by Newcastle-upon-Tyne and a small run (seven performances) at the RSC Courtyard Theatre in 2009 (although it has since been revived for the 2010 summer season). Here, unlike the other venues, members of the general public were able to attend – which noticeably extended the age-range of the audience upwards.

THE RSC'S AGENCY IN DETERMINING THE VALUE OF SHAKESPEARE AS THEATRE

The RSC is, by its very nature, an agent in presenting Shakespeare as theatre over other possibilities (Shakespeare as poetry, as artefact, or as the object of textual study). It determines Shakespeare's value as such and shares this valuation outside of the theatre realm through its education programmes. Its naturalization of Shakespeare as theatre is reinforced by its appropriation of certain strands of academic discourse, particularly the work of Rex Gibson, and establishing academic collaborations (with, for instance, the University Warwick's Capital Centre) to externally affirm the validity of such a value.

That the RSC's ethos of teaching Shakespeare as theatre draws strongly on the work of Rex Gibson was acknowledged at the 2010 International Shakespeare Conference by Jonothan Neelands.[12]

Gibson asserts that 'Shakespeare was essentially a man of the theatre who intended his words to be spoken and acted out on stage. It is in that context of dramatic realisation that the plays are most appropriately understood and experienced.'[13] He also encouraged the use of rehearsal-room techniques in the classroom on the basis that they offer a connection with the way Shakespeare would have worked with his acting company.[14] Divorced from their association with Gibson in the programme for the Regional Schools Celebration, these methods and discourse are implicitly rebranded as those of the RSC. The contributors to the programme, including the teachers and students quoted in it, praise the 'rehearsal-room techniques' and 'physical' 'work' involved in the production of this event.

The RSC's agency in constructing the value of Shakespeare as synonymous with theatre was also visible throughout the Regional Schools Celebration in their emphasis on the importance of taking a play from rehearsal to its realization on the professional stage. This focus was noticeably transmitted to the teachers it collaborated with: 'From understanding and dramatising the Shakespearean language in small groups, to working with the RSC practitioner, to actually performing at the Festival, has been an incredible journey. Now, the Courtyard Theatre!', enthuses teacher Tracey Bennett.[15] Additionally, the actor's journey – not always attended to in the experience of playing Shakespeare in the context of an English classroom – is praised as a useful part of the process by teachers: RSC methods, writes Steven Little, a head of department, have enabled 'students to fully get "inside" the characters'.[16] That the students involved, as well as their teachers, have picked

---

11 Told By An Idiot, 'Company History and Artistic Policy', www.toldbyanidiot.org/about/history/, accessed 6 September 2010.

12 Jonothan Neelands and Jacqui O'Hanlon, 'There is Some Soul of Good: An Action-centred Approach to Teaching Shakespeare in Schools', pp. 240–50 in this volume.

13 Rex Gibson, *Teaching Shakespeare* (Cambridge, 1998), p. xii.

14 Gibson, *Teaching Shakespeare*, p. 12.

15 RSC, 'Regional Schools Celebration', p. 3.

16 RSC, 'Regional Schools Celebration', p. 7.

up on and see value in RSC professional theatre is evident in their absorption and use of its discourse to describe their experience. They write of 'putting this fantastic play together', of 'going on stage',[17] and declare that 'acting is a great way to learn' and that 'the thing I most enjoyed was playing the trust games because they made it easier to act in role as we were thinking about the motivation of our characters'.[18] This discourse is arguably derived from that of the RSC itself, for example, their exhortation to 'do it on your feet' – a phrase deployed throughout their 'Stand up for Shakespeare' campaign. It is their experience of (personal) development through the activities of the RSC that is evidently in their minds, rather than Shakespeare's plays which are notably absent from many of these quotations. This signals the confusion of intrinsic value with instrumental, the value of Shakespeare with that of the methods used to teach him. These absences and confusions are problematic elements of the RSC's determination of Shakespeare's value which will be traced throughout this article.

The RSC has also been successful in turning ensemble casting into a hallmark, not only of its productions, but of its education programmes – being inspired to do so by the artistic direction of Michael Boyd.[19] Half of the ten teachers writing in the programme identified as particularly valuable the collaboration of, as teachers including Diana Lucas and Michelle Thresher termed it, their 'ensemble' or 'cast':[20]

Throughout the rehearsal process I have been impressed with the way in which these students have embraced the method of ensemble acting adapted from the Royal Shakespeare Company strategies. This has enabled them to take ownership of their scenes and work collaboratively to explore Shakespeare's language.[21]

Here, Thresher explicitly attributes the ensemble and collaborative methods with having positively impacted on her students' understanding and ownership of Shakespeare. Moreover, they become through her words branded 'RSC strategies', rather than Gibson's, or more generically, those belonging to 'active methods', 'practical' or 'dramatic' work.[22]

The transmission of an ethos from the RSC to teachers can be identified in the way this teacher picks up and deploys the term 'ownership': a term used by the RSC in much of their literature to capture their mission 'to give young people ownership of Shakespeare by unlocking the power of his language and exploring the contemporary relevance of his plays'.[23] Such examples illustrate the way in which a collective re-membering of Shakespeare is being successfully transmitted between 'survivors' through the use of a common discourse.[24] However, this mission statement also demands that some pressure be put on the sense in which the RSC is 'giving' 'ownership' of Shakespeare to students and teachers. Firstly, it must be remembered that although their website materials are freely accessible, as is some face-to-face contact, elements of the RSC's school education programmes are sold commercially through teacher training, INSET days and class excursions. Secondly, in claiming to be able to bestow ownership of Shakespeare on these groups, the RSC reinforces its ownership of a certain (in the above quotation, presentist) understanding of his works. It makes a public statement that Shakespeare is theirs to give, that they hold the key with which to 'unlock' his works. This imparting of ownership can also have a limiting effect on *which* Shakespeare is possessed: within the RSC's focus on Shakespeare as theatre, he is constructed, not as a wide range of knowledges and practices on which students will be assessed

---

[17] RSC, 'Regional Schools Celebration', p. 7.

[18] RSC, 'Regional Schools Celebration', p. 9.

[19] Jonothan Neelands and Jacqui O'Hanlon, 'There is Some Soul of Good', p. 247.

[20] RSC, 'Regional Schools Celebration', pp. 8–9.

[21] RSC, 'Regional Schools Celebration', p. 9.

[22] James Stredder, *The North Face of Shakespeare: Activities for Teaching the Plays* (Stratford-upon-Avon, 2004), p. 15.

[23] RSC, 'Education News: Activities for Students and INSET for Teachers' (Stratford-upon-Avon, 2009).

[24] On the dependence of artworks' and artists' survival and reputations on collective memory, see Taylor, *Cultural Selection*, pp. 2–6.

through coursework or examination, but primarily as performance and rehearsal.

A consequence of the RSC's emphasis on the value of teaching Shakespeare as theatre is that pedagogy and the plays are falsely elided; with the result that the non-Shakespeare-specific comes to be valued, perhaps unconsciously, over the Shakespearian. Physical theatre, ensemble work, the actor's journey and other elements of drama methods, portrayed above as the quintessential experience of Shakespeare, can all be used when studying other playwrights. If taken out of the context of the programme, the quotations cited in support of the RSC's education programmes – such as 'we all learnt to be more confident and join in more'[25] – could be testimonials to the benefits of staging any play, by any playwright. Furthermore, during the Regional Schools Celebration, the audience's enjoyment was occasionally divorced, if only humorously, from any Shakespeare-specific grounding in the plays at all. Singh Kohli, for example, joked that hosting last year's Regional Schools Celebration offered him 'genuinely new insight into writing that's four hundred years old but mainly what I wanted to come back for was the hairstyles'.[26] The lack of Shakespeare specificity here puts into question whether teachers and students are being given ownership of Shakespeare or of a set of techniques which can be applied equally well to other authors as they can to the bard.

DEFINING THE VALUE OF SHAKESPEARE THROUGH RSC PEDAGOGY

A second way in which the RSC exercises agency in defining the value of Shakespeare is by promoting his plays through performance outside the classroom as the ultimate experience of his works, both in terms of the potential for educational and personal development (a key component of C. B. Cox's rationale for English, and one which RSC education has made central to their own operations). This tenet of their education department has its origins in the RSC ethos, discussed above,

that first and foremost Shakespeare is theatre and he is 'active'. The RSC's belief that performance is not just a pedagogy, but *the* pedagogy through which to experience and with which to overcome barriers to, Shakespeare is made evident not only on stage but also in the pages of the Regional Schools Celebration programme. Michael Boyd explains, 'Through our manifesto for Shakespeare in schools, *Stand up for Shakespeare*, we want to see young people doing Shakespeare on their feet, seeing it live and starting it earlier. The schools taking part in our celebration today are the manifesto in action.'[27] Versions of the verb 'perform' appear seven times in sentences alongside 'Shakespeare'. For example, the Learning Performance Network is described as giving 'students the opportunity to explore and gain ownership of Shakespeare's work through performance'.[28] The emphasis on performance in the programme text is further reinforced by the high quality colour images from the productions which adorn most pages and many of which capture the movement of the student actors.

Alternative pedagogies are dismissed in testimonials to RSC practice by teachers and students alike: 'My own memory of Shakespeare was in the third year at high school studying *Macbeth*, sat behind a desk with no visual idea of what on earth was happening'[29] writes one teacher. Further anecdotal evidence of the RSC's superior pedagogies is drawn on from student participants in their programmes. The following opinions from students represent a unanimous majority in these materials: 'I enjoyed learning practically. It was challenging but it was fun';[30] 'I liked today because we approached the play through games rather than just reading the text';[31] 'Shakespeare is so much better on your feet'.[32] These students certainly

---

[25] RSC, 'Regional Schools Celebration', p. 4.
[26] RSC, Regional Schools Celebration, (Stratford-upon-Avon, 16 June 2009).
[27] RSC, 'Regional Schools Celebration', p. 1.
[28] RSC, 'Regional Schools Celebration', p. 2.
[29] RSC, 'Regional Schools Celebration', p. 8.
[30] RSC, 'Regional Schools Celebration', p. 4.
[31] RSC, 'Regional Schools Celebration', p. 9.
[32] RSC, 'Regional Schools Celebration', p. 8.

rate their RSC experience above other ways of learning Shakespeare and thus rank RSC constructions of Shakespeare (as practical, on your feet, and as games) above others. However, the RSC must be recognized as the agent in putting forward the superior value of Shakespeare experienced in this way: it chooses and uses these anecdotes and sound bites to confirm its narrative of desk-based, literary criticism as the proverbial 'bad old days'.

A related problem with the RSC's educational provision – premised as it is on the superiority of active pedagogies – is that prescriptivism is somewhat inevitable in trying to roll out any scheme, belief or pedagogy on a nationwide scale, however inherently liberal it might be. Richard Wilson has previously traced the way in which such unintentional prescriptiveness undermines not only the freedom to choose such pedagogies but also freedom within the teaching itself. Using pharmaceutical metaphors to explain the dominance of active approaches to Shakespeare, he writes that, 'Gibson's "Shakespeare in Schools" project is charismatically anti-intellectual in its exhortation to joy, though his instructions to pupils sound like *matron's most muscular instructions to swallow the medicine whole*' and 'Music and movement in the aisles is the *sugar that makes the bitter pill go down* in Gibson's regime, which seems a *perfect prescription* for schools compelled by law to study Shakespeare yet starved of funds for critical or historical support.'[33]

Rather than dismissing the value of active methods, I want to convey here a sense that the relationship in RSC education between prescription and progressivism remains troubled, over a decade after Wilson identified it as such. At the Regional Schools Celebration, the RSC was unquestionably keen to share the way it values 'doing' Shakespeare with the schools involved in the event (and the long lead up to it). Its eagerness to do so, however, creates a potential contradiction between its ideology and actual practice. A discourse of progressivism is evident, with explicit references to child-centred learning, exploration and play (a word frequently used in proximity to Shakespeare throughout the Regional Schools Celebration

programme) as well as overt criticism of traditional approaches, seen above. However, a more dogmatic, transmission-oriented approach was also discernible – in repeating relentlessly the 'Stand up for Shakespeare' motto (do it on your feet, see it live, start it earlier); having children in the audience chant 'what's happened to the Bard? I don't know'; and correcting children's responses to questions about their experience of Shakespeare. As an audience member, I witnessed one particularly striking incident in which a girl playing Cordelia was asked, on stage, what she had most enjoyed about the putting on of *King Lear*. She answered by saying she had enjoyed being given a main part. To this the RSC practitioner responded negatively, criticising her lack of 'ensemble spirit': 'there's no such thing as small parts, only small actors'. The value of Shakespeare for this girl (providing the opportunity to take a lead role) did not match the master of ceremony's idealized value for the company (providing the opportunity of ensemble work, supposed equality among actors). Thus her experience of Shakespeare was effectively invalidated because it did not fit the RSC paradigm. Sharon O'Dair suggested in her recent ISC paper that much online Shakespeare activity run by institutions represents a faux-democratization of the bard:[34] here, the gap between acknowledged values for and the implementation of a progressive ethos, combined with blatant prescriptivism. 'Stand up for Shakespeare', represents a faux-progressivism.

FOREGROUNDING PRODUCTION OVER PLAY IN RSC EDUCATION

The third way in which I want to discuss the RSC as an agent in equating the value of Shakespeare with the value of its organization is through the confusion of elements of the play

---

33 Wilson, 'NATO's Pharmacy', p. 63.

34 Sharon O'Dair, 'Against Internet Triumphalism', 34th International Shakespeare Conference (2010), and see revised version in this volume, pp. 83–96. See also Sharon O'Dair, *Class, Critics, and Shakespeare: Bottom Lines on the Culture Wars* (Ann Arbor, 2000).

with elements of the production, including slippages in the company's use of discourse concerning text/production. 'Play' and 'production' are often used interchangeably, making the location of the value hard to determine. The Young People's Shakespeare *Comedy of the Errors*, along with the Regional Schools Celebration and the Youth Ensemble's *Winter's Tale*, formed a cluster of RSC activities in 2009 aimed at engaging a school-age audience. This youthful target audience was evident in the programme, where traditional actor biographies were replaced with short actor interviews covering their 'favourite bit of this play' (not production), first experience of Shakespeare and favourite Shakespeare character. In answer to the first question, only three out of twelve actors named elements from the text of the play. These included Antipholus of Ephesus trying to enter his house when Adriana is inside with Antipholus of Syracuse; Antipholus of Syracuse hiding from Adriana in the priory; and the pursuit of Antipholus of Ephesus for debt. Noticeably, all these examples emphasize the potential for physical theatre afforded by the plot over other elements of the text. The other responses were all concerned with characteristics of this individual production including their participation in a whole-cast song worked up from the Courtesan's lines – 'My favourite bit is playing the double bass with dark glasses on during the Courtesan song because I think it looks funny and I like the music' (James Traherne/Solinus); slapstick violence between Dromio and Antipholus – 'I love doing the scene where I get to dunk Richard in the water'[35] (Dyfan Dwyor/Dromio); a slow motion chase; and a puppet show which summarizes the action before the reunions which end the play. What is being valued in the above quotations is not only production over play, but *added*-value, RSC-brand productions. Boyd's use of puppets has become a hallmark of his productions, while the RSC has enviable resources in its music department with which to create high-production value, big numbers. In addition, the RSC's style of production is increasingly associated, away from a tradition bent on verse-speaking, with the physicality of the actors' bodies, movement

and set as determined by the director's concept (in this case, cartoon violence).[36] To paraphrase British department store Marks & Spencer's now-infamous marketing of their chocolate pudding, it's not *just* Shakespeare, it's *RSC* Shakespeare. Admittedly, an assumption that, in talking about a play, one is referring to a specific production is natural in the realm of theatre. However, for the purposes of a theatre's education department – working with school students who will face examiners who insist on rigid distinctions between the two – such an elision is a potentially problematic element of their provision.

The need for a clear distinction of concepts in teaching students is further demonstrated in a story related in the programme for the Regional Schools Celebration. The ultimate confusion between author and company, between Shakespeare himself and as embodied by the RSC is jocularly expressed in the anecdote of a year 2 teacher, taken from the Regional Schools Celebration programme: 'Having got over the shock and initial disappointment that Shakespeare himself was not coming to work with them, they embraced Gemma [the RSC practitioner] as the next best thing.'[37] In these students' minds Shakespeare and the RSC had become one and the same.

THE CULTURAL CHEMIST IN
CONTEXT: THE RSC AND
GOVERNMENT POLICY

I have suggested above many implicit ways in which the RSC effects an amalgamation of its values for education with values perceived as inherent to Shakespeare, in ways that alter how students and teachers define him. It is also important to acknowledge the RSC's agency in transforming Shakespeare explicitly and deliberately through campaigns, like 'Stand up for Shakespeare', targeted at changing both teaching practice and

---

[35] RSC, 'The Comedy of Errors' (Stratford-upon-Avon, 2009).

[36] Jami Rogers, private conversation (4 August 2009).

[37] RSC, 'Regional Schools Celebration', p. 9.

government education policy. In 2009, the RSC could well have claimed some victory in the abolition of the testing of Shakespeare at key stage 3. This move, on the part of the government, marked the most radical change to the status of Shakespeare in education since he was rendered the only compulsory author in the 1989 National Curriculum for English. The RSC welcomed the decision as allowing more freedom for teachers to embrace RSC-style pedagogies.

Yet, the RSC not only lobbies to influence government education policy – another (even rival) agency in shaping Shakespeare – it also responds to it. This can be seen in the way the RSC fits its education activities to the requirements for attainment and programmes of study at each key stage, many of them non-Shakespeare specific. A catalogue of available RSC courses states that 'all our activities for young people are devised in line with the relevant curriculum requirements'.[38] More subtly, the company's adherence to the goals of the curriculum is visible in their adoption of its language in their own publications. The *RSC Education News*, for instance, echoes the curriculum's division of skills into reading and writing, speaking and listening.[39] Moreover, the RSC aligns itself with government objectives for National Curriculum English as elucidated initially in the Cox Report and reaffirmed in subsequent publications. For example, in terms of personal growth, RSC courses commit to developing 'social and emotional intelligence' as well as 'confidence and understanding'.[40] The Curriculum 2000's new attainment orders, AO4 and AO5, are reflected in the RSC's educational focus on awakening students to 'making interpretative choices' for themes, characters and current productions; seeing 'the play from different points of view'; and having them 'relate the plays to their social, cultural and historical context'.[41] These are only a handful of examples of the RSC's fit to government education policy.

In terms of arts policy, this massively subsidized organization is increasingly forced to justify its receipt of government funding in an environment where public value and the value of the arts is being hotly debated.[42] The organization needs to demonstrate its own worth – meeting criteria for funding, including increasing participation, widening access and improving their accountability for expenditure – as well as that of Shakespeare as a cultural icon. This perhaps explains, in addition to the use of anecdotes and sound bites, the recent surveying of students' attitudes towards Shakespeare resulting in the production of statistics with which to evidence the success of school groups' Shakespeare experiences of the RSC pedagogies.[43] Whether related to arts or education policy, the RSC's attempts to respond to government agendas demonstrate the way in which no chemist (cultural or scientific), especially one receiving significant government funding, works in isolation from their political and economic context.

---

[38] RSC, 'Education News', p. 1.

[39] RSC, 'Education News', p. 5.

[40] RSC, 'Education News', pp. 3–4.

[41] RSC, 'Education News', p. 5.

[42] See Tessa Jowell, *Government and the Value of Culture* (London, 2004); John Holden, *Publicly Funded Culture and the Creative Industries* (London, 2007); and Richard Ings, *Call it a Tenner: The Role of Pricing in the Arts* (London, 2007).

[43] Jonothan Neelands and Jacqui O'Hanlon, 'Some Soul of Good', Paper at the International Shakespeare Conference, Stratford-upon-Avon, 2010.

SHAKESPEARE AT THE
WHITE GREYHOUND

ADAM G. HOOKS

Edmond Malone was 'utterly incredulous' at the idea that Shakespeare launched his career by holding on to the horses of playgoers outside the theatre, in part because

it is not reasonable to suppose, that his countryman, Mr. Richard Field, the son of a tanner in Stratford, and a very eminent printer in London, whom our poet in 1593 employed to issue 'the first *heir* of his invention' to the world, would have suffered an amiable and worthy youth to have remained in so degraded a state, without making some effort to rescue him from it.[1]

Malone's immediate concern was to disprove the apocryphal story that young Will, new to London and in dire financial straits, started his professional life as nothing more than a servant, and he was interested in Richard Field only as a way to rescue Shakespeare from circumstances that were rather less than auspicious. But Malone's suggestive language – the 'very eminent' printer, 'employed' by Shakespeare to publish *Venus and Adonis*, which the poet himself had described in the dedicatory epistle as the '*first heire of my inuention*'[2] – reveals a further assumption based on this fortuitous Stratford connection that has since become axiomatic: that Shakespeare authorized and arranged for his own debut in print. Richard Field thus provides essential evidence of Shakespeare's own authorial intention and professional ambition, albeit an ambition he soon abandoned for the world of the playhouse. As David Scott Kastan has argued, using evidence that echoes Malone, '[c]learly, Shakespeare's commitment to print was reserved for his narrative poetry. His *Venus and Adonis* and *Lucrece* were

published in carefully printed editions by his fellow townsman, Richard Field, and to each volume Shakespeare contributed a signed dedication.'[3] The recent Arden 3 edition of Shakespeare's poems, the latest in what has been a welcome and concerted effort to relocate the poetry from the margins to the centre of both Shakespeare's career and our critical focus, likewise reiterates this conventional wisdom, describing the two poems as 'authorized by Shakespeare' and 'excellently printed by his Stratford contemporary Richard Field'.[4] When compared to the frequently disparaged state of the printed plays, these 'excellent authorized texts' confirm the view that Shakespeare's investment in print publication – that is, in an elite form of literary authorship separate from the popular business of the theatre – was restricted to the poems.[5] This standard account has lately been challenged by Lukas Erne, who argues that Shakespeare's commitment to print did indeed extend to the plays, and that he and his company actively sought to

---

[1] Edmond Malone, 'The Life of William Shakspeare', in *The Plays and Poems of William Shakspeare*, ed. Edmond Malone and James Boswell, 21 vols. (London, 1821), vol. 2, pp. 159, 165–6.

[2] *Venus and Adonis* (1593), [A]2ʳ.

[3] David Scott Kastan, *Shakespeare and the Book* (Cambridge, 2001), p. 6.

[4] Katherine Duncan-Jones and H. R. Woudhuysen, eds., *Shakespeare's Poems* (London, 2007), p. 3.

[5] Duncan-Jones and Woudhuysen, *Shakespeare's Poems*, p. 9. The Arden 3 editors place this comment in direct contrast to the phrase 'stolne, and surreptitious copies' used by John Heminges and Henry Condell to describe quarto editions of the plays that preceded the First Folio.

publish them. Erne questions a number of the accepted narratives of Shakespeare's career, with varying degrees of success, but Richard Field continues to play a crucial role in Erne's argument since his putative connection to Shakespeare provides the necessary documentary guarantee of authorized Shakespearian texts.[6] Indeed, as the editors of a recent essay collection have remarked, the presumed link between Field and Shakespeare provides the 'textual corroboration' as well as the 'aspirational context' to Erne's argument.[7]

Field undoubtedly provides a plausible basis upon which to build claims for Shakespeare's interest in publication. But to consider this potential relationship as an historical reality and, further, to use Field as a guarantor of Shakespeare's authorial status is to fall prey to what Leeds Barroll has identified as a tendency to canonize certain accounts of Shakespeare's career by the 'privileging of supposed events as basic facts'. Instead, Barroll stresses the 'multiple interpretive possibilities' of the evidence from which we construct historical narratives, possibilities that are not self-evident, and which are inevitably influenced by our own critical preoccupations.[8] In the first iteration of this argument some twenty years ago, Barroll was primarily concerned to evaluate certain methodological confusions of new historicism. In the revised and expanded version that appeared three years later, though, he began with a critique of what he termed the 'difficult art' of Shakespearian biography and the requisite, yet delicate task of reaching back in time through the surviving documents and records to 'some notion of the reality of the historical personage'.[9] The renewed interest in and production of Shakespeare biographies makes this a timely moment to reassess the manifold ways in which desires for and assumptions about the 'historical personage' both authorize and impinge upon our critical practices. The current biographical trend reclaims, and even resurrects, Shakespeare as an individual authorial agent that demands to be the central object of our attention, and Richard Field allows him to be rescued once again from 'so degraded a state', formerly represented by postmodern theoretical

discourse and the author-function, and now by the attention to the collaborative modes of textual and theatrical production that locate Shakespeare firmly within the institutional and material conditions of his time. Although employing the techniques of book history and bibliography, which seem to promise a measure of objectivity, much of this recent revisionist work continues to be motivated by an essentially biographical, if not romantic, interest in the individual: Erne positions his lengthy study as a biography, beginning with an anecdote that purports to provide a 'rare glimpse of Shakespeare's inner life', and one explanation given by the Arden 3 editors for their approach is that '[w]orking alone, Shakespeare was able for once to exercise complete control over the design of his artefacts'.[10]

Sidney Lee once remarked that 'Shakespeare's poem of *Venus and Adonis* has a peculiar fascination alike for the poet's biographer, critic, and bibliographer',[11] and in the case of Richard Field – the native of Stratford-upon-Avon and well-documented printer of texts apparently approved by Shakespeare – the raw materials and the methodologies of all three intersect. Like Lee himself, many of the most distinguished Shakespearian scholars, from Malone to Katherine Duncan-Jones (a co-editor of the Arden 3) have played all three roles. Rather than opening up interpretive possibilities, though, the convenient intersection represented by Field has given biographical speculation

---

[6] Lukas Erne, *Shakespeare as Literary Dramatist* (Cambridge, 2003), pp. 96–8.

[7] Richard Wilson, Jane Rickard and Richard Meek, eds., *Shakespeare's Book* (Manchester, 2008), p. 2.

[8] Leeds Barroll, 'Privileged Biographies, Marginal Shakespeare', in *Politics, Plague, and Shakespeare's Theatre: The Stuart Years* (Ithaca and London, 1991), p. 7.

[9] Baroll, 'Privileged Biographies', p. 3. For the earlier version of his argument see 'A New History for Shakespeare and His Time', *Shakespeare Quarterly*, 39 (1988), 441–64.

[10] Erne, *Shakespeare as Literary Dramatist*, p. 1; Duncan-Jones and Woudhuysen, *Shakespeare's Poems*, p. xvii.

[11] Sidney Lee, *Shakespeares Venus and Adonis Being a Reproduction in Facsimile of The First Edition 1593* (Oxford, 1905), p. 11.

the weight of bibliographical fact, and has been used to reinforce and capitalize on one of the most established and fundamental narratives of Shakespearian scholarship. Attractive as this narrative may be, it has obscured its own speculative basis and prevented us from acknowledging the existence of other important influences involved in creating and maintaining Shakespeare's reputation in print.

Richard Field was certainly one of the agents responsible for making Shakespeare the writer into 'Shakespeare' the author. But his presumed biographical link with Shakespeare has granted Field (and by extension Shakespeare himself) an exaggerated prominence in the creation of the poet's authorial persona, eclipsing the contributions of others by privileging a single moment in Shakespeare's textual life. By printing and publishing *Venus and Adonis* in 1593, Field became the first to invest in Shakespeare, but this investment was short-lived: his responsibility for and financial risk in Shakespeare's poetry were limited to two editions within a year, which were sold at the White Greyhound, the shop of his partner, John Harrison. While Field would continue for a brief time to print Shakespeare's poetry, thereafter it was Harrison who took on the responsibility of publishing and selling it, distinct and significant functions that played crucial roles in shaping and sustaining Shakespeare's career. For the next two decades, both of Shakespeare's narrative poems could be found at the sign of the White Greyhound: Harrison passed on *Venus and Adonis* to William Leake, the subsequent occupant of his shop, while holding on to *Lucrece* at his new location, also called the White Greyhound. By shifting our focus to the White Greyhound and to the stationers identified with it – that is, to the shops where Shakespeare's poetry was sold and to the people who ventured to publish and sell it – we can recover the multiple and intersecting forces that fashioned Shakespeare into one of the most famous and successful poets of his day, even while he devoted his energies to a career writing for his theatre company. Shakespeare may never have set foot in a shop called the White Greyhound, but he

would flourish there throughout his professional life.

I begin, then, by exploring the business of Richard Field and his known relationships with writers and with other stationers, in order to show that his potential interest in Shakespeare could have extended beyond a merely personal acquaintance. In this context, I go on to reconsider the title-page motto of *Venus and Adonis*, taken from Ovid's *Amores*. The motto, like the signed dedication, has been read as a direct statement by Shakespeare and interpreted as a bold claim to individual authorial status, marking his turn away from the popular stage towards a commitment to a certain kind of literary print publication. There are other possibilities, though: the motto circulated widely both before and after Shakespeare made his audacious assertion, and it is better understood within a broader Ovidian milieu which was visibly accessible in Field's printing house and in Harrison's bookshop rather than as the result of an isolated authorial ambition. Both Field and Harrison had a vested interest in Ovid which fostered and promoted Shakespeare's reputation as an Ovidian poet – a reputation on which William Leake would notoriously capitalize.

My goal here is not to relocate a singular agency from the poet to his publisher or bookseller, a move that would simply replace Shakespeare as the object of biographical or critical attention with a less familiar historical personage. Rather, my aim is to embrace the multiple agencies involved beyond Shakespeare and beyond Richard Field. What we gain is not only a more nuanced account of Field's contribution to Shakespeare's career, but an account of the crucial, if neglected, contributions of two stationers who play no part in conventional biographical narratives, even though their investment in Shakespeare was far more extensive, and ultimately more significant, than Field's. By attending to the publication of Shakespeare's poems without granting a preconception of biography, this approach allows us to rethink the ways that Shakespeare was defined by the field of print authorship.

I SHAKESPEARE'S TOWNSMAN

Edmond Malone was not the first to recognize that Richard Field hailed from Stratford-upon-Avon, but he was the first to make something of the Warwickshire roots he shared with Shakespeare.[12] Beginning in 1589, Field ran one of the most sophisticated and accomplished printing houses in London.[13] Unlike his townsman, though, Field seems to have had little to do with his hometown after becoming a successful London businessman.[14] The two families may have known each other, though: when Field's father Henry died in 1592, Shakespeare's father John served as one of the witnesses of the inventory taken of Henry's goods. John Payne Collier discovered the inventory in the 1840s and used it as documentary proof that the sons of Henry Field and John Shakespeare did indeed know each other.[15] This family connection allowed Collier to assign responsibility for Shakespeare's first appearance as a published author to the poet himself, and he concluded that Shakespeare had employed Field to print the poems simply 'because he was a fellow-townsman, and wished to render him a service'.[16] Field was busy enough by 1593 that he would not have needed anyone to 'render him a service' but Collier's formulation has been remarkably persistent, since it characterizes Shakespeare as a figure engineering his own presentation as a literary author.

While Collier labelled the connection between Field and Shakespeare a 'curious, though I cannot call it an important, circumstance in the history of Shakespeare and his works', he was soon to be proven wrong, for subsequent critics were willing to infer rather more. Andrew Murphy has recently surveyed some of these conjectures, from the plausible – that Shakespeare used Field and his shop as a source of books, particularly the editions of Plutarch and Ovid he printed – to the more fanciful, including that Shakespeare had not only proofread his own poems but had actually worked alongside Field as a printer himself.[17] These are undoubtedly good stories, but they are, as Murphy states, 'little more than wishful speculation', albeit speculation that does reveal a critical

investment in a learned Shakespeare deeply immersed, whether intellectually or literally, in the world of print. Shakespeare could of course have haunted Field's shop frequently, but there are equally likely alternatives that cast doubt on these conjectures: Shakespeare could have gained access to books in any number of ways, and since the

---

[12] Malone and Boswell, 2:159. In 1786, William Herbert included an entry for Richard Field, 'Son of Henry Field of Stratford on Avon, Tanner', in his revision of Joseph Ames's *Typographical Antiquities*, 3 vols. (London, 1785–1790), 2:1252. Two years later George Steevens first published the entries from the Stationers' Register pertaining to Shakespeare, including Field's entrance of *Venus and Adonis*; see Samuel Johnson and George Steevens, eds., *The Plays of William Shakspere*, 10 vols. (London, 1778), 1:253–68. Malone was the first to make an explicit connection between Field and Shakespeare.

[13] Field was bound as an apprentice to Thomas Vautrollier in 1579; when Vautrollier died in 1587, Field married the widow, and had taken over the business by 1589. Edward Arber, ed., *A Transcript of the Registers of the Worshipful Company of Stationers of London, 1554–1640 A.D.*, 5 vols. (London, 1875–94), 2:93. For an overview of Field's career, see A. E. M. Kirwood, 'Richard Field, Printer, 1589–1624', *Library*, 4th ser., 12 (1931), 1–39.

[14] In 1592, Field did take on his younger brother Jasper as an apprentice (Arber, 2:179), but no further contact with Stratford is recorded until his death in 1624, when he bequeathed a small sum to his niece. Henry R. Plomer, *Abstracts from the Wills of English Printers and Stationers, from 1492 to 1630* (London, 1903), p. 50.

[15] John Payne Collier, 'Life of William Shakespeare', in *The Works of William Shakespeare*, ed. John Payne Collier, 8 vols. (London, 1844), 1:cxliv. A full transcription of the Henry Field inventory can be found in Jeanne Jones, ed., *Stratford-upon-Avon Inventories 1538–1669*, 2 vols. (The Dugdale Society in association with The Shakespeare Birthplace Trust, 2002), 1:116–19. The inventory is currently housed in the Shakespeare Birthplace Trust Record Office, BRU 15/1/3. The heading refers to 'Mr John Shaksper', and 'John Shaksper senior' is listed by the scribe among the signatories. The designations 'Mr' and 'senior' distinguish Shakespeare's father from another John Shakespeare, a corviser (or shoemaker) who also lived near Field's house; see Edgar I. Fripp, *Shakespeare's Stratford* (Oxford, 1928), pp. 13–15. I would like to thank Robert Bearman of the SBTRO for discussing the various John Shakespeares of the Stratford area with me.

[16] Collier, *The Shakespeare Society's Papers, Vol. IV.* (Printed for The Shakespeare Society, 1849), p. 37.

[17] Andrew Murphy, *Shakespeare in Print* (Cambridge, 2003), pp. 15–17.

scant press corrections evident in the texts of the poems conform to routine printing practices, the myth that Shakespeare served as a proofreader was dispensed with long ago.[18]

The poems may be in better shape than several of the early plays but, despite, or indeed because, the poems are assumed to have been authorized by Shakespeare, they have not often received a thorough textual analysis. While they do not question the authorised status of the poems, the Arden 3 editors, in the most exhaustive examination to date, nevertheless conclude that it is impossible even to determine whether Field and his compositors set the poems from Shakespeare's autograph or from a scribal copy.[19] Field presumably worked from a clear and legible fair copy but his compositors often imposed their own orthography and punctuation, making it difficult to ascertain the specific kind of manuscript underlying the unquestionably well-printed early quartos.[20] In addition, the presence of printed commonplace markers throughout Lucrece points to an intermediate stage of transmission – an annotating reader with access to the manuscript copy – since Shakespeare was almost certainly not responsible for inserting them himself.[21]

Field may not offer us unqualified access to the true original copies, then, but he does continue to be used as a guarantor of Shakespeare's authorial status. As the recent Oxford editor of the poems writes, 'Field's shop produced books which looked good and which made claims to high literary status, as well as works which sought to define what high literary status was.'[22] The implication is that through an association with Field, Shakespeare would become just such an author himself. Field did have a hand in a number of works we now recognize as canonical, including Edmund Spenser's Foure Hymnes (1596) and the first complete edition of The Faerie Queene (1596), as well as the third edition of Sir Philip Sidney's Arcadia (1598). But these books were printed for William Ponsonby, who made his career serving the Leicester faction and its heirs.[23] Field's involvement with these books was limited to a business arrangement: he printed a number of books for Ponsonby, for the most part

large, complicated volumes that he was more than capable of producing. Of the books Field chose to publish himself, though, no discernible speciality arises: his output included a mix of political, religious, educational and scientific works but virtually no vernacular poetry.

The two works most often cited as evidence of Field's literary concerns are the exceptions and have been given a disproportionate importance considering Field's total output. The first, George Puttenham's Arte of English Poesie (1589), was published early in Field's career and was at the time the largest project he had taken on independently. Puttenham's extensive treatise was one of the early attempts to define the realm of English 'poesy', but Puttenham is just as concerned to laud the Protestant nation-state of Elizabeth and he shows little awareness of contemporary literary trends.[24] Although the Arte is at least in part a result of

---

[18] See Charles R. Forker, 'How Did Shakespeare Come by His Books?', Shakespeare Yearbook, 14 (2004), 109–20. On the proofreading myth, see Henry R. Plomer, 'The Printers of Shakespeare's Plays and Poems', Library, 2nd ser., 7 (1906), 151. For an analysis of the compositors' practices in setting the two poems, see Duncan-Jones and Woudhuysen, Shakespeare's Poems, pp. 471–89.

[19] Duncan-Jones and Woudhuysen, Shakespeare's Poems, pp. 482, 489.

[20] For further textual analysis, see A. C. Partridge, A Substantive Grammar of Shakespeare's Nondramatic Texts (Charlottesville, 1976), pp. 23, 44; and Orthography in Shakespeare and Elizabethan Drama (London, 1964), pp. 67–79.

[21] On commonplace markers in Lucrece, see Roger Chartier and Peter Stallybrass, 'Reading and Authorship: The Circulation of Shakespeare 1590–1619', in A Concise Companion to Shakespeare and the Text, ed. Andrew Murphy (Oxford, 2007), pp. 35–56; esp. p. 47. See also Zachary Lesser and Peter Stallybrass, 'The First Literary Hamlet and the Commonplacing of Professional Plays', Shakespeare Quarterly, 59 (2008), 371–420, esp. pp. 381, 400–1.

[22] Colin Burrow, ed., Complete Sonnets and Poems (Oxford, 2002), p. 6.

[23] On Ponsonby's career, see M. G. Brennan, 'William Ponsonby: Elizabethan Stationer', Analytical and Enumerative Bibliography 7 (1983), 91–110.

[24] On the date of composition for various sections of the Arte of English Poesie, see Frank Whigham and Wayne A. Rebhorn, eds., The Art of English Poesy by George Puttenham: A Critical Edition (Ithaca and London, 2007), pp. 42–3.

Puttenham's ambitions, both political and poetical, it appeared anonymously and it is clear that the presentation of the volume had more to do with Field's connections than with Puttenham's. Field claimed he did not know the author, and hence took the liberty of attaching a signed dedication to Lord Burghley, who had employed him the previous year.[25] The frontispiece engraving of Elizabeth – which Field would later reuse – was also a chance to showcase his handiwork.[26]

That Puttenham's *Arte* was considered out of date is demonstrated by the one author with whom Field certainly had an intimate working relationship, Sir John Harington. In the 'Briefe Apologie of Poetrie' prefacing his translation of *Orlando Furioso* (1591), Harington mocked not just the *Arte*, mentioning it by name, but Puttenham's skill as a poet as well. While Harington disapproved of the content of Puttenham's book, he certainly paid close attention to its appearance. The manuscript used as copy for *Orlando* survives, replete with instructions to Field concerning layout and typography in Harington's hand, including a note that refers specifically to 'Putnams book'.[27] Harington may also have helped initiate the patent that was granted to Field in 1592 for the sole printing of what would have been a laborious and expensive undertaking.[28] Harington continued his association with Field throughout the 1590s, employing him to print the notorious series of *Aiax* pamphlets. Again, the printer's copy survives and in one case shows Harington collaborating with Field, designing the title-page and supplying a Latin motto – a collaboration that will be examined in more detail in a moment. It is important to note here that Harington, the Queen's godson, is far from a representative case, though. The lavish volume of *Orlando* was intended for a court audience and Harington prepared a number of presentation copies designed to further his career (one of which was given to Lord Burghley).[29] His relationship with Field was unique in the printer's career and this relationship cannot serve as a model for Field's link with Shakespeare.[30]

To use Field as the foundation for or confirmation of the literary concerns often attributed to Shakespeare is thus no straightforward matter. Claiming Field as the guarantor of Shakespeare's cultural and authorial status both generates and conflates the supposed interests of the printer and the poet. The conventional critical and biographical narratives use Field as little more than a conduit through which Shakespeare fulfils his own literary ambition, neglecting his normal business model, as well as any potential reasons that Field may have found Shakespeare to be an acceptable investment. So what did Field have to gain, beyond rendering a service to a former neighbour? The answer could lie in the dedication to Henry Wriothesley, Earl of Southampton and the young ward of

25 Several issues of Burghley's famous Armada pamphlet *The Copie of a Letter sent out of England to Don Bernardin Mendoza* (1588) were printed by Field, in both French and English; see Conyers Read, *Lord Burghley and Queen Elizabeth* (New York, 1960), pp. 431–4. Field contributed a signed preface to another Armada pamphlet in 1589, *The copie of a letter sent from sea by a gentleman who was employed in discouerie on the Coast of Spaine*. Burghley had previously employed Field's master Vautrollier to print his pamphlet *The Execution of Justice* in 1583, which may in part account for Burghley's involvement with Field. See also Denis B. Woodfield, *Surreptitious Printing in England 1550–1640* (New York, 1973), pp. 22–5.

26 The engraving is identical to one that appeared in *A booke, Containing the True Portraiture of the Countenances and attires of the kings of England, from William Conqueror, unto our Soveraigne Lady Queene Elizabeth now raigning*, printed by Field in 1597.

27 '[I wowld have the allegory (as allso the appollogy and all the prose that ys to come except the table in the same printe that Putnams book ys[)]', British Library Add. MS 18920, fol. 336ʳ.

28 On 6 February 1592 there is recorded a 'Grant to Rich. Field, printer, of the sole license of printing Orlando Furioso, translated into English verse by John Harrington'. Mary Anne Everett Green, ed., *Calendar of State Papers, Domestic Series, of the Reign of Elizabeth, 1591–1594* (London, 1867), p. 179. See also W. W. Greg, ed., *A Companion to Arber* (Oxford, 1967), pp. 151–2.

29 See Jason Scott-Warren, *Sir John Harington and the Book as Gift* (Oxford, 2001), pp. 49–55.

30 The Arden 3 editors agree, stating that 'it is worth bearing in mind that what might have obtained for one author – Harington – in folio in 1591 (or in octavo in 1596) did not necessarily obtain for a different author – Shakespeare – engaged in different sorts of poetic practice in quarto in 1593 and 1594' (Duncan-Jones and Woudhuysen, *Shakespeare's Poems*, p. 472).

Field's sometime employer, Lord Burghley. Field may have seen the dedication as a convenient way to continue a connection with a powerful circle at court, and it has even been suggested that Field could have introduced Shakespeare to his prospective patron.[31] The Earl of Southampton was not yet well known as a patron – *Venus and Adonis* was only the second work dedicated to him – and as a ward living on a fixed income he had little in the way of monetary incentives to offer, so it is possible that Field played a role of some kind in suggesting Southampton for his own benefit. Nevertheless, Southampton was a suitable choice, since the first book dedicated to him – a Neo-Latin poem called *Narcissus* (1591), written by Burghley's clerk John Clapham – contains some structural and thematic parallels to Shakespeare's erotic epyllion, including a classical source in Ovid's *Metamorphoses*. Shakespeare would go on to dedicate *Lucrece* to the earl the next year, writing of the 'warrant I haue of your Honourable disposition', which seems to imply a connection to, or even a reward of some sort from, Southampton. The poem may have appealed to Southampton's nascent political interest in republicanism – an interest well represented in the books on statecraft produced by Field.[32]

At the very least, then, Field would have been comforted to know that there was a proximate precedent for his venture in contemporary Ovidian poetry, and that it was dedicated to a member of a circle with which he was associated. Field was by and large a trade printer hired by other stationers, and this was particularly the case for most of the literary works that issued from his press. He had very little to lose with *Venus and Adonis*, though: Shakespeare's slim pamphlet constituted only a small fraction of Field's considerable output, so the immediate financial risk was negligible. Field also chose to share the risk (not to mention the reward) with his partner John Harrison: although it was Field who initially registered and published *Venus and Adonis*, it is the location of Harrison's shop – the White Greyhound – that appears in the imprint, indicating that he was the primary distributor of Shakespeare's poem. This arrangement, by no means uncommon in the period, indicates that

as the wholesaler, Harrison had in effect helped to subsidize production by providing Field with a guaranteed outlet for his printing work.[33] This was a familiar role for Harrison, who had a longstanding relationship with Field's former master and who provided steady work for his junior associate Field in the crucial early years of his independent career.[34] Harrison was thus fully engaged in the enterprise, if only as a secondary partner – but he would not serve as such for long. Just over a year later, Field officially transferred *Venus and Adonis* to Harrison, not long after Harrison himself had registered *Lucrece*, thus giving Harrison full responsibility for the publication and distribution of the two poems.[35] The specific terms of the transfer are irrecoverable, but the simplest explanation is that Harrison agreed to hire Field in return for the title,

---

[31] For an overview of the possibilities, see Duncan-Jones and Woudhuysen, *Shakespeare's Poems*, pp. 26–30.

[32] See Martin Dzelzainis, 'Shakespeare and Political Thought', in *A Companion to Shakespeare*, ed. David Scott Kastan (Oxford, 1999), p. 107. The same year *Lucrece* appeared – 1594 – Field printed Petruccio Ubaldini's *Lo Stato delle Tre Corti*. A presentation copy with a manuscript note in the hand of the author was given to Burghley's son, Robert Cecil; see Woodfield, *Surreptitious Printing*, p. 38. On Clapham's poem, see Charles Martindale and Colin Burrow, 'Clapham's *Narcissus*: A Pre-Text for Shakespeare's *Venus and Adonis*?', *English Literary Renaissance*, 22 (1992), 147–76, esp. p. 151.

[33] For an analysis of the arrangements indicated by this form of an imprint, see Zachary Lesser, *Renaissance Drama and the Politics of Publication* (Cambridge, 2004), p. 29. Lesser elsewhere argues that 'even when a printer chose to publish a book "to be sold by" a bookseller, the printer was still at the mercy of the bookseller to take his product to market' (33).

[34] Vautrollier had printed for Harrison as early as 1580, during Field's apprenticeship, and Harrison took over several of Vautrollier's patents, including one for the publication of Ovid. Field first printed for Harrison in 1589, and over the next decade Field would print twenty of the thirty-four books Harrison published, including ten of the fifteen from 1589–92.

[35] Field had entered 'a booke intituled VENUS and ADONIS' on 18 April 1593 (Arber, *Transcript*, 2:630). Harrison entered 'the Ravyshment of LUCRECE' on 9 May 1593 (2:648); less than two months later, on 25 June 1594, Field assigned his rights in *Venus and Adonis* to Harrison (2:655).

since like most printers Field preferred stable earnings over the gamble of speculative publication. Harrison did indeed hire Field to print *Lucrece*, and Field would continue to print four editions of *Venus and Adonis* in quick succession, until Harrison sold his rights to the hot commodity in 1596. Harrison held on to *Lucrece*, eventually publishing it five times during his career, making it one of his most dependable titles. Harrison's stake in Shakespeare thus paid off handsomely, as he continued to supply the poems that remained very much in demand.

Shakespeare may have brought *Venus and Adonis* to Field because of his connections to potential patrons or simply because as a childhood acquaintance Field was more likely to grant Shakespeare's wish to become a man in print. While this remains the most plausible of explanations, to view Shakespeare – or the version of Shakespeare traditionally represented through Field – as the isolated impetus for the poems' publication not only privileges one instant and one agent to the exclusion of all others, it also simplifies and misrepresents the way the early modern book trade worked. John Harrison was also involved from the beginning, particularly with *Lucrece* and, if Shakespeare did rely on a personal relationship to get his poetry into print, he had to rely even more on the acumen and commitment of Harrison to make that poetry a success. Although critics have claimed that Field and Shakespeare maintained a lifelong relationship – a claim which conveniently corroborates conventional notions of Shakespeare's commitment to print – Field's documented association with Shakespeare was strikingly brief. After 1596, he would print only one more poem by Shakespeare, his contribution to the collection *Loves Martyr* (1601), but this volume was produced for Edward Blount, who was already becoming known as one of the leading literary publishers of the time.[36] It now seems nearly unthinkable that a printer – and a printer from Stratford, no less – would pass on the chance to be involved with Shakespeare's works but Field did exactly that. Shakespeare may be Field's claim to fame, at least among Shakespearians, but for Field the

budding poet seems to have been little more than a brief matter of business, conducted in conjunction with a stationer whose professional relationship with and dependence on Shakespeare's printed poems would ultimately last much longer. Shakespeare's fame was made at the White Greyhound, not in a single moment of ambition, inspiration or dedication, but over a number of years – and a number of sought-after reprints. Harrison did not merely benefit from or enable Shakespeare's best-sellers, though: he also provided a crucial context for understanding the poems within the Ovidian milieu of the 1590s, as well as the aspiration often attributed to the poet within this milieu.

SHAKESPEARE'S MOTTO

In the dedicatory epistle to Southampton that prefaces *Venus and Adonis*, Shakespeare christened the poem the '*first heire of my inuention*', an appellation that points to an awareness that this was his first published and dedicated work – an awareness admittedly accompanied by an anxiety that it may '*proue deformed*'. An altogether more confident appraisal appears on the title-page, which displays a Latin motto, taken from the first book of Ovid's *Amores*:

> *Vilia miretur vulgus: mihi flauus Apollo*
> *Pocula Castalia plena ministret aqua.*

Editors often use Marlowe's renowned rendition of the lines as a gloss: 'Let base conceipted witts admire vilde things, | Faire *Phoebus* lead me to the *Muses* springs.'[37] The statement is certainly bold

---

[36] For details on the publication of this volume, see Duncan-Jones and Woudhuysen, *Shakespeare's Poems*, pp. 498–503. The only other documented (albeit still circumstantial) contact between Field and Shakespeare occurred in 1596, when as a resident of Blackfriars Field signed the petition opposing the proposed indoor theatre for Shakespeare's company. For the text of the petition, see E. K. Chambers, *The Elizabethan Stage*, 4 vols. (Oxford, 1923), 4:319–20.

[37] Quoted from Roma Gill, ed., *The Complete Works of Christopher Marlowe*, 5 vols. (Oxford, 1987), 1:35. Marlowe's translation of the *Amores*, the earliest in English, was first published in the late 1590s, most likely between 1594 and 1599. For

and is usually interpreted as a boast whereby Shakespeare claims Ovid as his 'source of inspiration and his guarantor of high cultural status, his way of rising above the "vulgus"'.[38] Ovid's *Amores* as a whole do offer an unabashed celebration of love poetry, and the particular elegy from which Shakespeare's motto is taken does serve as an apt introduction to *Venus and Adonis*. In context, the lines appear in one of the programmatic poems in which Ovid's poetic persona both defends and declares the power of poetry. In elegy 1.15, addressed 'Ad invidos' [to those who are envious] the poet proclaims 'Thy scope is mortall, mine eternall fame, / That all the world may euer chaunt my name.'[39] This daring declaration certainly suits the image of a Shakespeare consciously crafting his career, albeit perhaps a bit prematurely. Although it does not mark a turn away from drama towards poetry – as Ovid outlines in other elegies – in the lines that follow the motto Ovid's persona dedicates himself once again to the myrtle associated with Venus, rather than the laurel traditionally associated with the poet's crown, thereby providing a fitting gloss for a poem starring the eponymous goddess.[40]

Critics have frequently equated the particular *vulgus* mentioned in the motto with the theatre, reading it as a 'career announcement for the famed man of the theatre's turn from stage to page'.[41] This reading has the benefit of distancing Shakespeare from the collaborative commercial world of the theatre, where he had recently been called an 'upstart Crow'.[42] For readers to make sense of Greene's infamous insult – the young upstart 'is in his owne conceit the onely Shake-scene in a countrey' – Shakespeare must have been a recognizable figure both within and beyond the professional theatrical community. For Shakespeare to mark a transition of some kind by choosing a clever motto would thus also make sense, although it is unlikely he would intend to denigrate the profession (and the audiences) that would eventually secure his livelihood. The theatres were closed due to an extended outbreak of plague when the narrative poems were first published and this has strengthened the notion that Shakespeare intentionally turned to poetry at this time, either for the

prestige it might offer an ambitious writer or for the income an aristocratic patron might provide in the absence of theatrical employment.

A desire for patronage, status or income during the plague years may have prompted Shakespeare to turn to poetry, but to enact any of these desires Shakespeare would have necessarily encountered and depended on a variety of factors out of his control. In Barroll's revisionist account, which resists an orderly and controlled progression to both Shakespeare's oeuvre and his social status, he suggests that, if Shakespeare did want a career as a patronage poet, he seems to have either quickly rejected it or failed to acquire it, since he returned to the business of the theatre in short order.[43] The actor and hitherto unpublished playwright was turned into a poet, but this transformation, which would define him as an author for years to come, was not accomplished single-handedly. Our focus on Shakespeare's personal or financial motivation for writing the poems has caused us to ignore the interests that actually shaped their reception. The motto has traditionally been paired with the signed epistles and characterized as a similarly revelatory assertion of Shakespeare's authorial aspirations and as such it has long played a crucial role in the narratives of his poetic career. However, the motto had a rich history both before and beyond Shakespeare

---

an overview of the tangled publication history, see 1:6–12. Editors often accompany Marlowe's version with a more literal translation: for example, the Arden 3 glosses the lines as 'Let common people gawp at common things: may golden-haired Apollo serve me with his goblets filled from the Castalian waters.'

[38] Jonathan Bate, *Shakespeare and Ovid* (Oxford, 1993), p. 2.

[39] Gill, ed., *Marlowe*, 1:34.

[40] 'About my head be quivering mirtle wound, | And in sad lovers heads let me be found' (Gill, ed., *Marlowe*, 1:35).

[41] Patrick Cheney, *Shakespeare, National Poet-Playwright* (Cambridge, 2004), p. 92.

[42] Robert Greene, *Greenes, Groats-Worth of witte* (1592), F1ᵛ. Muriel Bradbrook once called the motto a 'dignified bid for fame' designed as a direct refutation of this epithet. See 'Beasts and Gods: Greene's *Groats-Worth of Witte* and the Social Purpose of *Venus and Adonis*', *Shakespeare Survey* 25 (Cambridge, 1962), p. 62.

[43] Barroll, 'Privileged Biographies', pp. 8 and 11–13.

and it is more productively approached through a specifically Ovidian cultural tradition that was promulgated by none other than John Harrison and his favourite printer, Richard Field.

The only edition of the *Amores* printed in England had come from the press of Field's master Vautrollier in 1583, during the time Field was serving as his apprentice. Up to that point, English customers would have relied on copies imported from continental publishers such as Christopher Plantin, for whom Vautrollier had briefly worked as an agent.[44] When the production of Latin books in England started to take off, Vautrollier capitalized on the trend by acquiring ten-year patents for a number of authors, including Ovid.[45] Starting in 1582, Vautrollier produced a three-volume set of Ovid's complete works, copying the format of the Plantin editions.[46] The *Amores* appeared in one volume alongside the *Heroides, Ars amatoria* and *Remedia amoris* – that is, all of Ovid's love poetry in a single book. When Vautrollier's patent expired, Harrison and Field retained control of the titles; their first collaboration was in 1589, when Field printed an edition of the *Metamorphoses* for Harrison. Field would reprint the *Amores* for Harrison in 1594, within a year of the appearance of *Venus and Adonis*.

To find his motto, then, Shakespeare would not have had to look any farther than Harrison's shop or Field's printing house. Indeed, we know that Sir John Harington supplied just such a motto to Field a few years later. In the extant printer's copy for *An Anatomie of the Metamorpho-sed Aiax* (1596), we can see Harington once again collaborating with his printer, providing Field with a design for the title-page that included a Latin motto, taken from Horace's *Ars poetica*, that serves as an assertion of poetic licence.[47] Field would have recognized the source for the motto, since he had printed an edition of Horace's works for Harrison a few years prior (although Harington did interpolate a pointed phrase that may have been aimed at his critics).[48] If the aristocratic Harington cannot provide a model for the reception of and status accorded to Shakespeare's poems, his example does illustrate how Shakespeare may have

chosen his motto in collaboration with his printer. Both Field and Harrison surely approved of the choice of the motto: Field and his compositors were intimately familiar with Ovid's work and the motto's explicit association with the tradition of Ovidian love poetry would prove propitious for Harrison, who was primarily responsible for propagating this tradition in England. While writers often supplied a motto to their printer, it was common for the printer or the publisher – whose financial stake in a book was the greatest – to design the title-page, since they were often used as advertisements. As the publisher of *Lucrece*, Harrison may have dictated the design of its title-page, which was nearly identical to *Venus and Adonis*, making the two poems a distinctly matched set. Advertising and branding Shakespeare as an Ovidian poet would be a shrewd business tactic for Harrison but this brand would also have a profound impact on Shakespeare's poetic reputation.

Jonathan Bate has remarked that Shakespeare's two narrative poems are 'self-conscious Renaissance exercises in the imitation and amplification of Ovid' that 'demand to be read side by side

---

44 See Colin Clair, 'Christopher Plantin's Trade-Connexions with England and Scotland', *Library*, 5th ser., 14 (1950), 28–45, esp. pp. 31–2.

45 Vautrollier was granted the patent on 19 June 1574 (Arber, *Transcript*, 2:746–7). The best account of the patents remains T. W. Baldwin, *William Shakspere's Small Latine and Lesse Greeke*, 2 vols. (Urbana, 1944), 1:494–527.

46 See Baldwin, *Small Latine*, 1:512. Léon Voet remarks that Plantin 'often published the works of Ovid, each time in a number of volumes (generally three), which could be sold separately'. See *The Plantin Press 1555–1589: A Bibliography of the Works Printed and Published by Christopher Plantin at Antwerp and Leiden*, 6 vols. (Amsterdam, 1980–2), 4:1720.

47 BL Add. MS 46468, fol. 45ʳ.

48 As it appears on the title-page, Harington's motto reads as follows:

> Inuide quid mordes? Pictoribus at*que*; Poetis.
> Quidlibet audendi semper fuit aequa potestas.

The first phrase – 'Inuide quid mordes?' – does not appear in the *Ars poetica*. Cf. the edition Field printed for Harrison, *Quincti Horatii Flacci Poemata* (1592), Viijʳ. The remainder of the motto states that 'Painters and poets have always enjoyed an equal right to dare to do whatever they will.'

with the narratives upon which they improvise'.[49] And so they were, in the bookshop of John Harrison. Customers who expressed an interest in *Venus and Adonis* would be able to find not only the source for the poem in the *Metamorphoses* but a volume of Ovid's collected love poetry as well. The White Greyhound thus served as a nexus in which a nascent vernacular Ovidianism coexisted with the Latin originals that inspired it. But would customers in Harrison's shop, whether retail purchasers or other stationers, have been familiar enough with the *Amores* to recognize the source of the quotation and hence its significance for Shakespeare's poetic persona? Harrison could of course have made the connection clear to potential customers, but it is doubtful they needed to rely on a clever bookseller. As T. W. Baldwin noted, Ovid's elegy 1.15 served as a preface to Octavianus Mirandula's *Illustrium poetarum flores* (generally referred to as the *Flores poetarum*), an immensely popular printed commonplace book that was used in grammar schools throughout Europe.[50] In the *Flores*, the confrontational title 'Ad inuidos' is replaced by 'De Laude Carminum' [In praise of song], although the rest of the title remains the same: 'quod fama Poetarum sit perennis: ex Ouidii Eleg. lib. I' [that the fame of the poets is perennial, from Ovid, *Elegies*, Book I]. The text of the elegy follows, with one extraordinarily visible omission: the final six lines of the elegy are not printed.[51] The poem thus ends with the very couplet that appeared on the titlepage of *Venus and Adonis*, and its appearance in the *Flores* would ensure that anyone who had used this ubiquitous book would be likely to recognize the source of the lines.

Shakespeare's fate as a printed poet was inextricably tied to Ovid's fame – a fame sustained and exploited by Harrison, but a fame which was also far from uncontested in late Elizabethan England. Ovid enjoyed a reputation as a notoriously salacious author and so to be branded an Ovidian poet invoked particular cultural debates about the literary and ethical merits of this sensational classical antecedent. The year before Vautrollier first printed Ovid's love poetry on English soil,

the Privy Council actually approved a ban on teaching Ovid in schools, although it was manifestly unsuccessful.[52] Indeed, Ovidian poetry famously thrived in the 1590s and Shakespeare was seen as perhaps its leading representative, due to the runaway success of *Venus and Adonis*. The

---

[49] Bate, *Shakespeare and Ovid*, p. 83.

[50] Baldwin, *Small Latine*, 2:410. The *Illustrium*, a revision of Mirandula's earlier commonplace book *Viridarium illustrium poetarum*, was in print by 1538, and has been labelled by Ann Moss 'the most successful commonplace book of all time'. *Printed Commonplace Books and the Structuring of Renaissance Thought* (Oxford, 1996), p. 189. Although it was not printed in England until 1598, copies imported from the continent were widely available throughout the sixteenth century. Copies of 'Flores Poetarum' appear in seven inventories of Oxford scholars, dating from 1560 to 1586, in *Private Libraries in Renaissance England*, ed. R. J. Fehrenbach and Elisabeth Leedham-Green, 6 vols. (Binghamton, NY, 1992–2004), 3:181, 4:12, 5:7, 5:43, 5:89, 6:100, 6:235. Copies also appear in eighteen Cambridge inventories, dating from 1538 to 1609, in *Books in Cambridge Inventories*, ed. Elisabeth Leedham-Green, 2 vols. (Cambridge, 1986), 2:350. In the Latin comedy *Pedantius*, a satire on the academic pretensions of Gabriel Harvey performed at Trinity College, Cambridge, in 1581 (but not published until 1631), the title figure is mocked for relying on his '*Floribus Poetarum*' (F9[r]), and a frontispiece illustration shows a copy of 'Flores Poet' on the bookshelf of Pedantius. As part of their notorious quarrel, Harvey accused Thomas Nashe of relying too much on 'his good olde *Flores Poetarum*' in *Foure Letters* (1592), E2[v]. The book remained popular, especially in grammar schools, for educational treatises beginning with John Brinsley's *Ludus Literarius* (1612) listed the *Flores* among books suitable for use well into the seventeenth century.

[51] Most of the continental editions I have examined omit the final lines of the poem; however, the 1588 Antwerp edition in the British Library (11355.a.9) does print the entire poem, and thus does not end on the motto. The printer of the first English edition, Thomas Creede, must have used a continental edition that did omit the final lines for his copy, for his edition also ends on the couplet that served as the motto. However, there is one important variant in the lines as they appear in Mirandula: 'populus' is used, rather than 'vulgus', the reading that appears in every manuscript witness and in printed editions of the *Amores*, including the one produced by Field and Harrison, which confirms that their edition was likely the direct source for the motto. See E. J. Kenney, ed., *P. Ovidii Nasonis Amores, Medicamina Faciei Femineae, Ars Amatoria, Remedia Amoris* (Oxonii, 1961; rpt. 1994), p. 36.

[52] See Baldwin, *Small Latine*, 1:111–2.

density of allusions to both *Venus and Adonis* and its companion piece *Lucrece* demonstrates the extent to which Shakespeare was recognized as a distinctly Ovidian poet.[53] By the end of the decade, identifying Shakespeare with Ovid had quite literally become a commonplace, as the oft-quoted phrase of Francis Meres attests.[54] Shakespeare was not alone, though, for he was not the only one to claim an affinity for his favourite, widely circulated Ovidian elegy. Selections from Marlowe's translation of the *Amores* – including elegy 1.15 – were in print by 1599, when the volume in which they appeared was mentioned by name in the Bishops' Ban.[55] In the first scene of Jonson's *Poetaster*, Ovid himself quotes Marlowe's version of elegy 1.15, making a few conscious revisions along the way.[56] *Poetaster* epitomizes the contemporary literary debate over the appropriate classical precedent for vernacular poetry: Ovid is rejected by the play's end, while Jonson figures himself as Horace, thereby choosing to follow a different model. While the vogue for Ovidian epyllia had waned by the time of *Poetaster*, the popularity of Shakespeare's *Venus and Adonis* continued unabated and the motto remained, as it had been, a standard poetic commonplace that was identified with, but not exclusively connected to, Shakespeare.[57]

Shakespeare's fame may have spread far and wide, aided by the notoriety of his Ovidian slogan, but the primary location of his poetry stayed the same. John Harrison published the fourth edition of *Venus and Adonis* in the first half of 1596, before he assigned his rights to the title to William Leake, on 25 June.[58] That same year Harrison moved from the White Greyhound, in St Paul's churchyard, to a shop in nearby Paternoster Row, which he also called the White Greyhound.[59] Harrison kept shop there until he retired, in about 1614, during which time he published *Lucrece* an additional four times, making it one of the most profitable books of his career.[60] He sold *Venus and Adonis* at the height of its initial popularity, perhaps as a way to extract a good price for the rights; the transfer could also have been part of a larger transaction, since Leake took over Harrison's shop in

the churchyard, which he continued to call the Greyhound. Leake would move to a much larger shop two doors down, the Holy Ghost, in 1602, but he held on to *Venus and Adonis* at his new location until he retired.[61] At the turn of the century, there was no stationer more closely identified with Shakespeare than William Leake: in 1599, the year he first published *Venus and Adonis*, he also served as the bookseller for William Jaggard's collection of poetry, *The Passionate Pilgrime*, which he attributed to Shakespeare. This collection, which infamously intersperses a few genuine Shakespearian compositions with several spuriously ascribed to him, includes a number of poems which plainly imitate *Venus and Adonis*. The attempt to capitalize

---

53 See Sasha Roberts, *Reading Shakespeare's Poems in Early Modern England* (Basingstoke, 2003).

54 In his printed commonplace book, *Palladis Tamia* (1598), Meres wrote that 'As the soule of *Euphorbus* was thought to liue in *Pythagoras*: the sweet wittie soule of Ouid liues in mellifluous & hony-tongued *Shakespeare*, witness his *Venus*, and *Adonis*, his *Lucrece*, his sugred Sonnets among his priuate friends' (Oo1ᵛ). On Shakespeare's poems as sources for commonplacing, see Chartier and Stallybrass, 'Reading and Authorship', pp. 43–55.

55 Marlowe's translations were published together with the epigrams of Sir John Davies in a volume called *Epigrammes and Elegies. By I.D. and C.M.* For the order banning the book by name, see Arber, *Transcript*, 3:677–8.

56 *Poetaster* (1602), A4ᵛ. Jonson's rendition was printed directly after Marlowe's in the revised, complete edition of his translation, *All Ovids Elegies*.

57 For example, a version of the motto would appear much later on the title-page of John Day's *The Parliament of Bees* (1641), as well as on Robert Baron's collection of poetry *Pocula Castalia* (1650), the title of which alludes to a phrase from the motto.

58 Arber, *Transcript*, 3:65.

59 See *STC*, 3:77.

60 On 1 March 1614, Harrison transferred his four most dependable titles to Roger Jackson: *Lucrece*, Leonard Mascall's *The Government of Cattell* (published by Harrison in five editions), Robert Record's *The Ground of Artes* (twelve editions), and Arthur Dent's phenomenally popular *A Sermon of Repentance* (twenty-two editions). See Arber, *Transcript*, 3:542.

61 On the location of these bookshops, see Peter W. M. Blayney, *The Bookshops in Paul's Cross Churchyard* (London, 1990), pp. 28–31 and 33–4.

on the popularity and profitability of Shakespeare and his signature poem would be unmistakable – and all the more successful – in Leake's shop.[62] Leake's investment in Shakespeare would continue to pay dividends, both for himself and for one of his more dubious associates, Robert Raworth, who apparently pirated the undeniably profitable poem sometime around 1607.[63] Leake retained the rights to the poem until 1617, by which time it had been published six times under his auspices.[64]

Throughout his life, then, Shakespeare's poetry was owned and sold by stationers working at the sign of the Greyhound. These Shakespearian smash hits would have been available in any number of locations: as the principal investors and primary booksellers, Harrison and Leake would have been as interested in wholesale distribution as in retail sales. Shifting our focus to the Greyhound, as a crucial site for and representative of the continued circulation of Shakespeare's poetry, thus allows us to see the importance of that circulation, beyond the originary moment that has traditionally held our attention. By the time of his death in 1616, the two poems had appeared in a total of fifteen editions, ensuring his enduring reputation as a popular poet in print. In turn, Shakespeare's reputation provided a return on the stationers' prolonged and extensive investment, helping to ensure their own livelihood. As a published author, Shakespeare was known first and foremost as a poet, and the popularity of his poetry, particularly *Venus and Adonis*, inflected both his authorial reputation and the reception of his works – including his plays – for some time.[65] The initial impulse and authorial aspiration belonged to Shakespeare, but once he turned over his poems to Field's printing house (and reaped whatever momentary reward he might have received from Southampton) they belonged to the book trade, where they thrived, inside and undoubtedly beyond the White Greyhound. The poems may not have done much to enrich Shakespeare financially – his fortune was made in writing for the stage – but they continued to enhance his fame long after the brief moment of artistic inspiration in which he composed them.

SHAKESPEARE'S CAREER

In the dedicatory epistle to *Venus and Adonis*, Shakespeare promised the Earl of Southampton '*some grauer labour*', a promise that he presumably fulfilled the following year with *Lucrece*. The phrase does not necessarily demand this explanation; Shakespeare may or may not have been referring specifically to *Lucrece* and his description was not unanimously accepted. Dressed in similarly sparse title-pages and anchored firmly in an Ovidian source, the two poems were often read as analogously ardent examples of Shakespeare's work. If interpreted as Shakespeare's characterization of *Lucrece*, though, the epithet can become a rare and valuable statement about the trajectory of his own career, revealing his intent to turn towards the *gravi numero* that Ovid's *Amores* had explicitly rejected.[66] Critics have generally taken Shakespeare's hint, placing *Lucrece* in strict opposition to its more notorious precursor – John Roe,

---

[62] See Joseph Quincy Adams, *The Passionate Pilgrim* (New York and London, 1939), pp. xi–xv. Both volumes were published twice in 1599. When Jaggard reissued his collection in 1612 – without Leake's involvement – he made sure to retain the close connection to *Venus and Adonis*, advertising it as *The Passionate Pilgrime. Or Certaine Amorous Sonnets, betweene Venus and Adonis, newly corrected and augmented.*

[63] See Harry Farr, 'Notes on Shakespeare's Printers and Publishers with Special Reference to the Poems and *Hamlet*', *Library*, 4th ser., 3 (1923), 225–60, esp. pp. 229–45. See also Chartier and Stallybrass, 'Reading and Authorship', p. 38.

[64] On 16 February 1617, Leake assigned most of his titles, including *Venus and Adonis*, to William Barrett, the subsequent occupant of the Holy Ghost. See Arber, *Transcript*, 3:603; and Blayney, *Bookshops*, p. 34.

[65] For example, in the address to the readers included in the second issue of *The Famous Historie of Troylus and Cresseid* (1609), the publishers Richard Bonion and Henry Walley remark that '*such sauored salt of witte is in his* [Shakespeare's] *Commedies, that they seeme (for their height of pleasure) to be borne in that sea that brought forth* Venus' (¶2ʳ).

[66] The opening line of the *Amores* begins 'Arma gravi numero', a clever nod to the opening line of Virgil's *Aeneid*; however, Ovid rejects the 'gravi numero' of epic in favour of writing love poetry. See J. C. McKeown, *Ovid: Amores: Text, Prolegomena and Commentary*, 4 vols. (Leeds, 1989), 2:11–12.

for instance, calls it the 'antithesis' of *Venus and Adonis*.[67]

There are other reasons to make such a distinction, some of which may have originated with Shakespeare, most noticeably the prose argument that prefaces *Lucrece*. Derived from Livy, the argument emphasizes the political implications of Tarquin's crime ('*the state gouernment changed from Kings to Consuls*') rather than the travails of its protagonist, implications that have recently been attended to with increasing frequency. The echoes of *Lucrece* found in some of Shakespeare's later and more mature efforts such as *Hamlet* and *Macbeth* have further amplified the poem's significance to our view of Shakespeare and his creative process. The late play *Cymbeline* presents only the most obvious example: Imogen falls asleep reading Ovid's tale of Tereus and Philomela, a model for *Lucrece*, and, although he does not rape her, the intruder Iachimo does compare himself to Tarquin.[68] The story of Lucretia circulated in a startling number of forms (including Ovid's *Fasti*), so this is not necessarily a specific allusion to Shakespeare's own *Lucrece*, but the recurrence of an Ovidian myth that Shakespeare had explored in a lengthy poem written a decade and a half earlier may indicate that it was an enduring preoccupation of his career. *Venus and Adonis*, on the other hand, has generally been portrayed as the exuberant work of a relative novice, to the extent that the '*first heire of my inuention*' was once read quite literally as referring to Shakespeare's first composition, thereby dating the poem to his Warwickshire youth.

As a result of the recent Arden 3 and Oxford editions, which offer and embody powerful arguments for the value of and connections among all of Shakespeare's poems, this state of affairs is beginning to change.[69] *Venus and Adonis* and *Lucrece* are again companions of a sort, this time as the centrepieces of an accomplished non-dramatic oeuvre (including the sonnets and other occasional poems) that was recognized as such in Shakespeare's own time, if perhaps for different reasons than they are today. The poems can no longer be viewed as an early interlude in Shakespeare's theatrical career that merely prefigures concerns he would more fully develop later for the stage; rather, they are complex creations in their own right that reveal to us a Shakespeare imaginatively, and perhaps professionally, interested in poetry. This is a valuable corrective, one with the advantage of conforming more closely to Shakespeare's reputation among his contemporaries, reversing years of neglect by claiming the poems as a vital part of the Shakespearian canon. But it does have the potential to simply reinscribe a version of the traditional biographical narrative. It is an account that results not just from an editorial decision, historical investigation or critical deduction, for it also depends on an underlying sanction by Shakespeare himself. If Shakespeare authorized the printing of his first forays into poetry, then he has told us that he cared about print publication, and that he self-consciously helped to bring it about. Authorization becomes revelation; Shakespeare expediently endorses – and indeed shares – our own critical investment in and definition of his literary career.

The man to whom Shakespeare entrusted his poems thus remains indispensable, particularly if we can attribute an acknowledgement of his importance to Shakespeare himself. And there is one final detail from *Cymbeline* that is commonly read as Shakespeare's expression of gratitude to Richard Field, a tribute to the putative friend and fellow townsman who helped him launch his life's work. Imogen disguises herself as a page in order to avoid capture, calling herself 'Fidele'. Upon finding the decapitated body of Cloten, she mistakes

---

67 John Roe, ed., *The Poems*, The New Cambridge Shakespeare (Cambridge, 1992; updated edn 2006), p. 21.

68 Speaking of himself, Iachimo says that 'Our Tarquin thus / Did softly press the rushes, ere he waken'd / The chastity he wounded' (2.2.12–14); upon finding the sleeping Imogen's book he says that 'She hath been reading late, / The tale of Tereus, here the leaf's turn'd down / Where Philomel gave up' (2.2.44–5).

69 Burrow considers his edition a 'physical encouragement to readers to think about these poems together, and to explore what they might have in common' (*Complete Sonnets and Poems*, p. 2), and Duncan-Jones and Woodhuysen write that 'we believe the poems to be so closely connected' that 'we discuss them in tandem . . . rather than dealing with them sequentially' (*Shakespeare's Poems*, p. 1).

him for her beloved Posthumus. When confronted by this grisly scene, the Roman general Lucius asks 'Fidele' who the dead man was; she answers that this was her former master, a 'very valiant Briton' named 'Richard du Champ' (4.2.371, 379). The name received little attention until the 1950s, when it was suggested that 'Richard du Champ', which translates as 'Richard of the field', was an allusion to the Stratford-born printer.[70] 'Fidele' is the French term for 'faithful', chosen by Imogen to represent her own faithfulness to Posthumus, and Lucius remarks that 'Thy name well fits thy faith' (4.2.383), so there is some indication of wordplay here.[71] Richard Field used a literal translation of his name, 'Ricardo del Campo', in the imprint of several Spanish works he printed, and he was not averse to altering the location of his shop in the imprints for other foreign language books (although he never translated his own name into French or into any language other than Spanish).[72] That Field's first wife Jacqueline was French has only strengthened this identification. If this was an allusion or private joke on Shakespeare's part, it is somewhat surprising, a headless corpse being a rather unexpected substitute for an apparently close friend. The names of characters in *Cymbeline* do often hold special significance, and so 'Richard du Champ' does invite us to try to undo the puzzle, but Shakespeare's printer is by no means the most plausible answer. It is more likely a generic name with chivalric or militaristic connotations ('champ' was a term used for the field of battle),[73] a sober acknowledgement of the position and appearance of the body (it is on the ground and has been strewn with flowers),[74] or an evocation of a biblical metaphor that recurs throughout the scene ('The ground that gave them first has them again' (4.2.291)).[75]

That such a tenuous reference, indeed an almost wilful misreading, has gained acceptance points once again to Richard Field's standing in our critical consciousness and the lengths to which we will go to keep him there. The idea that Shakespeare would allude to Field in this way is desirable because it reaffirms his prominent role in Shakespeare's life, thereby providing coherence to an

otherwise fragmentary and resistant record: years after *Venus and Adonis* and *Lucrece* appeared,

---

[70] Robert J. Kane first published this suggestion in '"Richard du Champ" in *Cymbeline*', *Shakespeare Quarterly*, 4 (1953), 206. The allusion was independently discovered by Nosworthy, and noted in his Arden 2 edition that first appeared two years later; see his note to 4.2.377. Wilson, Rickard and Meek take this apparent allusion to Field as the central conceit in their editorial introduction to *Shakespeare's Book*.

[71] On the importance of names in *Cymbeline*, see John Pitcher, 'Names in *Cymbeline*', *Essays in Criticism*, 43 (1993), 1–16.

[72] The most thorough treatment of the early modern penchant for punning on translations of one's name is found in Laurie Maguire, *Shakespeare's Names* (Oxford, 2007), esp. pp. 34–5 for an analysis of Richard Field and his translated imprints. Woodfield discusses the Spanish imprints of Field and several other stationers (*Surreptitious Printing*, pp. 38–9).

[73] *OED* s.v. 'champ', (*n.*[1]), 1. Martin Butler, in his New Cambridge edition, notes that the name 'suggests the kind of knight regularly met with in Elizabethan dramatic romance – a chivalric anachronism in this context' (*Cymbeline* (Cambridge, 2005), p. 199). Likewise, Maurice Hunt suggests that the name is used by Imogen to express her regard for Posthumus: 'Giving her husband a knight's name, Imogen in a verbal phrase confers upon him the honor that his deeds in battle will show that he deserves' (*Shakespeare's Romance of the Word* (Lewisburg, PA, 1990), p. 64). In William Camden's *Remains of a Greater Worke, Concerning Britain* (1605; STC 4521), the name 'Richard' is defined as an 'antient Christian name' that signified 'Powerfull and rich disposition' or 'Powerfull in the Armie' (K3r). Cf. Richard A. Coates, though, who argues that the name connotes rusticity and prefigures the peasant disguise Posthumus later assumes, thus confirming the recurrent association of Posthumus with a non-aristocratic world. See 'A Personal Name Etymology and a Shakespearean Dramatic Motiv', *Names*, 24 (1976), 4.

[74] Belarius, Guiderius and Arviragus lay both Cloten and 'Fidele' on the ground, strewing them with flowers in a funereal ritual. Jodi Mikalachki reads the name as an analogy between the dead body and the ground in 'The Masculine Romance of Roman Britain: *Cymbeline* and Early Modern English Nationalism', *Shakespeare Quarterly*, 46 (1995), 319. Shakespeare used 'champaign', a variant of 'champ' that signified a field or open countryside, in *Lucrece*: 'a goodly champaine plaine' (I2v); in the First Folio *King Lear*: 'Champains rich'd | With plenteous Riuers' (TLN 69–70); and *Twelfth Night*: 'daylight and champain discouers not more' (TLN 1163–4). Cf. *OED*, s.v. 'champaign (*n.* and *a.*)', A.1–4.

[75] See Naseeb Shaheen, *Biblical References in Shakespeare's Plays* (Newark and London, 1999), pp. 708–11. Cf., for instance, Genesis 3:19, 'dust thou art and unto dust shall thou return', which is alluded to in the Burial Service of the Book of Common Prayer ('earth to earth, ashes to ashes, dust to

Shakespeare remains grateful to the man responsible for first putting them into print, thus starting him on the path to what was at the time an already considerable fame. It is telling, though, that one of the first to suggest this unlikely explanation was an editor of *Cymbeline* keen to prove that the oft-maligned play was indeed the product of Shakespeare's 'single creative activity'.[76] Once again Richard Field was used to confirm a preconceived, decidedly romantic notion of Shakespeare. At the same time, this narrative completely ignores the two stationers who, at the time Shakespeare wrote *Cymbeline*, actually remained responsible for publishing and selling Shakespeare's poems. Shakespeare's fame as a poet continued to be circulated and sustained by John Harrison and William Leake, who have been disregarded due to the distinct disadvantage of not having shared a hometown, or even an identifiable personal connection, with Shakespeare.

While we may no longer find it critically or theoretically tenable to speak of Shakespeare's 'single creative activity', the curiosity about and desire to explain it remains unabated, as the recent abundance of Shakespeare biographies attests. Biography does not, and indeed cannot, focus solely on the individual; however, even biographies which take the subject as the nexus of a broad array of cultural forces inevitably privilege a single agent to the exclusion of other agencies, whether individual or institutional. The structure of conventional biographies tends to subordinate and conflate the intentions of other historical actors with those of Shakespeare, producing a teleological narrative in which they play predetermined roles in the authorial career that brought them to our attention in the first place. It is only when the biographical impulse is allowed to appropriate the authority of other forms of history that it can become a hindrance,

by reproducing a familiar story through different means, to the exclusion of other stories of equal, if not greater, importance. The critical attention given to collaboration, both in the playhouse and the printing house, has changed – and will continue to change – the way we look at Shakespeare, as it challenges us to suspend belief in some of the powerfully attractive myths that surround him. But it has also evoked a compelling nostalgia for a more romantic, or at least a more firmly individuated, Shakespeare that is incompatible with the collaborative processes responsible for the creation of his authorial persona. My goal here has been to place one of these myths in the wider context provided by the early modern book trade, in order to provide an account of Richard Field's contribution to Shakespeare's career that is fairer to the printer's potential interests, and to recover the contributions of other stationers whose endeavours have been less evident, although no less essential. The financial investment of stationers such as Harrison and Leake has in part made possible our intellectual investment in Shakespeare. Attending to all of the factors that fashioned Shakespeare into an author need not reduce or diminish our appreciation of his art or his ambition. On the contrary, by doing so we gain a richer understanding of Shakespeare's value in his own time – and in our own.

---

dust'). Further echoes occur in this scene: 'So man and man should be; / But clay and clay differs in dignity, / Whose dust is both alike' (3–5); 'though mean and mighty, rotting / Together, have one dust' (246–7); and Arviragus asks Guiderius to help 'sing him [Fidele] to th'ground' (236), and the dirge's refrain is 'come to dust' (263, 269, 275).

76 J. M. Nosworthy, 'The Integrity of Shakespeare: Illustrated from *Cymbeline*', *Shakespeare Survey 8* (Cambridge, 1955), 52.

DARK MATTER: SHAKESPEARE'S FOUL DENS AND FORESTS

CHARLOTTE SCOTT

The forest in literature has a long humanist history. It dates from classical Greek and Roman writers to Hellenistic/Jewish philosophers and is reiterated through subsequent Christian texts and allegories.[1] The space of the forest as a setting was a popular place on the Elizabethan stage. The anonymous *Mucedorus*, in which the forest is central to the drama, was played frequently during the 1590s and revised in 1610; there are numerous references to 'trees' in the accounts for the Office of the Revels; and the tree or collection of trees often appears in plays that do not demand such scenic props.[2] Many of the allusions in Shakespeare's forests are Ovidian and particularly refer to Books IV and VI of the *Metamorphoses* and the tales of Pyramus and Thisbe and Tereus and Philomel.[3] But the forest can also represent a version of the pastoral, as exemplified in *Mucedorus*, as a place that supports the exploration of antithesis (the savage and the civilized), and the juxtaposition of containment and imagination. Although Shakespeare's forests are much indebted to this tradition and its translation by other contemporary Elizabethan writers, including Spenser, this article argues that there is something more parochial, more urgent, at work in Shakespeare's forests on stage. Such parochialism draws us back to how Elizabethan forests were being used, as well as abused, and how the forest stood in relation to the rest of the social community. The forest is not a comprehensive landscape; rather, it emerges as a habitat for multiple voices, which occupy a transitional space – literally and metaphorically – between action and thought. This space is haunted by the forest's history of danger, punishment and pleasure.[4] The following argument maintains that the Elizabethan forest is defined not as a physically bounded space but as a discursive construct,

---

[1] The forest's history is long and complex and my primary concern here is with Shakespeare's representational use of such a space. Forthcoming and recent work on this subject includes Anne Barton's book-length project on Shakespeare's forests; Jeanne Roberts's 'Falstaff in Windsor Forest: Villain or Victim', *Shakespeare Quarterly*, 26 (1975), 8–15, and *The Shakespearean Wild: Geography, Genus, and Gender* (Lincoln and London, 1991); Michael Pincombe's essay 'Classical and Contemporary Sources of the "Gloomy woods" of *Titus Andronicus*: Ovid, Seneca, Spenser', in John Batchelor, Tom Cain and Claire Lamont, eds., *Shakespearean Continuities: Essays in Honour of E. A. J. Honigmann* (London, 1997), pp. 40–55; Robert Watson's *Back to Nature, the Green and the Real in the Late Renaissance* (Philadelphia, 2006), esp. pp. 77–107; E. Thompson Shields Jr's 'Imagining the Forest: Longleaf Pine Eco-Systems in Spanish and English Writings of the South East, 1542–1709', in Ivo Kamps and Karen Raber, eds., *Early Modern Ecostudies: From the Florentine Codex to Shakespeare* (New York and Basingstoke, 2009), pp. 251–68; and, in the same collection, Todd Andrew Borlik's 'Mute Timber: Fiscal Forestry and Environmental Stichomythia in the *Old Arcadia*', pp. 33–54.

[2] On stage properties see G. F. Reynolds, '"Trees" on the Stage of Shakespeare', *Modern Philology*, 5 (1907), 153–68.

[3] In Book VI of Golding's translation of *Metamorphoses*, Philomel's beauty is compared to the fairies, who 'haunt' 'the pleasant woods and water springs'; 'yet in beautie far more riche' she delights the eye and desire of Tereus (VI, 579). Bent on his violent lust, Tereus takes her to 'woods forgewen', the 'shadie woods' (VI, 664, 807), and after the terrible deed, Philomel tells her assailant: 'If thou keepe me still / As prisoner in these woods, my voyce the verie woods shall fill, / And make the stones to understand' (VI, 698–8), *XV Books of Ovid's* Metamorphoses (London, 1567).

[4] Robert Pogue Harrison, in *Forests: The Shadow of Civilisation* (Chicago and London, 1992), explores the social and philosophical relations between disforestation and institutional order.

a linguistic practice that was subject to shifting civil and legal pressures. An examination of an influential Elizabethan treatise on the forest suggests that the concern is primarily with the use of and behaviour within the forest, rather than its organic matter. Shakespeare's shady landscapes are not dependent on their allegorical precedents but belong to an emerging, Elizabethan preoccupation with language: of orientation, of order, of emotion and of possession. The forest space trials a moral economy that will, as we move into the seventeenth century, become much more defined as a social landscape.[5] For the Elizabethans, however, the forest was a place of exploration that stood in conversation with the social world but also in conflict with it.

In 1598 John Manwood published a book entitled *A Treatise of the Lawes of the Forest*. Manwood was a legal writer, an MP for Sandwich, a gamekeeper for Waltham Forest and a justice for New Forest. Manwood's book was the first major book on the subject, although it was indebted to two widely circulated Inns of Court readings which had preceded it.[6] In an exposition to the reader, Manwood declares that not only does such a treatise contribute to the 'common good' but that it is necessary because the forests are so neglected and trespassed and that the laws 'are grown clean out of knowledge . . . partly, for want of use, and partly by reason that there is very little or nothing extant of it in any treatise by it self'.[7] Manwood sets out to redress this in his re-presentation of the forest laws and those who regulate them. He explains their place as the privilege of the king, their role in maintaining a landscape for hunting that is free from poaching or encroachment, and their symbolic value as demarcating a space that is distinct from common law and supported by custom. Manwood dedicates his book to Charles Howard, Earl of Nottingham, Knight of the Garter and, among other things, chief justice of the Queen's Forest south of the Trent. For Manwood the forests are abused through ignorance and stupidity and we are 'as well to revive in memory these laws being so ancient and learned prerogative laws, as also to satisfy the fond opinions and blind conceits that such

unlearned men do hold'.[8] Manwood's *Treatise* is a unique record not so much of the landscape of the forest but of the attitudes it absorbs and the emotions it sustains. He declares the space to be both discrete and ideal, since it represents and contains a unique order that works on the basis of pleasure (the king's hunting), punishment (the, often savage, penalties for breaking those laws), hierarchy (the system of justice that recognizes authority only in the shape of the monarch or nobleman) and reward (in the resurrection of 'history' as the path to 'merry' England).[9] Manwood reveals a much darker side to the maintenance of that pleasure, a darkness that emerges through pain, punishment, animal mutilation and an uncompromising 'justice' system based on the whim of a single authority.[10] Whatever crime is committed the perpetrator is turned over to the king, who deals with him or her at his will:

There is no certain fine set down for the same by the Laws of the Forest, but only that the same fine is arbitrable at the will and pleasure of the king.[11]

---

5 The metaphysical poets often draw on the tree as a way of exploring the relationship between man and his material world: Henry Vaughan, in 'The Book' (1646), for example, follows the tree through its timber to the leaves of a book, through the godly nature of creation and renewal to find faith in nature and nature in faith; Michael Drayton, on the other hand, travels the country in 'Poly-Olbion' (1612) where he looks plaintively at a landscape that has lost the beauty and resources of so much woodland.

6 These were by Richard Tresketh and George Treherne, which, as Baker says in his entry on Manwood for the *DNB*, are 'occasionally cited' by Manwood.

7 John Manwood, *A Treatise and Discourse of the Lawes of the Forrest* (London, 1598), sig.*3r-v.

8 Manwood, *Treatise*, sig.*3r-v.

9 In Manwood's earlier edition, which was printed for private circulation, he is much more explicit about the importance of the history of these laws, *A Briefe Collection of the Lawes of the Forest* (London, 1592), sig. 2.

10 This darker side to the forest emerges, for the most part, in Manwood's description of how forest justice systems should be implemented. The penalties for poaching are hard – dogs can have their paws cut off and men and women who commit any crimes in breach of forest law (including the harming of animals, trespassing, or cutting of timber) will be punished either by 'Imprisonment, Fine or Ransom' (p. 37).

11 Manwood, *Briefe Collection*, p. 47, cf. pp. 125–6.

It is with this arbitrariness, as well as ambiguity, that this article is concerned and the exclusive space that the forest provides for the coexistence of punishment and pleasure, beauty and horror. Although Shakespeare writes at least four plays in which the forest occupies a significant space, it is the woods of *Titus Andronicus* and *A Midsummer Night's Dream* that are most compelling in their exploration of Elizabethan anxieties.[12] Despite their different generic resolutions, *Titus Andronicus* and *A Midsummer Night's Dream* bring their action to a forest in which there is no certainty, moral, social or structural, and tragedy is always nearer than harmony. Invested in questions of authority and order, predicated on theories of pleasure, and haunted by images of abuse and punishment Manwood adumbrates a localized vision of Shakespeare's dramatic landscape. Although there is no doubt as to the classical influences in Shakespeare's forests there is also a more parochial forest in place. As Manwood's text attempts to authorize the Elizabethan forest, so Shakespeare's plays begin to explore it.

When, in *A Midsummer Night's Dream* (1594–6), the lovers return from their night amidst fairies and darkness in 'the wood, a league without the town' (1.1.165), Demetrius declares that 'These things seem small and undistinguishable, / Like far-off mountains turnèd into clouds' (4.1.186–7) and Hermia muses: 'Methinks I see these things with a parted eye / When everything seems double' (4.1.188–9).[13] Where they have been and what they have seen fade and divide as though, in trauma or in trance, they resist remembering. The wood in *A Midsummer Night's Dream*, like the forest in *Titus Andronicus*, is a space for the play's action to retire into horror or fantasy: 'double', 'dreadful', 'desert', 'ruthless', 'shadowy', 'indistinguishable' and 'green', this natural expanse secludes lovers and rapists, murderers and fairies. But the word 'forest' is an ambiguous one, referring to both a physical and a legal space – which were frequently neither the same size nor aspect. The forest could encompass marsh, bog, fen, pasture, cultivated and uncultivated land, as well as patches of woodland. First appearing in English in the fourteenth century to describe a tract of land covered in trees and undergrowth, the term synthesises Old French and Mediaeval Latin words for 'outside' (*forest-em*) or 'out of doors' (*forīs*).[14] According to the *Treatise*, however, what defined the forest was its deer, its ownership and, most significantly, its legal status and social ideology:

A Forest is a certain territory of woody grounds and fruitful pastures, privileged for wild beasts and fowls of forest, chase and warren, to rest and abide in, in the safe protection of the king, for his principal delight and pleasure, which territory of ground, so privileged, is meered and bounded, with unremovable marks, meers, and boundaries, either known by master of record, or else by prescription: And also replenished with wild beasts of venery or chase, and with great coverts of vert, for the succour of the said wild beasts, to have their abode in: for the preservation and continuance of which said place, together with the vert and venison, there are certain particular laws, privileges and officers, belonging to the same, meet for that purpose, that are only proper unto the forest, and not to any other place.[15]

As Manwood seeks definition for the forest, so he also seeks containment, betraying a profound anxiety as to the propriety of this space. Certain aspects of the forest are absolute, relating to who owns it and where the boundaries lie. The forest must contain particular animals – hart, hind, hare, boar and wolf – to be defined as such.[16] As a forest is a 'privileged' area of land, distinct from 'any other place', in which deer are kept as the property of the king or member of the nobility, the laws governing these areas of land extend beyond the wooded tracts of land where deer lived to where they roamed. Manwood's book emphasizes the order of the

---

[12] These are *The Two Gentlemen of Verona*, *Titus Andronicus*, *The Merry Wives of Windsor*, *A Midsummer Night's Dream* and *As You Like It*. In *Macbeth*, Burnham Wood has a very particular role both symbolically and literally.

[13] Shakespeare uses the words *wood* and *forest* interchangeably. The term 'wood', according to the *OED*, applies to 'a collection of trees' larger than a grove but smaller than a forest. The word emerges earlier than the term 'forest', around the eleventh century out of Old English and German.

[14] See the *OED*.

[15] Manwood, *Treatise*, pp. 40–1.

[16] Manwood, *Treatise*, pp. 43–4.

forest; it belongs to the king (or a nobleman), it is defined by its animals for hunting, it is subject to particular laws and its scope is mapped with 'unremovable marks' according to the ranging capacity of its beasts. The boundaries exist, as they are 'either known by master of record, or else by prescription'. Like the term 'privilege', Manwood uses 'prescription' in its legal context, meaning a title or right acquired through uninterrupted use or possession. The forest belongs to those who use it, 'possess' it and understand it. The forest is entirely self-reflexive; as discrete from the rest of the realm and accountable only to the king's will, the forest is a place of fantasy and, for Manwood, much of his fantasy is embedded in a sense of England's history. Yet according to Oliver Rackham's analysis of the forests, Manwood's text is misleading.[17] For Rackham, Manwood's text is a vision of 'merry England' which represents a nostalgic landscape of feudal order and customary relations. But this need to authorize the forest, as well as define it, exposes a relationship between organic and symbolic worlds. The anxiety expressed in Manwood's *Treatise* suggests a shift in the ways in which the landscape functions in relation to the social worlds. Again and again, Manwood tries to address the organic space through the language of possession and terms like 'wild', 'privileged', 'law' and 'sacred' are constantly being traded over the boundaries between the forest and the city.

Manwood's authorization of the forest as a legal space through terms that reflect both the spatial and the social exposes a landscape that appears to threaten as well as reflect its community. More prescient than the imagined forests of myth and metamorphoses, the Elizabethan forest comes to occupy a transitional place in the changing moral economy of the natural world. When, in *A Midsummer Night's Dream*, Egeus begs 'the ancient privilege of Athens' (1.1.41) over Hermia, he does so for the recognition that 'As she is mine, I may dispose of her' (1.1.41). This 'privilege' is a property right which, in Egeus's understanding of Athenian law, allows him to regulate the body of his daughter. However, for Manwood, the term is often used in conjunction with 'sanctuary', which, as Richard

Marienstras observes, alludes to the right of asylum.[18] Like the wood itself Hermia becomes caught up in competing notions of liberty and constraint; in Athenian terms her father's response declares her to be condemned by paternal law, and yet in terms of the wood into which she will enter, to be privileged is to be protected by law. In recognition of the different legal spaces, Manwood writes:

the laws of the forest, the reason and punishment, the pardon, or absolution of offenders, whether the same be pecuniary or corporeal, they are differing from other judgements of the laws of the Realm, and are subject unto the judgements of the king, to determine at his will and pleasure . . . Reason, Punishment, and Pardon shall not be tied to the order of the Common Law of this Realm, but unto the voluntary appointment of the prince; so that the same which by this law in that behalf shall be appointed or determined, may not be accounted or called absolute justice or law, but justice or law according to the laws of the forest.[19]

Whilst 'absolute justice or law' is statutory, the laws of the forest are subject to the 'will and pleasure' of the king.[20] The idea of a single figure of authority regulating and governing the forest space, as distinct from the rest of the realm, presents the forest as an alternative, yet reflective, model of the anthropocentric world. To determine 'Reason', dispense 'Punishment' and grant 'Pardon' within the forest is to allow it to exist as the shadow of the law, as experiential rather than essential. This practice is not, Manwood reminds us, 'absolute justice or law, but justice or law according to the forest'. His caveat makes the forest a rather remarkable place, for it is not fixed; or rather what goes on in the forest is not subject to fixed principles. Only a

---

[17] Oliver Rackham, *Ancient Woodland, its History, Vegetation and Uses in England* (London, 1980), p. 179.

[18] Marienstras notes that this right of asylum extended 'to churches, essentially, and a few sanctuaries': *New Perspectives on the Shakespearean World*, trans. Janet Lloyd (Cambridge, 1985), p. 20.

[19] Manwood, *Treatise*, pp. 486–7.

[20] Forest law is created under statute, despite its apparent fluidity, and is written down in 'a book remaining in the exchequer, called *Liber Rubrus*', Manwood, *Treatise*, p. 486.

recognized figure of authority can determine what the ethical and social codes of the forest are, and until they do so the forest is entirely independent of the community it borders. Manwood betrays an urgent need to demarcate this space; to express the separation if not necessarily to understand it.

Just after the lovers make their pact to escape into 'the wood, a league without the town' (1.1.165), where 'the sharp Athenian law / Cannot pursue us' (1.1.162–3), we become aware of the wood's pre-history: this place is not strange to the couples, since not only have Helena and Hermia spent time there together, but Lysander remembers the wood:

> Where I did meet thee once with Helena
> To do observance to a morn of May (1.1.166–7)

The context of May morning links the lovers to the wood under the auspices of festival and misrule. The wood in *A Midsummer Night's Dream* is frequently given the role of the pastoral or festive escapism; C. L. Barber writes:

The woods are established as a region of metamorphosis, where in liquid moonlight or glimmering starlight, things can change, merge, melt into each other. Metamorphosis expresses both what love sees and what it seeks to do.[21]

The wood becomes a 'literary' forest, a conventional place of projected perception, created by the imagination but endorsed by social fantasy; any materiality that the woods may represent is only necessary in support of the lovers' subjective journey. The wood begins as a region, a place, which requires the lovers to make a journey, but is sustained by the transcendental qualities of that journey. What supports Barber's construction of change is not the woods but perception and a 'glimmering' half-light in which anything can happen. Barber's description presupposes that, in order for metamorphosis to occur, the woods do not occupy or enable any organic, or at least consistent, reality. For Marienstras even when the forest is organic it is also emotional:

In Shakespeare, despite the role played by the forest in *Titus Andronicus*, the important initiatory space is located within man himself (*Hamlet*) or else it is abstract,

topographically ill-defined even if outside the city (*King Lear*, *Timon of Athens*, *Coriolanus*).[22]

Here the wood is a refuge from civil institutions but only as a place for 'licence' rather than destruction. It provides temporary relief from an order to which we must return. The forest endorses an apparently comprehensive notion of 'refuge' ('amorous licence', 'animality', discovery or romance) because it remains a part of human nature rather than in opposition to it. Yet as Manwood seeks to define the forest through its legal status and social bonds, so he also tries to separate the forest from the rest of the community and, indeed, the commonwealth. The Elizabethan forest is not a refuge from the community but a reflection of it, an alternative model of design fraught with the anxiety of status, boundaries, order and responsibility.

Although the wood in *Dream* appears to be an escape from the 'sharp Athenian law', soft with 'faint primrose beds' and sympathetic to the emotions of youth in Oberon's famous description of the bank on which he will lull Titania into 'hateful fantasies', the natural fabric becomes enmeshed in something more sinister:

> I know a bank where the wild thyme blows,
> Where oxlips and the nodding violent grows,
> Quite overcanopied with luscious woodbine,
> With sweet muskroses, and with eglantine.
> There sleeps Titania sometime of the night,
> Lulled in these flowers with dances of delight;
> And there the snake throws her enamelled skin,
> Weed wide enough to wrap a fairy in;
> And with the juice of this I'll streak her eyes
> And make her full of hateful fantasies. (2.1.249–58)

The soporific landscape with which Oberon begins to induce Titania into her corrupted passion turns on the image of the snake. The snake that creeps through gentle beauty and the fairy that wraps itself in the shining skin draws this nature into a

---

[21] C. L. Barber, *Shakespeare's Festive Comedy: A Study of Dramatic Form and its Relation to Social Custom* (Princeton, 1959), p. 133.

[22] Marienstras, *New Perspectives*, p. 15.

fragile paradise or a potential hell. This wood holds the vulnerable to ransom. When Demetrius and Helena enter the wood and find each other, the fabric of the place releases the violence of their determination: Demetrius to reject Helena at all costs, and Helena to subject herself to Demetrius at all costs. Having told Helena to 'Tempt not too much the hatred of my spirit; / For I am sick when I do look on thee' (2.1.211–12), he goes on:

> You do impeach your modesty too much,
> To leave the city and commit yourself
> Into the hands of one that loves you not;
> To trust the opportunity of night,
> And the ill counsel of a desert place,
> With the rich worth of your virginity (2.1.214–19)

Its distance from the city, 'the opportunity of night' and the 'ill counsel of a desert place' makes the wood, in collaboration with Demetrius's hatred, a profoundly hostile environment. It is, however, the idea of isolation that makes the wood so threatening. Demetrius tells Helena of her vulnerability; she is with a man who loathes her in a place that will not protect her. What becomes ambiguous is to what extent the seclusion and darkness of the wood make it a passive bystander to human cruelty or an active collaborator in both violence and hatred. Shakespeare's use of the wood seems to suggest that it moves, often seamlessly, between the two. Dramatic records show that trees and woods were used to invoke solitude and isolation. G. F. Reynolds explains that brutality lurks in,

> the wood scenes of Elizabethan drama, and . . . the scenes supposed to be located in solitary and desert places. In many cases these will coincide – the wood scenes are usually represented as solitary, the solitary scene usually mentions woods. One of the principal characteristics of the Forest of Arden, for instance, is its savagery and solitude.[23]

Reynolds's reference to Arden is not unusual: although an *idea* of the place has predominantly emerged through a Romantic perspective, A. Stuart Daley reminds us that *As You Like It* is dominated by the pastoral, and that sheep husbandry was an extensive Tudor business and, as such, the

Elizabethans would have recognized the different landscapes for grazing and hunting.[24] The Forest of Arden, however, when it appears, only does so in association with Duke Senior:

> Once we distinguish between these two Arden settings, we notice what must be a meaningful set of correspondences or parallels between their constituent elements. One features dark, perilous woods, hunters, native deer (and other, still more emblematic beasts), a brawling brook, and a cave of self-knowing. The other is characterised by sunny fields, shepherds, sheep (and goats), a murmuring steam, and a cottage fenced with olives. These features should suggest a plenitude of classical, Biblical, and Christian symbols.[25]

The coexistence of these two settings is an evocative reminder of the internal relations between comedy and tragedy that the forest space often suggests. Yet alongside the classical and Christian symbols is a more urgent place, the 'dark, perilous woods' that reflect a complex dynamic between punishment and pleasure, violence and entertainment. When Valentine arrives in the forest in search of Silvia, in *The Two Gentlemen of Verona*, he observes 'This shadowy desert, unfrequented woods' as distinct from both custom ('habit') and the 'flourishing peopled towns' (5.4.2, 1, 3). For Valentine this desert place is a release and a relief, and one in which he can 'sit alone, unseen of any, / And to the nightingale's complaining notes / Tune my distress and record my woes' (5.4.4–6). Yet this isolation will soon turn Valentine into an observer of violence, calling us back to the fateful nightingale and the haunting melody of Philomela. Proteus's attempted rape of Silvia reminds us of the potential danger that such isolation holds, and the nightingale sings in the shadows as a reminder of cruelty and violence. Whilst Valentine may see seclusion as a haven, both Demetrius and Proteus find the woods (as Titus calls them) 'deaf' and 'dull'. For these lovers the wood turns a blind eye to their hatred or violent desire, and in covering them in

---

[23] Reynolds, '"Trees" on the Stage of Shakespeare', p. 155.
[24] A. Stuart Daley, 'Where are the Woods in *As You Like It?*', *Shakespeare Quarterly*, 34 (1983), 173.
[25] Daley, 'Where are the Woods', p. 180.

darkness they are (temporarily) separated from the implications of their selves.

Yet the forest that is, at least according to how Titus read his Ovid, 'made for murders and for rapes', is also a refuge for the weary lover and the hunted beloved. Helena's response to Demetrius's threats is to submit herself to their implications; translating force into acquiescence and abuse into privilege, she declares,

Your virtue is my privilege, for that
It is not night when I do see your face;
Therefore I think I am not in the night,
Nor doth this wood lack worlds of company;
For you in my respect are all the world.
Then how can it be said I am alone,
When all the world is here to look on me? (2.1.220–6)

In ecclesiastical law, 'privilege' refers to the exemption from certain civil or canon laws as granted by the pope; in civil law it refers to a set of rights or immunities granted by a legislative body; and in forest law it refers to a certain sanctuary granted by the king. For Helena, Demetrius's virtue will grant her 'privilege' within the wood; in other words, she must believe that he has the virtue to give her sanctuary or safety within the wood and its night. Helena's belief that Demetrius's 'virtue' is her 'privilege' trades her body as the property of his honour, making him both the authority and the owner of the wood to which she submits. Helena's love for Demetrius dissolves any boundaries between honour and horror and transports her private kingdom into a 'detested vale'. Helena's beliefs are fantasy, Demetrius cares little for her 'privilege' or, it seems, her virtue, let alone his own. But as Helena recasts her wood from Demetrius's language of hatred into the topography of asylum, she offers herself as the possessed animal to his hunt. Where Helena makes herself a 'wood of worlds', Demetrius declares himself to be 'wood within this wood' (2.1.192). As Helena finds sanctuary Demetrius feels madness. For the lovers, the wood becomes a semantic landscape through which they can create either empathy or violence. Both lovers look for excuses in their environment and part of what makes the forest such an effective arena for the exploration of emotion – desire and violence, love and hate, loss and recuperation – is the auspice of Nature. Writing of the 'cosmic matrix' that Mother Nature was thought to govern, Robert Pogue Harrison explains:

Under the goddess's reign...earth and sky were not opposed, nor were life and death, animal and human, male and female, inanimate and animate, matter and form, forest and clearing. These unconditional distinctions (which the forest forever confuses) lie at the basis of 'civilisation' as opposed to mere 'culture'.[26]

As the human world seems to import such distinctions, the forest 'confuses' them. This confusion is vital in allowing the forest to support a sympathetic psychological arena for those in distress or seeking disorder. Manwood constantly seeks to manage or even erase this confusion. Paradoxically, his careful delineation of the space makes the forest a self-consciously unstable environment. For Shakespeare the arbitrariness of the Elizabethan forest sustains a dramatic landscape which can chart both journey and emotion. Demetrius tells Helena, 'I'll run from thee and hide me in the brakes, / And leave thee to the mercy of wild beasts' (2.1.227–8), then, 'I will not stay thy questions. Let me go; / Or if thou follow me, do not believe / But I shall do thee mischief in the wood' (2.1.235–7). For Helena, however, the place itself is merely symbolic, since her landscape is manifest only in relation to her beloved; first, she inverts tales from Ovid, 'the story shall be changed: / Apollo flies, and Daphne holds the chase' (2.1.230–1), and then she cries: 'I'll follow thee, and make a heaven of hell, / To die upon the hand I love so well' (2.1.243–4). Helena's 'wood of worlds' is always in motion as her self-reflexive drama takes on its multiple roles. Despite the turmoil of the wood, when Puck travels through it in search of the couples, he admits:

Through the forest I have gone,
But Athenian found I none
On whose eyes I might approve
This flower's force in stirring love.
Night and silence. Who is here? (2.2.72–6)

---

[26] Harrison, *Forests*, p. 19.

Although nature is the hobgoblin's domain, he finds only 'Night and silence'. The inability of the forest to register the prints of its inhabitants makes it a compelling space for the imposition of fantasy. The madness of Helena and Demetrius is erased and silenced by the time Puck travels through the forest's brakes and briars. Manwood similarly constructs a tension between these worlds of wood, between a semantic construction and an organic space. Seeking not only to define and animate but also to create the forests, Manwood repeatedly falls back on constructions of order and authority inherent not in the landscape itself but in organized perception. Where the 'five beasts of the forest' alert us to its status, the forest courts and the king's rights sustain the area through ideas of threat and punishment. The sinister synthesis between the materiality of the forest and how it is perceived pervades *A Midsummer Night's Dream*, *The Two Gentlemen of Verona* and *Titus Andronicus*. Puck's description of the moment Titania wakes to her desire for Bottom, the mechanicals' reaction to their asinine friend and 'Pyramus's translation' culminates in the fairy's delight as he 'led them on in this distracted fear' (3.2.31). The opportunities that both Oberon and Puck take in the forest for humiliation are based on the perversion of love, from the emotional into the absurd, under the cover of night. Inculcating this manufactured desire over the body of Titania, Oberon says,

> What thou seest when thou dost wake,
> Do it for thy true love take;
> Love and languish for his sake.
> Be it ounce, or cat, or bear,
> Pard, or boar with bristled hair,
> In thy eye that shall appear
> When thou wak'st, it is thy dear.
> Wake when some vile thing is near (2.2.33–40)

The pun on deer/dear returns Titania to her forest in abject humiliation. The deer is the only one of the animals that Oberon names that would permit the forest landscape to exist as such, and it is through Titania's manipulated vision that the viable becomes the vile. Oberon will subsequently compare himself to a forester, 'tread[ing]' 'the groves'

'with the morning's love' (3.2.390, 391), returning to the creative status with which his journey into the lives of the mortals began: 'We are their parents and original' (2.1.117).

Much of the arbitrariness of the forest resides in a destabilization of conventional ideas – to be wild is to be the property of the king, to be free is to be subject to different laws, to be secluded is to be under threat, and to be animal is to be safer than to be human. Unlike the park, the meadow or the field, the forest emerges from the language and imperatives of its inhabitants. Yet even if the wood had an authentic fabric or an organic reality it would resist – or at least remain unchanged by – the impositions of its lodgers. As *Dream* draws to a close, we return to the nature of the wood through hunting. Hippolyta and Theseus guide us to the pre-history of this wood where, much like *The Tempest*, the agency of sound charges the landscape to appear:

> Go, one of you, find out the forester;
> For now our observation is performed;
> And since we have the vanguard of the day,
> My love shall hear the music of my hounds.
> Uncouple in the western valley; let them go.
> Dispatch, I say, and find the forester.
> We will, fair Queen, up to the mountain's top,
> And mark the musical confusion
> Of hounds and echo in conjunction. (4.1.102–10)

As Theseus releases his hounds we are drawn back to the woods of man's nature, the woods of hunting, and the voice of Echo forever haunting the air with her love-lost cries. The majesty of the place is animated by the history of voices and the man-made 'privileges' in the creation of the 'wild'.

As Barber notes, there is little 'nature' in *Dream*, and what does come to us emerges through an interplay between the pathetic imagination and anthropomorphism. Similarly, the 'wood' is manifest as a place in which there may be 'brakes' and 'briars', 'tufts' and 'banks', but these terms are used to mark material moments of our journey with the play and not a stable landscape. The 'horrors' to whom Puck refers, who are compelled 'to wilfully themselves exile from light', seem to wander about the wood as they nightly escape from churchyards, crossways and floods where they 'have burial'. But, despite Puck's tricks and hobgoblin nature, he and Oberon 'are spirits of another sort', who can 'like a forester' 'tread' the 'groves' with the 'morning's love'; and here, briefly, the forest returns to a semblance of its man-made construction, under the morning light with the idea of the forester keeping its peace and paths as a substantial land. The story of the lovers, according to Hippolyta, 'grows to something of great constancy' and brings the reality of the wood to rest in the characters' memory of trauma. These woods are like those in *Titus*, 'dreadful', 'deaf', 'ruthless' and 'dull'; created by the emotions they absorb and the anxieties their images remember:

> O, why should nature build so foul a den,
> Unless the gods delight in tragedies? (4.1.58–9)

Where *Dream* imports the forest to explore the proximities between pleasure and punishment in the language of love, in *Titus Andronicus* the forest takes shape through the language of destruction. Our first experience of the forest begins with Aaron entering as the villain, contemptuous of the part he plays. Armed with his bag of gold he looks for a tree, under which he can bury his gold:

> He that had wit would think that I had none,
> To bury so much gold under a tree
> And never after to inherit it.
> Let him that thinks of me so abjectly
> Know that this gold must coin a stratagem
> Which, cunningly effected, will beget
> A very excellent piece of villainy.
> And so repose, sweet gold, for their unrest
> That have their alms out of the Empress' chest.
>   (2.3.1–9)

Dependent again upon the dramatic construction of isolation, the tree alerts us to Aaron's seclusion. Tamora then enters with her version of the landscape, fashioned like sixteenth-century tapestries with images of pleasure and delight, hunting, desire and elegance:

> My lovely Aaron, wherefore look'st thou sad
> When every thing doth make a gleeful boast?

The birds chant melody on every bush,
The snake lies rollèd in the cheerful sun,
The green leaves quiver with the cooling wind
And make a chequered shadow on the ground.
Under their sweet shade, Aaron, let us sit,
And, whilst the babbling echo mocks the hounds,
Replying shrilly to the well-tuned horns,
As if a double hunt were heard at once,
Let us sit down and mark their yellowing noise;
And after conflict such as was supposed
The wand'ring prince and Dido once enjoyed
When with a happy storm they were surprised,
And curtained with a counsel-keeping cave,
We may, each wreathèd in the other's arms,
Our pastimes done, possess a golden slumber
Whiles hounds and horns and sweet melodious birds
Be unto us as is a nurse's song
Of lullaby to bring her babe asleep.   (2.2.10–29)

As Tamora invests the scene with an exquisite tension between the aggressive and inert – the chanting melody of birds, quivering leaves, cooling winds and shadows – and the powerfully coiled, muscular nature of the snake, the mocking echo and the bellowing hounds, we move through the topography of the play, the forest that is created by stories and myths – Dido, Diana, Philomel – desire, revenge and authority. The dynamic that Tamora establishes in the landscape between the predatory and the precious, the tempter and the tempted, the secluded cave and the 'double hunt' looks forward to *Dream* and captures the dramatic ambiguity of the forest. This is the forest that can turn from the lovers' 'pastime' and their 'golden slumbers' to rape, mutilation and murder. The formal poetic mode that conjures both the aesthetic and emotional fabric of the scene is Ovidian, lending bitter irony to Titus's later description of the wood as having been 'patterned by . . . the poet' (4.1.56).

Aaron picks up Tamora's image of the snake and inhabits it:

> What signifies my deadly-standing eye,
> My silence, and my cloudy melancholy,
> My fleece of woolly hair that now uncurls
> Even as an adder when she doth unroll
> To do some fatal execution? (2.3.32–6)

The bodies, desires and fears of the predators who occupy its scenery create the forest: just as the 'wilderness of tigers' is sustained in Tamora. The metamorphic movement of the scene emerges as the characters change, occupy and generate their landscape through the snake, Venus, Diana, Juno and the hunt. As the predators are established so the prey enters and Aaron and Tamora retreat like snakes back into the grass, only to re-emerge once again changed. Nothing is stable and this instability makes the forest a frightening place: contrary to forest law, there are no boundaries and no limits, since the bodies of its visitors, dead or alive, constantly reinvent the space. When Bassianus enters he moves Tamora from the participant to the observer:

> Or is it Dian, habited like her
> Who hath abandonèd her holy groves
> To see the general hunting in this forest? (2.3.57–9)

As she has moved from Venus to Diana so she develops the images through Ovid's story and transforms Bassianus into the hart, only to be hunted by his own hounds.[27] The ways in which the characters move through the images associated with the forest and the stories that dwell in them centralizes the theme of metamorphoses – both literally and metaphorically – as we move ever increasingly towards Lavinia's 'transformation' and Ovid's Philomela. Lavinia now takes up the image of the hunter hunted and the rhythm of transformation sets the pace for the changing landscapes of the scene. Like a modern hologram the forest moves between horror and beauty, pleasure and danger depending on the body of the character through which we view it. A language heavy with anticipation sustains the fabric of the forest, pulling the very atmosphere into the story of Lavinia's destruction. Yet again the landscape changes as we move from the predators' – Chiron and Demetrius, Aaron and Tamora – forest to the 'valley' which supports Tamora's 'raven-coloured love'. Organically, a valley is a hollow or stretch of ground lying between hills; metaphorically, however, it is usually associated with death, darkness and dissolution in the image of the 'shadow'.[28] Lavinia seems to combine the two in her use of the term, suggesting a dark secluded area which is both foreboding and isolated. The substance that makes up the various forest landscapes of *A Midsummer Night's Dream* and *Titus Andronicus* includes a grove, valley, tree, bush, thicket, moss, mistletoe, vale and a 'secret hole'. What becomes clear from this nature is that the 'forest' is mercurial; less dependent upon its matter than its inhabitants.

When Tamora turns to her sons in mock humiliation she redefines the landscape that was once her loving ally:

> Have I not reason, think you, to look pale?
> These two have 'ticed me hither to this place.
> A barren detested vale you see it is;
> The trees, though summer, yet forlorn and lean,
> Overcome with moss and baleful mistletoe.
> Here never shines the sun, here nothing breeds
> Unless the nightly owl or fatal raven. (2.3.91–7)

The forest moves with the mood and scheme of the play from sensuous lustre to ravaged decay, where even the seasons cannot hold on to their sense. Summer is sterile, poisoned even, by the mistletoe which hangs where green leaves should be. Lavinia's 'valley' is now a 'vale' and the image of the vale of tears becomes complete.[29] The glittering backdrop to the lovers' desire is now barren, ominous and aggressive. Where is the melody of the chanting birds, the 'cheerful sun', the 'green leaves' and the 'cooling wind'? Tamora peoples the landscape with the noises and creatures of her imagined hell. The hunt and its yelping hounds are now replaced by a cacophony of misery – 'hissing snakes', 'swelling toads' 'urchins' with such 'fearful and confused cries' (2.3.100, 101, 102)

> As any mortal body hearing it
> Should straight fall mad, or else die suddenly. (103–4)

---

[27] Ovid's *Metamorphoses*, Book III.

[28] According to the *OED*, English versions of the Bible, from Coverdale's translation in 1535, have 'the valley of the shadow of death' (Psalm 23, 4).

[29] Although the phrase comes from the Catholic prayer, 'Salve Regina', it echoes Psalm 24 in its reference to the valley of the shadow of death.

The forest becomes a place of madness and horror; what was once gentle is now fatal. Much like the wood in *Dream*, the landscape can change, at the whim of its authority, the purpose of its place or the perspective of its inhabitants. The forest is never secure or stable; it is never essential or consistent but rather a map of the desiring or diseased mind, a backdrop for transformations and a space for the solitary – for the hunter and the hunted. We realize that beneath the lustful verdure of Tamora's landscape lies the dark, cavernous forest that Aaron described:

The woods are ruthless, dreadful, deaf, and dull:
There speak and strike, brave boys, and take your turns.
There serve your lust, shadowed from heaven's eye,
And revel in Lavinia's treasury. (2.1.129–32)

The isolation or solitude often associated with the forest is partly derived from the idea that it is densely 'shadowed' or canopied, hidden not just from the human but, more significantly, 'heaven's eye', both god and the sun. That the forest can shield the guilty from god's view is rooted in the system of thought that sees the human race as sky-worshippers, those who look up to god and heaven beyond the realm of their selves.[30] This is the reason that Aaron sends Tamora's sons into the wood: 'shadowed from heaven's eye'. The 'monstrous' forest presents an alternative site to the civilized space of social bonds and the moral responsibility of consensual institutions: as a refuge from law – personal or social – the forest can suppress crimes and conceal criminals. The fear and threat of the forest is predominantly due to its apparently amoral ability to obscure wrongdoing, yet within its darkness another version of the law exists and one that is absolutely based on a single authority and a punitive system of control. For Manwood, forest law is part of what defines the space as unique but also as essential to the wider fabric of the community. The strange, ambiguous woods of *Titus* that can reveal and conceal, permit and destroy are always fluctuating on the borders of civilization. Like Manwood's forest it begins as a province for hunting under the authority of the emperor. The forest's role, however, in the recognition of the boundaries

between power and play, pastime and patriarchy is almost instantly subverted by Tamora's assignation with Aaron. As Tamora transforms the sport of hunting into the 'pastime' of love-making, Aaron transforms the killing of the hart into the destruction of Lavinia. Despite the inevitable role of the forest in the destruction of Lavinia and Bassianus it will always remain an emotional space for the realization of desires and the dissolution of law. At the heart of the idea of the forest, according to Harrison, is the tension between the origins of social living and the threat of its destruction. What emerges from the forest is a desire to build out of its landscape: to clear the scrub and create the 'universal institutions of humanity': religion, matrimony and burial. As the forest gives birth to the social, so it becomes a metaphor for human institutions, but this metaphor is always provocative for as the forest returns us to our roots so it is also boundless. That the forest sits at the end of human institutions, lying 'outside' or beyond institutional order is what creates and sustains the eternal opposition between the topographies. Precisely because the forest is 'outside' (*foris*) it disturbs us, challenging our methods of orientation and our psychologies of community.[31] This anxiety lies at the heart of Manwood's text, his insistent need to determine the space of the forest and set its laws down marks the changing status of the forest in the Elizabethan imagination.

The plays' interest in order and chaos lies at the heart of their forests and exposes a profound anxiety of orientation. In the forests of *Titus* and *Dream* there is an unhinging of place and protection, law and order: if part of the necessity of boundaries is that they protect us, part of the threat of the forest is that it has none. Manwood repeatedly tries to set boundaries for the forest but they are always in flux since they depend not on design, enclosure or space but on the ever-shifting movements of the animals in habitation. The hunter and the hunted shape the forest, and as long as they do

---

[30] See Harrison on Vico in *Forests*, p. 6.
[31] See Harrison, *Forests*, p. 8.

it will remain a place of disorientation. The universal institutions that Harrison speaks of as rising out of the forest are central to the plays' exploration of social borders. As *A Midsummer Night's Dream* explores the social viability of marriage and the destabilization of authority, so *Titus Andronicus* explores the destruction of marriage, the failure of religion and the significance of burial. The human institutions that are born of the forest are tested to their limits, and where *Dream* tries to reinstate a version of natural law *Titus* can only turn to literary values in the face of its civil ruins. Burial rites are tied up with what it means to be Roman and Titus's interment of his sons and sacrifice of Tamora's establishes early on in the play how 'civilized' institutions work. But as the forest becomes the centre for the destruction of such values the boundaries dissolve and those civilizing institutions crumble. When Aaron is buried alive outside of the city walls, the forest has reached the absolute limit of its containment. As the forest moves figuratively closer to the city, the city raises its walls, but they are always contingent.

Titus ends with Lucius directing the interment of his father and sister:

My father and Lavinia shall forthwith
Be closèd in our household's monument.
As for that ravenous tiger, Tamora,
No funeral rite nor man in mourning weed,
No mournful bell shall ring her burial;
But throw her forth to beasts and birds to prey.
Her life was beastly and devoid of pity,
And being dead, let birds on her take pity. (5.3.192–9)

Lucius attempts to restore those boundaries through the bodies and burials of the dead: Tamora is thrown out of the city's walls with the beasts and returned to the wild to decompose as part of the 'wilderness' to which she belonged; Lavinia and Titus return to the tombs of Rome; and the forest and the city are safely removed from each other once again. But such a separation is always notional, and, as Marcus reminds us, 'O, why would nature build so foul a den, / Unless the gods delight in tragedies' (4.1.58–9). Tragedy lies at the edge of the city, ready to consume its waste.[32]

Yet despite the importance of limits in *Titus*, the woods are also boundless, shaped as much by the literary as the contemporary. As Lavinia reveals her ordeal through Ovid, so Titus makes sense of it through the poet. He exclaims:

Lavinia, wert *thou* thus surprised, sweet girl,
Ravished and wronged as Philomela was,
Forced in the ruthless, vast, and gloomy woods?
See, see. Ay, such a place there is where we did hunt –
O, had we never, never hunted there! –
Patterned by that the poet here describes,
By nature made for murders and for rapes. (4.1.51–7)

Titus turns to the *Metamorphoses* for the aetiology of his woods: nature has created the landscape and the poet gives life to it. Ovid animates the latent matter of the 'ruthless, vast and gloomy woods' and as the human and animal worlds come into contact with each other memory and emotion are born. Titus does not repudiate the landscape only his part in animating it: 'O, had we never, never hunted there!' The woods become meaningful only when they come into contact with human design, and hunting secures the ambivalence of the place as it moves between cruelty and pleasure.[33]

Part of *Titus*'s exploration of the civilized and the barbaric is negotiated through the use of space and time, and the psychology of place becomes fundamental in defining what these terms mean.

---

[32] In *Titus*, the ways in which Rome tries to define itself as separate and civilized, in defence of a chaos primarily associated with barbarism, become profoundly ironic in the play. Rome was founded as an 'asylum' out of the forest in which it began. Although Romulus and Remus found refuge in the forests of Latium in which they grew up, they were compelled to transform them once they discovered their true identities. The boundaries *Titus* tries to reinstate are always illusions – as Rome emerges from a forest so it can always return to one and, within the play, the spaces of civilized and barbaric become indistinct.

[33] This ambivalence is captured at a more playful level by the horticultural notion of the 'wilderness', when a wood is artificially created in a garden environment to suggest solitude or, as one seventeenth-century preacher puts it, 'a multitude of thick bushes and trees, affecting an ostentation of solitariness in the midst of worldly pleasures', as quoted by Keith Thomas, *Man and the Natural World* (London, 1983), p. 207.

The history of anxiety associated with the forest is predominantly universal (largely based on a primal fear of darkness and predators) but that sense of threat in darkness was translated by the church into a concept of spiritual blindness or removal from God. In Christian terms, forests were representative of both error and separation and their wandering paths were a challenge to those who had strayed and erred to find salvation.[34] But for Manwood, the Elizabethan forest is less about God and more about 'man': about authority and possession and the value systems that law and order presume to create as well as depend upon.

The trees on the stage of *Titus* are largely strategic: for Aaron the tree provides a space under which he can hide his gold; for Tamora, 'this dismal yew' – presumably the same tree – illustrates the specious tale she tells her sons to further incite them to the rape and mutilation of Lavinia.[35] The tree, like the forest landscape, changes to accommodate the psychological drives and emotional needs of its inhabitants.[36] The relationship between the mind and the forest is paralleled in the relationship between the tree and the body: the body is cut down, lopped, hewed and burned like the tree. The lover's arms as the branches of trees are distinctly Ovidian and feature in the image of Lavinia, severed – from loving and from life. The body as the tree literalizes the relationship between the human and the forest. As the status of the human falls into crisis in the forest we notice how versions of power are played out through the felling of the body, like the tree, in warfare – be it psychological or physical. As *Titus's* forest dehumanizes it also amplifies with horrid glory what human impulses have come to mean: Tamora's desire dresses the landscape through her encircling arms, Aaron's revenge sets the scene for destruction and the emperor's hounds howl as the hunt goes on. The idea of the forest – as a place of dehumanization – keeps the image of the body in constant motion as it moves, like the landscape itself, between pleasure and savagery, the animal and the human.

How the play uses the body and the tree is symptomatic of the ways trees were being dramatically explored on the Elizabethan stage. Yet the representation of the forest is ambiguous: we know that trees were often used as properties and that they are mentioned in stage records; forests, on the other hand, could be a collection of timber trunks, a painted cloth or simply one 'tree' strategically placed.[37] Woods were used to conjure danger and solitude – and presumably to evoke the danger itself of solitude, thus presenting isolation as a condition of weakness and vulnerability. What we begin to notice is that the isolation of the forest consistently reinvents the community as protective or safe; only the multiple gaze reflects institutional order and only the language of ownership imposes it. But woods were also used to create the emotional landscape of danger in isolation even when the practicalities of the scene did not demand them.[38] Manwood's *Treatise* attempts to record this landscape as it moves through the transition from allegory to improvement, from a customary habitat to private

34 Spenser writes of this in the trials of the Redcrosse Knight in the *Faerie Queene*. Spenser's 'wandering wood' and the monstrous Error is a synthesis of the allegorical and the mythical.

35 See Jonathan Bate's Arden edition, quoting E. M. Waith's Oxford edition p. 168, nn. 2.2 and 9.1.

36 *Titus* features both the material and the metaphoric wood, requiring the isolation to commit its deeds and the ground, twigs and briars to conceal them. But the *idea* of the wood as a place used to indicate error and anxiety is clearly at the forefront of contemporary productions. In his *Book of Plaies* Simon Foreman describes a production of *The Winter's Tale*, in 1611, in which 'Perdita was carried into bohemia & ther laid in a forrest.' Similarly, in *Macbeth* (1610), Foreman noted how 'Macbeth and Banquo . . . Two noblemen of Scotland, riding through a wood, there stood before them three women Fairies'. Reynolds notes, 'we have "trees for a wildernesse", and without a single hint of their presence in the text', see '"Trees" on the Stage of Shakespeare', pp. 147–58.

37 'Perhaps this "extended" use of woods . . . for any scene of desolation seems purely theoretical and impossible . . . Fortunately, however, direct proof of it exists in a single line of the Revels accounts (p. 41; 1572–3): "for this provision *and* carriage of trees *and* other things to the Coorte for a wildernesse in a playe, viij sh. vj d." No clearer statement could be desired: woods in 1572–3 were used at court to represent a wilderness', see Reynolds, '"Trees" on the Stage of Shakespeare', p. 156.

38 Reynolds refers to Greene's *Alphonsus* (1599) as 'full of references to woods' (p. 155).

property. Above all, however, Manwood's text tries to redress the intense anxiety that the forest creates by offering a legal framework through which the animal and social become distinct. However residual this anxiety seems to be, Shakespeare develops his forests through the multiple spaces of the material, the social and the mimetic that Manwood offers.

The wood signifies a point at which these multiple spaces intersect and metamorphoses takes place: the 'waylesse woods' as Golding translates them in Book III of Ovid's *Metamorphoses* (line 171) are the shadow of humanity, following it around not in antithesis but like 'a guilty conscience'.[39] Shadowing as well as engendering our human institutions, the forest holds the shape of natural form as we encounter the very limits of social law. Primarily a place of isolation – 'deaf' and 'dull' – the forest takes us into its shadows to explore the limits of social values: how we try to recover or represent those values becomes the site of human drama at the centre of both *A Midsummer Night's Dream* and *Titus Andronicus*. But as both plays encounter their forests so they also lose their memory and the distinctions that pre-existed this landscape collapse and fade: as Demetrius admits, 'These things seem small and undistinguishable, / Like far-off mountains turnèd into clouds', or, as Titus howls,

> O, had we never, never hunted there! –
> Patterned by that the poet here describes,
> By nature made for murders and for rapes.

The forest lurks beside us as the ghost of civilization – its birth and its forgetting.

---

[39] See Harrison's analysis of the law, *Forests*, p. 63.

WHAT WE HEAR; WHAT WE SEE: THEATRE FOR A NEW AUDIENCE'S 2009 *HAMLET*

BERNICE W. KLIMAN

In any production of a Shakespeare play what we hear and see is largely determined by the text, but individual productions can and do make surprising and sometimes enlightening choices that bring the text to life in unexpected ways. Theatre for a New Audience (TFANA) added visual images (through video and staging techniques) and sound effects to a text that, with almost all the unfamiliar words and images cut, rarely could trouble even a novice audience. By cutting the text in decisive ways, director David Esbjornson shaped a clear interpretation of a play that has seemed to contain too many possible interpretations. Esbjornson's was not, however, a heavy-handed imposition of a director's perspective on the play but a subtle enactment of the play's potential within a modern context. The production avoided the problematic Hamlet proposed by much critical literature from the eighteenth century through to the present and the potentially less than admirable Hamlet exposed in passages that undercut the character's nobility. It was a production that could please those who praise Hamlet as one of the most admirable characters in literature; it required no excuses for his inaction. Nevertheless, this Hamlet was as complex and deeply layered as the actor Christian Camargo could make him. Greeted by most reviewers as one of the best *Hamlet*s seen in many years, the production had at its heart superb acting and an innovative group of designers.

Entering the theatre, the Duke on 42nd Street, in New York City, audiences were immediately struck by the intimacy of the venue (180 seats for *Hamlet*). Arranged on three sides of a black, tiled platform stage, the audience was close to the action but shielded from each other most of the time by extreme darkness. The choice of a mixture of modern-dress costumes fitted the neutral setting. Penetrated by spotlights, the darkness focused attention where it was needed. The script eliminated lines that invite actors to speak directly to the audience, keeping Elsinore hermetically sealed within that black space. For example, Polonius does not urge the audience to share his perception of Hamlet's madness with lines often interpreted as asides, such as 'How say you by that' (2.2.189) and 'I'll speak to him again' (2.2.193).[1] The darkness of the production precluded any such intimacy between the actors and the audience and made the production insular and pressurized.

Hamlet's centrality is emphasized by the way the production begins and ends. In a visual prologue Hamlet stands next to what appears to be a pit in the obsidian stage's centre. The stage direction reads

Lights up on HAMLET's hand, outstretched; a steady stream of dirt falls through his fingers. Light grows to reveal his full body standing in a shallow grave.

But in performance, instead of standing within the grave he simply lifts a handful of dirt and

---

[1] The early seventeenth-century texts mark no asides, but several seem to be built in and are often interpreted so in performance.

lets it sift through his fingers into the opening.[2] An earlier plan to include a fuller prologue was dropped in rehearsal: 'When house goes to black, HAMLET goes into position. Sound: wind, rain, radio waves, static, snippets of text spoken by famous Hamlets of the past.' The next stage direction suggests that he is dressed 'perhaps in period clothes'. None of these choices made it as far as the previews.

The effect of the textual collage would have been to set this Hamlet against the best that had preceded him as well as suggesting that in his Elizabethan costume he embodied Shakespeare's vision – a pretentious and perhaps counter-productive ploy. Though there is something to be said for acknowledging the connections to the past, the production did better by beginning and ending the play with this particular Hamlet. The sombre, death-touched beginning casts its gloom on the opening of the first court scene, interwoven with the ramparts scene (the only scenes in this production thus entwined). The play ends with Horatio's eulogy over Hamlet's dead body ('good night, sweet prince', 5.2.312–14) followed by a fade to darkness. Thus the play begins and ends with its image of Hamlet. But this is not a morbid *Hamlet*: it is one that celebrates creative engagement with the script, with designers of all stripes, with deference to the audience.

David Esbjornson often makes his choices speak not only to the particular moment on stage but also to echoes in later scenes: they do so both for those familiar with the play who recognize the foreshadowing and for audience members new to the play who might recall the earlier reference when seeing a development in a later scene. For example, in the first scene as the sentries and Horatio await the ghost, a shift of lighting introduces the first part of the court scene announcing the coronation and marriage; each of the first and second scenes continues within the interstices of the other, with one grouping highlighted and active, the other frozen in darkness. With video projections of a lighted grid of 14-inch squares focused on the actors, framing them, as it were, the production suggests the constraints shaping action or the idea that the audience is viewing the court through a lens. Then in 1.4, as Hamlet, Marcellus and Horatio (and in this production Bernardo also) await the ghost on the ramparts, they are aware of and discuss the court's festivities that they overhear. Thus in both ramparts scenes, the blare of festivities contrasts with the dark, cold atmosphere.

In the first scene, right after Horatio's sceptical line, 'Tush 'twill not appear', the lights shift to the first court scene. 'It' will not appear, at least not yet, but what will appear is this self-satisfied new king. The costume palette is grey, silver and black modern dress, perhaps with nods to the 1950s. With the added huzzahs of all present after the first part of the king's speech and the silence of Hamlet, standing apart, we see immediately the tension between this court and Hamlet, the representative of the previous regime. Among the wine-drinking revellers is a priest, recognizable by his cassock, who will make an appearance later as the one called most often 'the second gravedigger' in cast lists (when the character is retained). While he drinks convivially with the rest of the court, joining them in their shout of 'Hear! Hear!' in response to the line 'taken to wife' (1.2.14), in the later scene he is something of a rebel who resents the intrusion of royal authority over death and burial. Having him there in the first scene is an example of the continuity the director builds; it's also an example of flexible role reassignment.

When Hamlet says 'I am too much i' th' sun' in the first court scene, the light shifts and returns us to the ramparts for the ghost's second appearance in the first scene. The script cuts 'Good now, sit down, and tell me, he that knows' (1.1.69) through to 'That was and is the question of these wars' (1.1.Add.A.1–4), eliminating the relaxation of

---

[2] The gesture is a possible echo of Zeffirelli's 1990 film when, during the added funeral ceremony, Mel Gibson as Hamlet pours a handful of dirt over the sarcophagus of his father. But Zeffirelli's emotional affect is different because all the other main players are there, including his weeping mother and an exultant Claudius whom Hamlet eyes suspiciously while the TFANA Hamlet mourns alone.

tension Shakespeare provides, the false trail of possibility for the appearance of ghosts and an opportunity for Horatio to show that he is non-committal about religion. He refers only to the 'high and palmy state of Rome' (1.1.Add.A.6), and the script avoids all his guesses about the reasons for the ghost's presence and both the historical and religious sensibility of the lines like 'And then it started like a guilty thing' (1.1.139) through to 'So have I heard, and do in part believe it' (1.1.146).

Like several directors, Esbjornson substitutes light and the actors' intent gaze towards the back wall of the house for the ghost in the first and fourth scenes.[3] All the more startling is his presence in the scene with Hamlet. We cannot deny that Bernardo, Marcellus and Horatio see the ghost, but it appears most fully to Hamlet, bursting forward from upstage sliders, lit by the now familiar grids of light which here are terribly distorted, the smooth squares collapsed and shapeless. Esbjornson introduces tormenting demons who hover at the threshold of the sliders, moaning and crying, impatient for the ghost's return – purgatory made visible and audible. When the ghost retreats as if pulled to the rear exit, the demons leap on his body: they have him in their grip. Later, though, when he returns in the closet scene, the demons are no longer with him. He is dressed the same way in both scenes, in a white military greatcoat: other productions sometimes use a costume change to signal a difference in the ghost's standing with heaven. For example, Gielgud as the ghost in the 1970 TV production with Richard Chamberlain as Hamlet began in a white Napoleonic greatcoat but re-entered in the closet scene in something more like Q1's nightgown.[4] Here, however, it is the absence of the demons rather than any other change that effects a distinction. The ghost calmly sits behind Gertrude on her bed listening to Hamlet's harangue (that is, once Hamlet lets her rise from his hold on her on the floor).

As in many productions, a sword is important, but unlike many Hamlets that extend the sword before them as they follow the ghost in 1.5, this sword is part of the ghost's military guise, tenting out his greatcoat. At the decisive moment that the ghost asks for his revenge, he reveals the sword for the first time. Taking it up, Hamlet keeps it with him through the closet scene with his mother, a constant reminder of why the ghost has given it to him. Hamlet's remoteness from his father is however suggested by the sword's incongruity in his hands. Its bulk is inappropriate to his slender physique and modest, more contemporary costume.

This ghost in the first act has quiet moments but also a disturbing amount of rant, emphasizing the contrast between father and son in that scene. As a result, Hamlet's waiting and thinking afterwards are not surprising. The ghost's revelations disturb him deeply, as a matter of course, but murder simply compounds for him the horror of the speedy marriage and the incest – the truth of which he had known before the revelations. When he rages it is from the pressures of his feelings for the two women in his life.

Esbjornson develops the second family, Polonius, Laertes and Ophelia, to create interest in them as a unit and as individuals as well as cogs in the wheels of the tragic outcome.

The character of Osric (Ryan Quinn), made into a member of the Polonius family, has an impressively realized through-line. In 1.3, until Laertes interrupts them, Quinn as Osric plays with

---

[3] Richardson 1969, stage and film, with Nicol Williamson; Gielgud, 1964, stage and film record, with Richard Burton. For film information and credits with photos, see Kenneth S. Rothwell and Annabelle Henkin-Melzer, *Shakespeare on Screen: An International Filmography and Videography* (New York, 1990). A revised and updated Internet edition by Kenneth S. Rothwell, José Ramón Díaz Fernández and Tanya Gough is available at http://internetshakespeare.uvic.ca/Theater/sip/spotlights.html. See also Bernice W. Kliman, *Hamlet: Film, Television and Audio Performance* (Rutherford, NJ, 1988), with illustrations. The book is available in full on *hamletworks.org*.

[4] See photo in *Hamlet: Film, Television and Audio Performance* on p. 184. Q1 line 1551 gives the stage direction '*Enter the ghost in his night gowne*' in the closet scene.

Ophelia and her white shawl, both of them pretending it is a bridal veil or a bridal dress, perhaps a signal of her hopes for her love for Hamlet (later a similar piece of white cloth is her shroud). By introducing this young Osric, Esbjornson gives Ophelia (Jennifer Ikeda) a friend, who later appears as the messenger who urges the queen to see the mad Ophelia (4.5) and the messenger who delivers letters to the king (4.7). Then, after pressing Hamlet to undertake the duel with Laertes, Osric connives with the king and Laertes to make sure the duel is fixed with a poisoned, unbated weapon. Quinn plays him as not quite the evil figure of some productions (like the ubiquitous presence in Peter Wirth's 1960 production with Maximilian Schell), but this Osric has ample motivation for his actions. Thus, instead of extraneous messenger-figures, the production offers a developed minor character. Because of the race-blind casting (as pioneered in the 1960s by Joseph Papp at the Public Theater in New York City) that nevertheless makes race a feature, this young African-American actor is easily recognizable as a continuing character. Dressed in Elizabethan costume with the other travelling players presenting the Mousetrap, he is also an entirely different character, the player queen.

Giving Ophelia a friend makes it possible for her to be somewhat stronger than the weak sister of so many productions. Similarly, less prolixity on Laertes's part makes him more sympathetic. When advising Ophelia, Laertes in several lines undercuts his own gravity by jokingly mimicking his father. Ophelia underlines her caution to Laertes to watch out for his own virtue by pulling from his rucksack a pill vial that could hold Oxycodone or some other street drug and waving it at him before returning it. Suddenly he's in a hurry to go, emphasized by his half-line 'I stay too long' (1.3.52), uttered before the entrance of Polonius.[5] His reaction helps to give the Ophelia character some heft. A few minutes later, she will happily surreptitiously take from Laertes some of the money that their father had handed to Laertes. This is an Ophelia who is not subservient to her father and brother.

5. *Hamlet*, 3.1, Theatre for a New Audience, New York, directed by David Esbjornson. Hamlet (Christian Carmargo) and Ophelia (Jennifer Ikeda).

The production enhanced both Ophelia's character and Hamlet's by inserting in the script Hamlet's quiet visit to her grave after the violence of the graveside encounter with Laertes. Alone, Hamlet kneels at the open grave, grieving. This addition is far more persuasive of his feeling for her than his rage had been. But it is not Shakespeare. It is telling that only by adding such a scene could Esbjornson convey feelings that in the text remain open to interpretation. The added scene also enhances Ophelia's presence: as Hamlet prays or mourns over her body, her spirit rises from the grave and dancingly exits through the same sliders through which the ghost had entered so ominously in scene 5. But here the projected video squares are whole and sound – as, we infer, is her soul. She dances off to meet a second version of herself at the portal, two Ophelias, one representing her pure soul. Music

---

5 Q2 places the stage direction for Polonius's entrance before Laertes's 'O fear me not', while F1 places it after, an immaterial diffence textually, but one that can be manipulated in performance for comic effect.

works here as it does at the boundaries of many
scenes to enhance the exalted mood. Thus the production lightens her character and her tragedy.

Though the director made choices to darken
Polonius's character, the native congeniality of the
actor Alvin Epstein as Polonius worked against that
purpose. The best the director could do was cast
Polonius as the bad guy after the play-within scene,
when he stalks after a soldier (Bernardo) escorting the players from the court. Menaced by the
large gun that the soldier wields, the players walk
backward upstage left and out. An audience could
believe that Polonius striding behind the guard may
have decided on his own to frighten off the players,
but it is eminently reasonable that the king would
have given orders for their forceful removal. Players
do not upset kings without repercussions; that was
probably something Shakespeare knew very well.
This interpretation of the players' exit is one of
the many visual additions to the script that makes
satisfying sense. In an earlier version of the script,
Bernardo, under orders from Polonius, shoots the
players dead. Removing this murder scene was
wise; it would have distracted from the ongoing
action – Hamlet's hilarity at his success with the
play-within, and the task before him – but in its
modified form it reminds the audience that Polonius is the king's man.

Because of the darkening of Polonius's character,
an audience must feel less sympathy for the accidental death Polonius soon suffers: thus the director
makes Hamlet less culpable. Similarly, to counteract the reaction some have to Hamlet's cavalier
dispatching of Rosencrantz and Guildenstern, the
script at one stage had them remain when the king
speaks his lines about killing Hamlet, from 4.3.65–
70, and including

<blockquote>

                    Do it, England,
For like the hectic in my blood he rages,
And thou must cure me. Till I know 'tis done,
Howe'er my haps, my joys were ne'er begun.
                    (4.3.67–70)
(Exit ROSENCRANTZ and GUILDENSTERN ...)[6]

</blockquote>

In rehearsal the exit was changed to the standard earlier position, after 'Pray you, make haste'

6. *Hamlet*, 2.2, Theatre for a New Audience, New York,
directed by David Esbjornson. Polonius (Alvin Epstein)
queries Hamlet (Christian Carmargo).

(4.3.59), but given Esbjornson's interpretation, it
would have made good sense for Rosencrantz and
Guildenstern to remain. Shakespeare, on the other
hand, whether by design or not, makes their guilt
ambiguous. If they are present during what is

---

[6] In the script sent to me this page is dated 6 March 2009. I
attended the production on 31 March 2009, a few days after
the opening. Previews began 17 March and the run ended 12
April. Unfortunately, Theatre on Film and Tape (TOFT) at
the Lincoln Center Performing Arts Library did not record
the show. For scripts and other assistance, my thanks to Jeffrey
Horowitz, TFANA's Artistic Director; Arin Arbus, Associate
Artistic Director and director of the award-winning *Othello*
that preceded *Hamlet*; Thomas J. Gates, the production stage
manager, who shared recollections of the production; Owen
Smith, assistant to the artistic and managing directors; Ryan
Quinn, who played Osric.

usually acted as the king's soliloquy, Hamlet can justify to Horatio his vengeance on them without an audience's revulsion:

Why, man, they did make love to this employment.
They are not near my conscience. Their defeat
Does by their own insinuation grow.
'Tis dangerous when the baser nature comes
Between the pass and fell incensèd points
Of mighty opposites.   (5.2.58–63)

And we can assent to his view if we have seen them participate in the plan to kill Hamlet. The final script returns their exit line to 4.3.59, removing their overt connivance, and the script cuts the most vicious of Hamlet's lines: that they are to be killed 'Not shriving-time allowed' (5.2.48).

Besides character-bending cuts like this one, many textual omissions are sensible concessions to what an audience can hear and grasp; some of these cuts occur in other productions, some are original. Avoiding excessive exits and entrances, the production has the king and guards enter to Hamlet and Rosencrantz and Guildenstern in 4.2 instead of changing to a new scene, and it does not have Ophelia exit and re-enter in 4.5 (instead she hides under a table, concealed by the tablecloth, and later reappears). Whole passages with difficult words or imagery are gone; those requiring more actors than the production employed are cut (no ambassadors, no crowd accompanying Laertes when he returns to menace the king at 4.5.110, F1 only). A few obscure words are changed: '*coted* them on the way' (2.2.319) becomes *encountered* them on the way. The script changes potentially offensive words, for example, the 'Polack' (4.4.Add.J.14) to 'poor Poland' in Hamlet's Q2-only soliloquy. The queen's 'He's fat and scant of breath' (5.2.240) becomes 'He's sweating, scant of breath'; this tall slim Hamlet could not have been described as 'fat' in any sense that a modern audience would understand. Similarly sensitive to the audience is such a change as making Osric, the messenger in 4.7 who has letters for the king, say that the person who gave them to him was Horatio (4.7.40) instead of the sudden Claudio of the early texts, a character never seen and mentioned only this one time.

We had heard Horatio reading the letter, but no one was with him, for the sailors in 4.6 had been omitted.

Such lines are not much missed, perhaps; on the other hand, many of the lines that make Horatio a fully rounded character are cut. Horatio's daring wit disappears with the line that suggests the king is an ass, that is, 'You might have rhymed' (3.2.273) in response to Hamlet's song, 'For thou dost know, O Damon dear' (3.2.269–72), and though the song and Horatio's rejoinder might have been difficult for an audience to understand, they could have grasped the playful, iconoclastic tone.

A major cut that does not have to do with difficult words or concepts is the praise of Horatio, 3.2.52–72. The lines not only flatter Horatio but also reveal Hamlet as a generous, gracious friend:

                    Give me that man
That is not passion's slave, and I will weare him
In my heart's core, ay, in my heart of heart,
As I do thee.   (3.2.69–72)

Both characters by their demeanour and obvious affection for each other help make up for the loss. It's possible the director thought – as Hamlet himself says – that there was 'Something too much of this' (3.2.72), but the praise compensates for Horatio's long absence in the whole of the text's second act.

Most cuts are smooth and unobtrusive. Though no ambassadors take the king's missive to old Norway, Polonius can still reasonably announce that the ambassadors have returned from their mission (2.2.40). Lines that essentially repeat what other lines have already said are not needed when actors clarify them through brisk and clear speech. Shakespeare often uses repetition with variation to emphasize a point; delivery can accomplish much the same effect. On the other hand, the script retains lines when repetitions are character-revealing, as they are for Polonius's verbosity.

Many of the cuts are traditional, such as the Polonius–Reynaldo scene at the beginning of Shakespeare's Act 2, deleted rather late, 12 March 2009, so that the actor playing him is still listed in the credits (he also plays the First Gravedigger). We miss both the Reynaldo scene's comic relief and its exposure of Polonius's immoral thinking.

Originally, the script had the actor appear as Reynaldo in the first court scene where he carries a tray and serves drinks, but audiences would not necessarily identify him as Polonius's servant because they never again see him playing this role. As Polonius's servant, he signals that the celebration is Polonius's event, and this explains the king's fulsome thanks to his host (1.2.47–9) and his turning to Laertes before addressing Hamlet (1.2.42–6). The scene, as in the original text, without the overt presence of Polonius's servant, is more complicated as it provides no reason for Claudius's snubbing of Hamlet, which performances often amplify.

Many productions eliminate Fortinbras. Here he is not only named as a source of worry in the first act, he also appears in 4.4 (in Q2 only), when Rosencrantz and Guildenstern are escorting Hamlet to England, and interestingly enough it is *he* rather than his captain to whom Hamlet unknowingly speaks. This switch in role is meaningful for several reasons.

Sean Haberle as Fortinbras, an impressive soldier, takes his measure of Hamlet as they speak. To an audience member familiar with the play as printed, it was an evocative decision: Fortinbras in Shakespeare's Act 5 eulogizes Hamlet without having known him.

> For he was likely, had he been put on,
> To have proved most royally; and for his passage,
> The soldiers' music and the rites of war
> Speak loudly for him. (5.2.351–4)

In the TFANA version, Fortinbras could have credibly uttered these lines because he has conversed with Hamlet in an intimate moment. Without this knowledge, the latter lines become merely a pro forma encomium. In the Act 4 encounter, Fortinbras, not the captain, expresses misgivings about the campaign:

> Truly to speak, . . .
> We go to gain a little patch of ground
> That hath in it no profit but the name.
> To pay five ducats, five, I would not farm it
> (4.4.Add.J.8–11)

Fortinbras's second guessing of his own action makes him a kind of Hamlet figure. In spite of the potential development of their interesting encounter, the production cuts the whole of the play after Hamlet's death, everything after 'And flights of Angels sing thee to thy rest' (i.e. 5.2.313–57), almost fifty lines. The main reason for this cut, often made in performance, was probably the play's length, but here the cut has the added effect of having Hamlet bracket the play, intensifying the focus on him. Fortinbras's conversation with Hamlet compensates for his absence at the end.

Other cuts suggest a shift in Gertrude's character from the version most often discussed by anti-Gertrude critics. This queen, played by Alyssa Bresnahan, is young (no more than 40) and beautiful, wearing high heels and dressed in a knee-length form-fitting silvery cocktail dress with cowl neck framing her face. The production cut several of Hamlet's most castigating lines to the queen in the closet scene; some are in Q2 only:

> . . . for at your age,
> The heyday in the blood is tame, it's humble,
> And waits upon the judgement; and what judgement
> Would step from this to this? Sense sure you have,
> Else could you not have motion; but sure that sense
> Is apoplexed, for madness would not err,
> Nor sense to ecstasy was ne'er so thralled
> But it reserved some quantity of choice
> To serve in such a difference. (3.4.67–70.Add.F.1–6)

and

> Rebellious hell,
> If thou canst mutine in a matron's bones,
> To flaming youth let virtue be as wax
> And melt in her own fire. Proclaim no shame
> When the compulsive ardour gives the charge,
> Since frost itself as actively doth burn,
> And reason panders will. (3.4.72–8)

The deep cuts remove Hamlet's unhealthy focus on the queen's sexuality (as interpreted by so many directors).

Though Bresnahan as queen is young enough to feel passion (and passion after all knows no bounds), she shows no special attachment to this king, especially since, after the king's announcement of their marriage in the first court scene, the lighting immediately returns the audience to the first ramparts scene. Esbjornson varies here from common interpretations of Gertrude's motivation. Bresnahan's remarriage does not seem to be driven by passion as it was so clearly in Richardson's 1969 stage and screen productions with a hard-drinking Judy Parfitt or in Zeffirelli's 1990 film with Glenn Close joyously revelling in her new marriage. The only queen similar in her absence of passion is in the stage and video productions of *Hamlet IV* by the Polish director Andrzej Wajda (on stage at Purchase, NY, 1990; made-for-TV film, 1991).

When Bresnahan's queen is alone with the king before the entrance of Rosencrantz and Guildenstern, and he attempts to caress her, she seems indifferent or even repelled. With this effect, Esbjornson raises questions about her decision to remarry quickly. Her sexual attraction to this king obviated, it seems to suggest a political choice: with this marriage she continues in power. She cares for Hamlet but for herself more. Since the ghost accuses his queen of lust and incest, it is interesting to see that her behaviour with her new husband contradicts both the ghost's and Hamlet's view of her. She is never anything but completely proper – as she always is in her words alone.

Gertrude's lack of feeling for the king is understandable given that, as played by Casey Biggs, he is a shallow politician; this interpretation makes it possible for Hamlet to tower over him. They are not 'mighty opposites' (5.2.63), as the text's Hamlet describes their agon on only one occasion; rather Claudius is the 'king of shreds and patches' (3.4.93) that Hamlet holds up to his mother in her closet and that he has in mind most often.

Though the script cuts many lines, her line that is most difficult to explain remains: 'But not by him' (4.5.127), *him* being the king: this is directed at Laertes who has burst into the court asking about his murdered father. It seems an answer that Shakespeare designed to expose the queen's loyalty to her new husband in spite of all the hectoring Hamlet has engaged in to divide the couple. Why does *this* Gertrude say it? She looks appraisingly at her husband as she speaks, almost as if she is musing, 'No, he has not killed Polonius, but whom *has* he killed?' Her look mitigates the effect of the words. She may feel she can safely divert Laertes's attention from Claudius to Hamlet because he is, after all, out of the country.

The director's choice for Gertrude's attenuated feelings for Hamlet and her capacity to put her own needs first is reflected by her lack of knowledge of her son. The old school-fellows Rosencrantz and Guildenstern, as played by Craig Patterson and Richard Topol, whom she flatters in the second act, are so far different from Hamlet, so lacking in Horatio's steadiness, loyalty and certainty, that one wonders how she could have thought them welcome companions, equal to Hamlet's wit. He sees through them immediately, from the moment they cavort towards him later in the scene covered with a cloth as if imitating a ghost. Their sophomoric games (they wear sneakers) disgust Hamlet.

The play-within is another opportunity to weigh the queen's feelings: she reveals nothing. As played, the scene has both traditional and unusual cuts. A traditional one is the dumb show, a feature that, when performed along with the fully acted version, makes for difficulties: why does the king not react to the first version? In the play-within, an important omission is Hamlet's remark upon the player queen's vow of eternal single life should her husband die, 'If she should break it now' (3.2.213), which calls attention to Gertrude's lack of loyalty when it is said aloud for all to hear. And when Hamlet says it as an aside, it shows what is important to him in this test. The script excises Ophelia's response to Hamlet's off-colour jokes about puppets dallying (3.2.234–5), cuts that are common enough in earlier, more prim times, but that serve to eliminate Hamlet's cruelty to her, softening his character. However, having been given a chance to hold her own in repartee with her brother, Ophelia might have been offered this opportunity to do the same with Hamlet. A little more sprightliness on Ophelia's part would have gone far to explain Hamlet's attraction to her.

A major cut is Hamlet's revelation of the plot of the play-within: he declares in the early texts

A poisons him i'th' Garden for 's estate. His name's Gon-
zago. The Story is extant, and writ in choice Italian.
You shall see anon how the murderer gets the love of
Gonzago's wife.   (3.2.249–52)

And at that point the king rises. As in F1, Hamlet
asks in this production 'What, frighted with false
fire?' (3.2.254), a line that commentators have wondered at, given Hamlet's prior speech. But without
his summary of the ending, the inscrutable line is
credible. The players' performance has not given
away the whole resemblance to Claudius's murder
of his brother; the lines this Hamlet has added to
the play have presumably not yet been heard.

A transposition places Polonius's call for the end
of the play (3.2.256) *after* the king's demand for light
(3.2.257), which follows right after the queen asks
him how he fares (3.2.255). The king thus instigates
the retreat from the scene. In another example of
transposition, in the closet scene Hamlet's three-
times repeated 'mother' (3.4.6) is interspersed real-
istically within Gertrude's and Polonius's dialogue.
A more significant transposition is the decision to
place 'To be' at the beginning of the production's
second act, after the soliloquy that ends 2.2 and
an intermission. The intermission masks the close
proximity of two soliloquies. Displacing 'To be' is
not uncommon; what the shift accomplishes here
is its detachment from the nunnery scene. Without
the audience's awareness of the king and Polonius
as well as Ophelia close by, with Hamlet alone on
stage, the focus is entirely on him.[7] More importantly, perhaps, the displacement allows Hamlet to
say later, when he mourns at her grave, the lines
that end his soliloquy:

> Soft you now,
> The fair Ophelia! – Nymph, in thy orisons
> Be all my sins remembered.   (3.1.90–2)

Placed here, after her death, his lines express his
love for her. Gertrude continues to be a problematic character in the later scenes. After the second
intermission, Act 3 (i.e. 4.5) opens with the queen
downstage right, at one end of a long table that is
canted slightly upstage left, and with the king a long

distance away at the other end. She suffers miserable thoughts, revealed in soliloquy after she agrees
to see Ophelia:

> To my sick soul, as sin's true nature is,
> Each toy seems prologue to some great amiss.
> So full of artless jealousy is guilt,
> It spills itself in fearing to be spilt.   (4.5.17–20)

What is not clear is whether she is describing herself, full of suspicion (the meaning of *jealousy*), or
the suspicion that the king has acted upon in sending Hamlet away. However her soliloquy is understood, her delivery underscores the evil that will
come.

The king, in contrast, eats hungrily, uncon-
cerned about and oblivious to Gertrude's feelings.
He has taken care of everything in dispatching
Hamlet, and can now relax. Even when Laertes
bursts in, the king feels satisfied that he has disposed of Hamlet, the only barrier to his earthly
contentment. This king, however, does not say to
Gertrude and Laertes

> There's such divinity doth hedge a king
> That treason can but peep to what it would,
> Acts little of his will.   (4.5.122–4)

This famous speech is evidence of Shakespeare's
king's impudence in claiming divine protection
for kings when he had murdered a king who
should also have been protected by divinity. But
the TFANA king is too diminished a character to
have the nerve to say these lines.

The script cuts the king's response to Laertes's
vow of revenge for his father's death 'Who shall
stay you?' (4.5.135), which would be a problematic
one for a Gertrude to overhear in any production,
like this one, that has her loyalty shifting to Hamlet. Similarly for the king's following lines, which
TFANA did include: Gertrude according to the
script remains in the scene all the way through
to the line most ominous for Hamlet, 'and where
th'offence is, let the great axe fall' (4.5.216). But

---

7 Olivier, like many others, had also moved the soliloquy, but
in his 1948 film Ophelia was the proximate cause of Hamlet's
angst.

in the performance that I saw she follows Ophelia out at 'God b'wi' ye' (4.5.198), as she does in most productions, avoiding most of the direct threats to Hamlet. There is no problem with these threats when a Gertrude has colluded with her brother-in-law/husband for power: such a Gertrude willingly – if perhaps reluctantly – sacrifices her son.

The Hamlet that the king and Laertes encounter next is far different from the one we have seen before. Hamlet at the end of the ramparts scene had suggested that he will put on an antic disposition. His subsequent costume, with one pant leg jammed into a tube sock and a bathrobe (with piping) loosely tied around him, is a minimalist sort of code for craziness. When he returns from England, he is no longer all in black as at the beginning nor in his antic garb. Instead he wears trim black trousers and an open-necked white shirt with sleeves rolled up from the wrists. Whatever the extremes of emotion this Hamlet experiences up to the last scene, at the end, knowing he is dying and that, with his mother dead, he can complete his task, he shows not a speck of regret or even sadness. He is content to die. This is the ending that Joseph Pequigney proposes on *hamletworks.org*, in his note for line 3847 (5.2.311), discussing the Folio's four 'O' groans:

Hamlet, in dying, has a calm and clear mind; he is in full possession of his faculties; he is busy preparing for the succession; he gives no sign of anguish or melancholy or of mental disturbance of any kind. What would he be sighing about? He could perhaps be groaning from the pain of his wound and/or the poison in his system. But hitherto he has given no indication of suffering physical pain. Most editions and productions omit the O sound(s).

While the 'O' groans might work in some performances, in this version, they would have been, as Pequigney argues, misleading. This is a *Hamlet* that does not wrench the heart; instead it presents a clear view of a valid interpretation. The death of Ophelia is not without its consolation: she goes to heaven; she has been loved. Several others deserve their deaths. Camargo's Hamlet triumphs, in spite of a few wild moments in the nunnery and closet scenes, in that he never violates his humanity.

Still, it is important to note that the upbeat interpretation comes with the cutting of interfering lines and the additions of images that enhance the themes. Shakespeare's play as we have it in the earliest texts is much more complicated, a mine from which directors as talented as Esbjornson can draw diamonds like this TFANA production.

NARRATIVE OF NEGATIVITY: WHIG HISTORIOGRAPHY AND THE SPECTRE OF KING JAMES IN *MEASURE FOR MEASURE*

KEVIN A. QUARMBY

Traditional criticism of *Measure for Measure* has long noted a similarity between the fictional Duke Vincentio and the real King James. Indeed, some critics of *Measure for Measure* have insisted that the Duke and James are one and the same. Providing a cautious warning against such analogous readings, the 1991 Oxford editor N. W. Bawcutt advised that one 'would best be sceptical about excessive claims for royal presence' in the Duke's role.[1] Bawcutt's scepticism appeared in sharp contrast, however, to that of his Cambridge counterpart Brian Gibbons who, also in 1991, proclaimed 'no doubt' that aspects of the Duke's personality were 'intended to be recognized as allusions to the new king'.[2] Gibbons's comments echoed those of his Cambridge forebears, Sir Arthur Quiller-Couch and John Dover Wilson, who, in their 1922 Cambridge edition (and repeated in editions as late as 1950), maintained that 'James I's dislike of crowds' was a 'historic fact', and that 'any doubt upon the matter... should be laid to rest'.[3] As is evident, for these early twentieth-century editors, analogous similarity between Shakespeare's Duke and the real King James was based irrefutably on 'historic fact', with Shakespeare attempting a lifelike portrayal, or topical caricature, of the personality or political opinion of his Scottish king and patron. Biographical analogy held the key to appreciating the contextual topicality of Shakespeare's dramatic creation, with the spectre of King James residing firmly in the Duke of *Measure for Measure*.

In this article, I will refer to this specific instance of biographical analogy, focusing as it does on certain negative aspects of James's personality and reign whilst searching for parallels in the Duke, as the 'Duke-as-James' theory. That the 'Duke-as-James' theory should remain relatively unchallenged in criticism of *Measure for Measure* is surprising, not least in the light of revisionist historical research that has, ever since the 1950s, offered an alternative, more sympathetic view of James and his reception in England in 1603–4. Unfortunately, a culture of critical conservatism among Shakespeare scholars, especially those who follow the hegemonic/subversive model of new historicist practice, continues to uphold the 'Duke-as-James' theory as irrefutable 'historic fact'. By refusing to respond to longstanding revisionist historical research, new historicist scholars continue to nurture a traditionally held view of *Measure for Measure* as topical political commentary, with Shakespeare offering decidedly negative or apologetic opinions about the qualities and intentions of his new king. This article seeks to redress the imbalance caused by such critical conservatism by interrogating our tacit acceptance of the 'Duke-as-James' theory in relation to *Measure for Measure*, and by highlighting the anachronistic historical construct at the theory's core.

The almost universal belief that the disguised Duke in *Measure for Measure* represents a barely disguised caricature of James is based on two famous

---

[1] N. W. Bawcutt, ed., *Measure for Measure* (Oxford, 1991), p. 5.

[2] Brian Gibbons, ed., *Measure for Measure* (Cambridge, 1991), p. 22.

[3] Sir Arthur Quiller-Couch and John Dover Wilson, eds., *Measure for Measure* (Cambridge, 1922; rev. edn 1950), p. 118n.

passages in the play. The first contains the Duke's brief explanation to Escalus about his secretive plans to travel 'privily away' from Vienna:

> *Duke.*   I love the people,
> But do not like to stage me to their eyes:
> Though it do well, I do not relish well
> Their loud applause and *aves* vehement:
> Nor do I think the man of safe discretion
> That does affect it.   (1.1.67–72)

The Duke's excuse is that he hopes to avoid both the public 'staging' and the consequent 'loud applause and *aves* vehement' (a hendiadys that combines loud clapping with the excessively loud 'hails and farewells') of his adoring public. Not only does the Duke fail to 'relish' these noisy public farewells – 'relish' either referring to being 'pleased or satisfied with' (*OED v.*[1]3.b.) or, more intriguingly, to his 'appreciating' or 'understanding' them (*OED v.*[1]3.d.) – but he also expresses concern over the 'safe discretion' (judgement or prudence) of any man who does 'affect it' (who ostentatiously shows a liking for such displays (*OED v.*[1]5.a.)).

The second supposed allusion to James occurs in Angelo's description of the physical effect of his meetings with Isabella:

> *Angelo.* So play the foolish throngs with one that swoons,
> Come all to help him, and so stop the air
> By which he should revive – and even so
> The general subject to a well-wished king
> Quit their own part and, in obsequious fondness
> Crowd to his presence, where their untaught love
> Must needs appear offence.   (2.4.24–30)

Like the subjects who rush to greet their king, Angelo's blood rushes uncontrollably to his swooning (and lusting) heart, so stifling the metaphorical 'air' that will aid his moral recovery. Angelo likens this onrush of blood to the 'untaught' (ignorant) masses who, from 'obsequious fondness' (unduly servile and foolish affection) and spurred on by seeing the kingly object of their veneration, are prone to 'quit' (relinquish) their 'own part' (their allotted role in society) and crowd into the royal presence, thus unwittingly causing offence with their coarse behaviour. As Angelo's contemplation of his

physical and emotional response to Isabella's proximity suggests, the 2.4 dialogue is more subjective and introspective in its imagery. Although Angelo pointedly refers to a 'king', this royal presence in the metaphor, like a king's presence in a court, is a necessary factor in Angelo's expression of uncontrollable lust and unexpected passion; reference to a 'king' need not imply Shakespeare's conscious allusion to his own ruler, King James. Subjectivity and introspection remain the true focus of Angelo's concern.

The Duke's 1.1 'privily away' comment appears, however, far more specific in its self-analysis. Nevertheless, and despite the wholly acceptable and logical explanation for the Duke's secretive departure, the true reason for his travelling 'privily away' (as the audience soon discovers) is to embark on an adventure of subterfuge and surveillance, with the intention of observing the actions of his deputy: 'Hence shall we see / If power change purpose, what our seemers be' (1.3.53–4). Indeed, the likelihood that the Duke's original explanation represents no more than a diplomatic excuse for his disguised adventure is confirmed by his later choice 'To enter publicly' (4.3.93) on his return to Vienna with all the pomp and ceremony appropriate to his rank. The Duke's command to Angelo to 'Give [him his] hand / And let the subject see, to make them know / That outward courtesies would fain proclaim / Favours that keep within' (5.1.13–16), appears both ironic and politically astute. For a Duke who has earlier claimed to dislike 'staging' himself to his people's eyes, his decision to 'enter publicly' in 5.1 implies a confidence and ease with the spectacle of state that belies the 1.1 reference to self-conscious avoidance of the public gaze. As Steven Mullaney suggested in the late 1980s, such spectacle was particularly suited to Queen Elizabeth's 'theatricality of power'.[4] Likewise, Jonathan Goldberg had already argued that James adopted and adapted Elizabeth's theatricality on his accession to the English throne, fashioning it to suit his

---

4 Steven Mullaney, *The Place of the Stage* (Chicago, 1988), pp. 10–15.

more distanced, representational attitude to kingship and display.[5] In consequence, and in the light of his staged return, the Duke's original excuse for hurrying away in secret appears at best spurious, at worst defensive and obfuscatory. It likewise suggests the Duke's skilful manipulation of his deputies and of events as they unfold.

Any suggestion that the Duke might be manipulating his deputies – claiming a desire to avoid his people and then returning to Vienna with all the spectacle of state for the public exposure of Angelo's misconduct – is, however, contrary to traditional occasionalist readings of *Measure for Measure*. Belief in the occasionality of *Measure for Measure* (its composition as a direct result either of the 'occasion' of James's accession to the throne or of a royal command performance at court) presupposes that the play represents Shakespeare's direct engagement in Jacobean social and political debate; in effect, that Shakespeare had a specific agenda in highlighting his monarch's presence in the play. Quiller-Couch and Wilson's comment, that the 1.1 and 2.4 passages appear to have been '*additions*, written expressly*' for the play's royal auditor at the 'Court performance of 1604', is a specific example of occasionalist commentary (*Measure*, 118n.). In the late 1970s, however, Richard Levin expressed his derision for those who interpret Shakespeare's plays as 'compositions directed at a special audience', in *Measure for Measure*'s case, King James.[6] Levin was particularly scathing about one aspect of the 'Duke-as-James' theory that had come to dominate critical consideration of *Measure for Measure*: the quest for suggestive parallels between the Duke's character and James's famous political writings, especially *The True Lawe of Free Monarchies* (1598) and *Basilikon Doron* (1599 and 1603).[7] This quest had resulted in the creation of what Levin termed a 'King James Version' of *Measure for Measure*. For Levin, this personality-nuanced 'King James Version' of critical study, based, as it appears, on the 'Duke-as-James' theory which represents its extreme expression, threatened to elide alternative readings of the play.

Despite Levin's comments and possibly because of the date of his writing being so close to the advent of new historicist practice in the early 1980s, such caution has received only passing consideration from literary scholars intent on analysing *Measure for Measure* as an occasionalist text.[8] It is, of course, wholly understandable why occasionalist readings of *Measure for Measure* appear so attractive, not least considering the famous Revels Account record of a performance 'By his Ma[tis] plaiers': 'On S[t] Stiuens night [Boxing Day 26 December 1604] in the [Banqueting] Hall [at Whitehall] A play caled Mesur for Mesur' by 'Shaxberd'.[9] This reference provides the earliest and only evidence for the play's existence prior to publication in the 1623 Folio. Important as this historical evidence undoubtedly is, the fact that other Shakespeare plays presented at Court in the same Christmas Revels season (*Comedy of Errors* and *Henry V*) are equally well documented appears to counter any claim that *Measure for Measure* represents a unique example of court-specific play presentation. As Goldberg first noted, there are no extant plays irrefutably known to have been written specifically for court performance; all seem already to have appeared in the public repertory.[10] Nevertheless, the continued acceptance of a specific occasionality for *Measure for Measure*, which has proved most valuable when considering the play's chronological situation in the Shakespeare canon, has only served to confirm the 'Duke-as-James' theory as literary 'fact' for those who believe the character of King James lurks in the character of the Duke.

---

[5] Jonathan Goldberg, *James I and the Politics of Literature* (Baltimore, 1983), pp. 30–1.

[6] Richard Levin, *New Readings vs. Old Plays* (Chicago, 1979), p. 167.

[7] King James, VI & I, *The True Lawe of Free Monarchies* (Edinburgh, 1598) and *Basilikon Doron* (Edinburgh, 1599; repr. London, 1603). See Jenny Wormald, 'James VI & I, *Basilikon Doron* and *The Trew Law of Free Monarchies*: the Scottish Context and the English Translation', in Linda Levy Peck, ed., *The Mental World of the Jacobean Court* (Cambridge, 1991), pp. 36–54.

[8] Ivo Kamps and Karen Raber, *Measure for Measure: Texts and Contexts* (Boston, 2004), pp. 124–7.

[9] Public Records Office AO3/908/13.

[10] Goldberg, *James I*, p. 231.

Of significant importance for our understanding of the 'Duke-as-James' theory as an anachronistic historical construct, rather than as 'historic fact', is the actuality that the theory's heritage can be traced to a critical tradition that gained strength not in the seventeenth century in the immediate aftermath of either Shakespeare's, King James's or King Charles's death, but in the mid-eighteenth century. Indeed, what is generally accepted as the earliest mention of the 'Duke-as-James' theory in relation to *Measure for Measure* was not made until 1766, when Thomas Tyrwhitt claimed that Shakespeare's intention in writing the Duke was 'to flatter ['to represent too favourably' (*OED v.*[1]9.a.)] that unkingly weakness of *James the first*, which made him so impatient of the crowds that flocked to see him, especially on his first coming'.[11] Tyrwhitt offers apparently irrefutable historical evidence about James's public persona to justify this comment. This evidence, however, is itself potentially flawed and, like so much eighteenth-century commentary on James, is reliant on partisan hearsay rather than objectively gathered 'historic fact'. Stemming from historical commentary by individuals actively participating in a post-regicide, pro-Parliament narrative of negativity directed against all aspects of the Stuart monarchy, such partisan historicizing, full of half-truths and gossip, scandalous fictions and downright lies, was to become known as Whig historiography.[12] First identified by Herbert Butterfield as a principle 'introduced for the purpose of facilitating the abridgement of history', Whig historiography presented a grand narrative of historical events that was biased in favour of an inevitable progression towards liberal democracy and constitutional monarchy. Whig historiography was also to become the defining historical principle for describing James's personality and rule, reaching its apotheosis with Thomas Babington Macaulay's *History of England* of 1848.[13] It was in direct response to eighteenth-century Whig historiography, therefore, that Tyrwhitt introduced the 'Duke-as-James' theory into the vocabulary of *Measure for Measure* criticism.

Preceded in 1765 by Samuel Johnson's obvious displeasure at *Measure for Measure*'s morality, being particularly outraged by '*Angelo's* crimes' and believing that 'every reader feels some indignation when he finds him spared',[14] Tyrwhitt's 1766 'Duke-as-James' comments about the 1.2 and 2.4 dialogue demonstrate how far Shakespeare's play had captured the imagination of the age. Citing the opinion of 'some of our Historians' (a comment which, as we shall later see, is particularly relevant when considering the source for his ideas), Tyrwhitt discusses how James 'restrained' the crowds who flocked to him and offers 'A Manuscript in the *British Museum*' as primary evidence:

> Sir *Symonds D'Ewes*, in his Memoirs of his own Life, has a remarkable passage with regard to this humour of *James*. After taking notice, that the King going to Parliament, on the 30th *of January*, 1620–1, 'spake lovingly to the people, and said, '*God bless ye, God bless ye*'; he adds these words, '*contrary to his former hasty and passionate custom, which often, in his sudden distemper, would bid a pox or a plague on such as flocked to see him*.'[15]

For Tyrwhitt, the most convincing proof of James's 'unkingly weakness' comes not from the early years of James's reign when *Measure for Measure* was first performed, but from a manuscript describing a reminiscence about the year 1621 (old-style calendar 1620) written by the parliamentarian and procedural historian, Sir Simonds D'Ewes. D'Ewes relates this experience in his handwritten *Autobiography* (*c.* 1637), a self-edited though unpublished account of his life up to 1635 (based on memory and personal documents) intended for the private edification of his family.[16] D'Ewes's *Autobiography* was not published, therefore, until 1845, over two centuries after his meticulous and

[11] Thomas Tyrwhitt, *Observations and Conjectures upon some Passages of Shakespeare* (Oxford, 1766), p. 36.

[12] Herbert Butterfield, *The Whig Interpretation of History* (London, 1931), pp. 24–6.

[13] Thomas Babington Macaulay, *History of England from the Accession of James II*, 5 vols. (London, 1848–55), vol. 1 (1848).

[14] Samuel Johnson, ed., *The Plays of William Shakespeare*, 8 vols. (London, 1765), vol. 1, p. 378.

[15] Tyrwhitt, *Observations*, pp. 36–7.

[16] BL Harley MS 646, fols 53–4.

steady hand first drafted it.[17] In his discursive narrative style, which embraces personal, national and international affairs and anecdotes in chronological sequence, D'Ewes recalls how once, as an onlooker and 'not without some danger', he had positioned himself in a throng of well-wishers to see 'his Ma[tie] passe to Parliament in state' on his 'short progresse from Whitehall to Westminster' (Harley 646, fol. 54). This fleeting moment in the young D'Ewes's life is seized upon by Tyrwhitt to explain two passages in Shakespeare's *Measure for Measure*.

Primary evidence as D'Ewes's testimony undoubtedly is, it is also worthy of a certain circumspection, especially since it recalls an event towards the end of James's life that occurred when D'Ewes was obviously an impressionable nineteen-year-old observer and newcomer to London. As recently as September 1620, four months prior to the state occasion he recalls, D'Ewes had been forced by his overbearing father to leave Cambridge University and embark on a career at the Inner Temple. Only a year old when James acceded to the English throne, and educated variously in Dorset and Suffolk, D'Ewes's only experience of the metropolis or of the pomp of state came from occasional sojourns with his father and grandfather, whose legal duties kept them in London for the seasonal Terms.[18] D'Ewes's 1620s comment about James's customary behaviour must, by necessity, be considered at best a response to, at worst an interpretation of, family hearsay and gossip about James's early reign; it cannot be considered objective personal observation conducted over a number of years.

Closer inspection of this particular memory also negates Tyrwhitt's emphatic stance about its significance. The same anecdote continues with D'Ewes's observation (not included in Tyrwhitt's commentary) that King James, on 'looking upp to one window as hee passed full of gentlewomen or Ladies all in yellow bandes hee cried out aloud, A pox take yee are yee there; at which being much ashamed, they all withdrew themselves suddenlie from the window' (Harley 646, fol. 54). Tantalizing as this picture of an elderly, disgruntled and possibly paranoid monarch might be, or for what reason these specific onlookers (or perhaps, more intriguingly, one special 'onlooker' among many) were recipients of James's ire, D'Ewes's reminiscence hardly proves some newly found desire in the king to speak 'lovingly' to his subjects, nor does it confirm a general displeasure with the wider crowds who flocked to see him. Indeed, the whole procession, as described by D'Ewes, is one of pomp and public display. Likewise, with the cheering crowds and 'danger' of the throng, D'Ewes was fortunate to have heard *anything* the king had to say, let alone be in a position to interpret his meaning or compare it with his 'former' behaviour.

Of final significance, when considering Tyrwhitt's reliance on this eminent 'witness', is D'Ewes's own anti-Stuart predisposition and, as his Victorian editor J. O. Halliwell accurately described it, his insufferable pedantry.[19] In 1643, six years after penning his autobiography, D'Ewes famously aligned himself with the parliamentary side.[20] As a parliamentary sympathizer and (albeit private) commentator on political history (his first published work on Elizabethan parliaments appeared in 1682, thirty-two years after his death), D'Ewes's observations were to become of particular relevance to later Whig historians who recognized the value of his unsympathetic portrait of the Stuart monarchy.[21] Even so, these same observations and notes did not enter the public domain until long after the sale of D'Ewes's private papers in 1705, their acquisition for the Earl of Oxford's library, and, following the earl's death in 1741, their relocation to the British Museum as part of the Harley

[17] J. O. Halliwell-Phillips, ed., *The Autobiography and Correspondence of Sir Simonds D'Ewes*, 2 vols. (London, 1845), vol. 1, pp. 169–70.

[18] Andrew G. Watson, *The Library of Sir Simonds D'Ewes* (London, 1966), pp. 2–3.

[19] Wallace Notestein, ed., *The Journal of Sir Simonds D'Ewes* (New Haven, 1923), p. x.

[20] See J. M. Blatchly, 'D'Ewes, Sir Simonds, first baronet (1602–1650)', *Oxford Dictionary of National Biography* (2004) www.oxforddnb.com/view/article/7577, accessed 26 September 2010.

[21] Sir Simonds D'Ewes, *The Journals of All the Parliaments During the Reign of Queen Elizabeth Both of the House of Lords and House of Commons* (London, 1682).

MSS.[22] Writing some twenty years after a select few finally gained access to these documents, Tyrwhitt was responding to evidence only recently being read and recognized by his contemporaries as valuable materiel in their arsenal of Whig propaganda. Tyrwhitt was also responding to evidence from a man whose youthful response to an ailing monarch could not mask the fact that D'Ewes was describing memories from his early impressionable days in London, long before his legal and political skills had made him an invaluable though pedantically self-important asset to the nation's government.

Implicit in Tyrwhitt's description of James's personality and his use of D'Ewes's reminiscence as a key to interpreting aspects of *Measure for Measure* is an underlying acceptance of nuanced Whig historiography disseminated by contemporary commentators who pored over newly available manuscripts for the least sign of any publicly or privately expressed anti-Stuart feeling. D'Ewes's memoirs (and his comments about the Stuarts), having remained in private libraries for nearly a century, were now open to scrutiny by partisan eighteenth-century Whig historiographers. Nevertheless, partisan historiography was by no means restricted to the eighteenth century, nor was Tyrwhitt's awareness of James's personality and rule necessarily restricted to D'Ewes's newly discovered testimony. Ralph Houlbrooke has recently traced the genesis of Whig historiography to the period that accompanied the fall of the Stuart monarchy (Charles I's execution in 1649) and the subsequent publication of memoirs that 'purported to uncover James's personal weaknesses and the more unsavoury aspects of his regime'.[23] The dry, ironic and cynical character assassination of James as 'a Slave' to his 'Favourites' in Sir Anthony Weldon's memoirs of 1650 set the tone for subsequent moralizing exposés about the king's supposedly unrestrained homosexual proclivity.[24] Like Weldon, Francis Osborne (1658) also attacked James's sexuality, claiming that the king openly and 'amorously conveyed' his affection to his '*Favorites* or *Minions*' as if he had 'mistaken their Sex, and thought them Ladies'.[25] With anti-theatrical homophobic

fervour, Osborne describes James's propensity for 'kissing [his favourites] after so lascivious a mode in publick, and upon the Theater as it were of the world, [which] prompted many to Imagine some things done in the Tyring-house [a barely-disguised euphemism for anal intercourse], that exceed my expressions no less then they do my experience' (128).[26] Weldon's and Osborne's prejudiced, inaccurate and rabidly anti-Scottish 1650s polemics were to have a lasting influence on subsequent histories of James.

Character assassinations they undoubtedly are, but Weldon's and Osborne's testimonies at no time introduce the theme of James's avoidance of crowds or unwillingness to stage himself to public gaze. Indeed, in another of his anti-Stuart, anti-Scottish polemics, *A Cat May Look Upon a King* (1652), Weldon describes the 'Entrance of King James into this Kingdome, with as much pomp and glory as the World could afford', a description which belies any claim for kingly reticence towards public display.[27] Similarly, Osborne (intending only to demonstrate the sexual duplicity of both James and Queen Anne) cites a specific occasion when James made a very public show of affection as an apparent political statement to his English subjects. Osborne recalls how, when next he saw the King's 'Progress after his Inauguration' (his state procession sometime after the 25 July 1603 coronation), James was 'dres'd' in an outfit, 'as *Greene* as the grasse he trod on, with a *Fether* in his Cap, and a *Horne* instead

---

[22] Watson, *Library*, p. 62.

[23] Ralph Houlbrooke, 'James's Reputation 1625–2005', in Ralph Houlbrooke, ed., *James VI and I: Ideas, Authority, and Government* (Aldershot, 2006), pp. 169–90 (p. 171).

[24] Sir Anthony Weldon, *The Court and Character of King James* (London, 1650), fol. A3v.

[25] Francis Osborne, *Traditionall Memoyres on the Raigne of King Iames* (London, 1658), p. 127.

[26] For recent study of Stuart Court effeminacy, see Thomas Alan King, *The Gendering of Men, 1600–1750* (Madison, 2004), pp. 70–6. Also: Michael B. Young, *King James and the History of Homosexuality* (New York, 2000), pp. 36–63; David M. Bergeron, *King James and Letters of Homoerotic Desire* (Iowa City, 1999), pp. 147–219.

[27] Sir Anthony Weldon, *A Cat May Look Upon a King* (London, 1652), p. 85.

of a Sword by his side' (54). James's flamboyant huntsman's attire, evoking as it would the English folklore hero Robin Hood, is accompanied by an unusual degree of political awareness for the expectations and wants of the gathering spectators:

He that evening parted with his Queene, and to shew himself more uxorious before the people at his first coming than in private he was, he did at her Coach side take his leave, by Kissing her sufficiently to the middle of the Shoulders, for so low she went bare all the dayes I had the fortune to know her. (55)

James's overtly sexual public display of affection towards his wife and queen, as well as the ostentatious employment of an English mythical figure for his processional costume (as described by a commentator who had already shown little regard for the monarch), displays none of what Tyrwhitt was, a century later, to describe as James's 'unkingly weakness'. Unsavoury as Osborne's character assessment of James might be, neither he nor Weldon appear responsible for later comments about James's antisocial, politically incompetent or reclusive behaviour.

Although Weldon and Osborne are representative of the negative responses to the House of Stuart that were voiced in the aftermath of Charles I's execution, alternative views about James's personality were also being expressed at the time. Sir William Sanderson's 1656 description of James as a wise and intelligent monarch, who was by nature more reserved than popular, is representative of this alternative pro-Jamesian polemic.[28] As Houlbrooke notes, the diverse opinions expressed by Weldon and Osborne on one hand and Sanderson on the other meant that, by 1660, 'two sharply opposed views of James had been established':

In the eyes of his admirers, he was a wise, far-sighted, eloquent, open-hearted king who had given his realms and their churches peace and stability. His English critics saw him as a monarch whose mistaken policies towards Roman Catholicism at home and abroad had contributed to his quarrels with his parliaments, along with his extravagance, his elevating of his undeserving favourites and his attempted stretching of the crown's prerogatives.[29]

Two sharply opposed views indeed, but neither the arch-vilifiers Weldon or Osborne nor the arch-apologist and supporter Sanderson offer any suggestion that James was a king who avoided or feared all public display. Quite the reverse; their comments suggest a reserved and intellectual statesman who, through manipulation of his public persona (whether attractive or not), was fully aware of the spectacle of state as an adjunct to successful rule.

As Sanderson's positive appraisal of James's character confirms, bipartisan attitudes towards the Stuart king remained the norm throughout the closing decades of the seventeenth century. By the early eighteenth century, James was finding further support from royalist or 'Tory' apologists such as the Earl of Clarendon (1702) and Laurence Echard (1707), who both describe his great perspicacity and sound judgement.[30] Unfortunately for James, however, the predominant eighteenth-century stance was to become one of Whig animosity towards the king and his regime, as epitomized by the Whig historian John Oldmixon, whose *The History of England* (1730) not only accuses James of abusing English law and custom 'notoriously' for his personal political gain but also nurtures a conspiracy theory that the Gunpowder 'Plot was of the King's own making', with James 'privy to it from first to last'.[31] What seems apparent, therefore, is that Tyrwhitt's 1766 'memoir' evidence is written in the critical tradition not of the royalist or 'Tory' apologists but of that anti-Stuart Whig historiography of which Oldmixon's *History* is such a significant example. Tyrwhitt's comments

---

[28] Sir William Sanderson, *A Compleat History*, 2 vols. (London, 1656), vol. I, pp. 507–13; Sir William Sanderson, *Aulicus Coquinariae: or a Vindication [of] The Court and Character of King James* (London, 1650), pp. 200–5.

[29] Houlbrooke, 'James's Reputation', p. 176.

[30] Edward Hyde, 1st Earl of Clarendon, *The History of the Rebellion and Civil Wars in England*, 3 vols. (Oxford, 1702–4), vol. I, p. 9; Laurence Echard, *The History of England*, 3 vols. (London, 1707–18), vol. I, p. 979.

[31] John Oldmixon, *The History of England* (London, 1730), pp. 14 and 27. See Pat Rogers, 'Oldmixon, John (1672/3–1742)', *Oxford Dictionary of National Biography* (2004), www.oxforddnb.com/view/article/20695, accessed 26 September 2010.

also demonstrate how 'Whiggish' influences had begun to permeate contemporary consideration of Shakespeare, at least with regard to *Measure for Measure*.

Towards the end of the eighteenth century, Edmond Malone (1790) was to develop Tyrwhitt's argument in a similar 'Whiggish' tone. Writing twenty-four years after publication of Tyrwhitt's *Observations*, Malone comments that the same 1.1 and 2.4 'passages...seem intended as a courtly apology for the stately and ungracious demeanour of King James I...written not long after his accession'.[32] For Malone, there is no doubt that Shakespeare, rather than flattering James, was in fact apologizing for his monarch's unattractive 'demeanour' (his bearing or outward behaviour (*OED* 2)), with 'stately' used in its pejorative sense of 'haughty, domineering, arrogant' (*OED* A.*adj*.2.a) and 'ungracious' as 'ungraceful, unattractive' (*OED* a.5.a). Apparently calling upon Osborne's unflattering description of James's personal appearance, Malone's uncomplimentary remark, which complements Tyrwhitt's own interpretation, also represents a turning point in critical consideration of *Measure for Measure* as topical political commentary and Shakespeare's overt attempt to acknowledge his patron's less attractive attributes. For Malone, *Measure for Measure* could now be read as actively engaged if not in the inexorable decline of the Stuart monarchy, then at least as justification for the inevitable bloody outcome of later years.

That Malone's 'courtly apology' theory was generally accepted by his contemporaries is suggested by its repetition in George Steevens's 1793 edition of *Shakspere*.[33] Even so, the Malone theory also had its detractors, as is evident from George Chalmers's scathing 1799 rebuttal of those 'commentators' (Malone and Steevens) who offer their argument for the apparent '*stately* and *ungracious* demeanor of King James': 'No,' exclaims Chalmers, '[t]he fault of this prince was *too much familiarity*, and not stateliness; he was good natured, and not ungracious; he did not like to *stage* himself to the people's eyes; because he delighted in retirement, in the company of a few, in study, and in writing.'[34] For Chalmers,

there appears no doubt that Shakespeare's Duke is correlative to James. Indeed, he expresses his belief 'that the character of *the Duke*, is a very accurate delineation of that of King James, which Shakspeare appears to have caught, with great felicity, and to have sketched, with much truth' (404). The debate about *Measure for Measure*, according to Chalmers, revolves not around whether Shakespeare intended to caricature his king but whether such caricature should be considered offensive or complimentary. As if pre-empting the twentieth-century 'King James Version' controversy and its fascination with textual negotiation, Chalmers adds the rejoinder that, '[k]nowing that King James's writings; his *Basilikon Doron*; his *The True Lawe of free Monarchies*; and other treatises; had been, emulously, republished, in 1603, by the London booksellers, in many editions, Shakspeare could not fitly give a closer parody' (404–5). What is evident from Chalmers's interpretation of the supposed allusions to James is that he considers *Measure for Measure* a 'parody' of contemporary Jacobean political thought and, more importantly, that such parody does not imply Shakespeare's condemnation of his king: 'Shakspeare did not intend to make an apology, but merely to give *traits of character*' (409). Whether those '*traits of character*' are derogatory or not, the critical analysis of Malone, Steevens and Chalmers demonstrates how entrenched the concept of the 'Duke-as-James' theory had become by the beginning of the nineteenth century.

By the mid-nineteenth century, Charles Knight (1849) could reaffirm that Chalmers had made a 'random hit' with his description of the Duke's character traits, claiming them an 'accurate' though good-natured 'parody' of James.[35] Knight's subsequent comparison of the Duke with James nevertheless betrays his own 'Whiggish' distaste

---

[32] Edmond Malone, ed., *The Plays and Poems of William Shakspeare*, 10 vols. (London, 1790), vol. 1, p. 344.

[33] George Steevens, ed., *The Plays of William Shakspeare*, 15 vols. (London, 1793), vol. 1, p. 568.

[34] George Chalmers, *A Supplemental Apology for the Believers in the Shakspeare-Papers* (London, 1799), p. 408.

[35] Charles Knight, *Studies of Shakspere* (London, 1849), p. 319.

for the Stuart monarch. Despite the fact that 'James was a pedant, and the Duke is a philosopher,' Knight observes, 'there is the same desire in each to get behind the curtain and pull the strings which move the puppets' (319). Knight implicitly scorns the pedantry of James's personality. For Knight, the underlying factor that links both Shakespearian character and historical reality is the 'desire' (a particularly emotive word which implies heightened sexual appetite) of both Duke and King to manipulate situations and subjects to their advantage and whim. That Knight should make these less-than-flattering observations is not surprising since his *Studies of Shakspere* was published a year after the first two volumes of Macaulay's *History of England* (1848) first appeared in print. Recognized as the archetypal Whig historian, Macaulay writes an unashamedly partisan history that (following Weldon's and Osborne's lead) describes James's implicitly homosexual 'fondness for worthless minions . . . [his] cowardice, his childishness, his pedantry, his ungainly person and manners, [and] his provincial accent, [which all made] him an object of derision'.[36] Macaulay's distinctive 1848 reference to James's 'pedantry' is reflected in Knight's own 1849 description of James as a 'pedant'. Indeed, the resurgence of interest in the 'Duke-as-James' theory in Shakespeare criticism from the 1850s onwards appears directly linked to the prevailing popularity of Macaulay's partisan Whig history.

The pervasive negativity towards James of Macaulay's Whig history, and its implicit application by Shakespeare scholars to *Measure for Measure*, set the standard for subsequent consideration of the Duke's role in Victorian criticism. It was not, therefore, until the first decade of the twentieth century that serious doubts were expressed about the 'Duke-as-James' theory. Charlotte Porter and Helen A. Clarke, Bostonian editors of a famous complete works based on the First Folio (1903–5), argue that the 'dislike of public adulation' in *Measure for Measure* is more reminiscent of *Coriolanus*, 'rather than James'.[37] Porter and Clarke's American comments, apparently immune to the partisan excesses of British Whig vitriol (a

possible reason why their notes were unceremoniously dropped from the thirteen-volume British edition published in 1906), are contemporaneous with historical reappraisals of James's character.[38] Most notable among these was P. Hume Brown's scathing 1902 description of Macaulay's Whig history as 'false and cruel and vindictive'.[39] Nevertheless, the twentieth century also saw a growing interest in the social implication of *Measure for Measure*, as exemplified by George Bernard Shaw's 1898 comment that Shakespeare was, with *Measure for Measure*, 'ready and willing to start at the twentieth century if the seventeenth would only let him'; in effect, that *Measure for Measure* was coming of age.[40] Heralding the transition from Johnsonian moral outrage to Shavian social commentary, Shaw's remark is indicative of a new climate in which *Measure for Measure*, and thus the 'Duke-as-James' theory, could develop its own topical and socially oriented literary and historical specificity.

'Duke-as-James' specificity is likewise evident in the occasionalist source study of the German scholar Louis Albrecht (1914), which describes *Measure for Measure* as specifically '*vorschwebte*' ('envisioned') by Shakespeare to be '*Huldigungsakte für den neuen König bei seiner Thronbesteigung in England zu gestalten*' ('shaped as a homage for the new king on the occasion of his accession in England').[41] Albrecht also explicitly champions the argument of Chalmers that the play was directly influenced by *Basilikon Doron* (131). Even so, Albrecht is at no time judgemental about the personality of James, believing instead in Shakespeare's analogous intent to flatter his monarch.

---

[36] Macaulay, *History of England*, 11th edn (1856), vol. 1, p. 73.

[37] Charlotte Porter and Helen A. Clarke, eds., *The Complete Works of William Shakespeare*, 12 vols. (New York, 1903–5).

[38] Only seventy-five copies were printed of Porter and Clarke's 1906 *Works* for the British market.

[39] P. Hume Brown, *History of Scotland*, 3 vols. (Cambridge, 1900–9), vol. 2 (1902), p. 186.

[40] George Bernard Shaw, *Plays: Pleasant and Unpleasant*, 2 vols. (London, 1898), vol. 1, p. xxxi.

[41] Louis Albrecht, *Neue Untersuchungen zu Shakespeares* Mass für Mass (Berlin, 1914), p. 164.

Albrecht's non-judgemental pre-First World War comment is countered by the post-war remarks of the first Cambridge editors, Quiller-Couch and Wilson, whose 1920s 'historic fact' about Shakespeare's complicity in providing topical sociopolitical commentary is itself suspiciously dependent on the partisan 'facts' disseminated by earlier Whig historians.[42] Nonetheless, their commentary confirms the extent that the 'Duke-as-James' theory had become entrenched in twentieth-century British criticism, setting the tone for such theorizing for the next thirty years.

It was not, therefore, until 1953 that Mary Lascelles could express cautious doubt about the 'Duke-as-James' theory's validity.[43] Lascelles's caution coincides with a notable shift in historical focus, exemplified by D. Harris Willson's 1956 treatment of James, which suggests that the Scottish king made an unusually favourable impression on observers in 1603, only losing their faith and adulation after perceived failures in his government and foreign policy after 1612.[44] Willson's modest reappraisal of James's reception was subsequently developed by William McElwee, who, in 1958, embarked on the first of many revisionist historical treatments of the Scottish king.[45] McElwee notes that, rather than deriding the 'loud applause and *aves* vehement' of the 'mobs of wellwishers' that greeted his journey to London, James actually enjoyed his new-found popularity (111). As example, McElwee cites James's first 'Speach to Parliament', 19 March 1603, where the new king appears to express genuine 'thankefulnes' for the 'ioyfull and generall applause' he received on entering Parliament, and from his English subjects:[46]

[S]hall it euer bee blotted out of my minde, how at my first entrie into this Kingdome, the people of all sorts rid and ran, nay rather flew to meet mee? their eyes flaming nothing but sparkles of affection, their mouthes and tongues vttering nothing but sounds of ioy, their hands, feete, and all the rest of their members in their gestures discouering a passionate longing, and earnestnesse to meete and embrace their new Soueraigne.

(King James I, 'Speach to Parliament', 19 March 1603)

According to McElwee, there is little here to suggest that James, at this early stage in his rule, was perceived as reticent or unwilling to receive the adulation of his people; on the contrary, such adulation appeared a welcome change from the relative inattention of James's Scottish subjects and perfectly in accord with a widespread optimism and general English relief that the 'tired, old queen' had finally gone.[47]

Despite the alternative historical interpretation of James's political standing by Willson, and despite McElwee's subsequent historical evidence about his reception by the nation, these factors were systematically ignored by Shakespeare critics. In consequence, by the late 1950s, David Lloyd Stevenson was still rehearsing a negative debate about the 'Jamesian' character of the Duke in *Measure for Measure*, even though a decisive sea-change in historical appreciation of James's skill as a ruling monarch was to be announced by Mark H. Curtis's 1961 reappraisal of the 'Hampton Court Conference and its Aftermath'.[48] Explicit in Stevenson's analysis is a full expression of the 'King James Version' of *Measure for Measure* according to Chalmers's late-eighteenth-century model and Albrecht's subsequent early-twentieth-century source study. Likewise, Ernest Schanzer (1963) comments that, 'taken

---

[42] Quiller-Couch and Wilson, eds., *Measure for Measure*, p. 118n.

[43] Mary Lascelles, *Shakespeare's 'Measure for Measure'* (London, 1953), pp. 108–9.

[44] D. Harris Willson, *King James VI & I* (London, 1956), pp. 166–8 and 196.

[45] William McElwee, *The Wisest Fool in Christendom: The Reign of King James I and VI* (London, 1958).

[46] Neil Rhodes, Jennifer Richards and Joseph Marshall, eds., *King James VI and I: Selected Writings* (Aldershot, 2003), pp. 293–4.

[47] Keith M. Brown, 'Monarchy and Government in Britain, 1603–1637', in Jenny Wormald, ed., *The Seventeenth Century* (Oxford, 2008), pp. 13–50 (p. 14).

[48] David Lloyd Stevenson, 'The Role of James I in Shakespeare's *Measure for Measure*', *English Literary History*, 26 (1959), 188–208, later included in David Lloyd Stevenson, *The Achievement of Shakespeare's 'Measure for Measure'* (Ithaca, 1966), pp. 134–66 (p. 134); Mark H. Curtis, 'The Hampton Court Conference and its Aftermath', *History*, 46 (1961), 1–16.

together', the 'idealized image' in the various character traits of the Duke seem 'too uniquely characteristic of James to be dismissed as mere accidental likenesses'.[49] In his Arden 2 edition (one yet to be replaced in the Arden canon), J. W. Lever (1965), although cautious not to suggest the Duke was an 'exact replica' of James, agrees that 'a number of [James's] personal traits went to the making' of the Duke.[50]

By the beginning of the 1970s, therefore, Lever's opinion held sway, despite over a decade's revisionist rethinking of James's personality and political legacy.[51] The eventual 'demolition' of the Whig version of Stuart history was completed, however, by Conrad Russell (1976) and Kevin Sharpe (1978).[52] It is perhaps no coincidence that, at the same time revisionist historians were restoring James's reputation as a skilful king and politician, Levin (1979) could be found wryly coining his phrase 'the "King James Version" of *Measure for Measure*'.[53] Levin's argument against the false occasionality of such 'King James Version' criticism is fiercely contested, however, by Goldberg (1983), who brands Levin a 'skeptic' who 'attacks straw men'.[54] For Goldberg, *Measure for Measure* is undoubtedly a political 're-presentation', whereby the 'power of theater bears a royal stamp'; as such, Shakespeare has written the Duke not as an occasionalist caricature of his king, but as a 'role that represents [Shakespeare's] powers as playwright as coincident with the powers of the sovereign' (232). Likewise, the Duke, according to Goldberg, is representative of Shakespeare's 'coincidence' (his exact agreement) with Stuart divine-right rule as expressed in James's political writings. Goldberg's commentary on *Measure for Measure* appears, however, to rely on traditional negative readings of James's politics and regime. As an early new historicist, Goldberg seems unaware of contemporary developments in revisionist historical thinking, exemplified by the studies of Maurice Lee, Jr and Jenny Wormald, whose respective analyses highlighted the achievement of James's Scottish government, as well as James's energy, informality and accessibility, whilst demonstrating a contemporary belief by the English nation that they were

adopting a new king whose experience far outweighed any negative opinion about their ruler's personal demeanour.[55] Goldberg does not address these issues, concentrating instead on his single fact: that the 'Duke represents James's Divine Right claims' (236).

Echoes of a 'Whiggish' mistrust of James are likewise evident in Leah Marcus's description (1988) of the Duke's 'mythos of power' as synonymous with that adopted by James.[56] Although Marcus argues that the 'King James Version' of *Measure for Measure* has often been 'dismissed as impossibly reductive', she still suggests that 'many parallels' exist between the Duke and James (164). This 'Duke-as-James' parallelism is sufficient to introduce a 'remarkably Jacobean *style* [to] the duke's activities' (177). Implicit in Marcus's description of James's 'Jacobean *style*' is her unquestioning acceptance of the same 'Whiggish' facts that had created the 'King James Version' of *Measure for Measure* and which she finds so reductive. For Marcus, the argument against a 'King James Version' of

---

[49] Ernest Schanzer, *The Problem Plays of Shakespeare* (London, 1963), pp. 123–4.

[50] J. W. Lever, ed., *Measure for Measure*, Arden 2 (London, 1965), pp. l and xlix. Less cautious is Josephine Waters Bennett, *'Measure for Measure' as Royal Entertainment* (New York, 1966), who argues that the likeness to the playwright's patron was because Shakespeare played the part of the Duke himself (p. 137). Goldberg, *James I*, describes this as 'literalistic fantasy' (p. 232).

[51] For the change in historical attitudes towards James that began in the 1960s, see Marc L. Schwarz, 'James I and the Historians: Towards a Reconsideration', *Journal of British Studies*, 13 (1974), 114–34.

[52] Houlbrooke, 'James's Reputation', p. 185; Conrad Russell, 'Parliamentary History in Perspective, 1604–1629', *History*, 61 (1976), 1–27, and Conrad Russell, *Parliaments and English Politics 1621–1629* (Oxford, 1979), pp. 85–203; Kevin Sharpe, ed., *Faction and Parliament* (Oxford, 1978).

[53] Levin, *New Readings*, p. 167.

[54] Goldberg, *James I*, p. 286n.

[55] Maurice Lee Jr, *Government by Pen: Scotland under James VI and I* (Urbana, 1980); Jenny Wormald, *Court, Kirk and Community: Scotland 1470–1625* (London, 1981), pp. 143–59; Jenny Wormald, 'James VI and I: Two Kings or One?', *History*, 68 (1983), 187–209.

[56] Leah Marcus, *Puzzling Shakespeare* (Berkeley and Los Angeles, 1988), p. 163.

the play rests solely on her assumption that Shakespeare would have been foolhardy to admonish his king so openly. In a similar vein, Gary Taylor and John D. Jowett (1993) also implicitly agree with the theory when claiming that, '[c]learly, James's distaste for crowds became visible, at least to discerning observers, very early'.[57] Taylor and Jowett base their conclusion not on James's public speeches to Parliament, nor on D'Ewes's memoir evidence, but on a private letter from Thomas Wilson of 22 June 1603, which refers obliquely to public dismay at James's inaccessibility, and equally private journal entries by Queen Elizabeth's Master of Requests, Sir Roger Wilbraham (written sometime between April and July 1603), which comments on the 'offence' caused to James by those who 'thronge at Court' (172–3).[58] Taylor and Jowett do not note, however, that these same references also share a common complaint. Wilson's letter claims that the 'people . . . desyre some more of that generous affabilitye wch ther good old Queen did afford them' (Nichols, 1, 188). Likewise, Wilbraham's journal complains that the queen would 'labour to entertayne strangers and sutors & her people', a 'courtlie courtesie' no longer proffered by the king (Wilbraham, *Journal*, 59).[59] Both Wilson and Wilbraham recognize a difference in court practice following the death of Queen Elizabeth that apparently accords with the 'Duke-as-James' theory of kingly reserve and distance; they also privately bemoan this new circumstance, in Wilson's case understandably, since in 1601 he had penned a lengthy justification for James's right to accede to the English throne.[60]

The privately expressed grievances of two English courtiers, apparently reacting to a refusal by their king to 'entertayne strangers and sutors' and expressed in the aftermath of James's arrival with his privileged Scottish entourage, might be read not only as biographical observations about their new monarch but also as personal complaint about changes in the distribution of privilege and power.[61] Wilbraham, as Master of the Court of Requests since at least 1600 (the post was transferred in 1603 to Wilbraham's rival Sir Julius Caesar), was in a privileged position to observe

unscrupulous courtiers abusing the non-fee-paying benefit of (what originally had been envisioned as) the nation's tribunal for the poor.[62] Unwilling to pander to the 'thronge' of wealthy petitioners who appeared at 'every back gate & privie dore', the new king, as Wilbraham declares, showed great 'wisdome' in avoiding suitors whose outlandish requests might have caused 'the damage of the crowne & government' (Wilbraham, *Journal*, 56–7). Wilbraham's comments (ignored by Taylor and Jowett) confirm the opinion of revisionist historians who, arguing against traditional Whig interpretations of James, describe the new king as far less amenable towards those wealthy suitors who sought further to line their pockets at the expense of the nation. As Peter R. Roberts has recently noted, two such suitors, Richard Fiennes (Lord Say and Sele) and the ex-Irish campaigner Francis Clayton, separately pleaded to the king for respective monopolies to tax playgoers and performances at the public playhouses.[63] Fiennes's request to impose a poll-tax on playgoing and Clayton's equally audacious tax on individual performances

---

57 Gary Taylor and John D. Jowett, *Shakespeare Reshaped, 1606–1623* (Oxford, 1993), p. 173.

58 Thomas Wilson's letter appears in John Nichols, ed., *The Progresses, Processions, and Magnificent Festivities, of King James the First*, 4 vols. (London, 1828), vol. 1, p. 188. For Sir Roger Wilbraham see Harold Spencer Scott, ed., *The Journal of Sir Roger Wilbraham*, The Camden Miscellany, 10 (London, 1902), p. 56.

59 Also Robert Ashton, ed., *James I by his Contemporaries* (London, 1969), p. 7.

60 A. F. Pollard, 'Wilson, Sir Thomas (d. 1629)', rev. Sean Kelsey, *Oxford Dictionary of National Biography*, www.oxforddnb.com/view/article/29690, accessed 26 September 2010. See F. J. Fisher, ed., *'The State of England, Anno Dom. 1600' by Sir Thomas Wilson*, Camden Society Miscellany, xvi, 3rd series, 52 (London, 1936).

61 See Curtis Perry, *The Making of Jacobean Culture: James I and the Renegotiation of Elizabethan Literary Practice* (Cambridge, 1997); W. B. Patterson, *King James VI and I and the Reunion of Christendom* (Cambridge, 1997); Keith M. Brown, 'The Scottish Aristocracy, Anglicization and the Court, 1603–38', *The Historical Journal*, 36 (1993), 543–76 (pp. 548–9).

62 Scott, *Journal of Sir Roger Wilbraham*, p. xii.

63 Peter R. Roberts, 'The Business of Playing and the Patronage of Players at the Jacobean Courts', in Houlbrooke, ed., *James VI and I*, pp. 81–105.

were, as Roberts suggests, 'either abandoned in the face of insuperable obstacles or rejected by the king as unacceptable' (102). If categorically refused by James, such refusal would no doubt result in equally disgruntled private correspondence and journal entries from the snubbed pair. Whether the result of policy or direct intervention, this refusal implies a less self-serving, disinterested or reclusive stance for James and/or his regime.

Whatever our own response to the theatrical implications of this brash attempt to tax playgo-ers and performances, this episode provides fur-ther proof that the supposedly easily recognizable 'style' of James's rule, as one of unlimited patron-age and favouritism, can be countered by revisionist historical study. Likewise, contemporary responses to James's sixteenth-century writings suggest con-fused and inconsistent opinions about the king's perceived personal 'style'. Available in print prior to and immediately following his arrival in Lon-don, political texts like *Basilikon Doron* and *The True Lawe* might have provided a flavour of his tech-nique of power; their diverse and contradictory nature ensured that they could never be read by Shakespeare and his contemporaries as a blueprint for a Jacobean 'style' of government.[64] Similar revi-sionist considerations should be given to comments about James's lack of political interest and dedica-tion. On 26 December 1604, the date of *Measure for Measure*'s court performance and the day after Christmas Day, no less than twenty-one documents were signed by James, a workload matching previ-ous and subsequent working days, and one which appears counter to the perceived 'style' of a lax and disinterested ruler.[65] If the 'style' of James's reign could, as early as 1604, not be pinpointed by contemporary complainants, it seems particu-larly unlikely that a playwright at the Globe should have developed so close a relationship with govern-ment and with his royal patron as to parody, satirize or comment on its/his efficacy or direction.[66]

Our continued critical engagement with 'Duke-as-James' parallelism, with its belief in the supposed subversion of a Jacobean political 'style' as funda-mental feature of *Measure for Measure*, effectively relies on, and implicitly upholds, those partisan

falsehoods about James's government that suited the bias of earlier Whig historians. Literary crit-ics who recognize a 'Jacobean style' for *Measure for Measure* thus unwittingly and almost impercepti-bly accept this partisan appraisal of James and the inevitable failure of his regime. As Diana New-ton has recently argued, however, it is 'only by taking a holistic view of James's early years, and considering all the aspects of his first years in Eng-land simultaneously, that [we can] get closer to an understanding of his English reign'.[67] A 'holistic view' permits James to emerge as 'energetic, vig-orous, intelligent and flexible', managing his new kingdom 'shrewdly, effectively, and even innova-tively' (Newton, 146). Newton's comments would have been inconceivable to a Whig historian. They likewise appear inconceivable to Shakespeare com-mentators wishing to detect an anxiety-inducing, 'divine-right' patriarchal principle in the Jacobean 'style' of *Measure for Measure*'s Duke – a parallelism and subversion in Shakespeare's message. It is only when the Whig interpretation of James's rule is finally expunged from critical appraisal of *Measure for Measure* that the Duke's disguised adventure can and will be appreciated in its true Jacobean context.

Since Whig historiography appears to hold the key to 'Duke-as-James' theorizing and its applica-tion to *Measure for Measure*, then might Whig his-toriography also offer an alternative, earlier source for Tyrwhitt's 1766 observation, calling as it does upon the evidence of 'some of our Historians', and generally regarded as the first to liken Shakespeare's Duke to James? To answer this question we must

---

[64] Jenny Wormald, 'James VI and I (1566–1625)', *ODNB* (2004) www.oxforddnb.com/view/article/14592, accessed 26 September 2010.

[65] *Calendar of State Papers Domestic: James I, 1603–1610* (1857), pp. 164–82 www.british-history.ac.uk/report.aspx?compid=14995, accessed 21 September 2010.

[66] Daniel Fischlin and Mark Fortier, eds., *Royal Subjects: Essays on the Writings of James VI and I* (Detroit, 2002), stress the 'contradictions' in James's writings that guaranteed the mis-interpretation of his political views by contemporary hear-ers/readers (pp. 22–3).

[67] Diana Newton, *The Making of the Jacobean Regime* (Wood-bridge, 2005), pp. 141–6 (p. 146).

return to that early and significant exponent of Whig historiography, John Oldmixon, whose anti-Jamesian interpretation of the Scottish monarch's character, written thirty-six years before Tyrwhitt's discussion of *Measure for Measure*, appears itself to rely on aspects of Shakespeare's language as analogous indicators with which to explore the personality traits of the Stuart king. A likely candidate for being one of Tyrwhitt's praised Whig 'Historians', it is Oldmixon who demonstrates a specific interest in Shakespeare as an accessible reference point for his anti-Stuart, anti-Scottish and pro-Parliament history.

As already noted when discussing the eighteenth-century bias of anti-James propaganda, Oldmixon, in his 1730 *History of England*, is representative of the Whig historiography that took issue with pro-Stuart 'Tory' historiographers like Clarendon and Echard. Repeating the oft-used soubriquet of the new or second 'Solomon' to describe James's learning, knowledge and wisdom, Clarendon and Echard had defended the king's memory.[68] For Oldmixon, this 'glorious Title of second *Solomon*' represented a falsehood and one that was anathema to his Whig sensibilities (Oldmixon, *History*, 10). Oldmixon's intention, what he describes pointedly and significantly as 'My Design', was 'to show' not James's inherent wisdom and learning, but 'how he and his Posterity . . . made this once flourishing and glorious Kingdom, a Scene of Misery and Disgrace' (11). With his 'Design' firmly established, Oldmixon proceeds to describe James's accession to the English throne with imagery more befitting a fallen angel than a philosopher-king:

Such a Beginning of a Reign promis'd very little Good in the Course of it, but so much Care was taken to gild the Appearance that the Darkness had not its full Effect on the Minds of the people (17).

It is significant that Oldmixon is commenting not on the negative reception of James by his new nation but on the way the king's supposed satanic 'Darkness' was carefully 'gilded', effectively shielding the truth of his evil intent from his adoring subjects' 'Minds'.

Oldmixon's crusading 'Design', to show the devastation James supposedly wreaked on his unfortunate new kingdom, also develops the concept of a suspicious and reclusive monarch, one which better suits those aspects of the Duke's behaviour in *Measure for Measure* that proved of such import to Tyrwhitt in his observations on the play. Having made, as part of his grand character assassination, a particularly scathing condemnation of James's appearance as 'far from being handsome' (10), Oldmixon describes how 'The King had been almost ten Months in *England*, but had not been seen much abroad':

He naturally did not love to be look'd at, for, as has been said, he was not very handsome, and had no Relish of the Formalities of State. Some attribute it not to the Disagreeableness of his Person, but to the Shyness of his Temper, and some to his Timorousness, there being more Danger in a Crowd than in a few attendants (21).

Oldmixon's analysis of James's attitude to the 'Formalities of State', based as it appears on his acceptance of the unflattering portrait of James painted by the post-regicide polemics of Weldon and Osborne, is significant because it echoes the Duke's excuse for travelling 'privily away' because he does not 'relish well' the 'loud applause' of his people. Disagreeable to behold, shy, timorous and threatened with danger by the 'Crowd', James bears a demeanour which, according to Oldmixon, accords with a monarch whose outward 'Appearance' has been altered to 'gild' the true 'Darkness' of that which lurks beneath. It also implies Oldmixon's conscious or unconscious reliance on imagery derived from passages in a Shakespeare play.

A similar description of James's timorousness and irascibility occurs a few lines later, when Oldmixon

---

[68] Clarendon, *History of the Rebellion*, calls James 'a Prince of . . . Learning and Knowledge' (vol. 1, p. 9). Echard, *History of England*, describes James as 'the *Solomon* of the Age for Knowledge, Learning and Wisdom*' (vol. 1, p. 979). For James's iconography as the second 'Solomon', see James Doelman, *King James I and the Religious Culture of England* (Woodbridge, 2000), pp. 76–9.

discusses the King's procession through the City of London:

Having summon'd a Parliament to meet the 19th of *March* [1604], he went on the 15th with his Queen and the Prince to the *Tower*, riding through the City amidst the continu'd Acclamations of the Multitude, which did not affect him as they affected his Predecessor Queen *Elizabeth*. Whether it was that the Noise disturb'd him, or that he did not think them real, 'tis most certain, when the People have been impatient of Access to him, he has often had them dispers'd with Force, and sometimes with Curses. (21–2)

Oldmixon is describing the first procession of the king and his family through the streets of London following the awful plague that had greeted his arrival a year earlier. This very public pageant, complete with ornate triumphal arches designed and erected by Stephen Harrison and with speeches supplied by Thomas Dekker, Ben Jonson and Thomas Middleton, had been delayed until it was deemed safe for the royal family to emerge from self-imposed and wholly understandable plague-induced quarantine within the Tower of London.[69] Again, following the descriptions of James by Weldon and Osborne and perhaps influenced by recently discovered commentary by D'Ewes (who could not have been an eye-witness to this particular episode since he was at the time a two-year-old toddler), Oldmixon nevertheless adds to an image of James that is uncannily reminiscent of Shakespeare's Duke.

If Oldmixon was making a conscious or subconscious analogy between a Shakespeare character and the real King James, what in this Whig historian's background might account for this particular circumstance? Significant for our understanding of Oldmixon and his appreciation of Shakespeare is his 1728 literary study, *An Essay on Criticism*, published two years before his *History of England*.[70] In *An Essay on Criticism*, Oldmixon attacks not only Alexander Pope, but also the 'Royal Historiographers' Clarendon and Echard (Oldmixon, *Essay*, 55). His most intense derision, however, is reserved for John Dryden, who, along with the likes of Sir William D'Avenant (whose 1662

version of *Measure for Measure* was staged as *The Law Against Lovers*), Colley Cibber and Nahum Tate, had famously written Shakespeare-based adaptations, 'in Imitation of *Shakespeare's* Stile', in an effort to make them more palatable to contemporary Restoration tastes.[71] Oldmixon claims to be particularly scornful of Dryden's observation 'that *Shakespear* himself did not distinguish *the blown puffy Stile from true Sublimity*' (Oldmixon, *Essay*, 45), although he does accept Dryden's negative description of France's poetic heritage, agreeing that the 'Latter is incontestable': 'They [the French] have nothing of *Epick* Poetry so good as our King *Arthur*; neither are their *Corneille* and *Racine* a Match for our *Shakespear* and *Otway*' (54).[72] That Shakespeare was, according to Oldmixon, the nation's supreme dramatist had earlier been confirmed by his description of how:

Our *Shakespear* shone on the Stage, with all the Qualities of a Dramatick Poet, and *Diction* in particular, when the . . . *French* Stage was Barbarous. His Style has its Beauties now, and is newer than many who have since Writ, and for a while with Reputation. (29)

For the Whig historian Oldmixon, Shakespeare's dramatic skill was as commendable as James's personality was despicable. That Oldmixon should have such a knowledge and appreciation of Shakespeare is not surprising. Oldmixon was, at the turn of the century, himself an aspiring though self-confessedly less than successful playwright, with several plays performed professionally on the

---

69 Stephen Harrison, *The Arches of Triumph* (London, 1604); Thomas Dekker, *The Magnificent Entertainment* (London, 1604); Ben Jonson, *Part of the Entertainment, through the Cittie of London, Given to James I. 1604* (London, 1604).

70 John Oldmixon, *An Essay On Criticism* (London, 1728).

71 As stated on the frontispiece to John Dryden's *All for Love; or, The World Well Lost* (London, 1678). Also William D'Avenant and John Dryden, *The Tempest, Or, the Enchanted Island* (London, 1670); D'Avenant, *The Law Against Lovers*, in *The Works of Sr William D'avenant K^t*, 3 vols. (London, 1673), vol. 1.

72 Dryden's comments appear in his *Essay of Dramatick Poesie* (London, 1668).

London stage spanning a variety of formal genres.[73] Regardless of how these were received, the plays that Oldmixon presented demonstrate his passion for drama, whilst equally explaining his passion for, and informed opinion about, Shakespeare.

Oldmixon's unfortunate early experiences as a playwright, and the glowing admiration for Shakespeare expressed in his critical studies, represents far more than a passing interest in drama. There seems little reason to doubt, therefore, that Oldmixon, when writing his *History* in 1730, was aware of Shakespeare's plays, especially in their unadapted form. A revival in interest in performing unaltered or relatively complete plays by Shakespeare from the 1720s onwards heralded the birth of the national obsession with the Bard.[74] That *Measure for Measure* was an important part of this revival is confirmed by its ranking sixth of the nine most-performed Shakespeare plays up to 1730.[75] When Oldmixon was writing his *History of England*, and describing James's lack of 'Relish of the Formalities of State', he was doing so in the immediate aftermath of this explosion of interest in *Measure for Measure*. Whether from seventeenth-century editions of Shakespeare or from reprinted examples of individual Shakespeare plays offered by London's booksellers (the 1727 catalogue of books printed for and sold by Thomas Astley from his establishment in St Paul's Churchyard lists *Measure for Measure* in a single play-text edition), Oldmixon would undoubtedly have had access to *Measure for Measure* in one form or another.[76] Obviously in tune with his contemporaries, and with his publicly avowed interest and respect for Shakespeare, Oldmixon appears perfectly situated to respond to aspects of a play that could be adapted to suit his particular 'Whiggish' preconceptions about a discredited Stuart king.

Regardless of whether Oldmixon was consciously employing imagery derived from *Measure for Measure*, or was adopting Shakespeare's language in the belief that his favourite playwright was sending a coded message about the Globe's kingly patron, Oldmixon's description of James bears sufficient similarity to the dialogue isolated by Tyrwhitt over thirty years later to suggest a source for this specific observation. Tyrwhitt's 'Whig' interpretation of *Measure for Measure*, and his expression of the 'Duke-as-James' theory as an explanation for Shakespeare's dialogue, might represent not only his own response to the play but also his response to an idea first suggested by the equally 'Whiggish', equally partisan commentary of Oldmixon, whose literary opinion about Shakespeare has largely gone unnoticed. More famous as a Whig historiographer than as a failed playwright and literary commentator, Oldmixon nevertheless confirms how Shakespeare was viewed as a playwright who was free from 'Whiggish' suspicion that his plays represented the work of an apologist for the despised patron of the King's Men. Oldmixon also provides a plausible prelude to Tyrwhitt's 'Whig' analysis of *Measure for Measure*; like the later Whig historiography of Macaulay that fuelled Charles Knight's reaffirmation of the opinions of Steevens, Malone and Chalmers, Oldmixon's Whig historiography provides similarly accessible fuel for the partisan criticism of Tyrwhitt.

To conclude, the recognition of an occasionalist portrayal or caricature of James in *Measure for Measure* has, for the most part, relied on interpretation of two passages from the play that, in retrospect, have been read as negative appraisals of King James's personality and style of leadership. These passages form the backbone of subsequent literary studies of *Measure for Measure* in an occasionalist Jacobean context. As successive generations of Whig historiographers destroyed the character of James, these 'Whiggish' factors were seized on and integrated into contemporary critical studies of *Measure for Measure*. Although Tyrwhitt

---

[73] See John Oldmixon, *Amintas. A Pastoral* (London, 1698); *The Grove, or Love's Paradice. An Opera* (London, 1700); *The Governour of Cyprus: A Tragedy* (London, 1703).

[74] Robert D. Hume, 'Before the Bard: "Shakespeare" in Early Eighteenth-Century London', *English Literary History*, 64 (1997), 41–75 (p. 60). Also Katherine West Scheil, *The Taste of the Town: Shakespearian Comedy and the Early Eighteenth-Century Theater* (Lewisburg, 2003).

[75] Hume, 'Before the Bard', p. 60.

[76] Thomas Astley, *Books Printed For and Sold By Thomas Astley* (London, 1727), p. 8.

has long been acknowledged the first overtly to describe the 'Duke-as-James' theory in relation to these two passages, an example of anti-James propaganda by the Whig historiographer, Oldmixon, written over thirty years earlier than Tyrwhitt's, suggests a possible source for this later literary conjecture. As with the 'Whiggish' dismissal of James implicit in subsequent analysis of *Measure for Measure*, Oldmixon's account of the much-maligned Stuart monarch acts as precedent for Tyrwhitt's, and thus Malone's, comparison of a fictional Duke with a real king.

Nineteenth-century studies of *Measure for Measure* continued to follow the prevailing fashion for 'Whiggish' historical discourse, exemplified by Macaulay's 'cruel and vindictive' invective. Indeed, much of the partisan flavour of Macaulay remains evident in historicized studies of *Measure for Measure* to this day. Since the 1960s, however, revisionist historians have systematically reappraised James's skill as a king, so casting serious doubt on traditional readings of his reign. Among historians, 'Whiggish' distaste for James has been replaced by a more tolerant and accepting appreciation of his skill as a statesman and writer. The revision of James's history has also led to a reappraisal of his reception in England following the death of Elizabeth; contrary to the traditional Whig narrative, James's accession appears to have been greeted warmly by many of his English subjects, grateful for the peaceful transition to rule by an experienced and erudite monarch. In consequence, James is no longer viewed as the harbinger of court immorality, or as the vanguard of an inexorable decline in the English monarchy that leads inevitably to the execution of Charles I. Likewise, contemporary responses to James's sixteenth-century writings have suggested confused and inconsistent opinions about the Scottish king's perceived personal 'style'.

Revisionist history's reappraisal of James's early political career in England appears only now to be entering the critical vocabulary of literary commentators in their studies of *Measure for Measure*.[77] This somewhat belated acknowledgement of James's political skill is no doubt due to the overriding strength of the parallelism and subversion model that has dominated new historicist criticism from the mid-1980s onwards, and which, although seemingly revisionist in its radical interpretation of *Measure for Measure*, appeared unaware of the old-style conservative historicism that underpinned its arguments. Traceable back to the failed playwright and ardent supporter of Shakespeare, Oldmixon, and predicated on Whig historiography, anti-James attitudes inherent in new historicist studies of anxiety, hegemony and subversion in *Measure for Measure* unwittingly engage in such partisan pursuits. Only by acknowledging the implicit heritage of partisan, anti-James Whig historiography residing undetected in new historicist studies of *Measure for Measure* can the play's complex engagement with the social and theatrical culture of its time truly emerge.

---

[77] Andrew Hadfield, *Shakespeare and Renaissance Politics* (London, 2004), pp. 182–200, argues that Shakespeare and his contemporaries were less critical of James's rule; also Andrew Hadfield, *Shakespeare and Republicanism* (Cambridge, 2005), pp. 205–6.

QUÉBÉCOIS SHAKESPEARE GOES GLOBAL: ROBERT LEPAGE'S *CORIOLAN*

ROBERT ORMSBY

Speaking in advance of the Montréal performances of his *Cycle Shakespeare*, staged at international venues between 1992 and 1994, Robert Lepage described the tour stop in his home province as a response to the double colonization that Québec has historically experienced within Canada.[1] Explaining that, in an effort to defend French culture, Québécois theatres have traditionally staged Molière and Racine more frequently than Shakespeare, Lepage remarked, 'Shakespeare, jusqu'à présent, était réservé au Canada anglophone. Il nous était toujours présenté comme un auteur de luxe que l'on pouvait lire mais pas monter' [Shakespeare, until now, has been reserved for Anglophone Canada. He has always been presented to us as a de luxe author who can be read but not staged].[2] As he would later relate, his solution to this situation, in which loyalty to one former colonial power compounds the inequalities caused by obedience to another, was to redeploy Shakespeare as a product of transnational culture. He believed that, by including performances at Montréal's Festival de Théâtre des Amériques (FTA) in the *Cycle* tour, he was allowing 'the French-speaking public [to] discover a repertoire that it virtually never gets to see', and thus he could bring global culture to Québec *through* Shakespeare.[3] At the same time, by touring the *Cycle* – comprised of *Coriolan*, *Macbeth* and *La Tempête* – to numerous countries, he implicitly validated an outward-looking image of Québec while incidentally helping to ensure the viability of international Shakespeare theatre.

The tone of Lepage's comments actually seem, politically, rather moderate, considering that the *Cycle*'s two-year tour overlapped with the highly charged political events of the early 1990s, events that harked back to Québec's nationalist movement of the 1970s in their divisive effect on Canadian federalism. In October 1992, shortly after the Paris run of the *Cycle*, Canadians voted in a bitterly debated referendum, rejecting the national government's Charlottetown Accord, which would have enshrined in the Constitution Québec's status as a distinct society within Canada. The following autumn, at the mid-point between the Montréal *Cycle* performances and the Québec City tour stop,

I would like to thank John Astington, Barbara Hodgdon, Alexander Leggatt and Jill Levenson for their helpful advice on an earlier version of this article. I would also like to thank the anonymous reader from *Shakespeare Survey* and Peter Holland for their insightful feedback on this article; their suggestions allowed me to improve it significantly.

[1] The *Cycle* was co-produced with the Am Turm Theatre in Frankfurt, La Manège in Maubeuge (France), the Festival d'Automne in Paris, the FTA and Théâtre Repère, the Québec company with which Lepage often worked. *Coriolan* was co-produced in Nottingham with the Nottingham Playhouse. For an account of the *Cycle*, see Denis Salter, 'Between Wor(l)ds: Lepage's Shakespeare Cycle', in Joseph I. Donohue and Jane M. Koustas, eds., *Theater Sans Frontières: Essays on the Dramatic Universe of Robert Lepage* (East Lansing, 2000), pp. 191–204.

[2] Quoted in Christelle Prouvost, 'En Québécois dans le Texte', *Le Soir*, 23 September 1992, 35.

[3] Robert Lepage, *Connecting Flights: Robert Lepage in Conversation with Rémy Charest*, trans. by Wanda Romer Taylor (Toronto, 1998), p. 117.

the Bloc Québécois party, newly formed to defend Québec's interests, became the official opposition in Parliament, sitting across the floor from Prime Minister Jean Chrétien, a man disliked by many Québécois for his strong centralizing approach to federalism. Within two years, Canada seemed poised to come apart: in September 1994, Québec's provincial government promised to hold a referendum on negotiating sovereignty from Canada; one year later, Québec voters turned down this proposal by a margin of only 1 per cent.

Given these circumstances, *Coriolan* offers an especially significant illustration of why intercultural Shakespeare, and Lepage's work in particular, has become a crucial site for investigating the relationships between global performance, local identities and the playwright's traditional literary authority.[4] The plays in the French-language *Cycle* were based on 'tradaptations' by Québec poet Michel Garneau, who ostensibly rendered each of the three dramas in a different register of Québécois.[5] Although Garneau began tradapting Shakespeare in the 1970s to establish the viability of a distinct national Québécois culture and language, Lepage's *Coriolan* had a markedly global identity. Not surprisingly, with their international co-producers and touring schedule, *Coriolan* and the *Cycle* complicated efforts to establish a specifically Québécois identity for the productions.[6] Lepage's *Coriolan*, furthermore, did little to suggest specific associations between Shakespeare's cultural cachet and the linguistic and political hegemony of Anglophone Canada. That is, while the director's combination of inventive blocking and his placement of a 'letter-box' cloth frame around the stage action, which, as Lepage noted, put '*everything* – including the fragmented body – into parentheses', may have challenged Shakespeare's textual authority, *Coriolan*'s scenography was not overtly topical and did not appear explicitly to comment on Québec's place within Canada.[7]

I wish to examine in this article how *Coriolan* embodies the competing influences that help define Lepage's Shakespeare production. The complexity of these influences is neatly captured by the questions that Margaret Jane Kidnie poses of Lepage's *Elsinore*: 'Is home something Shakespeare returns *to*, or that Lepage departs *from*? Or is the idea of the "local" best represented by a set of relations that exceeds both Britain and Canada?'[8] The answer to the latter question is, I suggest, yes: these relations are not simply those existing between Québec and England or English Canada but result from interaction amongst local–national Québécois concerns, the traditional authority of Shakespeare, and global theatrical performance. By examining Lepage's scenography and comparing the very different British and Québécois critical response to the production I hope to describe these sets of relations in detail. I argue that *Coriolan* reveals not

---

[4] For discussions of Shakespeare and globalization, see Sonia Massai, ed., *World-Wide Shakespeares: Local Appropriations in Film and Performance* (London and New York, 2005); Krystyna Kujawinska-Courtney and John M. Mercer, eds., *The Globalization of Shakespeare in the Nineteenth Century* (Lewiston, 2003); W. B. Worthen, *Shakespeare and the Force of Modern Performance* (Cambridge, 2003). For discussions of Lepage's Shakespearian work, see Barbara Hodgdon, 'Macbeth at the Turn of the Millennium', in Jay L. Halio and Hugh Richmond, eds., *Shakespearean Illuminations: Essays in Honor of Marvin Rosenberg* (Cranbury, NJ, London, and Mississauga, ON, 1998); Barbara Hodgdon, *The Shakespeare Trade: Performances and Appropriations* (Philadelphia, 1998); Margaret Jane Kidnie, 'Dancing With Art: Robert Lepage's *Elsinore*', in Sonia Massai, ed., *World-Wide Shakespeares*; Ric Knowles, *Shakespeare and Canada: Essays on Production, Translation and Adaptation* (Brussels, 2002); Leanore Lieblein, 'Theatre Archives at the Intersection of Production and Reception: The Example of Québécois Shakespeare', in Edward Pechter, ed., *Textual and Theatrical Shakespeare: Questions of Evidence* (Iowa City, 1996); Salter, 'Between Wor(l)ds'; Shannon Steen and Margaret Werry, 'Bodies, Technologies, and Subjectivities: The Production of Authority in Robert Lepage's *Elsinore*', *Essays in Theatre / Études théâtrales*, 16 (May 1999).

[5] FTA large program, pp. 6–8, states that the plays are written in three different types of Québécois. All references to *Coriolan* are from William Shakespeare, *Coriolan*, trans. by Michel Garneau (Montréal, 1989).

[6] For an account of the dual Québécois and international identities of Lepage's current company, ExMachina, see Jennifer Harvie and Erin Hurley, 'States of Play: Locating Québec in the Performances of Robert Lepage, ExMachina, and the Cirque du Soleil', *Theatre Journal*, 51 (1999).

[7] Denis Salter, 'Borderlines: An Interview with Robert Lepage and Le Théâtre Repère', *Theater*, 24 (1993), 76.

[8] Kidnie, 'Dancing', p. 133, emphasis original.

only how local identity is shaped by international performance contexts and histories of colonial subservience, but that it also demonstrates how globalization can spur the reinvention of the local and that such reinventions operate in global theatrical events to sustain Shakespeare's cultural prestige.

Garneau's *Coriolan* was an appropriate script for Lepage's *Cycle* tour insofar as it demonstrates a shift from local-national contexts to international ones. The internationalizing effect that Lepage's actual touring would eventually have on *Coriolan* was already discernible in the differences between Garneau's first and last tradaptations. Garneau's 1978 *Macbeth* is quite evidently a product of the Québec nationalist movement of the 1960s and 70s; as Annie Brisset puts it, the translation 'vouch[ed] for the existence of a [distinct Québécois language and] "people"' by replacing the historicity of Shakespeare's Jacobean language with the quasi-historicity of a dialogue based on a vocabulary from the Gaspésie region of Québec, where Jacques Cartier first landed and laid claim to the territory.[9] For Brisset, Garneau's *Macbeth* thus 'ties the search for identity to the myth of origins, a myth that the language itself helps to create . . . It is a perfect vehicle for reconstructing a past . . . when the language and those who spoke it owed nothing to anybody.'[10] Garneau's printed text of *Coriolan*, however, does not immediately reflect such markedly nationalist goals. Unlike *Macbeth*, for instance, the published version of *Coriolan* makes no claim to be 'traduit en Québécois', and Garneau's omission of nearly 350 Shakespearian lines from his translation in *Coriolan*, as well as his lowercase lettering of all the dialogue and virtual lack of punctuation embody not so much a pointed linguistic-political agenda as a general insouciance or sense of freedom from the need to translate Shakespeare 'faithfully'.[11]

Moreover, the register of Garneau's *Coriolan* makes the translation easy to 'travel' or to be understood in different parts of the globe. In addition to removing virtually all references to the Classical world, Garneau diminishes the challenge of Shakespeare's complex figurative language for his Francophone audiences.[12] Typical of this strategy is Garneau's prosaic translation of Cominius's 'You shall not be / The grave of your deserving' (1.10.19–20), Coriolanus' 'and at all times / To undercrest your good addition / To th' fairness of my power' (1.10.71–3), and his 'For they do prank them in authority / Against all noble sufferance' (3.1.24–5), which he renders, respectively, as 'je ne te laisserai pas enterer tes mérites' (1.8.29), 'je porterai le nom que tu me donnes / avec fierté' (1.8.74–5) and 'parce qu'ils font croire / aux pauvres gens / qu'ils ont quelque chose à dire / sur la conduite du monde' (3.1.39–42).[13] There is nothing especially Québécois about such language; like the vast majority of the translation, these lines are not in 'joual', the distinctly Québécois dialect, but are written in standard French. Thus, while Garneau's *Coriolan* generally challenges the notion of fidelity to Shakespeare's poetry, the ordinary quality of the French in his translation, along with his removal of much of the play's explicit Graeco-Roman context, eliminate two main sources (Elizabethan and Roman) of historico-linguistic analogues that might serve to 'vouch for' a specific nation with a particular geographic origin, such as Brisset claims he tried to establish in *Macbeth*.

Lepage's treatment of the script followed Garneau in its general disregard for Shakespeare's textual authority (and Garneau's, for that matter). By cutting nearly a third of the published translation that resulted in a performance which ran to just over two hours, Lepage simplified the drama considerably; eliminating more than two dozen

---

[9] Annie Brisset, *A Sociocritique of Translation: Theatre and Alterity in Quebec, 1968–1988*, trans. by Rosalind Gill and Roger Gannon (Toronto, 1996), p. 167.

[10] Brisset, *A Sociocritique*, p. 182.

[11] William Shakespeare, *Macbeth*, trans. by Michel Garneau (Montréal, 1978), front cover.

[12] Garneau either deletes or alters Graeco-Roman gods, myths, offices, locations and luminaries from forty-two places in Shakespeare's text.

[13] All of the English quotations in this paragraph are from William Shakespeare, *Coriolanus*, R. B. Parker, ed. (Oxford, 1994); all of the French quotations in this paragraph are from Garneau's published script.

roles, he foregrounded Coriolan's struggle with Volumnia, Aufidius and the Tribunes.[14] Perhaps Lepage's most significant alteration was his virtual eradication of the Plebeians from the production; they simply never appeared on stage. This omission greatly reduced the play's debate and literal struggle over political enfranchisement, conflicts that could easily be interpreted as an analogy for the historical and contemporary relationships between Québec and Anglophone Canada. What remained of the Plebeians might be understood as a metaphor for the production itself. Menenius still had a (shortened) exchange with the people at the play's opening, but rather than rioting citizens, he delivered the 'Tale of the Belly' (as though from a radio studio) to a few unseen offstage voices. Coriolan still asked for the people's voices (as though from a television studio), but the citizens were, again, represented by unseen offstage voices and, when they 'acclaimed' him consul, their voices were represented by honking horns, becoming even more anonymous. Similarly, when Brutus and Sicinius questioned the Plebeians after Coriolan's election as Consul, the Tribunes spoke to them on the telephone; their lines cut here, the people were neither seen nor heard at all. Elsewhere, the Plebeians' political concerns were voiced entirely by the Tribunes, whom Lepage understood to 'hate the people as much as the elite [patricians] do'.[15] In other words, as the *Cycle* productions' local identity might have been jeopardized by touring extensively to elite theatre venues, so the Plebeians in the production became disembodied and anonymous, and the danger they represented was contained, made symbolic and turned into a debate amongst elites, with the Patricians on one side and the Tribunes (privileged political representatives) on the other.

Indeed, despite the fact that Lepage had called the language in *Coriolan* 'clearly Québécois', he was not necessarily interested in devising a specifically Québécois identity for the production.[16] Certainly, there was nothing in the set, costume or sound design of *Coriolan* that would readily signal 'Québec' to international audiences. Like the soundscape of horns, sirens and alarm bells, the costuming derived from post-war Western culture: the women wore evening frocks, the Tribunes had business suits, and the other men alternated between military dress and formal attire. Most scenes were staged against a black curtained background, while others occurred in contemporary settings, including the aforementioned radio and television studios, a bar, a motel bedroom, a locker-room and a restaurant. All aspects of the scenography belonged to the visual and aural lexicon of North American and European modern-dress Shakespeare production and modern Western culture more generally; none of the individual design elements are especially foreign to that elite 'Western, Northern, and metropolitan' part of the globe (including Québec) to which Lepage primarily tours.[17]

Instead of directly addressing the particular historical relationships that affected Québécois cultural nationalism, *Coriolan*'s simple yet innovative scenography reflected Lepage's talent for experimenting with canonical character-based approaches to Shakespearian performance. Such approaches, which circulate across national boundaries among mainstream Western practitioners and journalistic theatre critics, are grounded in traditions of psychological realism that elide the body of the performer and the character and privilege the dramatic text by linking the act of embodiment to the author's purportedly transhistorical intentions regarding character.[18] As is typical of Lepage's Shakespearian production, *Coriolan* disrupted the effort to create the effect of subjectivity by putting that effect into competition with the materiality of the performers' bodies.[19] The riveting first-act battle between Coriolan (Jules Philip) and Aufidius (Gérald Gagnon) best illustrates *Coriolan*'s competition between the performing body and character.

---

14 Because no prompt-book exists for the production, all information about cuts and scenography are derived from the video of a 1993 performance in Montréal at the FTA, now in the archives of ExMachina in Québec City.
15 Salter, 'Borderlines', p. 73.
16 Salter, 'Borderlines', p. 72.
17 Harvie and Hurley, 'States of Play', p. 307.
18 See also Steen and Werry, 'Bodies', p. 146.
19 Barbara Hodgdon, '*Macbeth*', p. 160.

The scene began in darkness, the sound of drums pounding to the rhythm of a rapid heart-beat. As the lights came up, an upstage mirror was angled into position, revealing Philip and Gagnon rolling nude into the frame (though they remained on the stage floor throughout the scene). They appeared to be crouching and, with their arms slightly raised like wrestlers, they angrily addressed each other, very much 'in character'. Still, their speeches were brief and the scene's impact resulted from the captivating spectacle of their hand-to-hand combat: bathed in a golden light, the men's stocky muscular bodies glistened with perspiration as they punched, grappled, spun, and rolled over each other in slow motion.

However, Lepage typically achieved richly meaningful effects in *Coriolan* by ostentatiously manipulating the relationship between his actors' bodies and the technology of the theatre. He accomplished this through his use of the playing space's cloth frame, the signature effect of which was its cropping of the spectators' view of the actors' bodies. When the aperture of the frame was lowered or performers stood on the tables that were frequently pushed into place in the middle of the stage and thereby moved their heads out of sight, Lepage denied his spectators access to the actors' faces, conventionally the most significant physical feature in conveying psychologically 'realistic' characters. While Lepage thus depersonalized or dehumanized the actors, *Coriolan* did not enact the 'Death of the Character' in any simple way.[20] Instead, the director put the fundamental goal of conventional mainstream Shakespearian acting – producing the effect of interiority – 'into parentheses', frequently by contrasting actors whose faces were visible with those whose were not. For instance, in 5.3, when Volumnia (Anne-Marie Cadieux) harangued her son not to invade Rome, she was kneeling on the table, the angry desperation visible in her eyes; Coriolan, meanwhile, stood, his face covered by the frame and he seemed an anonymous, immovable force. When Volumnia stood to exit, Coriolan dropped kneeling into the frame's opening, and his eyes registered the despair in his voice as he addressed his mother,

who had become the impersonal, superior figure. Lepage's use of the frame here thus actually intensified the emotional impact of the power shift from son to mother by reversing the contrast between one faceless, 'characterless' performer and the other whose face was visible and whose emotions the audience could track.

The action immediately preceding Coriolan's and Aufidius' single combat represents Lepage's most creative and extended staging of the *process* of the performers' bodies becoming and unbecoming characters, a process he staged throughout the production. Here the Roman troops massed before the walls at the Volscian town of Antium were represented by marionettes and the puppeteers who manipulate them. The frame was lowered so that only the puppeteers' legs and their hands were visible. This image of the faceless, characterless puppeteers, whose dark-trousered legs partly blended into the black background and seemed to be growing out of or into the top edge of the frame, is characteristic of Lepage's larger body of work where the performer becomes merely another element of the theatre's technology that the director can draw on in devising his image-driven *mise-en-scène*.[21] Yet, when Philip's Coriolan, who had been battling off stage behind Antium's closed gates, tumbled into the frame from stage left with his bare upper body wet and blood-stained like a new-born infant's, spectators witnessed what might be called the 'Birth of the Character'. Once his face was in view his body assumed an individual personality, especially in comparison to the anonymous puppeteer's legs and the marionette, which he addressed in his crouching position. Unlike the legs and marionettes, his body was not part of the theatre apparatus: Philip's ribcage heaved in unison with his angry speech that the audience could now see him mouthing and the muscles in his naked torso duplicated the intense emotion visible in his eyes, thereby eliding the performer's body with

---

20 Hodgdon, '*Macbeth*', p. 161.
21 For a thorough examination Lepage's approach to *mise-en-scène*, see Aleksandar Saša Dundjerović, *The Theatricality of Robert Lepage* (Montréal and Kingston, 2007).

the character. Lepage immediately repeated and embellished the process. Philip first embraced the marionette that represented his general Cominius; then, standing up to embrace the puppeteer, his body became an extension of the frame as his face was invisible. A second later Philip twirled the puppeteer around, pulled him crouching into the frame with him, and two characters came into being as both actors' now-visible faces gave their bodies individual subjectivity. Lepage thus treated the playing space as a kind of chamber for transforming actors' bodies, a chamber that alternately generated psychologically realistic personalities and interred these characters within the theatrical apparatus.

By experimenting with and supplanting canonical, character-based Shakespearian theatre with vaguely 'global' staging techniques that arguably blunt the production's local identity, *Coriolan* encouraged what Denis Salter refers to as the *Cycle's* 'hyperaestheticisation of political difference'.[22] To a degree, British critical reaction to the production's November 1993 tour stop at the Nottingham Playhouse helped to decontextualize *Coriolan* by restricting its identity to its relationship to Shakespeare's text. Ironically, this exclusive reliance on Shakespeare, which validates Lepage's own belief in an Anglophone preference for the verbal text over scenography in performance, entailed a narrow focus on the visual.[23] British reviewers – even those who admired Lepage's scenography – typically assessed *Coriolan* according to a rhetoric of loss in which modish but hollow spectacle is substituted for the fullness of Shakespeare's 'original': the 'minimalist precision' of Lepage's 'images' may have been admirable but the director 'replaces the richness of the original *Gesamtkunstwerk* with a thin and desiccated deconstructionist chic'; *Coriolan* is a 'chicly staged but shallow, unexploratory account of the play'; '[m]any of Lepage's pictures stay in the mind' but '[t]he great rhetorical set-pieces of Shakespeare's play . . . are miserably unexplored' giving 'the production a gutless feeling'.[24]

Not surprisingly, this rhetoric of loss usually cohered around the contrast between actors' (in)ability to produce the effect of interiority and the disposition of the performers' bodies in relation to the frame. Much of this discussion concerned the supplication scene in which Coriolan's family begs the exiled general not to invade Rome with the Volsces to whom he has defected. On one side were Charles Spencer, who lamented the 'fatuousness' of leaving Philip's face invisible during most of his mother's supplication which rendered 'one of the most moving scenes in Shakespeare . . . a ludicrous farce' and Paul Taylor, who found it 'hilarious' that the 'only glimpse of the hero's son is a bit of blazer and a pair of freakishly long legs'.[25] By contrast, Tom Morris admired Lepage's ability to demonstrate the process of creating the effect of subjectivity, writing that Volumnia 'begins her entreaty headless at the right-hand edge of the slot, then gracefully kneels into view before her son – surrendering the power of inscrutability for that of irresistible emotional presence'.[26] Benedict Nightingale picked up where Morris left off: 'we see her kneeling figure and Coriolanus, impersonal in his uniform, up to the shoulders only. When she prevails, the situation is reversed and a hand descends from a long black dress contemptuously to rumple his hair as he droops before her.'[27] The disagreement between the two pairs of critics regarding the actors' success in producing the effect of interiority is less important than the fact that all the reviewers followed the logic that Shannon

[22] Salter, 'Between Wor(l)ds', p. 192.

[23] See Collette Godard, 'Les branches de l'arbre', *Le Monde*, 29–30 November 1992; Robert Lepage, *Connecting Flights*, p. 57; Robert Lepage, Interview with Alison McAlpine in Maria M. Delgado and Paul Heritage, eds., *In Contact With the Gods? Directors Talk Theatre* (Manchester and New York, 1996), pp. 148–9.

[24] Michael Billington, 'The Shallow Side of Chic', *The Guardian*, 26 November 1993, 4; Paul Taylor, 'Crowded Out', *The Independent* 26 November 1993, 23; Tom Morris, 'The Hopeful Boxer', *Times Literary Supplement*, 10 December 1993, 17.

[25] Charles Spencer, 'Coriolanus Lost in a Sea of Gimmicks', *Weekend Telegraph*, 27 November 1993, 23; Taylor, 'Crowded Out'.

[26] Morris, 'Hopeful Boxer'.

[27] Benedict Nightingale, 'Power Play Through a Peephole', *The Times*, 26 November 1993, 35.

Steen and Margaret Werry identify in criticisms of *Elsinore*: when the actors were fully visible, they were deemed fully present as characters because their bodies were sutured to those of their characters; when their faces were invisible, their bodies were read as being decoupled from character, as being part of the apparatus of theatre and therefore less than human (inscrutable, impersonal, freakish, ludicrous).

If such comments decontextualized *Coriolan* by limiting its identity to a mere contest between traditional transatlantic modes of Shakespearian production and more contemporary international theatrical practices, other aspects of the response suggest the opposite, the localization of the production's aesthetics. It is in such comments that we witness what Roland Robertson calls 'the "invention" of locality', a manifestation of those forces − most evident in the significant differences between Québécois and British reviewers' reaction to *Coriolan* − that constitute the supposedly homogenous nature of global culture.[28] The operation of these forces upon *Coriolan* produced, to use Robertson's phrasing, 'something like an "ideology of home" which has in fact come into being partly in response to the constant repetition and global diffusion of the claims that we now live in a condition of homelessness or rootlessness'.[29] The ideologies of home produced by *Coriolan*'s reception not only challenged the notion that the 'elite festivals' which host Lepage's work are, strictly speaking, 'remarkably homogenous', but lent the production its heterogeneous identity, which became much more complex over the course of its touring.[30]

Coriolan provoked locally meaningful response from a segment of the British critics who identified the actors' failure to elide their characters with their own bodies as an excess that signalled an assault on the national poet by colonial mimicry. The reviewers sexualized the performers and either displaced their bodily excesses by a foreign analogy or corrected them according to British cultural models. Taylor coded the very frame as sexual, writing that it offers 'a peeping Tom's perspective on the proceedings'. From this voyeuristic position, he regarded the battle between Coriolan and Aufidius

as 'a nude love wrestle that makes the one in *Women in Love* look like a bad case of mutual indifference', employing a domestic standard of homoerotic performance to demean Lepage's preference for 'a more narrowly psycho-sexual drama'.[31] Nightingale, meanwhile, associated the voyeuristic aspect of the framed action with illicit foreign sexuality: 'When Volumnia, Virgillia, and Valeria (who doubles as a sexy radio producer) are seen sewing away in their negligees, they resemble tarts in a window in Amsterdam.'[32] He reinforced what Hodgdon calls in another context this 'xenophobic blocking' strategy by invoking Tyrone Guthrie's production that opened the Nottingham Playhouse thirty years earlier.[33] Suggesting that the current *Coriolan* 'would have even raised that great innovator's [Guthrie's] eyebrows a yard or so', Nightingale chastened Lepage with a 'proper' British example of Shakespearian innovation. Billington, too, employed the Playhouse's inaugural production as a domestic example of how archetypal sexuality served Shakespeare with canonical performances that did not threaten the playwright's textually inscribed meaning: 'Volumnia's Freudian lust and the homo-eroticism of warfare are ideas that have informed more conventional productions, including Guthrie's where [Ian] McKellen's Aufidius swooped on the dead body of his adversary.'[34] Such comments not only demonstrate the power of the body to disrupt Shakespeare's textual authority but they re-localized *Coriolan*'s disruption of those 'global' performance techniques that sustain this authority by reinforcing a sense of British cultural superiority.

In comparison to British reviewers, who recontextualized *Coriolan*'s engagement with global

---

[28] Roland Robertson, 'Glocalization: Time-Space and Homogeneity-Heterogeneity', in Mike Featherstone, Scott Lash and Roland Robertson, eds., *Global Modernities* (London, 1995), p. 35.

[29] Robertson, 'Glocalization', p. 35.

[30] Harvey and Hurley, 'States of Play', p. 308.

[31] Taylor, 'Crowded Out'.

[32] Nightingale, 'Power Play'.

[33] Hodgdon, *The Shakespeare Trade*, p. 182.

[34] Billington, 'Shallow Side'.

or canonical performance techniques to advance a rather limited range of local, nationalist sentiment, Québécois critical response provides a fuller, more nuanced image of the diverse local concerns at stake in the performance of globalized Shakespeare. This is not to say that Québec critics necessarily had a more accurate understanding of *Coriolan* than British critics did, though, as Francophones, they had greater access to the subtleties of Garneau's language. Rather, their comments reflect the struggle that Lepage outlines in the quotations at the start of this essay: the urge, on the one hand, to take part in global culture through an international repertoire that includes Shakespeare and, on the other, the powerful sense of Québec's double colonization by France and England and English Canada. In negotiating such conflicting influences, Francophone Québécois response to *Coriolan* did not so much embrace Lepage's global theatrical style as it localized the production's transnational identity by re-inscribing it with both the French and English colonial pasts that the director had hoped to surmount.

The Québécois media's diligent tracking of the director's career abroad during the *Cycle*'s tour embodies a particular type of tension between the global and local identities of Lepage's Shakespearian enterprise. At one extreme, the celebration of the director's success with both the *Cycle* and other original productions in France in the autumn of 1992 displayed very little tension between the global and the local.[35] Louis-Bernard Robitaille, for instance, echoed Lepage's optimism that intercultural, international Shakespeare is an entirely liberating phenomenon, enthusing that the director had joined a club where 'L'appartenence est éminemment cosmopolite' [the 'affiliation is eminently cosmopolitan'] and, consequently was at the edge 'd'un cercle magique où tout lui est permis, où ses fantaisies se réalisent' ['of a magic circle, where all is permitted, where his fantasies are realized'].[36] Robitaille argued that *Coriolan* would secure Lepage's place within this transnational elite in part because it did not possess 'une once de local, de régional' ['an ounce of

the local, the regional'] and that the production's cosmopolitan identity was also partly the result of Garneau's idiomatic script and the actors' vocalizations, both of which reflected the impact of standard or international French on the Québécois spoken within Canada's official French-language broadcaster (Radio Canada): 'Contrairement à *Macbeth*, où Michel Garneau a recherché une version en "français archaïque", le *Coriolan*, vigoureusement adapté et amputé du tiers de son texte, est en français "standard", où certains comédiens ont l'air français et d'autres "radio-canadiens"' ['Contrary to *Macbeth*, where Michel Garneau sought out a version in "archaic French", *Coriolan*, vigorously adapted and with a third of its text amputated, is in "standard" French, where certain actors seem to be French and others "'Radio-Canadiens'"].[37] Thus Robitaille's enthusiasm for Lepage's entry to a liberating realm of elite international theatre artists was commensurate with a flattening of the production's local, nationalist elements by the adoption of a homogenizing 'standard' French.

However, most Québécois response reflected a deeply ingrained sense that home is an historically determined locale that Lepage had departed from and to which this response, metaphorically, returned him. Like Robitaille, all Québécois correspondents who wrote about Lepage's Paris tour stop celebrated his French success, but most did not merely praise the vague cosmopolitanism of the *Cycle*. Rather, the majority of Québécois reviewers who carefully analysed the director's Parisian reception localized and re-contextualized the global sphere in which Lepage operated and, in doing so, expressed their own sense of colonial inferiority to France. A tone of relieved joy at gaining the former colonial power's approval characterizes Michel Dolbec's series of articles on the

---

[35] In addition to the three *Cycle* plays, Lepage also toured his *Le Polygraphe* and *Les Aiguilles et L'Opium* to France.

[36] Louis-Bernard Robitaille. 'Robert Lepage à Paris, dans les ligues majeures', *La Presse*, 25 October 1992, B12.

[37] Robitaille, 'Robert Lepage à Paris'.

Paris run of the *Cycle*, which were picked up by various Québec newspapers. '"La France va enfin découvrir le plus allumé des Québécois", annonçait le Nouvel Observateur dans un article dithyrambique'. ['"France will finally discover the brightest Québécois [director]" the *Nouvel Observateur* announced in an enthusiastic article'], wrote Dolbec in the first piece.[38] Similarly, Jean Saint-Hilaire emphasized the significance of the director's success by stressing the prestige of Lepage's Parisian judges: '"Le Festival d'automne lui a fait une fête et il a fait du Festival d'automne une fête", a écrit Olivier Schmitt dans le très respecté Le Monde.' ['"The Festival d'Automne fêted [Lepage] and he turned the Festival d'Automne into a celebration", wrote Olivier Schmitt in the highly respected *Le Monde*'].[39] Such commentary does not simply celebrate Lepage's international achievements, but marks the supposedly homogenous space of globalized locales like the Festival d'Automne in Paris with the very local historical loyalties to French culture that Lepage described as a hindrance to internationalizing Québécois culture. Specifically, by appealing to the authority of the Parisian media, the Québec journalists returned the director to the role of a subservient provincial whose success, as Dolbec (quoting Lepage) came close to saying, depended upon the approval of a scrutinizing colonial authority: 'Pendant un mois et demi, le théâtre du metteur en scène-acteur-auteur québécois a été soumis à un "véritable examen aux rayons X" qu'il a passé avec succès' ['For a month and a half, the theatre of the Québécois director-actor-author was subjected to a "veritable X-ray exam", which he passed with success'].[40]

Set against British reaction, moreover, Québécois response suggests how Shakespearian authority is articulated 'in different ways in the different locations in which' intercultural Shakespeare is performed.[41] Like the British critics, Francophone Québécois journalists, who reviewed the production's tour stops at the Festival de Théâtre des Amériques in Montréal and in Québec City, judged *Coriolan* according to its supposed adherence to or deviation from Shakespeare's scripted intentions. Unlike their British counterparts, Québécois critics focused less on the production's scenography than on the relationship between the playwright and national linguistic identity embodied in Garneau's translation. Such reaction frustrated Lepage's stated desire to deploy Shakespeare as a product of transnational culture by reinforcing the old colonial relationships to England and English Canada that the director saw embodied in the deference to Anglophone censure of Québécois performance of his drama. The harshest criticism came from Robert Lévesque, who, in one review, called Garneau's *Coriolan* 'une traduction pesante' ['a ponderous translation'], and who went out of his way in a second review to attack Garneau's scripts, concluding that, as a group, 'Ces traductions-là sont faibles, elles diminuent et abrutissent Shakespeare' ['These translations are weak, they diminish and stultify Shakespeare'].[42] He furthermore equated this failure to serve Shakespeare with what he regarded as the dated and insular nationalism of recent Québec theatre, stating that the translations 'appartient au passé ingrat et malhabie de la langue théâtrale québécoise des années nationalistes, et relève de la vision complaisante d'un poète qui ne sort pas de son clos linguistique' ['belong to the old arid and clumsy Québécois theatrical language of the nationalist era and are part of the vision of a poet who never ventures out of his own linguistic enclosure'].[43] Although no other reviewer so vehemently denied Garneau's script the universality that 'authentic' Shakespeare translation supposedly achieves, a majority of francophone Québécois

---

38 Michel Dolbec, 'Robert Lepage débarque à Paris avec sa trilogie Shakespearienne', *Le Soleil*, 26 October 1992, B5.

39 Jean St-Hilaire, 'Lepage séduit la critique parisienne', *Le Soleil*, 15 January 1993, A9.

40 Michel Dolbec, 'Robert Lepage s'impose à Paris', *Le Soleil*, 5 December 1992, C7.

41 Worthen, *Shakespeare and the Force*, p. 127.

42 Robert Lévesque, 'Shakespeare en *Sitcom*', *Le Devoir*, 29 May 1993, A12; Robert Lévesque, 'La trilogie des abrutis', *Le Devoir*, 7 June 1993, B8.

43 Lévesque, 'La trilogie'.

critics gauged the translation according to its perceived fidelity to Shakespeare's authoritative original, whether they understood Garneau to have respected the text or to have flattened the complexities of narrative and character.[44]

While comparing Québécois and British response reveals how Shakespearian authority was used to imagine the local differently in the different countries to which *Coriolan* toured, Québécois reaction suggests that the set of relations amongst national concerns, global touring and Shakespeare's traditional stature did not produce a stable or singular sense of the local but a variety of local perspectives. Certain Québécois critics, for instance, proposed a symbiotic relationship between Shakespeare's and Garneau's scripts, either by arguing that Garneau honoured Shakespeare by liberating him from the deadening category of the classics or that the translation made Shakespeare speak with North American rhythms without losing his poetry.[45]

However, no one so vociferously employed Shakespeare to buttress Québécois nationalist sentiment as Guy Marchand did in his polemical response to Lévesque. Although Marchand's comments (which were reprinted in the Québec theatre journal, *Jeu*) are unique in their extensive defence of Lepage, they are worth reviewing because they so clearly illustrate what was at stake in the *Cycle* plays for Québec audiences.[46] Comparing Lévesque to the proverbial ape which shut its eyes and covered its ears against that which displeased it, Marchand questioned the critic's right to determine Shakespeare's intentions, while self-consciously needling him with a Québécois turn of phrase: 'ce qui est comique, c'est la prétention du critique de savoir ce que doit être Shakespeare mieux que "toute le monde, y compris sa mère", comme on dit en bon québécois, ce québécois que M. Lévesque trouve si peu à sa place chez Le Grand Will' ['what is comic is the critic's pretension to know what Shakespeare should be, better than "the whole world, including his mother", as we say in good Québécois, this Québécois that M. Lévesque finds so out of place chez Le Grand Will'].[47]

Despite his mocking tone, Marchand did not declare independence from a Shakespeare who is no longer relevant to Québécois nationalism, but used the authority that the playwright's ostensible intentions confer to defend Lepage's production. Marchand praised the director for revealing Shakespeare's hidden intentions with a modern parallel: 'Il a fait ressortir de ce "drame sec" le vieux fond du boulevard qui s'y cachait, en le transposant dans les milieux d'une haute bourgeoisie de ce siècle qu'on ... rencontre ... dans toutes les capitales du monde' ['He brought to light the ancient foundation of the boulevard that is hiding within this "dry drama", in transposing it to the milieus of a *haute bourgeoisie* of this century that we ... encounter ... in all the capitals of the world'].[48] He then applauded Lepage for exposing the linguistic pretensions of this ubiquitous class of social climbers:

Dans cette bourgeoisie, pour mieux se distinguer de la plèbe, on y châtie sa langue (ma chaêre!) en singeant ce français international, on ne peut plus artificiel, qui ne se parle que dans les minuscules archipels médiatiques flottant à la dérive sur l'océan fantomatique de la francophonie. Plusieurs scènes étaient donc transposées dans un studio de radio.

[In this bourgeoisie, the better to distinguish oneself from the plebs, language is refined (ma chaêre!) by aping an international French, one cannot be more artificial than those who only speak to others on tiny floating mediatized archipelagos drifting on the phantom ocean of the *francophonie*. A number of scenes are thus transposed to a radio studio].[49]

---

[44] See, for instance, Jean St-Hilaire, 'Le Coriolan de Lepage: ironique et d'une pure virtuosité', *Le Soleil*, 31 May 1993, B6; Luc Boulanger, 'Bilan du FTA', *Voir*, 10 June 1993, 23.

[45] Rémy Charest, 'Trilogie Shakespearienne de Robert Lepage', *Le Devoir*, 28 January 1994, B6; Jean Baunoyer, 'Le Coriolan de Lepage, un spectacle captivant!', *La Presse*, 31 May 1993, E2.

[46] The piece appeared originally as Guy Marchand, 'Ne touchez pas à mon héros', *Le Devoir*, 22 June 1993. I cite from the *Jeu* version.

[47] Guy Marchand, 'Lévesque et la trilogie de Lepage: comme Alonso dans l'Île de Prospéro', *Cahiers de Théâtre Jeu*, 67 (June 1993), 63.

[48] Marchand, 'Lévesque et la trilogie', 65.

[49] Marchand, 'Lévesque et la trilogie', 65.

Thus, while Marchand relied upon the authority of Shakespeare's intentions, he also drew the production into the negotiation between Québécois linguistic identity – captured in joual pronunciation of 'chère' ('ma chaêre!') – and those, like Robitaille, who dismissed local language in celebrating the homogenizing and rootless French of the 'radio-canadiens'. At the same time, by using the verb 'aping', he managed to conflate this rootless global bourgeoisie with Lévesque, who, like the unseeing and unhearing ape, rejected the Québécois language and culture that displeased him in favour of a decontextualized reverence for Shakespeare.

Scrutinizing the various points of historical reception in *Coriolan*'s touring life brings into focus important aspects of global Shakespearian theatre. *Coriolan*'s production history is comprised of a series of geographically and chronologically discrete events and, perhaps, as Kidnie writes about 'the idea of "'local'" concerning *Elsinore*'s touring, 'in such a mobile geographical context', the production's significance 'breaks free of national boundaries associated with the author (Shakespeare) or auteur (Lepage) to attach itself instead to the particular *locales* at which' it was performed.[50] Yet *Coriolan*'s relative freedom to cross national boundaries – its apparent lack of specifically 'Québécois' identity and its literal international touring – does not *necessarily* entail 'vanish[ing] down the memory-hole of revisionist history' or the production of 'absent identit[ies] from which absolutely *nothing* of value can ever be salvaged'.[51] Québécois and British critics may have invoked Shakespeare's traditional literary authority, based on his supposed ability to portray transhistorical characters, but they both used this trope to evoke specific national identities. Experimental Shakespeare may have increased Lepage's prestige as a global theatre artist but Québec critics incorporated this prestige into narratives about local identity. What such 'returns' to the local indicate is that the kind of intercultural theatre that *Coriolan* represents is caught up in a set of relations in which 'home', the global and Shakespeare are not mutually exclusive entities but sustain each other through the production of identities that may not be firmly fixed but are nevertheless shaped by numerous and competing histories.

---

[50] Kidnie, 'Dancing', pp. 133–4, emphasis original.
[51] Salter, 'Between Wor(l)ds', p. 193, emphasis original.

ENDLESS MORNINGS ON ENDLESS FACES: SHAKESPEARE AND PHILIP LARKIN

PETER HOLBROOK

I don't want to transcend the commonplace, I love the commonplace . . . Everyday things are lovely to me.

Philip Larkin[1]

For Shakespeare, in the matter of religion, the choice lay between Christianity and nothing. He chose nothing; he chose to leave his heroes and himself in the presence of life and of death with no other philosophy than that which the profane world can suggest and understand.

George Santayana, 'The Absence of Religion in Shakespeare' (1899)[2]

The critic in search of Larkin's 'sources' will have a tough time of it. It is hard to imagine Larkin himself enthusiastic about such a quest: he thought poetry should issue out of what he called 'unsorted experience' – 'I tried to keep literature out of my poems', he said.[3] His literary personality was defined against that of modernist scholar-magpies like Eliot and Auden – poets he respected, but warily. In a review of 1960 he reproached Auden for intellectualism and arch literary game-playing – implicitly, the antithesis of his own poetry, which was to be understood as a record of personal experience.[4]

Of course Larkin looked to other writers for inspiration: Christina Rossetti, Thomas Hardy, D. H. Lawrence, A. E. Housman. But the poetry is not thick with allusion. Larkin meant what he said: poetry should grow out of personal experience, not books. 'Poems don't come from other poems' he declared, 'they come from being oneself, in life. Every man is an island, entire of himself, as Donne said.'[5] One of the reasons he liked Wilfred Owen was because, in that poet's words, he was

'not concerned with Poetry'.[6] The significance of at least two of Larkin's literary heroes, Hardy and Lawrence, was their licensing Larkin to speak in his own voice about those things that mattered to him. Hardy showed it was possible to write poetry without drawing on what Larkin called the 'myth-kitty' that had weakened, by rendering artificial, the work of so many English poets.[7] Lawrence taught a similar lesson: the importance of sincerity, of being yourself and not someone else. In his essay on Benjamin Franklin, Lawrence wrote that 'To be sincere is to remember that I am I, and that the other man is not me.'[8] Larkin spoke about his own poetry in this way. In response to Raymond Gardiner's complaint that his art lacked 'the humanity of comfort', he observed that

---

[1] 'An Interview with John Haffenden', in *Philip Larkin: Further Requirements – Interviews, Broadcasts, Statements, and Book Reviews, 1952–1985*, ed. Anthony Thwaite (London, 2002), p. 57.

[2] *Interpretations of Poetry and Religion* (New York, 1924), p. 152.

[3] 'Interview with John Haffenden', p. 86.

[4] See 'What's Become of Wystan?', in *Philip Larkin: Required Writing – Miscellaneous Pieces, 1955–1982* (London, 1983), p. 126 (criticizing the 'rambling intellectual stew' of *New Year Letter* and 'literary inbreeding' of *The Sea and the Mirror*) and p. 128 (claiming 'Auden . . . has now become an unserious' poet for whom 'poetry is a game'). Auden's poetry improved when it became 'more personal' (p. 126).

[5] 'Interview with John Haffenden', p. 54.

[6] 'The War Poet', *Required Writing*, p. 163, quoting Owen.

[7] 'Statement', *Required Writing*, p. 79.

[8] 'Benjamin Franklin', in *D. H. Lawrence: Selected Essays* (Harmondsworth, 1950), p. 239.

The drift [of such objections] seems to be that I shouldn't be myself, I should be somebody else. Well, there may be something to be said for that, but it's not a thing I can do anything about. I don't want to turn other people into me, I'm only saying what I feel . . . [P]eople don't want you to be yourself.[9]

In 1942 Larkin claimed that Lawrence was to him as Shakespeare was to Keats.[10] Lawrence's insistence on authenticity – the urgency of acknowledging that I am I and not the other man – is central to understanding Larkin.

As Larkin saw it, then, Hardy and Lawrence liberated him from the pitfall of imitation. It is therefore probably not, as Simon Petch suggests, very productive to look for specific echoes of these two in Larkin's work. Their influence was negative: teaching him it was acceptable *not* to be them – or anyone else.[11] In 'I Remember, I Remember' Larkin portrays his childhood as bereft of 'Blinding theologies of flowers and fruits'. Lawrence helped Larkin make poetry out of the *absence* of Lawrentian epiphanies – helped him become himself.[12]

My point is that Larkin affiliated himself to a line in English literature we might call 'empiricist', one rooted in common life and the everyday. This tradition understands itself to be unlearned and demotic, at least not 'difficult' and recherché in the way modernist poetry often is; sees itself as natural rather than artificial, conventional or derivative; and regards the essence of poetry, and art generally, as the communication of powerful emotion rather than glib displays of cleverness, erudition or irony.[13] (In a letter, Larkin conceded that George Bernard Shaw was 'superior' to Shakespeare 'as a thinker', but only in the sense that 'Beavers are superior to elephants as nibblers. But whereas a beaver nibbles the thing down in a day, the elephant uproots it bodily in a second.'[14]) This empiricist tradition is oriented towards reality rather than suave or pedantic evasions of the real. It puts pathos above polish, life above literature, sensation above scholarship. Larkin's preferences in other art forms show a similar predilection for the empirical. His love of jazz was based on his belief in that music's rootedness in the painful emotional experience of

America's blacks; he switched off when it became academic, cerebral and self-quoting – 'postmodern', if you will. Feeling was the *sine qua non* of significant art. Approvingly, he noted A. E. Housman's sense of poetry as 'a physical thing, like tears'.[15] Likewise Larkin admitted he'd never had '"ideas" about poetry. To me it's always been a personal, almost physical release or solution to a complex pressure of needs.'[16]

This empirical tradition in English literature is, I think, an actual one rather than something concocted by Larkin in order to help himself write (though it did that). For Larkin, the greatest English writers shared a quality he designated as 'sanity': the ability to look at things directly and get them right.[17] He scoffed at what he called 'the look-at-me-I'm-round-the-bend school' of postwar poets like Plath and Berryman – Chaucer and Shakespeare didn't belong to that camp.[18] Another aspect of the empiricist tradition in English letters

---

[9] 'Interview with John Haffenden', pp. 53, 55.

[10] *Philip Larkin: Selected Letters, 1940–1985*, ed. Anthony Thwaite (London), pp. 34–5.

[11] '[T]he significance of Hardy to Larkin was a matter of giving him confidence in himself and his personal feelings as subject-matter for poetry': Simon Petch, *The Art of Philip Larkin* (Sydney, 1981), p. 7.

[12] Quotations from Larkin's poetry are from the *Collected Poems*, ed. Anthony Thwaite (London, 1988). Some Larkin poems do, of course, display Lawrence's intense feeling for nature: 'Cut Grass', 'The Mower', and 'The little lives of earth and form', for example.

[13] Cf. Hardy: 'The Poet takes note of nothing that he cannot feel emotively': *The Life and Work of Thomas Hardy, by Thomas Hardy*, ed. Michael Millgate (London, 1984), p. 369.

[14] *Selected Letters* (23 June 1941), p. 17. Cf. his charge that Auden had 'become a reader rather than a writer' in 'What's Become of Wystan?', p. 125.

[15] 'All Right When You Knew Him', *Required Writing*, p. 264. It could be a physical thing for Larkin too: the Immortality ode was almost the death of him when he heard it on the radio while driving, eyes awash with tears: 'An Interview with the *Observer*', *Required Writing*, p. 53.

[16] 'An Interview with *Paris Review*', *Required Writing*, p. 76.

[17] 'Poetry is an affair of sanity, of seeing things as they are': 'Big Victims: Emily Dickinson and Walter de la Mare', *Required Writing*, p. 197.

[18] 'Poets in a Fine Frenzy and Otherwise', *Further Requirements*, p. 259.

is impatience with theory, with thought that is less than red-blooded. To the objection that the poem 'Solar' was inconsistent with the kind of argument about life his poetry was generally supposed to have developed, Larkin retorted sharply 'It's a feeling, not a thought.'[19] Lawrence's vitalism is relevant here ('My great religion is a belief in the blood, the flesh, as being wiser than the intellect. We can go wrong in our minds. But what our blood feels and believes and says, is always true'[20]), as is Keats ('O for a life of sensations rather than of thought!').

For Larkin, the greatest writers in English since Shakespeare were Hardy and Lawrence.[21] We could fill out what I am calling this empirical tradition with other names – Chaucer, Bunyan, Wordsworth; dialectal poets (William Barnes); rural ones (Crabbe, Clare). But in Larkin's estimation the three summits are Shakespeare, Hardy, D. H. Lawrence.

I have specified some of the features we might associate (or Larkin seems to have associated) with this line in English writing: emotional power, directness, lack of theoretical abstraction from life, lack of an academic, or generally footling concern with literary decorum. It is a tradition exemplifying the value Keats named as 'energy' ('Though a quarrel in the streets is a thing to be hated, the energies displayed in it are fine') and William Hazlitt 'gusto' ('Gusto in art is power or passion in defining any object').[22] These values can, I think, be redescribed in political terms, as a commitment to individual freedom – having the audacity to be, as Lawrence put it, who you are and not another person. As I've said, this notion was fundamental to Larkin, and is connected to what he acknowledged, with regard to one of his masterpieces, 'High Windows', to be a universal human need for freedom: 'one wants to be somewhere', he said, 'where there's neither oppressed nor oppressor, just freedom'.[23] Commitment to individual freedom seems to me at the heart of Larkin's poetry.

If that proposition is true it rather complicates the received image of Larkin as a buttoned-up, aesthetically timid, tradition-bound conservative – as does, for that matter, his liking for the Beats, whom he saw as 'debased Whitman' (but

better that than 'debased Ezra Pound').[24] In fact his poetry is full of what he called, in a discussion of Andrew Marvell, 'sudden sincerities'[25] – shocking moments of self-exposure. Larkin's poetry has a freedom of demeanour, an unliterary indecorousness (the image in 'Dockery and Son' of the poet eating 'an awful pie' on a railway station platform can serve as a not wholly serious emblem of that aspect of his work) that makes its natural home the empirical, quotidian, convention-spurning tradition I've invoked.

What interests me is that Larkin should see only Shakespeare as matching the genius of Hardy and Lawrence. The mention of Shakespeare could of course be a meaningless honorific (to whom else compare a writer when you want to make the case for greatness?). And saying something is as *good* as something else is not, of course, necessarily to say it *resembles* it. Nevertheless, I feel the invocation of Shakespeare is not casual. Larkin would, I believe, find the qualities he was attracted to in Hardy and Lawrence abundantly present in Shakespeare. I certainly find an affinity between the two.

Needless to say, this is not a matter of specific allusions, of which there are perhaps a scant three. In 'Letter to a Friend About Girls' Larkin signs himself '*Horatio*', thus casting himself as the duller (but also less narcissistic?) sidekick to Kingsley Amis's glamorous Hamlet (the poem takes a slyly subversive view of Amis's self-satisfied

---

[19] 'Interview with John Haffenden', p. 61.

[20] Letter to Ernest Collings, 17 January 1913, vol. 1 of *The Letters of D. H. Lawrence*, ed. James T. Boulton (Cambridge, 1979), p. 503.

[21] Hardy was 'the most considerable English writer since Shakespeare before D. H. Lawrence': 'Poets in a Fine Frenzy and Otherwise', p. 260.

[22] *Letters of John Keats*, ed. Robert Gittings (Oxford, 1975), p. 230; William Hazlitt, 'On Gusto', in *Selected Writings*, ed. Jon Cook (Oxford, 1991), p. 266; gusto is the product of 'truth of feeling' (p. 266).

[23] 'Interview with John Haffenden', p. 59.

[24] 'A Conversation with Ian Hamilton', *Further Requirements*, p. 26.

[25] 'The Changing Face of Andrew Marvell', *Required Writing*, p. 253.

womanizing).[26] The poem 'Deceptions', printed in the volume *The Less Deceived*, alludes to Ophelia's reply to Hamlet's cruel avowal that he loved her not – 'I was the more deceived' responds Ophelia pathetically.[27] The other allusion is to a famous passage in *The Tempest*, in Larkin's much-quoted poem about work, 'Toads': 'Why should I let the toad *work* / Squat on my life?' The speaker's desire to shout '*Stuff your pension!*' to his employer is undone instantly by the rueful awareness that 'that's the stuff / That dreams are made on'. Prospero's sentence concludes with the words 'and our little life / Is rounded with a sleep' – a reminder, if we ever needed one, that Larkin's defining subject was death and the fear of death. I will suggest that this is also a peculiarly Shakespearian preoccupation.

For the remainder of this article I shall note some of the ways Larkin's poetry might be compared to Shakespeare's, which, as suggested, seems to have been for Larkin part of an imaginative tradition encompassing those writers most important to him. I will discuss in particular the *Sonnets*, which seem to me especially close in theme, outlook and tone to Larkin's work. It surprises me that this connection has been neglected. As far as I can tell, the only critic to explore it has been James Booth, who has discussed the early poem 'Two Portraits of Sex' in the context of Shakespeare's famous meditation on lust, Sonnet 129.[28] The Larkin poem, Booth observes, takes a perspective similar to Shakespeare's, one in which sated desire runs out into stark disappointments and deprivations: after '[t]he wet spark', and the 'collapse' of 'the bright blown walls',

. . . what sad scapes we cannot turn from then:
What ashen hills! what salted, shrunken lakes!

But before turning to the poems I should note that Larkin's relation to Shakespeare is instructively different from that of another great twentieth-century poet, T. S. Eliot. For Eliot Shakespeare was part of the problem a modern secular-liberal – which is to say, for Eliot, a decadent – culture confronted. True, the Elizabethans were our only begetters – and so much the worse for us: 'the philosophical basis, the general attitude towards life of the Elizabethans, is one of anarchism, of dissolution, of decay'.[29] The modern chaos arrived with them, with the Reformation and the splintering of medieval Christendom. Eliot's view of Shakespeare as the poet of the West's fall into atheism, individualism, democracy and rebellion makes his appreciations of him guarded and chilly: in Shakespeare he recognizes the genius of modern liberalism. Larkin's attitude is different. He spoke on only one occasion at length about Shakespeare, and then to stress, in approving tones, the intimate bond between audience and playwright in the Elizabethan period. Unlike modernist authors, and their heirs in creative writing courses since, Larkin observed, Shakespeare had had to please a paying, impatient, unlettered audience.[30] 'Poetry', Larkin wrote elsewhere, 'like all art, is inextricably bound up with giving pleasure, and if a poet loses his pleasure-seeking audience he has lost

---

[26] For the rather amazing facts on that, see Zachary Leader's recent biography (London, 2006).

[27] *Hamlet* especially seems to have a ghostly yet pervasive presence in Larkin's poetry, in particular in his general preoccupation with failure (something I discuss later in this article), with neurotic self-doubt and self-contempt, and with states of painful psychological blockage. There is a moment (one hesitates to call it an 'allusion') in Larkin's great extended meditation on the fear of death, 'Aubade', which seems to bring *Hamlet* into focus, in particular 'To be or not to be'. The speaker's characterization of our awareness of death as 'a standing chill / That slows each impulse down to indecision' recalls Hamlet's indecisiveness in the play and in his soliloquy's musing on how fear of what may lie after death 'puzzles the will' and 'turn[s] awry' or 'sicklie[s] o'er' one's 'resolution', so that it 'lose[s] the name of action' (3.1.82, 86–90). A just possible allusion to *Hamlet* lies also in the title of 'The Old Fools', a poem which, like Shakespeare's play, meditates on death as 'oblivion' or 'silence'; cf. Hamlet's 'These tedious old fools!' (2.2.221). Overall, *Hamlet* is the Shakespearian play we can most readily imagine Larkin having written, because it bundles together so many of his characteristic obsessions, especially death, sex and individuality.

[28] James Booth, *Philip Larkin: Writer* (New York, 1992), pp. 104–6.

[29] 'Four Elizabethan Dramatists' (1924), in T. S. Eliot, *Selected Essays*, 3rd edn (London, 1951), p. 116. Cf. 'The Art of the Elizabethans is an Impure Art' (p. 114).

[30] 'Subsidizing Poetry', *Required Writing*, pp. 91–2.

the only audience worth having.'[31] Larkin, then, invoked Shakespeare to attack what he saw as the increasingly academic and elitist character of modern poetry. Here again Shakespeare is a writer in the Hardy–Lawrence line of empiricism, a popular tradition rooted in common life, the real 'Movement' Larkin signed up to. The cultural politics of this allegiance are interestingly liberal-democratic, populist, English and Protestant as against Eliot's authoritarian, elitist, Latin and crypto-Catholic loyalties.

If Shakespeare belongs to an empirical tradition in English writing – and the concreteness and actuality of his writing has always drawn praise – it ought to embolden us to seek for closer connections between the two poets. For me these revolve around a few common preoccupations and a certain shared style of self-presentation.

First, as mentioned, the treatment of death. Larkin saw Hardy (and, I think, Lawrence) as 'worldly' writers. Of Hardy he wrote: '[h]e's not a transcendental writer, he's not a Yeats, he's not an Eliot; his subjects are men, the life of men, time and the passing of time, love and the fading of love'.[32] This aspect of the empiricism of Hardy and Lawrence – a fundamental irreligiousness – has long been attributed to Shakespeare. In a lecture of 1889, A. C. Bradley commended the tragedies for their deep worldliness, which made them modern:

the special significance of Shakespeare's tragedies in literary history lies in this: that they contain the first profound representation of life in modern poetry which is independent of any set of religious ideas. Chaucer had represented life directly, but on the whole had not represented it profoundly. Dante's view had been profound, but it had taken a theological shape. Shakespeare was the first great writer who painted life simply as it is seen on the earth, and yet gave it the same tremendous significance that it has to religion. In doing so, he, perhaps . . . produced the most universal of all modern poems; universal in the sense that no set of religious ideas forms a help or a hindrance to the appropriation of his meaning.[33]

Similarly, Eliot's teacher, George Santayana, in 'The Absence of Religion in Shakespeare' (1899), observed that 'Shakespeare's world . . . is only the world of human society. The cosmos eludes him; he does not seem to feel the need of framing that idea. He depicts life in all its richness and variety, but leaves that life without a setting, and consequently without a meaning.'[34] Santayana's view anticipates Eliot's: Eliot's conviction that Shakespeare lacks a transcendental or spiritual commitment explains why he could never speak as warmly about Shakespeare as he could about Dante, who, he asserted, drew upon a complete theology – Dante 'wrote when Europe was still more or less one'.[35] It is the absence of 'any coherent view of life' or doctrine in Shakespeare, specifically a religious one, that explains Eliot's astounding lack of enthusiasm for the greatest poet in English.[36] It is Shakespeare's empiricism, materialism and pluralism – in short, his modernity – that he objects to. By contrast it is Shakespeare's 'negative capability' and commitment to ordinary life – the *absence* of any complete transcendental doctrine, any theoretical abstraction from experience – that links Shakespeare to Larkin. The first three stanzas of the 1946 poem 'Many famous feet have trod' are a gloss of Keats's negative capability remarks (themselves of course a tribute to Shakespeare):

Many famous feet have trod
Sublunary paths, and famous hands have weighed
The strength they have against the strength they need;

---

[31] 'The Pleasure Principle', *Required Writing*, pp. 81–2.

[32] 'The Poetry of Hardy', *Required Writing*, p. 175.

[33] A. C. Bradley, 'The Nature of Tragedy with Special Reference to Shakespeare: Paper Read before the Warrington Literary and Philosophical Society, 19 February 1889' (Warrington, 1889), pp. 14, 25–6.

[34] Santayana, 'The Absence of Religion in Shakespeare', pp. 154–5.

[35] This sentence comes in a comparison with Chaucer but Eliot thinks exactly the same of Shakespeare. See 'Dante' in *Selected Prose of T. S. Eliot*, ed. Frank Kermode (London, 1975), p. 209, and cf. his statement 'I prefer the culture which produced Dante to the culture which produced Shakespeare' in 'Second Thoughts About Humanism' (1929), in *Selected Essays*, p. 488. Such distinctions acknowledge Shakespeare's greatness but also demote him as a less than complete poet.

[36] 'Shakespeare and the Stoicism of Seneca' (1927), *Selected Essays*, p. 135.

And famous lips interrogated God
Concerning franchise in eternity;
And in many differing times and places
Truth was attained (a moment's harmony);
Yet endless mornings break on endless faces:

Gold surf of the sun, each day
Exhausted through the world, gathers and whips
Irrevocably from eclipse;
The trodden way becomes the untrodden way,
We are born each morning, shelled upon
A sheet of light that paves
The palaces of sight, and brings again
The river shining through the field of graves.

Such renewal argues down
Our unsuccessful legacies of thought,
Annals of men who fought
Untiringly to change their hearts to stone,
Or to a wafer's poverty,
Or to a flower, but never tried to learn
The difficult triple sanity
Of being wafer, stone, and flower in turn.

The stanzas defend the Protean, multifaceted consciousness long attributed to Shakespeare, and attack rigid exclusive conceptualizations of life – systematic yet 'unsuccessful legacies of thought' that are of no help to us here now, for whom the trodden ways (and the received doctrines) have run out. Each day, the poem asserts, we start anew – there is nothing for it but to make our own paths, construct our own meaning. 'Days', as Larkin wrote in a better-known poem, 'are where we live': there is no getting outside time; each temporary, makeshift truth or code must be contrived again, for 'endless mornings break on endless faces'. This anti-dogmatic Shakespeare is Lawrence's as well. To Lawrence, Shakespeare seemed, like 'the novel' in general, to be part of what he called 'the bright book of life'. Thus Plato, Lawrence argued, spoke to the ideal part in D. H. Lawrence, the Sermon on the Mount to the 'selfless' bit, the Ten Command-ments to the quivering guilt-ridden portion, and so on. But only 'the novel' appealed to 'the whole man alive' in him. The novel, he asserted, is the enemy of the 'ugly imperialism of the absolute', which always speaks in the end only to a part of the whole human being, and is therefore ultimately *against* life (because privileging one value over all others is to exclude large parts of life – life by def-inition being *all* values). Lawrence, like Nietzsche, wanted to be able to affirm all of life, even the immoral parts. The 'imperialism of the absolute' is for Lawrence precisely what Shakespeare, who is one 'of the supreme old novels', along with the Bible – but, note, 'all the Bible' – stand against. The old novels 'set the whole tree trembling'; they don't 'just stimulate growth in one direction'.[37] This is another way of saying Shakespeare is a poet of freedom. The anti-transcendental, irreligious or non-absolutist understanding of Shakespeare I am attributing to Keats and Lawrence is, I suspect, also Larkin's understanding of him. This is not (quite) to say that Shakespeare was an atheist but it is to say that the texts have lent themselves to such a con-struction, Eliot's hostile interpretation being a case in point. In any case, as we have seen, it is com-mon to think of Shakespeare as a worldly writer who agrees with Larkin that 'Days are where we live' and have our being: i.e. as one who holds that there is no getting beyond mutability to some more perfect perspective.

Larkin's obsession with death, from the 1946 poem 'Going' ('There is an evening coming in / Across the fields, one never seen before, / That lights no lamps') to the late masterpiece 'Aubade', is, of course, shared by those poets who most influenced him, Rossetti, Hardy, Housman among them. He didn't need the *Sonnets* to write about what was evidently a deeply personal preoccu-pation. Nevertheless they do form an intriguing paratext for reading Larkin. Their sense of life as *essentially* ruin – Shakespeare's 'Nature' being 'sovereign mistress over wrack' (Sonnet 126) – is shared by Larkin, as is Shakespeare's sense of life as death's quarry: 'Only one ship is seeking us, a black-/ Sailed unfamiliar', Larkin writes in 'Next, Please',

---

[37] See the excerpt from Lawrence's essay 'Why the Novel Mat-ters', in Richard Ellman and Charles Feidelson's The *Modern Tradition* (New York, 1965), p. 705.

> towing at her back
> A huge and birdless silence. In her wake
> No waters breed or break.

And, in 'Unfinished Poem', death is described as he 'Who covets our breath, who seeks and will always find'; just as Shakespeare's Nature must eventually yield up her 'treasure' (the Young Man) to Death: 'Her audit, though delayed, answered must be, / And her quietus is to render thee' (Sonnet 126). (In 'Unfinished Poem' it is not death who appears at the end but, dazzlingly and bewilderingly, love: 'Nothing like death has such hair, arms so raised. / Why are your feet bare? Was not death to come? / . . . What summer have you broken from?').

In a brilliant and provocative study, Robert N. Watson has argued that English Renaissance culture was increasingly beset by annihilationism – the fear that 'Our little life is rounded with a sleep' and that 'The rest is silence', i.e. the Larkin-esque fear (Watson uses some lines from 'Aubade' as an epigraph) that death may be simple oblivion.[38] In the *Sonnets*, it seems to me, death performs a function precisely like that which it performs in Larkin's work, reminding us of all that is beautiful in life, the more beautiful because transient. This is a way of experiencing the world – as inhabiting death, and as having its value and beauty heightened through vulnerability to death – that, I suggest, is shared by Larkin and Shakespeare (as well as by Hardy and Lawrence). Like Shakespeare in the *Sonnets*, Larkin is fond of using the hackneyed or proverbial imagery of the seasons; and, like the *Sonnets* again, every summer in Larkin is haunted by an approaching autumn and winter. In 'An April Sunday brings the snow', a poem written on the death of his father, Larkin contemplates the wondrous quantity of jam ('a hundred pounds or more') his father had made last summer – 'your final summer – sweet / And meaningless, and not to come again'.[39] The sweetness of that great vivid jam-making summer is dependent partly on its contingency (it is part of no larger meaning-giving scheme of things but is simply and entirely itself) and partly too its sweetness is dependent on its unrepeatability – that

summer will never come again.[40] Likewise, in 'Mother, Summer, I' Larkin describes himself as 'summer-born / And summer-loving'. Yet, he confesses, he is not unlike his mother, who anxiously scans summer skies for 'grape-dark clouds', and who is somehow more at ease when August brings the 'brittle frost' and 'bird-abandoned air'.[41] 'Show Saturday' describes a brilliant life-packed scene; but the end of the day inaugurates a movement 'Back . . . to autumn' and 'winter coming'; it is 'the ended husk / Of summer that brought them here for Show Saturday'. And in 'All catches alight', a jubilant poem about spring, in which 'Every one thing, / Shape, colour and voice, / Cries out, Rejoice!' a barebones refrain sounds: '*A drum taps; a wintry drum*'. It is as if Larkin cannot imagine spring or summer without his mind running ahead at once to their extinction in winter and autumn – and it is this proleptic movement that gives his summers their aching sadness. The *Sonnets*, of course, use an exactly similar strategy:

> For never-resting time leads summer on
> To hideous winter, and confounds him there,
> Sap checked with frost, and lusty leaves quite gone,
> Beauty o'er-snowed, and bareness every-where. (5)

> Then let not winter's ragged hand deface
> In thee thy summer ere thou be distilled (6)

> When lofty trees I see barren of leaves,
> Which erst from heat did canopy the herd,
> And summer's green all girded up in sheaves (12)

---

[38] Robert N. Watson, *The Rest is Silence: Death as Annihilation in the English Renaissance* (Berkeley, 1994).

[39] For the biographical context, see Andrew Motion, *Philip Larkin: A Writer's Life* (London, 1993), p. 177.

[40] The jam is stored under 'cellophane' and, as a trace of the person who made it, may conjure up the image of distillation Shakespeare uses in the *Sonnets*: 'Then were not summer's distillation left / A liquid prisoner pent in walls of glass' (5), etc.

[41] The image of decay or death as 'bird-abandoned', as here, or as entailing 'A . . . birdless silence', as in 'Next, Please', almost inevitably brings to mind the most famous image in the *Sonnets*: 'That time of year thou mayst in me behold / When yellow leaves, or none, or few, do hang / Upon those boughs which shake against the cold, / Bare ruined choirs where late the sweet birds sang' (73).

And summer's lease hath all too short a date (18)

O how shall summer's honey breath hold out
Against the wrackful siege of battering days (65)

Like Larkin, Shakespeare in the *Sonnets* shows every summer haunted by 'hideous winter' (5) – shows life itself as a kind of epiphenomenon of death, a doomed 'inconstant stay' (15) against what Larkin, in his own last words, is said to have called 'the inevitable'.[42] In 'Ambulances' bystanders watch someone taken off to hospital, and at that moment 'sense the solving emptiness / That lies just under all we do / And for a second get it whole, / So permanent and blank and true'. In 'The North Ship', the speaker's 'sleep is made cold / By a recurrent dream / Where all things seem / Sickeningly to poise / On emptiness'. Shakespeare's *Sonnets*, it seems to me, are simply the most famous example in English literature of this way of looking at the world – of seeing life itself as *founded on* nothingness. It is this quality that gives every description of beauty in Shakespeare's *Sonnets*, as in Larkin's poetry, its heart-rending emotional power.

An example is Larkin's lovely poem 'The Trees':

> The trees are coming into leaf
> Like something almost being said;
> The recent buds relax and spread,
> Their greenness is a kind of grief.
>
> Is it that they are born again
> And we grow old? No, they die too.
> Their yearly trick of looking new
> Is written down in rings of grain.
>
> Yet still the unresting castles thresh
> In fullgrown thickness every May.
> Last year is dead, they seem to say,
> Begin afresh, afresh, afresh.

What makes the trees beautiful, and noble (the word 'castle' is significant in that connection), is their participation in death, which is the ultimate cause of their yearly 'trick' of pretending that they are born anew, pretending that they do not simply grow old and die, like every other created being, but instead die only to be reborn each year. There is something heroic but also touchingly vulnerable about this determination of the trees (as of all nature) to pretend that they begin 'afresh', that they live outside of days. But the sombre truth is there, marked down in melancholy 'rings of grain' – each day, and year, the trees come a little closer to extinction. What makes them beautiful is their defiance of this reality, which is of course testimony to a desperate love of life. Larkin wrote that 'Man's most remarkable talent is for ignoring death... Truly... ignorance – in the sense of ignoring – is the necessary condition of life.'[43] Nature ignores death, or attempts to, and in doing so acquires a sort of grandeur. Had the trees been created for eternity the seriousness and tragic nobility of their existence would have been taken from them: it is after all their vulnerability to time that is the basis for that annual heroic 'trick' of pretending that they will not die.

Seeing life as inhabiting death is closely connected, I think, with another persistent and prominent theme in Shakespeare and Larkin: sexual desire. For Shakespeare in the *Sonnets* sex is a way of standing against time and its insults – not simply in the sense that heterosexual lovers beget children who will call back the lovely April of their prime, but also in the sense that, as Larkin puts it in 'An Arundel Tomb', 'What will survive of us is love'. In loving the young boy Shakespeare presents himself as waging a war against death: it is his love for the boy that has moved him to write these anti-death poems, and it is this love too, it turns out, which is the best thing about the speaker's life, the one part of him that deserves to survive, and that offsets his rather pathetic and seedy identity as it emerges in the poems as a whole. Like the couple in effigy on the tomb, what will remain of Shakespeare is his selfless devotion to the boy. What survives of us is love.

Selflessness and selfishness are of course large themes in the *Sonnets*, as in Larkin. It seems odd

---

[42] Motion, *Philip Larkin*, p. 521.

[43] 'Point of No Return', *Further Requirements*, p. 345. Cf. 'The costly aversion of the eyes from death' ('Wants') and of course the closing lines of 'Aubade'.

no one has noticed the close connection between Larkin's persistent interest in these themes – in particular, his poems' exploration of his own real-life reluctance, as 'An indigestible sterility' ('Spring'), to marry and have children – and the opening sequence of the *Sonnets*, in which Shakespeare portrays the Young Man as selfish for precisely this reason ('who is he so fond will be the tomb / Of his self-love to stop posterity?' (3)). Larkin's poetry frequently confesses an incapacity on his part to give himself to another; and where Shakespeare criticizes his Young Man for a narcissistic perversion of love ('Unthrifty loveliness, why dost thou spend / Upon thyself thy beauty's legacy?' (4)) Larkin's poems are often wary of the costs of love – costs to one's autonomy, to one's ability to be oneself and not another. 'None of the books have time' makes explicit a theme encountered throughout Larkin's poetry:

> None of the books have time
> To say how being selfless feels,
> They make it sound a superior way
> Of getting what you want. It isn't at all.
>
> Selflessness is like waiting in a hospital
> In a badly-fitting suit on a cold wet morning.
> Selfishness is like listening to good jazz
> With drinks for further orders and a huge fire.

This is not in the least ironic; and one of the tougher aspects of Larkin's poetry to come to terms with is this realistic, and consciously selfish, view of what love demands of one.[44] To be sure, the celebrations of selfishness that Larkin vents often let on more about the speaker than he would like to have known, telling us of something inside him – a simple disability – that bars him from committing to another. In 'Dockery and Son' the speaker, in contemplating Dockery's career, comes to sudden awareness of all that he, the speaker, has missed out on in life: wife, son, etc. But the poem is finely poised: there is the realization of loss but also the stubborn awareness (as if in direct reply to the argument of the first seventeen of Shakespeare's *Sonnets*) that the life Dockery has led is not for him: what amazes the speaker, as he reflects upon what he now knows of how Dockery's life has turned out,

is 'how / Convinced' Dockery must have been that 'he should be added to! / Why did he think adding meant increase? / To me it was dilution.'[45] Shakespeare urges his Young Man to breed and augment himself: spending oneself, it turns out, is a mode of self-preservation; by contrast, 'having traffic with thyself alone' is 'of thyself thy sweet self' to 'deceive' (4). For Larkin this is unconvincing: love, children, relationships simply *do* diminish one's freedom[46] and sweet-talking that reality away won't wash: in 'Afternoons' the young children play in the park; 'Summer is fading' and 'The leaves fall in ones and twos / From trees bordering / The new recreation ground'; the young mothers who watch the children (who will soon demand and 'Expect to be taken home') are perhaps vaguely aware, in their quiet undramatic unhappiness, that 'Something is pushing them / To the side of their own lives.' That something is the life of children and family that they have created for themselves (or which was created for them). At the end of 'Dockery and Son' the speaker realizes how sadly conditioned our choices can be: did he choose bachelorhood, as Dockery (apparently) chose marriage and family, or is it always rather a matter of 'what something hidden from us chose'? Whatever the answer to that question, the poem is starkly clear: Dockery's life could never have been the speaker's, because the speaker simply is not Dockery. '[H]ow we live', writes Larkin in 'Mr Bleaney', 'measures our own nature'. For good or ill, the speaker of 'Dockery and Son' is who he is. There was never an alternative.

---

44 The poem 'Love' distinguishes between two sorts of selfishness. The first (good) sort involves 'upset[ting] an existence / Just for your own sake'; the second (bad) type involves simply not getting involved with others: 'My life is for me'. The *Sonnets* are likewise interested in the complicated ways love, selfishness and selflessness interact.

45 Larkin's use of the word 'increase', in the context of a discussion of the merits of having (or not having) children, may put us in mind of the opening line of *Sonnets*: 'From fairest creatures we desire increase . . .'.

46 See 'Counting': 'But counting up to two / Is harder to do; / For one must be denied / Before it's tried'.

What I am emphasizing is this non-ironic side to Larkin's celebration of selfishness – or, to put it in more positive terms, of solitude – and I'm interested in the way it forms an extended argument with Shakespeare's *Sonnets*. Again and again Larkin expresses the need to be alone, which is to say to be oneself. In 'Vers de Société' the speaker sarcastically intones the common wisdom: '*All solitude is selfish*'; '*Virtue is social.*' 'Reasons for Attendance' features a man standing outside a dance-hall, looking at the couples moving within. His reasons for non-attendance are cogent: he devotes his life 'to that lifted, rough-tongued bell / (Art, if you like) whose individual sound / Insists I too am individual'. So the speaker needn't merge with the throng inside who 'maul to and fro'; he has his own mission. This subtle, intelligent poem keeps in play two contradictory views. The ending suggests that the speaker fatally misjudges his own needs: is what perhaps stops him from connecting with other people, what bars him from the dance of love, not any lofty summons of art and ideal of individuality but some more inscrutable, and destructive, force? Yet the speaker's commitment to self-preservation is not merely un-self-knowing; it is also serious and stubbornly individual. He cuts a ridiculous figure (he knows this) and will remind us of the similarly pretentious and emotionally stultified Gabriel Conroy in Joyce's famous story, a figure also incapable of connection. But no such awareness can change for a moment the reality that this is who the speaker is. While his identity may not be a happy, even a morally defensible, one, he cannot simply transform himself into those other people there. He is who he is. Larkin's emotional parsimony – the care he takes not to waste himself in others – constitutes an on-going reply in his poetry to the argument of the *Sonnets*, which asserts that to waste oneself by having children is actually to preserve oneself, an idea explicitly mocked in 'Marriages': most people will end up with a 'partner – / Some undesirable, / With whom it is agreed / That words such as liberty... / Shall be unmentionable'. Nevertheless the sacrifice is worth it, or so the world says anyway: 'So they are gathered in; / So they are not wasted'.

The persona of Larkin's poetry is related to that of Shakespeare's *Sonnets* in another key respect: the theme of failure and, paradoxically enough, of self-assertion. 'Failure', along with 'oblivion' and 'death', is one of the most hard-worked words in Larkin's oeuvre. One quite terrifying poem is addressed 'To Failure' ('You have been here some time'); in 'Vers de Société' the speaker's resolve to stay home by the lamp is undermined by feelings of 'failure and remorse'. The stranded speaker in 'Autobiography at an Air-Station' eagerly anticipated the 'Assumption' of aeroplane travel – 'Now it's failed'. In 'Toads Revisited', ne'er-do-wells turn 'over their failures / By some bed of lobelias'; 'Unfinished Poem' begins at dusk, or 'the failure of evening'. Larkin's speakers are appalledly aware of how failure infects every part of their lives ('Continuing to live' he observes in the poem of that name, 'Is nearly always losing'); but such everyday failures are merely a foretaste of the true and final failure, which awaits all of us: death itself. In 'Tops' it is that almost imperceptible 'falter' and 'stumble' that signifies that the spinning top is 'starting to die'. Failure, Larkin perceives, as does Shakespeare in the *Sonnets*, is an ineradicable part of life because *life itself is part of nothingness*. What is repeatedly insisted upon in Larkin is how one does not make oneself. Instead, something obscure and dark in oneself is 'doing the damage' ('The Winter Palace') and knowing what that something is, and the failure it is responsible for, won't stop its poisonous work.[47] In 'As Bad as a Mile' the apple-core misses the bin – but the bungled throw began well back, in the arm and in the life that arm is part of:

Watching the shied core
Striking the basket, skidding across the floor,
Shows less and less of luck, and more and more

Of failure spreading back up the arm
Earlier and earlier, the unraised hand calm,
The apple unbitten in the palm.

---

[47] The poem 'Continuing to Live' speaks of 'the blind impress / All our behavings bear'. Knowing about this 'impress' will make no difference.

Larkin's poetry gives us a view of life as *essentially* failure – as always defeated by 'the inevitable'. The *Sonnets*, I think, are built on precisely this tragic insight.

For the *Sonnets* are one of the most startling explorations of human failure in English, and the breath-taking openness of their self-exposure (exposure of moral, erotic, existential failure) makes them directly comparable to Larkin's work. The *Sonnets* chronicle a failed, dingy life. The speaker is an ageing lover ('Beated and chapped with tanned antiquity' (62)), a man 'made lame by fortune's dearest spite' (37), impotently envious of others' abilities (29) and pained by the unspecified 'vulgar scandal' (112) attached to his name. He has made a public fool of himself, become 'a motley to the view' (110). He is 'bar[red]' by 'fortune' from the 'triumph' of 'public honour and proud titles' (25); the world 'is bent [his] deeds to cross' (90). He adores a beautiful young boy who treats him badly and is obsessed with a woman ('the bay where all men ride' (137)) manifestly unworthy of his desire – another failure, this time of his better self. The poems' description of the speaker's descent into madness, lust and disease seem to me unparalleled in Renaissance literature as far as the extent of their self-exposure goes.[48] And, hovering at the edge of all these failures described in the *Sonnets* is that 'small unfocused blur', as Larkin described our sense of death in 'Aubade' – the great failure of inevitable oblivion.

Like Larkin's poems, then, the *Sonnets* are among the bleakest documents in our language. But there is another side to them that makes them exhilarating, notwithstanding their melancholy grasp of life as inevitable failure. I mean their defiant self-assertion, the way in which they insist upon the speaker's identity as, if not exemplary, at least his own. The speaker is in the end simply and sincerely himself; he can be no other. In his biography of Larkin, Andrew Motion says Larkin's 'powerful self-esteem was matched by an equally virulent self-disparagement'.[49] This seems to me absolutely right of Larkin's poetic persona, which, even as it is conscious of personal failure, remains true to itself. And it is a psychological

characterization equally applicable, I think, to the speaker of the *Sonnets*, who, just as he acknowledges his tawdry, ridiculous, scandal-plagued identity, nevertheless accepts himself, in the way that Hardy, Lawrence or Larkin might have applauded him for doing. He knows his unworthiness yet

> Sin of self-love possesseth all mine eye,
> And all my soul, and all my every part;
> And for this sin there is no remedy,
> *It is so grounded inward in my heart.* (my italics)

The speaker in this sonnet (62) goes on to assert, with extraordinary pugnacity, that he will be the judge of his own worth: '*for myself mine own worth do define*' (my italics). What comes through this poem, despite the unconvincing let-out at the end, in which the speaker claims that in loving himself he is actually loving the friend (his 'self'), is this virtue of 'Sincerity' in Lawrence's (and Larkin's) sense: the stubborn insistence on being oneself – whatever that self is – rather than another. Sincerity in this sense seems to me the key virtue of the *Sonnets* – cumulatively, they have the same effect, in the audacity, even shamelessness, of their confessional impulse, as Rousseau's self-exposure in the *Confessions*. Shakespeare seems to say in them, with Rousseau, 'I may be no better than other men, but at least I am different.' That commitment to individuality is thrilling and is one of the modern features of the *Sonnets* that reminds us of Larkin. In Larkin's poem 'Schoolmaster', a kind of failure infinitely more appalling than the worldly one is described – the loss of one's own self. The character described in the poem has got his job as a schoolmaster: 'He was safe . . . / . . . he would never fail.' The 'unreal life' that follows – one of blandly fitting in with others – is the consequence of his ignoring

---

[48] Note that the poems are presented as autobiographical (the 1609 volume's title-page is *Shakespeare's Sonnets*) whether they are in fact or not. On this point see Katherine Duncan-Jones's discussion in *Ungentle Shakespeare* (London, 2001). Perhaps only Montaigne's *Essays* compare with Shakespeare's *Sonnets* in terms of this rhetoric of self-exposure.

[49] Motion, *Philip Larkin*, p. xviii.

those who speak in elevated Lawrentian tones of 'the claims / Of living: they were merely desperate'. The result is that 'though he never realised it, he / Dissolved'. All Larkin's poetry is directed against such self-dissolution. So, I would argue, are Shakespeare's *Sonnets*. 'No, I am that I am' Shakespeare declares aggressively in Sonnet 121; he can be no other, and those who preen themselves on being better than he, and who scorn him on account of his follies (his 'sportive blood'), are likely no better in reality: 'By their rank thoughts my deeds must not be shown'. Larkin's 'Best Society' concludes with the speaker 'Viciously' locking his door against the world to find 'Uncontradicting solitude', in which 'cautiously / Unfolds, emerges, *what I am*' (my italics). Shakespeare's 'I am that I am', with its half-ironic, half-blasphemous tone, expresses an intransigent insistence on being oneself and not someone else – not fitting in, like Larkin's Schoolmaster. It is a declaration that places their author in the same empirical, worldly and libertarian-individualist tradition of English writing to which Hardy and Lawrence – and Philip Larkin – belonged.

SHAKESPEARE PERFORMANCES IN ENGLAND 2010

CAROL CHILLINGTON RUTTER

6 January 2010. Snow in Stratford-upon-Avon. Thick snow. Snow such as hasn't been seen for thirty years. Drifts down Sheep Street. Black ice along Waterside. The town in grey gloom and muffled silence except for the hooting of boys from Shakespeare's grammar school, let out from classes early to get home before the next ice age sets in, pelting snowballs at each other, setting off mini-avalanches from snow-laden bare-branched chestnut trees in the Bancroft Gardens. I'm positioned on the tramway footbridge, looking across the frozen boat basin at a white wilderness towards the construction project I reported on two years ago (*Shakespeare Survey 62*). I'm taking stock. Then, I described the site of the demolished Royal Shakespeare Theatre as a rubble-strewn wasteland that put me in mind of post-war Warsaw. Now I'm looking at something like present-day Bruges, where twenty-first century architecture must fit a conservation agenda in a medieval town substantially invented in the 1900s with neo-Gothic in-fills, extensions and retro-renovations. I'm looking at pastiche and can't decide whether it represents a triumph of best-of-British provincial conservatism or a world-class failure of nerve. Left, beyond the snow-plastered construction hoardings, the 'new' riverside elevation is brand spanking *old*, restored to Elizabeth Scott's 1932 design, complete with metal-frame windows built to original specifications. Looking that way, I'm in the past. Looking right, though, towards the town-side, there's the future, ultra-modernity, an attention-seeking brick and glass observation tower, set slightly 'off' the main building, thrusting up higher than the theatre's new fly tower, with multi-level connecting corridors still open to the weather where workmen in yellow waterproofs are busy. (On a day like today, I muse, construction is a 'dreadful trade', worse than gathering samphire.) And between these two, facing me, the new RST's front façade is an architectural cut-and-paste job. The preserved ground floor and two storeys of Scott's foyer and dress circle are topped with a final half storey lifting the roof line, a postmodern flourish in glass, steel and brick. It's an odd cap on a matronly head – as though my twenty-something daughters had talked fifty-something me into an Amy Winehouse quiff.

Is this vision bold enough? Will it produce the town planner's *ne plus ultra*, a 'destination building'? Is it overburdened with the past, too much memorial reconstruction? (The project director has talked about leaving 'scars' from 'the removal of the later additions' visible on the façade; 'the theatre's "ghosts"', he calls them, a kind of bricks-and-mortar 'remember me'.) Or is this structural tie-in of memory and moment a canny metaphor of theatrical practice, a wearing on its sleeve of a constitutional paradox? This state-of-the-art theatre is designed, after all, to stage early modern plays – but to postmodern audiences; to be today 'the best possible performance space for Shakespeare' (as the publicity has it), restoring us and Shakespeare to (some of, but not too many of) the conditions of early modern playing – a thrust stage, with spectators on three sides, a 'one room' playhouse that bids for intimacy, complicity and collaboration, putting no spectator further than 15 metres from the stage.

(But there won't be any pesky 'groundlings'. And there will be miles of modern plumbing.)

It's too early to tell. More significantly, it's too early to tell whether the building will work *as a theatre*. We won't get a proper look inside – at the stage, at the auditorium – until November. For now, though, in the snow on the bridge, I'm prepared to be simply beguiled by the structure, both its materiality and promise: bricks + risk. And I don't know it yet, but the building is putting into my head thoughts that will direct my viewing in a year when I'll be fascinated by structures – and not just the architectural structures of theatre buildings (though nothing I'll see of them this year will thrill me as much as standing on scaffolding over an excavation in Shoreditch in August, looking down at a short length of stonework, the exposed foundations of all that survives of London's first purpose-built playhouse, the Theatre). This will be a year when casting decisions will invite me to think of actors' bodies as performance structures. When production rhythms will demonstrate the structural force of Shakespeare's play-wrighting, the genius of the way he puts plays together. When local audiences watching Shakespeare in local theatres will create structures of community viewing. And when, not a little ironically, back in Stratford at the Courtyard (in its final season as stand-in and working prototype for the under-construction RST), technicians will produce increasingly ingenious devices to overcome the structural limitations they're already encountering in the very innovation – the thrust stage – that is the still-unfinished new building's most hyped retro-feature.

HISTORIES

Last year, history was entirely absent from the repertoire. This year, it's back, the Globe opening its 'Kings and Rogues' season with a Tudor-dressed *Henry VIII* directed by Mark Rosenblatt, making his Shakespeare debut in this theatre. *Henry VIII* is an important play for any who still want the reconstructed Globe to work (sometimes) as a laboratory for understanding how early modern scripts worked on early modern stages, not

least because it's a play definitely assignable to the Globe, given that an accident with a production effect gone wrong (subsequent designers: take note) involving a cannon, some wadding and the roof thatch was responsible for burning the playhouse to the ground in June 1613. Reporting that disaster, Harry Wotton (as usual, seriously mischievous) critiqued the play, getting to the nub of the problem of attempting to stage awe-fullness. If you try in a measly cock-pit to represent 'some Principal Pieces' of a reign that you 'set forth with many extraordinary circumstances of pomp and majesty, even to the matting of the stage', you risk making 'greatness very familiar, if not ridiculous'. That problem of 'ridiculous' familiarity persisted here.

Now, it wasn't as if Rosenblatt needed to cultivate familiarity – to find ways of making the slippery ins-and-outs of this least performed Shakespeare (and Fletcher) history play accessible to today's audience. Familiarity was handed him on a plate. Last year, you couldn't swing a cat in England without hitting a Tudor. Exhibitions across the kingdom remembered the 500th anniversary of Henry's coronation. In the cinema, there was *The Other Boleyn Girl* and, on the best-sellers' list, Hilary Mantel's superb *Wolf Hall*. All of this worked like advance publicity, making this play's cast of characters *open* in close-up. Their crises of conscience, dynastic anxieties couldn't help but be politically hot topics in weeks following months of electioneering in Britain that had dynastically anxious politicians staging their own crises of conscience on platforms up and down the land. International audiences who, in June, stood in the yard of the Globe listening to Peter Hamilton Dyer's politic Norfolk ram down Buckingham's throat (Anthony Howell) a report on a cross-channel junket that made him splutter with indignation had themselves swallowed, in the past twelve months, a belly-full of sour news about banking collapse, taxpayer bail-outs and the unimaginable extravagance of the London City traders' bonus culture. So a director didn't have to do very much to make this play's opening scene, with its account of macho swaggering, inventory of conspicuous waste on a field turned sartorially into a 'cloth of gold', and gripes about who'd be paying for these 'fierce vanities', relevant to the day's groundlings. With all that going for him – plus a full range of eye-dazzling Tudor costumes (designed by Angela Davies) lavished on his actors' bodies – Rosenblatt might have done what the script actually needed: found with his company a performance style that played *against* familiarity, distancing greatness by heightening formality. This would have provided a platform for Shakespeare-and-Fletcher's writing, which gives actors a 'weighty . . . / Sad, high, and working' rhetoric to play with in political speeches that rise to climaxes like pyramid-high steps up a hangman's scaffold, so making the spectacular falls that come hard on each other's heels in Henry's court terrible. Instead, we merely got the 'very familiar'. We got (with important exceptions) a kind of colloquialism of speech and movement that made Anne Boleyn (Miranda Raison) less Tudor courtier than footballer's WAG – hardly a temptation to make the anonymous Gentleman excuse the king, 'I cannot blame his conscience.' And we got Dominic Rowan's flop-haired, pudding-faced Henry, who first appeared in shirt and Tudor trainers, playing *real tennis* on a virtual court. (Could something have been made of this concealed pun on game-playing as a metaphor for Harry's *modus operandi*? It wasn't.) In another life he might have made a decent enough 'suit' holding his own in televised election debates against the likes of Gordon Brown and Nick Clegg – other wrinkle-free 'suits'. Here, though, vocally underpowered and not, as an actor, taking the bait his playwrights offer him, the stunning inconsistencies in Henry's tangled impulses that can't be ironed out (his conscience over Katherine, his lust for Anne), he never lived up to the rhetorical expectations troped by his super-size codpiece. (Late on, when Rowan's Henry strode on to meet his baby Elizabeth in the christening scene and struck the iconic wide-legged, hands-on-hips Holbein portrait pose, he just looked silly: simultaneously overblown and about ten stone underweight.)

Once again, the Globe's 'improvers' had put the company's carpenters to work fixing up the stage –

wrecking my notional 'laboratory' and the chance to see how the play, built episodically of 'Pieces', played in something like original conditions. But other ideas took shape in the built structure. Connecting to the platform in a T-junction, a broad runway thrusting out into the middle of the yard served as Tudor exhibition space: Henry's male-strut masque, Anne's gilded coronation (staged 'authentically', with the new queen six months pregnant), Katherine's defiant exit from her show trial. Much more interesting was how Rosenblatt used the platform itself. Almost always empty of furniture, the space inside the (for once, structurally useful) Globe pillars was marked out as a square, accessed by the central upstage double-doors. Outside it, running around the rim of the stage and accessed by the upstage doors left and right of centre, a red strip marking the perimeter gave the effect of carpeted corridors – suggesting, beyond the stage, a warren of lobbies and narrow passages and endless halls. This was a design that could cut from interior to exterior with the slam of a door. It gave us Henry's private presence chamber where 'insider' deals were cut, hairs split, arguments heard, lives decided; but outside, on the edge, the corridors of (dissident) power that drove fault-lines through Henry's court. Subjects who exited smiling through one set of doors instantly re-entered snarling through the other. The presence was the place for nodding yes-men; the corridors, for rumour-rattled subjects to huddle in twos and threes to whisper, gossip and conspire, and for the reign's Icaruses, fallen dizzily, to pause, to stand for a quiet time and get their bearings – like Howell's Buckingham, betrayed 'by [his] servants, by those men [he] loved most'; like Wolsey (Ian McNeice), who'd 'ventured' in 'a sea of glory' 'far beyond my depth' 'like wanton boys that swim on bladders' – before continuing their doomed exits down a blood-red corridor that troped their deaths. What this spatial arrangement marked clearly was the structure of *Henry VIII* as a *progress macabre*.

Finally, the production managed – just – to snatch a comic ending with a birth, a baby, and a prophecy ('This royal infant . . . / promises / . . . a thousand thousand blessings'). That triumph, crowded with nurses, bishops, cheering attendants spilling off the gangway, might have been interestingly undercut by the textual ambiguity of Henry's response: 'Oh lord Archbishop, / Thou hast made me now a man.' Did Henry mean that the revelation of her future had transformed his baby daughter into the man-child he needed as heir? Or that his conscience would no longer be routed through his groin, paternity transforming his adolescence 'now' – a little late – into 'a man'? Such potential edginess at the end was swamped by the Holbein pose.

The most compelling stories (and watchable performances) were Wolsey's and Queen Katherine's (Kate Duchêne). McNeice played the Wolsey of Buckingham's phrase, the jumped-up 'Ipswich fellow', a tradesman in scarlet. Magnificently imperturbable in his self-regard, oozing lines, he was awesomely ugly, his bull's head sunk into the folded fat of half-a-dozen chins. This was a man whose mountain belly archived men's accusations, so it was no hyperbole but the truth: 'his very bulk' *could* 'Take up the rays o'the beneficial sun / And keep it from the earth'. That he was finally brought down by something as footling as a mis-sent email McNeice was able to make tragic. In his steadfast farewell to Cromwell, not even his jowls wobbled.

Duchêne's wronged queen saw him as 'mine enemy'. But in this production, where, at her trial, accused, she was fearlessly indomitable, and later, divorced, wasn't broken, Wolsey wasn't her nemesis. That part went to an invented character, Amanda Lawrence's cross-dressed Will Sommers-type Fool – a disturbingly insinuating jack-in-a-box who popped up to speak the play's prologue and epilogue; who shadowed Henry's throne; and who went everywhere with a mockingly lifelike puppet: the boy Katherine couldn't produce. In her Act 4 dream sequence, Duchêne's queen didn't see a sublime vision of golden-vizarded, white-robed 'personages' (as the stage directions have it) offering her peace, apotheosis, a celestial crown. She saw a nightmare: the leering Fool, the jigging puppet-boy, a phantom Wolsey appearing to grab the crown from the infant's head, before laughing in her face and vanishing. Duchêne's queen woke

up screaming. And it was this fantasy, replaying the truth of her everyday life, that killed her.

Except for one hilarious sequence that had Michael Bertenshaw's harassed Porter and his deeply uncertain Man (John Cummins) like truncheon-armed Tudor lollipop ladies attempting crowd control (where the Globe's groundlings were cast as the 'fry of fornication' that Shakespeare's script imagines thronging the court, coming to see some lewd peep show, some 'Indian with the great tool', instead of a christening), *Henry VIII* gave us history-without-plebs, top-down history as magnificent entertainment on a stage that instantiated high-level intrigue.

Coming into the Globe season next, directed by Dominic Dromgoole, the two parts of *Henry IV* turned the perspective, saw history as low-down shenanigans, its *vox* raucously *pop*. Its celebrities were a trashy rogue's gallery of shifters and shysters, lousy drunks and gluttons, irritating, delinquent youths and beguilingly disgraceful geriatrics, all dressed out of pre-Tudor Oxfam, set on a stage (designed by Jonathan Fensom) that materialized two-nation England. On view, covering the upstage façade, was the kingdom's 'official' face: hanging like a floor-to-ceiling tapestry from the heavens, an ochre-coloured canvas backdrop blazoned England's heraldic arms. Pulled aside, this cover-up discovered the nation's back passage, a rickety wooden scaffold rising up stairs into crazy galleries, a snakes-and-ladders structure identified by a tatty, worsted banner: its blazon, a snaggle-toothed boar's head.

Where the rogues were kings, the kings (the actual, the aspirational, the apparent) were something of a washout. Oliver Cotton – grizzle-bearded, a big man just beginning to slip into his sixth age where his 'youthful hose' would flap around his 'shrunk shank' – certainly looked the part of King Henry, but didn't appear to have studied it (or hadn't been directed in it). 'So shaken as we are, so wan with care', he bellowed. (But isn't there a performance clue somewhere in the line?) 'Here is . . . / Sir Walter Blunt . . . / Stain'd with the variation of each soil / Betwixt that Holmedon and this seat of ours.' Enter Blunt, fresh as a daisy. For his part (and for all his period gear and knee-high boots), Sam Crane's thin-chested Hotspur looked like a DIY flat-pack mis-assembled without a central strut. Physically, he had two positions. Bent forward, legs wide and weak-kneed, pigeon-toed, hands on hips: 'I'm saying something important.' Bent forward, legs wide and weak-kneed, pigeon-toed, fingers splayed Edward Scissorhands-fashion in the air: 'I'm saying something very important.' (But why wasn't anybody listening? Why didn't words like 'betray'd' and 'traitor' in scene 2 sting anyone into a reaction?) Narrating his 'impatience' at the 'popinjay' who'd shown up on his reeking battlefield with a pouncet-box and 'new reap'd' chin, this Hotspur *was* the popinjay, his own caricature, a gesticulating human parenthesis in doublet and hose with an adenoidal voice and strange tea-kettle lisp (Crane's take on Hotpur's 'thick' speech?). But then, when Crane returned in Part 2 as Hal's swaggering sidekick, the casting, the body and the vocal delivery suddenly clicked into place. Hotspur was Pistol.

Just as Crane couldn't help having a body built for comedy, so Jamie Parker, playing a posh-accented Hal, couldn't help bearing an uncanny resemblance to the Tory party's Pigling Bland, David Cameron. (And, vocally, sounding not dissimilar, so that weirdly this Hal kept bringing the cadences of recent Tory electioneering to mind: 'I know you all . . . ') I'm guessing that Parker wasn't entirely responsible for Hal's utterly miscalculated first entrance, emerging through the trap, breeches around his ankles, tossing a coin downstairs to the tart who'd been servicing him. (But doesn't Dromgoole get it? Shakespeare's bright youth, Malcolm, Romeo, Claudio: they're virgins. Slumming at the Boar's Head Hal is as much aspirational raver as Hotspur, among the rebels, is aspirational usurper, delinquency an act, not action.) Both Cotton and Parker were at their best – and showed the performances another director might have got out of them consistently – in the stand-off between father and son in Part 1's 3.2. The prince, at first, was all adolescent twitch and shrug and humping folded arms and pursed lips and lame excuses. When the relentless paternal hammering

(Cotton hardly drawing breath) got to the 'shallow jesters' and 'rash bavin wits', the comparison to deposed Richard through 'vile participation', Hal had frozen, head bowed almost into his lap. But his dad – resting for only a half beat after 'Not an eye / But is a-weary of thy common sight' on 'Save mine', a half beat that gave the father (caught out by love) and the son (stunned, hearing it) a second to exchange looks surprised by feeling – still went on and on about Douglas and Northumberland, Mortimer and Percy, Percy, Percy. And it was the banging of that name onto his battered sense of self that finally provoked the interruption, 'Do not think so'; then, 'I AM YOUR SON.' This production needed more work of that quality.

I understand that, as a camera, the Globe really gives spectators only one viewing lens – wide angle. There's no directional lighting to close down areas of the stage, to create intimacy. But textually, Shakespeare's scripts *do* zoom into close-up – like the scene in Part 2 that replays the row in Part 1, that has the son wrangling with the crown over the body of the father he thinks it killed. On the evidence of a number of seasons watching Globe performances I'd say that actors on this stage need much more direction on Shakespeare's speech-craft, on the rhetoric of theatre speech (as opposed to that old chestnut reviewers regularly complain about, 'verse-speaking'): how he locates interruption to redirect focus, how he builds speeches to grab attention (frequently with some sort of rhetorical sucker punch), conducts argument (speech plateauing out into discursive thought), then trips the switch from speech into action. There was a brilliant example in Part 1. Crane had been mouthing Hotspur's put-down of Worcester's second thoughts in 4.1 – from this actor, a wash of unpointed sound and fury, emotion without sense – when he turned on Vernon with a tossed-off comment about the 'madcap Prince of Wales'. Kevork Malikyan's Vernon cut him dead. Then used this speech like Muhammad Ali pulping some hapless palooka. 'All furnish'd' (Jab). 'All in arms' (Jab). Now the left–right sequence, building up rhythm, pace: 'All plumed like . . . '; 'Bated like'; 'Glittering . . . like'; 'As full . . . as'; 'gorgeous as';

7. *Henry IV Part 1*, 2.5. Globe Theatre, directed by Dominic Dromgoole. Roger Allam as Falstaff, Jamie Parker as Prince Hal.

'Wanton as'; 'wild as'. Then the combination. Stiff jabs: 'I saw young Harry with his beaver on'. Power punches: 'arm'd'; 'Rise'; 'vaulted'; 'dropp'd'; 'To turn and wind . . . / And witch . . .' Taking this verbal beating, Hotspur had just enough wind left to throw in the towel: 'No more, no more!' In speeches like Vernon's (as played by actors like Malikyan) you can hear Shakespeare not just making the story but making his audience, structuring ways of listening in the theatre. I'd happily stand for another three hours in the Globe yard to listen to Malikyan do that speech again.

Of course, the role in *Henry IV* for which the wide-angle lens might have been invented is Falstaff, and here Roger Allam's 'trunk of humours', 'huge hill of flesh' filled the viewfinder. His knight's tale was proleptically appropriated by the plebs. This production opened in the theatre's courtyard (before invading the pit and overrunning the stage), with Brueghel-esque commoners putting on a rowdy mummers' play involving plenty of knock-about, daggers of lath, exaggerated death and miraculous resurrection – anticipating the end of Part 1. But the mumming was also reprised at the opening of Part 2, when Falstaff, metamorphosed in the popular imagination into St George killing the dragon, Hotspur, appeared as their national hero and subject of ballads sung in the street (which dropped into whispers and low murmurs that emerged as a chorus of gossip, then crescendoed into full-blown Rumour clamouring in the street). In Part 1, Allam's Falstaff was first discovered dead drunk and snoring behind King Henry's heraldic arras. In Part 2, he entered, beaming, bejewelled, nodding left and right to his paparazzi.

This was a Falstaff whose greasy grey hair and food-slicked doublet made him the walking embodiment of the 'obscene . . . tallow-catch' Hal calls him; whose voice (Roger Allam possessing

8. *Henry IV Part 2*, 5.1. Globe Theatre, directed by Dominic Dromgoole. Roger Allam as Falstaff,
William Gaunt as Shallow, Christopher Godwin as Silence, Phil Cheadle as Davy.

the second-best voice currently on the English stage – and 'first-best'? For me, Simon Russell Beale) could slide from bald-faced effrontery ('I knew ye') to wheedle ('kill the heir apparent') on the banana skin of a single sentence; who could pause for refreshment on the battlefield, taking out a leather lunch box; who, for all his girth, could dance like Orpheus's leviathan on shore around Barbara Marten's wonderful scrag-end Mrs Quickly (played here, for once, not as some anachronistic male fantasy of a glamourised silk-and-taffeta bodice-breaker but a greyed, wool-and-dowlas pot-scrubber), 'forgiving' her for picking his pocket, ordering yet more linen, promising yet more golden futures. He came to Shrewsbury with his alibi stashed in his kit bag, a leather bottle of blood that, when he needed it to cover his perfidy, he dowsed liberally over himself and Hotspur before killing the rebel 'for real' – a counterfeit that momentarily gruesomely trapped him in the lie as, toppling over, he was pinned to the ground by the corpse. But this reprehensible craven also hit raw nerves point-blank. 'What is honour?' he asked an audience who that day had heard more news of casualties in Afghanistan – ending the speech on a loud raspberry of empty air. (Later, though, he didn't hesitate to pilfer dead Blunt's pockets.) He could be heart-stoppingly moving. In Part 2, in his address to sack, when he got to that climactic hypothetical, 'If I had a thousand sons . . .', the never-never of that word 'son' dropped out from under him like a crater. And such is Allam's generosity as an actor that this Falstaff could play – could *under* play – straight man to the geriatric clowns in Gloucestershire, scenes in which Shakespeare invents Alzheimer's, and scenes that were played definitively here by William Gaunt as Shallow, all woofling, whistling, tottering busyness ('Davy, Davy, Davy, Davy, Davy') and Christopher Godwin (anorexic but somehow lumpen) as Silence: performances I wish I could've captured in a bottle to let out on rainy days. Most impressive of all was how Allam showed the structural point of Falstaff's soliloquies, standing on the verge of the platform, taking in the whole wooden O, addressing us on the topic of honour, 'my soldiers', or the 'better part of valour', doing big what Vernon would in little: making us listeners, an audience. In lean times under a regime headed by a Cameron look-alike that had already loosed the Fangs and

9. *Richard III*, 1.4. Propeller on tour, directed by Edward Hall. Full company,
John Dougall as Clarence.

Snares on London even before the ink on the coronation invitations was dry, Allam's Falstaff wasn't – in today's political language – 'sustainable'. He had to go. But oh, the pity of it.

As a bracing antidote (even purgative) to 'heritage history' as staged at the Globe, Propeller's touring *Richard III* (directed by Edward Hall, designed by Michael Pavelka) reassigned the nation's storytelling from the early modern to the postmodern, from the plebs and aristos to the 'No-bodies'. In a fifteen-minute-long pre-show, eerily identical figures in knee-length dirty-white coats (sprouting dapper black bow ties at the neck) hung motionless as death around a grey set lined with metal gantries, fitted up with mobile hospital screens and plastic abattoir curtains on wheels. They might have been meat-packing inspectors or morgue stewards or the squad sent in to clean up the basement in a Stieg Larsson novel, their faces covered in stretched fabric, like gas-masks with eye and mouth holes, their hands casually holding rusty tools from a century ago's tinker's bazaar, ugly implements for ragged cutting, punching, slicing.

The programme called them 'Orderlies', a nice joke because in this fourteen-strong all-male company where cross-casting and continuous doubling define both the company's aesthetic and practice, this constantly self-substituting anonymous gang were the fixers behind the mayhem who made misshapen Richard's anarchy orderly. They could transform Edward's throne into a hospital gurney with the slip of a bolt. Change scenes like film cuts with the sideways slide of a screen (making Richard Clothier's hunchback Richard first suddenly materialize in empty space). Act as faceless extras handling the next gleeful assassination (by sulphuric acid to the eyes or poison in the drink; by dismemberment by chainsaw or disembowelling by scythe). Run the plastic curtain between viewers and the killings, catching the spewing blood in Rothko-esque murals. Then come back as named parts, prim in Edwardian frock coats and tailored skirts, black, grey and white (except for Chris Myles's stocky bank-manager Buckingham's red leather gloves).

This was an irreverently bustling *Richard* that wanted spectators to see what the deliciously twisted mind at the centre of operations was talking about. So as, centre stage, Richard – played by Clothier as a peroxide-blond charmer, more sleek

10. *Richard III*, 4.4. Propeller on tour, directed by Edward Hall. Tony Bell as Queen Margaret,
Dominic Tighe as Queen Elizabeth and Kelsey Brookfield as the Duchess of York.

Count Dracula than 'bunch-backed toad' – began 'Now is the winter . . . ', his big brother Edward (Robert Hands) entered (stage right). He shed his fur-collared overcoat, placed the tinselly crown on his head, grabbed his giddily laughing queen (Dominic Tighe) and posed for a photo whose garish flash seemed to make the confetti thrown at the couple stick in the air, acting out the whole family story – which brought on Kelsey Brookfield's Lord Rivers, weaving drunkenly across the background, and Edward again, sprawling, sucking alcohol out of a blood transfusion bag – before 'But I . . . ' doused the party lights and turned the focus of the soliloquy back onto Richard.

Playing the action alongside speech set up tropes of metatheatricality that presented the York family as a kind of music-hall troupe on the skids and worked to release the pure, conscienceless, comic performativity of Richard's *Kind Hearts and Coronets* manoeuvres. But if Richard's suave clown was the genius of the place, he had loads of competition from other stand-up turns, each black joke more outrageous than the last. 'Set down, set down your honourable load', ordered Jon Trenchard's gorgeously poised Anne, grief straining her

voice. An Orderly obeyed, thwumping onto the throne-turned-funeral-gurney the body that was slung over his shoulder, bagged up in a black bin-liner. Later, Anne and Richard staggered to his coronation down a path of those steadily accumulated body-bags, nearly toppled by the corpses he'd made. Hastings (Tom Padden), chain-sawed into quarters, was delivered back on stage sandwich-packed in a *square* body-bag. (The disposed-of got the last laugh, though: like grave worms, splitting open their black cocoons in 5.3 to release their contents as ghosts.) In 2.1, to make their peace, the warring family lined up to present their arms to Orderlies flashing hypodermics – then toasted each other, cheerfully exchanging their phials of blood samples and knocking them back. In 1.4, Clarence's murderers (Sam Swainsbury, Richard Frame) were a pair of chirpy bowler-hatted cockney song-and-dance spivs who whistled as they worked – but didn't survive the scene. (Clothier's Richard regularly slipped in unannounced to kill the hired killers.) Tyrell (Wayne Cater) wore a tool-belt hung with weapons and stuffed toys, and Catesby (David Newman) realizing with a fluttering little 'oooh!' that he'd failed to 'clear evidence from the latest murder, draped himself around the incriminating chain-saw like a boa constrictor in a morning suit. In 4.3, the murder of the princes (here played by puppets sprouting the kinds of heads you see on dummies modelling school clothes in Mothercare, making these kids precocious, unnerving and deeply irritating, so ripe for infanticide) was set to the tick-tock of the nursery clock, which – stopped. Their heads returned floating in a specimen jar. Throughout, Richard Ratcliffe (Dugald Bruce-Lockhart) was the man who kept time on the comic timing, immaculate, a human cultured pearl, gazing at his gold pocket watch. When he clicked it shut, time's up. You're dead.

So there was plenty of boys' own knock-about in this production, buckets of blood, eviscerated guts and a chomped-off finger (Richard needing Anne's wedding ring to give to his next bride). But what kept it from collapsing into a goon/buffoon show or bloody farce was, first, the company's serious self-interrogating commitment to the conceit of violence as comically grotesque excess; then, more significantly, their astonishing ability to act upon the formal instructions of Shakespeare's writing. This is a company full of brilliant metre-readers (perhaps because, to a man, they're musicians, ears tuned to timing, cadence, the shape of a phrase, the beat of a line, syncopation). They found in the structures of the verse the counterweight to the slapstick, voices mourning, accusing, remembering, re-citing, layering this *Richard* with a plangent chorus of formal reckoning. We heard it in the funereal beats of Trenchard's 'Set down, set down . . .' and 'Poor key-cold figure . . .' before Anne gave way to Richard's wooing, increasingly breathless, in tight little staccatos ('Well well'; 'To take is not to give'). And in Tony Bell's Margaret's pounding curses, she appearing like some out-sized death-watch beetle swathed in crêpe. In John Dougall's Clarence's telling of his dream, he in a hospital gown, the brother confined to the loony bin, where only under the pressure of mounting hysteria (and eyes blinded with acid) was he discovering conscience: ('Methought . . . /Methought . . . /Methought . . . ').

And in Tighe's Elizabeth's womb-wailing lament for her dead children: 'Ah . . . ah . . . ah'.

But we heard it too in the music this *Richard* produced, arranged by Jon Trenchard as a parallel acoustic text to Shakespeare's, nearly all of it produced by the actors. So the weirdness of that opening paralysed scene was transformed as, on a single note, it came to life with the Orderlies in gorgeous close *a cappella* harmony singing lines from the 'Dies Irae' – that would return at the end. In between, Richard was crowned in plainsong, the princes murdered to the 'Coventry Carol' ('Herod the king / In his raging . . .'), the Welshman Richmond acclaimed to 'Rhuddlan' ('purge the realm . . . cleanse the nation'). And Clarence bumped off to the eighteenth-century catch, 'Down among the dead men . . . down . . . down . . . down . . . down.' This was a production where the audios and the visuals were in perfect, productive tension, the profundity of the one wiping the smirk off the bloody face of the other.

COMEDIES

Three productions of *A Midsummer Night's Dream* interested me less for anything they were saying about the play than for the great deal the theatres that staged them were saying about the local communities they're reaching around them.

At the Octagon Theatre, Bolton, David Thacker, finishing his first year as Artistic Director, set his *Dream* in 1967, a 'best-of-times, worst-of-times' year giving him tropes for re-imagining the law and lunacy the play explores. It was the year of the 'Summer of Love' in San Francisco; of hippies and sitars; experimentation with mind-expanding drugs; domestic skirmishes across the 'generation gap'; draft cards burned; militarism mocked (on the cover of) and psychedelic rock invented (in the tracks of) *Sergeant Pepper's Lonely Hearts Club Band*. It was also the year the so-called 'Greek Colonels' staged a coup that installed in Athens the brutally repressive regime accused of outlawing not just the Fab Four but Aeschylus. Seeing Shakespeare

11. *A Midsummer Night's Dream*, Epilogue. Octagon Theatre, Bolton, directed by David Thacker. Full company.

as proleptically inventing flower-power, Thacker put these cultural references on view.

His opening scene was seriously militarized. Even Demetrius (Jake Norton) and Lysander (Nick Underwood) were in uniform – though to judge by his slouch, Lysander had probably been on the point of dodging the draft when he was conscripted. This Athens was presided over by a wall-sized poster of King Constantine in uniform as one of the colonels. (Sensationally bad history; but probably nobody in the theatre under fifty would have known it.) When 'General' Theseus (Rob Edwards) entered, at a clip, surrounded by uniformed flunkies ('Colonels' in the cast list), the sense that they'd been mobilized for military manoeuvres went comically awry. Theseus had to hang around *for ages*, nervously checking his wrist-watch, before a deputation of high-heeled, sheath-dressed women entered opposite, heavily veiled, in mourning, like chic war widows who, showing

no inclination to fraternize, held aloof. Hippolyta (Paula Jennings) snatched her hand away when Theseus took it, turning smartly on a stiletto and exiting, leaving him to wail 'What cheer, my love?' and chase after her, before returning, abashed, to face Egeus and the rest. This was a place you believed capable of summary executions; also a place where everything was under control – except the women. (In the pre-show, the backing track had Aretha Franklin shrilling 'R-E-S-P-E-C-T'.)

We arrived in the woods on an acid trip. The poster boy was still there, but his epaulettes were made of liquorice All-sorts and his cheek was splodged with paint. The place (designed by Ashley Shairp) was like a kid's climbing frame built for dodg'ems – stairs, high-level catwalks, runways curving along back walls – imagined under the influence of hallucinatory substances: all psychedelic purple, lime green and orange, with trees growing upside-down canopies, beach balls in a dozen over-grown sizes rolling around, and, staring from the walls, dozens of vibrantly coloured bulls' eyes – a signature design of the late 60s. (Or were they human eyes optically challenged by having ingested a drug distilled from a purple flower: 'I would my father looked but with my eyes'?)

Given this set-up, the transformations in the wood were obvious enough (to any who remember the 60s – and Peter Brook). The 'Colonels' doubled as fairies: their uniforms translated into Oz-like garish greens and yellows; their medals, into Christmas tree baubles bouncing on their chests. Hippolyta returned as Titania: a blonde Bond girl in white mini-dress, hip boots, performing leggy 60s dance routines. Leo Atkin's pension-aged Puck in electric-blue bowler hat and steward's coat had one gag, but it was a good one: too old for this lark, he kept pausing – mid earth-girdling – for breath. What got lost in this visual scheme was a relevant sense of who the Mechanicals were: not what they should have been, the kind of bolshie trades unionists who, in the 60s were reframing UK labour relations, but nostalgic throwbacks to a Hovis age, in button-fly trousers and braces. (Bizarrely, Kieran Hill's Bottom was transformed by the addition of ears and black-face: a kind of hippy Al Jolson.)

What also went missing was much of anything that Shakespeare's script might have been contributing to this love-in. Half of Thacker's company this season was very young, and he's known to help poetry-anxious actors with blank verse by telling them to treat it as prose cast off into manageable chunks. Here, we got theatre speech at its most prosaic: the lovers' duet in scene 1 without sparkle because, treated like naturalistic conversation, without the delicious wit of the shared couplets pointing both the pain and the deep silliness of – 'Ah me!' – being young and in love. Even a veteran like Edwards as Oberon seemed to have been directed to underline every image as though issuing instructions to a slightly dim office boy who was having a hard time keeping up with the plot: 'I know a <u>bank</u> where the wild <u>thyme</u> blows.' The 'compulsive art' of the actor was almost entirely absent, or any notion that characters in Shakespeare speak verse because, as Robert Butler

once put it, 'it's the fastest way to make themselves understood' (*Shakespeare Survey 56*, p. 249). So this was the slowest *Dream* in living memory – three-and-a-half hours of *Dream*, the result not just of plodding speaking and indulging *Pyramus and Thisbe*, where productions regularly add on extra time long after the final whistle should have blown. Here, there was an absurd amount of deferred death from a Pyramus who looked not like the Ovidian boy-next-door but a Roman general. Interpolated 'business' also stretched things out: actors having to negotiate their way around those balls that turned the stage into a human pachinko machine. So did casting, where considerations were more politically charged. Kiruna Stamell – La Petite Princesse in Baz Luhrmann's *Moulin Rouge*, who describes her disability as dwarfism – was given dance sequences as 'Amazon/Fairy', almost as scenic cross-cuts. Making his stage debut as 'Snout/Colonel', Laurence Clark (whose biog credits 'his latest controversial show, *Spastic Fantastic*') played Wall with wheelchair extensions. Stamell and Clark were just the first of several performers who challenged me to think differently about actors' bodies this year – and not entirely comfortably. Was his speech disability meant to characterize Snout as stammering and slow? Was her inability, three feet shorter than Quince, to get his attention, running round his ankles like a terrier, a joke? Is disability meant to 'play' on the stage or not?

There were moments of delight – Puck 'haunting' Bottom by chucking at his head 'invisible' balls that really hurt; Theseus directing traffic at the end of Act 4; Thisbe (Brendan Quinn) dropping her voice on 'what, dead?', throat-catchingly moving. Mostly, though, the drug this production was on was Seconal, not speed.

And the audience didn't care. They clearly loved every minute. The Octagon sits smack between Bolton's Victorian Town Hall (a grotesquely overblown monument to its cotton-mill boomtown past) and its covered market (teeming, with a slightly fevered air of no-frills bargains and 'end of line' discounts). On the day I saw Thacker's *Dream*, the theatre was a heaving 'space between'. Its foyer felt like a community drop-in centre, thronged with kids, pushchairs, Elsie Tanners having tea, adolescents on their way to Activ8 sessions. In the auditorium the demographic was one the RSC would kill for. Half the audience was 'yoof', lads in that ostentatious slouch position, lasses holding up their market purchases, in greens and pinks, silk roses in their hair, like tropical birds. A couple of years back, Alan Plater (who died this year) said that the Octagon should be a place for 'talking to each other about things that matter', 'a workshop and a shop window'. On this season's evidence, both shops are doing cracking business.

One of the past-production photographs featured in Thacker's programme showed Ian Holm's Puck eavesdropping on the lovers in Peter Hall's 1959 *Dream*, a revival of which, three years later, had Judi Dench taking over from Mary Ure as Titania in a theatre Hall had recently renamed the 'Royal Shakespeare'. Nearly half a century later, Hall, Dench and *Dream* this year staged a reunion at the Rose Theatre, Kingston. A gimmick? Of course. Hall co-founded the two-year-old Rose. He's now 'Director Emeritus'. The Rose gets no Arts Council subsidy. Dench's name sold out the run the day bookings opened – bankrolling the theatre's survival for another year. (Theirs wasn't the only Shakespeare reunion. Less touted was another meeting across five decades: Rachel Stirling here played Helena, the part her mother – Diana Rigg – played in 1962.)

The gimmick, though, was cannily managed. The production's opening conceit situated the action in the court of Elizabeth I, where to the sounds of a tabor, courtiers promenaded in gorgeous period dress (far beyond the Rose's costume budget; borrowed from the Benjamin Britten *Dream* Hall directed at Glyndebourne in 1981). But when the music abruptly stopped, they dropped, kneeling in two straight lines, a human corridor for a formal entrance: the Queen, a.k.a. Dame Judi, in full early modern rig-out, at once an Elizabethan impersonation and herself, the reigning female monarch on today's English stage. (Since *Shakespeare in Love*, we somehow see these two as one.) But Dench's Elizabeth was also visibly an aged 'Imperial votaress', this 'Virgin Queen'

no longer a contradiction in terms. Patrolling her genuflecting ranks, she raked a severe eye along them, stopping before one hapless, dazzling and *young* lady-in-waiting. She thrust out a withered hand; demanded to see what the girl had anxiously concealed. Some writing. She read it over. As motionless as a cobra. (Some reviewers took the paper for a script; I saw it as contraband, a love letter, those 'verses of feigning love' Lysander would shortly be accused of, this petty confiscation setting up ideas of sexual jealousy in the court of a geriatric queen who still fancied herself the sole object of all who 'dote . . . in idolatry'.) She turned – ignoring the stricken girl's gesture, wanting her property back. But as she exited, a courtier – hardly more than a youth, Essex, say, when he first came to Court – lunged forward impetuously and kissed her hand. Her pause, the slight bow of head, the radiance of her smile astonished. This septuagenarian diva exuded an erotic charge capable of turning toadying courtiers into princes (this one would return as Oberon) or indeed mechanicals into immortals.

It's no wonder reviewers read the invented prologue as a rehearsal setting up a play within a play with the Queen silently appropriating the role of her alter ego. For when Dench re-entered, this *Dream* was very evidently all Titania's. She couldn't help stealing the show. She's one of the most generous actors on the English stage. (In a pre-show talk-with-the-audience, she stood up four times to shift her bulky armchair further upstage – so spectators in the seats with the bad sightlines could get a view of *the interviewer*.) But listening to Dench speak Shakespeare is like watching Ronaldo kick a football. Dribbling, passing, tackling, heading, shooting, attacking, defending: she can just do so much more with the play-thing Shakespeare gives her than anyone else on the side. When she squared-up opposite her philandering fairy partner, 'What, jealous Oberon?' had the brittleness of sheet ice breaking up. 'Then I must be thy lady' looped silken knots of irony around his shrill neck – and yanked them tight. 'These are the forgeries of jealousy' took us on a journey into human apocalypse, terrible for the discrete images of loss she made

12. *A Midsummer Night's Dream*, 3.1, Rose Theatre, Kingston, directed by Peter Hall. Judi Dench
as Titania, Oliver Chris as Bottom (translated).

us see (broken oxen, rotted corn, a season-altered world, cheerless, sick, 'mazed') and for the grief we heard darkening the voice – 'this same progeny of evils . . .' – then hardening: 'We are their parents and originals.' It made a difference that this was spoken by a Fairy Queen who'd clearly reigned over the mortal world for as long as a human lifetime. She'd lived her analysis. And it was sobering. (Not least because she seemed to be talking about us, now.)

Falling for the ass, though, she simply shed years, gravity, turned deliciously giddy. (Only Dench and Peggy Ashcroft can do that thing of metamorphosing from pensioner to schoolgirl with the tilt of a chin.) Since Brook (1970), one line of *Dream* productions (Lepage, 1992; Noble, 1993; and so on to Thacker, 2010) has, ever more explicitly, tiresomely and/or nastily, imagined between the beauty and the beast kinky sex in kinky locations – a porn star's pink umbrella; a hash-head's hallucinogenically tumescent phallic tree. Fantasies, perhaps, dreamed up by male directors facing their Viagra years? This *Dream*, though, produced rapture, not raunch, and a delicate but big-hearted love story of sublime, if improbable, affections. Woken

from her 'flowery bed' by the din of the 'ousel cock', Dench's Titania was hearing the music of the spheres. Her adoration was wondrous: 'I *do love thee*.' (Thus, as in our best dreams, this *Dream* was 'true' to 'life', where we're all gods and donkeys, in love.)

Still, it was perhaps too bad, in a year when the National Theatre was exhibiting Harriet Walter's 'Infinite Variety', her collection of full-on photographic portraits celebrating the ageing female face, and when 50-something Juliet Stevenson was, wrinkles-and-all, cover-girl on *Equity*, the acting industry's trade mag, publicizing her article about the absence of good parts (*any* parts) for older women, that so much was done in Hall's *Dream* to evade the issue of Dench's age. An evasion that was diplomatic? Or misogynistic – of that old-fashioned kind that passes as 'gallantry'? In any case, Dench's Titania could've been a campaigner. And wasn't. Her gormlessly wet-behind-the-ears Bottom (Oliver Chris) was forty years her junior, but since we lost any sense of his youth when he was transformed by a full ass's head, we never got a scene of gender-reversed January–May loving. Given that the theatre is one of the places where culture learns to 'do' love and sex and death, the scene we were denied was a real loss to an audience that, national demographics show, is on a steep age-ing curve.

For the rest, Hall's production was workman-like: not under-cast – with actors of the cali-bre of James Laurenson (Quince), William Chubb (Egeus/Starveling) and Tam Williams (Lysander) on side. But certainly under-imagined. Cut-out trees in silhouette against the upstage wall gave the effect of the wood and left the Rose's lim-ited stage space free for actors. But Peter Mum-ford's lighting plot seemed to have only two cues – gloomy and gloomier – and Elizabeth Bury's mobile fairy bower, hardly big enough for two, moved like a kid's scooter (making me wish that Titania, like Bottom, was wearing protective head-gear). The mechanicals were decent, harmless buf-foons: nostalgic throw-backs to Hardy's Wessex (or more recently, the Archers' Ambridge, since they spoke with Brummie accents), in smocks and straw hats as though come from farm labouring instead of city jobs as city traders making city things for city buyers in Athens. The fairies were uni-sex period-dressed court flunkeys, and performa-tively invisible. (Compare the brilliantly devised anarchists of Propeller's *Dream*, exploding with attitude and pulp fiction back-stories (*Shakespeare Survey 63*)). Puck (Reece Ritchie) was a pretty-boy cipher who managed to wreck the best toy Shakespeare gave him, the 'wild geese . . . / Rising' speech. Charles Edwards's whey-faced, Jedward-haired Oberon experienced neither pleasure nor repentance at the 'fierce vexations' he'd engi-neered. And not even the four-handed lovers' rammy in the woods packed much of a punch. There was 'designer dishabille' – a bodice slightly ripping, a button on some breeches slipping open – but nothing full-throated, full throttle that got at the true miserable awfulness (and hilarity) of that scene when the young pups turn into bitches – and savage each other. In short, this was a *Dream* without mischief or malice, danger or edginess, the only rough edges the torn petticoats. But for the local audience – and the Rose, like the Octagon, is full of locals (okay, they're wearing Jigsaw and

13. *A Midsummer Night's Dream*, 5.1. Shakespeare at the Tobacco Factory, directed by Andrew Hilton. Byron Mondahl as Flute-as-Thisbe, Chris Donnelly as Bottom-as-Pyramus.

Hunters that will never see mud) – Judi's Titania was magic enough.

Dream is a play, as John Peter has said, that tells you more – much more – about actors and acting than Hamlet ever got round to. But it's also a play that gives you shrewd instruction on the business of being an audience – which is where Andrew Hilton's production at the Tobacco Factory began, with Jay Villiers's dark-suited Theseus alone on stage, sole audience to Philostrate's (Christopher Staines) *a cappella* recital. The minor-keyed dirge went dragging on, deadly stanza by stanza and, just when Theseus thought it had droned out its last depressing observation about the moon, melan-choly and folly – a ditty to distract a groom from premarital nerves, or to make him want to cut his throat? – it gasped a breath and started all over again. What's an audience to do? How much pain should they endure? Theseus finally sent Philostrate packing – an opening that nicely anticipated the play's ending where *Pyramus and Thisbe* would sig-nificantly challenge the patience of its audience, but an opening, too, that worked like prophylaxis, fairy blessing, to ensure 'fortunate' 'issue' from a *Dream* producing that magic thing almost entirely absent at the Rose: laughter.

As always at this reclaimed factory address – a venue where spectators on four sides crowd around a stage that measures six paces by four, whose main design feature is its structural pillars – the company produced Shakespeare on a shoe-string. And the theatre poet was clearly thriving on the 'less' that was here being filled up with the 'more' of actorly imagination. The pillars – how actors moan about them at the Globe! – became collaborators: lined with ladders that, scaled, gave fairies surveillance posts, instantly creating a two-tier, parallel world of seeming doubles where the metaphysical could dive-bomb the haplessly real and throw subjectivity into existential crisis. ('Am I not Hermia?' wailed Ffion Jolly's dumped girlfriend – and the question was genuine.) Everybody doubled: snubbed Philostrate became a truculent Puck; Hippolyta (Amy Rockson) stewed in Amazonian defeat but returned flaming as Titania in red; Mechanicals added bits of kit to become Titania's henchmen – like Byron Mondahl's tubby Flute (joke #1), transformed into Peaseblossom (joke #2) by miles of tulle skirting. Fairies in bowler hats and braces (Nadia Williams, Kay Zimmerman) went invisible by putting on dark glasses – a gag that worked delightfully with all the imagery about sight and blindness and with scenes where folk were constantly making spectacles of themselves. One of the fairies rolled around in a wheelchair, knitting: Cobweb (Jonathan Nibbs). Another, antennae on springs bobbing out of his hat, held a lantern that he kept smacking with his head: Moth (Alan Coveney). The Mechanicals were belt-and-braces tradesmen who wouldn't have looked out of place in any northern working-men's club – and who took this new work called 'play' very seriously indeed. Snug (David Plimmer), dead keen to get it right, turned up to rehearsal, bumbling out of the bushes, in his lion costume, terrifying the life out of his mates who were, later, not about to be caught out a second time by Bottom (Chris Donnelly) larking around in a donkey head. So it took a hilarious age of shuffling and joshing before the penny dropped and they fled like 'russet-pated choughs' 'rising and cawing' at a 'gun's report', leaving poor little lion-headed Snug, who'd earlier fallen fast asleep waiting for his cue, to wake up all alone, very alone, scarily alone in the moonless woods. There was just enough nightmare in this *Dream*-ing to make waking the better alternative.

For all this living on their (creative) wits, these were also actors who delighted in Shakespeare's writing. One marker: Bottom-as-Ass had splendid ears exploding out of his hat – but a muzzle made, *Equus*-style, of open-work metal, *so we could hear his lines*. Helena (Rebecca Pownall) may not have had the extraordinary quality of dark vocal colour that Rachel Stirling produced at the Rose, but she was always hearing things for the first time, stunned by the dizzying turns of events and stung into speech when her (former) best friend ripped into her. Their ding-dong ('juggler'; 'puppet'; '"Puppet"!'; 'vixen') had Tamburlaine taking on Herod the Great and, although – because they were in high heels, pony tails and frou-frou dresses – there was plenty flapping around to undercut them as Amazons-in-the-making, they demonstrated, smacking those speeches into each other, such spirited likeness of mind that I longed for them to ditch their dopey boyfriends and head not to Athens but arm-in-arm to Lesbos.

And so, back to the audience. It's a well-known theatrical fact that the 150-or-so lines of *Pyramus and Thisbe* can add, as Bottom might say, 'in the true performing of it', a good three-quarters-of-an-hour onto the playing time of Shakespeare's *Dream* (viz. Doran, 2008). The temptation for actors to interpolate more and more outrageous business, to milk laughter from not one but two audiences, must be fierce. But when invention tips into indulgence (viz. Doran, 2008), actors need to be pulled up. (Mind you, if Shakespeare, and not just Hamlet, had seriously wanted his clowns 'to speak no more than' was 'set down for them' he might have 'set down' his performance text much more explicitly.) Watching this latest *Pyramus and Thisbe* I felt a little like Theseus in the opening scene. The trouble was Felix Hayes's Snout-as-Wall. The gag in rehearsal must have looked like such a winner. Snout would turn himself into a mural caryatid by balancing a stone slab on his head. The problem was, once the conceit was introduced, this weight-lifting palaver had to be conducted in real time and with physical acting that mimed the effect of real avoirdupois. Watching him, eyes bulging, grunt and sweat and totter dangerously before – huge physical effort – bracing his legs and heaving the stone into position was very funny; even funnier when, getting enough breath to speak, he reached the end of the second couplet, the bit about this Wall having 'in it a crannied hole, or chink', and realised, astonished horror freezing on his face, that both potential chink-making hands were otherwise engaged. So: try to balance the stone to free one hand. Careful. Careful. It's falling! Stumble. Recover. Brace. Steady. Other hand. No! (And so on, for the next fifty lines.) We eventually extracted ourselves from the gag – but not until long after its 'brief' had become 'tedious'.

The Tobacco Factory's other production in a season billed 'Art to Enchant' was *The Tempest*, a play, the director ventured in a programme note, about 'vengeance, forgiveness and contrition'; about 'a man to whom Shakespeare awards private spirits and the power of wish-fulfilment'; a play, he thought, 'more likely to be looking inward to the dark and turbulent recesses of the mind, than outward to political debate'. Good thing I read that after the event. For *The Tempest* I saw in this barebones production (ladders against pillars for ship masts; a rope strung catty-corner for rigging; some flashes of lightning; basic Elizabethan wardrobe) was an outward-looking play that told three big political stories: Prospero's, the courtiers', the grotesques'. All of them had to do with inheritance (or its spoil), managed by marriage or murder, or mis-managed by comically mis-timed mayhem, and the centre they met in was a crop-haired, huge-eyed Miranda, played by Ffion Jolly as the embodiment of her name. She was a lass who saw wonder everywhere she looked; who had amazement written on a face that was open to the next miracle that was already on its way. This Miranda's artlessness had power to enchant – but also to redeem, to make the 'brave' world she saw 'new'.

What I didn't get was the story Andrew Hilton aimed to tell, the one that looked 'inward to the dark and turbulent recesses of the mind', maybe because Ian Barritt's resolutely un-cerebral Prospero had no sealed-off cranial rooms stashed with memories he couldn't bear to meet in daylight. He

had no books. And seemed to have no thoughts. White bearded, booted, burly, he told his daughter their past in the flat tones of an emotional amnesiac ('sea sorrow' pitched the same as 'Providence divine'), or more problematically, in this actor-friendly theatre, of a player who didn't relish this script, who spoke every line like prose. Because I couldn't see in this Prospero a mind working – a mind working either like an engine motored by speech that could split ideas across antitheses and test possibilities by pursuing linked images; or a mind working like a library archiving memory – I missed the point of Hilton's big directorial concept: Ariel and Caliban were played by the same actor. The doubling was meant to establish them as symbolic proxies for the psychic dualism that (going along with the concept) constitutes Prospero's self: Prospero has a 'born devil' residing cheek by jowl with a 'delicate spirit' in those 'turbulent recesses' I didn't see.

Now, it's hard enough for any actor to play a concept, but to pull this one off, Hilton needed an actor equipped with a much bigger toolkit than Christopher Staines carried. A barefoot skin-head in chopped off trousers, Staines could 'do' the obvious: Ariel ('brave spirit') on tip-toe and Caliban ('deformed slave') an arm-swinging simian, one with a whistling voice, the other a grumbling growl (though even this wasn't sustained – when the ape also had to play drunk). But Staines couldn't perform the imaginative turn Shakespeare's writing produces for these roles, the eccentric curves of their mental and material beings: one the 'chick', the other the 'tortoise'; one the fire-diver and cloud-rider, the other, the shoe-licker and curse mutterer; the one who goes, the one who stays, the both who break our hearts.

Hilton's *Tempest* started with a flash and a bang – and sprinted to the interval in just fifty minutes, taking it after 2.2. Sam Mendes's *Tempest* for the Bridge Project at the Old Vic started almost in slow motion. A broken-down dosser in an even more broken-down pinstriped suit – with hair like that, once perhaps a mad professor, but now the kind of geezer who shuffles into public libraries to get out of the weather – stood up from behind a music stand where he'd been peering through spectacles into a thick sheaf of dog-eared papers. Grudgingly, he draped himself in a cloak, cinched it with a frayed belt of feathers and began a ritual, a shamanistic performance. He walked the circumference of an island of sand he found centre stage. He marked around it a circle of water dumped from a bucket. A staff he'd picked up was used like a cosmic storm-catcher, to summon the elements of earth, air and water into Katrina-sized collision, then he stood back, releasing the staff into other hands that stumbled into the space, where it became a ship's guy rope, held on to for dear life, then a bow splitting, throwing castaways in all directions, clinging to virtual wreckage. Once it had raised the storm, this *Tempest* didn't let up until all the squalls had blown themselves out, two-and-a-quarter hours later.

If what Hilton's *Tempest* showed me was a play about possession, built on an elegant, double three-part structure (in the first half, heading for ruin; in the second, resolving disaster in the wonder of those three endings that make everybody in this play a 'foundling'), Mendes's was more meditative. What the director seemed to be thinking about here was relationship, marriage, the rituals of social binding – and love pulled gasping out of a sea of sorrows like maritime salvage and given the kiss of life. Gonzalo (played wonderfully as a Nestor-like 'good old chronicle' by Alvin Epstein), seeing Miranda, the baby he'd handed into the boat uncertainly (but certainly into the hands of death) all those years ago, folded her in a bear hug. Oh miracle! She, not dead! And he, *not guilty*! Seated in the sand to watch their wedding masque, Ferdinand (Edward Bennett) and Miranda (Juliet Rylance) saw not goddesses in stately dances but images of childhood: projections like juddery home movies of a couple of toddlers. Themselves before the coup that made their fathers enemies? Images from a dead past – or photographic evidence of the hope Prospero had nursed in exile along with his child? (This concentration on relationship: was it perhaps because *The Tempest* was double-billed with *As You Like It*; or because Mendes's own marriage was (very publicly, painfully) hitting the rocks?)

This was the second season of the Bridge Project, Mendes's collaboration with Kevin Spacey at the Vic bringing together a part-US, part-UK company to perform in New York and London (and elsewhere on tour). It was also Mendes's second go at the play. As a 27-year-old at the RSC in 1993 he directed an irreverent 'young man's' *Tempest*, 'after Magritte', that had 'disgusted, Tunbridge Wells' writing in to squawk indignantly about Simon Russell Beale's Ariel: the perfect (perfectly inscrutable) Mao-jacketed colonial civil servant who welcomed his freedom by spitting in Prospero's face. Nothing so audaciously in-yer-face happened here but, if not directly quoting himself, Mendes seemed sometimes to be reminiscing.

The outside edges of the stage were piled with junk – broken chairs, a victrola, smashed instruments, an empty bookcase – that made the stage itself a kind of cultural midden (*pace* Mendes's *Troilus and Cressida*, 1990) or perhaps a raft with, bumping up against it, the teasingly allusive flotsam of a dozen European wrecks. Inside that, a wooden platform was set with chairs, randomly placed in deep shadows. And inside that was the circle of yellow sand. Mid-stage stood two stunted trees, out of *Godot*. And beyond that, a blank wall, plastered in bruise-red and purple, cracked. A door set high on the face was reached by a ramp running onto the platform across a strip of water that crossed the stage: light playing off it turned the plaster façade into a dark surface of shifting waves (designed by the 'light fantastic' Paul Pyant, who's been working with Mendes since *Richard III* in 1992; lit the 1993 *Tempest* and last year's gorgeous *Winter's Tale* that settled light like a haze of dreams over the opening).

The set by Tom Piper drew eyes to the circle, making a space for performance – elsewhere, that sandpit would have been a wooden O – but also, in the shadows, for spectatorship. Once they entered, characters remained on stage, retreating to those chairs to observe or, like Christian Camargo's barefoot, black-suited and blank-faced imitation-Beale Ariel, to stand coldly aloof on the ramp before re-entering the action, as when he passed across the sand, the invisible butler, putting weapons into hands the conspirators were unsurprised to find armed. So far, then, this was a production that confirmed Mendes's reputation as a director who constructs in space powerful images that work like physical poetry in conversation with Shakespeare's writing.

The problem was a Prospero who seemed to want to have nothing to do with it. While on the sand the lovers loved or the conspirators conspired, you could catch Stephen Dillane at his music stand in the shadows absorbed in his papers, leaning forward every once in a while to mark up the text – less Prospero-the-director than Prospero-the-Arden-editor, wanting to niggle with words but not to speak them. This was a Prospero who made Camargo's sullen Ariel sound garrulous, a Prospero so inward as to be absent, played by an actor who appeared to be mumbling his way through a first read-through. Undoing his power – 'this rough magic / I here abjure' – Dillane flung his papers away. That was the most effort he put into the script all night.

There were places where a sense of watching a heart monitor go flat was desperately poignant. 'We are such stuff as dreams are made on' was one. And: ''Tis new to thee.' And those lines near the end, whose force I'd never heard before: 'To comfort' 'dear loss', Prospero advises 'patience' – and calls 'patience' the 'soft grace'.

But Dillane's constitutionally reclusive Prospero was certainly making a big mistake leaving the island. He should have given Ron Cephas Jones's Caliban his passage home. Skin-headed, hollow-eyed, cheeks tribally marked (like Atandwa Kani's Ariel last year, *Shakespeare Survey 63*) this lanky Caliban had a feel for power. In his first entrance, he erupted through the sandpit's surface like a landmine exploding: clad in earth-colours, shaking off sand with every move, he seemed almost to be 'that earth' that Prospero calls him. When he dug it up, shook it under Prospero's nose to claim, 'This island's *mine*', Caliban didn't persuade just on the evidence he held in his gold-clawed right hand. The evidence was in the voice. Jones comes from the American-accented side of the company. And we couldn't help but hear in that 'foreign' voice –

the voice of the 'slave', the 'lying slave', the 'abhorred slave' – a legacy evoking the original sin out of which a new-world nation was built upon old-world bodies, but also resistance. After his failed coup, wrecked by white-boy supremacist dolts he could see were his mental inferiors, this Caliban had important experience he could have turned to political advantage running Milan. How disturbing, then, to see him brushed off as a 'thing of darkness', not even much acknowledged 'mine', and dismissed – to housework.

And now for a spot of late night cabaret. The man opposite me on the train heading home after the Bridge Project's *Tempest/As You* double bill was bemused by my comic turn, watching me struggle with my programme. First idly inspecting it, front cover, back cover. Then performing a quick double take, followed by an increasingly agitated flip flop. It took me from Paddington to Slough to be sure: the man in the tight close-up portrait on the front cover – green eyes, stubbly beard, frown line, mean-and-moody – *wasn't* the same man (slightly younger) in the tight close-up portrait on the back cover – green eyes, five o'clock shadow, mean-and-moody. One was Dillane. The other Camargo. How could I have taken them for the same – like, mistaking Prospero and *Orlando*? Was it perhaps because the Orlando I'd earlier watched Camargo play for three hours as a walking black hole (his Ariel, I would realize, had *risen* to inexpressiveness) was the kind of Orlando who'd grow up to be Dillane's Prospero? (Come to think of it, surely I was suckered. Why bookend this programme with images that made them uncanny twins if you didn't want to make punters see them as doubles?)

Mendes's *As You Like It* opened in gloom against a black, rough board wall: no sight of the (ordered) orchard that in Shakespeare's script tropes postlapsarian man's attempt to reclaim Eden and makes sense of a character called 'Adam' and a flight to a forest wilderness by someone called 'Orlando', but a couple of blighted trunks any respectable orchardman would long ago have grubbed up. Cut to more gloom. Celia's (black) bedroom: the cousins' tête-à-tête (Michelle Beck: Celia; Juliet Rylance: Rosalind) broken up by men (in black) barging in on them. Cut to deep gloom: 2.1 and 2.2 transposed; the bad men in black who'd ordered a search party to track down the runaways turning upstage, collecting bits of costume from boxes to dress themselves as 'good' (if ragged) exiles as the black board wall flew out to reveal behind *another black wall*, the forest of Arden, set somewhere near Chernobyl: snow blanketing the upstage area, more acid-rain blighted trees. One wag described Tom Piper's set as a 'post-apocalyptic squash court'. But a squash court would at least have troped ideas of *play*. This set – maybe the antidote to the glare-white, dismantle-your-own-Elizabethan-IKEA-Arden Piper designed at the RSC last year – was like an actor's mausoleum. Poor Old Adam (another lovely performance from Alvin Epstein) didn't survive the 2.7 forest banquet, but quietly expired before the interval, and before Camargo's Orlando had finished his upstage confab with Michael Thomas's Duke.

I'd have liked to have gone with him – because Camargo was having the same effect on me. He was good in the really ugly fist fight that replaced the wrestling. But for the rest, he was the actorly impersonation of that bottomless Bay of Portugal Rosalind calls to mind to measure the depth of her love. Bottomless?, mocks Celia. Like a broken bucket: 'as fast as you pour affection in, it runs out'. So the wooing scenes were like some perverse acting exercise: 'You're Thisbe and your objective is to make Wall fall for you.' The more stonily unreceptive he, the more desperately hyper-expressive she, hurling herself at him.

Rylance's Ganymede arrived in Arden – clearly not having read any ecological disaster reports – dressed for Eton: tie, plus-fours, boots. After the interval, and after 3.1, that, in business 'borrowed' from Tim Supple's *As You* last year (*Shakespeare Survey 63*) had Oliver (Edward Bennett) waterboarded by nasty Duke Frederick's goons (Michael Thomas, again), both Arden and Ganymede were changed. She'd gone in to buff-coloured chinos, off-white open-necked shirt and vest, Converse trainers, jaunty trilby and cotton jacket – gear that colour-coordinated her to 'new' Arden: all yellow light, warm brown floorboards, willow baskets

and – weirdly – what looked like mini-savannah grass, wall to wall, upstage. So we got the design point. 'Bad' Arden, like 'bad' Court, produced black thoughts and black images. (In 'bad' Arden, Stephen Dillane's Jaques was a deadpan mortician's assistant who spoke the Seven Ages of Man speech as if describing seven sizes of coffin and sent up 'Blow, blow thou winter wind' with a mournful Bob Dylan harmonica riff. He spent his time in 'bad' Arden looking for somewhere to lie down, acting like an actor on strike.) 'Good' Arden captured folk for a golden idyll in a golden world, so *everybody* changed into warm yellow-and-brown (Thomas Sadoski's Touchstone holding on to his 'I'm a black comic' black jacket until he arrived for his wedding). In 'good' Arden, lit wonderfully by Pyant as a Manet picnic, when Dillane's Jaques hunkered down in the savannah to scan what the locals were up to, he looked like a seedy ornithologist.

And what *were* the locals up to? Ganymede did lots of 'acting'. Remember that early Aardman Animation short *Next* (directed by Barry Purves, 1989), the one that has a look-alike Peter Hall 'director' sitting in the third row of some stalls conducting auditions when a look-alike Shakespeare comes on and starts acting some parts of Shakespeare, then, when the director's not impressed, faster and faster, with more dazzle and the acrobatic skills of the top circus performer, *all* his parts, at the end of which the director languidly calls 'Next'? That's what this Ganymede/Orlando double act was like. Rylance's Ganymede swaggered; stood manly, straddle-legged or foot planted (do men do that?) on a box; pouted; pretend-swooned; impersonated every image ('proud, fantastical, apish, shallow'; 'now like him' (high squeak), 'now loathe him' (low boom)); bounced on lines like trampolines ('Do you hear, forester?'); used them like the verbal equivalents of magicians' hats to pull out rabbits ('I'll tell you . . .'); and mostly fixed a big, big grin on her face. And for what? Since Camargo's Orlando showed less personality, being wooed, than Ganymede's snail, these scenes were only interesting as studies in what hadn't happened in rehearsals.

Was there compensation elsewhere for the gaping hole at the centre of this production? Not a lot. Mendes fell into the same trap here as in *The Winter's Tale*'s Bohemia scenes, allowing his American actors to behave like they were auditioning for *Oklahoma!* – all 'gee-shucks' hokey-ness, hats pushed back ('I'm a regular joe') and cowgirl plaits. But the real problem was how they worked with Shakespeare's writing. It's not a matter of accent – Anglo v. Yankee – but of a different *pulse* of speaking. The metronome of English speaking is just set faster than theirs. More laid back, the Americans frequently mis-timed the rhythms of blank verse in this play, but also got the pulse of the prose wrong (which is always calibrated as finely by Shakespeare as his iambic pentameter). And if the *timing* of the prose, which is built into the *structure* of the prose, isn't observed, jokes fall flat – to be replaced as too often here with physical gags.

Except for one beautiful moment – beautiful not least because it came out of nowhere. 'Good shepherd,' thundered Phebe (Ashlie Atkinson), swinging her ample weight behind the command, 'Tell this youth what 'tis to love' – a cue that normally sets off four-part droning ('And so am I... and I... and I') that really does sound like 'the howling of Irish wolves against the moon'. Here, when Aaron Krohn's sweetly gormless Silvius began 'It is to be made all of sighs and tears', the simplicity of the utterance, its tonal limpidness, its perfect pitch was not just magical in itself but drew the others in to the kind of layering of voice that you hear in Mozart quartets. It was as if time stood still and all the 'confusion' that had been banging around in Arden dropped away as we heard 'what 'tis to love' declared for human truth and human miracle: ''tis' all 'fantasy', 'passion', 'wishes', yes; but also 'duty', 'humbleness', 'patience', 'trial', 'observance'. Hymen and Jaques would ultimately make and remake the play's marriages to blessèd and farcical specifications; but it was Silvius, the shepherd, who told us what marriage was.

Time stood still in Mendes's Arden figuratively; in Roxana Silbert's Ephesus, in the theatre-in-the-round of the Royal Exchange, Manchester, it did literally. The playing area for *Comedy of Errors*, designed by Anthony MacIlwaine, was a set of two concentric white discs faintly scored with white lines, like the dial of a 24-hour clock. Above it hung a Perspex cube, and inside it sat a body, eyes closed, an oriental satrap in black and gold, like a Damien Hirst exhibit, animation suspended. This strange object anticipated what was to come. It gave us a life (as Egeon's would, shortly) hanging by a thread. It evoked (as in Antipholus-of-Syracuse's life story) a human being as water drop. Its weirdness put on view visual 'cozenage', the work of 'nimble jugglers that deceive the eye'. And it suggested that physics – and metaphysics – would operate in Ephesus by laws all their own.

Once the cube descended, once the Duke (Munir Khairdin) set time going, giving his prisoner the 'limit... of this day' to find a ransom, once Egeon (Fred Ridgeway, almost killing the *Comedy* before it got going with a criminally dull rendering of the magnificent life story Shakespeare gives him) finished his 'hopeless... helpless' narrative, Ephesus went into over-drive. The place filled with a teeming, noisy, story-full bazaar. Some of the absolute best work on this production was done by Anna Morrissey, the choreographer, who, with only twelve actors, managed to mob the stage, moving traffic in all directions that had twins constantly passing shoulder to shoulder while gazing in opposite directions. These people – traders, hawkers, cozeners, mountebanks – looked like they'd been dressed by Vivienne Westwood high on Turkish Delight: ottoman slops, vibrant Mediterranean yellows and golds, oriental robes, batik prints, and corsets with Elizabethan lacing. Just arrived (and already out of his depth) Samuel Collings's earnest Antipholus-of-Syracuse was a tourist with a guidebook who didn't care to be fooled by the locals – and just had been. 'Soon at five o'clock', promised the dreadlocked 'Merchant' (Huss Garbiya) who'd 'befriended' him, 'I'll meet with you upon the mart', so launching the action into those missed, mistaken meetings that make mayhem in Ephesus. And we noticed that the outer circle of the playing space had made a move: time was ticking.

The doubles were emotionally and visually satisfying: Jack Farthing's choleric Antipholus-of-Ephesus – all irascible bluster, handsomely edgy – was his sanguine (equally handsome, equally young) brother's psychic mirror. Both chunky, both shock-haired, the two Dromios, Michael Jibson and Owain Arthur (distinguishable from his twin by his Welsh voice in Ephesus) endearingly shared habits. Seriously biffed by masters who pulled no punches punishing faults they hadn't committed, they suffered anxiety attacks and pulled out inhalers they had to suck on hard to regain composure. Both of these actors made debuts at the Royal Exchange and, on this showing, they're a pair to watch out for, clearly performers who delighted in the comic turns Shakespeare wrote for them, where each gets to 'star' in half the play. You can see the playwright warming up for the future here. Adriana/Luciana in 2.1 is surely a first go at Desdemona/Emilia in 4.3 of *Othello*. Dromio-of-Syracuse in 3.2 on the subject of Nell the greasy Kitchen Wench drafts both Falstaff (the tallow catcher) and Thersites (the wise-cracker): 'If she lives till doomsday she'll burn a week longer than the whole world.' (And doesn't Antipholus-of-Ephesus, on Pinch-the-mountebank, invent the 'dead parrot' joke with that line of epithets that ends with 'a living dead man'?)

This is comedy that depends not just on the audience hearing the words, but on actors phrasing the line so we get the set up (in that outrageous Nell joke, the hypothetical, 'if she') followed by the consequence ('she'll'), timed to land the line's punch with just enough pause to let us take the hit. Both Dromios inhabited the prose rhythms of this play like natives to the manor born. But they also made jazz with the play's physical rhythms. Stood on opposite sides of Antipholus's locked front door – here, made of Perspex, a courtesy to an audience in the round that intensified the joke of the Dromios's blind incomprehension – they were like a couple of daft game birds shadow-boxing themselves in a mirror.

Finally, the excellent Jan Chappell, who'd doubled as a truly alarming Dr Pinch, descended from the flies like Glinda the Good Witch of the North as the Abbess to preside over the ending. Time stood still. Then suddenly time dropped out from under the Ephesians' feet as the double dials on the clock, which they didn't know was the surface of their world, shifted, tilted vertiginously, and momentarily knocked them all off balance – but only as a prelude to the physical, time-healing recognitions that made all things even.

The Vienna of Michael Attenborough's modern-day *Measure for Measure* at the Almeida gave out mixed signals. In the foyer, on posters and publicity materials, the city branded itself under the sign of that reverend lady, Justicia, sword raised in one stiff-stretched arm, scales in the other, spikey crown on her head (like thorns, topping a body arranged, significantly, cruciform). But this lady was made in screaming pink neon tubing, the kind that flashes down the Strip in Las Vegas: a curvy broad, not so much icon as pop-art fetish. On stage, Vienna had antique gravitas, its signature a formal audience chamber in near dark, black floor, black chair, black table. Oddly, though, the sole occupant (greying, dishevelled, like some tramp who'd mistaken his way from the servants' entrance; actually, Vienna's Duke, Ben Miles) padded around the elegant furniture in his sock feet, smoking, nervy, restless, stubbing out one fag then instantly lighting another, a silent prologue lasting some ten minutes. The place was a pig-sty: a dump of overflowing ashtrays, scattered papers, half-drunk wine glasses, collapsing piles of books. Behind the mess, rising above it, on the wall was a splendid floor-to-ceiling late Renaissance fresco showing a teeming cityscape and people busy in it: da Cortona's 'Rape of the Sabine Women'.

Given this range of visual reference, how did material Vienna read? What did this city think about women? Sex? The majesty of the law? Violence as civic project? (Those Sabines, we remember, were raped to populate Rome.) And that solitary man who couldn't sit still: what was eating him?

We seemed to be watching his nervous breakdown. Low notes played vibrato on a cello were suddenly drowned out by a throbbing, deafening disco beat. Da Cortona vanished. Behind, we saw pole dancers in cages dressed mostly in lurid snatches of light offering themselves in acts of indecency, a bizarre dissolve that seemed to position spectators to look through walls, into the city's grotty dives and flesh markets where 'corruption' would 'boil and bubble / Till it o'er run the stew', but also to peer into a brain, one psychically printed with da Cortona, at an imagination polluted with images and contradictions it couldn't keep at bay that revealed themselves in flashes as garish as neon signs. (Later, the back wall – the set was designed by Lez Brotherston – would split and revolve, to show behind the solemn glamour of the Duke's office Vienna's smoke-blackened streets as a Dickensian slum.)

Usefully, the notion of mental meltdown worked to motivate this Duke's sudden departure, but also made available from the off ideas about 'seeming' and 'seemers', that there might be more than one devil, horns tucked tidily inside a cowl or a cap of justice, operating here under the masquerade of the 'good angel'. Ironically, it also normalized the existential crisis that would hit Angelo later, since existential crises were what happened to men in this city: the walls of their known worlds dissolved, the 'sanctuary' in the foreground proving just a front prettying up the 'waste ground' beyond.

Problematically, however, this opening meant that the rest of the play would have to operate on Miles's bonkers Duke as therapy, curing him to make his decisions appear sane at the end. And that didn't work. Indeed, I've never seen so unresolved an ending to *Measure* as this one gave us: the Duke restored to authority, gleefully dealing destinies from a chair of state set centre stage, all schoolboy delight that he'd stuck the wheels back on his go-cart, all jolly thriving wooer offering himself to Isabella – while the others stood around in a semi-circle, stupefied. Gazing at a madman.

So Miles's Duke was a fixer who couldn't fix. (The measure of his hare-brained ineffectuality registered in David Annen's phlegmatic Provost, a decent flunkey who knew himself to be one, driven to finger-knotting fits so as not to strangle the do-gooder who kept turning up at his prison.)

Worse though Miles's Duke was an empiricist who didn't appear to be learning anything from his experiments on human subjects: 'thus shall we see if . . .'. Miles has spent most of his career in front of TV cameras that tell spectators what a character is thinking. The filmic opening to this production, then, suited him down to the ground. But big 'think' speeches like 'Be absolute for death' that might have shown his Duke groping for the next analogy or reflecting on his own mortality came out as a series of thoughtless platitudes, platitudes that didn't go on to be radically re-thought as *live* considerations under pressure of, say, 'Sweet sister, let me live.' (The fault there, though, was as much the director's, placing his actor in 3.1 where he couldn't be seen, so cutting the Duke/Friar's reaction to what was happening between brother and sister – and 33 per cent of the scene's meaning.)

The fascination of this *Measure for Measure* wasn't, then, the Duke's journey; still less, the low-lifers' (though Lloyd Hutchinson's whining Irish wideboy Lucio with his purple tie and Tony Blair grin was a smarmy grotesque who comprehensively trashed any notion of honour among thieves). It was the throwing about of brains and bodies that happened in 2.2 and 2.4, scenes that emerged here as like the heavy-weight grappling of *Othello*'s Act 3.

To begin with, Rory Kinnear's Angelo was a lightweight who, like David Killick's excellent Escalus before him, entered 1.1 running – combing his forelock over a receding hairline with his fingers, noticing his shirt sleeves were still rolled up and that there was nothing he could do about it now. He was a backroom nerd, a bookish paper pusher in wire-rim spectacles and beard, who never expected to speak to the CEO, never mind get promoted to his job. And he didn't want it: 'Let there be made some more test of my metal,' he insisted, aghast, sincere – to a Duke who was already out the door. In the silence, Escalus's rather stiff, 'I shall desire you [slight pause], sir . . .' made him spin round, barking a laugh. No one had ever called him 'sir'! Realization dawned. His steep learning curve, also a power trip, had just gone vertical.

When he next appeared – suit, tie, briefcase, document files – he was a different man, diffidence gone, talking like he'd taken a crash course in spitting nails ('We must not make a scarecrow of the law . . . He must die'). He'd already made an impact on the city. The office was cleared. The desk, immaculate. The fresco, removed. But it turned out that handling papers was more straightforward than handling people – with all their odd angles, dog-eared corners, non-standard sizes: hard to stack people in piles. And then there was their sheer bloody-mindedness, refusing to 'be said', to let go of an argument. Squat Pompey (Trevor Cooper), who, except for the earring and leather biker's jacket, looked like the Friar Tucks you see on Toby jugs, simply routed Kinnear's Angelo with his mulishness, his dogged story of the prunes, the china dish, the pregnant Mrs Elbow. The deputy exited, snapping his briefcase smartly shut. But he should've hung around. Pompey, defending (the indefensible) Froth, was as canny a pleader as any Middle Temple barrister. He juggled Justice and Iniquity – as Escalus observed – so fast-and-loose that they merged into a smokescreen. Attending to his rhetoric might have served Kinnear's Angelo as a warm-up exercise, a mettle workout before he faced the test of that next self-confessed defender of the indefensible: Isabella.

As much of a nerd as Angelo, Anna Maxwell Martin's Isabella entered possessing the unselfconscious audacity, invulnerability, *sexlessness* of the woman who knows herself to be plain. This production's version of modern dress did her no favours. She wasn't in the contemporary clothes of today's working-in-the-community nun (which makes Isabella look like a hospital auxiliary and her religious absolutism, in a secular age, somewhat hysterical), nor in the still-surviving traditional retro-fashion of the enclosed order (that, if it makes Isabella look like a throw-back to a redundant past, at least makes sense of what grounds her uncompromising principles). Her costume was both a fudge and a smear. In an interpolated sequence between 1.3 and 1.4, as the revolve turned to give sight of the mortifying brick interior of the nunnery, Miles's Duke moved downstage

right; Maxwell Martin's Isabella, downstage left; he, helped into a friar's habit, over his clothes; she, undressed to knickers and bra, then re-dressed in long black velvet cassock. For her, then, no recognizable female monastic 'order', but a kind of dour puritanism; a body 'voyeurized' in the undressing; and a change of clothes that, transacted simultaneously, analogized her to the Duke's 'seeming', offering her, too, as a hypocrite. It's a measure of this actor's achievement that she out-acted the costume.

Like Pompey, she wouldn't let the argument go; like Pompey, she worked by lateral thinking, and her thinking was fast and fearless. In her first interview with Angelo it wasn't that she was cool, only tongue-tied because compromised defending her (by the letter of the law, justly condemned) brother. But what really heated her blood and loosed her into vehemence was when the debate moved from the specific, from the local penal code, to the theoretical, to principles of natural, eternal justice: questions of judgement, mercy, the remedial offices of forgiveness, human faultiness tried in a spiritual court. Her turn to the *ad hominem*, needling the deputy ('So you . . .'; 'Go to your bosom . . .'), was like injecting a live virus under his skin. Like 'sir' earlier, no one had ever talked to Kinnear's Angelo like this before. The manoeuvrings, the meticulous listening and picking up of words that turned, in their repetitions, to new directions ('too late', 'too late?'; 'forfeit', 'forfeit'; 'remedy', 'remedy!'), the excruciating hair-splittings ('I will not do't'; 'But can you if you would?; 'what I will not . . .'; 'But might you?') were like rhetorical kick-boxing. He couldn't shut her up, this Sabineesque virgin who was mind-fucking him. 'Ask your heart what it doth know': it was as though she could see right through him. And she couldn't see it.

The curtain raiser to their second interview was a fumbled comic routine – Angelo dashing around his office, setting up props (a desk crucifix), trying to transform himself into Peter Finch's Dr Fortunati (jamming contact lenses into squinting eyes with trembling hands). Ironically, it was Isabella-the-absolutist's concession to human

14. *Measure for Measure*, 2.2. Almeida Theatre, directed by Michael Attenborough. Rory Kinnear as Angelo, Anna Maxwell Martin as Isabella, Lloyd Hutchinson as Lucio.

frailty – responding to Angelo's outburst making fornication and murder equivalent crimes, that ''Tis set down so in heaven, but not in earth' – that opened up the space that gave Kinnear's Angelo his way through her defence. 'Say you so?' (He sat on the seat behind her.) 'Then I shall pose you quickly.' (He slid a hand onto her thigh.) Isabella froze, but *with pleasure*: no one had ever touched her like that! Then she snapped; the game got vicious; she shrilled her accusation but wound up pinned underneath him to the desk; he retreated from the rape he was somehow too fastidious to commit; and in the long, long, long silence after he exited (straightening his tie with his parting shot, 'Say what you can: my false o'erweighs your true') she slowly got back on her feet, as though re-articulating every bone in her body.

These were two terrific performances of brilliantly matched *agon*-ists. And the pity of it was that, in this Vienna, at the end, these two – who eyed each other warily across the Duke's 'happy' dispensations – would never speak to each other again, but would always be in each other's fantasies, would always be what would lie, when it dissolved, behind their psychic wall. The pity of it was that in another life, this Angelo and Isabella might have been Beatrice and Benedick.

TRAGEDIES

The sign fixed to the playhouse door warned: 'Please note: this is a gruesome production of a brutal play.' No it wasn't. It was a sensationalist serving up of a deep-thinking play as spooks-and-ghouls twaddle, directed by Lucy Bailey whose shock-tactic experiments with design at the Globe, if they used to look interesting, are now merely gimmicky. And worse, operate like self-parody. In 2006, for *Titus Andronicus*, she wrapped the Globe in black and put a lid on the playhouse – a vast black circular awning with a hole in the middle – that put *Survey*'s reviewer in mind of Roman arenas where Christians were fed to the lions. And she made the violence so realistic that a St John's ambulance had to be on permanent call to deal with the half dozen spectators the production turned into casualties at every performance (*Shakespeare Survey 60*). In 2008, for *Timon of Athens*, Bailey stretched black netting across the Globe's roof, trapping spectators inside an aviary where, above their heads, half a dozen black-clad extras performed continuously as bungie-jumping birds of prey (*Shakespeare Survey 62*). But whereas in 2006 the design and all the activity that Bailey staged in the yard worked 'genuinely' to 'redefine . . . the space' (as against other directors who used the yard in a 'desperate bid for attention or a vote of no confidence in the stage proper'), in 2008 the design had 'replaced most of the acting': 'the aerial parallel play pulled focus from anything happening on stage where the story seemed to have been kicked into the corner and forgotten'.

This year, directing *Macbeth*, Bailey's bright idea was to turn the Globe's yard into Dante's hell. (I'm not making this up: the Gustave Doré illustration of the frozen Lake of Cocytus that was her 'inspiration' was reproduced in the programme.) So the yard was covered in stretched black fabric, held taut, four feet or so above the ground, perforated with holes. If you wanted to be a groundling, you had to duck under the cloth, find a hole, and stick your head up through it. The yard, then, presented a black sea of the 'decapitated' – like Macbeth at the end: get it? – who were also, of course, stuck to the spot, which killed any idea of the groundling as active play-maker, mobile and on the hoof.

Worse, though, the design killed the script (which is why, reportedly, actors hated it) by deadening the acoustic, so that 'If it were done . . . ' and 'Yet here's a spot' had to be bellowed out like auctioneers crying prices in Smithfield. In any case, reconceiving *Macbeth* as early modern slasher narrative, Bailey wasn't much interested in Shakespeare's script beyond 'What bloody man is that?' She was going for Halloween effects (that would keep the ambulance men on standby). The pre-show 'performance' fixed the noise of this production in the mindless shrieks of the groundlings. It had the witches (Janet Fullerlove, Simone Kirby, Karen Anderson) – in whiteface, eyes hollowed into red pits, mouths gashed vampirically ear-to-ear, wearing medieval skull caps, filthy skirts and, over them, stiff with dirt, the dried-blood-red tabards of the Globe's army of volunteers, the still faintly legible word 'steward' printed on the back (get it? witches = stewards of hell?) – running like rats under the

cloth, touching up spectators. And when you spun round you either found yourself nose to nose with one of these gruesomes, or staring into air before you realised you had to drop your gaze: the third witch was 'a little person', three feet tall. The Bloody Captain (Michael Camp) erupted from the cloth, screaming, as though escaped, post-flaying, from an abattoir, while the dead, around him, writhed up out of the battleground, like blood-maggots. Dead Duncan (James Clyde) was carried on in a blood-soaked sheet. So was Lady M (Laura Rogers) at the end – and unrolled to show she'd committed suicide by do-it-yourself hysterectomy.

The actors did manage to salvage something from this freak show. Elliot Cowan's Macbeth was momentarily, desperately poignant, sitting on his throne, rocking, silent, a terrified child, having realized that 'to be thus is nothing'. Keith Dunphy's great big Macduff, gutted by grief, was simply heartbreaking: 'all my pretty chickens?' And Fleance's (Josh Swinney) induction into violence was genuinely shocking, at the banquet entertaining Duncan with a ballad in Gaelic that turned into a drinking song that degenerated into a rowdy scrum, a male-bonding ritual, blooding the child.

But what actually saved the show for me was entirely accidental: a pair of blackbirds. They were nesting in the Globe thatch, utterly oblivious to the Grand Guignol happening below. And their performance – unwitting casting as 'temple-haunting martlets' ducking and diving graciously over Globe air space – was just what this *Macbeth* needed: 'sweet oblivious antidote'.

As it happened, Cheek by Jowl, playing at the Silk Street Theatre in the Barbican, fixed a warning to their *Macbeth* this season, too. It said: 'This production is suitable for 16 +'. But then, that's the notice they put on *every* show – because Cheek by Jowl aim to produce Shakespeare for grown-ups.

As a strapline, this production meditated on the thought that 'present fears are less than horrible imaginings'. It made theatre the means of that imagining, using theatrical resources to probe the monumental failure to imagine that lies at the heart of the Macbeths' project: 'who would have thought . . . ?' (In a podcast on the company's website, the director Declan Donnellan talked about *Macbeth* as a tragedy of realization, 'not so much about the doing' of the murder but 'all about the realisation of what [they] have done', and spoke about imagination as an aspect of that realization. To see 'thing as they are', he remarked drily, 'reality needs a lot of imagining'.)

To put spectators in parallel play with the Macbeths, to make *them* imagine, Donnellan stripped out the literal. There was no blood. No daggers. No witches. No letter. No banquet. They had to be imagined. Designing black-on-grey and flanking the stage with slatted boxes of various heights that produced, in imagination, primitive stone tors as much as objective metaphors of boxed-in enclosure and, by extension, a kind of *camera obscura* inside which it was the words of the script that produced the images spectators saw on their retinas, Nick Ormerod created a space that was simultaneously wide open and claustrophobic. This eerie location-in-nature – also a weird landscape of the mind; void-space for 'terrible dreams' – was lit by Judith Greenwood with expressionist effect, like film noir, to cast long, looming shadows, as if literalizing 'thought . . . fantastical', where 'nothing is, but what is not'.

Twelve actors – dressed in minimalist black uniform: T-shirts, military tunics, combat boots, a plain floor-length dress for Lady M – did all the work of this production. Most of them remained on stage as watchers for the duration of the play, silent witnesses of the action, played at a relentless hugger-mugger pace without the let-up of an interval in just under two hours. Some of that work, particularly by the ensemble making physical, expressive sculpture out of actors' bodies, was superb. After Duncan's (David Collings) murder, as the thanes surrounded young Malcolm (Orlando James), ostensibly comforting him, transferring to him fealty in the sacred ritual of touch that had defined his (blind) father's rule, the laying on of hands turned monstrous, tentacular, a scrum of bodies closing in, pawing, groping, claiming the youth who struggled and twisted out of their killing embrace. Equally good, and employing Cheek by Jowl's signature

technique of overlapping scene upon scene, was the superimposition of the portrait of the Macduffs at home upon Macbeth's instructions to the murderers to slaughter the whole household. This picture, Macduff (David Caves) embracing his wife (Kelly Hotten) and son (Vincent Enderby), dissolved into the tense scene following, which had the wife accusing the husband of desertion, and him performing it, exiting on her line as the killers stepped into the light. His stunned grief, a man who, in his owlish black spectacles looked more like the company paymaster than a warrior, hearing of their deaths, made palpable in his near silent reaction the 'horrible imaginings' this Macduff was witnessing in his mind that he would try to exorcise in hunting down their killer.

The company work, then, was strong – particularly Ryan Kiggell's Banquo, who made a terrifying spectre at the feast by simply rising from an invisible table and turning his countenance on Macbeth. But the pair at the centre were disappointingly one-paced, delivering their entire performance in their first scene. Both Will Keen's Macbeth and Anastasia Hille's Lady were headcases from the off: nervy, strung-out, brittle; constitutionally given to twitches, to hyper-active lunges across diagonals as if simultaneously magnetically attracted and repelled by each other's words (while never really appearing to *listen* to each other), and to strange gaps in speaking as though gulping images that were mentally choking them. Which was fine (sort of) for them experiencing the gagging; but impenetrable to an audience not hearing what they were 'seeing'. Sleepwalking, Hille went through the motions of miming her memories, but without showing their terrible psychic effect, 'eyes . . . open', 'sense . . . shut'. Soliloquizing, Keen conveyed a kind of frantic mania, illustrated with compulsive hand-clenches, that made him a borderline hysteric from the first – but not what the speeches require of Macbeth, a thinker thinking the 'horrible'. While I admired much of the company's stylization, particularly of the fight sequences and deaths, I found some of it simply too abstract, and wondered what narrative sense a first-time viewer would make of, for example,

15. *Macbeth*, 2.3. Cheek by Jowl at the Barbican Theatre, directed by Declan Donnellan. Kelly Hotten as the Porter.

Lady Macbeth, after the sleepwalking, moving to sit at her husband's feet, he cupping her chin while he confessed that he had 'supp'd full of horrors', and exiting when Seyton entered to announce her death, to return, finally, to curl up with her dead husband at the end. A haunting image? Or just baffling?

That said, there was nothing abstract about the delicious vulgarity of the Porter scene. (Cheek by Jowl holds the theatrical monopoly on this line of iconoclastic outrageousness.) No tired piss-in-bucket gags here (viz. the Globe). Kelly Hotten was the receptionist from hell, backcombed flame-coloured hair stacked on her head and detonating in all directions, lipstick sliding down her chin, stuck in a wooden booth with an intercom to the front gate whose buzzing she backchatted ('Knock, knock, knock!') and cut dead in a

Glaswegian growl as she flipped through her *Heat* magazine and filed her nails. Only when she finally, flouncingly picked up the phone and heard it was MACDUFF! at the gate did she shift from the shiftless into overdrive – grabbing an atomizer from somewhere to squirt under arms and up her skirt; bursting out of her box to shimmy and squirm like a besotted schoolgirl under Macduff's disconcerted gaze. Hilarious – but also a time-out we spectators were grateful for. The only colour in this production, Hotten's *Heat*-seeking Porter was a lurid flash of tawdry brilliance before the dark clamped down on this *Macbeth* and turned all life's lights off.

Last year, reviewing the RSC's *Julius Caesar*, I idly speculated (before it was announced for this year's repertoire or he, cast in the part) on the sequel, wondering what kind of figure Darrell D'Silva's 'sprawling, joyless reveller-turned-brutal-thug' of an Antony might cut in Cleopatra's deliciously pranked-up and prank-addicted Egypt. This year, I found out.

Early news leaking out of Michael Boyd's rehearsal room reported his original concept: to make the Egyptians Spanish of the time of Philip II (which just about makes sense, if Alexandria's gypsies translate into Andalusian gitanos), the Romans no-more-cakes-and-ale English Roundheads. (But wait a second, didn't we see something of that reductive reading hitting a brick wall at the Tobacco Factory last year (*Shakespeare Survey* 63)?) Eventually (thankfully) Boyd scrapped those ideas – but put nothing better in their place. This *Antony and Cleopatra* was a modern-dress fashion parade that conceived Cleopatra's 'infinite variety' as a sequence of *haute couture* costume changes – the blue gown, the red gown, the black gown, the other black gown – absurdly coordinated in her sidekicks, making Iras and Charmian (Samantha Young, Hannah Young) each a mini-me and the queen's apotheosis ('give me my robes'), anticlimactic down-dressing. And none of this did anything to cover the disastrous miscasting of Kathryn Hunter as Cleopatra.

Hunter is an extraordinary performer, capable of prodigious physical transformations: doubling Paulina with Mamillius in Complicite's *Winter's*

16. *Antony and Cleopatra*, 2.5. RSC at the Courtyard Theatre, directed by Michael Boyd. Kathryn Hunter as Cleopatra.

chain-smoked her namesake Gitanes. But even more disconcerting, given this actor's biog, there was almost nothing physical animating Hunter's performance. She reproduced the same flat-palmed hand gestures over and over. The same scowl-furrowed brow. The same foot tapping and jaw dropping. And, when she wasn't acting the almost dementedly mood-swinging diva (as in the 2.5 messenger scene), a kind of monotony of speaking (broken up by a strange, growly 'heh, heh, heh' passing for mirth) that was unequal either to the breath-taking coarseness of Cleopatra's kitchen-wench lewdness or to the soaring journeys of imagination such as she takes Dolabella (and us) on, effecting one last seduction, aural arousal to climax, in telling her dream of Antony. Almost worst of all, in a script that gives the Egyptian queen some of the funniest and saltiest wisecracks Shakespeare ever wrote, this Cleopatra produced no laughter from the audience either time I saw the performance. (Perhaps Boyd's aim was to kill laughter; he cut the asp man in Act 5 who plays the Clown – and all those jokes about eating and being eaten. A giveaway?)

Sad to report, this car-crash wasn't a single vehicle incident. Behind it came a multiple pile-up that left wrecks everywhere. John Mackay's strangle-voiced Caesar, like the rest of the killjoy Romans (the lot of them, Malvolios in grey suits), was by turns prissy and smutty, a hysteric who showed an unhealthy attitude towards his sister and whose reasons for promoting her marriage were opaque. Political? Cynical? Promotional? Reconciliatory? Greg Hicks's Soothsayer looked (and acted) like he'd wandered in from a Hassidic production of *Fiddler on the Roof*; Tunji Kasim's Mardian, in a Michael Jackson wig, from a turn on 'Celebrity Look-alike'; Brian Doherty's slouching, mumbling, dullard hands-in-pockets NCO Enobarbus, in Afghanistan desert war fatigues but trendily 'dissident' in necklace and non-U panama hat, from a bad episode of *M*A*S*H*, expiring by numbers like Bottom's Pyramus ('die, die, die . . . ').

Then there were the interpolations. Actium was represented by Cleopatra and her girls (black berets; sunglasses; trenchcoats – presumably against wet

Tale years ago; playing King Lear, Kate Minola, *and* Kafka's ape; and telling all those stories with physical power – and *fearlessness*. But on any reckoning, the body itself (and indeed, what makes it acrobatically mesmerising) is a weird structure, scarcely bigger than a child's but with a face deeply wrinkled in late middle age; wiry; made up of arms that appear to be attached to the wrong shoulder; all double-jointed; legs of different lengths that give her an uneven gait (not helped by here being put into ridiculously high heels that made her galumph across the stage like Peg-Leg the Pirate). No director, least of all Boyd, could have been ignorant, casting the play, of the signifying presence of that body. Or indeed, of the acoustically narrow waveband of Hunter's voice: gravelly, as though this seeming kid-Cleopatra had, since weaning, weather on shipboard; patent leather knee boots – silly footwear for sea) crossing the stage in a kind of two-step march holding toy boats over their heads while around them a blue silk sheet billowed, a dazed Antony following, looking as gobsmacked by this charade as I felt. The line 'It is my birthday' (3.13) produced a queen-sized cake, party poppers and a chorus of 'happy birthday to youuuuu'. The end of the messenger scene dissolved into a rendition of the Tom Jones classic 'Delilah' as 'O, O, O – Octavia!'. Earlier the 'I'm bored alone in Egypt' scene had introduced a new line for Cleopatra, 'Act like a fish, Alexas.' Crass in themselves, these distractions were bought with cuts elsewhere: the Parthia scene (3.1), just about acceptable; the Clown, unforgiveable.

It wasn't all bad news. Tom Piper's set was both handsome and versatile, an up-scaled version of his design for the 2007–9 histories season that gave the actors plenty of space to move around the open platform stage, and for entries, a burnished metal rotunda, split by double doors at the centre, that shone gold in certain lights; in others, rusty, flakey, like a serpent sloughing dead skin. Clarence Smith was a dangerously bipolar Pompey, aggrieved and emotionally hair-triggered ('Antony, you have my father's house'), wearing his chip on his shoulder like the high explosive body pack of a suicide bomber. And Peter Shorey was a wonderfully diffident Schoolmaster-turned-ambassador, blinking through his wire-rims as though plucked from a dim library and spruced up in a linen suit to appear before Caesar's celebrity. In a sudden movement, he told us everything we needed to know about Antony's future when, dismissed, he threw himself on his knees in the young man's path, grabbed his hand, and fervently kissed it.

And what of D'Silva's Antony? In 3.1 he wore a silly sailor's hat. In 3.4, his bathrobe (while Octavia appeared in his pyjamas). That is, he was no magnificent head-of-pride 'old [lion] dying', raking his claws across the fresh face of youth to wound history with his memory. He was a flabby buffer, speech after speech, blustering bow-wow, giving the distinct impression, as an actor, of wishing he were elsewhere. (During final technical rehearsals,

D'Silva mishandled a prop gun and wounded himself in the hand; the gossip from one company insider being that he was aiming for his foot, to invalid himself out, and missed.)

Watching Boyd's work over the past two seasons, I can't get rid of the awful thought that keeps surfacing: burn-out. Having master-minded the Herculean labour of the Complete Works Festival (2006–7) and the 'transformation of our theatres' that is on the point of opening the new RST, is Boyd just exhausted? His fund of artistic ideas bankrupted? Certainly the ensemble he prides himself on having reconstituted is too big to be usefully employed, and he seems at a loss to know what to do with it. Witness the line of six actors-as-extras playing aides-de-camp in 2.2, silent stenographers taking down the generals' words. Is it time to hand over the Artistic Directorship of the RSC to some next-generation Ventidius?

Where Boyd's production opened with lights up on Burton-meets-Taylor, with no sign of Philo's caustic comment ('Nay, but this dotage') but with the glam couple in evening wear canoodling ('If it be love . . . '; 'There's beggary . . . '), Janet Suzman's modern dress *Antony and Cleopatra* at the Liverpool Playhouse gave spectators an altogether less clichéd first shot, simultaneously iconographic and iconoclastic. Leaning over an open-railed bridge suspended above the main playing area, Philo (Alex Blake) – whose uniform clearly hadn't been through the laundry in *months* – spat resentment ('Those his goodly eyes . . . ') onto the head of a monumental figure posed like a statue below. On 'tawny front', the statue turned, showing Cleopatra (Kim Cattrall), the icon, as earthy Isis, in a gold mask that was tugged off as laughter erupted and she stepped down from the plinth, more lights coming up to show Antony (Jeffery Kissoon), the ruin, sprawled at her feet, half-naked, drunk, snoring, nudged into consciousness by the prod of her toe and hoots of mockery from Cleopatra's retinue.

Suzman was once a famous Cleopatra (directed by Trevor Nunn in 1972), and perhaps that history inclined her as a director to 'show a little bias for her sex' (as Jane Austen might have it) and privilege the queen over the general, making Cleopatra a political pragmatist, a working monarch in thick-rimmed spectacles in 2.5 signing stacks of memos, and therefore genuinely interesting as a chancer in the final scenes with Octavius (Martin Hutson). Kissoon's Antony was a drunk, but a dangerous one; a warrior whose knees had given out, for the knacker's yard, but still powerful in the shoulders, bull-necked and blundering into speeches hunched forward like a wrestler. (In the three-way Mexican stand-off in Rome in 2.2 ('Sit'; 'Sit sir'; 'Nay then') Lepidus (Martin Herdman) blinked first; Antony grabbed his chair by its throat, swung it round to plonk it eyeball to eyeball with Octavius, and, spreading his crotch, straddled it.)

Perversely, given the histories Shakespeare writes in this play where Egypt is clearly racially black, Suzman's casting produced a white Cleopatra presiding over a black Alexandria; a black Antony in an all-white Rome. Vocally, this worked for Antony, for while Kissoon was given to various odd inflections and a wobbling vibrato whinny on some words – 'betraaaayed'; 'gaudy nnnnight' – when it came to Antony's black Herculean tempers, he had a voice to pull bamboozled rage out of the Roman's knotted bowels. There was still enough of the 'plated Mars' about him to be stopped dead in his tracks when the nameless Soldier blurted out, fiercely, 'Do not fight by sea!' – but not enough to resist Cleopatra's beckoning, muttering 'Well, well,' and turning his back on masculinity, on the mob of men attending him, to chase her swishing skirts. The greatness Kissoon's Antony achieved was in decay, conveying the isolating pain of betrayal in moments of stillness that plumbed deep interiority. After Actium he crouched, as Plutarch has him, 'alone', 'clapping his head betwene both his hands'; in 4.14, almost narcotic, he sat on the earth splay-legged, looking up at the clouds, wondering how it was possible that 'I am Antony / Yet cannot hold this visible shape'.

By contrast, Cattrall, returning to her hometown (and to the stage) after years of playing the man-eater in *Sex and the City* on television (and despite dying her signature blonde hair black), was so vocally 'white' and underpowered that her Cleopatra felt like the erotic equivalent of a vegan. In 5.2 it was a measure of his priggishness, not her seductiveness, that Octavius found her disgusting – shaking off her, and her sincere (therefore shocking) ingratiation ('My master and my lord!') with contempt. That pulling away of the imperial hand operated like a nice *quid pro quo* on a Cleopatra who in Act 3 was already calculating next moves, tired of Herculean histrionics. 'Not know me yet?' (3.13) had been flatly inscrutable; 'if I be so...' ended with Antony 'satisfied', his head in her lap – but she drawing away her hand, averting her gaze, distaste curdling her smile. Only when Antony was dead – here, the scene reversed Shakespeare's directions, lowering the dying warrior into the monument rather than, in all its grotesque awkwardness, lifting him – did this Cleopatra find utterance that put emotional flesh on thought. 'This case is cold' was shattering because so simple – and because the line connected to her hands, cradling the cooling skull of dead Antony.

But such moments were rare. And Cattrall's bleached-out performance wasn't helped by the constant (if wholly unintended) distractions of her excellent Iras (Gracy Goldman) and Charmian (Aïcha Kossoko), the one who held stillness in the body as though she were a sculpture of the sphinx, the other who, every time she opened her mouth and let loose the dark vocal register, the compulsive rhythms of Africa, made me long for an instant recasting of Cleopatra. Whether they were playing board/bored games far upstage in the shadows or, straight men, feeding lines to their mistress, they were compulsive viewing.

Watching this production, it struck me that these days – what with the military (especially the military dressed in Iraq campaign desert fatigues) discredited and the 'riggish' no longer sensationally, deliciously scandalous but common, sex being what every chit gets up to in the city – the only easy part to cast in *Antony and Cleopatra* is Octavius. As Hutson cannily played him, he was the kind of emotional ectomorph we recognize from the front benches on both side of the Commons: a man in a suit, with lips like a cut-throat razor, who ostentatiously wiped surfaces before he sat down, and decided Lepidus's fate when, drunk on Pompey's galley, Lepidus suddenly pitched forward vomiting into Octavius's lap. He was the bureaucrat as politician, promoting mean policies to nudge the plebs into a well-ordered, intimidated herd of sheep for the slaughter: 'Plant those that have revolted in the van / That Antony may seem to spend his fury / Upon himself.'

But it also struck me that, as at the RSC, practically the best thing about this production was the set. There's a spit-and-sawdust tawdriness to the Playhouse that somehow remembers its days as a music hall and that nicely evoked the sleazy imagery the play's Romans constantly mouthed. The stage itself, though, was both elegant and splendid, Peter McKintosh designing space that worked like a set of cultural Chinese boxes, nestling Egypt inside Rome, feminine curves inside male lines and squares. The back and side walls were constructed of red brick and arches that evoked the Coliseum. Inside that, a sleek lining of glass and steel felt like the architectural equivalent of trapped water. Inside that, a warm wood floor shaped like an oval, surrounded by black reflecting tiles, gave the heat, haze and laze of Alexandria. Above it all, an open gantry allowed for simultaneous staging, male surveillance and mobility along the vertical axis. The surfaces of this space seemed to dissolve and re-solidify under Paul Pyant's lighting, creating mirages. One example: during Octavius's speech in 3.6 condemning Antony's performance 'I'th'marketplace', handing out crowns and titles to Cleopatra and her children, light passing through the meshed gantry floor threw onto the stage shadows that spectators could see as the very thrones Caesar was talking about.

Where Michael Boyd seemed to have no ideas beyond dress-up for tragedy at the RSC this year, his associates came bogged down with concepts and evidently determined to push around actors-as-manikins to embody them. A case in point was Rupert Goold, whose past form as a director of Shakespeare has shown him to be distinctly hit (*Macbeth*, Chichester 2007) or miss (*King Lear*, Liverpool 2009), occasionally in the same production (*Tempest*, RSC 2006): it all depends on how he pulls

off what he calls the 'conceptual buggering around' he 'normally' does with Shakespeare's script. For this year's RSC *Romeo and Juliet* at the Courtyard, I'd give him, marks out of ten, two: his 'buggering around' embarrassingly crude and the concept frankly dim.

In fact, there were two concepts. The first, that *Romeo and Juliet* is a 'timeless tragedy' of doomed but oh-so-modern youth: so Goold put the lovers (Sam Troughton, Mariah Gale) in hoodies and Converse trainers and T-shirts blazoned with a motif of copulating skeletons, but surrounded them with Elizabethans. Verona's lads were in doublets; Ma Capulet (Christine Entwisle) was strapped into an iron farthingale. Then at the end, this scheme was time-reversed, Juliet dressed for marriage in an early modern high-ruffed gown; Romeo, like a monk; Verona re-dressed in suits and jeans. In between, time frames collided. Romeo rode a bicycle (fast becoming a production cliché on the Courtyard stage); Capulet's ball, farthingales notwithstanding, was a head-banging rave (and excruciatingly embarassing, as always when the RSC tries to act streetwise and dance dirty); doubleted Benvolio (Oliver Ryan) snapped shots on a digital camera, then later, caught by the rival street gang (swords notwithstanding), was doused with petrol and only just saved from torching.

That last pointed up Goold's other concept, that *Romeo and Juliet* is (*pace* the programme) a tragedy 'written for a Protestant audience' 'set in a Catholic world'. So: a 'lurid' play 'luridly' evoking the imagery of 'prayers', 'sins', bleeding hearts, confession and 'heretics' 'luridly' burned at the stake. The lines Goold evidently took for gospel were Romeo's from 1.2 – you know, the ones he swears to just before he sees Juliet and recants: 'When the devout religion of mine eye / Maintains such falsehood, then turn tears to fire, / And these, who often drowned could never die, / Transparent heretics, be burnt for liars.' What we know about Shakespeare's Romeo is that he grows up. Conceptually, Goold's production didn't.

What Goold gave us, in a bid to link secular modernity to a traditional language of religious extremism that works equally well applied to love or death, was an opening conceit that had a wide-eyed youth, camera slung around his neck (tourist, journalist?) rushing as though seeking sanctuary into a dark incense-clouded space where the shadow of a rose window fell dimly on the floor (designed by Tom Scutt). Outside was the sound of sirens wailing; closer, monastic voices in plainsong. He picked up the audio guide, clicking through several languages before getting the English voice that started, 'Two households . . . ', then tentatively he pushed through the metal sanctuary gates upstage – and was captured for the play, returning as Romeo, still 'mod' in that otherwise 'early mod' Verona.

There was plenty of the lurid in this Verona – flames shooting out of the floor in the street fight that would have done any Marian torturer proud; Capulet (Richard Katz, pulping oranges) the patriarch-as-psychopath prepared in 3.5 to martyr his daughter; a peroxide-blond Mercutio (Jonjo O'Neill) literally disappearing up his own backside in a hideous example of actorly self-indulgence, taking 'Poor Romeo . . . his heart cleft with the blind bow-boy's butt-shaft' as cue for a ten minute mime that had him simulating his friend sodomising Rosaline then, sucked up her anus, travelling touristically through guts and privities, taking tea along the way – like some Mad Hatter in a vaginal Wonderland – before climbing, kicking and elbowing, 'birthed' from her cunt. I've never been so delighted to see a Mercutio die. Not least because his solipsism, his misogynist narcissism were allowed to make the running, to be performatively coercive in a production that wasn't able to produce wonder to counterbalance this trashy imaginary.

Gale's Juliet was a sullen teenager swinging a toy on a string in time with her moods; Troughton a Romeo arabesquing into balletic postures at ends of lines ('vow!'; 'emperor!'); both of them, excellent actors, adrift in these parts as though never having done the basic work on this gorgeously wrought script, reciting words, words, words in the wooden fashion of reading around a classroom. I minded, too, the basic directorial incompetence of this production: the way Romeo had already shown in 2.2 he could scale the balcony (so why the song and dance about the rope ladder?); the way, post-coitally, in the morning-after scene Juliet was in Romeo's hoodie which he hadn't been wearing the night before. This production, in a year when there was lots of competition, also takes the prize for the worst directorial abuse of an actor in performance: Goold's decision to make Gruffudd Glyn's Balthasar suddenly burst into castrato song to warble out the speech that begins 'I brought my master news of Juliet's death . . . ' What can he have been thinking of?

But in this season of RSC duds, worse was to come, David Farr's *King Lear*, set by designer Jon Bausor in a post-apocalyptic, post-industrial Britain, a vast space of abandoned manufacturing, broken skylight windows running the width of the stage and dripping pipes, like a derelict jam factory (a nod at the building project going on down the road from the Courtyard?) populated by characters whose costumes located them variously in prehistoric Albion, socialite Edwardian London, the trenches of the Somme, the Russian revolution, a medieval convent. On the one hand, these visuals were a canny response to a script that feels sometimes located at the time of Stonehenge, sometimes in the Renaissance, sometimes in a future nuclear winter. But they also betrayed a team much more interested in technical production than in whatever actors might have been doing to tell *King Lear*'s story.

Here, the lighting plot was the star of the show: industrial neon strips that fizzed as though about to short, electrocution in the air; a chandelier that weirdly crackled and dimmed, proleptically the ghost in the machine that predicted the family power-out to come; a battery of some fifty lamps, six hanging like high-intensity interrogation lights aimed straight down, others stacked in a lighting grid angled (at first) in the audience's eyes; at the end, more lamps, like car headlights, packed in an industrial-sized metal box suspended by industrial arms over the thrust of the stage, lowering robotically, forensically down upon the bodies of dead Lear and Cordelia like some mechnical pathologist intent on anatomizing them under the searing scrutiny of white light. In the storm, light exploded as the walls of this place caved in (Bausor quoting himself from *The Winter's Tale* last year, the designer-doyen of collapsing worlds), giving the heath as horizonless, weirdly one-dimensional in a grey wash of gloom.

Nothing the actors did seemed as interesting as the performance the machinery was giving. First wrong-footing the rest of the family who'd assembled at a run (doors in the echoing distance clunking like metal vaults shutting) and fallen on their knees looking upstage to reverence the patriarch, Greg Hicks's Lear came on from the side, his mirthless laughter eventually alerting them to the joke. That was the kind of sense of humour he had, this king who looked like a primitive tribal warrior, a mountain of dead animals, furs and feathers: a dad who (time-travelling) put his daughters up on soapboxes to speak their pieces and who mouthed 'I love you' against their utterance in a kind of incestuous karaoke. Stringy (in shirt, trousers and braces once he'd shed all that artificial bulk), whiney, with a vibrato quiver to the voice that moved between the peevishly splenetic and the geriatrically querulous, Hicks was Lear-the-prankster putting on the grotesque little shows of a flyweight domestic despot. So he bowed and scraped idiotically playing out 'Your name, fair gentlewoman' to Kelly Hunter's Goneril, but really playing to the audience of his hooting male retinue who were still laughing when he reprised his 'unsightly tricks' with 'age is unnecessary' to Regan (Katy Stephens). By then, however, he himself had been silenced, his incredulous 'Ask her forgiveness?' met with Regan's frigid stare and calmly nodding head, forcing him for the first time in his life to consider admitting fault, asking forgiveness.

It was on Dover Beach with Geoffrey Freshwater's blind Gloucester that Hicks finally got beyond mannerism and superficial actorly technique to probe the mass of contradictions that lay at Lear's centre – his grief, his heart, his unchildedness. Stripped naked to the waist, he'd finished that tedious piece of business that seems to have become standard since McKellen's Lear in 2007, shoving his hand down his pants to masturbate

his way through his misogynist fantasy ('Down from the waist they are centaurs . . . there is the sulphurous pit . . . stench, consumption!') then, when Gloucester begged to kiss it, needing to 'wipe it first' for 'it smells of mortality'. But when the two old wrecked geezers propped themselves up against each other, the one heaving off the other's boot, the ruined king finally cradling his faithful servant in his skinny arms and in a flash of lucidity recognizing that 'I know thee well enough' – a recognition that was the beginning of a world of love redeemed – this Lear and *Lear* hit greatness.

In no small part, it was Freshwater who enabled the poignancy and profundity of that moment, on the back of the stunned near-recognition his decent, blundering frock-coated dad of a Gloucester had achieved earlier. Much earlier, in the opening scene with Darrell D'Silva's leering Kent, a bluff soldier who clearly relished smut, Gloucester had simpered this way through the bastard Edmund's nasty little history. Now, in the storm in the hovel, looking at the tortured, emaciated figure of the bedlam beggar (played in a loincloth by Charles Aitkin as a figure out of El Greco), he'd suddenly thought about 'my son'. He showed us a *Lear* that was much more about the personal than the political, about fathers discovering their children and, too late, the truth that 'life's a miracle'.

His stirling work was matched by Stephens's brittle Regan, a girl with a grin like the cat in the cartoon who twangs the incisor just before pouncing on Tweetie Bird, and Hunter's stony Goneril who, when she took the safety catch off her gagged emotions, launched into a tirade against her father ('This admiration . . . your new pranks') that had her turbo-propelled and stumbling with the volcanic ferocity of that rage.

But given that Farr had worked with most of these actors the previous season, and given the great hoo-ha the RSC has been making about the value of the three-year-contracted ensemble as continuous actor training, how is it possible that some performances were barely amateur, and others (even among the principals) frequently inaudible? Tunji Kasim's Edgar had none of the dangerous chemistry, seductive tug or political cunning the

17. *King Lear*, 4.6. RSC at the Courtyard Theatre, directed by David Farr. Greg Hicks as King Lear,
Geoffrey Freshwater as Gloucester.

part requires; Samantha Young's Cordelia looked luminous but like Kasim hardly knew what to do with Shakespeare's writing; Kathryn Hunter's cross-dressed Fool in motley, cap and bells, with two expressions of pucker-browed concern, was an irrelevance. Clearly, this Lear didn't need a fool, didn't connect to Fool, so Fool, though watchful, was merely mouthing taglines to the wind. Then there were the 'extras', eleven of them in a bloated ensemble of twenty-three, recycled in different period costumes, having to be kept busy as singing nuns [sic], starched uniformed ward sisters, soldiers in tin hats, ruffian knights (peculiarly well-ordered, sitting on a bench). What continuous training can actors like Hannah Young and Ansu Kabia be getting, acting as RSC scene-dressing for three years?

There was an early moment in Nicholas Hytner's *Hamlet* at the National Theatre that precisely spelled out Hamlet's future. The prince, in black suit and rumpled shirt, had sat huddled in misery, hands pinched between knees, on a chair, off, while the lights and cameras were set up for a press conference, and the make-up girls flapped around Gertrude and Claudius, 'at home' in Elsinore, smiling imperial-sized smiles on an imperial-sized sofa, the background a full-length military portrait of the dead king, to address the nation on the death, the funeral, the marriage, blah, blah, blah. He waited when the arc lights switched off, when the cameras and smiles vanished, when his hatchet-faced uncle gave off-the-record instructions to a couple of flunky ambassadors to deal with Norway. Then he sprang to his feet, slammed down his open passport face up on Claudius's desk – who daffed it aside to ask, 'And now Laertes, what's the news with you?' Rory Kinnear's Hamlet would be a prince who just wanted out – and who wouldn't be allowed to go.

This Elsinore operated as a surveillance state, Hytner, as against Boyd *et al.* at the RSC, making brilliant use of his extras as an in-house army of wired-up goons, earpieces like implants, whispering into their lapels, shadowing every scene. Vicki Mortimer's set felt like the palace at Blenheim that Vanbrugh designed so the toffs would never have to cross paths with the servants: a National Trust grey place of sliding monogrammed panels and moving walls that reconfigured apartments from formal reception salons to dingy backroom offices, giving both the glitter and grunge of an antique pile occupied by modern royals. David Calder's terrifyingly formidable Polonius, Walsingham trained by MI5, was a spymaster who commanded operations from one of those grey offices, from a desk dominated by a personal PC and littered with wire baskets full of files; who could move men around with the barest flick of a finger; whose surveillance of his son in Paris was routine; who had a file to hand his daughter (handed him by a minder) when he started grilling her about the 'private time' ''Tis told me' that Hamlet was devoting to her; and who could set up that daughter for the fishing scene – with her as 'bait' – by handing her a Bible we'd seen one of his goons planting with a listening device. His kids (Laertes: Alex Lanipekun; Ophelia: Ruth Negga) were the kind of teenagers you see on university open days, she stuffing something under a cushion when he sat beside her on the family sofa (in a service wing of the palace where the sofas weren't so deep as in the royal apartments) and began on the big brotherly advice; then stuffing the same cushion into her mouth to keep from shrieking with laughter when he, all po-faced, got to that bit about opening her 'chaste treasure'. Clare Higgins's raddled, puffy Gertrude lived on the gilt-and-champagne side of the world, wobbling from sofa to sofa on six-inch leopard-skin heels, her alcoholic's bloat sheathed in tight black linen, a woman used to giving commands in a voice like a metal saw ripping through tin. Patrick Malahide's skull-faced Claudius wore suits from Savile Row but eyes by Bram Stoker, and had the signature accoutrement of the top CEO: a desk big enough to perform autopsies. Its surface, completely clear.

For them all, Elsinore furnished their tragedies. The desk was the site of Claudius's prayer, a coldly unrepentant statement that made God, angels and the 'limed soul . . . struggling to be free' dupes of his latest politicking. In the closet scene, urged by Hamlet to 'look, . . . look', 'on him', 'my father', Gertrude started in the direction he pointed as though seeing the ghost, but actually staggering dazedly across the portrait of her first husband, removed from public display, lying on the floor. At the end of the nunnery scene, Negga's Ophelia, furious that she'd been her father's unwitting stooge, seeing the minder extract the contents of the Bible, seeing Polonius yank his earpiece out, declared UDI from the family, shoving the 'remembrances' into his stunned hands and storming off. The civil servant couldn't go after; couldn't repair his family, get his lost daughter back; the king was at his ear. But when he fell through the curtain onto Gertrude's floor, stabbed through neck by the prince as happy assassin, he was clutching Ophelia's letters. She, driven mad by being goon-restrained from grabbing his body as it passed through the palace on a gurney, replayed the scene in parody, wheeling on a whole shopping trolleyful of stuff to distribute to 'remember' her dad, quietly promising 'My brother shall know of it.' She wasn't mad enough to be safe. She was reading alone when the goons found her, hustled her off (as earlier they'd rounded up the 'subversives', the players, and marched them away). Gertrude knew the girl had been assassinated. She addressed 'There is a willow' to Claudius, irony splintering the cover-up she was colluding in. As she raised her latest glass, saluting him, you knew she was the next troublesome dame for the chop.

Kinnear's Hamlet moved through this imperial charnel house like a self-alienated exile, knowing himself no Hercules, but no satyr either, *just wanting out*. In 2.2 Polonius tracked him to his room, like a dosser's bedsit in an attic, with a mattress on the floor and a grey duvet he hid under, not bothering to take off his trainers. When the irksome intruder asked blandly about his reading, Kinnear's

18. *Hamlet*, 2.2. National Theatre, directed by Nicholas Hytner. Rory Kinnear as Hamlet, David Calder as Polonius.

Hamlet climbed into the half-filled school trunk he'd been packing for Wittenberg, turning one of the books that littered the floor into a flapping bird cawing 'Words, words, words', a joker with a patter-line in desperation strung out on a high-pitched maniacal laugh. For by now he knew all his exits were sealed. On the battlements the night before he'd been wittering on to Horatio and the others about the new king's rouses, local customs, moles of nature, blah, blah, blah, oblivious to their tensing, seeing what was approaching behind him but prevented by etiquette from interrupting the prince until he caught the terror in their eyes, slowly turned, and dropped to his knees. That encounter slammed all his doors. The Ghost (a magnificent performance by James Laurenson, who doubled the Player King as the avuncular flip-side to this fearsomely stern revenant) looked like he'd travelled in his trenchcoat from purgatory, cooling as he exited the flames, ash-grey, and, only two months into an eternity of fasting in the fire, so *weary* of the pain, a torment his son took upon

his own body, reaching out but unable to touch his father. The story he told broke the son's heart, who heart-breakingly tracked with the flat of his palm the Ghost's departure down the far side of a wall of smokey windows, the panes of glass between it and his empty hand. Then he turned anguish into a laugh, scrawling the goonishly smiling face of a villain onto the wall, a logo that would return as his political signature, stencilled on T-shirts he'd force everyone at *The Mousetrap* to put on like uniforms.

Dozens of performance details like these made this *Hamlet* a constant revelation. But it was Kinnear's living through Hamlet's speech that made this not just an astonishingly inventive but a very great performance, soliloquies belonging to a meditative mind surprised by words – 'dead'; 'mother'; 'player'; 'Hecuba' – that forced the pace of thought until it was racing, slamming the brain out of the cranium; exchanges that brought him smack up and in the flesh against the appalled images that pestered his imagination. (He nearly retched when, dragging a finger across Ophelia's face he found the cosmetic 'face' of her 'paintings' under his nail.) That, against all the odds, he'd travelled so far and yet never left Elsinore was conveyed by Horatio's (Giles Terera) shocked 'HOW?', learning that he'd contrived the 'sudden death' of Rosencrantz and Guildenstern, 'Not shriving-time allowed'. That he saw his own death – 'Thou wouldst not think how ill all's here about my heart' – but held that 'ill' at bay – 'no matter . . . Let be' – restored this ravaged consciousness to sweetness. I don't weep for Hamlet. I wept for this one.

That said, I don't want to end this year's survey with tears; rather, with a reviewer's version of the lollipop at the end of the concert, brief mention of some of the best work I saw all year (certainly, the best RSC work this year), 'reduced Shakespeare' touring productions of *The Comedy of Errors* and *Hamlet* at the RSC and Propeller's *Pocket Dream*. Aimed at young audiences, but delighting wrinklies like me, these shows were 'reduced' only in terms of running time, not direction (Tarrell McCraney directed *Hamlet*), personnel (members of the permanent ensembles played all these productions) or production values. They had kids on the edges of their seats looking out for pirates (pirates? yup; no Yorick in this *Hamlet*; it did pirates instead); or twisted around to see where the next fairy would come from; wincing at violence (Hermia kicked in the face) or laughing dementedly (the Dromios clearly proxies for every playground bashing they'd ever experienced); rapt with attention (watching Hamlet – a delicious performance by Dharmesh Patel – fall in love as his paper dart letter was wafted across the stage into Ophelia's hands on wind made by a flapping umbrella; watching death come with the exhalation of the ensemble's collective breath); engrossed with the theatricality of the theatre, the actorliness of actors' bodies, and above all, the wonder of 'words, words, words' telling fleshified stories. Looking at those faces looking at Shakespeare, I could see the future, and it made me smile.

PROFESSIONAL SHAKESPEARE PRODUCTIONS IN THE BRITISH ISLES, JANUARY–DECEMBER 2009

JAMES SHAW

Most of the productions listed are by professional companies, but some amateur productions are included. The information is taken from *Touchstone* (www.touchstone.bham.ac.uk), a Shakespeare resource maintained by the Shakespeare Institute Library. Touchstone includes a monthly list of current and forthcoming UK Shakespeare productions from listings information. The websites provided for theatre companies were accurate at the time of going to press.

ALL'S WELL THAT ENDS WELL

National Theatre Company. Olivier Theatre, London, 19 May–30 September.
www.nationaltheatre.org.uk
Director: Marianne Elliott
Countess: Clare Higgins
Bertram: George Rainsford
Helena: Michelle Terry

ANTONY AND CLEOPATRA

Shakespeare at the Tobacco Factory. Tobacco Factory, Bristol, 1 April–2 May.
http://sattf.org.uk
Director: Andrew Hilton
Cleopatra: Lucy Black
Antony: Alun Raglan

Adaptation
The Roman Tragedies
Toneelgroep Amsterdam. Barbican BITE 09, 20–22 November.
www.toneelgroepamsterdam.com
Director: Ivo van Hove
Translator: Tom Kleijn
Coriolanus, *Julius Caesar* and *Antony and Cleopatra* adapted and played consecutively without an interval in a six-hour epic.

AS YOU LIKE IT

Dash Arts at the Curve Theatre, Leicester, 3–28 March.
www.dasharts.org.uk
Director: Tim Supple
Rosalind: Tracy Ifeachor

Royal Shakespeare Company. Courtyard Theatre, Stratford-upon-Avon, 28 April–3 October.
www.rsc.org.uk
Director: Michael Boyd
Rosalind: Katy Stephens

Principal Theatre Company. Forty Hall, London, 10–18 July.
www.principaltheatrecompany.com
Director: Paul Gladwin
Set in the 1960s' 'Summer of Love'.

Shakespeare's Globe, 8 June–10 October.
www.shakespeares-globe.org
Director: Thea Sharrock
Rosalind: Naomi Frederick

Heartbreak Productions. UK tour, June–August.
www.heartbreakproductions.co.uk

THE COMEDY OF ERRORS

Royal Shakespeare Company Young People's Shakespeare and Told By An Idiot. Courtyard Theatre, Stratford-upon-Avon, 25 June–15 August, and on tour.
www.rsc.org.uk
Director: Paul Hunter

Shakespeare's Globe Touring Company. June–November UK tour.
www.shakespeares-globe.org
Director: Rebecca Gatward

CORIOLANUS

Adaptation
The Roman Tragedies
Toneelgroep Amsterdam. Barbican BITE 09, 20–22 November.
www.toneelgroepamsterdam.com
Director: Ivo van Hove
Translator: Tom Kleijn
Coriolanus, *Julius Caesar* and *Antony and Cleopatra* adapted and played consecutively without an interval in a six-hour epic.

CYMBELINE

Theatre Set-up. UK tour, June–August.
www.ts-u.co.uk

Richmond Shakespeare Society. Mary Wallace Theatre, Twickenham, 24–31 October.
www.richmondshakespeare.org
Director: Stephen Oliver

HAMLET

Royal Shakespeare Company. Novello Theatre, London, 3 December 2008–10 January 2009.
www.rsc.org.uk
Director: Gregory Doran
Hamlet: David Tennant

Tower Theatre Company. Theatro Technis, Camden, 12–23 May.

http://home.btconnect.com/theatrotechnics/framset
Director: Martin Mulgrew
Hamlet: Paul Jacobs

Donmar Theatre Company at Wyndham's Theatre, 3 June–22 August.
www.donmarwarehouse.com
Director: Michael Grandage
Hamlet: Jude Law
Gertrude: Penelope Wilton

Lodestar Theatre Company. St George's Hall, Liverpool, 8–15, 17–23 August, 12–13 September.
http://lodestartheatre.co.uk
Director: Max Rubin
Played in rep with *Rosencrantz and Guildenstern Are Dead*.

The Factory. Theatre Royal, York, 22–26 September, and tour.
http://web.mac.com/factorytheatre
Director: Tim Carroll
An ensemble of seventeen actors with casting determined by the audience just before the show starts.

Adaptation
Ha Ha Hamlet!
Jaime Wilson Productions Ltd. Pavilion Theatre, Worthing, 27 June, and tour.
Playwright: Ben Langley
Comic version.

Humble Boy
London Classic Theatre. Haymarket Theatre, Basingstoke, 29–31 January and tour January–May.
www.londonclassictheatre.co.uk
Playwright: Charlotte Jones
Director: Michael Cabot

Rosencrantz and Guildenstern are Dead
Lodestar Theatre Company. Novas CUC, Liverpool, 1–5, 8–13 September.
http://lodestartheatre.co.uk
Playwright: Tom Stoppard
Director: Max Rubin
Played in rep with *Hamlet*.

Shakespeare Bingo – Hamlet!
Running Torch Theatre Company. The Space
@ Venue 46, Edinburgh, 8–21 August.
The audience are given bingo cards for a truncated version of *Hamlet*. The winning audience member gets to play Laertes in the last
scene.

JULIUS CAESAR

Shakespeare at the Tobacco Factory. Tobacco Fac-
tory, Bristol, 18 February–21 March.
http://sattf.org.uk
Director: Andrew Hilton
Mark Antony: Alan Raglan
Brutus: Leo Wringer
Julius Caesar: Simon Armstrong

Royal Shakespeare Company. Courtyard Theatre,
Stratford-upon-Avon, 26 May–2 October.
www.rsc.org.uk
Director: Lucy Bailey
Julius Caesar: Greg Hicks
Brutus: Sam Troughton
Mark Antony: Darrell D'Silva

Lazarus Theatre. The Blue Elephant Theatre,
London, 13 October–7 November.
www.freewebs.com/lazarustheatrecompany
Director: Ricky Dukes

Adaptation
Caesar
Instant Classics. Broadway Studio Theatre, Cat-
ford, 4 February–1 March.
www.broadwaytheatre.org.uk
Playwright: Charles Marowitz
Director: David Cottis.

The Roman Tragedies
Toneelgroep Amsterdam. Barbican BITE 09,
20–22 November.
www.toneelgroepamsterdam.com
Director: Ivo van Hove
Translator: Tom Kleijn
Coriolanus, *Julius Caesar* and *Antony and Cleopatra* adapted and played consecutively without an
interval in a six-hour epic.

KING LEAR

Young Vic, in association with Headlong The-
atre and Liverpool Everyman. Young Vic, 4
February–28 March. Transfer from Liverpool
Everyman.
Director: Rupert Goold
King Lear: Pete Postlethwaite

Adaptation
The Cordelia Dream
Royal Shakespeare Company. Wilton's Music Hall,
London, 11 December–10 January 2009.
www.rsc.org.uk
Playwright: Marina Carr
Director: Selina Cartmell
Two-hander with echoes of *King Lear*.

LOVE'S LABOUR'S LOST

Shakespeare's Globe, London, 28 September–
10 October, and tour.
www.shakespeares-globe.org
Director: Dominic Dromgoole

MACBETH

Royal Exchange Theatre Company, Manchester.
25 February–11 April.
www.royalexchange.co.uk
Director: Michael Dunster
Macbeth: Nicholas Gleaves
Lady Macbeth: Hilary Maclean

The Faction. Brockley Jack Pub, London,
10 March–4 April.
www.thefaction.org.uk
Director and Lady Macbeth: Mark Leipacher
All-male ensemble.

Love & Madness. Riverside Studios, 21 May–
22 July.
www.loveandmadness.org
Director: Neil Sheppeck
Macbeth: Will Beer
Lady Macbeth: Lucia McAnespie

Bard in the Botanics. Glasgow Botanic Gardens.
17 July–1 August.

www.bardinthebotanics.co.uk
Director: Jennifer Dick
Macbeth: Paul Cunningham
Lady Macbeth: Beth Marshall

Hull Truck Theatre Company. Hull Truck Theatre, Hull, 12–28 November.
www.hulltruck.co.uk
Director: Gareth Tudor Price

Adaptation
King MacBeth
Reveal Theatre. Lyceum Theatre, Crewe, 4–5 March, and tour.
www.revealtheatre.co.uk
Playwright: Deborah McAndrew
Using historical sources to produce a positive portrayal of Macbeth.

National Theatre. Cottesloe Theatre, London, 10–20 February, and tour.
www.nationaltheatre.org.uk
Director: Carl Heap
65-minute production for younger audiences.

Macbeth: Who Is That Bloodied Man?
Biuro Podrózy, Poland. Belfast Festival at Queen's. 22–31 October.
www.teatrbiuropodrozy.ipoznan.pl

MacDeath or, What's in a Name
Landor Theatre, London, 28 May–9 June.
www.landortheatre.co.uk
Playwright: Delores Tremens
Director: Rob McWhir
Comic adaptation.

Max and Beth
YPT Urban Arts. The Egg, Bath, 24–25 July; Tobacco Factory 1 August; Edinburgh Festival 9–15 August.
Debut play by UK rapper Lowkey.

Opera
Edinburgh Festival Chorus and BBC Scottish Symphony Orchestra. Usher Hall, Edinburgh Festival, 23 August.
Composer: Verdi

MEASURE FOR MEASURE

Lights of London Productions. Upstairs at the Old Blue Last and the Rose Theatre, London, 24 January–7 February.
www.lightsoflondonproductions.co.uk
Director: Darrie Gardner

Theatre Royal Plymouth. Yvonne Arnaud Theatre, Guildford, 24–8 March and on tour.
www.theatreroyal.com
Director: Jamie Glover
Duke: Alistair McGowan
Isabella: Emma Lowndes

THE MERCHANT OF VENICE

Propeller Acting Company. Liverpool Playhouse, 30–1 January and on tour.
www.propeller.org.uk
Director: Edward Hall
Shylock: Richard Clothier
All-male production with a prison setting.

The Festival Players. UK tour 6 June–30 August.
www.thefestivalplayers.co.uk
Director: Michael Dyer

Adaptation
Taiwan Bangzi Theatre Company at British Shakespeare Association Conference, Greenwood Theatre, King's College, London, 11 September.
Director: Po Shen Lu
Chinese-style opera production.

THE MERRY WIVES OF WINDSOR

Adaptation
The Merry Wives of Wedza
The Oval House, London, 30 June.
www.ovalhouse.com
Playwright: Sarah Norman
Set in rural Zimbabwe. Part of the First Bites work-in-progress season.

Opera
Falstaff
Glyndebourne Opera, 4–11 July.
www.glyndebourne.com
Director: Richard Jones
Composer: Verdi

A MIDSUMMER NIGHT'S DREAM

Royal Shakespeare Company. Novello Theatre, 20 January–7 February. Stratford transfer.
www.rsc.org.uk
Director: Gregory Doran

Propeller Acting Company. Liverpool Playhouse, 30–1 January and on tour.
www.propeller.org.uk
Director: Edward Hall
All-male production.

Middle Temple Hall, London, 5 May and broadcast on Radio 3.
Director: Tim Carroll
Includes incidental music by Mendelssohn.

British Shakespeare Company. Rose Theatre, Kingston, 5–6 June and tour to August.
www.britishshakespearecompany.com
Director: R. J. Williamson

Shakespeare's Globe Touring Company. City Museum, Portsmouth, 19–21 June and on tour.
www.shakespeares-globe.org
Director: Raz Shaw

Illyria Theatre Company. UK tour June–August.
www.illyria.uk.com

Chapterhouse Theatre Company. UK tour June–August.
www.chapterhouse.org

Ballet
Independent Ballet Wales. UK tour May–June.
www.welshballet.co.uk
Director: Darius James
Composer: Felix Mendelssohn

The Dream
Birmingham Royal Ballet. The Lowry, Salford, 1–2 July.
www.brb.org.uk
Choreography: Frederick Ashton
Composer: Felix Mendelssohn

Opera
Benjamin Britten International Opera School. Royal College of Music, Britten Theatre, 29 June–4 July.
Director: Ian Judge
Composer: Benjamin Britten

The Fairy Queen
Glyndebourne Opera, June; Royal Albert Hall, 21 July.
www.glyndebourne.com
Director: Jonathan Kent
Composer: Henry Purcell
Bottom: Desmond Barritt

MUCH ADO ABOUT NOTHING

New Shakespeare Company. Regent's Park Open Air Theatre, 1–27 June.
http://openairtheatre.org
Director: Timothy Sheader
Beatrice: Samantha Spiro
Benedick: Sean Campion

Antic Disposition. St Stephen's Church, London, 25 June–19 July.
www.anticdisposition.co.uk
Director: Ben Horslen

British Shakespeare Company. Gawsworth Hall Open Air Shakespeare Festival, 3 July and tour to August.
www.britishshakespearecompany.com
Director: R. J. Williamson

MDCC Theatre Company. Forge Mill Needle Museum, Redditch, 27–28 June and tour to August.
www.mdcctheatre.com
Director: Tim Ward

Veni Vidi Theatre Company. Lauderdale House, London, 26–8 August.
www.venividitheatre.com
Director: Natalie-Anne Downs

OTHELLO

Royal Shakespeare Company. Warwick Arts Centre, 30 January–7 February; Hackney Empire, 10–14 February and on tour.
www.rsc.org.uk
Director: Kathryn Hunter
Othello: Patrice Naiambana
Iago: Michael Gould

Northern Broadsides and West Yorkshire Playhouse. West Yorkshire Playhouse, Leeds, 18 February–14 March, and tour.
www.northern-broadsides.co.uk
Director: Barrie Rutter
Othello: Lenny Henry
Iago: Conrad Nelson

Creation Theatre Company. New Road Baptist Church, Oxford, 17 April–30 May.
www.creationtheatre.co.uk
Director: Charlotte Conquest

Mad Dogs & Englishmen Theatre Company. Tour 1 August–11 September.
www.mad-dogs.org.uk

Icarus Theatre Company. Tour 18 September–25 November.
www.icarustheatre.org
Director: Max Lewendel

Citizens Theatre, Glasgow. 23 October–14 November.
www.citz.co.uk
Director: Guy Hollands
Othello: Jude Akawudike
Iago: Andy Clark

Opera
Otello
Birmingham Opera Company. Argyle Works, Birmingham. 5–7 December.
www.birminghamopera.org.uk
Composer: Verdi

Community outreach project with a cast of over 250 actors, singers and dancers.

Otello
London Symphony Orchestra. Barbican, London, 3–6 December.
http://lso.co.uk
Composer: Verdi

PERICLES

Blotto Theatre. Greenwich Playhouse, Greenwich, London, 24 February–22 March.
www.blottotheatre.co.uk
Director: Benjamin Henson
A company of three actors.

RICHARD III

Bute Theatre, Cardiff, March–April.
Director: Iqbal Khan
Richard III: Tom Cullen

Oddsocks Theatre Company. Tour 19 June–27 August.
www.oddsocks.co.uk

Bard in the Botanics. Glasgow Botanic Gardens. 18 July–1 August.
www.bardinthebotanics.co.uk
Director: Gordon Barr
Ninety-minute version played by three actors.

Adaptation
African Company Presents Richard III
Greenwich Theatre, London, 17–21 February.
www.greenwichtheatre.org.uk
Playwright: Carlyle Brown
Set in New York in 1821, two competing theatre companies perform *Richard III*.

ROMEO AND JULIET

Royal Shakespeare Company. The Courtyard Theatre, Stratford-upon-Avon, 27 November 2008–24 January 2009.
www.rsc.org.uk
Director: Neil Bartlett

Shakespeare's Globe, 30 April–23 August.
www.shakespeares-globe.org
Director: Dominic Dromgoole
Juliet: Ellie Kendrick
Mercutio: Phil Cumbus
Romeo: Adetomiwa Edun

Iris Theatre. St Paul's Church Gardens, Covent Garden, 29 May–13 June.
www.iristheatre.com
Director: Dan Winder
Promenade performance.

Chapterhouse Theatre Company. Tour 13 June–31 August.
www.chapterhouse.org

Oxford Shakespeare Company. Gray's Inn, London, 16–19 June and tour to 22 August.
www.oxfordshakespearecompany.co.uk

Exeter Northcott and the Ludlow Festival. Ludlow Castle, 22 June–4 July; Rougemont Gardens, Exeter, 17 July–9 August.
www.exeternorthcott.co.uk
Director: Kate Saxon

Adaptation
Opening Night of the Living Dead
Obstacle Productions. C Cubed, Edinburgh, 6–31 August.
www.obstacleproductions.co.uk
A performance of *Romeo and Juliet* is interrupted by zombies.

People's Romeo
Tara Arts. Tara Studio, London, 16–18 April.
www.tara-arts.com
Director: Mukul Ahmed
Inspired by Bangladeshi theatre and performed in English and Bengali.

Imperial Productions. Baron's Court Theatre, London, 2–13 June.
www.imperialproductions.org
Director: David Phipps-Davis
Set in a girl's school where pupils plan to stage a secret production.

Compagnie Papierthéâtre. Little Angel Theatre, 5 November.
Playwright: Edward Gordon Craig
Suspense London Puppetry Festival.

Romeo and Juliet Docklands
Admiration Theatre Company. Space Theatre, London, 29 January–14 February.
www.admirationtheatre.com
Director: John Seaforth
Set in contemporary Docklands with a cast of six.

Shakespeare Goes Bollywood – Popo Gigi
Jolliwood Productions. Ashcroft Theatre, London, 15–26 September.
Playwright: Sam Sterling
Director: Anthony Shrubsall
Musical about an actor staging a Bollywood-inspired *Romeo and Juliet*.

West Side Story
Ambassador Theatre Group. Donald Gordon Theatre, Cardiff, 6–17 January and tour, August–June 2009.
Choreographer: Joey McKneely
West Side Story 50th anniversary production.

Ballet
Northern Ballet Theatre. Sadler's Wells, 21–23 May.
http://northernballet.com
Choreography: Kenneth MacMillan
Director: Christopher Gable

Moscow City Ballet. Derngate Theatre, Northampton, 19–21 January and tour.
Composer: Sergei Prokofiev
Choreography: Victor Smirnov Golovanog

Mariinsky Ballet. Royal Opera House, 3–6 August.
www.mariinsky.ru
Composer: Sergei Prokofiev
Choreography: Leonid Lavrovsky

THE TAMING OF THE SHREW

Royal Shakespeare Company. Novello Theatre, 17 February–7 March. Stratford transfer.
www.rsc.org.uk

Director: Conall Morrison

Bard in the Botanics. Glasgow Botanic Gardens, 26 June–11 July.
www.bardinthebotanics.co.uk
Director: Gordon Barr

Crescent Theatre Company. Tour 30 June–19 July.
www.crescent-theatre.co.uk

Rain or Shine Theatre Company. Tour 2 July–31 August.
www.rainorshine.co.uk

THE TEMPEST

Royal Shakespeare Company in association with Baxter Theatre Company, South Africa. Courtyard Theatre, Stratford-upon-Avon, 18 February–14 March, and tour.
www.rsc.org.uk
Director: Janice Honeyman
Prospero: Antony Sher

Platform4. Dorchester Arts at Thomas Hardy School, 18–19 September and tour until 11 November.
www.platform4.org
Director: Simon Plumridge
A company of three, doubling Miranda and Ariel, and Ferdinand and Caliban.

Adaptation
Caliban's Island
Somesuch Theatre Company. Old Joint Stock Theatre, Birmingham, 16 May.
www.oldjointstocktheatre.co.uk
Caliban, abandoned on the island, recounts the story from his perspective.

Lanternfish Theatre Company. Salisbury Playhouse, Salisbury, 12–14 March, and UK tour February–April.
www.lanternfish.org.uk
Adaptor: Anthony Peters

Tempest in a Teacup
Side By Side Theatre Company. Augustine's, Edinburgh, 11–15 August.

www.sidebysidetheatre.co.uk
Director and Choreographer: Susan Wallin
Includes mime and dance. Performed by actors with learning difficulties.

The Tempest: Re-imagined for Everyone Aged Six and Over
New Shakespeare Company. Regent's Park, London, 5–28 June.
http://openairtheatre.org
Director: Liam Steel
Adapted for children, including a 20-minute prologue.

A Tempest – Such Signs as Dreams are Made On . . .
Krazy Kat Theatre Company. Warwick Arts Centre, Coventry, 1–2 November and tour.
www.krazykattheatre.co.uk
Adaptor: Nick Wood
Director: Caroline Parker
Designed for 8–11-year olds and incorporating signing for deaf/hard-of-hearing children.

Opera
Prospero
Llandudno Festival of Music and the Arts, Venue Cwmry, Llandudno, 11 July and Welsh tour.
Composer: Owain Llwyd
Libretto: Peredur Davies and Claire Jones
Director: Annabel Chalk
Opera based on the artist Rex Whistler's designs for the 1935 Stratford production of *The Tempest*.

TIMON OF ATHENS

Timon
Cogs Theatre. Barons Court Theatre, London, 1–12 September.
www.cogstheatre.com
Director: Matt Beresford

TITUS ANDRONICUS

Derby Shakespeare Theatre Company. Guildhall, Derby, 10–14 November.
www.derbyshakespeare.org.uk
Director: Chris Scott

TROILUS AND CRESSIDA

Shakespeare's Globe. 20 July–20 September.
www.shakespeares-globe.org
Director: Matthew Dunster
Pandarus: Matthew Kelly

TWELFTH NIGHT

Donmar at Wyndham's Theatre. Wyndham's Theatre, London, 5 December–7 March 2009.
www.donmarwarehouse.com
Director: Michael Grandage
Malvolio: Derek Jacobi

Shochiku Grand Kabuki. Barbican Theatre, 24–28 March.
Director: Yukio Ninagawa
Samurai-themed production in Japanese.

Unicorn Ensemble. Unicorn Theatre, 13 May–7 June.
www.unicorntheatre.com
Director: Rosamunde Hutt
Viola/Sebastian: John Cockerill
Sir Toby Belch: Samantha Adams

Creation Theatre Company. Said Business School, Oxford, 14 July–5 September.
www.creationtheatre.co.uk
Director: Heather Davies

Lord Chamberlain's Men. Ham House, Surrey, 2 August and on tour.
www.tlcm.co.uk
Director: Andrew Normington
All-male production.

The Faction. Tabard, 22 September–10 October; Brockley Jack, 13–24 October.
www.thefaction.org.uk
Director: Mark Leipacher

The Royal Shakespeare Company. Courtyard, Stratford-upon-Avon, 21 October–21 November; Duke of York's, London, 22 December–27 February 2010.
www.rsc.org.uk
Director: Gregory Doran

Malvolio: Richard Wilson
Sir Toby Belch: Richard McCabe
Viola: Nancy Carroll

THE TWO GENTLEMEN OF VERONA

Guildford Shakespeare Company. Guildford Castle Grounds, Guildford, 12–27 June.
www.guildford-shakespeare-company.co.uk
Director: Joanna Read

C Company. Bridewell Theatre, London, 23 June–10 July.
www.ccompany.cc
Director: Aileen Gonsalves
45-minute version, played at lunchtimes.

Adaptation
Vakomana Viviri ve Zimbabwe
Two Gents Productions. Arena Theatre, Wolverhampton, 6 October.
Director: Arne Pohlmeier
Fifteen roles played by two actors.

THE WINTER'S TALE

Shakespeare at the Tobacco Factory. Tobacco Factory, Bristol, 1 April–2 May.
http://sattf.org.uk
Director: Andrew Hilton
Leontes: John Mackay
Hermione and Perdita: Lisa Kay

The Royal Shakespeare Company. Courtyard, Stratford-upon-Avon, 9 April–3 October.
www.rsc.org.uk
Director: David Farr
Leontes: Greg Hicks
Autolycus: Brian Doherty
Hermione: Kelly Hunter

Theatre Delicatessen. Cavendish Gate, Theatre Delicatessen, 16 April–16 May.
www.theatredelicatessen.co.uk
Director: Jessica Brewster

The Bridge Project. Old Vic, London, 9 June–
15 August.
Director: Sam Mendes
Leontes: Simon Russell Beale
Autolycus: Ethan Hawke
A company combining American and British
actors.

Nuffield Theatre, Southampton with Schtanhaus
and Headlong Theatre, 10–26 September and
on tour.
www.nuffieldtheatre.co.uk
Director: Simon Godwin

POEMS AND APOCRYPHA

The Rape of Lucrece
British Shakespeare Company. Rose Theatre, Bankside, London, 14 December, and
tour.
www.britishshakespearecompany.com;
www.therapeoflucrece.co.uk
Performer: Gerard Logan
Director: Gareth Armstrong

Venus & Adonis
Transition Opera Company. Wilton's Music Hall,
London, 11–14 February.
www.transitionopera.com
Composer: John Blow
Director: Netia Jones

MISCELLANEOUS

The Dresser
Geoffrey Whitworth Theatre, Dartford, 7–14
February.
www.thegwt.org.uk
Playwright: Ronald Harwood
Director: Vanessa Coatz

For All Time
Theatre by the Lake, Keswick, 23 July–
7 November.
www.theatrebythelake.co.uk
Playwright: Rick Thomas

Director: Stefan Escreet
Biodrama, focusing on Shakespeare and Fletcher's
collaboration on *The Two Noble Kinsmen*.

Seven Ages
Kepow Theatre Company. Tristan Bates Theatre,
London, 9–28 November.
www.kevintomlinson.co.uk
Performer: Kevin Tomlinson
Improvised theatre combining Shakespeare with
input from the audience.

Richard
La Compagnie des Chemins de Terre. The Brew-
ery, Bristol, 5 September.
http://www.cdcterre.be
A spoof academic lecture interspersed with extracts
from *Hamlet*, *Romeo and Juliet*, and *Richard III*.

Such Stuff As Dreams are Made
Mustardseed Theatre Company. Etcetera Theatre,
London, 23–28 June.
www.mustardseedtheatrecompany.co.uk
Prospero summons characters from the works of
Shakespeare.

The Man Who Was Hamlet
Vital Theatre Company. The Maltings, St Albans,
29 January and tour.
www.georgedillon.com
Playwright: George Dillon
Suggests the real author of *Hamlet* was Edward de
Vere.

Time Out of Joint
Heart Productions. C SoCo Venue, Edinburgh, 5–
31 August.
www.heartproductions.net
Playwright: Frank Bramwell
Director: Arnaud Mugglestone
A love story between Shakespeare, Katherine
Hamnet and the Dark Lady.

The Tragedian Trilogy
Prodigal Theatre. Theatre Royal, Brighton, 3 May,
and tour.
www.prodigaltheatre.co.uk
One-man show about the life of Edmund Kean.

THE YEAR'S CONTRIBUTION TO
SHAKESPEARE STUDIES

1. CRITICAL STUDIES
reviewed by JULIE SANDERS

It might seem somewhat perverse of me to open with a discussion of a study that is in most respects *not* about Shakespeare, but Andrew Gurr's *Shakespeare's Opposites*, which offers a 'biography' of the Admiral's Company that played at the Rose and at the Fortune, rival playhouses to those used by Shakespeare's King's Men, is in some sense rich proof of Emma Smith's point in another essay this year (on 'Shakespeare and Early Modern Tragedy' in *The Cambridge Companion to English Renaissance Tragedy*, ed. Emma Smith and Garrett A. Sullivan, Jr) that Shakespeare is always the 'elephant in the room' (p. 132) when talking about early modern drama in its wider sense.

Gurr has of course written many of the seminal works of recent decades on the early modern playhouse and its playing and staging practices. *Shakespeare's Opposites* is an elegant disquisition on one particular company, echoing in its focus the move of recent repertory studies to turn our attention to the company and its repertory as categories for understanding. Gurr draws our attention with consummate skill to the ways in which the Admiral's Company dealt with the 'daily routine of performing a different play each day to much the same body of customers', facing 'the fact that the same familiar faces had to appear on stage each playing a different role every afternoon' (p. 1). Thinking in particular through the charismatic and entrepreneurial performances of Edward Alleyn (contemporary responses and accounts indicate as much), Gurr explores how doubling and also knowing use of

disguise became a positive tactic or strategy in the company's approach to this practical dilemma. Leads were constantly given roles involving quick-change disguises and audiences in turn became well trained in the art of noticing and understanding these swift transformations of identity and costume. Gurr's stress is very much on novelty and innovation within the Admiral's Company's repertoire; other innovations made by the company included the introduction of contemporary London as a setting for plays, an approach inaugurated by William Houghton's *Englishmen for My Money*. What is brilliant about this book is that it connects with the stage in such real ways, with the fragmentary records of 'theatrical brilliance' rather than just linguistic pyrotechnics on the page, and in this way it does offer new modes for understanding and reabsorbing Shakespeare (not least as a collaborative and entrepreneurial author) within the wider early modern context. In this respect, Gurr's book connects in important ways with Emma Smith's aforementioned essay which speaks about the problematic ways in which institutional culture has caused the separation of Shakespeare and his plays from their time of production, as if texts like *Hamlet* were somehow produced *sui generis* rather than from within the complexities of the revenge drama tradition (p. 132). Smith's essay, which focuses in on issues of form, character and tone, demonstrates the relationship of *Hamlet* to *The Spanish Tragedy* and the kinships of *Othello* and *Macbeth* with domestic tragedy. In a striking comparison of

Webster's *The Duchess of Malfi* and in particular its deployment of soliloquy, she also draws out differences between Shakespeare's reputation for soliloquies that confide and build shared intimacies with audiences and Webster's 'alienating tragic aesthetic' (p. 141), which means that the Duchess herself conceals as much as she reveals in these peculiar moments of 'aloneness' on the stage. Nevertheless, Smith makes the crucial point that this version of Shakespeare is itself only partial and does not account for the radical dissonances of early tragedies like *Titus Andronicus*, which she explores partly through the lens of modern performances and interpretations. This is a smart-thinking essay which does important work in terms of repositioning Shakespeare's plays 'in dialogue, forward and back, with other contemporary tragedians' (p. 134). Gurr's book, too, I think achieves this 'repositioning' dialogue as we are forced, by studying his 'opposites' and rivals, to understand Shakespeare from within the societal contexts of early modern crowds, plague and touring regimes, and commercial enterprise. There is, in the process, a superb analysis of the collaborative writing practice (pp. 104–6) as well as expert analysis of the archaeological finds from early modern theatre sites and what they might tell us about the staging practices and conditions within which Shakespeare worked and wrote.

Among the archaeological residue that Gurr trains his lens upon is foodstuffs of various kinds: hazelnut shells, walnut shells, the seeds of raspberries and sloes, various grains, plums, figs and cherries (p. 127). It suggests, he notes, early modern playgoing as a version of the picnic. These kinds of details would surely be grist to the particular mill of the contributors to Joan Fitzpatrick's edited collection *Renaissance Food from Rabelais to Shakespeare*. The editor herself contributes an essay on 'Shakespeare's Foods from Apples to Walrus' examining in detail Caliban's references to his dining habits in *The Tempest* and in the process exploring the status of wild and introduced fruits in the early modern diet. Diane Purkiss contributes a particularly welcome essay to the same volume on 'Bakers and the Poor in Early Modern England', offering a material

culture of bread which she begins with a quotation from *Henry V*. Purkiss's investment in the labour and craft of breadmaking in this essay is palpable and persuasive.

If Andrew Gurr found scholarly raw material residing in the residue and detritus of the Rose excavations, so too does Elizabeth Williamson who starts her book *The Materiality of Religion in Early Modern English Drama* with the very tangible example of a bone rosary found during the same theatre excavations (and now in the Museum of London collection). This object may constitute evidence of the continuing practice of Catholicism after the Reformation or be an example of a stage property. Rosaries were officially banned from the 1540s onwards but would still have been found in the context of private homes and chapels. Middleton certainly has several references to characters and their 'beads' (Williamson mentions *Your Five Gallants* in 1607 where two young lovers exchange rosary beads as loaded love token). Williamson uses the object as a springboard for her own ruminations on early modern theatre's engagement with 'the shifting status of religious objects' at this time (p. 2) and on the ways in which worship was dramatized on the Elizabethan stage. Building on previous work on stage properties, not least by Natasha Korda and Jonathan Gil Harris, and Andrew Sofer, Williamson makes the fascinating observation that the 1620s–40s are the high watermark of the use of traditional religious objects on stage. It would be interesting to pause longer to consider the ramifications of this statement; what are the impacts of Laudianism on this? To what extent was this a marker of a more public form of tolerance of Catholic ritual and practice under the influence of Henrietta Maria's theological leanings and practices at Somerset House and elsewhere? Williamson is more interested in a wider question, perhaps, about the 'basic sympathy' as she sees it between theatre and religion (p. 12) and here she makes useful recourse to the work of Anthony Dawson and Peter Lake among others. Her research brings her to conclude that there is 'compelling evidence for the claim that the binaries such as Catholic/Protestant or even sacred/secular were far less meaningful during this period than critics have previously supposed' (p. 31). This is a big, bold assertion and one which studies by Adrian Streete among others (discussed later) might find themselves in serious dispute with, but where I found real strengths in Williamson's approach was in her engagement with theatre as a working, flexible form and her acknowledgement of its capacity to engage with theological issues in a 'complex, and highly adaptable' way (p. 31).

In specific chapters, Williamson unpacks the particular resonances of tomb properties, highlighting in the process important inheritances from medieval cycle plays and 'shared theatrical technologies' (p. 35) which are themselves evidence that the English Reformation did not effect some clean or complete break with the past and its practices, cultural or religious. Props in her story have genuine agency, resisting period labels like 'medieval' or 'early modern' by the very nature of their operations; stage objects for her function as 'traces of a continuous set of cultural and theatrical practices' (p. 36). In her discussion of tomb scenes, several Shakespeare plays feature (though again in helpful conversation with other early modern drama): *Romeo and Juliet*, *Much Ado About Nothing*, *Pericles* (in the latter she traces a 'resurrection motif', p. 63). Elsewhere Williamson considers various 'stagings of the cross' in plays as diverse as *The Knight of Malta* and *The White Devil*. I enjoyed her interweaving of stage and real-life examples; this chapter, for instance, took us as readers inside Henrietta Maria's private chapel but also made a direct link to the staged representations of Catholic ritual practice in the observation that 'As patron of the Queen's Men, [the Queen Consort] oversaw the revival of *The White Devil* at the Cockpit in 1630–31' (p. 147). The time-span as well as the historical detail of this study is consistently impressive.

A subsequent chapter focuses on the religious book as property, examining prayer scenes in both *Hamlet* and *Richard III* in the process. Interestingly, Williamson turns to later performance history for some of her 'evidence' here: 'Although we know relatively little about the actual book properties used in the early modern theatre, we do have evidence that such properties played an important role in Shakespearian performances during subsequent centuries as actors continued to experiment with the implications of bringing sacred books on stage' (p. 155). The methodology here is perhaps open to question but the discussion that follows of particular scenes involving characters reading books on stage (for example, Ophelia: 'Nymph in thy orisons be all my sins remembered' 3.1.88–9) is engaging. Ophelia's scene is of course 'staged' by her father and Claudius and another famous Shakespearian scene with a prayer book is equally artificially constructed: Richard III before his people at 3.7. Williamson invites us to reflect on this 'pointed' use of the prayer book as prop by Shakespeare at this time (p. 163). The shock value of the sacred book on stage should not be underestimated and Marlowe's plays prove a particularly rich repository of shock in this regard. Williamson discusses the burning of the Qu'ran on stage in part 2 of *Tamburlaine* but notes that the book would have been an 'unfamiliar icon of Islamic culture' (p. 181) at the time of first performances. It was, she says, 'an example of the kind of sacred text that could be burned on stage without exciting controversy' (p. 181), a suggestion that registers its own kind of shock today; she accords to Marlowe in the process a radical kind of atheism that is reflected in his treatment of such properties on the stage. A real strength of Williamson's study is the range and the genuine depth of knowledge she brings to the Caroline portions of the discussion; in this case she notes that by the 1620s and 1630s references to the Qu'ran in public theatre contexts had become 'both more casual and more overtly negative' (p. 188). Elsewhere she weaves Brome, Shirley and others effortlessly into the conversation, making the Caroline cultural moment a central part of discussions rather than a brief add-on as it occasionally suffers from being.

In her coda, Williamson returns to the familiar Greenblattian theme of the 'circulation of stage objects' and their stage afterlives. She draws, as many other scholars of early modern stage properties have done, on the propensity in cognate disciplines towards the 'cultural biography of things'

(p. 201), citing the work of Igor Kopytoff in particular. Othello's handkerchief proves a particularly potent facilitating example as Williamson demonstrates the ways in which objects accrue meaning 'both affective and economic' (p. 205). She builds to a closing discussion of theatre 'relics' and the particular resonance of Shakespearian objects and traces in this context. Relics are in the end valued, she states, for the stories they tell; Williamson's own study is a story well told and one which I have returned to on several occasions this year to test and re-examine its arguments and case-studies.

PHILOSOPHIZING SHAKESPEARE

If a number of the books considered thus far attend to a material Shakespeare there has also been a significant cluster of work this year around the contact zone between Shakespeare and philosophy and it is to these that I now turn.

Shakespeare and Moral Agency is a stimulating collection which, as one referee's report on the back cover suggests, offers a fresh perspective, post-Bradley as it were, on character criticism through the frame of moral philosophy; this in many respects means it acts as a complement to Continuum's own series on Character Studies which I reviewed last year (*Shakespeare Survey 63*).

The editor Michael Bristol, who, judging by the deference of contributors to his specialist knowledge and influence in this area, was the perfect choice for the role, offers in his introduction a spirited defence of character criticism in the context of what he terms 'vernacular criticism', that is to say engaging with Shakespearian characters 'using the same means that one would use to engage in familiar conversations with actual people' (p. 1). Bristol is not advocating a complete rejection of the historicist or cultural materialist criticism that has dominated in recent decades but suggests that the pursuit of these scholarly modes ought not to close off the opportunity for ethical and cognitive speculation in relation to Shakespeare's canon and its characters and their actions. Bristol is particularly interested in agency and the capacity for action in individuals and suggests

that 'Shakespeare's characters inhabit a contingent world where they are faced with novel, unpredictable, and unprecedented situations that require evaluation and judgement' (p. 5).

A first section on 'The Agency of Agents' includes an essay by Hugh Grady which also suggests the need for a valid critical alternative to the historicist mode, while acknowledging the tendency of post-structuralism to neglect agency as a category. Grady's observation that 'Typically, agency for major Shakespearian characters is mixed or "mediated"' (p. 16) finds kinship with a later essay in the volume by Sharon O'Dair which insists on the social context for individual action. Whereas O'Dair focuses her discussion on *Macbeth* as a particular kind of political and socio-political analysis, Grady's essay concentrates on plays from Shakespeare's so-called 'Machiavellian moment', in particular *Julius Caesar*. It's interesting to reflect overall on the plays that attract most attention in the context of this polyvocal discussion of moral agency; the Roman plays are clearly one important cluster, but so too are what used to be called the 'Problem Plays' – several essays make recourse to *Measure for Measure* or *The Merchant of Venice*, and indeed to that romance that is also so often deemed a problematic play to unpack and to categorize, *The Winter's Tale*. Philosophical Shakespeare appears in this way to have its own working canon or repertoire of texts.

James Knapp, via brief recourse to cognitive psychology, considers the process that characters go through in the act of making ethical decisions. Discussions of Leontes and Prince Hal lead him to conclude that 'Shakespeare's plays allow us to reflect on the way particular experiences arouse passion, generate moral conviction and complicate moral agency' (p. 39). In an extremely thought-provoking essay that made welcome attempts to bridge the world of cognitive linguistics and stylistics with more conventional literary critical close reading practices, Keira Travis explores the ethics of wordplay in Shakespeare's mature tragedies. She unpacks 'intricate networks of wordplay' (p. 43) that work across characterizations and allow characters to be understood contrapuntally

(Travis builds here explicitly on previous work by Margreta de Grazia). I was particularly struck by her interest in how Shakespeare's wordplay functions to bring 'dead' or 'stale' metaphors back to life, reviving in a dramatic context the figurative root of words like 'explain' or 'unpack' (she offers a particularly cogent analysis of Hamlet's soliloquizing in the process).

Sharon O'Dair's previously mentioned essay, which deploys important findings from interactionist sociology, opens the second section on 'Social Norms'. I appreciated her insistence (sometimes lacking elsewhere in the collection) on the potential differences between read and performed Shakespeares. Katherine R. Finin in her essay on ethical questions in *Measure for Measure* and *The Merchant of Venice* pays complementary attention to the effects of soliloquy in drawing us into the ethical dilemmas of characters like Isabella. She also draws on anthropological distinctions between 'thick' and 'thin' relationships – where 'thick' relations would be close or intimate belongings such as family – to think about ethics in terms of the 'spaces between people'. The gaps and distances or indeed the dangerous proximities between different characters seem particularly compelling in her chosen texts, where Isabella struggles to choose between a brother's life and her virginity and her faith, or where Portia finds herself overseeing the 'pound of flesh' trial on behalf of ostensible strangers but fully in the knowledge that everything, emotionally and ethically, is at stake. I was drawn most deeply to this central cluster of essays, perhaps revealing my own leanings towards the sociological rather than the more purely philosophical discussions. Naomi Conn Leibler offers a suggestive discussion of old age and the function of memory in relation to *King Lear* that manages to be as astute on the deterioration of the mind in the ageing process as it is about the play *per se*. I was struck by her suggestion that a twenty-first-century empathy towards old age is not to be found in the Shakespearian canon, where on the whole the reminiscences of old men are given very short shrift (she cites the 'Chimes at Midnight' sequence of *2 Henry IV* as well as *Lear* itself to make this claim).

Scholars from the discipline of Philosophy, including Tzachi Zamir and Gregory Currie, contribute essays to the third section on 'Moral Characters'. Mustapha Fahmi considers questions of perspective in relation to ethical thinking; he too notes the 'contrapuntal' tendency in Shakespeare where an opposite perspective to one character's particular habit of thought is often proffered. Like O'Dair he sees the creation of individual identity as a profoundly social act: 'We become selves... through a continuous exchange with other people, real or imagined, especially those whose views matter to us, whether they are friends or enemies' (p. 132). The sense that Shakespeare's plays are a crucial part of this exchange is a view shared by all of the contributors to this collection and Fahmi also manages to suggest in the process the profoundly social operations of drama as a form. His notion of 'quoting the enemy' reminded me a great deal of earlier responses to Shakespeare, and indeed to tragedy, by anthropologists like René Girard, which paid attention to Shakespeare's predilection towards the trope of 'enemy brothers' like Hal and Hostpur in the construction of his plays; this was, I see in retrospect, an earlier version of the 'contrapuntal' argument so beautifully crafted by de Grazia and which seems to have been so influential for the contributors here. It is a literary scholar, Sarah Coodin, who gets the last word, however, in this thought-provoking collection; she asks what it actually means to 'philosophize Shakespeare' suggesting that 'moral character is a principle that helps us to get closer to Shakespeare's most complex fictional agents' (p. 184). It occurred to me that there was a missing essay that would actually pose the question as to why we even feel the need or imperative to 'get close' to Shakespearian characters in this way but Coodin and her colleagues have without a doubt put moral philosophy firmly on the agenda for Shakespearian scholarship with this collection.

The gauntlet these essays throw down is picked up pretty promptly by a grouping of substantial monographs by Peter Holbrook (*Shakespeare's Individualism*), Hugh Grady (*Shakespeare's Impure Aesthetics*) and Stanley Stewart (*Shakespeare and*

Philosophy). Holbrook's opens with the confident claim that 'Shakespeare is an author for a liberal, individualistic culture' (p. 1) and sets out to prove that Shakespeare's world view was an entirely 'modern' one in that it focused on 'freedom, individuality, self-realization, authenticity' (p. 23) by means of sections on *Hamlet* and selfhood (where he views authenticity as Hamlet's 'keynote'), on 'Shakespeare and evil' (which encompasses discussions of *Titus Andronicus*, *Coriolanus* and *King John*, among other plays), and on the *Sonnets*. Stewart's book is interested in the ways that philosophers attend to Shakespeare in their work and in this respect his study has most in common with the essays in Michael Bristol's collection. Stewart erects a brusque defence of the academy's deep attention to Shakespeare while at the same time (and he shares much with Holbrook and Grady in this respect) offering a trenchant critique of the dominance of new historicism and cultural materialism in recent decades. It's interesting how often those who seek to 'philosophize Shakespeare' do so in tandem with claims to be offering a more 'vernacular' version of him than that created by historicists. I'm not sure how convinced I am by those claims but the debate certainly felt to be hotting up this year in terms of the number of publications from the 'phil-lit' end of the spectrum. Stewart's book, despite its objections to 'Moral posturing by cultural materialists', is actually an exercise in historicism itself, moving as it does from Hume to Derrida, through Enlightenment Shakespeare and Enlightenment Philosophy to its end.

Hugh Grady is more forgiving in his analyses of new historicism and cultural materialism, crediting Stephen Greenblatt in particular with the retention of the aesthetic as 'an important and autonomous category for critical analysis and for understanding the interactions of the work of art and its larger social and cultural context' (p. 2). He later explores in suggestive ways the interaction of new historicism as a practice with aesthetics, citing in particular the work of Patricia Fumerton, which, in his words, fell prey to the 'anthropological lure of turning society itself into an aesthetic space' (p. 38). Grady himself is insistent that the aesthetic is not simply a category of the beautiful but has a political aspect. I found his suggestion that art should be understood as a 'form of labour' (p. 31) particularly compelling. In a cogent analysis of *A Midsummer Night's Dream*, Grady demonstrates the complexity of the 'fictive space' of that play and its mixing of material and fairy worlds. Its self-conscious play is for him a sign of its 'meta-aesthetics' and this is most obviously played out in the space of the forest or the Athenian woods, to be more precise: 'This already complex neo-Spenserian space is itself soon subject to the even more complex aesthetic distancing brought into existence by metadramatic devices, including the play-within-a-play' (p. 57). As a result Grady sees the fairy world less as a mirror of the human than as a consciously aesthetic space of possibility. Another play that engages with the space of the Athenian woodlands is *Timon of Athens*, to which Grady turns in the next chapter. He sees a dialectic between commodification and aestheticization being worked through in this text (*Timon*, he notes, depicts an 'emptied world ruled over by commodification and devoid of other values', p. 133) and connects it directly to the blurred status of early modern commercial theatre in Shakespeare's time. If an important theme to Grady throughout is 'autonomy', it is autonomous space that he finds, at least to an extent, in the playhouses for which Shakespeare laboured and crafted.

The second section of the study concentrates on the aesthetics of death and mourning and opens, unsurprisingly, with a sustained discussion of *Hamlet* as a 'mourning-play' (p. 133). Walter Benjamin is the presiding genius of this chapter (whereas in earlier discussions Theodor Adorno was more to the fore) and in particular his 1928 study *The Origin of German Tragic Drama*, which, in Grady's opinion, provides 'a quarry of ideas little discussed in Anglo-American Shakespeare studies' (p. 134). Grady indicates that 'For readers of Shakespeare, this book presents fresh ideas and analysis about Shakespeare's relation to his historical moment and to the dramatic form in which he wrote his non-comic plays' (p. 135). Re-presenting *Hamlet* through the filter of Benjamin's theories, Grady argues for the play as a '*Trauerspiel*', that is to say as akin to a lesser known category of German seventeenth-century baroque drama that deployed fragmented allegory and aesthetic in potent combination. In the process he unpacks a series of the play's governing metaphors (for example, unweeded gardens) as well as its metadramatic structures. In the final chapter of the study, Grady applies aesthetics to the 'beautiful death', as he suggestively terms it, of *Romeo and Juliet*. I cannot do the subtlety of the arguments full justice here but this is a stimulating and challenging book that places Shakespeare not only within the context of aesthetics *per se* but at the heart of a European philosophical tradition that is sometimes too readily neglected in mainstream publishing trends.

In an alternative version of philosophizing Shakespeare, Adrian Streete's *Protestantism and Drama in Early Modern England* argues for 'a new understanding of the political and philosophical import of Reformed theology in early modern England' (p. 3). Shakespearian scholars will find particular purchase in the chapter focused on *Richard II*, which, intriguingly, Streete also opens by positing a Shakespeare in dialogue with contemporary forms and aesthetics; this play is, he argues, a 'reply' to Marlowe's *Edward II* (p. 162). In an insightful reading, Streete analyses the ways in which *Richard II* 'examines the political as well as the interior difficulties inherent in pursuing an analogue between a secular ruler and Christ', returning in newly informed ways to an older 'King's two bodies' argument. 'Richard can either be a Christlike figure or a man; he cannot be both simultaneously, and this realisation heralds a political breakdown that impacts upon the political utility of the identity of monarchy generally' (p. 163). Streete's readings are acutely tuned to metaphor in the play as he observes how both Bolingbroke and Mowbray's opening lines 'invoke the monarch's temporal contingency' (p. 177), thereby preparing the way for the time-soaked metaphors of Richard's speeches in prison towards the close. In a further chapter that reads Shakespeare in dialogue with contemporary writers and forms, Streete illuminates *The Revenger's Tragedy* by reading it against

Hamlet and vice versa. He finds in *The Revenger's Tragedy* a 'deeply uneasy juxtaposition of images and words' and in striking cross-reading of the symbol of the skull in both plays, he notes: 'In *Hamlet* the audience has to wait until Act V of the drama to get a glimpse at the skull beneath the skin; but in *Revenger's Tragedy* the skull is unapologetically revealed to the audience as the play begins' (p. 210). If Yorick's skull provokes 'philosophical disquisition', says Streete, then Gloriana's is part of a 'complex strategy of memorialisation' which both remembers and echoes those of *Hamlet* and radically diverts them. Once again, then, in Streete's erudite and thoughtful study, we have a deeply intertheatrical and networked account of early modern drama practices, in which Shakespeare is part of a much larger picture, being offered to the reader; this for me was one of the most welcome tropes of this year's published scholarship.

There was a philosophical bent too to Joel Altman's monumental study *The Improbability of 'Othello'*, which applies 'rhetorical anthropology' to a sustained close reading of that play across 375-plus pages with insightful detours into other plays by Shakespeare and contemporaries such as Jonson (there are some striking readings of *Volpone*, for example). Altman has a seductive turn of phrase; Iago is described, for example, as 'the connoisseur of probabilities' (p. 7). But this is also a study acutely attuned to issues of language and performance. Altman explores the ways in which Shakespeare subjects probability to critique in this play and others, presenting the rhetorical discourse of Renaissance humanism as a kind of spiritual backbone to the canon, underwriting as it were Shakespeare's 'poetics' at all times. As well as charting the classical roots of rhetoric, not least through Plato, Cicero and Aristotle, Altman seeks to 'reconstruct the psycholinguistic environment in which Shakespeare wrote his plays' (p. 89). There is admirable attention here to space, both linguistic space and the physical space of the playhouse in which the words are given life. There is a particularly brilliant discussion of the relationship between Iago and his theatrical forebear the medieval Vice (see, for example, pp. 158–9); Iago is, in Altman's terms, 'a Vice morphing into human' (p. 161) and in this way the character on stage mobilizes a whole set of complex associations and cultural memories.

Altman is, it must be said, particularly good on the villains. He offers a brilliant insight into Mosca's function in Jonson's *Volpone* as 'working', 'placing', and 'giving words' (p. 256). In that cluster of phrases he neatly opens up a whole space of interpretation for that play and its self-conscious dramaturgy. What Altman conveys at all times is the way in which characters are 'rhetorically situated' and how that provides keys for unlocking both behaviour and effect. Equally pertinent are his readings of Richard of Gloucester's propensity towards confiding soliloquy as a mode of speech (p. 268). Students of dramatic discourse could do worse than invest in this book as course companion. While Altman is rightly interested in the cognitive and the behavioural he never forgets that these have dramaturgic implications. That awareness of the dramatic moment extends to considerations of the actor when, towards the close of the study, Altman thinks through what it might have been like for Richard Burbage to play the part of the beleaguered Moor of Venice. In a brilliant riff on identity, he notes: 'We know that [Burbage] . . . was informed by the various discourses of his culture in which he occupied, as occasion hailed him, different socially inflected subject positions: joiner's son, backstage bully, common-law litigant, theatrical entrepreneur, actor, company sharer, liveried servant, housekeeper, painter, and limner . . .'. He goes on in particular to think about the craft of the painter in relation to Burbage's onstage creation of the role. This is not an easy book to categorize but I have included it in this section because it struck me as deeply, profoundly even, philosophical in its arguments and in the demands it makes on its richly rewarded readers.

I'd have been interested to see a similar list of cultural identities to that which Altman fashions for Burbage gleaned from the multiple biographies that are the focus of David Bevington's survey of *Shakespeare and Biography*, the latest contribution to Oxford's well-conceived series of 'Oxford Shakespeare Topics'; I suspect it would be highly instructive about the multiple Shakespeares we construct and which are fashioned by the playwright himself through his plays and poetry. Bevington's introduction erects a spirited defence of the relevance of biography for Shakespeare studies and indicates how Shakespeare himself fashioned particular versions of his life story to suit. The importance of Stratford-upon-Avon as a site and place in that narrative is emphasized by Bevington in ways that were suggestive; I wondered as a result if the book might have paid more attention to this construction of Shakespeare through resonant spaces and places. Charles Nicholl's *The Lodger*, an interesting study for me not least due to its resonant and innovative methodologies adopted from archival scholars and cultural geographers (recreating Shakespeare from a room as it were in much the same way that Iain Sinclair and Rachel Lichtenstein reconstructed David Rodinsky's 1960s London life from his abandoned apartment in *Rodinsky's Room*, (Granta, 2000)), might have provided an important bridging text in this regard though as it is it received relatively brusque mention here. What Bevington does attend to with great skill, however, is shifting of biographical emphases across time to the present day. Early chapters are organized thematically under such resonant umbrella terms as 'Sex', 'Politics' and 'Religion'; in the latter Bevington inevitably has to tackle the recent controversy over Shakespeare's presumed Catholicism which he does with considerable grace and even-handedness. We come right up to date with the more 'speculative' biographical writing of Stephen Greenblatt in *Will in the World* (Greenblatt himself contributes an essay this year on imaginative biography to *The New Cambridge Companion to Shakespeare*, which is discussed in the next section) and en route Bevington gives us much to ponder about the 'man from Stratford' and our ongoing obsessions with him. Bevington perhaps needed more space than the format of this series allowed to reflect on the new movements within the sphere of biographical writing itself; where would the group biography fit into the discussion, for example (we might think of Stanley Wells's 2007 *Shakespeare and Company* as an early intervention in this field)? Or indeed the relevance of cultural geography, which can be found in new attentions to collaborative and societal networks as embodied by the forensic mappings conducted by Nicholl on the back of a single manuscript reference? These questions are part of a whole series of new disciplinary and interdisciplinary applications throwing fresh light on the Shakespearian canon and on our attitudes to the man himself and it is to works in this vein that I now turn for the final section of this review essay.

NEW SHAKESPEARES?

Shakespearian criticism is often a useful cultural and critical barometer; through emergent subgenres and trends in Shakespeare publishing we can chart the turns that particular disciplines, not least literary criticism and performance studies, are undergoing and actively undertaking. One buzz area of study in North American and UK higher education institutions at the moment is certainly 'digital humanities' – Katherine Rowe makes a very welcome contribution to that area in her essay in *The New Cambridge Companion to Shakespeare*, co-edited by Margreta de Grazia and Stanley Wells. Rowe's essay, on 'Shakespeare and Media History', thinks about how new technologies are changing the way we receive, encounter and indeed study Shakespeare. A particular beneficiary of this has been adaptation studies, as Rowe observes: 'New genres such as the remix and video mashup make audio-visual sampling, quotation and interpretation a popular form of artistic play' (p. 303). She generously offers various approaches to adaptation in the course of this discussion which have applicability both within and beyond Shakespeare studies, noting that new technologies have 'transformed the phenomenon of adaptation as the normative way that Shakespeare's works have always been transmitted' (p. 304). Moving far beyond outmoded fidelity arguments, Rowe takes us firmly into the discursive arena of remixes, recycling and remediations, offering a very active notion of audiences in her case-study examples. The volume as a whole is somewhat patchy in how readily it

responds to the challenge of the 'new' of the title; the collection was less cutting-edge in research terms than I thought it might be in terms of seeking to switch on a whole new generation of students to Shakespeare in the innovative ways that Rowe is proposing. Nevertheless, there are some excellent essays here: Stephen Greenblatt, as previously noted, extends the biographical discussion we effectively began with the reading of Bevington's survey volume earlier in this review. In 'The Traces of Shakespeare's Life' he makes the case for the role of imagination on the part of the biographer. Greenblatt resists those who might wish to question Shakespeare's existence by using as his evidence base Jonson's poem for the First Folio which constructs him as for 'all time' and as the 'sweet swan of Avon'. Once again, the cultural and literal landscape of Stratford, carefully framing both the beginning and the end of the Shakespearian literary career, is seen to be a crucial trace for a forensic biographer seeking to recapture 'Shakespeare' from the past.

Other essays take on important topics such as 'Shakespeare's Reading' and 'Shakespeare's Writing'. In the latter Henry Woudhuysen makes welcome recourse to more recent scholarship on the collaborative production of early modern drama in which Shakespeare's position is still hotly contested. Place and space is at the centre of Tiffany Stern's typically lively essay on 'The Theatre of Shakespeare's London' in which she carries us from Southwark as a site of popular entertainment and towards the court as a possible site of influence. Andrew Murphy considers transmission and Jonathan Hope looks at language, noting in particular the sociable contexts for understanding linguistic practice in this period (p. 77). I particularly enjoyed the close-ups Hope offered here on monosyllables and lexical stress and the 'optionality of stress on monosyllables in performance' (p. 87), which seemed to take us in to the heart of the matter which is performance. This is a very useful, pithy piece of work which I can imagine my students using a great deal in the years to come.

Colin Burrow attends to 'Shakespeare the Poet' and pays particular attention to the *Sonnets* and the 'peculiar social and intellectual space' the form inhabited in early modern England (and Scotland?) (p. 99). Subsequent chapters also adopt a generic approach: Stanley Wells himself writes on the comedies and Michael Neill on the tragedies. I liked Neill's nod to the ways in which popular culture invaded or permeated tragic space; one particularly resonant example is the bear-baiting references of *Macbeth* (p. 127). Ton Hoenselaars addresses the histories and Shakespeare's interest in the late medieval past, Heather James considers the classical plays, and Janette Dillon the tragicomedies. These are all excellent pieces of work in themselves and perhaps the 'newness' rests simply in the new scholarship all of these significant critics are able to bring to bear on their subjects, but another approach to the *Companion* could have taken the remit of the innovative more to heart and offered a more up-to-date field guide of Shakespeare studies today in the way that Rowe's essay seemed to be attempting. Gender, race and sexuality are also covered topics and there are overviews of Shakespeare in performance in terms of critical history that will no doubt be of use to the new undergraduate student, but I was left thinking there would have been space for more variation, more diversity of approach towards a writer who has inspired such a polysemous global and multicultural response in recent decades. Anston Bosman does write on the latter topic in his essay on 'Shakespeare and Globalisation', but as an approach this seemed to 'ghettoise' the subject and I would have liked the idea of the 'New Shakespeare', and indeed the 'Global Shakespeare', to have permeated the volume as a whole. It is all admirably solid, reliable scholarship, it will be well read; I just thought there were other roads worth travelling.

One interdisciplinary encounter currently taking place within Arts subjects is in the sphere of Medical or Health Humanities. Kaara L. Peterson's *Popular Medicine, Hysterical Disease, and Social Controversy in Shakespeare's England* is a contribution to that area and has a wonderful frontispiece from the 1636 publication, *The Sick Woman's Privat Lookingglasse*, with a herb garden clearly in view; it is a visual stimulus to the discussions which follow in the book and which focus on the ongoing conversations within early modern culture about popular medicine and the significance of print culture within those debates (p. 4). One specific chapter of this well-researched, solid, if slightly dry, study concentrates on *King Lear* and the feminizing of Lear's *hysterica passio* that takes place in that play. Women and melancholia were traditionally linked, not least in early modern drama (earlier Peterson has had cause to evoke the Jailer's Daughter in *The Two Noble Kinsmen* as a particular case study), and the discussion here allows Peterson to build on this in the subsequent chapter's extended focus on female illness (with mention of *Romeo and Juliet* and Juliet's 'greensickness', p. 95). A further chapter on 'Revivification in Jacobean Tragedy' allows for discussion of Desdemona and the Duchess of Malfi who are both figured as sexual transgressors within their respective playtexts. *The Winter's Tale* also features in a chapter on 'The Theatrics of *Hysterica Passio*'.

Adaptation studies, as already noted, has been a vibrant field of interdisciplinary encounter not least within Shakespeare studies for some time now. It has also occasioned fresh work within the sphere of literary criticism itself: Neil Corcoran's *Shakespeare and the Modern Poet*, for example, is a genuinely thought-provoking and compelling study. Starting out with the idea that 'writers flow into each other like waves' (p. 1) he explores the particularly rich relationship between modern poets and Shakespeare. Especially striking is the correlation he finds in the focused case studies of his later chapters (the opening chapter is a white-water-rapids journey through the many and several modern poets from H. D. to John Berryman to Thom Gunn) on W. B. Yeats, T. S. Eliot, W. H. Auden and Ted Hughes between what he describes as their 'critical and creative work'. All of these poets were, intriguingly enough, practising playwrights as well as poets and critics of considerable merit on Shakespeare among other things; the creative synergies that Corcoran identifies in this heady mix are engaging and persuasive and suggest that in one respect all critics are also already practitioners. In a particularly insightful analysis building on work by Hugh Grady, Corcoran makes the case that T. S. Eliot was a 'co-creator' of work with G. Wilson Knight and the influence of each man can be seen in the other's literary and literary-critical output. In turn he offers one of the better readings I have come across of Eliot's hugely influential essay on 'Ben Jonson', noting, as many previous critics have failed to do, that 'The extra dimension possessed by Shakespeare's characters does not mean that Jonson's do not also spring from an emotional source' (p. 73).

Each case study is structured by means of paired chapters looking in turn at the critical and creative outputs of these writers as shaped and pervaded by Shakespeare. Some deeply meaningful readings of Eliot's Shakespearian allusions are offered in the chapter concentrating on the presence of Shakespeare in his poetry; for example, Corcoran says of 'Marina' that: 'Eliot's poem is, in part, a tissue or patchwork of words recurrent in *Pericles*: seas; shores; daughter; wind; breath; pulse' (p. 117). The coupled chapters on Auden enable a welcome return to Auden's essays on Shakespeare in *The Dyer's Hand* and in his striking introduction to the 1964 Signet edition of the *Sonnets*. Here, just as Knight's criticism was seen to register in Eliot's readings of Shakespeare, so A. C. Bradley can be seen standing behind a number of Auden's observations and insights. A strong close reading of 'The Sea and the Mirror' follows in the adjacent chapter and in turn flows into the section on Ted Hughes, whose versions of Shakespeare are seen to be filtered through the work of others, Eliot not least. Though I found myself quibbling with the comparison of Hughes's output as Poet Laureate with the seventeenth-century court masque towards the close of this section, an analogy that was not explored in enough detail to be entirely persuasive, overall this is a beautiful book, a profound mixture of poetic appreciation and critical insight, providing its own perfect model-mirror of the blending of the creative and the critical that surely represents the Arts as a disciplinary field at its very best.

Shakespeare and the Irish Writer, edited by Janet Clare and Stephen O'Neill, is an equally rich collection of essays looking at the particularities of Irish responses to Shakespeare across time. As the essays demonstrate, Ireland has made major contributions to the Shakespeare industry from the seventeenth century onwards. The essays here are testimony to the 'centrality of Shakespeare in Irish culture' (p. 8) but also the ambiguities of that centrality. Key figures like W. B. Yeats, George Bernard Shaw, James Joyce and Oscar Wilde are discussed at length but new respondents including Elizabeth Bowen and Frank McGuinness are also brought into the frame. Homage and parody are handled in equal measure and the complexities of colonial and post-colonial attitudes to the English bard are explored. Philip Edwards commences the volume with an examination of the mixed inheritance of Shakespeare in the Irish context and alternating attitudes of acceptance and resistance, a debate Brian Cosgrove picks up on in the juxtaposed chapter comparing and contrasting Dowden and Yeats. Tadhg Ó Dúshláire notes in an essay on Shakespeare and Gaelic how claims were made in the twentieth-century that 'translating Shakespeare might enhance the Irish language' (p. 71). Matthew Creasy engages with parody and satire as forms, exploring the 'allusive transformations' of Joyce and others (p. 92). In a superb essay on 'Hamlet in Kildare Street' Declan Kiberd looks at the presence of Shakespeare in Joycean narrative, paying deep attention to form and aesthetic in the process: 'For Joyce, *Hamlet* the play as well as Hamlet the character was a dire warning that interior monologue may displace action rather than enable it' (p. 95). He unpacks the thick presences of *Hamlet* in *Ulysses* not least through the trope of father-son relations, concluding that: '*Hamlet*, like *Ulysses*, is not so much a celebration of a son's fidelity to his father as a lament for the lost integrity of the father-son relationship' (p. 102).

Cary DiPietro, in a lively discussion of George Bernard Shaw's vexed and 'combative' relationship with Shakespeare throughout his career, places welcome focus on Shaw's late puppet show *Shakes versus Shav* in which the playwrights encounter each other head-on. It is an example, he stresses, of a 'playful, but very serious iconoclasm' that can be traced through the Shavian canon, not least in Shakespearian response works like *Caesar and Cleopatra* or *The Dark Lady of the Sonnets* or even the reaction to the Jeanne d'Arc of *1 Henry VI* in *Saint Joan*. Shaw's theatre reviews of Shakespeare are, in my opinion, an untapped source of thinking that might also have figured in these analyses, but I welcomed the relocation of Shaw's objections within a wider cultural context: 'Not unlike many of his later modernist contemporaries in England', notes DiPietro, 'from T. S. Eliot to L. C. Knights, when Shaw took aim at Shakespeare, he took aim at romanticist conventions of performance and criticism' (p. 116).

Noreen Doody contributes the first of two strong contributions on Oscar Wilde. Stressing Wilde's 'deep knowledge' of Shakespearian drama (p. 125) she describes *The Portrait of Mr W. H.* as a 'subtle, close critical reading of the *Sonnets*' (p. 125). That knowledge would be replayed from the dock in his 1895 trial, an indication of the ways in which for Doody Wilde makes 'demands' on Shakespeare at crucial moments in his life. Richard Meek moves away from the often discussed *Mr W. H.* to look in detail at the Shakespearian allusions in *The Portrait of Dorian Gray*, describing that text as an exploration of the 'perils of influence'. In a particularly fine essay Heather Ingman brings into view the Shakespeare-steeped novels of Elizabeth Bowen, indicating her role as a 'precursor' (pp. 153, 161) to many twentieth-century women novelists who have appropriated Shakespeare, not least as a means to re-explore and reconfigure gender relations. *Twelfth Night* proves a core text in Bowen's relationship to the Shakespearian canon and traces of its influence in *The Last September* and *The Big House* are elegantly mapped.

Drama provides the raw material for the final two chapters of this engaging collection. David Wheatley revisits the long-held associations between Samuel Beckett's *Endgame* and *King Lear* filtered through the theoretical writings of Jan Kott, while Helen Heusner Lojek provides a fascinating analysis of Frank McGuiness's *Mutabilitie*, a play in which Shakespeare is washed ashore in Ireland and, in the company of two actors Richard and

Ben (named to provoke memories of Burbage and Jonson), encounters Edmund Spenser in his colonial castle. The play is described as a 'bricolage of erudite references' but also as one whose very dramaturgy maps the Shakespearian association: it is intended to be performed, says the author, on a 'fluid, open space reminiscent of Elizabethan stage spaces' (p. 179). The criss-crossing of early modern and contemporary allusions (Ben the actor refers to what can only be the riots that occurred at first performances of Synge's *Playboy of the Western World*) is deftly sketched as Lojek explores McGuinness's uses of history in his play.

Shakespearean Gothic, a varied response to the theme in the form of a series of essays edited by Christy Desmet and Anne Williams, makes the fascinating point that canonical Shakespeare and eighteenth-century Gothic came into being at the same time. Gothic was emerging as a vibrant and challenging form at the same time that a 'sublime' Shakespeare was being constructed as a conscious response to French neoclassicism. The editors stress the importance of female subjectivity in this particular adaptational narrative and suggest that Gothic writing's obsession with 'family romances' creates an affinity with Shakespeare (p. 10).

Anne Williams herself opens with an essay on Horace Walpole's readings of Shakespeare. In this account Walpole's particular version of Gothic becomes a veritable bricolage of references, though the sustained response of *The Castle of Otranto* (1764) to *Hamlet* is notable within that. Rictor Norton follows with an essay on Anne Radcliffe and romance, suggesting that Radcliffe actually established the pattern for Gothic writers to allude to and quote from Shakespeare. I was struck by the details of Radcliffe's practical and experiential playgoing and how attendance at the Haymarket and Covent Garden theatres may have shaped her particular version(s) of Shakespeare, in particular as responses to the specific interpretations of Sarah Siddons and her brother John Philip Kemble, leading actors of the day. Other essays produce parallel close readings of Thomas Love Peacock and Jane Austen (and in particular their parodic approaches to Gothic as filtered through Shakespeare) and of

Mary Shelley. Marjean D. Purinton and Marliss C. Dessens, writing on Peacock, also refer to the specific conditions of eighteenth-century theatre productions of Shakespeare, noting how these in turn became inflected by Gothic tradition with productions of *Hamlet* at Covent Garden deploying scenery with a Gothic aesthetic (interestingly this was a Kemble production, effecting a link with Anne Radcliffe's previously cited reception of Shakespeare in the theatre). David Garrick's adapted Shakespeares also become an important factor in the particular Gothic versions of Shakespeare that in themselves become quasi-canonical in Yael Shapira's account of 'The Gothic Abduction of *Romeo and Juliet*': Lewis's *The Monk*, for example, offers a 'perverted' version of Romeo strongly inflected by Garrick (p. 143). Shapira notes the irony here of adaptation becoming a marker of 'fidelity' (p. 149). Elsewhere we are asked to see Gothic afterlives of plays including *King Lear* and *Richard III* (the latter also cited as a shaping subtext for Walpole's *Castle of Otranto* in Jessica Walker's contribution).

Christy Desmet, always a valuable commentator on the processes of adaptation, focuses on Shakespearian citation in *Dracula*. Suggesting that citation is an essential part of the Gothic novel's mode and method and using important work by Doug Lanier (from his 2002 *Shakespeare and Popular Culture*) on the way in which citation turns Shakespeare into 'freely applicable cultural truisms' (p. 199), she reveals how Shakespeare appears in 'bits and pieces' throughout Bram Stoker's novel and how *Hamlet* in particular pervades the first half of that text. There is some brilliant linking here to contemporary visual culture, not least through the work of Henry Fuseli, but also once again to actual theatre productions. I thought one of the great triumphs of the scholarship here was the grounding of the accounts of Shakespearian adaptation in detailed theatre history and it should provide a model for this way of working. Desmet draws our attention, for example, to Tom Mead playing the ghost in Henry Irving's Lyceum production of *Hamlet* in 1874 and 1876 where the ghost was 'bathed in a moonlight created by

combining green footlights with blue footlights' and how this feeds in to the descriptions of the blue flames witnessed by Jonathan Harker in his passage along the road in Chapter 1. Similarly, Ellen Terry's 1892 Lyceum performance as Lady Macbeth, which was itself informed by her earlier interpretation of Ophelia, informs the female characterizations of the novel in profound ways. Desmet goes so far as to suggest that Stoker's novel is a part-tribute to Terry. In a closing chapter Susan Allen Ford takes us into the more recent medium of cinema, demonstrating ways in which the Gothic aesthetic informs Kenneth Branagh's 1996 film version of *Hamlet*. She discusses Branagh's 'Gothic ghost' and the 'Gothic vocabulary' at work in his epic wide-screen production: 'This *Hamlet*', she notes, 'mines the Gothic not only for its trapping and suits but also for its tactics, vision and effects' (p. 217). This is a collection that is full of exciting and sometimes surprising detail; textured and engaged in its response to Shakespeare in textual and theatrical modes, it is always admirably sensitive to the Gothic genre within which it is operating. It is an example of the most sophisticated kind of adaptation studies and, quite simply, a stimulating read.

A rather different edited collection this year, *Shakespeare and Early Modern Political Thought*, edited by David Armitage and Andrew Fitzmaurice, describes itself as a 'collaborative attempt to situate Shakespeare's works within the landscape of early modern thought' (p. 1). It is a collaboration that engages historians, political scientists and literary scholars in a suggestive and significant collection which openly acknowledges the influence of the 'contextualist' work of Quentin Skinner (who provides an afterword on 'Shakespeare and Humanist Culture') on its working practices and principles. David Armitage begins by suggesting the shadowy nature of Shakespeare the man and the difficulties that poses for scholars seeking to identify any clear political line or position in association with him. In an intelligent move, Armitage deploys social history to unpack a version of the Shakespearian biography; invoking research on office-holding by Steve Hindle, Mark Goldie and others, he is struck by Shakespeare's veritable 'absence from formal civic life' (p. 30), in marked contrast to contemporaries such as Ben Jonson or Robert Armin, who were guild members. Several contributors continue this attempt to locate Shakespearian politics by exploring Shakespeare's association to Renaissance moral thought, theories of the commonwealth and other positions familiar from more standard histories of Renaissance political thought or humanism. Susan James's essay takes a more unexpected tack by thinking about 'Shakespeare and the Politics of Superstition' with particular reference to *Macbeth* and *Julius Caesar*, arguing that the politics of these plays are inseparable from an understanding of the operation of the passions. Jennifer Richards reflects on the politics of co-authorship, turning to *Henry VIII* as a template text and Cathy Shrank offers a fascinating account of the *Sonnets* and of sonneteering more generally as a humanist activity.

In what was for me a highlight of this ambitious volume, Phil Withington contributes a significant essay on Shakespeare's city comedy which asks to what extent his plays can be read through some of the recent scholarship (by Steve Hindle and others – Hindle is a common touchstone for contributors and his absence as a contributor from the volume is perhaps marked as a result) on the 'politics of the parish' and the 'political nature of urban citizenship' (p. 199). Thinking about early modern participation in the institutions of urban life such as assemblies, courts and councils, Withington suggests that this social practice provides a key context for the political vocabulary with which Shakespeare engages even if, as Armitage's opening essay indicated, he appears as a person to have eschewed engagement with those institutions in the form of practical office-holding. What follows is a superb reading of *The Merry Wives of Windsor* from this vantage point, in which Withington suggests Shakespeare's wives take on the role of protecting their community, not through the obvious space of the guildhall but by means of the 'quintessentially feminine space of the household' (p. 210). This is an original and persuasive essay which asserts that the households and neighbourhoods of urban England were on a 'discursive

continuum with common councils and guildhalls' (p. 215); in this way Withington's method connects the political science approach of this volume and the spatially informed studies I turn to next in the discussion.

The 'spatial turn' is another area of interdisciplinary enquiry that is beginning to make its mark in significant ways within Shakespeare scholarship. Janette Dillon's *The Language of Space in Court Performance, 1400–1625* is an elegant study that sets out to look at 'accounts of movement in or through a given space' in historical documents, but Dillon also pays close attention to plays, Shakespeare and Fletcher's *Henry VIII* in particular, as repositories of 'kinesics and proxemics' (p. 2), the movements and spatial dispositions in which she is rightly so interested. *Henry VIII* provides Dillon with a facilitating starting point. She notes the ways in which Shakespeare and Fletcher as professional dramatists were 'habituated to thinking about how to script the movement of, and distances between bodies in the restricted space of the stage' (p. 4). In dealing with the court scenes for this play, however, she argues that they were also consciously drawing on the careful documentation of that space and the events and ritual performances that took place there. The playtext is then juxtaposed with a series of other spatial events, from court revels to trials, in a significant book that makes a major contribution to the spatial debate that is currently generating energy in a range of disciplines from architecture to archaeology, from dance and drama through to practical geography.

Continuing this interest in space and place as sites of enquiry, Geraldo de Sousa's *At Home in Shakespeare's Tragedies* (Ashgate, 2010) examines in detail the ways in which domestic space and dwelling places are mediated through the medium of Shakespearian tragedy. Describing his project as, in part, an 'anthropology of home' de Sousa demonstrates the ways in which tragedy's destructive effects on households and families can be registered spatially. The first chapter looks at *King Lear* and the concept of what de Sousa terms the 'vanishing castle' of that play as Lear is successively unhoused both in his self-willed exile from his own rule and through the rejection of his elder daughters. The deconstruction of the normal or assumed conventions of hospitality in this play are noted and the hovel is understood as a 'survivalist space'. De Sousa is good, I think, on the mobility and restlessness of this play's dramaturgy as a result of this lack of a sustained or sustainable domestic space at his heart, though at various turns in the study I found myself looking for a deeper engagement with the 'spatial turn' that has taken place within literary and performance studies as well as in adjacent disciplines such as geography. The chapter on *Othello* is more satisfying in these respects as de Sousa engages at length with James Clifford's notion of travelling cultures and the interconnectedness of dwelling and travelling. The discussion of *chiaroscuro* that followed was something of a digression for me but the study again finds its feet in an excellent chapter on *Hamlet* which understands the play through a spatial prism. The dynamic aspect of the play is beautifully conveyed: 'In *Hamlet*, walls seem to shift: space expands and contracts, as a matter of perception' (p. 116). De Sousa makes a convincing case for the play in performance as a competition for space between Hamlet, Claudius and Laertes. I also liked his account of the first and second scenes of the first act as 'contrapuntal', generating 'differently textured' notions of light and dark, inside and out, wintry and warm.

The chapter on *Macbeth* begins with a lovely epigraph from Gaston Bachelard on doors and this leads de Sousa on to a discussion of architecture as a form that both defines boundaries and makes connections. Using sixteenth- and seventeenth-century accounts of travel in Scotland, the author explores the concept of wildness and wilderness in the play, going on to demonstrate how the witches move out of that locale to invade and permeate domestic space. De Sousa captures the restlessness and mobility that characterizes this play in performance. The volume concludes with a wider reflection on the generic enactments of space and the way in which tragedy in particular 'hinges on the emplacement of embedded tragic subjects in houses and home spaces' (p. 167). There is much

to commend this book; while I might have wanted more engagement with spatial theory and with ideas of phenomenology that hover at the edges of some of the discussions, de Sousa unpacks new ways of thinking about his focus plays and his focus genre.

Archipelagic studies and new literary geographies is an outgrowth of the spatial and geographical encounters that literary criticism has been undertaking in recent years. One particular collection this year, Willy Maley and Philip Schwyzer's *Shakespeare and Wales: From the Marches to the Assembly* offers new and revisionist 'national' histories of Shakespeare in the wake of this research. The editors describe this collection of essays as a 'Welsh correction' in that they are attending to the often neglected presences of Welsh issues, identities and geographies on the Shakespearian stage. They suggest that Welsh locales and characters are far more common within the canon than usually presumed.

Kate Chedgzoy's opening essay on 'Shakespeare's Welsh Grandmother' revisits her earlier published work on Welsh women's writing. She makes the important observation that Stratford-upon-Avon was on the route for Welsh migrants and operated like a 'regional magnet' in this period (p. 7). While some representations of Welshness might be seen as no more than myths and fantasia, Chedgzoy makes the persuasive case that through Welsh culture Shakespeare had access to cultural practices, not least in terms of the sophisticated practices of Welsh poetic culture, which involved and engaged women far more than is usually acknowledged. Chedgzoy continues her scholarly good work in this chapter of 'making audible' voices from the geographical, cultural and literary margins and along the way raises key issues about mobility and discourse.

Philip Schwyzer alludes to the poetry of Wallace Stevens in his title 'Thirteen Ways of Looking Like a Welshman' and argues that Welshness for many of Shakespeare's contemporaries was merely a form of 'ventriloquism' (p. 22). David Baker challenges the sense that Shakespeare's understandings of Welsh culture were derived solely from reading

Holinshed and argues instead, in ways that connect to Chedgzoy's narrative of migration and influence, that there was a rich social memory within London's migrant communities that he could draw on. Megan Lloyd also detects pro-Welsh sentiments in Shakespeare, quoting as does Chedgzoy the Lady Mortimer scene of 3.1 of *1 Henry IV* in the process. Christopher Ivic looks at hybridity in *Henry V* and Margaret Tudeau-Clayton examines accent and dialect on the Shakespearian stage in ways that reveal a dual attitude to Wales; its beautiful landscapes are aestheticized but its peoples and communities are parodied. Marisa Cull zooms in on the specific year of 1610, presenting a comparative discussion of *Cymbeline* and its Milford Haven sequences with R. A.'s *The Valiant Welshman*. The specific political context for these plays in 1610 was the investiture of Prince Henry as Prince of Wales (also celebrated that year in Ben Jonson's *Prince Henry's Barriers*). Intriguingly, both these commercial plays feature a theatrical double for the Prince of Wales and Cull gives a useful account of how different stories get told depending on which side of the River Severn you come from. Milton's 1634 *Masque at Ludlow Castle* would be an obvious text to turn to at this point. Lisa Hopkins and Andrew King also have *Cymbeline* in view. Hopkins returns to the duality raised by Tudeau-Clayton's essay when she remarks that 'For the Tudors and the Stuarts, Wales [was] both safe and dangerous' (p. 143), while King in an engagingly written essay looks at performativity in the play. Co-editor Willy Maley offers his own case for the 'Welshness of Shakespeare' (p. 181) and Richard Wilson examines 'Shakespeare's Welsh Roots' through a range of allusions and characterizations including the Welsh parson Sir Hugh Evans in *The Merry Wives of Windsor*.

In an informative afterword, Katie Gramich looks at 'Welsh Shakespeares', that is to say the act and art of translating Shakespeare into the Welsh language. She brings things full circle with an analysis of a Welsh reworking (for the purposes of a Cardiff City performance in the FA Cup final in the UK that year) of the St Crispin's day speech from *Henry V* in which Crispin becomes the Welsh saint Ninian and the names of players echo the list of soldiers in the Shakespearian original. It's a witty end to a lively and provocative set of essays.

Ecocriticism and cultural geographies have also responded to the 'spatial' turn, with environmental habitats themselves constituting spaces for exploration. The nature of that encounter has itself become a subject of critical debate with varying cases made for mediated experience and immediate sensory perception. Bruce R. Smith has been at the vanguard of historicized responses to this debate and he has now published his 'manifesto' on the theme, *Phenomenal Shakespeare* (the study appears as part of Wiley-Blackwell's Manifesto series which has elsewhere looked at topics such as the state of the novel, the future of society and the uses of literature). Smith's case is that an 'historical phenomenology' is both viable and desirable; and in the course of the book he lays out ways and methods to do it as well as the rationale as to why we might want to and what we might gain from it. As well as having recourse to seminal figures within phenomenological philosophy, not least Husserl and Merleau-Ponty, though in many respects his historicized approach finds it deepest associations with Sir Francis Bacon and his seventeenth-century experiments in and with perception, Smith insists on a sustained engagement with the Shakespearian text *in performance*. That latter phrase and concept is surely at the heart of this study, though Smith is judicious in thinking about private reading as a performative act, not least in a very fine chapter on reading the *Sonnets* which treats with sign language, gesture and embodiment. He begins, though, with an ending: with that most metatheatrical moment of engagement, Rosalind's epilogue at the close of *As You Like It*. A rigorous examination of the 'situatedness of the observer' (p. 17), not least in the theatrical experience, is being expounded here with Shakespeare as a facilitating lens; in this respect Smith's work has many correlations with recent moves within cognitive psychology and cognitive linguistics to think about the moment of reception in terms of physiological and emotional *affect*.

The helpfully illustrated chapter on the *Sonnets* asks us to think about the performance of hands in all kinds of suggestive ways, moving outwards from the body and labour of the signer in a series of informing circles to the early modern hand manuals like John Bulwer's *Chirologia* (1644), which have been the focus for analysis by theatre historians from Andrew Gurr to Joseph Roach but which now in Smith's capable hands become the impetus for a consideration of a canon of hand gestures that do not just represent but in some sense 'embody' the passions. Readership and the act of 'seeing' are also a driving concern in the following chapter on sexuality which focuses in the main on *Venus and Adonis* and versions of 'carnal knowledge' in the early modern period. In this section his book connects in intriguing ways with the social and cultural contexts for understanding sexuality that Stanley Wells deals with in another book this year, *Shakespeare, Sex, and Love* which blends cultural history (not least some fascinating reflections on the role of the bawdy court in everyday Stratford life) with readings of key genres and texts in the canon. The final chapter of Bruce Smith's study concentrates on touch as a medium of interpretation and understanding. There was much to admire here in the individual readings and case studies of *Phenomenal Shakespeare* but I did feel that there remains a bigger book yet to be written on historical phenomenology, one that engages with methodologies, and strongly hope that Bruce Smith finds the time and energy to do that. The cross-disciplinary dialogue between cognitive poetics, psycholinguistics and performance studies is still at very embryonic stages and would itself benefit from the input of cultural geographers exploring their own versions of somatic experience.

Another evolving sub-field of interest in the new 'literary geographies' has been the 'new thalassology', or the more pronounceable 'blue cultural studies', and Steve Mentz's book *At the Bottom of Shakespeare's Ocean*, part of Continuum's 'Shakespeare Now!' series, is a lively and energizing contribution to this emergent and evolving area. In a hugely poetic response to the presence of sea and ocean in Shakespeare's canon (the chapters are interspersed with collages of quotations from a wide range of watery sources), Mentz suggests that 'the dramatist's engagement with the sea was neither casual nor simply metaphoric' (p. x). New attention is paid to oft-quoted phrases such as *The Tempest*'s 'sea-change into something rich and strange' in an exploration of the sea as non-human agent, and that play becomes itself a kind of choric refrain in the discussions here. Picking up on some of the writers explored in Corcoran's monograph, Mentz reflects how the oceanic is often a keynote or 'keystone' (p. 7) in modernist adaptations and appropriations of Shakespeare, from the drowning motifs of T. S. Eliot's 'The Waste Land' or his exquisite 'Marina' or indeed in W. H. Auden's 'The Sea and the Mirror', an extended response to *The Tempest*. Practical seamanship and the opening scene of that late romance is analysed but so too is the metaphorical idea of fathomless depths in *King Lear* and not least the Dover Cliff imaginings of Edgar as Poor Tom (p. 16). In a suggestive opening sentence to a chapter on *Othello* Mentz declares that 'It's sea water that mads Othello' (p. 19), moving on to a brilliant description of the geographical structuring of that play by means of a storm at sea that marks the movement between Venice, and the happy optimism of the Venetian general's marriage to Desdemona, and the heated entanglements and jealousies, sexual and professional, that rise to the surface on the island of Cyprus.

Storms and shipwrecks also propel the plotlines of the subjects of the next two chapters: *The Comedy of Errors* and *Twelfth Night*. Water and identity become inextricably intertwined in these discussions ('The ocean changes people' declares the opening sentence of the chapter on *Twelfth Night* (p. 50)), during which Mentz makes fruitful digressions to other seminal sea-texts such as Melville's *Moby-Dick* to give weight to his point-making. The Mediterranean emerges in these accounts as a crucial geography for Shakespeare's cultural imaginary, much as the Pacific was for Melville. The Illyrian coastline of *Twelfth Night* in particular – that liminal space between land and water where Viola is cast up in the second scene of the play, 'What country, friends, is this?' (1.2.1) – occasions in turn an evocative rumination on limens more generally, between gender, people and places. In a chapter on *Pericles* and 'Fishing', Mentz commences with a thought-provoking word list presented in two columns on the page, the first presenting us with words from Shakespeare's play, the second with cognate terms from *Moby-Dick*. Caliban and Moby-Dick he argues by extension are 'fish' who have spread themselves out over literary culture. These kinds of fresh and unexpected comparisons of canonical texts which become a kind of method in Mentz's book occasioned in my experience genuine space for free thinking in ways that I found truly productive. He moves out from the shock of the first comparison to a more historicized consideration of fishing in *Pericles* but we have nevertheless been invited to enter the text in new ways and with new eyes.

The final focus text is *Timon of Athens* where drowning becomes the poetic focus, but it is in the afterword on 'Blue Cultural Studies' that Mentz makes his most radical suggestions for the value of Shakespeare in a world facing peak oil and climate change. This may not be a rallying cry that everyone feels they can or want to respond to (or at least if they do they may not necessarily wish to argue that Shakespeare is the best means of doing so) but Mentz is brave in asserting the value and usefulness of stories at this time. It feels right to end this chapter pondering the value of the arts and humanities in a new age of global crises and wondering what it says that it is still Shakespeare to whom we are turning to help us to think about where we are now and where we might want to be decades down the line. The rights and wrongs of that particular 'Shakespearian turn' I will leave readers to decide about for themselves . . . the value of the stories and the stories we in turn choose to tell about them, I suggest, remains compelling.

BIBLIOGRAPHY

Altman, Joel B., *The Improbability of 'Othello'* (Chicago and London, 2010)

Armitage, David, Conal Condren and Andrew Fitzmaurice, eds., *Shakespeare and Early Modern Political Thought* (Cambridge, 2009)

Bevington, David, *Shakespeare and Biography* (Oxford, 2010)

Bristol, Michael D., ed., *Shakespeare and Moral Agency* (London and New York, 2010)

Clare, Janet, and Stephen O'Neill, eds., *Shakespeare and the Irish Writer* (Dublin, 2010)

Corcoran, Neil, *Shakespeare and the Modern Poet* (Cambridge, 2010)

De Grazia, Margaret, and Stanley Wells, eds., *The New Cambridge Companion to Shakespeare* (Cambridge, 2010)

Desmet, Christy, and Anne Williams, eds., *Shakesperean Gothic* (Cardiff, 2009)

de Sousa, Geraldo, *At Home in Shakespeare's Tragedies* (Farnham and Burlington, VT, 2010)

Dillon, Janette, *The Language of Space in Court Performance, 1400–1625* (Cambridge, 2010)

Fitzpatrick, Joan, *Renaissance Food from Rabelais to Shakespeare: Culinary Readings and Culinary Histories* (Farnham and Burlington, VT, 2010)

Grady, Hugh, *Shakespeare's Impure Aesthetics* (Cambridge, 2010)

Gurr, Andrew, *Shakespeare's Opposites: The Admiral's Company, 1594–1625* (Cambridge, 2010)

Holbrook, Peter, *Shakespeare's Individualism* (Cambridge, 2010)

Maley, Willy, and Philip Schwyzer, eds., *Shakespeare and Wales: From the Marches to the Assembly* (Farnham and Burlington, VT, 2010)

Mentz, Steve, *At the Bottom of Shakespeare's Oceans* (London and New York, 2009)

Peterson, Kaara L., *Popular Medicine, Hysterical Disease, and Social Controversy in Shakespeare's England* (Farnham and Burlington, VT, 2010)

Smith, Bruce R., *Phenomenal Shakespeare* (Oxford, 2010)

Smith, Emma, and Garrett A. Sullivan Jr, eds., *The Cambridge Companion to English Renaissance Tragedy* (Cambridge, 2010)

Stewart, Stanley, *Shakespeare and Philosophy* (London, 2010)

Streete, Adrian, *Protestantism and Drama in Early Modern England* (Cambridge, 2010)

Wells, Stanley, *Shakespeare, Sex, and Love* (Oxford, 2010)

Williamson, Elizabeth, *The Materiality of Religion in Early Modern English Drama* (Farnham and Burlington, VT, 2009)

2. SHAKESPEARE IN PERFORMANCE
reviewed by PASCALE AEBISCHER

Theatre history, this year, has been even more than usually concerned with the material traces left by early modern theatre practices. Julian Bowsher and Pat Miller's *The Rose and the Globe – Playhouses of Shakespeare's Bankside, Southwark: Excavations 1988–91* takes this trend to an extreme and brings together all the significant strands of archaeological evidence unearthed in digs, richly and informatively illustrated with maps, sketches and photographs of documentary sources, sites and finds. The book minutely documents excavation data and finds that have been re-examined using the latest technologies. The result is a remarkable and important report that would like to 'appeal to a wide audience'. Because of the uncompromisingly technical approach and style it adopts not only in the specialist appendices that fill a third of the volume but also in its discursive account of the excavations, however, it will probably find a more specialist readership amongst archaeologists and materialist critics in search of the telling piece of archaeological evidence in support of an argument about the social practices affecting the early modern theatre industry. Somebody working on early modern fashions in the theatre is sure to find something intriguing to say about the decorative trimmings and the 'most unusual' number of glass beads that were found and which may have represented 'a special fashion statement on the part of a few of those attending the playhouse' or even been part of 'highly ornate stage costumes'.

Most of all, *The Rose and the Globe* will be compulsory reading for anyone exploring early modern theatre architecture, whether sitting at a desk or through original practices performance in one of the reconstructed theatres: this is a book which, in its quiet, factual way intervenes in ongoing debates about the exact shape of the theatres and the performance spaces within them. The reconstructed Shakespeare's Globe (referred to in this book as 'the third Globe') has twenty sides to its polygon – Jonathan Greenfield here concludes that the building was more likely to have had sixteen or eighteen sides. No criticism of the new building, which is also briefly discussed, is made at any point, but those who are aware of the heated debates and their implications for how we understand the spatial relationships in the original Globe(s) will find their views challenged and/or confirmed by the carefully laid-out facts and foundation plans. The evidence collected here also intriguingly suggests that the first Globe could not have been largely based on the same dimensions as the Theatre, disturbing a convenient and widespread ontological myth. But certainty is impossible: as Jonathan Greenfield writes of the second Globe, 'the actual dimensions of the overall structure are still open to discussion, and, until further remains are revealed, will remain so'. Furthermore, Greenfield cautions against the practice of 'using evidence from any one of the playhouses to support conclusions about any other one', since what the partial excavations clearly show is that there were significant divergences between the different public theatres. It will take a full excavation of these playhouses and the exploration of 'other areas of Tudor Bankside, other playhouses, baiting arenas, inns, taverns and shops' to convey a full archaeological picture of early modern playgoing practices and theatres. In the meantime, what this book does quite brilliantly is provide the raw materials on which years of scholarship and debate will be based.

Even for those without an investment in theatre architecture and without the background in archaeology that is needed to properly appreciate the information about the geology and topography of the area and the chronology of the digs, this book is an eye-opener. Christopher Phillpotts's account of the Bankside in the sixteenth century fills that neighbourhood, otherwise characterized by ditches and fishponds, with businesses and trades, from tanning to brewing and the sex industry. His section on 'Theatre History' is an excellent, very concise, summary of current knowledge about innyard, private and public theatres in early modern London. Later sections of the book build on this account and fill some of the gaps in our knowledge. Thus, for example, it is only thanks to the excavations that Henslowe's expenditure of over £105 for building costs in 1592 can now be put down to the remodelling of the Rose's northern half, including a new stage with a roof over it. Spectators must, it seems, have been thronging around that stage, since the floor around it is heavily eroded. For the Globe, the archaeological find that intrigued me most was the discovery of what may have been seventeenth-century theatrical props, including a sword. In the appendix, a brief section on 'Arms' reveals that the large number of items associated with weaponry found in the digs 'suggests this was an era with a particular potential for violence arising from weapons that were regularly being carried around'. The chapter on 'Plays, Players and Playgoers' adds some fascinating details, not only about the fact that the blade of the potential prop sword was never sharpened, but also about playgoers' dubious toilet habits and the use of clay tobacco pipes in the theatre. The book may be a rather demanding read but it is a treasure-trove of information.

Tiffany Stern's *Documents of Performance in Early Modern England* is also a fount of knowledge but it certainly is not a dry read. Stern takes the raw materials of surviving playbooks, plots, bills, title-pages, 'arguments', prologues, epilogues, songs and masques and turns them into a compelling, fresh narrative of how plays were patched together out of disparate texts. To build her argument, Stern moves between the fields of theatre history and textual criticism, harnessing masses of documentary evidence (much of it new), which she manages to order in such a way as not to overwhelm her reader, helped by her talent for telling a good story. Having heard several conference and seminar-paper versions of the material presented here, I was struck, when reading the book, by the extent to which Stern has been able to preserve the lightness of tone, love of anecdote and obvious enthusiasm for her discoveries and conclusions in the written version. Sometimes, in fact, her stories are so compelling and well told that it is difficult to remember Stern's warning, in her introduction, that hers 'is a book of tendencies, trends and likelihoods' rather than certainties. Significant amounts of evidence are garnered from Restoration and eighteenth-century texts that are used as a complement to scarcer earlier documentary traces, allowing Stern to spot patterns where otherwise we would be able to see nothing but disconnected textual fragments. The conclusions she arrives at may thus not be definitive, though they will be the operative truths for some time to come.

One thing Stern establishes beyond doubt is the fragmentary nature of the early modern play-text. This is not only because, as she argued with Simon Palfrey in *Shakespeare in Parts*, actors learned their lines from separate 'parts', and because, as she showed in *Rehearsal*, prologues and epilogues were separate pieces of text cued to specific performances, but also because right from the start, the play was conceptualized as, and created from, a string of textual fragments. The plot, she tells us, was not only considered by early critics and playwrights themselves as separate from the dialogue of a play, but it was actually a separate piece of writing: what Stern calls a 'plot-scenario' (as opposed to a 'backstage-plot') was a piece of writing that sketched the outline of the action before the dialogue was filled in. Fascinatingly, one of the ways in which various writers could collaborate in composing a play would involve a plotter working with one or several dialogue-writers. A good plot was a valuable commodity, purchased separately by a theatre long before the play based on it existed. Like all valuable commodities, plots may also have been stolen or at least reused: Stern draws attention to the ways in which Shakespeare's *King John* and *The Troublesome Reign of King John*, two very dissimilar plays, share their structure and narrative organization and even contain a couple of very similar stage directions that may have been lifted from the same, shared, plot. Another important document was the playbill, which, pinned to some kind of post (tethering post, 'pissing post', door-post or even a whipping post), advertised forthcoming performances. The problem, here, is that although Stern has no trouble proving that playbills were printed from at least 1587 onwards, no such bill survives today. Picking up this gauntlet, she does a great job supplementing the missing material witness to this practice by looking at cognate texts. These include other types of poster advertising entertainments and the title-pages that may bear traces of playbills in them and may themselves have been posted as advertisements. Stern argues here for a much closer relationship between playhouse and printing-house, between the experience of watching a play and reading it, than commonly assumed.

The 'Argument' is yet another part of the play-text that is not often examined. Stern argues that this paratext, which seems entirely literary rather than theatrical, was in fact 'a frank piece of theatre available to a particular tier of audience and reproduced in some playbooks'. Arguments were often printed for masques and plays, mediating performances for their elite spectators, much in the way Middleton portrays the masque scene in *Women Beware Women*, which is preceded by the argument that is read out loud for the benefit of its courtly audience. As a consequence, '[t]he division between play as printed text and play as enacted performance is not as stark as it is often said to be, and Arguments provide one of the thrilling moments at which the two intersect, belonging to a strange textual hinterland where performance is most bookish and, conversely, where the playbook is most performative'. Other parts of the play, like prologue, epilogue and songs, were first performed and then circulated amongst readers as texts separate from the play. Stern shows how these texts' separate existence, and that of the letters or scrolls featuring as theatrical properties in plays, resulted in their odd placement within printed playtexts. The peculiar layout of scrolls or letters in printed playtexts, Stern argues, was designed to help the scribe responsible for creating the property scroll incorporate all the features necessary for that letter to do its work on stage: what look like bizarre stage-directions may in fact be 'scribe-directions'. An important point Stern makes in relation to prologues and epilogues is that 'it can never be assumed that the author of a prologue or epilogue (or chorus) is the author (or are the authors) of the play',

since stage-orations were written for specific occasions, may have been written much later than the rest of the play, and may have been reused for different plays. Songs, too, are an interesting category of text, for they seem to have been one of the first things affected by theatrical revision, as easily added to pad out a scene or 'update' it as excised to shorten the running time.

Theatrical revision and the traces it left becomes the focus of the end of the book, as Stern revisits her own earlier work and debates about censorship and questions whether the words spoken on stage, memorized as they were from individual parts transcribed by more or less reliable scribes, actually corresponded to the book approved by the Master of the Revels. Concluding with a section on the improvisation expected of early modern clowns, Stern adds hers to the choir of voices warning us not to confound written plays with spoken plays in the early modern theatre. Even with that warning in mind, however, this must-read for theatre historians and textual critics alike takes us tantalizingly close to witnessing an early modern play in performance and succeeds in reassembling the pieces of the documentary jigsaw in new ways that make excellent theatrical sense.

Brian Walsh's *Shakespeare, the Queen's Men, and the Elizabethan Performance of History*, which shares some of Stern's concern with extemporizing clowns, takes theatre history as its starting point, uses performance studies for its theoretical framework, and dedicates itself to a reassessment of how the *idea* of history (as opposed to actual history) was represented in Shakespeare's Elizabethan history plays and plays in the repertory of the Queen's Men. The Queen's Men are set alongside Shakespeare because they were the first company to 'stage the English past in the popular theatres', paving the way for Shakespeare's own dramatizations of the past and the theoretical engagement with notions of history which Walsh traces in these plays. What makes Walsh's study appropriate for inclusion in a review of Shakespeare in performance is its methodology, which adapts present-day performance theories to the specificities of the early modern theatre: the thinking of Phelan,

Roach, Blau, States and Taylor underpins Walsh's richly suggestive readings of the ways in which Elizabethan history plays produce a past that is both desired and always already on the point of vanishing; theatre can only revive history on 'borrowed time'. In the theatre, the realization of historians like Camden that history is necessarily discontinuous and 'not a naturally occurring form of knowledge' was embodied in plays that '*enact* historicity as a sense of discontinuity and all the while reflect on the strategies through which historical representation, particularly *corporeal* representation, addresses that discontinuity'.

In his chapters concerned with the Queen's Men's *Famous Victories of Henry V* and *The True Tragedy of Richard III*, Walsh works through the traces of performance that can still be detected in these texts. As he goes on to demonstrate, these early history plays use the company's charismatic clowns (Tarlton, Wilson, Singer and Lanham) to draw attention to the absence of history in the present moment of performance: the clowns disrupt the historical narrative and highlight the rupture between past and present. Just like the figures of Truth, Poetry and Report in the frame of the *True Tragedy of Richard III*, whose debate prompts the spectator to appreciate the crafted nature of witness reports and the construction of historical truth, the clowns' anachronisms, in Walsh's readings, are not a sign of the playwright's clumsiness but contribute to the metatheatrical effects through which the Queen's Men's histories self-consciously reflect on the impossibility of historical representation.

In his chapters on Shakespeare's histories, Walsh continues this line of enquiry, analysing the plays for the ways in which they probe and puncture the notion that historical truth can be staged while simultaneously contributing to the creation of 'history' – as Walsh notes in his chapter on *Richard III*, Shakespeare's play is responsible for fixing Thomas More's negative image of this king in our historical imagination. Walsh finds that *1 Henry VI* enacts a 'critique of genealogy as a mode of historical organization' because the play reveals genealogies to be 'self-interested forms of historical knowledge'.

Richard III, on the other hand, is notable for the ways in which it represents history as a memory rooted in earlier history plays, since the characters keep reminding their on- and offstage audiences of key visual moments in the *Henry VI* plays that depend, for their full effect, on audiences remembering performances of the earlier plays. Thus, for example, the corpse of Henry VI over which Richard woos Lady Anne is a prop that recalls the beginning of *1 Henry VI* more than it does actual history: as Walsh explains, '*Richard III* aligns history with a memory of theater.' Grisly corpses are also key to Walsh's exploration of *Henry V*, which links the onstage bodies of the actors, to which Princess Katharine in her language lesson and Henry in his meditation on the eve of Agincourt draw attention, to the extratheatrical mummified corpse of Katharine of Valois which lay openly in Henry V's tomb in Westminster Abbey, for the curious and morbid to touch. Extratheatrical references such as this draw attention to the discontinuities between the present and the past and prompt audiences to experience the present, in the shape of the tombs and chantries at Westminster Abbey, in new ways. The book certainly managed to make me experience history plays as theoretical engagements with the production of history and I only wish that Walsh had included chapters on the *Henry IV* plays and concluded with a consideration of *Henry VIII*.

Abigail Rokison's *Shakespearean Verse Speaking: Text and Theatre Practice* is a very different sort of book from Walsh's, even though both are animated by the dual preoccupation with history and performance. Rokison targets a mixed readership of performers and critics and takes an academic approach to investigate how Shakespeare's verse is spoken in present-day theatre practice. For this, Rokison researches acting handbooks by famous directors and voice coaches designed to help the actor find the hidden cues Shakespeare wrote into his scripts. She then goes on to compare the practitioners' assertions with the findings of theatre historians, 'contest[ing] some of the claims made by leading theatre practitioners and reiterated by actors and students looking for guidance in speaking Shakespearean verse'. One of the book's stated aims is to alert 'theatre practitioners to diverse editorial and compositorial methods' that will have an impact on the Shakespearian line, on which many manuals base their advice to actors and their claims to an 'authentic' approach. At the same time, Rokison hopes to be read by editors and to make them aware of 'the way in which actors may interpret editorial emendations'. All too often, as she demonstrates in this book, the decisions of actors and directors are based on editorial decisions that have little to do with early modern punctuation or dramatic significance and are grounded in a desire to make the text easier to read for the modern user.

One of the things that makes Rokison's argument so persuasive is the thoroughness and up-to-date nature of her research into present-day practical approaches, early modern rhetoric, theatre history and textual scholarship (her scholarly weakness is in performance studies, where she ignores William B. Worthen's seminal, and in many ways analogous, work on actors' handbooks in *Shakespeare and the Authority of Performance*). Rokison's scholarship is combined with a close attention to the plays themselves, which she examines with a view to establishing the dramatic functions of metrical irregularity as an indicator of a character's emotional condition. Her book is an antidote to the earnestness with which many leading practitioners, from directors Peter Hall and John Barton through to voice coaches Cicely Berry and Patsy Rodenburg, argue for a single, authentically Shakespearian, way of speaking verse, while each of them advocates a slightly different method. It is also a courageous book that, for example, takes issue with some of the statements about speech units in Stern and Palfrey's *Shakespeare in Parts*, which Rokison otherwise relies on quite heavily: Rokison's criticism is certainly not confined to the prescriptive methods of theatrical stars but also offers correctives to the conclusions of leading theatre historians. Noting the central role played by the Folio text in discussions of Shakespeare's verse, she delves into textual criticism to examine the various compositorial and scribal interventions, theatrical revisions and the censorship that shaped this text. Neither this, nor the material on early

modern punctuation, will be news to the scholarly community, but it ought to be compulsory reading for all practitioners basing their work on the Folio text, as should her examination of the internal evidence of Shakespeare's plays, which demonstrates variations in his verse lines across his career that make fixed rules unworkable. Together with *The Rose and the Globe* and *Documents of Performance*, *Shakespearean Verse Speaking* dismantles many of the critical assumptions underpinning the original practices performance movement. Theatre practitioners might seize on Rokison's chapter on 'Historical Evidence', which covers prosody, Elizabethan education and whatever evidence can be scraped together about actors' delivery in order to find more authentic approaches to the verse line, but they will find in that same chapter a powerful corrective to the tendency to read too much into the presence of shared, single, final or initial short lines.

In the final parts of her book, Rokison directs her criticism at the blindness of current editorial practices to the ways texts are used in the rehearsal room. Her section on modern edited texts explores how present-day editors render features such as short verse lines or shared lines and reveals significant variations of practice within a single series, such as the Arden Shakespeare. In her final chapter Rokison builds a strong case for what she calls 'a "theatrical" text, for use in the rehearsal room, which makes apparent the unambiguous metrical connection between certain lines, emends obvious errors, and modernizes spelling for ease of use, whilst not obscuring ambiguities inherent in the lineation and punctuation'. To illustrate what she means by such a text, she provides an example of *Measure for Measure*, Act 2 scene 4, edited according to her proposed principles in her appendix. Actors are alerted to the problems caused by Ralph Crane's scribal interventions and are left to make up their own minds about how to deal with punctuation in the light of that information. Lines with an 'amphibious structure' are highlighted and annotated, offering explanations about the lineations chosen by various editors and adding commentary by practitioners like Juliet Stevenson or Patrick

Tucker on how they interpret the lineation. While there is some doubt about how practical actors would find such an edition, which substitutes the usual gloss on words with substantial material on various ways of dividing verse lines, Rokison's suggestions are provocative and well worth keeping in mind. The conversation between practitioners and editors that she is thus opening up is an important one and I rather hope that both communities will indeed read this book.

Although Adrian Noble's *How to Do Shakespeare* does not feature in Rokison's critique (being published in the same year, it couldn't be), this is exactly the sort of actors' manual by a famous director which her book dissects so intelligently. Noble's cover blurb warns us that 'whether you are an actor or a student, you will miss [this book] at your peril', a message that is reinforced by Ralph Fiennes's Foreword, which tells us that 'any actor will find this book invaluable. For any student of Shakespeare it should be essential.' This acting manual is thus misleadingly marketed as also aimed at students, when the guidance it provides is exclusively aimed at budding actors. For students, Noble's book provides examples of inaccurate information (the chapter on metaphor discusses similes as metaphors) and of poor critical practice (there is no critical apparatus to support assertions about early modern theatre practice). For young actors, on the other hand, this will be a helpful and readable addition to a library well stocked with books on Stanislavskian method acting, since Noble's overt goal is to marry that method to the more verse-centred approach of the Lord Chamberlain's Men (note, here, the desire to root present-day approaches in early modern theatre practice – Rokison will enjoy seeing yet another confirmation of the accuracy of her analysis in this book). For Noble, 'one of the great excitements of rehearsal is to watch an actor approach a scene from both a Shakespearean and a Stanislavskian angle. This is the ideal: a marriage of the two traditions.'

In order to allow his reader to achieve such an ideal marriage of traditions and understand 'Shakespeare's genius', Noble takes his readers by the hand and gives them a guided tour through various aspects of Shakespearian verse and structure, inviting them to read long passages aloud while focusing on specific features to discover how Shakespearian verse 'works'. Didactic, gossipy, vivid and patronizing in turn, Noble manages to convey his passion for Shakespeare's language and characterization. I did not find much in this book that I had not heard or read before in acting manuals and at drama college, but Noble livens things up with rare but precious anecdotes about his own work as a director that provided brief glimpses of a life steeped in the working practices of the RSC and the late twentieth-century stage. Thus we read about Simon Callow's declaration that the role of Titus is unactable, about the tittering of French audiences at a production of *Malfi* that had been received with great acclaim and seriousness in Britain and about the way Jonathan Pryce changed his manner of delivering soliloquies in response to a preview performance. It is a shame that Noble did not yield to his instinct for storytelling more often in this book, since it is a mode that suits him well.

More storytelling would also have benefited Elizabeth Schafer's edition of *Twelfth Night* for Cambridge's 'Shakespeare in Production' series. The series itself is possibly responsible for the somewhat plodding nature of Schafer's impressively researched introduction, which starts by sketching some large trends in the production of the play from the early modern period to the present. Five strands structure Schafer's narrative: 'the attempt to locate a production geographically, culturally and politically by means of its vision of the world of Illyria; the treatment of the Malvolio narrative; the treatment of the Viola narrative; the radical change in the theatrical fortunes of Feste, and the implied commentary on theatrical practice offered by recorded *Twelfth Night*s'. The strands are very helpful in allowing Schafer to align productions with specific trends, but they are inevitably also reductive, as are the little vignettes about individual productions which are too short to give a rounded picture of any one production. This edition is wonderful in that it opens up so much theatrical history that we don't know enough about, but each page in it left me yearning for more detail: I wanted to know what songs Hannah Pritchard and Kitty Clive sang in the 1741 production, I would have enjoyed seeing the painting of Dora Jordan as a late eighteenth-century Cesario 'in a hussar's high hat and regimental coat, but with delicate, feminine features', more context about Samuel Phelps's larger agenda to situate the discussion of his prompt-book would have been welcome and, being a lover of salacious detail, I would have enjoyed a quotation to illustrate how exactly Leigh Hunt 'spent thirteen lines of his review [of Maria Tree's performance of Viola] salivating over the display of her legs'. In the section on recorded *Twelfth Nights*, I felt short-changed by the absence of any discussion of Tim Supple's 2003 adaptation for Channel 4. Most of all, having just come from reading Schafer's lively discussion of the lesbian genealogy of Lydia Lopokova's Olivia for Harcourt Williams's revival of 1933 in *Shakespeare in Stages* (of which more below), I would have relished it if Schafer had felt able to bring that same sense of controversy and queer rereading of theatre history to this edition. Comments about the 'femininity police' Vivien Leigh apparently ran foul of with her fearless Viola punctuate the introduction with reminders of the sharpness Schafer is holding in check much of the time. Even without that edge, though, this will be a very valuable, because thoroughly researched, referenced and annotated addition to our libraries: what I am regretting here is that the 'Shakespeare in Performance' series is missing out on one of its contributors' talent for seeing theatre history in ways other than the chronological procession of productions we are offered here.

If the 'Shakespeare in Performance' *Twelfth Night* is conspicuously following the imperatives of first generation performance criticism, Stephen Purcell's *Popular Shakespeare: Simulation and Subversion on the Modern Stage* is a hybrid coming out of a mixture of theatre history, performance studies and theatre practice. The book ends with a personal narrative about the 'rough magic' of a performance of *The Tempest* which had begun rather roughly and concluded in a magical moment as Ariel's spirit was released in the shape of balloons

rising to the sky and the audience cheered in communal approval. This narrative itself, with its final refusal to attempt to deconstruct the experience, is one of the more magical moments of a book which is energetic, thoughtful, well written and rough in turns. The ups and downs of the book are partly due to the book's idiosyncratic structure: personal narratives are juxtaposed with scholarly chapters so as to combine Purcell's 'subjective experience (both as a playgoer and as a maker of theatre) with the more formal registers of academic writing', without imposing a synthesis that would obscure the conflicts between emotional and critical modes of response to theatrical events. There is also an unevenness in tone within and between the analytical sections of the book, as Purcell's sharply observed critical appraisal of the present-day cultural phenomenon of popular Shakespeare gradually gives way to advocacy for a specific way of performing Shakespeare for a popular audience which, it turns out, corresponds closely to Purcell's own partly improvisational theatre practice.

Purcell is at his very best when discussing Shakespeare's changing cultural status and his own experience as a keen, highly culturally literate and articulate theatregoer. There is much in *Popular Shakespeare* that made me want to explore the work of companies I had not come across before and I am entirely convinced by Purcell's argument that stagings of Shakespeare plays in recent years have frequently taken issue with the perceived pretentiousness of Shakespeare productions in mainstream theatres. Ad-libbing, deliberately disruptive anachronisms and the use of theatrical spaces that enhance a sense of *communitas* between performers and spectators (and between spectators) are all ways in which theatre practitioners have been contesting Shakespeare's cultural authority. Purcell's discussion of the ways in which Shakespearian clowns have improvisation scripted into their roles provides a seamless link with Brian Walsh's analysis of Richard Tarlton's tendency to ad-lib in the early modern theatre, and his appraisal of the way the improvisational practices of present-day performers of Shakespeare's clown roles turn performances into 'theatresports' is compelling. What is problematic here, however, is Purcell's paradoxical desire to lend authority to what he terms 'unofficial speech' and irreverence by linking present-day practices to the ways Shakespeare scripted the clowns' roles: surely, if irreverence is authorized in this way, then it is no longer irreverent. There is something disingenuous in criticizing Peter Brook's belief in the timeless and unchanging truths communicated by Shakespeare's plays while suggesting that there is something timeless and unchanging about the way in which Shakespearian clowns communicate with their audiences.

At several other points in this study, Purcell's desire to taxonomize popular Shakespeare runs directly counter to the phenomenon's inherent transgression of norms and boundaries – it seemed to me to be a peculiarly fruitless exercise to attempt to categorize different types of parody or configurations of space. Purcell often seems aware of the futility of trying to pin down the ideological work performed by some of the performances he discusses. Of the Beatles' version of 'Pyramus and Thisbe', for example, he admits that 'ultimately the cultural meanings of the broadcast are impossible to fathom . . . there is no way in which one might attempt to pin down such a nebulous phenomenon'. On the other hand, it is often when Purcell is struggling to define terms and practices that he finds ways of saying important things about modes of adaptation, about the pitfalls of 'relevance', about how 'straightness' is more a matter of attitude than of textual fidelity, or about the ways in which parody, instead of being subversive, can end up being 'culturally elitist in itself, appealing as it does only to those with enough knowledge of the parodied text to understand its references'. Rough this book may be at times, but there is magic in it, too.

Picking up Christie Carson and Christine Dymkowski's *Shakespeare in Stages: New Theatre Histories*, I was discouraged by the blurb on the back, which announced that 'no individual volume provides an in-depth consideration of the stage histories of a number of plays, chosen for their particular significance within specific cultural contexts. *Shakespeare in Stages* addresses this

gap.' My scepticism about how such a book might cohere so as to make its whole larger than the sum of its constituent parts was hardly allayed by the editors' very brief introduction, which offered no overarching theoretical framework or rationale, but which announced that the volume would steer 'a course between the Scylla of homogenising generalisation on the one hand and the Charybdis of eclectic and unrelated essays on the other'. I was the more surprised to find that the book works very well – works best, in fact, if read cover-to-cover rather than in a piecemeal fashion, for the case studies do, almost without exception, pick up strands of previous arguments. This is made possible by the chronological organization of the essays within each of the volume's three parts that focus on notions of authenticity, attitudes towards sex and gender, and questions of identity.

As the case studies in the first part illustrate, Carson and Dymkowski make no attempt at compiling a comprehensive historical narrative – this, as Coleridge might put it, is reading theatre history by flashes of lightning. An essay by Andrew Gurr on the King's Men's choice to open a 'private' indoor theatre alongside their 'public' amphitheatre is followed by Elaine McGirr giving us a glimpse of Whig politics at work in the reception of Colley Cibber's *King John*. The next flash of lightning takes us to Lucy Munro's account of William Poel's 'inauthentic' production of *Coriolanus*, with which the volume begins to slow down and gain in interest. Munro brings aspects of the repertory approach she honed in her earlier work on the Children of the Queen's Revels to an analysis of Poel's repertoire in the 1920s-early 1930s, seeing coherence and a political stance where others had seen discontinuity and inauthenticity. It is only when Poel's production of *Coriolanus* is viewed alongside his productions of non-Shakespearian plays in the same period, Munro argues, that we can properly understand his directorial decisions. Neil Carson picks up the Poel strand and discusses his influence on Tyrone Guthrie's collaboration with Tanya Moiseiwitsch to design the stage for the Shakespeare Festival in Stratford, Ontario. There is a vividness to Carson's account which stems from the fact that he himself, as his biographical note tells us, played a part in Guthrie's first Canadian production of *Richard III*, and I just wished he had allowed himself to shed more of the distance of the academic to acknowledge his involvement in this important moment of theatre history and design. Abigail Rokison follows this with a comparison of the various claims to authenticity made by Ed Hall's all-male theatre company Propeller and Mark Rylance's work with 'original practices' during his period as Artistic Director of Shakespeare's Globe. While I would question the need for quite so strong an argumentative thrust to the essay – Rokison clearly thinks the work of Propeller superior because it 'seeks to "rediscover" the plays for a modern audience by emphasizing the text and stimulating the audience's imagination' – her contrasting of the two companies' approaches to the staging of *Twelfth Night* brings the different artistic enterprises and their ideological underpinnings into sharp relief.

The second part, 'Attitudes towards Sex and Gender', returns us to the early modern theatre with Farah Karim-Cooper's essay on 'Performing Beauty on the Renaissance Stage'. The essay builds on Karim-Cooper's earlier work on cosmetics and spins it in a new way, focusing less on make-up and more clearly on the period's attitudes towards male adolescent and female beauty, which she describes as both semiotic and, potentially, prosthetic. Her reading of Olivia's speech about her 'natural' beauty brings a new resonance to Rokison's earlier reading of Rylance's original practices performance of the role. Fast-forwarding to the mid-eighteenth century, Fiona Richie's essay shifts our attention away from male actors and the dominant figure of David Garrick to reinstate Hannah Pritchard and Kitty Clive, two eighteenth-century actresses about whom we know too little, as seminal figures in the creation of the 'Shakespeare' of the Westminster Abbey monument. Invigorating, here, is not only the revisionary nature of Richie's theatre history, but also the range of evidence she relies on, using salary figures and notices about book publications to establish the wealth and social standing of these actresses. Jan

McDonald's reading of nineteenth-century women writing about Shakespeare's women fades by comparison: Pritchard and Clive's energy rather overpowers the Victorian women's attempts to co-opt Shakespeare in the creation of the ideal of the 'angel in the house'. Elizabeth Schafer's essay on the performance of *Twelfth Night*'s Olivia by Lydia Lopokova, a Russian prima ballerina, in 1933 is more energetic again, and certainly more controversial, as she traces her antecedents back to Charlotte Cushman's 1846 performance opposite her sister. Providing a depth of analysis absent from her discussion of the same production in her edition of *Twelfth Night*, Schafer identifies 'the potentially lesbian dynamic in the physicality of Lopokova's performance' that would have been 'very close to home for [Virginia] Woolf', who reviewed the production at a time when she was involved with Vita Sackville-West. This part of the book concludes with Christine Dymkowski's essay on *Measure for Measure* in the late twentieth century, which could have stuck more closely to the theme of sex and gender but which superbly brings into dialogue a very wide-ranging number of productions, including Sue Dunderdale's radical feminist and socialist Avon Touring Theatre production of 1978 and Declan Donnellan's 1994 Cheek by Jowl staging.

After such a strong middle section of thematically interlocking case studies, the concluding part of the book on 'Questions of Identity' coheres less convincingly. The strong essays in this section include Susan Bennett's analysis of the communities visited by the Montana Shakespeare in the Parks touring company. Bennett reveals the existence of highly Shakespeare-literate audiences far away from urban centres – a form of '"foreign Shakespeare" within a terrain – North America – that seems otherwise overdetermined in its relationship to, and promotion of, Shakespeare-as-culture'. I also much enjoyed Lynette Goddard's focus on the 'Binglish' productions of Yvonne Brewster's Talawa theatre company, which takes account of Brewster's desire 'for the right to tackle European plays without being required to render them "black"', but which nevertheless goes on to read her 1997 production of *Othello* with a view to uncovering how this colour-conscious and gender-aware production helped 'refigure the racial and gender dynamics' in this play. Brian Pearce's reading of post-Apartheid South African productions directed by British directors worked well in tandem with Goddard's essay and brought a South African perspective to bear on the productions of Gregory Doran, Janet Suzman and Paige Newmark. What I missed here was an acknowledgement of the sensitive criticism of these stagings by the likes of Virginia Mason Vaughan and Barbara Hodgdon: while Newmark has not received sufficient critical attention, Doran and Suzman have accumulated a significant critical heritage. The volume concludes with Christie Carson's searching essay on the politics behind the educational outreach work of the RSC and Shakespeare's Globe. Carson's concluding remarks keep the early promise made by the editors that they would '[raise] the question that all of the other essays ask either implicitly or explicitly: when we respond to a performance, when we try to understand its context, when we decode its meanings, when we feel it addresses or ignores our concerns, who are "we"?' *Shakespeare in Stages* is valuable because each of its case studies articulates a different, provisional answer to this fundamental question.

Weyward Macbeth: Intersections of Race and Performance, a collection edited by Scott L. Newstok and Ayanna Thompson, complements the strand of essays in *Shakespeare in Stages* concerned with race but narrows its focus to the role of a single play in shaping American racial formations. The choice of *Macbeth* as a lens through which to study race, as Thompson is aware, may itself seem weird/wayward, but she argues for a recognition that this is 'not an un-raced, non-raced, or normatively-raced play (you see how the English language bucks the sense that something is not raced!)'. Its preoccupation with blood and staining, she argues, 'unnervingly coincides with early American debates about the nature – the essence – of race', as the bloodstains on Lady Macbeth's hands come to stand for the indelible blots on America's history. As the essays by Heather S. Nathans, John C. Briggs, Joyce Green

MacDonald and Nick Moschovakis go on to show, *Macbeth* haunts America's history as much as the play itself is haunted by the rhetoric of race. Central to this history of haunting is Orson Welles's 'voodoo' *Macbeth*, which Thompson and Marguerite Rippy resist reading as unequivocally progressive (Rippy denounces the production's 'trade in stereotypical fantasies of the primitive'). *Weyward Macbeth*, with its twenty-six essays ranging from Celia R. Daileader's analysis of early modern racial and gender prejudice in Shakespeare's and Middleton's contributions to the play all the way to Richard Burt's tellingly titled epilogue 'ObaMacbeth', and its appendix listing over one hundred productions using 'non-traditional' (read: racially mixed or black) casting for the play, succeeds in making it impossible, henceforth, to ignore *Macbeth*'s racial resonances, both within its text and its deployment on North American stages and screens.

The body of the volume is organized into sections on early American intersections, Federal Theatre Project(s) (a section dedicated to Welles's production, its predecessor and its successors), other stagings (from the Asian-American to Alaskan Tlingit), music (from Verdi to Jazz and Hip-Hop), the play on screen and in cinematic allusions, concluding with *Macbeth*-inspired plays and poetry. What I like about these sections is not just their combination of range with internal coherence, but also the way that each is prefaced by an arresting image – whether an 1856 cartoon of 'A Proslavery Incantation Scene', a production photograph from Teatro La Tea's *Macbeth 2029* or the dust-jacket image for Langston Hughes's *Shakespeare in Harlem* – that could, in conjunction with one or two essays from that section, provide a fabulous starting-point for a classroom discussion. I have no doubt, since this scholarly yet accessible book is published as a paperback, that it will indeed feature prominently in classrooms, particularly in North America, since it so urgently speaks about and to North American politics and culture.

Amongst the many excellent contributions, I was particularly captivated by Bernth Lindfors's essay on Ira Aldridge's mid-nineteenth-century whiteface performances as *Macbeth*, for which he unearths many more reviews in European news-papers than I was aware existed, resulting in a sat-isfyingly rounded picture of Aldridge's ever more complex take on the murder scene. Scott L. New-stok's essay builds on Marguerite Rippy's account of Welles's 'voodoo' *Macbeth* with an intriguing discussion of the ways in which this production has achieved such an iconic power as to occlude other black *Macbeth*s and force subsequent produc-tions into fantastical contortions as they attempt to '[draw] upon familiarity with the 1936 produc-tion at the same time [as] they distinguish them-selves from it'. In turn, Lenwood Sloan's narra-tive of his own 'revival' of Welles's *Macbeth* as *The Vo-Du Macbeth!* slots in perfectly after Newstok and Rippy's essays while taking on a much more personal, immediate tone. As it turns out, with a new libretto and script, this must have been a pro-duction that ended up being quite different from Welles's and that drew heavily on the locale of New Orleans in 1863, only to be destroyed by Hurricane Katrina in the New Orleans of 2005. Thank goodness other black *Macbeth*s seem to have fared better, as we find out in Harry J. Lennix's – again, very personal – account of his own perfor-mance as Macbeth at the Lillian Theatre in Los Angeles in 2007. This is no mere 'I played this scene this way' narrative: Lennix discusses colour-blind casting, which he describes as 'avoid[ing] the realities of race' and therefore irresponsible and explains how the production was dramatically specific to African-American experiences even as Lennix himself apparently drew on the writings of white nineteenth-century actors to shape his per-sonal approach to the role.

In the sections on musical and poetic appropri-ations, an essay that stood out was Douglas Lanier's appraisal of Duke Ellington's 1957 *Such Sweet Thunder*, a suite of twelve musical vignettes on Shakespearian themes that 'self-consciously pushes against the way Shakespeare had been used in nineteenth-century minstrel shows to ridicule the cultural aspirations of black performers'. In Elling-ton's 'Lady Mac', 'Lady Macbeth, a Shakespearean voice of aspiration traditionally evaluated as a fig-ure of moral darkness, is transposed . . . into an

affirmational key, making her into an icon for the strivings of those who are racially dark.' Thanks to Courtney Lehmann's essay, I now know that Nina Menkes's *The Bloody Child: An Interior of Violence* is a film I ought to watch, if only I can muster the courage to subject myself to a viewing experi-ence that sounds like a true ordeal. Much more palatable and equally interesting are the poems by African-American women who 'conjure' with *Macbeth*, making the play feed into their portrayal of African-American childhood, prostitution and the Salem witch trials (in Charita Gainey-O'Toole and Elizabeth Alexander's joint contribution). Philip C. Kolin and Peter Erickson, in separate essays, also bring to our attention a number of contemporary African-American plays that enter into a dialogue with Shakespeare's play.

The part of *Weyward Macbeth* that will go on haunting me, however, is Francesca Royster's oppositional (weyward?) reading of whiteness in Roman Polanski's *Macbeth*. Royster's most personal moment is one which will speak to the experiences of many of her readers: 'I may have been told by my professors, by editors, and anonymous readers to produce a view that is "historicized" and objec-tive, but I have always understood that directive deep down as meaning that I should bring some forms of knowledge to the table while silencing others.' Royster's work is characterized by the need to denounce the assumption of whiteness as a neu-tral category, drawing attention, in this essay, to the ways in which Polanski's film undermines the idealization of whiteness, showing white bodies as fleshy, vulnerable, imperfect. Her worrying at the meanings of race in Polanski's film is representa-tive of the volume as a whole: urgent, political, personal, controversial, intelligent.

A sense of urgency and political engagement is also what characterizes Kim Solga's monograph *Violence Against Women in Early Modern Performance: Invisible Acts*, a book that is best read in tandem with Roberta Barker's 2007 *Early Modern Tragedy, Gender and Performance, 1984–2000*. My resistance to viewing the violence against women Courtney Lehmann describes in her discussion of *The Bloody Child* is unequivocally denounced by Solga. Her book is an eloquent, highly theoretically sophisticated and passionate call for an ethics of performance and ethics of spectatorship that relies on trauma theory and performance studies (in particular the work of Phelan, Bennett, Blau, Taylor and Schneider) to problematize the staging and viewing of early modern acts of violence against women in present-day performance. Solga notes that violence against women is, in early modern England, subject to simultaneous erasure and culturally choreographed performances. To convey a flavour of Solga's style and the core of her argument it is perhaps best to let her speak for herself: Solga wants to

imagin[e] performance as a witness to what I want to call the 'in/visible' act of violence against women. The in/visible act is both/and: it enters representation as invisible, as elided within representation, but quickly becomes palpable as such, as a missed and missing story of loss *within the frame of the very performance that would complete the process of its effacement.* The in/visible act is a guerrilla performance gesture that erupts from within the spectacle of violence's elision at its most critical moment – that interrupts, messily, violence's own forgetting . . . The in/visible act is the performance of violence against women as critical forgetting; it charges its witnesses to come to terms with what we've missed but also with *how* we've missed – with how we have failed to see the suffering before us, hidden in plain sight. (16–17)

Most urgently, perhaps, the performance of early modern in/visible acts of violence in present-day performance highlights the erasure of violence in the present. For Solga, reading violence as a trope, as has become the norm in feminist gaze theory, obscures the material presence of violence and women's suffering on our stages and in our lives. The challenge she poses is to 'witness women's violence and its elision in a way that pays attention to theory but doesn't simply reduce violence against women *to* theory, that pays attention to history but doesn't simply trope violence against women as a metaphor *for* history'.

In the body of the book, Solga rises to this challenge, using theory with a lighter touch as she analyses the performances of four plays, reading them

against early modern conduct and religious literature to tease out the ways in which they render the violations of their female protagonists 'in/visible'. Some Shakespeare scholars might end up confining their reading to her incisive and thoughtful analysis of the performance of rape – and the need for the rape victim to perform her rape so that it be acknowledged by the authorities and become readable in court – in *Titus Andronicus*. But they would be wrong to do so, not because the chapter isn't good (it *is*, and revises much recent thinking about the play and the paradigm-changing performances of Sonia Ritter in Deborah Warner's staging in 1987 and Laura Fraser in Julie Taymor's 1999 film), but because part of what makes Solga's work so significant is the way she puts Shakespeare's play alongside plays by Shakespeare's contemporaries. The fact that she does not feel the need to highlight that hers is one of the very rare single-authored performance studies (together with work by Kate McLuskie (1989), Susan Bennett (1996) and Roberta Barker (2007)) to analyse the performance of Shakespeare's contemporaries in present-day culture should not obscure the sea-change in the field this book might be registering: it is remarkable that this should be unremarkable. Shakespearian performance studies has been lagging far behind theatre history and historicist/materialist criticism in acknowledging that Shakespeare's plays do not exist in an historical vacuum but are deeply embedded in their historical and dramatic context. What Solga's book achieves is a recognition that this is true not only of the early modern period but also of the present: the representation of 'in/visible' acts of violence against women in performances of Shakespeare's plays are surrounded by performances of plays by his contemporaries, often by the same theatre companies, that pose analogous problems, that force us to reflect in similar ways on the ethics of our spectatorship and on the uses to which we put early modern drama in our theatres.

Solga shows how, in Katie Mitchell's 1992 production of *A Woman Killed with Kindness*, the director's naturalistic approach to the staging of Anne's 'kind' treatment by her husband (in which loving gestures turned shockingly violent) made her body a puzzle and revealed something of the difficulties involved in adhering to the cultural script for the battered wife's performance of salvation. Crucially, Solga juxtaposes Saskia Reeves's performance as Anne not only with performances of Lavinia but also with Mitchell's staging of Euripides' *Iphigenia*: the context for stagings of early modern drama in our theatres, Solga seems to suggest, is not confined to that canon. The painful submission of Heywood's Anne contrasts with the Duchess of Malfi's angry refusal 'to stage-manage her body's destruction' in Webster's play. The Duchess's resistance, Solga argues, creates problems for those who witness it in the theatre and demands that we pay attention to Act 5 of the play, where her refusals to play along are recuperated and her rage at her violation is erased. Looking at Peter Hinton's Stratford Festival production of 2006 and Phyllida Lloyd's staging for the National Theatre in 2003, Solga investigates how these productions involve their audiences in the act of witnessing. Of Janet McTeer's performance of the Duchess's enraged curses in the National Theatre, she gives us a chilling account that conveys the force of that performance's rejection of the prescribed modes of behaviour for the female martyr and the way it 'cast doubt upon the social and political efficacy' of its National Theatre audience's 'passive, consumptive watching'. Finally, noting how Middleton and Rowley's *Changeling* is 'the story of a woman undone first by architecture, and then by us', the book's concluding chapter argues for a reading of Declan Donnellan and Nick Ormerod's 2006 Cheek by Jowl production of *The Changeling*, which deprived its spectators of physical comfort and emotional distance, as creating 'an architecture of feminist performance'. Here, as Solga sets the play's obfuscation of Beatrice-Joanna's rape alongside present-day prejudices against rape victims, *Violence Against Women* more than ever asserts itself as a work of deeply politically committed scholarship. Solga demands that we adopt a politicized mode of viewing that involves 'a willingness on our part to be unsettled.' Her work certainly has the power to challenge and discombobulate (her word!) its readers and shake us out of our pleasurable habits of complacent spectatorship.

One of the things I have argued Solga's *Violence Against Women* does through practice rather than theory is advocate the need for the field of early modern performance studies to expand its scope beyond Shakespeare and consider the work plays by other early modern dramatists do in our theatres. What is implicit for Solga becomes increasingly explicit in a cluster of three edited collections that push at the boundaries of the field, opening it up in different directions and asking new questions about performances, methodologies, ideologies. The volumes are characterized by curiosity, intellectual energy and the sort of risk-taking and danger that can lead to critical disasters as much as to genuine discoveries, as a new field is sketchily mapped out and unusual approaches are tested. Together, the collections of essays by Melissa Croteau and Carolyn Jess-Cooke, Greg Colón Semenza and Sarah Werner do succeed in demonstrating the need for *New Directions in Renaissance Drama and Performance Studies*, as Werner's title so aptly puts it.

Melissa Croteau and Carolyn Jess-Cooke's *Apocalyptic Shakespeares: Essays on Visions of Chaos and Revelation in Recent Film Adaptations* is the volume in this group which is most troubled by the implications of its decisions. As it struggles to find a way of articulating its revision of the boundaries of the field, *Apocalyptic Shakespeares* exposes both the stranglehold Shakespeare still has on our imaginary and critical language and the need to escape it. The primary intertexts for the 'apocalyptic' film adaptations of Shakespeare's plays, it turns out, are not other adaptations of Shakespeare, but rather the Hollywood blockbusters whose (post-)apocalyptic visions have tapped into anxieties about climate change and the post-9/11 world order. Furthermore, the volume includes a chapter on Alex Cox's *Revenger's Tragedy*, which Gretchen E. Minton sees as related not only to Taymor's *Titus* and Almereyda's *Hamlet* (2000) but also to the films of Tarantino, Kubrick's *A Clockwork Orange* (1971), Ridley Scott's *Blade Runner* (1982) and George Miller's *Mad Max Trilogy* (1979–85). The volume's inclusion of a Middleton adaptation pushes Melissa Croteau's introduction, and its desire to put Shakespeare at the centre of her discussion ('this book is predicated upon the eminence and significance of Shakespeare in our culture'), into crisis: at one point she even describes Cox's *Revenger's*, alongside Luhrmann's *William Shakespeare's Romeo + Juliet* (1996), Jean-Luc Godard's *King Lear* (1987) and Almereyda's *Hamlet*, as an adapted Shakespearian narrative through which 'these filmmakers are able to comment simultaneously on the Bard, narrational modes, the apocalyptic, and contemporary cultures'. Later, a potted history of early modern England in a single paragraph begins to make a little room for other playwrights, as Croteau explains how 'Shakespeare and his contemporaries lived in a vibrant time fraught with tensions and fears regarding the realities of catastrophic disease, religiously and politically motivated violence, and even natural disasters.' Towards the end of the introduction, in the chapter-by-chapter outline of the volume, at last Croteau admits that, in the shape of the 'intensely post-apocalyptic adaptation of *The Revenger's Tragedy*, a play written by Thomas Middleton', there is some 'decidedly *not* Shakespeare' in this book. Clearly unsure of whether her readers know who Middleton is or was, Croteau adds: 'a contemporary of Shakespeare'. Coming after an involved discussion of the properties and functions of apocalyptic stories, I was half expecting an eclipse of sun and moon at this admission. As the book shows in several of its essays, however, the postmodern moment is one in which master narratives and stale approaches can be relinquished; what looks like the end of the world may simply herald a new era of hope and redemption.

With the introduction thus fraught with a barely acknowledged, yet tangible, anxiety about the boundaries of the Shakespearian canon, I found it difficult to read my way through *Apocalyptic Shakespeares* without seeing, in several of its essays, marks of exclusion alongside signs of boundary erosion. Ramona Wray's opening essay combines four examples of 'Contemporary Shakespearean Filmmaking' that allow her to build a strong argument about the apocalyptic world view, hovering between dystopian and redemptive scenarios, that informs them. Wray shows how Derek Jarman's *The Angelic Conversation* (1985), Miroslaw Rogala's '*Macbeth': The Witches' Scenes* (1988), Michael Bogdanov's *Macbeth* (1997) and Kevin Costner's *The Postman* (1997) all have 'a tendency to invert or unmoor any stable point of reference'. It is Wray's inclusion of Jarman's film on the Sonnets and the exclusion of his other apocalyptic works – *Jubilee* (1977), *The Last of England* (1988) and, most importantly, *Edward II* (1991) – which haunted my reading of her essay and unmoored Shakespeare as a stable point of reference: the presence of *Angelic Conversation*, the only film not to contain elements of *Macbeth*, ghosted the absence of Jarman's brilliantly apocalyptic adaptation of Marlowe's play about killing a king. Later in the volume, Adrian Streete, in an incisive investigation of conversion and anti-Semitism, manages a greater break from the Shakespearian stranglehold, comparing Michael Radford's *The Merchant of Venice* (2004) to Mel Gibson's *The Passion of the Christ* (2004) and giving the latter as much room as the former. The result is a reading of the Shakespeare adaptation that opens it up to a larger debate about the promulgation of anti-Semitic ideology in present-day culture than confining the discussion to Shakespeare would have allowed.

Other contributions to *Apocalyptic Shakespeares* bore traces of a different type of boundary erosion, as the corpus of supposedly 'apocalyptic' films appeared to include films (and essays) that had little in common with that category. There was nothing apocalyptic to speak of in Courtney Lehmann's enjoyable appraisal of Christine Edzard's *The Children's Midsummer Night's Dream* (2001) and her critique, informed with characteristic theoretical sophistication by cybernetic theory, of Adrian Noble's use of the boy actor Osheen Jones in his *Midsummer Night's Dream* (1996). In Julie Taymor's use of the same actor to portray Young Lucius in *Titus* (2000), Lehmann sees a feminist answer to Noble's patriarchal *Dream* in which the boy follows the maternal rather than the paternal role model as he walks into the sunrise with Aaron's baby in his arms. The next essay, in which Kim Fedderson and

J. Michael Richardson (anachronistically) set Julie Taymor's *Titus* against the background of 9/11, at least attempts a return to the topic of apocalyptic violence. The opening connection to the Apocalypse seems contrived, however, and the essay only acquires a sense of purpose towards the end, as the authors voice a sharp critique of Taymor's all-too-easy assimilation of difference, her ability to block out politics and her 'indifference to the otherness of the other'. By the time we arrive at Melissa Croteau's own essay on Almereyda's *Hamlet*, 'generation X' and 'postmodernity' rather than 'visions of chaos and revelation' have become the dominant strands of the argument. Carl James Grindley's discussion of the plague in films of *Romeo and Juliet* and *Twelfth Night* uses 'apocalyptic' as a synonym for 'bleak' and/or 'dangerous'; the author's tangible dismay at the 'plague-sized holes' he finds in the films brings the essay dangerously close to the widely discredited 'fidelity discourse' that has been the bane of adaptation studies. When, with Carolyn Jess-Cooke's concluding exploration of Kristian Levring's Dogme *The King Is Alive* (2000), we return to the topic of apocalyptic Shakespeare, the 'Shakespeare' in question is a memorial reconstruction of a text that is treated as a 'manifesto-document' authorizing new, oppositional, modes of film-making.

What unites many essays in *Apocalyptic Shakespeare*, then, is a sense, as Richard Vela puts it in his analysis of *William Shakespeare's Romeo + Juliet*, that we are in 'a post-Shakespearean world', in which 'Shakespeare the author is dead and survives as advertising copy and brand name.' This is an extreme view and is belied by the importance Shakespeare as an authorizing figure has in most of the films discussed here (a fact which Alfredo Michel Modenessi deplores in relation to the all-too-easy appropriation of 'Shakespeare' to authorize the dubious politics of *The Lion King*), yet the volume repeatedly registers an unspoken unease with its own use of Shakespeare as its organizing framework. It is because of this, perhaps, that Gregory Colón Semenza's *The English Renaissance in Popular Culture: An Age for All Time*, while comparable in many ways and sharing some of the same authors as *Apocalyptic Shakespeare*, is a much more successful volume. Vela's sentiments are echoed in this book by Donald Hedrick's comments on the era of 'late Shakespeareanism' that we have entered. The title-page illustration by Semenza features a Union Jack onto which the Folio engraving of Shakespeare is superimposed. Pasted over Shakespeare's eyes is the slogan 'God save the Queene', with the word 'Queene' crossed out and the much larger 'Shakespeare' substituted. The title-page, with its allusion to the Sex Pistols' album cover, its multiple substitutions and erasures and its invocation of competing authorities that oscillate between the early modern and postmodern moments conveys something of the complexity of this collection. Semenza seeks to address 'the fact that Shakespearean appropriations are merely part of a wider popular culture interest and investment in the Renaissance as an imagined historical period'. There is a problem with 'how the scholarly industry governs inquiry', leading to the critical neglect of noteworthy films and texts just because they are not 'Shakespeare-centric' enough. To Semenza's credit, his collection does not, in a knee-jerk reaction, exclude Shakespeare. Not only does Semenza include Deborah Cartmell's essay on Sam Taylor's 1929 landmark 'talkie' *Shrew* (starring Mary Pickford and Douglas Fairbanks), but his own contribution to the volume zooms in on John Lydon's Olivier and Richard III-inspired Sex Pistol persona Johnny Rotten and demonstrates the profound dependence of the British punk movement on the 'rhetoric of anarchy' of Shakespeare's villain in punk's negation of 'official versions of British history'. In the rich reflections that fill the volume, Shakespeare adaptations also repeatedly feature as part of a complex answer to the vital questions Semenza asks in his introduction:

To what ends do moderns seek to portray, adapt, or appropriate the English Renaissance? . . . In what ways have popular adaptations of Shakespeare's plays . . . informed popular ideas about what the Renaissance was 'actually' like? Have they promoted an author-centered industry in spite of a largely postmodern scholarship? How have they in turn limited or enabled our teaching and our students' learning about early modern literature and history?

That our focus on the Anglophone world and Shakespeare has indeed limited our understanding of modern appropriations of the Renaissance is especially clear in the essays on film adaptations of Middleton that are bunched together under the somewhat arbitrary heading 'Renaissance Cinemas' at the end of the book. This is the section of the book which is most marred by numerous proof-reading errors: Richard Burt even has a typo in his title and one unfortunate author in the list of contributors is described as a 'cow-riter'. While intensely conscious of the outmodedness of the historicist narrative, Burt shows no such self-awareness in his use of the deconstructionist punning coinage, as he conflates the names of New Wave film director Jacques Rivette and Guy Debord's *dérive* to form the compounds 'dérive-ation', 'dé-rive-iates', 'dérive-vative' and, worst, 'Dériv(e-i)ation'. This shouldn't put the reader off, however, for Burt's essay is, to my knowledge, the first by a Shakespeare scholar to consider the groundbreaking experiments with *Pericles* (which, according to a character in *Paris Belongs to Us* (1960) 'wasn't Shakespeare's work') and *The Revenger's Tragedy* by one of France's most important film-makers of the 1960s and 1970s. The essay begins to fill the vast gap in our knowledge of European engagements with early modern English drama, some of which is being filled by collections like *Shakespeare and European Politics* (2008, see last year's review), but much of which remains unexplored. Rivette's compulsive reiteration of fragments of early modern English drama is linked to his experimental practice and anticipates the concern with fragmentation, memory and theatricality of twenty-first century adapters such as Kristian Levring, Mike Figgis (who is given the sort of footnote that is really an essay) and Alex Cox. Fittingly, Burt's essay is followed by James Keller's investigation of Cox's *Revenger's*, the second of three essays on this film this year. Keller is more finely attuned to the class registers governing the film than Minton in *Apocalyptic Shakespeares*,

but the essay resembles Minton's in its emphasis on the film's apocalyptic framework and leaves much unsaid about the specific ways in which the film speaks to twenty-first century (cultural) politics.

That absence of politics is made up for by a cluster of essays that skewer the conservatism at the heart of several blockbuster portrayals of the Renaissance. Adrienne L. Eastwood is concerned with the way in which popular representations of Queen Elizabeth I portray this figure in a way that deprives her of the masculine attributes she associated with her body politic, defining her 'primarily by her natural body and its relation to men'. It's chilling to find that Shekhar Kapur's *Elizabeth* (1998, 2007), no less than the older *Elizabeth R* mini-series (1971) and *The Virgin Queen* and *Elizabeth I* (both 2005), again and again portray the queen as 'in varying degrees, mediated and, politically, reduced by her relationship to men'. As Courtney Lehmann suggests, a film like Kapur's *Elizabeth: The Golden Age* may go in search of the Renaissance, but what it finds in the end is 'us', with all our present-day prejudices and anxieties. Period film, for her, 'is the escapist genre *par excellence*', allowing us to 'project the present geopolitical travesties in the Middle East onto the palimpsestic figure of Elizabeth I'. It's a compelling argument that makes a lot of sense, but the politics of the film Lehmann and Eastwood expose in their essays are alarming in their intractable conservatism. The politics of twentieth and twenty-first century fictionalizations of the Renaissance in the cinema – whether in the graphic novel and film *V for Vendetta*'s versions of the Gunpowder Plot analysed by Melissa Croteau, or in 1960s and 1970s horror films centring on witch persecutions Deborah Willis discusses – are seemingly always at risk of being deeply reactionary, even when they show sympathy for the victims of patriarchal or state power.

For Ramona Wray, understanding a broadcasting phenomenon like the BBC's *The Tudors* (2009) requires an appreciation of the complex, *knowing*, intertextual web that connects the series to 'the glut of "Shakespeare" films of the 1980s and 1990s'. The series posits itself as a prequel to the other film representations of the life of *Henry VIII*, and is marketed as a response to HBO's *Rome* and *The Sopranos* in the anniversary year of Henry VIII's ascension. *The Tudors* may look like nothing more than a savvy exploitation of Jonathan Rhys Meyer's sex appeal (David Starkey memorably referred to the film as a 'shameful . . . bonkorama') but Wray, in her witty and energetic article, contends that it is much, much more than that: nothing less than 'the most definitive and eloquent expression of a sea change, a radical revision of the ways in which the origins of the Tudor dynasty, the Reformation and the long-standing ramifications of religious change are explained and understood in the popular imaginary'. Key to this are the series's stress on personality, its 'what if' narrative strategy that unsettles the audience's pre-knowledge of history, and the 'fast-paced yet intimate camera work' that allows the viewer access to Henry's 'Hamletian' inner psychology and follow his maturation into the king we all know about. This is combined with brutal visuals that portray the Renaissance as 'a graphically traumatic and physically immediate event' – a noticeably 'anti-nostalgic' angling of history that goes against the grain of late twentieth-century heritage Shakespeare while invoking this tradition.

The extent to which, in Wray's words, '"Shakespeare" on screen comes to the aid of the popular explanation of history, and history defers to an elaboration of "Shakespeare" in the search for a ready style and grammar of representation' is also evident in the essays of Kevin J. Wetmore, Jr and Amy Rodgers. Wetmore exposes the 'misrepresentation of medieval violence as Renaissance practice' in North American Renaissance fairs and demonstrates the extent to which the fairs' view of Renaissance combat is dependent not only on Renaissance knight lore but at least as much on Shakespeare, fantasy narratives and American history. What troubles Wetmore is the question of 'why period violence has such an important place in the recreation of the Renaissance'. He surmises that the answer might lie in our fetishization of the Renaissance sword as 'nostalgia and wish fulfilment combined in a single piece of material culture' and suggests that Renaissance fairs in fact carry on the romanticization of medieval combat which was a characteristic of Shakespeare's own theatre practice. Rodgers turns her attention from participants to spectators and investigates the role the figure of the 'groundling' plays in a variety of discourses, ranging from present-day scholarship through popular fiction, film and the ticket arrangements for Shakespeare's Globe. Hers is a strong new voice that accuses scholars of being influenced by popular nostalgic representations of the groundlings as 'the site where longings for our interpretative past and anxieties about its present and future begin to coalesce into legible forms'. Scholars no less than writers of historical fiction or film-makers like Al Pacino 'share the fiction of the noble spectator', a post-Enlightenment fantasy that enables an articulation of our yearning for an embodied, immediate spectatorial experience that belies the reality of class privilege underpinning present-day access to Shakespeare. Rodgers's essay packs a punch that makes me eager to see more of her work on spectators and spectatorship.

Even more than that I would like to see much more writing of the type and quality of Sarah Werner's *New Directions for Renaissance Drama and Performance Studies*, a book worth dwelling on because of the significance of the new avenues it sketches with lucidity and exemplary control. The volume is arranged into sections on 'Working with the Ephemeral', 'Reconnecting Literary Criticism and Performance Analysis', 'Resituating Shakespeare' and a 'Postscript' in which Courtney Lehmann takes this year's criticism of Alex Cox's *Revenger's Tragedy* to a new level of sophistication, using the film as a starting-point for a reflection on the status of the 'live' in theatre and cinema. As Lehmann puts it, '[s]uch a uniquely positioned figure like Thomas Middleton, an independently successful playwright who also worked closely with Shakespeare, may provide an unexpected window onto new ways of theorizing not just Shakespearean drama but, more importantly, Renaissance drama at large' – and it is this drive towards a new, theoretically informed, understanding of 'Renaissance drama at large' that characterizes the volume as a whole. That this is the goal of the volume is apparent right from the start, in Werner's smart, crisp introduction to the field in its current state. Werner asks us to learn the lessons taught by the 'multiplicity of approaches to studying Shakespeare and performance' in its first and second generations and seeks to identify the omissions in the field. She is especially alert to the implications of 'the near-exclusive attention paid to Shakespeare's plays', which 'has shaped the field's concerns in ways we do not yet fully understand. Our assumptions about the dramaturgy of Renaissance theater, about the power of performance, about theatrical languages – all these assumptions are rooted in Shakespeare's canon. What would happen if we were to move our attention away from this singular focus?' Changing our focus in this way is an imposing task and Werner's collection begins to tackle it with impressive force.

Robert Shaughnessy opens the conversation about the ephemerality of performance with a beautifully poised reflection piece on the experience of watching and recording live theatre. There is a difference between theatregoing and theatre history that points 'towards a more fundamental division between vicarious and authentic experience'. The theatre historian finds her/himself in a 'liminal position', both inside and outside the performance and the archival traces it has left behind. '[W]riting about performance', Shaughnessy reminds us, 'is an activity that takes place after the event', undermined by 'the partiality and fallibility of the human memories that attempt to preserve' the performance. The project of theatre history is therefore destined to fail. Yet theatre's 'never fully accomplished work of self-erasure' is also what makes Shakespeare in performance 'both viable and bearable'; forgetting is central to the experience of theatregoing. Note-taking, while assisting in the reconstruction of memories, results in Shaughnessy's/the viewer's dislocation from the onstage action as he addresses a future version of himself, losing his connection with the present. Watching Shakespeare in performance, for Shaughnessy, is tantamount to 'watching ourselves watching Shakespeare', which crucially involves watching others watching and reacting to the performance. Rarely have I read something that spoke quite so directly to my own experiences and anxieties as a theatre historian and, while Shaughnessy does not offer a simple answer to the ethical conundrum he raises, I took solace from hearing it articulated with such clarity.

William N. West, in the next essay, takes issue with the rhetoric of loss in Shaughnessy's reflection and in performance studies more generally. For him, this rhetoric is inseparable from English theatre's 'retrospectively defining trauma', the closure of the theatres in 1642 'which fixed "Shakespeare's theater" as a moment of plenitude decisively foreclosed by history'. West proposes that we counteract theatre history's rhetoric of loss with a recognition that performances record, in their gestures, script, props, and the memories of performers and spectators, earlier performances. 'Performance points out that every present is full of the past and full of the future'; a powerful performance 'gathers and multiplies the force of other performances that have preceded it', so that instead of speaking of loss we should be talking about what we gain by replaying performances. The critical pessimism and sense of loss is also examined by Christopher Cobb, who suggests that we need to become more attentive not only to performance but also to its contexts. If I was somewhat underwhelmed by Cobb's patronizing account of his students' reactions to a performance of *Othello* and his outline of a semiotic mode of analysis that distinguishes between signs that build a metonymy and those that are transformed into a metaphor (is this really necessary?), his illustration of his method through a reading of the Chicago Shakespeare Theater's *Macbeth* (2009) almost won me over with its meticulous attention to the workings of the theatrical sign.

The essays grouped in the middle of the book are concerned with unpacking the relationship between modern performances and the literary criticism of the plays. Andrew James Hartley opens this section with an essay that builds on his preoccupation with character in his contribution to *Shakespeare and Character* last year. For him, performance – and the actors' and spectators' bodies during a performance – are key to understanding character. Taking *The Revenger's Tragedy*'s Vindice as his example, he demonstrates how a character who is notorious for his discontinuity on the page becomes a coherent person when personated on stage: 'What in reading seem to be empty and inexplicable blanks in Vindice's character are, in performance, filled by the actor's presence.' This is the most eloquent rejoinder to Alan Sinfield's questioning of the existence of 'character' in early modern drama I have come across to date and it is a splendid illustration of how modern performance can still teach us something about the texts in spite of second-wave performance studies' critique of Styan's 'Shakespeare Revolution'. That 'revolution' and the impact it had on the construction of the Blackfriars in Staunton, Virginia, and Shakespeare's Globe in London is the object of Paul Menzer's sharp critique. Menzer argues that the revolutionary zeal that animated the building of these theatres has been contaminated by the need to secure funding, leading to a privileging of architecture over 'the less material, more ephemeral products and processes of playing which are harder to package and resell for grants and cash'. The original practices movement that started as an idealists' project has now, in its 'expansionist phase', become an attempt 'to reap the profits of nostalgia'. Figureheads like Sam Wanamaker, Ralph Alan Cohen, Peter Cockett and Tina Packer are the equivalent of 'the James Burbages and Philip Henslowes, not the actors who inhabited their buildings'; what is lost in their quest for real estate is the place of the player. This is why Menzer advocates the need for a counter-insurgency that opposes the forces of capitalistic enterprise and architecture by putting the actor back in the centre of the stage. We need to search for traces of performance not in archaeological digs but in what we can recover of 'the perceptual perspective of those involved in the event' of early modern performance, which we must acknowledge in all its mobility and ephemerality. Instead of spaces, we ought to be privileging bodies; not the stable, but 'the provisional, the ad hoc, and the occasional'. Academic theatre reviews are the most obvious way of recording the event

of performance, in all its ephemerality, today, but they are not neutral tools even when they attempt transparency. Jeremy Lopez, in a chapter that will disturb theatre reviewers (and that disturbed me, writing this review), is troubled by 'the proselytizing gesture – the apparently irresistible urge felt by reviewers of Shakespeare productions to promote and celebrate the ever-wider, ever-more accessible dissemination of the works of Shakespeare to less fortunate people elsewhere' – a gesture that is oddly uncritical. For Lopez, *Shakespeare Quarterly* and *Shakespeare Survey* are guilty of complicity in perpetuating the dissemination of information about productions that are simply not worth recording, with the proliferation of valueless reviews feeding the proliferation of valueless productions and vice versa. Many readers of this article, while recognizing Lopez's (deliberate?) underplaying of the value of reviews for theatre historians, will no doubt wince at his justified lambasting of the patronizing and self-serving politics behind the desire to bring Shakespeare to children and/or underprivileged people. It's refreshing to think that, in his role as theatre reviews editor for *Shakespeare Bulletin*, Lopez will be bringing these insights to his job and might be able to effect, if not a change in the volume of reviews, then at least in the tone and purpose of the genre.

With Genevieve Love's chapter, 'Performance Criticism Without Performance: The Study of Non-Shakespearean Drama', the volume returns to the problem of the rhetoric of loss underpinning performance criticism. Love proposes that 'perhaps plays utterly lacking a performance tradition are an apt site of inquiry for a field that has come to acknowledge loss as central to its motive and method'. Initiating the collection's section on 'Resituating Shakespeare', thus, is an invitation to use imaginary performances of non-Shakespearian drama as a way of rethinking the work of performance criticism not as something based on a specific performance, but more as 'a habit of mind, a positioning, an almost bodily attentiveness to the *idea* of performance'. This is a method she goes on to illustrate with a reading of Heywood's *A Mayden-head Well Lost*, whose textual gaps she imaginatively and very effectively fills with details of the effect of (imagined) stage actions in performance. I was amazed to see how well this method works to animate the reading of a play with no performance history through 'fantasy performance'. This is the more exciting since, as Emma Smith notes in her chapter, 'the study of non-Shakespearian early modern drama in performance is a more fragmentary and elusive object' than that of Shakespearian drama, partly because 'the emerging protocols for discussing Shakespeare onstage are implicitly comparative'. When there is no other performance to compare a performance to, our criticism of performances 'cannot so readily serve the liberal agenda of multiple literary interpretations'. Furthermore, the nature of our critical engagement with non-Shakespearian drama is often historicist rather than presentist, so that modern productions of those plays become 'marginal to our own readings' since they – like any performance – will be geared towards relevance to the present. Smith offers a creative solution to this problem: she proposes that we should read analogically, as she proceeds to demonstrate with a reading of Ben Jonson's plays as formally related, *analogous* to the films of Alfred Hitchcock. Again, what may seem an odd methodology works remarkably well in practice, as Smith links Jonson's parabastic appearances in his own plays to Hitchcock's analogous 'anti-narrative and anti-diegetic' cameos in his own films. In a way entirely different to Love, Smith succeeds in creating 'an awareness of performance possibilities in early modern plays which does not require the literal performance of these texts in order to be activated'.

It is only a small step from Smith's analogous methodology to Bridget Escolme's suggestion that Shakespeare's plays themselves need to be thought of in relation not to the theatrical practices of his contemporaries but ours. Escolme urges us to think of recent Shakespeare production in terms of contemporary theatrical trends: Brook's *Lear*, with its 'clear and conscious links to Beckett', is only an extreme example of the interdependence of Shakespeare and twentieth-century drama in performance. She argues for 'a historically

situated Shakespeare performance study, one which acknowledges that the historical play text is rendered meaningful within contexts of actor training, staging convention, and cultural pleasures and anxieties that are not of the playscript's time'. Specifically, the recent development at the RSC of a hypertheatrical performance style, Escolme contends, is best understood as a response to the audience-centred performance practices that have evolved at Shakespeare's Globe on the one hand and, on the other, to Lecoq-influenced physical theatre practitioners and their approach to Shakespeare via clowning. Ayanna Thompson, in the final chapter aimed at resituating Shakespeare, also looks at Shakespeare performance through the lens of contemporary theatre, urging us not to leave race out of the equation when we seek for new ways of discussing early modern drama. Race in Shakespearian performance is vitally important because, '[a]s these plays are constantly restaged, they not only reflect Renaissance constructions of race in/as performance but also inform, influence, and create modern constructions of them'. Her chapter is thus a theoretical, and *Othello*/Iago-centred, complement to the discussion of racial casting and its implications which she reignited this year with *Weyward Macbeth*. For Thompson, the new direction Renaissance drama and performance studies need to move towards consists in 'noticing and commenting upon race in/as performance' and 'then enabling the recognition of the metatheatrical intertexts that fuel the dialectical nature of restagings of classical texts'. Once more, in this provocative, thoughtful volume, Shakespeare, while still crucial to the enquiry, is resituated within a wider theatrical context that allows us to ask better questions and find more complex answers to questions new and old.

Escolme ends her contribution to *New Directions* with the following injunction:

an important next stage for Shakespeare performance criticism is . . . to endeavor to ensure that Shakespeare work outside of mainstream, Anglophone, subsidized production is seen and written about by contributors to the Anglophone Shakespeare criticism industry: Shakespeare work that is inevitably inflected by contemporary practice because it is created by theater practitioners whose work is not primarily Shakespearean.

Judging from this year's publications on Shakespeare's plays in performance, that call is already being heeded. As becomes apparent when reading these publications, however, Escolme's desire for this work to be performed by 'contributors to the Anglophone Shakespeare criticism industry' is not entirely unproblematic if it means that non-Anglophone voices are excluded in the discussion of their own performance traditions. This year, three edited volumes and one monograph powerfully argue for the need to pay closer attention to performances of Shakespeare in Asia. Significantly, these publications are heavily weighted in favour of Asian scholars and Westerners with extensive experience of living in Asia: the field asserts itself as too complex, and too locally embedded, to be done justice to by a touristic approach. Reading these books, I was struck by the strong resistance to received post-colonial paradigms, as one author after another insisted on the need to refine the critical approach to make it fit the specificities of the location and production under discussion. Very distinct local histories, performance traditions and intracultural relationships need to be taken into account in order to grasp the work Shakespeare does – and the work that is done through Shakespeare – in local communities across the Asian continent. Only occasionally does this work reach out to the West, and when it does so, it is motivated by the performances under discussion, as when various authors consider the work of directors like Ninagawa Yukio, Tim Supple and Ong Ken Sen, whose touring productions or intercultural approach require that Western responses be taken into account. In view of this, it will be interesting to see whether the forthcoming publication of Minami Ryuta's *Shakespearean Adaptations in East Asia: A Critical Anthology of Shakespearean Plays in China, Japan, Korea, and Taiwan*, which will span 1,600 pages and give Anglophone scholars access to twenty-five newly translated adaptations, will succeed in inviting Western scholars to join in the discussion.

Dennis Kennedy and Yong Li Lan's collection *Shakespeare in Asia: Contemporary Performance* is the most handsomely produced of this remarkable cluster of books on Asian Shakespeares. With twenty black-and-white illustrations and a striking cover, this is an attractive book which will be on many order lists for university libraries, especially since it presents itself as a sequel to Dennis Kennedy's 1993 *Foreign Shakespeare: Contemporary Performance*. That collection had a major impact on the field of Shakespeare studies, challenging its Anglocentrism with accounts of non-Anglophone Shakespeares throughout the world. Or, to be more specific, throughout the Western world: only two essays in *Foreign Shakespeare*, including Kennedy's own Afterword, had considered Asian Shakespeares. Now, with Yong's help, Kennedy is making up for the omissions of the earlier volume by dedicating an entire collection to Asian Shakespeares. Notwithstanding the insistence of the editors, in their introduction, on the 'diversity of Asia', the book's principal focus is on Shakespeare on Japanese stages, punctuated by essays that look at Chinese productions and Indian films.

The editors' forceful introduction underpins the volume with provocative – if somewhat vague – statements (e.g. the assertion that 'intercultural Asian performance ... asks its spectators about our foreignness to ourselves'). The editors also call for 'discursive terms for thinking about "imitation" that do not oppose it to "authentic" or "original", in order to understand the re-creation of Shakespeare in a different cultural aesthetic'. This gesture towards a theorization of the field is, however, not supported by quite a few of the essays, which are more descriptive than theoretical. The contradictions between the various standpoints of the volume's contributors that do embrace a theoretical standpoint are embraced by the editors, who pitch John Russell Brown (an author carried over from *Foreign Shakespeares*) against Rustom Bharucha in a debate about the ways in which Eastern performance practices may be appropriated by Western practitioners, without attempting to find a theoretical framework that can accommodate those opposed views. Only in her own essay on Ong Ken Sen's intercultural Shakespeares, for which 'a different performance style and language' were used for each character or group of characters, does Yong offer a strong and consistent theoretical position that is in dialogue with some of the other contributors to the volume.

As a critic, I usually have a lot of time for contradictions that resist reconciliation, yet at the end of this book, the contributors' irreconcilable positions, the lack of explicit dialogue between individual essays and the editors' deliberate avoidance of comprehensiveness or a balanced representation of Shakespeare production in the region left me feeling frustrated. I didn't feel that the book had made me learn much that helped me make sense of the role of Shakespeare in Japanese culture, let alone Asian culture more broadly. What I was left with instead was a sense of the sheer vastness of my gaps of knowledge, of my inadequacies as a reader and a craving for a strong guiding narrative. Being relatively new to the field, I needed someone to steer me from one case study of Shakespeare in Asia to the next and create a sense of texture, of interconnections between the various Shakespeares discussed and of the ways that they fit into a larger cultural context (the question of why and how Shakespeare matters in Asia often appeared irrelevant to the authors). Such interconnections between chapters as there were – as when an essay on Shojo Manga, Japanese comic strips for girls, was followed by another essay in which there was a reference to that genre, or an essay late in the book mentioned the translations of Tsubouchi Shoyo that had been described by an earlier contribution, or when different essays discussed Ong Keng Sen's work without entering into dialogue – depended entirely on the reader's ability to remember vast amounts of unfamiliar information. More could certainly have been made of the connections between Chinese and Japanese productions that emphasized the foreignness of Shakespeare: instead, compartmentalized into different chapters, the wider theoretical reflection this similarity seemed to call for did not take place. Even when

concentrating on the dominant Japanese strand of the book, I was struggling to piece together a coherent picture that would allow me to make sense of its individual components. Left in the dark about the relationship between the Tokyo-centric and local dialect Japanese translations of Shakespeare, sometimes in Kabuki style, discussed by Daniel Gallimore, the all-female Takarazuka Revue company (in Minami Ryuta's essay), the Shogekijo (Little Theatre) movement described by Kumiko Hilberdink-Sakamoto, and the break-up of the Shingeki 'monopoly hold on Shakespeare' analysed by Suematsu Michiko, I found myself unable to distinguish mainstream from fringe or to assess the cultural importance of the productions and styles described. To my discomfort, I felt myself yearning for a narrative history, an organizing framework, for the kind of generalization which as scholars we are trained to shun.

And yet I learned a lot from this book. Richard Burt's obsessively punning essay on Indian Shakespeare-plays-within-the-film introduces us to a group of films in which theatrical Shakespeare is used to signify the old and colonial leftover while framing the new. Helpfully, Burt sets these films side-by-side with the Shakespeare films of the Indian diaspora, warning us to remember that 'flows of capital and migrations of directors and actors link Asia to Shakespeare in the UK and US as much as they link Shakespeare and Asia in India': looking at Indian-made films in isolation risks distorting the global, diasporic nature of the phenomenon. What we need, as Burt points out in a footnote, is a full history of Shakespeare in Bollywood instead of the mere snapshots, however intriguing, that can be offered in such an essay. Films such as *Kuch Kuch Hota Hai*, with its citation of the press book for Luhrmann's *William Shakespeare's Romeo + Juliet* 'in which Shakespeare, the movie press book trumps both Shakespeare, the movie and Shakespeare, the book', sounded as though they would benefit from a much fuller treatment than they could be giving within the scope of this essay, however much leeway the author seems to have been given for his word count and his subject matter – his was by far the longest contribution, and the only essay to concern itself exclusively with either film or India.

Placed halfway through the volume, Suematsu Michiko's lucid assessment of the import/export dynamic operative in Japanese Shakespeares would have benefited from being placed at the beginning of the book, because it finally provided some of the organizing framework that allowed me to make better sense of some of the other essays. I enjoyed her discussion of Suzuki Tadashi's 'bicultural' *The Tale of Lear*, with its mutually challenging appropriation of western themes and eastern performance styles. Particularly provocative, in this essay, was Suematsu's opposition between Japanese directors' sense that they need to exploit Japan's '"foreignness" in order to sell its Shakespeare as an export commodity for the West', and the way Tokyo audiences found 'the torrent of *japonaiserie* and the exploitation of native theatrical traditions' in Ninagawa's *Macbeth*, which had been such a success in the West, 'extravagant and false.' It's fascinating to learn that, for the British version of his *Hamlet*, 'Ninagawa made sure that the Japanization of the production became more visible by making the design, especially the costumes and hairstyles, appear more Japanese', and to realize that Suematsu is probably right in her assertion that, with cultural traffic expanding to include more negotiations with other Asian cultures, the distinction, for Japanese Shakespeares, 'between importation and exportation lost its significance in the 1990s' as 'Shakespeare became one of the intersections for cultural exchange within and beyond Asian boundaries.'

Li Ruru's essay on Shakespeare in the Chinese-speaking world also makes itself accessible by providing a rich contextual backdrop to its discussion of three productions staged in 2001, in the midst of uncertainties about the country's social and economic future. What makes her essay particularly poignant is the way she allows her personal voice to come through at times, giving a vivid sense of the rapid changes China has undergone in the past two decades (something which is also true of Shen Lin's essay on China and globalization, which includes a discussion of

Lin Zhaohua's *Coriolanus* that pinpoints the angry political debates surrounding popular vs. elite culture in present-day China). As Li puts it, '[t]he story of Shakespeare in China is more about China than Shakespeare'. Accordingly, this essay gripped me not only because of the elegant evocativeness of its descriptions of performances, but also because it conveyed a sense of urgency about the need to understand the cultural moment and Shakespeare's role in articulating change and reflecting on the politics of the present and the recent past. The essay sits well alongside Yong Li Lan's searching assessment of Ong's radical intercultural theatre practice, most evident in *Search: Hamlet*, staged in Kronborg Castle, Elsinore in 2002. The theoretical sophistication of her essay (and of its subject matter, to be fair) singles it out from most of its peers and allows her to refine our understanding of the intercultural: as she reminds us, these days, 'it is the global movements of people and media that actually define' Shakespeare and Asia; 'so-called discrete cultures', Yong explains, 'are themselves the ongoing product of continuing intercultural movements'. It's to her credit that she allows the last word in the volume to go to Rustom Bharucha in a combative mood, since for him intercultural performance is driven by a Eurocentric agenda, if not by a desire to recolonize Asia through an appropriation of Asian performance styles for performances of Shakespeare. I did end up enjoying that particular unresolved contradiction in the book, though to get to that point was hard work.

It was with relief, therefore, that I picked up the next book, Alexander C. Y. Huang's *Chinese Shakespeares: Two Centuries of Cultural Exchange* and found, before I could even get to the introduction, a note that advised me that any gaps in my knowledge about Chinese cultural history and the critical field would be filled by the book's Select Chronology and chapter notes. Immediately flicking to the back of the book, I indeed found a very helpful table that mapped historical events against the growth of worldwide Shakespeares in general and Shakespeare in China in particular. It took just a few minutes for me to feel I had some sense of the relationships between what I already knew and what was news to me – I was excited to find out that China's first minister to England, Guo Song-tao, attended Henry Irving's *Hamlet* in 1879 and that that play was the first to be translated into Chinese in its entirety in 1921, or that Brecht's *Verfremdungseffekt* was inspired by a Moscow performance by Mei Lanfang and his Beijing opera troupe which he attended in 1935. In no time, I got a sense of texture and of the reciprocal exchanges that form the subject of this book. The laconic note, for 1966, the beginning of the Cultural Revolution, 'All foreign writers banned in China', also managed to convey some of the odds against which Shakespeare had to contend in this country, making the entry for 1999, 'Chinese premier Zhu Rongji quotes *The Merchant of Venice* to endorse the legitimacy of market law', the more surprising. As its title announces, the Chronology is selective and I would have included some different events for the parts I knew something about (I would especially have liked an acknowledgement of Karin Beier's 1996 production of *A Midsummer Night's Dream* in nine European languages to have been set side-by-side with Ong's similar experiments with Asian languages in his 1997 *LEAR*, which Huang's text describes as 'uniquely multilingual'), but it was a most effective way of giving me an entry point into the book.

Going back to the beginning, the Prologue continued this good work of setting the scene, providing a potted history of the development of Chinese Shakespeares that included a very welcome discussion of the specificities of Taiwan and Hong Kong as sites of cultural production (I was interested to find out that in Hong Kong, Shakespeare seems not to have been resisted as an image of colonization, for example). If the narrative rehearsed here about Shakespeare's expansion to become a cliché in the present-day global marketplace is, as Huang is quick to admit, 'old news', it was still important as a starting-point for his exploration of how 'Shakespeare has evolved from Britain's export commodity to an import industry in the Anglo-European culture, giving birth to Asian-inflected performances outside Asia.' What I liked here was the way the reassertion of what we know

is accompanied by an interrogation of the ideological work performed by the Chinese Shakespeares under discussion. Huang asks important questions about intercultural performances, probing cultural tourism and the effect of subtitling performances and drawing attention to the ways Chinese artists often insist on Shakespearean 'authenticity'. He also differentiates, in what seemed to me a particularly productive way, between Chinese Shakespeares that universalize him, productions that localize him for political purposes and adaptations that 'truncate and rewrite Shakespeare's plays so as to relate them to images of China'.

If Huang's aim is to counter the type of scholarship he satirizes as '[t]his is how they do Shakesepare over there; how quaint', he succeeds admirably, especially in the individual case studies that make up the body of the book. The theorization of 'locality criticism' which precedes them may be somewhat jargon-ridden and handled clumsily at first, but it opens up important debates and allows Huang to voice his call for a 'more capacious and polymorphous sense of China or Shakespeare as a continually evolving repository of meaning rather than a fixed textual corpus'. What is impressive here and throughout the volume is Huang's extensive scholarship that bridges Anglophone and Sinophone critical communities and is coupled with an equally impressive historical and generic range. He analyses how Shakespeare was seen as 'a symbol of the superiority of Anglo-European cultures' in China before any of his texts were available in translation, let alone performance; Lin Shu's vastly influential 'translation' of the Lambs' *Tales from Shakespeare* in 1904, which managed to exaggerate the 'potential for moral instruction in Shakespeare' yet all the while cutting references to Christianity; a silent film of *Merchant of Venice* focusing on Portia; the boom of Chinese Opera (*jingju*) adaptations of Shakespeare since the 1980s, all the way to recent productions of *King Lear* by Wi Hsing-kuo and Stan Lai (Lai Sheng-chuan). In the process, he traces an evolution from a Shakespeare used to express ideas about the modern age, morality or the nation, to a Shakespeare that has become more intimate, individual, personal. China, Shakespeare and Chinese Shakespeares come alive through Huang's text and its ample illustrations: this is a book whose Epilogue I will use in my teaching of Feng Xiaogang's *The Banquet* (2006) – a film Huang describes as being analogous to *Shakespeare in Love* in its myth-making – in the hope that students will want to read, learn and understand more.

Turning to *Shakespeare in Hollywood, Asia, and Cyberspace*, a collection co-edited by Huang with Charles S. Ross, it becomes obvious that a lot of the research for *Chinese Shakespeares* found its first outlet in Huang's work for the collection. For one, Huang's 'Chronology of Shakespeare in Hollywood, Asia, and Cyberspace' which is appended to the book looks remarkably familiar and does just as good a job of conveying the larger contextual picture here as its more Sinocentric equivalent does in *Chinese Shakespeares*. As this collection's title indicates, its twenty-odd essays are thematically very wide-ranging and, however much the editors strive, in their introduction, to impose order and a rationale on the contributions, this is not the sort of book anyone will want to be reading cover-to-cover. The disparate provenance of the contributions – some from a thematic online journal issue dedicated to Shakespeare in Asia originally edited by Ross, others from various events organized by Huang, still others commissioned specially for this collection – explains much of the volume's eclectic feel and its variant spellings (e.g. of General Ao, aka General Aw, in discussions of *Throne of Blood*). The essays, not surprisingly, are uneven: very young Asian scholars who are completing their Ph.D.s jostle for space with established Western scholars, and some of the essays could have done with much more rigorous editorial intervention.

I nevertheless found that there was fun to be got out of dipping into various parts of the volume. In the 'Hollywood' part of the book (otherwise the feeblest of the volume), Charles Ross's little essay on 'Underwater Women in Shakespeare on Film' investigates the bizarre 'Hollywood trope of the underwater woman'. In a move that surprised and delighted me in equal measure, Ross links the drowning/soaked Shakespearian women in 1990s film to Homer's description of Helen, medieval French literature and Jane Campion's *The Piano*, establishing a long history of the use of water as a symbol for female oppression.

The volume's second part, dedicated to 'Shakespeare in Asia', is more consistently interesting. David Bevington's account of what Shakespeare knew about Asia seems oddly disconnected from the other essays in this section, which contains two essays on Kurosawa by Yuwen Hsiung, who shows how Asian *Macbeth*s (including the Taiwanese *Kingdom of Desire* that is later discussed by Huang) draw on their cultures' codes of heroism, and Lei Jin, who investigates the role of silence (and the influence of silent film) in *Throne of Blood*. As in *Shakespeare in Asia*, here, too, I was drawn to the essay by Suematsu Michiko, which describes the enormous impact the first Tokyo Globe had on Japanese Shakespeares from 1988 to 2002, when it closed for refurbishment. She portrays the theatre as 'a liberated and exciting space' that hosted an astonishingly large number of English touring productions alongside Japanese productions in varying genres. As Japanese productions became more adventurous in their 'fantasizing' of Shakespeare, the Tokyo Globe helped dispel 'the last remains of Japan's century-long servitude to the authority and authenticity of the West'. Leaving Japan behind once more, it was refreshing to read about Shakespeare in countries such as Korea, Malaya, Cambodia and Indonesia, where traumatic colonial and war-torn pasts have led to Shakespeare taking on very distinct meanings in the present. I also enjoyed Elizabeth Wichmann-Walczak's observations about the rehearsal methods for the Shanghai Jingju Company's 1990s production of *King Lear* (*Qi Wang Meng*), which benefited from the directorial input of both *huaju* (spoken text) director Ouyang Ming and Ma Ke, whose work is in the *xiqu* (stylized theatre) tradition. 'I found it ironic', she wryly notes, 'that the *huaju*-based director invited for his enriching new methods in fact made effective use of traditional *xiqu* approaches, while the experienced *xiqu* director enriched the performances of his more experienced actors with Stanislavsky-based methods from *huaju*.' Adele Lee's essay on the Hong Kong film adaptation of *Romeo and Juliet* as *One Husband Too Many* (1988) will probably be more widely read, and she convincingly argues for the film to be read as a challenge to the 'British cultural hegemony by means of the Shakespearean text', as the film shows the failure of Shakespeare's play to engage the attention of rural audiences.

The most fun essay, though, has to be Peter Holland's, in the volume's section on 'Shakespeare in Cyberspace', who, in the guise of 'Peter Leonsbane, a good cleric avatar (because there was not one of a Shakespeare professor)', entered the world of Ted Castronova's *Arden: The World of William Shakespeare* online game, assisted by the figure of Peaseblossom. Lack of fake Elizabethan diction notwithstanding, this game apparently proved to be a hit only with Shakespeare experts: for play testers, there was '[t]oo much reading, not enough fighting'. Holland opens up the brave new world of Shakespeare's life on the internet, peeking at the work of the Second Life Shakespeare Company before stopping to consider YouTube clips and to muse on the types of viewing experience these clips afford and on the parasitic nature of the fragments on offer. His sense of amazement at some of the materials is contagious, and I found myself looking for some of the clips myself, wanting to share in his laughter. In his account of the ways in which sites such as *Stagework* document rehearsal, Holland questions the validity of some clips as a representation of actual rehearsals and speaks of the simultaneous excitement and frustration of this type of mediated access to hitherto inaccessible rehearsal spaces. It's a great essay on which to end a very uneven book.

Travelling back from Cyberspace to Asia, Poonam Trivedi and Minami Ryuta's *Re-playing Shakespeare in Asia* takes us back to stagings of the plays in various Asian locales. Trivedi's introduction to the volume is forbiddingly prefaced by no fewer than five epigraphs but turns out to be more readable than I was led to expect. For Trivedi, globalization has the positive side-effect of expanding the range of Shakespeares we may consider; the volume's stated aim is to investigate 'how Asian theatres, like Asian societies . . . engage

with Western and Shakespearean theatre on more equitable and interrogative terms than before; and how they produce innovative work which is forging new meanings and arresting imagination beyond the "local," hereby changing the equation between East and West'. The Asia represented in this volume is even more inclusive than in either the Kennedy–Yong or the Huang–Ross volumes, encompassing sixteen essays on Shakespeare performances in China, Japan, India, Bali, Indonesia, Korea, Taiwan, Malaysia and the Philippines. What is interesting here is the volume's dual emphasis on *inter*activity (of the East with the West) and *intra*activity (between different Asian locations) and its near-total rejection of Western authors in favour of 'voices which are rooted in their perspective of a first-hand experience'. This is the book that most explicitly privileges Asian voices to avert charges of orientalism. In the process, it introduces us to some very established authors whose work is too little known in the West.

Trivedi's introductory outline of the volume is complemented by James R. Brandon's helpful overview of 'Other Shakespeares in Asia', which, in subdividing Asian productions into the categories of canonical, indigenous and intercultural Shakespeares, provides a useful – if necessarily generalizing – taxonomy for the productions analysed in the rest of the volume. In particular, his 'tentative' definition of Richard Schechner's term 'intercultural' is valuable because it is underpinned by several examples and counter-examples that allow him to foster a refined understanding of a buzz word that risks being attached to any collaboration of Asian and Western practitioners. Already in the next chapter, in which Brian Singleton talks about Ariane Mnouchkine's Théâtre du Soleil and its dependence on Asian theatre forms 'to create a pictorial and formalist landscape of the imagination', having Brandon's taxonomy in mind proves helpful. Trivedi herself follows this up with a sharp critique of Tim Supple's acclaimed multilingual production of *A Midsummer Night's Dream* in 2006, whose claims to speak for India seem to have been more strategic than genuine. In India, the multilingualism that gave the production its edge for European critics led to different parts of the audience tittering at different moments, creating tensions in the auditorium: hardly the desired effect. Taking no prisoners, Trivedi condemns the multilingualism as 'a superficial tokenism towards authenticating a kind of fractional and bitty "Indian-ness"' and uses it as a springboard for an altogether more positive appraisal of Chetan Dathar's more modest Marathi adaptation of the same play in 2004. Minami Ryuta's essay on the ways in which, after more than a hundred years of Japanese Shakespeares, producing a Shakespeare play in Japan involves 'remembering, reviewing, and revising (the memories of) its preceding counterparts', has a less combative tone and offers a welcome insight into the limits of the *shingeki* movement as a background for a discussion of Ninagawa's *kabuki Twelfth Night*.

With Ian Carruthers's essay on the performance history of Suzuki Tadashi's *King Lear*, the location remains Japan but the focus shifts towards textuality and theatricality as Carruthers considers Suzuki's 'incisive but respectful cutting' of Shakespeare's play between 1984 and 2006. Carruthers's essay culminates in a fascinating appraisal of Suzuki's Moscow Art Theatre production (2004–6) that brought his method into contact with the custodians of Stanislavski's approach, 'wedding... two powerful theatrical languages'. Carruthers's close attention to the text is also characteristic of Li Ruru's inspired consideration of the difficulties of translating 'To be, or not to be, that is the question' into Chinese, a language which does not have an equivalent for 'to be'. Li's analysis concentrates on how six Chinese productions, in both *huaju* and *xiqu* styles, dealt with the problems posed by Hamlet's soliloquy.

The solemnity of the *xiqu* arias on which Ruru ends finds a refreshing contrast in Yoshihara Yukari's analysis of the pop Shakespeares produced by Inoue Hidenori in Japan (which resonates with Bi-qui Beatrice Lei's concluding essay on camp *Romeo and Juliet*s in Taiwan), before a return to solemnity with Tapati Gupta's discussion of Utpal Dutt's *Romeo and Juliet* and Bengali theatre history. In quick succession, the collection then takes us

to the Philippines, (Judy Celine Ick), Korea (Kim Moran), Malaysia (Nurul Farhana Low Abdullah and C. S. Lim), Taiwan (Wu Peichen) provincial China (Alexander C. Y. Huang) and Bali (John Emigh). Low Abdullah and Lim's essay, with its two beautiful illustrations, was my first introduction to the Malay art of *wayang kulit* or shadow puppetry, making me want to jump on a plane to see this form of theatre for myself. It is difficult to do justice to these essays, except to say that each opens the door onto a different complex post-colonial situation which complicates received ideas in post-colonial studies. Ick, for example, describes the Philippines as a country whose status as a 'territory' rather than a 'colony' 'forces a re-examination, if a [sic] not a reconfiguration, of postcolonial paradigms. Multilayered, conflicted, and conflicting, the history of colonialism in the Philippines disturbs simplistic analysis as it demands a more complex reworking of commonly deployed concepts like "hybridity," for instance, to account for the various elements that make up its colonial and postcolonial cultures.' Clearly, the work of directors like Ricardo Abad, whose 2002 *Shrew* allegorized American colonialism in the Philippines, or Tae-seok's Korean *Romeo & Juliet*, which responds to Asian traditions via their reception in the West (Moran) have a lot to teach us not only about the uses to which Shakespeare is put in these locations but also about our need to refine our critical categories when approaching Asian Shakespeares.

What these essays on the various, very locally specific, Asian art forms have in common is a desire not so much to speak of Shakespeare's translation into those forms as to translate the forms for the Western reader. At times, this is accompanied by a good degree of impatience with clumsy attempts to view Asian Shakespeares through the lens of 1990s post-colonial criticism. This is particularly obvious in Paromita Chakravarti and Swati Ganguly's chapter on 'Dancing to Shakespeare' which asks that we renounce 'the notion of a single, unified "Indian" dance' and accept that Saibal Basu's *Wheel of Fire* (2000) and Vikram Iyengar's *Crossings* (2004–5), two dance appropriations of Shakespeare, use distinct dance styles, one classical, the other derived from folk dance theatre, and 'their own internal logic to understand the tragedies that they choose to work with'. Chakravarti and Ganguly combine theoretical sophistication with an emphasis on the performance and subversion of gender within a mode of dance that has 'a fixed mode of performing femininity and masculinity'. The essay invites us to move beyond a study of Shakespeare to a consideration of how 'the Shakespearean text acts as a catalyst which draws out both the range and the specificities of the resources of classical and folk dance and theatre forms in India and initiates an intracultural dialogue between them'. Chakravarti and Ganguly's passionate rejection of 'the ready-made, postcolonial, or "intercultural" critical grid' and call for an understanding that 'emerges from the changing concerns, resources, and sites of work of contemporary cultural practitioners working with local forms and Shakespearean texts', while making it much harder for Western scholars to even begin to discuss Asian Shakespeares with any degree of confidence, demand to be heard.

As is clear from the publications reviewed this year, the trend towards setting Anglophone Shakespeare within a larger theatrical context, which I noted in my last review, is continuing. It is significant that the excavations that form the subject of Bowsher and Miller's book should have been concerned not just with the Shakespeare-identified Globe but also with Henslowe's Rose. The history of the early modern theatre, as written by Stern and Walsh, is using evidence from a large range of plays to illuminate Shakespeare's work. What has been even more obvious this year than last is that this trend is also influencing performance studies concerned with present-day performances. Shakespeare is absolutely central to traditional projects such as the 'Shakespeare in Production' series and he is also key for many theatre practitioners, as we can see from the work of Rokison, Noble and Purcell. At the exploratory frontiers of performance studies, however, where this year's most risky and exciting work has happened, a significant shift is occurring that repositions Shakespeare. Shakespeare is not marginalized, by any means, but rather, to use Werner's brilliant term, 'resituated',

placed *beside* contemporary films and theatre practices, performances of other early modern plays, or theatre practices belonging to other cultures. Not all the work at the frontiers of the field is polished, but there is a drive, energy and intellectual curiosity behind even the roughest work in this area that gives it an excitement which some of the more traditional modes of enquiry are lacking. The conversation about new directions in Renaissance drama and performance studies has well and truly begun.

BOOKS REVIEWED

Bowsher, Julian, and Pat Miller, *The Rose and the Globe – Playhouses of Shakespeare's Bankside, Southwark: Excavations 1988–90* (London, 2009)

Croteau, Melissa, and Carolyn Jess-Cooke, eds., *Apocalyptic Shakespeare: Essays on Visions of Chaos and Revelation in Recent Film Adaptations* (Jefferson, 2009)

Dymkowski, Christine, and Christie Carson, eds., *Shakespeare in Stages: New Theatre Histories* (Cambridge, 2010)

Huang, Alexander C. Y. *Chinese Shakespeares: Two Centuries of Cultural Exchange* (New York, 2009)

Huang, Alexander C. Y., and Charles S. Ross, eds., *Shakespeare in Hollywood, Asia, and Cyberspace* (West Lafayette, 2009)

Kennedy, Dennis, and Yong Li Lan, eds., *Shakespeare in Asia: Contemporary Performance* (Cambridge, 2010)

Newstock, Scott L., and Ayanna Thompson, eds., *Weyward Macbeth: Intersections of Race and Performance* (New York, 2010)

Noble, Adrian, *How to Do Shakespeare* (London, 2010)

Purcell, Stephen, *Popular Shakespeare: Simulation and Subversion on the Modern Stage* (Basingstoke, 2009)

Rokison, Abigail, *Shakespearean Verse Speaking: Text and Theatre Practice* (Cambridge, 2009)

Schafer, Elizabeth, ed., *Twelfth Night. Shakespeare in Production* (Cambridge, 2010)

Semenza, Greg Colón, *The English Renaissance in Popular Culture: An Age for All Time* (New York, 2010)

Solga, Kim, *Violence Against Women in Early Modern Drama: Invisible Acts* (New York, 2009)

Thanks to Mark Thornton Burnett, Kathryn Prince, Philip Schwyzer and Charlotte Welch for conversations about several of the books reviewed here: your expert views were precious.

Stern, Tiffany, *Documents of Performance in Early Modern England* (Cambridge, 2009)

Trivedi, Poonam, and Minami Ryuta, eds., *Re-playing Shakespeare in Asia* (New York, 2010)

Walsh, Brian, *Shakespeare, the Queen's Men, and the Elizabethan Performance of History* (Cambridge, 2009)

Werner, Sarah, ed., *New Directions in Renaissance Drama and Performance Studies* (New York, 2010)

3. EDITIONS AND TEXTUAL STUDIES
reviewed by ERIC RASMUSSEN

My first *Shakespeare Survey* review, over a decade ago, drew attention to a handful of errors in the collations of Katherine Duncan-Jones's Arden 3 edition of Shakespeare's sonnets. This year saw the publication of a revised edition 'improved by the correction of a number of errata listed by Eric Rasmussen'. However, something went wrong during the production of the revised edition and certain italic letters unaccountably did not print. Some of the resulting phrases are easily made out ('*Oxf d E gli Dic i y*'), while others take a bit more work: '*T R f L c*' (poem by Pope) and '*i P ili id y: C u i P*' (previous book by Duncan-Jones). A further corrected edition has now been produced, with a substantially reworked introduction that may well justify the purchase of the revised edition even by those who own the 1997 original.

Barbara Hodgdon's Arden 3 edition of *The Taming of the Shrew* opens with a wonderfully engaging analysis of the book's cover photo (which apparently went through several versions). In its final state, Katherina extends a hand towards another hand, visible just at the frame's edge, that reaches for hers. Hodgdon nicely observes that the Katherina figure 'almost seems to be dancing in tune to the play's perennial questions: shrew or not shrew? Un-tamed or tamed?' Hodgdon's introduction offers what may be the most lucid account yet produced of the play's multiple textual versions, finely characterizing *Shrew* as a '*texte combinatoire*' of 'textual, sexual, social, political and performative difference(s)'.

There are so many facets in a 400-page critical edition that it may seem ungenerous for a review to fixate, as mine often do, on a feature as relatively minor as textual notes. And yet, there are more than two dozen errors in Hodgdon's collations,[1] and further slips throughout that combine to make the edition somewhat frustrating to use. The running head on page 204 reads '2.2.188' rather than '2.1.188' (there is no 2.2 in the play). The discussions on pages 312 and 323 of the stray speech-prefix '*Par.*' (which may refer to the actor William Parr) repeatedly provide an inaccurate line reference, '4.2.73' instead of '4.2.72'; this is especially confusing because there's a speech-prefix issue at line 73 as well, where Hodgdon has emended Folio '*Ped*' to '*Merchant*'. Folio's '*servingmen*' at 4.1.93.1 is

With thanks to my ever perspicacious editor, Arthur Evenchik.

[1] Induction 1.129 SD F reading for '*Seruingman*' read '*seruing-man*'; Induction 2.0.2 lemma for '*three* Servants' read '*and three* Servants'; Induction 2.0.2 collation for '*attendants*' read '*with attendants, some*'; Induction 2.17 F reading for '*Burton-Heath*' read '*Burton-heath*'; Induction 2.63 F reading for 'o'errun' read 'ore-run'; Induction 2.133 F reading for 'it is not' read 'it is'; 1.1.25 F reading for '*pardonato*' read '*Pardonato*'; 1.1.47.2 F reading for 'Hortensio' read '*Hortensio*'; 1.1.71 F reading for '*Maids*' read 'Maids'; 1.1.106 F reading for 'love' read 'loue'; 2.1.75–86 for 'beene.' read 'beene'; 2.1.75–6 F reading for 'neighbours' read 'neighbors'; 2.1.77 F reading for 'kindness' read 'kindnesse'; 2.1.198 F reading for 'joyn'd' read 'ioyn'd'; 2.1.207 F reading for 'Should be' read 'Shold be'; 3.1.74 F reading for '*cfaut*' read '*Cfaut*'; 3.1.76 F reading for '*Ela, mi*' read '*Ela mi*'; 3.2.16 F reading for 'invite, and proclaim' read 'inuite, and proclaime'; 3.2.181 SD for '*opp.* 56' read '*opp.* 182'; 3.2.210 F reading for 'tomorrow' read 'to mor-row'; 4.1.126–8 F reading for 'Kate,' read '*Kate*,'; 4.2.7 F reading for 'master' read 'Master'; 4.5.27 F reading for 'company' read 'Company'; 4.5.39 F reading for 'whether' read 'Whether'; 5.2.0.3–4 F reading for '*Biondello, Grumio*' read '*Biondello Grumio*'.

silently changed to 'Servants' and the '*and*' in the stage directions at both 1.1.47.3 and 5.1.56.2 should be bracketed. Readers may be distracted by Hodgdon's practice of regularizing '*Kate*' to '*Katherina*' in the stage directions but referring to '*Katherina*' and '*Kate*' interchangeably in the commentary, often in the same note. At 5.2.141, for example, she writes, '*Kate* and Petruccio must exit and return immediately ... *Katherina* and Petruccio might simply join the others'.

More seriously, Hodgdon claims that the emendation 'o'er-ran' for Folio 'ore-run' at Induction 2.63 is 'a reading adopted for the first time in this edition'. In fact, this emendation was first adopted by Theobald, who was followed by many subsequent editors, including Johnson, Reed, Knight, Singer, Chalmers and Collier.

I've always admired Hodgdon's work, but I confess that I'm genuinely perplexed by some of her prose here. She says, for instance:

> The Comedies section of the First Folio begins with *The Tempest*, the play whose date of composition is closest to F's publication; four other plays, also apparently transcribed by the professional scrivener Ralph Crane, precede *The Shrew*, which is followed by plays already in print, and finally by the remaining F-only comedies.

If I understand this passage correctly, the assertion is that the Comedies section begins with *The Tempest* and four other Ralph Crane plays (*TGV, MW, MM, CE*). The naïve reader might be forgiven for assuming that *Shrew* then follows, but this is not the case, as there are five intervening plays (*MA, LLL, MND, MV, AYLI*). Hodgdon says that *Shrew* is then followed by plays already in print, but, again, this is not the case: not one of the comedies that follow *Shrew* in the First Folio had been previously printed (*AW, TN, WT*), nor had the play that immediately precedes it (*AYLI*).

Providing a happy counterpoint to the unfortunate number of slips in the Arden *Shrew*, John Pitcher's Arden 3 *Winter's Tale* offers an immaculate text of the play and a nearly perfect set of textual notes. The only significant error I found is the claim that the speech-prefix emendations at 5.2.3 and following are unique to this edition (the emendations were previously made by Craig's Oxford edition).[2]

Pitcher is finely attuned to the play's alternative possibilities ('Did Hermione die, and this is her reanimation? Or was she just hidden, waiting, numbed and dead to the world?') and its dualities ('The Bear is terrible and ridiculously funny, its explosive entry nearly unstageable but the best pantomime around'). Although the introduction is decidedly 'old school' in its focus on grand themes (Death, Tragedy, Knowledge, Nature, Wonder, Time), Pitcher's modern analogies are charming. He is at pains to correct the widespread impression that Shakespeare made a geographical blunder by conferring a coastline on Bohemia, insisting that it 'clearly wasn't Shakespeare's mistake, but a joke. Alluding to Bohemia's coastline would raise a laugh, as do modern jokes about the Jamaican ice hockey team or the Swiss Navy.' Pitcher also dismisses the revisionist argument that the production of *The Winter's Tale* that Simon Forman saw at the Globe in 1611 was an early version for which Shakespeare hadn't yet written the scene of Hermione's resurrection. To Pitcher, Forman's failure to record the climactic event in his diary is of dubious significance: 'perhaps he left early (like a crowd leaving a football match before a goal in the final minute), never expecting the statue to come to life'.

One of Pitcher's most significant contributions to the study of the play may be his novel idea that Shakespeare conceived and wrote *Cymbeline, The Winter's Tale* and *The Tempest* as a group, beginning at the end of 1610 and finishing in the summer of 1611. As Pitcher observes, apart from revisions to *King Lear*, these plays represent 'Shakespeare's only sustained writing' during the five years 1609–1614. The catalyst for his remarkable productivity,

---

[2] For the record, the emendation of F's speech-prefix '*Gent. 3*' to '*Steward*' at 5.2.30 should not be claimed by Pitcher, since it was first made in the *Viola Allen Acting Version of The Winter's Tale* (New York, 1905) as was the emended *Exeunt* direction at 5.2.110. Also, there is a minor error in formatting in the collation at 2.1.153 SD, where for 'Hamner subst.' read '*Hamner subst.*'

Pitcher suggests, may have been the 1608 theatrical flop of Fletcher's *The Faithful Shepherdess*. That is, 'Shakespeare may have taken the failure of *The Faithful Shepherdess* as a challenge – he could write a popular tragicomedy even if Fletcher couldn't.'

The bold headlines that announced the publication of *Double Falsehood* in the Arden 3 series ('ARDEN PUBLISH CONTROVERSIAL PLAY "BY SHAKESPEARE"') did little to prepare us for Brean Hammond's measured, undogmatic and carefully considered edition, based on Lewis Theobald's eighteenth-century adaptation of a purported Shakespeare play, presumably Shakespeare and Fletcher's lost *Cardenio*. Where one might have anticipated that the move to include *Double Falsehood* in the Shakespeare canon would be accompanied by heavy-handed claims about authorial attribution and assertions of dramatic worth, we get instead the bearable lightness of Hammond's rationale for his project: 'I hope that this edition reinforces the accumulating consensus that the lost play has a continuing presence in its eighteenth-century great-grandchild.'

Hammond observes that in the case of *Cardenio*, we are in much the same position we would occupy in relation to *The Two Noble Kinsmen* if the 1634 Quarto had never been published but we still had Davenant's 1664 adaptation, *The Rivals*: 'We would be forced to reconstruct the Shakespeare–Fletcher play as a missing intermediary stage between Chaucer's "Knight's Tale" and Davenant's abbreviated revision.' Similarly, *Cardenio* represents a missing intermediate stage between Shelton's 1612 translation of *Don Quixote* (over eighty pages of which are provided in facsimile here) and Theobald's adaptation. It remains to be seen whether Hammond's edition will spark further efforts to reconstruct the lost play.

Hammond's text is supremely well edited, leaving a reviewer only a few occasions for quibbling. The many instances in which Hammond prints an '*aside*' direction at the beginning of a line, where the 1728 copy-text prints the '*aside*' at the end of the line, do not really deserve to be flagged as emendations 'adopted for the first time in this edition'. The heading 'ROYAL LICENCE' does not actually appear on the Royal Licence, so probably should have been bracketed. It is unclear to me why the lapidary capitals in line 33 of the prologue, 'When great AUGUSTUS fills the British throne', are retained in a modernized edition that does not otherwise preserve typographic forms. I wonder, too, why the paragraph break at line 78 of Theobald's 'Preface of the Editor' has *not* been retained. Finally, given that Hammond breaks with Arden 3 convention in using elided –'*d* rather than –*ed*, it might have been helpful to delete the passage from the General Editors' Preface that outlines the standard procedure.

In an important new study, *Shakespeare's Errant Texts: Textual Form and Linguistic Style in Shakespearean 'Bad' Quartos and Co-authored Plays*, Lene B. Petersen takes methodologies that folklore philologists such as Albert Lord and Milman Perry employed to analyze oral poetry and applies them to a study of the quarto versions of Shakespeare's plays. Petersen points out that the omission and transposition of textual segments has long been considered evidence of folk material that was transmitted by an oral culture, and that these same sorts of textual tangles have been seen as indicative of the memorial reconstruction of Shakespeare's texts. Her book poses the genuinely provocative question, 'Is textual "suspectness" a stylistically significant factor?' That is, have editors and critics been suspicious about certain texts because they have features of oral transmission?

Petersen ably demonstrates that just as oral folktales tend to follow a set format in which each episode features two characters, the Q1 versions of both *Romeo & Juliet* and *Hamlet* scale down scenes with multiple characters so that only two appear on stage. Thus, the Q2/F direction '*Enter Mercutio, Benvolio and men*' becomes '*Enter Benvolio and Mercutio*' in Q1; Q2's '*Enter Prince, olde Montegue, Capulet, their wiues and all*' becomes an entrance for only the Prince and Capulet's wife in Q1.

Petersen is especially good about reminding us (or, perhaps more probably, informing us) of the many versions and offshoots of Shakespeare's plays that were in circulation during the early seventeenth century. These include ballads about

Titus Andronicus, King Lear, Romeo and Juliet, and Hamlet, as well as German derivative dramas of *Romeo & Juliet* and *Hamlet*. Moreover, early seventeenth-century stage performances of *Titus*, *Shrew*, *Romeo and Juliet* and *Hamlet* are recorded in Dresden, Leipzig and Frankfurt. In 1592, a contemporary observed that 'despised stage players come out of England into Germany . . . having neither a complete number of actours, nor any good Apparell, nor any ornament of the stage verifiable'. If these players lacked apparel and ornaments, they may have lacked scripts as well. Petersen's thesis is that a variety of dramatic texts may have been re-created from memory and reproduced through oral transmission, factors that ought to be considered in understanding all theatrical texts of the period.

Although Petersen is certainly breaking new ground here, the constant reminders that she is doing so are surely unnecessary ('theatre history seldom makes the leap into full-scale philology'; 'I can think of no currently available early modern authorship attribution study where the verbal effects of players' memories . . . are sufficiently considered'). More significantly, there are a number of errors in the scholarship, some of them serious. For instance, Petersen's claim that 'Jonson was particularly averse to the collaborative practice' is not true. Jonson co-authored a number of plays, although he chose not to include such collaborative works as *Eastward Ho*, *Hot Anger Soon Cold*, *Page of Plymouth*, *The Scot's Tragedy* (*Robert II*) and *The Isle of Dogs* in the 1616 Folio; in publishing *Sejanus*, Jonson claims to have removed material that had been written by a collaborator and replaced it with his own. Petersen's statement that 'unfortunately, the De Witt drawing shows us the playhouse without an audience' somehow manages to overlook the audience members who are indeed depicted sitting in the gallery above the stage in the famous drawing. Readers intrigued by the assertion that '*Edward II* is likely to be collaborative' and perhaps expecting a new attribution for Marlowe's play will be disappointed when they realize that Petersen is actually referring to *Edward III*. Petersen claims that 'the title-page of Q1 [*Titus*] indicates the likelihood of prior performance by no fewer than four companies', but I can find only three ('The righte honourable The Earle of Derbie, The Earle of Pembroke, and Earl of Sussex their Seruants'). The generalization that 'textual economy is a shared feature of all the currently designated "bad" texts, some of which approximate almost half the length of the folio and "good" quarto texts' is challenged by Q *Richard III*, which tips the scales at over 3,400 lines. Mark Turner's book *The Literary Mind*, a central study in cognitive science, is referred to as *The Literary Brain* in Petersen's text but is cited correctly in a footnote on the same page. Finally, *Shakespeare's Errant Texts* is punctuated by odd statements that either assert the painfully obvious ('the Rose, Globe, and Swan were all three-dimensional spaces') or border on the nonsensical ('Methodologies now exist that can virtually restore the human author to the written text').

AMS Press has issued a volume of essays by Akihiro Yamada that surely wins the prize for longest sub-title of any Shakespearian study published this year: *Secrets of the Printed Page in the Age of Shakespeare: Bibliographical Studies in the Plays of Beaumont, Chapman, Dekker, Fletcher, Ford, Marston, Shakespeare, Shirley, and in the Text of King James I's 'The True Lawe of Free Monarchies', with an Edition of 'Arcadia Restored', Egerton MS 1994, Folios 212–23 in the British Library*. The expansive title is a testament to the breadth of Yamada's bibliographical work during his distinguished fifty-year career. Previously published articles are usefully collected here along with previously unpublished essays. Given that some of Yamada's articles have appeared in Japanese journals that are sometimes difficult to obtain, their reprinting in this collection is especially welcome. The volume includes an old-spelling edition of *Arcadia Restored*; a modern-spelling edition, also edited by Yamada, has been published separately this year.

With the publication of *The Tragedie of Romeo and Juliet: A Frankly Annotated First Folio Edition*, Demitra Papadinis intends to fill the gap left by Shakespearian editors who 'abide eternally in the Never-Never-Land of the seventh grade classroom' and 'would never dream of expounding on lewd, deplorable, filthy language – probably for fear of getting the venerable Mr. Shakespeare kicked out of school'. It would appear that Papadinis is unaware of the Bate–Rasmussen edition of the RSC Complete Works, memorably reviewed by Peter Holland in the *TLS* under the heading 'Sexy Shakespeare'. Holland observes that the edition's heightened awareness of Shakespeare's sexual language may well 'provoke protests from American parents, so overanxious and overprotective about sex'.[3] For reasons I cannot fathom, this prediction has yet to be borne out.

Holland is no doubt correct that our commentary occasionally 'states unequivocally the presence of a sexual meaning that may or may not be there', but we are certainly outclassed by Papadinis in this regard. Her commentary manages to find sexual meaning in even the most unpromising of Shakespeare's words. Although it's possible (just) that Lady Capulet's 'By my count I was your mother' could be heard as 'By my cunt . . .', the suggestion that her following line, 'And see how one another lends content', should be read as 'Paris's loins will give pleasure when he probes Juliet's cunt' is so far beyond the realm of linguistic and philological possibility, to say nothing of its context, as to be ridiculous. Unfortunate students who find

themselves having to use Papadinis's edition really do have something about which to protest.

WORKS REVIEWED

Anonymous, *Arcadia Restored: An Edition of an Anonymous Play*, ed. Akihiro Yamada (Brooklyn, 2010)

Petersen, Lene B., *Shakespeare's Errant Texts: Textual Form and Linguistic Style in Shakespearean 'Bad' Quartos and Co-authored Plays* (Cambridge, 2010)

Shakespeare, William, *The Tragedie of Romeo and Juliet: A Frankly Annotated First Folio Edition*, ed. Demitra Papadinis (Jefferson, NC, and London, 2010)

Shakespeare, William, and John Fletcher, *Double Falsehood or The Distressed Lovers*, ed. Brean Hammond, Arden 3 (London, 2010)

Shakespeare's Sonnets, ed. Katherine Duncan-Jones, Arden 3 rev. edn (London, 2010)

The Taming of the Shrew, ed. Barbara Hodgdon, Arden 3 (London, 2010)

The Winter's Tale, ed. John Pitcher, Arden 3 (London, 2010)

Yamada, Akihiro, *Secrets of the Printed Page in the Age of Shakespeare* (Brooklyn, 2010)

---

[3] *TLS*, 15 August 2007.

INDEX

NOTE: Locators in italics denote the pages on which illustrations are to be found.

INDEX

INDEX

INDEX

INDEX